THE CROWN AND CONSTITUTIONAL LAW IN CANADA, SECOND EDITION

THE CROWN AND CONSTITUTIONAL LAW IN CANADA, SECOND EDITION

Peter W. Noonan

Magistralis
Ottawa, Canada

Magistralis Cataloguing in Publication Data

Noonan, Peter W. (Peter William), 1956-, author
The Crown and constitutional law in Canada, second edition/ Peter W.Noonan.

Includes bibliographical references.
Issued in print format.
ISBN 978-0-9683534-4-8 (hardback).

1. Monarchy–Canada. 2. Constitutional law–Canada. I. Title.

JL88.N66 2017   342.71 N817

Published by Magistralis, Ottawa, Canada

Contents

HIERARCHICAL TABLE OF CONTENTS

TABLE OF ABBREVIATIONS

I. Case Citations

Australia

ALR — Australian Law Reports

CLR — Commonwealth Law Reports

NSWLR — New South Wales Law Reports

QSCR — Queensland Supreme Court Reports

Canada

Admin LR — Administrative Law Reports

AR — Alberta Reports

BCLR — British Columbia Law Reports

CanLII — Canadian Legal Information Institute

CPC — Carswell's Practice Cases

CRC — Canadian Railway Cases but if used in connection with regulations it means Consolidated Regulations of Canada

CRR — Canadian Rights Reporter

DLR — Dominion Law Reports

Ex CR — Exchequer Court Reports

FC — Federal Court Reports

FTR — Federal Trial Reports

Man LR — Manitoba Law Reports

NR — National Reporter

Nfld & PEIR — Newfoundland and Prince Edward Island Reports

OAR — Ontario Appeal Cases

OR — Ontario Reports

Sask R — Saskatchewan Reports

SCR — Supreme Court Reports

WWR — Western Weekly Reports

Newfoundland (pre-confederation)

Nfld LR — Newfoundland Law Reports

New Zealand

NZLR — New Zealand Law Reports

United Kingdom (and English Reporting Series)

AC — Appeal Cases

All ER — All England Law Reports

All ER Rep — All England Law Reports Reprint

Co Rep — Coke's Reports

Cowp — Cowper's Reports

Cur. Mil. — Curia Militaris

ER — English Reports

Exch. Rep. — Exchequer Reports

Her. Cas. — Heraldic Cases

H & C — Hurlstone and Coltman's Exchequer Reports

LR — Law Reports

LRC — Law Reports of the Commonwealth

LRC (Const) — Law Reports of the Commonwealth (Constitutional)

PRO — Public Record Office (United Kingdom)

LT — Law Times

P — Law Reports – Probate, Divorce and Admiralty

State Tr — State Trials

State Tr (NS) — State Trials (New Series)

WLR — Weekly Law Reports

United States

US — United States Reports

II. Court Abbreviations

AD — Appeal Division

CCJ — Caribbean Court of Justice

Ch — Chancery Division

Comm. of Priv. — Committee of Privileges of the House of Lords

CP — Common Pleas

CA — Court of Appeal

Ct. Chiv. — High Court of Chivalry

CTC — Canadian Transport Commission

DC — Divisional Court

EWHC — England and Wales High Court

Ex. Ct. — Exchequer Court (Canada)

Exch. Pleas — Court of Exchequer Pleas (England)

FC — Federal Court

FCA — Federal Court of Appeal

GD — Ontario Court General Division

G.Ct. — Grand Court

HL — House of Lords

JC — Judicial Committee of the Privy Council of the United Kingdom

KB — Court of King's Bench

NUCJ — Nunavut Court of Justice

ONCA — Ontario Court of Appeal

ONSC — Ontario Superior Court

QC — Quebec Court

QCCS — Quebec Superior Court

QB — Court of Queen's Bench

Sup. Ct. — Superior Court

SC — Supreme Court

UKSC — United Kingdom Supreme Court

III. Judges and Officers of a Court

DPP — Director of Public Prosecutions

D.C.J — District Court Judge

J.A. or JJ.A. — Associate Justice or Associate Justices

J.C.Q. — Judge of the Court of Quebec

K.C. — King's Counsel

M.R. — Master of the Rolls

Q.C. — Queen's Counsel

IV. Other

affd. — affirmed

P.C. — Privy Council (or Privy Councillor if applied to a person)

R — *Regina* (Latin for the Queen) or *Rex* (Latin for the King)

rep. and repl. — repealed and replaced

revd. — reversed

sub. nom. — under name of

U.K. — United Kingdom of Great Britain and Northern Ireland

U.S. — United States of America

THE MONARCHY AND THE CONSTITUTION

1.0   THE MONARCHY

The monarchy is Canada's oldest constitutional institution, having existed since the inception of the state more than four hundred years ago. Although European claims to Canadian territory were made as early as the fifteenth century, the Canadian state cannot be truly considered to have come into existence prior to the founding of Quebec by the French explorer Samuel de Champlain in July 1608, during the reign of France's King Henri IV. From the time of the founding of Quebec however, Canadian territory was continuously inhabited by European migrants, who brought with them their European law, and their conception of the state as a political entity whose institutions derived their legitimacy from monarchical authority.

Prior to the European discovery the aboriginal peoples of Canada enjoyed an absolute sovereignty and even subsequent to the European discovery title to aboriginal territory was vitiated only by the surrender of aboriginal title to the Sovereigns pursuant to a treaty of cession.[1] Aboriginal political institutions, although quite sophisticated in some areas, particularly amongst the Iroquoian-speaking peoples, were supplanted by the constitutional institutions of the European settlers.

1.1   The Monarchy in the French Colonial Period 1608 – 1763

Since the original migrants to Canada from Europe came from France, it was the political institutions of that country which influenced the early development of state institutions in Canada. The Royal House of France became the Royal House of Canada (then called New France) and at that period of political development in France the monarchy was absolutist in its political philosophy. All power was vested in and flowed from the Sovereign, who ruled without the benefit of a Parliament. Indeed, as noted by one early authority on Canadian constitutional history, Parliament was unknown in France or Canada:

> The very name of the parliament had to the French colonist none of the significance it had to the Englishman, whether living in the parent state or in its dependencies. The word in French was applied only to a body whose ordinary functions were of a judicial character, and whose very decrees bore the continual impress of royal dictation. In Canada as in France, absolutism and centralization were the principles on which the government was conducted.[2]

Absolutism meant that the King, ruling by divine right, as the representative of God, was immune to any judicial process and thus French monarchical government could not be restrained by the law courts. As in Great Britain, the royal prerogatives of the Sovereign were not subject to the ordinary laws of the realm. Although in principle the King could not dispose of the Crown of France, nor alter the laws of succession to the Throne to defeat a legitimate male heir's right to succeed to the Throne, such principles were incapable of being enforced by judicial process and could only be enforced through political measures, usually after the preceding King's reign had ended.

The early Royal Instructions to the first Governors of New France invested them with wide law making authority over the affairs of the country. Later, from 1627 until 1663, King Louis XIII, acting on advice from his chief minister, Cardinal Richelieu, placed the development of Canada in the hands of a trading company, the Compagnie des Cent-Associés, although the Governor continued to exercise all of the necessary civil and military powers of the government. In 1663, King Louis XIV, advised by his chief minister, Colbert, dissolved the Compagnie des Cent-Associés and placed Canada under the direct rule of the Sovereign in Paris. From that point in time Canada was essentially administered as a royal province of France.

Subsequent to 1663, Canada was administered on behalf of the Sovereign by two important officials, the Gouvenner et Lieutenant – Général en Canada, Acadie, Isle de Terre Neuve, et autres payes de la France Septentrionale, (the Governor-General) and the Intendant de la Justice, Police et Finance du Canada (the Intendant). Both officials reported directly to the Sovereign.[3] To assist his officials the Sovereign established by decree a Conseil Souverain, consisting of the Governor General, the Intendant, the Bishop of Quebec, an Attorney General, and first five, then seven, and later twelve Councillors. Subsequently, the name of the Conseil Souverain was changed to Conseil Supérieur, due to concerns on the part of King Louis XIV that the word "sovereign" might imply a greater measure of independence from the actual Sovereign than he was prepared to permit.

Although the first Conseil was chosen by the Governor General and the Bishop later appointments to the Conseil were made by the Sovereign himself, acting on the recommendation of the Governor General and the Intendant.[4] The Conseil exercised legislative and judicial powers and issued decrees for the civil, commercial and financial management of the country. It also issued judgments in civil and criminal law cases in accordance with Royal Ordinances and the *Coutume de Paris*, the customary law of the City of Paris, which was also applied in Canada.

The social structure in Canada during this period reflected the traditional divisions which existed between classes, although the social divisions were not as pronounced as they were in metropolitan France. The Governor General was typically an aristocrat from France who often possessed a military background. He stood at the apex of the country's political and social structure. As the Sovereign's representative, the Governor General presided at state functions, acted as the commander in chief of the armed forces, and was responsible for Canada's relations with the British and the aboriginal peoples in the Americas. The Intendant, who effectively administered the government, was the most important official in the civil administration. He was usually drawn from amongst the minor nobility of France. The Bishop also held a significant post since the Roman Catholic Church was the established state church in both France and Canada.

A local Canadian nobility arose as the Sovereign began to ennoble Canadians for distinguished services. The King granted letters of nobility to a number of Canadians, often following the purchase or grant of a seigneury, which entitled them to the use of the honorific title of écuyer, or squire.[5] A Canadian corps of military officers was drawn from this local pool of nobility. Although the Sovereign ceased to grant peerages to Canadians during the French colonial period after 1700, a distinct Canadian aristocratic elite with strong links to the military had developed. Patronage, from either the Governor General or the Intendant, was important in the Canadian society of this era. The result was the development of a courtier-elitist society which nevertheless retained its stability until the state was finally overwhelmed by foreign military invasion in 1759-60.[6]

Society in Canada was organized under the French seigneurial system, a semi-feudal system which established a hierarchy of duties. At the apex was the King who granted tracts of land to men known as seigneurs in return for the seigneur providing duties and services to the Sovereign. The primary duties of a seigneur in Canada during the French colonial period included fealty and homage to the King, an obligation to build and maintain a manor house on the seigneurial lands granted to the seigneur, a requirement to grant concessions to settlers on the seigneurial lands, the provision of a map of the seigneury, the making of reports to royal officials concerning the efforts made the seigneur to develop his seigneury, and to pay fees to the Crown for any alienation of the seigneury other than to the seigneur's direct heirs.

The settlers who received concessions to settle on a seigneury obtained the right to exercise the incidents of ownership while the legal title remained with the seigneur. The settlers, or concessionaires as they were known, were responsible for paying dues and rent to the seigneur, to provide free labour for defined periods of time during the course of a year, to use the seigneur's grist mill, and to pay fees to the seigneur for any alienation of the concessionaire's lands. Upon a failure by the concessionaire to pay the dues owed the lands held by the concessionaire could revert back to the seigneur's control. Although it was possible for a concessionaire to obtain a clear title to land under the French landholding system that was not a typical outcome in Canada. This rigid structure survived until the end of French colonial rule in Canada and beyond. The final abolition of the seigneurial system was not accomplished until 1854, long after the Sovereign of France had ceased to exercise any sovereignty over Canada.

Despite France's control of the heartland of Canada, Great Britain was able to establish itself in the American colonies south of Canada, to the north along Hudson's Bay, and in the littoral provinces of Newfoundland and Nova Scotia (excluding, for a time, Cape Breton Island). The long struggle for domination in North America between those two eighteenth-century world powers ended with the final collapse of the French monarchial regime in Canada under the pressures of the Seven Years War. With the capture of Quebec City in 1759, the military position of the state became untenable. The Canadian-born Governor General, Pierre de Rigaud, Marquis de Vaudreuil, was forced to capitulate to the British commanders at Montreal on September 8, 1760. In the *Capitulations* signed at Montreal the government sought to preserve the position of the inhabitants as subjects of the King of France by proposing that they should owe only a strict neutrality to the British Sovereign. To this the British commander did not agree, stipulating that the inhabitants of Canada would become the subjects of the King of Great Britain.[7]

1.2   The Monarchy in the British Colonial Period 1763-1867

For almost three years following the capitulation, Canada remained under British martial law. With the signing of the *Treaty of Paris* on February 10, 1763, all of Canada, except for the islands of St. Pierre and Miquelon off the coast of Newfoundland, was ceded by France to Great Britain and the Sovereign of France ceased to be the Sovereign of Canada from that date. Article 4 of the treaty provided that His Most Christian Majesty, the King of France, renounced all of his claims to Nova Scotia or Acadia and ceded Canada and all of its dependencies "with the sovereignty, property, possession and all rights acquired by treaty or otherwise" to the British Sovereign.[8]

The legal consequences of the cession were explained by Lord Atkinson in 1906, in *Attorney General of Canada v Cain*, [1906] AC 542 (Canada, JC) at 545:

> In 1763 Canada and all its dependencies, with the sovereignty, property, and possession, and all other rights which had at any time been held or acquired by the Crown of France, were ceded to Great Britain. Upon that event the Crown of England became possessed of all legislative and executive powers within the country so ceded to it, and, save so far as it has since parted with these powers by legislation, royal proclamation, or voluntary grant, it is still possessed of them.[9]

The Treaty of Paris was soon followed by the *Royal Proclamation of 1763*,[10] which was issued on October 7, 1763, and which established civilian government in Canada, including a provision for locally elected assemblies. The governmental structure established by the *Royal Proclamation 1763* provided for the Governor General to be advised by an executive council, and for an assembly authorized to make laws for the peace, welfare, and good government of the country. However, no assembly was ever summoned in Canada pursuant to the *Royal Proclamation 1763* because the Roman Catholic inhabitants of the country were unable, by reason of their faith, to swear the Protestant-based test oath which was then required by law.[11]

Between 1763 and 1774, Canada was administered by a Governor General who was assisted by an Executive Council consisting of the Lieutenant Governors of the district administrations at Montreal and Trois Rivières, the Chief Justice, the Surveyor General of Customs, and eight leading residents selected by the Governor General. However, a great deal of constitutional uncertainty remained as a result of the *Royal Proclamation, 1763*, not the least of which was the question of which system of law, French or English common law, was to apply in the country.

In 1774, with the approach of the American Revolution, the Imperial Parliament enacted the *British North America (Quebec) Act 1774*[12] which was designed to secure for Britain the favour of the largely Francophone inhabitants of Canada, and to obtain for the Imperial government some leverage against the public agitation which was then beginning to swell in the American colonies to south. Under the *Quebec Act*, the borders of Canada were radically extended to encompass large territories that the American colonists looked upon as virtually their own. The Canadian government was entrusted to the Governor General and an appointed Legislative Council of between 17 and 23 members, who were charged with making ordinances for the peace, welfare, and good government of the country. Roman Catholics were guaranteed the free exercise of their religion and were relieved of the requirement to take the test oath before assuming public office, although they were still required to take the oath of allegiance to the British Sovereign. The traditional Canadian law (*Coutume de Paris*) was confirmed as the civil law of the country, with the law of England supplying the country's public and criminal law.

The *Quebec Act* served one of its purposes admirably well. The Canadian population remained loyal to the British Sovereign during the Revolutionary War despite entreaties by both General Washington, the American commander in chief, and by the French naval commander. After the war and the resulting loss of the American colonies there was an influx into Canada of loyalist refugees, particularly into the western part of Quebec, which changed its demographic composition and led to agitation for a division of the country into Anglophone and Francophone components. That agitation led to the enactment by the Imperial Parliament of the *Constitutional Act 1791*[13] which separated Canada into two provinces, Lower Canada in the east, and Upper Canada in the west.

Like the littoral colonies of Nova Scotia, New Brunswick, Newfoundland, and Prince Edward Island, Lower and Upper Canada were granted representative government. Under representative government the administration of the country remained in the hands of the Sovereign, represented by the Governor General, who was advised by an appointed Executive Council. The Governor General also appointed the upper house of the Legislature, the Legislative Council, while a lower house, known as the Assembly, was popularly elected. A Lieutenant Governor appointed by the Governor General exercised the gubernatorial powers in Upper Canada.

At first, representative government brought a modicum of harmony to the British North American colonies. With the passage of time however, public tension and agitation erupted between the elected assemblies on the one hand, and the appointed Executive and Legislative Councils on the other, over the control of government finances and indeed of the government itself. Eventually rebellion broke out in both Lower and Upper Canada, although cooler heads prevented violence in the maritime provinces. It appeared that Canada might reprise the American colonial disaster of 60 years before, in which popular rebellion was the chosen means of compelling political change.

This time, however, the Imperial authorities were well served by Lord Durham, a statesman who was despatched in the aftermath of military suppression to investigate the causes of the rebellions and to report about them to Parliament. Dufferin, after a brief tour of duty as Governor General in Canada, prepared a report for the imperial authorities in which he laid down the foundations for responsible government in Canada.

Responsible government is that form of government in which the administration of the country is placed in the hands of the people's representatives – in other words a parliamentary democracy. The long and sometimes violent struggles between the British Sovereigns and the Parliaments of England and Great Britain had finally established responsible government as the bedrock principle for the conduct of the British government. Lord Durham now proposed that responsible government be extended to those colonial possessions of the United Kingdom which were capable of exercising it. Stating the case for responsible government in the colonies boldly, Lord Durham said:

> I know not how it is possible to secure harmony in any other way than by administering the government on those principles which have been found perfectly efficacious in Great Britain. I would not impair a single prerogative of the Crown; on the contrary, I believe that the interests of the people of these provinces require

the protection of prerogatives which have not hitherto been exercised. But the Crown must, on the other hand, submit to the necessary consequences of representative institutions; and if it has to carry on the government in unison with a representative body, it must consent to carry it on by means of those in whom that representative body has confidence.[14]

The Imperial Parliament received Lord Durham's report in 1839 but no action was immediately taken with respect to it. Nevertheless, it became a blueprint for constitutional development not only in Canada but in other British colonies which had been settled by migrants from Europe.

New Royal Instructions first issued to Nova Scotia's Governor Sir John Harvey but subsequently issued to all governors in British North America opened the way for a new democratic form of government by requiring the colonial governors to refrain from dismissing their ministers so long as the latter could command the confidence of the colonial assemblies.[15] Those instructions reflected what is perhaps the most significant development in Canadian constitutional history. By the late 1840s, the practice of responsible government became established throughout British North America.[16] Thus it became an accepted principle of Canadian constitutional law that the powers of monarchial government would be subject to the political control of the people's own representatives.

As a result of the initiation of responsible government political leaders acceptable to the population achieved positions of power and eminence from which they were able to shape the national destiny of the country. In the early 1860s those leaders, men such as John A. Macdonald and George Etienne Cartier, perceived the need for expansion into the Hudson's Bay Company's lands to the west and, being sensitive to the enormous economic and military might marshalled by the government of the United States in its civil war with the Confederate States of America, began to think of a broader Canadian confederation. At constitutional conferences held in Charlottetown, Quebec City, and finally London, England, in the mid 1860s, a constitution for a federated Canada was agreed upon.

In the spring of 1867, at the request of the representatives of the Canadian colonial possessions, the Imperial Parliament enacted the *British North America Act 1867*[17] which provided for the creation of a union of the British provinces in North America.

On July 1, 1867, Canada came into existence as a constitutional monarchy enjoying responsible government. Initially the country consisted of the provinces of Ontario, Quebec, New Brunswick, and Nova Scotia. Ruperts Land, previously held by the Hudson's Bay Company under a Royal Charter, was surrendered and transferred to Canada in 1869, and the province of Manitoba was severed from it and joined confederation in 1870, followed by British Columbia in 1871, Prince Edward Island in 1873, the Arctic island territories in 1880, Saskatchewan and Alberta in 1905, and finally Newfoundland and Labrador, which completed the Canadian union in 1949.

Although not exercising *de jure* independence from 1867, Canada rapidly developed into an autonomous state within the British Empire and became a model within the Commonwealth for the evolution of British possessions from colonial status to modern statehood.

1.3   The Reception of European law into the Law of Canada

Before discussing the constitutional foundations of the monarchy in Canada, it is desirable to explore the manner in which the laws of France, England, or of the United Kingdom were subsumed into Canadian law. Defined legal principles exist that provided for the transfer of European laws to Canada during in the colonial period. In particular, a number of Acts of the Parliaments of England, Great Britain or of the United Kingdom of Great Britain and Ireland, as well as the common law of England relating to the constitutional position of the monarchy, form part of the laws of Canada under the doctrine of reception. The basis of the reception doctrine is the theory that English settlers take with them the law of England when they settle an uninhabited country, and that the laws of England follow the military conquest of an inhabited country by British armies.[18] The Judicial Committee of the Privy Council, the highest court of appeal for British dependencies and some Commonwealth states, has noted with respect to settled colonies ". . . the common law rule by which the English law taken by the settlers is both the unwritten law (common law and equity) and the statute law in force at the time of settlement".[19] The body of English law that was transferred from England to a colony included those public and private laws that could apply in the colony but those English laws that were peculiar to specific localities in England, or were of a private nature, were not susceptible of transfer under the reception doctrine.

The transfer date for the laws of England to the laws of a British colony (the laws of Scotland or Ireland were never transferred) is commonly referred to as a reception date. Reception dates are sometimes fixed by the date of a colonial conquest, as in the case of Quebec, which received the English law of 1763 (although French civil law based on the *Coutoume de Paris* was subsequently restored by the terms of the *Quebec Act, 1774).* The restoration of French civil law by the *Quebec Act, 1774,* did not affect the reception of the English public or criminal law into the colony which occurred on October 7, 1763 (the date of the *Royal Proclamation, 1763).* The territory that eventually became Upper Canada, and later Ontario, formed with Lower Canada, or Quebec, a single colony between 1763 and 1791, and thus in 1774 Upper Canada received by statute the French civil law which prevailed prior to the cession of Canada to

Great Britain, as well as the English public and criminal law as it stood on October 7, 1763, under the reception doctrine. When the *Constitutional Act 1791* separated Ontario from Quebec, the first statute of the Legislature of what then became known as Upper Canada established October 15, 1792, as the reception date for the transfer of both the common and statute laws of England to Ontario.

In other situations, the courts have held that the date of the first meeting of the colonial legislature marks the date of the reception of the law of England into the laws of a colony. Thus Nova Scotia's reception date is October 3, 1758, Newfoundland's reception date is January 1, 1833, and British Columbia's reception date is November 19, 1858. New Brunswick should have a reception date of 1758, as it was annexed to and formed part of Nova Scotia after New Brunswick's cession by France in 1763, but curiously the New Brunswick Supreme Court, Appeal Division, ruled in *Scott v Scott* (1970), 15 DLR (3rd) 374 (New Brunswick, AD) that the reception date in New Brunswick is 1660, which was the date of the restoration of the monarchy in England following the English civil war.

Similarly, Prince Edward Island should have a reception date of 1758, as it too was annexed to Nova Scotia after the cession but other dates have been suggested.[20] Manitoba, Saskatchewan, Alberta, the Northwest Territories, the Yukon Territory and Nunavut all received the law of England as it stood on July 15, 1870, by Federal enactment in the case of the Saskatchewan, Alberta, and the territories, and by dual Federal and Manitoba enactments in the case of Manitoba.

English or British statute law of general application became part of the laws of Canada in one of two ways, either by an express enactment of the Imperial Parliament or by the reception of the laws of England. Thus, some enactments of the Parliaments of England and of the United Kingdom are applicable to Canada because of an express reference within those enactments to the royal dominions possessed by the Crown of England or Great Britain. Where such references are not made within a statute, the reception dates will nonetheless have the effect of importing English or British statutes into the laws of Canada if it is apparent on the face of those statutes that they were not merely local statutes, or statutes peculiar to metropolitan Britain, but were intended to be public acts binding throughout the empire. This is particularly true in the case of that branch of Canadian law relating to the monarchy, described as Crown Law. As Chief Justice Laskin noted in *Quebec North Shore Paper Company et al v Canadian Pacific Limited et al*, [1977] 2 SCR 1054 (Canada, SC) "It should be recalled that the law respecting the Crown came into Canada as part of the public or constitutional law of Great Britain . . .".

After the passage of a reception date however, no further imperial statutes applied to Canada unless the imperial statute was made expressly binding on Canada, or was made applicable to it by necessary implication. Furthermore, from a constitutional law perspective, autonomy almost amounting to a *de facto* independence was achieved by Canada in the years subsequent to Confederation in 1867, although *de jure* independence was not formally granted until the enactment by the Imperial Parliament of the *Statute of Westminster, 1931*[21]. Section 4 of that Act is instrumental with respect to the application of imperial laws to Canada, as it provided that no Act of the Imperial Parliament enacted after the *Statute of Westminster 1931* would be binding upon Canada unless it was expressly enacted by the Imperial Parliament that Canada had expressly requested and consented to the application of an imperial statute to Canada. The sole exception to that provision, made upon the request of Canada itself, was that any amendment to the *Constitution Act 1867* (then named the *British North America Act 1867*) would continue to take the form of an imperial Act. That exception recognized the elusiveness of an amending formula for the constitution that was acceptable to the provinces, and to the Federal Government. Thus, while the Imperial Parliament continued to retain exclusive jurisdiction to amend the *Constitution Act, 1867*, after 1931, in practice the Imperial Parliament only exercised that power at the request of Canada, thereby acknowledging the sovereignty of Canada with respect to its own constitution.

That state of affairs continued until the enactment of the *Canada Act*,[22] by the Parliament of the United Kingdom, which provided in section 2 for the *de jure* independence of Canada by stating that:

> No Act of the Parliament of the United Kingdom passed after the Constitution Act, 1982 comes into force shall extend to Canada as part of its law.

Therefore, from 1982 onwards, no Act of the Imperial Parliament can purport to extend or have any application to Canada as part of Canadian law. Although it is theoretically possible for the Parliament of the United Kingdom to repeal both the *Canada Act 1982* and the *Statute of Westminster 1931*, the House of Lords has said in connection with the prospect of a repeal of the *Statute of Westminster 1931*; ". . . the Imperial Parliament could, as a matter of abstract law, repeal or disregard s. 4 of the Statute. But that is theory and has no relation to realities"; *British Coal Corporation v The King*, [1935] AC 500 at 520 (England, HL).

Lord Denning M.R. adopted a similar view in *Blackburn v Attorney General*, [1971] 2 All ER 1381, at 1382 (England, CA):

> Take the Statute of Westminster 1931, which takes away the power of Parliament to legislate for the dominions. Can anyone imagine that Parliament could or would reverse that statute? Take the Acts which have granted independence to the dominions and territories overseas. Can anyone imagine that Parliament could or

would reverse those laws and take away their independence? Most clearly not. Freedom once given cannot be taken away. Legal theory must give way to practical politics.

Thus, even if the Imperial Parliament could be motivated to repeal the statutes by which *de jure* sovereignty and independence was granted to Canada, it seems certain that any repeal of those statutes would not be recognized by the courts of law in Canada. Therefore, it may be safely concluded that the future extension of the laws of the United Kingdom to Canada is not possible, under any realistically conceivable circumstances, except perhaps by way of persuasion.

1.4   The Canadian Constitution

The monarchy occupies a central place in the constitutional law of Canada, but in order to fully understand its position it is essential to devote some attention to the nature of Canada's constitutional framework.

The Canadian constitutional framework is a complex creation reflecting much about the history and political tensions of a country that in many respects resembles a transcontinental empire, containing diverse peoples and cultures within its borders with all of the cultural and regional tensions thereby entailed. Unlike some other countries, no single document or series of documents can encompass the whole constitution of Canada. At the present time the entirety of the Canadian constitutional framework can be said to consist of following components:

1) the written *Constitution of Canada* consisting of the *Canada Act*, the *Constitution Acts 1867-1982*, as amended, and including the statutes and orders set out in the Schedule to the *Constitution Act 1982*, together with any amendments thereto, which operate as an entrenched written constitution possessing supremacy over every other law of Canada;

2) the unwritten principles of the constitution of the United Kingdom, and the principles underlying English constitutional statutes, which are incorporated into the *Constitution Act, 1867*, through its preamble, which mandates that Canada shall have "a constitution similar in principle to that of the United Kingdom";[23]

3) imperial, federal or provincial laws that address constitutional subject-matter but which are not entrenched within the *Constitution Acts 1867 – 1982*, including imperial statutes forming part of Canadian law under the reception doctrine, or enacted with reference to Canada, as well as ordinary statutes enacted by the Parliament of Canada, or the legislatures of the provinces, which pertain to constitutional subject-matter;

4) the conventions, customs and usages of the constitution which are unwritten but consist of commonly understood and applied rules for governance that are accepted by those to whom responsibility for the conduct of the affairs of state is entrusted, and without which the constitution would be dysfunctional; and

5) certain elements of the common law, particularly those aspects which concern the status of the Sovereign and those which govern the relations between Sovereign and subject, as well as some branches of English law received under the reception doctrine that were not historically conceived to be part of the common law, such as the royal prerogative powers, the law of parliament, and the law of arms.

Much of the law, conventions, and traditions of the Canadian constitutional monarchy have evolved from the monarchy as it exists in the United Kingdom. Unlike the constitution of the United Kingdom however, the supremacy of the written constitution in Canada can and does alter the effects of constitutional statutes and conventions, as well as the common law, in a variety of ways.

Many amendments have been made to the written constitution since the enactment of the *Constitution Act, 1867*, the most important one being the *Constitution Act 1982*[24]. The latter Act is of particular importance, for a number of reasons that will arise later in this text. At this point however, it is worth noting that the *Constitution Act, 1982* provides for the supremacy of the written constitution (described as the *Constitution of Canada*) over the general statutory, common, and civil law[25] of the country. Section 52(1) of the *Constitution Act, 1982*, states:

> (1) The Constitution of Canada is the supreme law of Canada, and any law that is inconsistent with the provisions of the Constitution is, to the extent of the inconsistency, of no force or effect.

Therefore all law, the common and civil law, as well as all of the statutes which are not entrenched in the written constitution (including constitutional statues received into Canadian law from England, or the United Kingdom, constitutional statutes enacted by the Parliament of Canada or by the provincial legislatures, and all laws that emanate from the exercise of the Sovereign's Royal Prerogative powers) are subordinate to the *Constitution Acts 1867 – 1982*.

In order to apply the supremacy clause in section 52 of the *Constitution Act 1982* it was necessary to define what is meant by the expression *Constitution of Canada*. Subsection 52(2) of the *Constitution Act 1982* does that by stipulating that the *Constitution of Canada* includes the *British North America Act 1867* (now the *Constitution Act 1867*), a series of amendments to that Act that were enacted by the Parliament of the United Kingdom at Canada's request, as well as certain imperial orders-in-council. Several acts of the Imperial Parliament are also included, notably the *Statute of Westminster, 1931,* and any future amendments to any of the constitutional documents recited in the *Constitution Act, 1982,* all of which can be collectively cited as the *Constitution Acts 1867 – 1982,* are also included.[26]

The most important entrenched element of the Canadian constitutional framework from the perspective of the organization and administration of government in Canada is the *Constitution Act, 1867.* In the first clause of the preamble of that Act, and especially in its final phrase, there is a succinct declaration of an intention by the founders of the modern Canadian state to possess what is sometimes referred to as a Westminster style constitution. The preamble states:

> WHEREAS the Provinces of Canada, Nova Scotia and New Brunswick have expressed their Desire to be federally united into One Dominion under the Crown of the United Kingdom of Great Britain and Ireland with a Constitution similar in Principle to that of the United Kingdom . . .

That portion of the preamble reflects the desire of the founders to possess a particular form of monarchical government and it is through the preamble that many parts of the unwritten British Constitution, particularly those relating to constitutional conventions, were adopted as an integral part of the constitution of Canada; *Reference Re Resolution to Amend the Constitution,* [1981] 1 SCR 753, at 883 (Canada, SC)

The ninth section of the *Constitution Act, 1867,* is of particular importance for an understanding the Canadian monarchy. It states:

> The Executive Government and Authority of and over Canada is hereby declared to continue and be vested in the Queen.

The effect of these constitutional rules was to provide that the person who held the Throne of the United Kingdom of Great Britain and Ireland by virtue of the law of that kingdom at time of the confederation of the Canadian provinces became, by virtue of the *Constitution Act, 1867,* the Sovereign of Canada. The subsequent application of the laws of royal succession have continued to maintain the Canadian Throne in the line of the Sovereigns of the United Kingdom. Thus, the United Kingdom and Canada have preserved and maintained a common personal monarch, notwithstanding that through the evolution of Canadian constitutional independence they have become separate states, each legally and politically independent of the other.

Next in legal importance to the entrenched provisions of the written constitution are those statutes of England, the United Kingdom, Canada, and the provinces which are of a constitutional character but which are not entrenched in the

Constitution Acts 1867 – 1982. These include a substantial number of statutory provisions scattered through the statute books.

Although constitutional law statutes can have an important bearing on the role of the monarchy in Canadian constitutional law and practice, they may be readily altered by the Parliament of Canada, or by the legislatures of the provinces, wherever those bodies possess constitutional jurisdiction over the subject matter of these statutes. Thus, alterations of statutes of a constitutional character which are not entrenched in the *Constitution Acts 1867 – 1982* may be made without recourse to the complex amending formulas necessary to alter the written constitution itself.

1.5   Constitutional Principles

The *Constitution of Canada* can undergo evolutionary change over time. It is not a static document but has been compared to a living tree that can change in its particulars though not in its essential elements, as times change. The Judicial Committee of the Privy Council said as much in its landmark decision on the status of women in the *Constitution Act, 1867*, in the case of *Edwards et al v Canada (Attorney General)*, [1930] AC 124 (Canada, JC) commonly known as the Persons Case where Lord Sankey stated that:

> ". . . their Lordships do not think it right to apply rigidly to Canada of today the
> decisions and the reasons therefor which commended themselves, probably rightly,
> to those who had to apply the law in different circumstances, in different centuries,
> to countries in different stages of development."

This has led in more recent times to a reliance by the courts on constitutional principles as a source of constitutional law. Constitutional principles are derived from ". . . an understanding of the constitutional text itself, the historical context, and previous judicial interpretations of constitutional meaning".[27] The source of constitutional principles is found in the unwritten part of the *Constitution of Canada*, which flows into the written constitution itself through the preamble to the *Constitution Act, 1867*. The preamble mandates that Canada shall have a constitution similar in principle to the constitution of the United Kingdom, which itself is largely an unwritten constitution. Certain organizing principles or rules of the constitution have been held to have emerged from Canada's constitutional history, such as adherence to a democratic form of government, and government accountability, and these principles animate the structure of the written constitution; *Reference Re Secession of Quebec*, [1998] 2 SCR 217 (Canada, SC).

Constitutional principles may be legally binding on constitutional actors and unquestionably they serve an important purpose where they are used to enhance the interpretation and application of existing constitutional provisions, or to bridge a gap in the written text of the constitution by reference to historic constitutional experience. However, their inchoate form precludes them from supplanting or diminishing the principles of the *Constitution of Canada* that are reduced to written form.[28]

The importance of constitutional principle as a source of constitutional law has increased since the patriation of the written constitution by the *Canada Act, 1982*, because the supremacy clause of the written constitution excluded certain constitutional statutes that were inherited from England under the reception doctrine from the formal written constitution itself. Unlike, for example, New Zealand, which formally incorporated underlying English constitutional statutes within its constitutional framework during its constitutional patriation process,[29] Canada did not incorporate certain fundamental statutes of English constitutional law such as the *Magna Carta*, the *Petition of Right, 1627*, the *Bill of Rights, 1689* or the *Act of Settlement, 1701* into the *Constitution of Canada*. While these important constitutional statutes were received into Canadian law under the reception doctrine their exclusion from the formal description of the written constitution in section 52(2)(b) of the *Constitution Act, 1982*, means that they are not supreme over other laws. However, many of the principles expressed in the ancient English constitutional statutes remain vital to the Canadian constitutional framework.

Although the express words of section 52(2) of the *Constitution Act, 1982*, were inclusive, and thus provided an opening for the Supreme Court of Canada to include omitted historical constitutional statutes within the *Constitution of Canada* the Court has been reluctant to do so since the omission of those historic statutes could not have been inadvertent. Faced with a conundrum in cases such as *Reference Re Secession of Quebec*, [1998] 2 SCR 217 (Canada, SC) and *New Brunswick Broadcasting Company v Nova Scotia (Speaker of the House of Assembly)*, [1993] 1 SCR 319 (Canada, SC) the Court opted instead to derive underlying principles from those historic English constitutional statutes and to incorporate those principles into the *Constitution of Canada* through the preamble, which mandates that Canada shall have a constitution similar in principle to that of the United Kingdom. As a consequence, those underlying principles of British constitutional law can be applied via the supremacy clause to prevail over other, non-constitutional laws. Although in the final result it has produced a rather torturous intellectual process it is one that balanced a respect for the choices made by Parliament with the need to ensure constitutional continuity in Canada.

1.6 Constitutional Convention, Custom and Usage

In addition to the formal laws of the constitution, there exists another special component of the constitution, without which the constitution could not operate efficiently. That component consists of the conventions, customs, and usages of the constitution. These consist of unwritten rules that allow the constitution to function in a manner that is acceptable to the citizens of a democratic society. All forms of political organization may be considered to operate in accordance with at least some political conventions, and thus conventions, customs, and usages are not unique to a Westminster style constitutional structure. Nevertheless, they are of perhaps greater importance in a constitution of the Westminster model where so much of the constitutionalism emerged in unwritten form from conventions, customs, and political usages.

Of these three aspects of the constitution, the most important by far are conventions. A well-known description of the difference between a law and a convention was provided by Professor Dicey in his landmark work entitled *The Law of the Constitution* where he distinguished between a constitutional law, which is something that the courts of law will recognize and enforce, and constitutional conventions, which consist of maxims and practices of statecraft that regulate the conduct of state officials but which are not characterized as law, and which Professor Dicey equated with "constitutional morality".[30] A modern description of constitutional conventions was provided by Justice Shore of the Federal Court in *Conacher v. Canada (Prime Minister)* (2009), 311 DLR (4th) 678 (Canada, FC) (affd. *Conacher v. Canada (Prime Minister)* (2010), 320 DLR (4th) 530 (Canada, FCA):

> Constitutional Conventions are non-legal rules that modify the strict legal rights of political officeholders. They emerge through political usage and become political rules once the relevant officeholders view them as obligatory. As a result of their non-legal status, conventions, *per se*, have not been enforced by the courts and no legal sanction exists for their breach.[31]

In *Reference Re Resolution to Amend the Constitution*, a majority of the Supreme Court of Canada adopted the following characterization of conventions given by Chief Justice Freedman of Manitoba in the Manitoba Court of Appeal ((1981), 117 DLR (3d) 1 (Manitoba, CA)):

> Thus there is general agreement that a convention occupies a position somewhere in between a usage and custom on the one hand and a constitutional law on the other. There is general agreement that if one sought to fix that position with greater precision he would place convention nearer to law than to usage or custom.[32]

In the same case, the nature of the constitution of Canada as an amalgam of law, convention, custom and usage, and the particular importance of convention, was remarked upon by Justices Martland and Ritchie in an illustrative passage in their dissent:

> The constitution of Canada, as has been pointed out by the majority, is only in part written, i.e., contained in statutes which have the force of law and which include, in addition to the *British North America Act* the various other enactments which are

listed in the reasons of the majority. Another, and indeed highly important, part of the constitution has taken the form of custom and usage, adopting in large part the practices of the Parliament of the United Kingdom and adapting them to the federal nature of this country. These have evolved with time to form with the statutes referred to above and certain rules of the common law a constitution for Canada. This constitution depends then on statutes and common law rules which declare the law and have the force of law, and upon customs, usages and conventions developed in political science which, while not having the force of law in the sense that there is a legal enforcement process or sanction available for their breach, form a vital part of the constitution without which it would be incomplete and unable to serve its purpose.[33]

Today we can characterize the constitutional law of Canada as a system of fundamental or ultimate law, which is justiciable and enforceable by the courts in accordance with judicial process. Conventions, on the other hand, while parallel in constitutional importance to constitutional laws, consist of rules that are not justiciable, and which are not amenable to enforcement by the courts of law through judicial process. They depend for their observance on the willingness of state officials to follow them and, in default of that obedience, on the willingness of the electorate to insist upon the adherence of state officials to such constitutional conventions.

It might be thought absurd to the ordinary citizen that any constitutional rules would be beyond the purview of the courts of law, but as the majority of the Supreme Court of Canada explained, in *Reference Re Resolution to Amend the Constitution*, there are sound reasons why conventions are not justiciable. The Justices of the majority stated:

> The conventional rules of the constitution present one striking peculiarity. In contradistinction to the laws of the constitution, they are not enforced by the courts. One reason for this situation is that, unlike common law rules, conventions are not judge-made rules. They are not based on judicial precedents but on precedents established by the institutions of government themselves. Nor are they in the nature of statutory commands which it is the function and duty of the courts to obey and enforce. Furthermore, to enforce them would mean to administer some formal sanction when they are breached. But the legal system from which they are distinct does not contemplate formal sanctions for their breach.

> Perhaps the main reason why conventional rules cannot be enforced by the courts is that they are generally in conflict with the legal rules which they postulate and the courts are bound to enforce the legal rules. The conflict is not of a type which would entail the commission of any illegality. It results from the fact that legal rules create wide powers, discretions and rights which conventions prescribe should be exercised only in a limited manner if at all.[34]

Although the conventions of the constitution are non-justiciable, the courts do have the ability to recognize and define them, at least to the extent of the precision afforded by a judgment of law. In defining a convention, the Courts apply an objective test. The Supreme Court of Canada discussed this process in *Reference Re Resolution to Amend the Constitution* where the Court held that not only must there be precedents to establish a convention, and a recognition by state officials that they are subject to that constitutional convention but there must also be a rationale for that convention.

A further opportunity for the Supreme Court to refine the role of the courts of law when they are called upon to identify and define a convention arose in *Reference Re Objection To A Resolution To Amend The Constitution*, [1982] 2 SCR 793 (Canada, SC), another reference emanating from the patriation of the *Constitution of Canada* from the United Kingdom. In that case, the Court stated:

> It should be borne in mind however that conventional rules, although quite distinct from legal ones, are nevertheless to be distinguished from rules of morality, rules of expediency and subjective rules. Like legal rules, they are positive rules the existence of which has to be ascertained by reference to objective standards. In being asked to answer the question whether the convention did or did not exist, we are called upon to say whether or not the objective requirements for establishing a convention had been met. But we are in no way called upon to say whether it was desirable that the convention should or should not exist and no view is expressed on the matter.[35]

Later in that judgment, the Supreme Court opined that the key factor for determining whether a convention exists is the participation of the political actors in a conventional process. The Court stated:

> Recognition by the actors in the precedents is not only an essential element of conventions. In our opinion, it is the most important element since it is the normative one, the formal one which enables us unmistakably to distinguish a constitutional rule from a rule of convenience or from political expediency.[36]

While the violation of a convention may not be amenable to judicial process, in the sense that the courts of law would provide a remedy for a breach, a violation of a constitutional convention is nonetheless an unconstitutional act. It differs from a breach of constitutional law only in that the remedies available for a breach of a convention are to be found within the political domain as opposed to the judicial.

A convention can become justiciable if it is incorporated into statute law. Even then, the incorporation of a convention into statute law does not entrench a convention into constitutional law in the absence of a constitutional amendment. A statute codifying a convention retains its status as an ordinary statute which is subordinate to the *Constitution of Canada*; *Osborne v The Queen* (1991), 82 DLR (4th) 321 (Canada, SC).[37] However, such a statute is a constitutional statute, and therefore it becomes part of Canadian constitutional law, broadly defined, although it does not become part of the entrenched and supreme *Constitution of Canada* itself.

Conventions differ from law both in the manner in which they arise and by the fact that conventions are mutable. Old conventions may be discarded and new ones may arise depending upon the exigencies of the times.

Customs and usages in the constitution resemble conventions in that they too are non-justiciable. We are not concerned here with custom in the sense of customary law, but rather with customary constitutional practices. Custom and usage in the constitutional sphere represent established ways of performing a constitutional function. However, unlike conventions, state officials may not regard themselves as necessarily bound by a custom or usage. Thus, custom and usages are of much lesser importance than conventions in constitutional principle, although they do afford guidance in the form of precedents. They have an even greater propensity to change over time than do constitutional conventions. Like conventions, they may be recognized but will not be enforced by the courts of law.

1.7   The Conventions of Responsible Government

The Canadian constitutional monarchy operates through the constitutional conventions of responsible government, which means that the Sovereign reigns but does not rule. While the formal legitimacy of the state is vested in the Sovereign, and the Sovereign's representatives, the political legitimacy of the government is vested in the political party that can command a majority of the votes in the House of Commons on any matter that resolves itself into a question of the confidence of that legislative body. The primary constitutional conventions that are applicable to government in Canada are:

a)   The Sovereign's Representatives will only appoint members of a Ministry from among those persons who have been elected to Parliament or a provincial legislature. Exceptionally, Ministers may be appointed who are not members of a legislative body provided that they seek and obtain a seat in Parliament or a provincial legislature at the earliest opportunity;[38]

b)   The Sovereign's Representative will only appoint and retain a Ministry that is capable of demonstrating that it has the confidence of the House of Commons or of a provincial legislature;

c)   The Sovereign or the Sovereign's Representatives will formally act in relation to matters of state only upon the advice of a ministry that commands the confidence of Parliament or a provincial legislature;

d)   Cabinet Ministers will share collective responsibility for sustaining a ministry in Parliament or a provincial legislature and any Ministers who are outside Cabinet must support the decisions taken by Cabinet Ministers; and

e)   A ministry that has lost the confidence of the House of Commons or a provincial legislature (or has been unable to obtain its confidence upon meeting the legislative body following a general election) must resign to allow a new ministry to be formed or must ask the Sovereign's Representative to dissolve the legislative body and call a new election.

The convention of responsible government is acknowledged in the *Constitution of Canada* by section 13 of the *Constitution Act, 1867,* which makes it clear that the monarchy cannot operate independently of a Canadian Ministry that can command the loyalty of an elected Parliament. Section 13 provides a rule for interpreting the role of the Sovereign's representative in Canada by stating:

> The Provisions of this Act referring to the Governor General in Council shall be construed as referring to the Governor General acting by and with the Advice of the Queen's Privy Council for Canada.

The operative element of the Privy Council in Canada is that portion of its membership that consists of the current Ministers of the Crown and therefore the interpretative rule set out in section 13 essentially confirms that actions taken in the name of the Governor General will be the political responsibility of the current Canadian Ministry.

Essentially, under a system of responsible government there is a constitutional division between what the English essayist Walter Bagehot described as the dignified and the efficient components of the constitution, or in more modern language, its formal and the substantive elements. The constitutional monarchy represents the dignified or formal aspect of the constitution. Thus the legal powers of the realm are vested in the Sovereign who provides constitutional legitimacy but the Sovereign and the Sovereign's representatives are not responsible for the exercise of those powers. Rather, constitutional advisors selected through a democratic election process are clothed with the political legitimacy necessary to make the requisite substantive or "efficient" decisions on behalf of the Sovereign. Under a system of responsible government the Sovereign and the Sovereign's representatives only act on the formal advice of constitutional advisors selected through a democratic election process. The result is a system of government that marries the constitutional legitimacy of the monarch with the political legitimacy of the democratically elected government. The only exception to the principle that the Sovereign and the Sovereign's representatives act on the advice of their democratically elected constitutional advisors concerns the rare exercise of the reserve powers. In that case the elected officials cannot give advice to the Sovereign or to the Sovereign's representatives because they would, in most circumstances, be in a self-serving position if they attempted to do so.

Responsible government is government by convention under which the legal powers that are vested in the Sovereign and the Sovereign's representatives in Canada are actually exercised by elected officials upon whose advice the Sovereign and Sovereign's representatives alone will act. These principles of responsible government enter the Canadian constitution through the preamble to the *Constitution Act, 1867*, which expresses the national desire for "a Constitution similar in Principle to that of the United Kingdom". Because the principles of responsible government are based on conventions rather than laws however, they are not by themselves entrenched and supreme principles that are capable of application by the courts. They remain political principles around which Canadian government is organized by the constitutional actors. Nevertheless, despite the fact that constitutional conventions are not law in the traditional sense, they can be partially protected by constitutional law. In *Public Service Employees Union v Ontario (Attorney General)*, [1987] 2 SCR 2 (Canada, SC) the Supreme Court considered that despite the exposure of convention to potential legislation the fact that certain legal powers were constitutionally entrenched offered a measure of constitutional protection to the principles of responsible government. Justice Beetz stated:

> Thus it is uncertain, to say the least, that a province could touch upon the power of the Lieutenant Governor to dissolve the legislature, or his power to appoint and dismiss ministers, without unconstitutionally touching his office itself. The principle of responsible government could, to the extent that it depends on those important royal powers, be entrenched to a substantial extent.

[1] See *Calder v Attorney General of British Columbia* (1973), 34 DLR (3d) 145 (Canada, SC) and in particular the landmark judgment of Justice Hall, who relied on earlier judgments by Chief Justice Marshall of the United States in *Johnson and Graham's Lessee v M'Intosh* (1823), 21 US 240 and *Worcester v State of Georgia* (1832), 31 US 530.

[2] *Manual of the Constitutional History of Canada*, Sir J G Bourinot, Toronto, Copp Clark, 1901, at page 5 (afterwards *"Bourinot"*)

[3] *Bourinot*, p.2

[4] Prior to the revocation of a Royal Charter in 1675, some nominations to the Conseil were also made by another chartered trading company known as the West Indies Company, see *Bourinot*, at page 3.

[5] *Beddoe's Canadian Heraldry*, Alan Beddoe (rev. by Strome Galloway), Belleville (Ont.), Mika Publishing, 1981, at page 44 (afterwards *"Beddoe"*)

[6] *The Illustrated History of Canada,* Craig Brown, ed., Lester & Orpen Dennys, Toronto, 1987, at page 162 (afterwards *"Illustrated History"*)

[7] *British North America Acts and Selected Statutes,* Maurice Ollivier Q.C., Queen's Printer and Controller of Stationary, Ottawa, 1962, at page 12 (afterwards *"Ollivier"*)

[8] *Documents of the Canadian Constitution 1759-1915,* W P M Kennedy, Oxford University Press, Toronto, 1918, at page 15 (afterwards *"Kennedy"*)

[9] The Crown in the Parliament of the United Kingdom abdicated its remaining powers over Canada by section 2 of the *Canada Act 1982,* c. 11 (UK).

[10] RSC 1985, Appendix, No. 1

[11] The test oath originated in an Imperial statute which required adherence to the established protestant Church of England. Practising Roman Catholics could not subscribe to that oath in good conscience.

[12] 14 Geo. III, c. 83, Imp.; RSC 1985, Appendix, no. 2.

[13] 31 Geo III, c. 31; RSC 1985, Appendix, no. 3 (Imp.).

[14] Quoted in *Bourinot,* p. 25, n.1.

[15] *The Pax Britannica Trilogy; Heavens Command, An Imperial Progress,* James Morris, The Folio Society, London, 1992, at pages 116-117 (afterwards *"Morris"*).

[16] In the Province of Canada responsible government was established from the commencement of the governorship of Lord Elgin in 1847.

[17] 30 & 31 Vic. c. 3 (Imp.) [now the *Constitution Act, 1867* (RSC 1985, Appendix, no. 5)].

[18] *Campbell v Hall* (1774), 1 Cowp. 204; *Bancoult v Secretary of State (Foreign and Commonwealth Affairs),* [2008] 5 LRC 769 (England, HL)

[19] *Christian et al v R,* [2007] 1 LRC 726 (Pitcairn Islands, JC) Per Lord Hope at 755.

[20] viz. 1763 – see *The British Tradition in Canadian Law,* Bora Laskin, Stevens and Sons, London, 1969, at page 6 (afterwards *"Laskin"*)

[21] 22 Geo. V, c. 4 (Imp.).

[22] 1982 c. 11 (UK).

[23] *New Brunswick Broadcasting Company v Nova Scotia (Speaker of the House of Assembly)*, [1993] 1 SCR 319 (Canada, SC) per McLachlin J: ". . . it is clear that, absent specific reference, the wording of the preamble should not be understood to refer to a specific article of the English *Bill of Rights*. This is not to say that principles underlying art. 9 of the English *Bill of Rights* of 1689 do not form part of our law and inform our understanding of the appropriate relationship between the courts and legislative bodies in Canada: *Reference re Resolution to Amend the Constitution*, [1981] 1 SCR 753, at p. 785."

[24] RSC 1985, App. II, No. 44.

[25] The reference to civil law in this context is to the civil law system applied in the Province of Quebec.

[26] In this text the expression *"Constitution of Canada"* refers to the written constitution defined by section 52 of the *Constitution Act, 1982* and the expressions "Canadian constitution" or "the constitution" refer more generally to both the written constitution defined by section 52 and non-entrenched constitutional statutes, common law, convention, practice and usage.

[27] *Reference Re Secession of Quebec*, [1998] 2 SCR 217 at para. 32 (Canada, SC)

[28] For a discussion of constitutional principle and the risks of a too dramatic adoption of constitutional principles as a source of constitutional law see Newman, Warren J., *Grand Entrance Hall, Back Door or Foundation Stone? The Role of Constitutional Principles in Construing and Applying the Constitution of Canada*, (2001), 14 SCLR (2d) 197.

[29] The *Imperial Laws Application Act, 1988* of New Zealand formally incorporated English statutes such as the *Magna Carta*, 1297, the *Bill of Rights, 1689* and the *Act of Settlement 1701* into New Zealand constitutional law.

[30] *Introduction to the Study of the Law of the Constitution*, A V Dicey, Liberty Classics, Indianapolis, 1982 (reprint of the eighth edition, at page cxl (afterwards *"Dicey"*).

[31] at para. 11.

[32] at pp. 13-14.

[33] at p. 852.

[34] at p. 880.

[35] at p. 803.

[36] at p. 816.

[37] ". . . statutes embodying constitutional conventions do not automatically become entrenched ... but retain their status as ordinary statutes" per Sopinka, J.

[38] In 1945, the Defence Minister, General Andrew McNaughton, was appointed without holding a seat in the House of Commons and thereafter he twice unsuccessfully sought election, to the House of Commons. Unable to secure a seat, he resigned as a Minister in August, 1945.

THE MONARCHY IN LEGAL THEORY

2.1   The Legal Personality of the Sovereign

At common law the Sovereign is both a natural person and a body politic, or a corporation sole as it is described in more modern legal usage. In the sixteenth century, the writer Plowden said that the King had in him:

> a body natural and a body politic together indivisible, and these two bodies are incorporated in one person and make one body and not divers, that is, the body corporate in the body natural et e contra the body natural in the body corporate . . . [1]

Under a theory developed in the common law during the medieval period, it was the Sovereign's politic or corporate personage which contained the office, government, and royal majesty of the Sovereign. When combined with the natural personage of the man or woman on the Throne the corporate element magnified the natural personage of the monarch.

By the time of *Calvin's Case* (1608), 7 Co. Rep. 1a, the common law had fully incorporated the theory of the Sovereign's duality. The court in that case stated:

> It is true that the King hath two capacities in him; one a natural body, being descended of the blood royal of the realm; and this body is of the creation of Almighty God, and is subject to death, infirmity, and such like; the other is a politic body or capacity, so called, because it is formed by the policy of man and in this capacity the King is esteemed to be immortal, invincible, not subject to death, infirmity, infancy, nonage etc . . . [2]

The principles espoused in that case have continued to resound in Canadian law. In *Attorney General of Quebec v Labrecque*, [1980] 2 SCR 1057 (Canada, SC) Justice Beetz took note of the difference between the twin aspects of the Sovereign's existence, and how that duality provided the executive component of government with an ability to use the agency of a natural person, recognized by the common law, to carry out many of the functions of government, including entering into contracts. Justice Beetz stated:

> It is also important to note that in Anglo-Canadian law, the relationship between a civil servant and his employer is not, strictly speaking, a relationship with an abstract being, the State: it is a relationship with a relatively concrete entity, the Crown, which "personifies the State," . . . The Crown is also the Sovereign, a

physical person who, in addition to the prerogative, enjoys a general capacity to contract in accordance with the rule of ordinary law. This general capacity to contract, like the prerogative, is also one of the attributes of the Crown in right of a province.[3]

The union of the Sovereign's natural body and the body politic leads to a proposition that, in law, the Sovereign never dies.[4] As a body politic, or corporate, the Sovereign is said to be perpetual, and for this reason any reference to the Sovereign in statute law includes all those persons who subsequently succeed to the throne.

As a perpetual body politic, the Sovereign is a non-statutory corporation sole, as well as a natural person; *Madras Electric Supply Corporation v Boarland*, [1955] AC 667 (England HL). In the modern law, a corporation sole at common law is a natural person who also possesses an artificial legal personality. The position of the Sovereign as a non-statutory corporation sole thus permits those acting under her authority to do whatever things a natural person might do, including entering into contracts without specific authority.

The Sovereign possesses all of the capacities applicable to a natural-born person under Canadian law. In *J.E. Verreault & Fils Ltée v Attorney General of Quebec*, [1977] 1 SCR 41 (Canada, SC), Justice Pigeon of the Supreme Court of Canada acknowledged that the Sovereign was a natural person subject to the ordinary civil law of Quebec in the following words:

> Her Majesty is clearly a physical person, and I know of no principle on the basis of which the general rules of mandate, including apparent mandate, would not be applicable to her.[5]

Sometimes confusion has occurred concerning whether a royal act was performed in the exercise of the Sovereign's natural capacity, or in the capacity of the Sovereign's corporate capacity. In *Smith v Attorney General (Canada)* (1977), 81 DLR (3d) 324 (Canada, FC) it was alleged that portions of Canada (primarily contained within the Yukon Territory) that had been surrendered by France pursuant to the Treaty of Paris in 1763 were acquired by the Sovereign in his natural capacity, rather than in his political, or corporate capacity. However, Justice Mahoney found that the lands had been ceded by the Sovereign of France to the Sovereign of Great Britain and had been received by the latter Sovereign in his corporate capacity, stating:

> . . . the basic proposition that the reigning Monarch's relationship to overseas territorial acquisitions was in a private, rather than an official, capacity during and after the 18th century is unsupportable. If one accepts that the land in question was ceded by the Treaty of Paris, 1763 then it plainly was acquired by conquest. That being so, among the propositions which Lord Mansfield held, in *Campbell v Hall*

(1774), 1 Cowp. 204 at p. 208, 98 E.R. 1045 at p. 1047, to be "too clear to be controverted", the following is particularly pertinent:

> "A country conquered by the British arms becomes a dominion of the King in the right of his Crown; and, therefore, necessarily subject to the Legislature, the Parliament of Great Britain."

> ... If, as appears most probable, the land now within the Yukon Territory became British by settlement, it was at a time when the Monarch did not, by the law of England, exercise sovereignty over England in the personal or private, as opposed to institutional, capacity which the Plaintiff seeks to ascribe to the Crown's sovereignty over the territory in issue.[6]

Case authority also holds that of the two capacities, the natural body and the body corporate, it is the latter which is the greater of the two, and which magnifies the natural body. In the *Duchy of Lancaster Case*, [1558-1774] All ER Rep 146 (England, Assembly of Judges and Others) it was said that:

> ... yet to this natural body is conjoined his body politic, which contains his royal estate and dignity, and the body politic includes the body natural, but the body natural is the lesser, and with this the body politic is consolidated. So that he has a body natural, adorned and invested with the estate and dignity royal, and he has not a body natural distinct and divided by itself from the office and dignity royal, but a body natural and a body politic together indivisible, and these two bodies are incorporate into one person, and make one body and not divers ... [7]

Royal privileges and prerogatives apply to the Sovereign in both the Sovereign's corporate and natural capacities. However, as discussed earlier, the prerogatives and privileges attaching to the Sovereign in the political or corporate capacity are the greater of the two and subsume the frailties of the Sovereign's natural capacity. That has, in turn, required the creation of certain legal fictions surrounding the position of the Sovereign.

Thus, it became a central legal fiction of our system of constitutional law that the Sovereign never dies. Nor is the Sovereign ever a minor under the law. The Sovereign's lack of a minority was settled as long ago as 1561-62, in the *Duchy of Lancaster Case* in which it was held that a lease of lands granted by the child-King Edward VI could not be defeated by his lack of majority. The issue in that case turned upon the relationship between the natural body and the body politic or corporate with the court finding that:

> ... the King has in him two bodies, *viz.*, a body natural, and a body politic. His body natural (if it be considered in itself) is a body mortal, subject to all infirmities that come by nature or accident, to the imbecility of infancy or old age, and to the like defects that happen to the natural bodies of other people. But his body politic is a body that cannot be seen or handled, consisting of policy and government and constituted for the direction of the people and the management of the public weal, and this body is utterly void of infancy and old age, and other natural defects and

imbecilities, which the body natural is subject to, and for this cause what the King does in his body politic cannot be invalidated or frustrated by any disability in his natural body. Therefore, his letters-patent, which give authority or jurisdiction, or which give lands or tenements that he has as King shall not be avoided by reason of his nonage.[8]

It is another fiction of our constitutional law that the Sovereign is perfect and can do no wrong. By reason of that fiction the Sovereign's person was immune from all suits or actions at common law.[9] That is also one basis for the constitutional convention that the Sovereign's public acts must be performed on the advice of constitutional advisors (i.e., the members of the Queen's Privy Council for Canada). It is those advisors alone who may be held accountable for any improper act performed in the name of the Sovereign.

2.2   The Sovereign as a Divisible Legal Entity

The subject of the divisibility of the Crown is important for an understanding of Canada's evolution to independence from its former status as a British colonial possession. It is also important in order to understand the relationship between the several monarchies within the Commonwealth that share the same personal Sovereign as well as to understand the nature of the monarchy within the Canadian federation. In this topic we are concerned with the divisibility of the Sovereign's body corporate as only one natural person can be the Sovereign in Canada, the Canadian provinces, and in the territories of the Sovereign's other realms beyond the seas. We turn first to the divisibility of the Sovereign in international relations, and Canada's ascension to independent membership in the family of nations.

2.3   Divisibility of the Sovereign in International Relations

After Confederation in 1867, the Sovereign continued to be perceived both internally and externally as indivisible within the Empire. With the passage of years, a growing maturity and self-confidence accrued to Canada and as a self-governing state it was joined in that status by other parts of the Empire, notably Australia, New Zealand, Newfoundland, and the Union of South Africa. However, despite the fact that a small external affairs function was created in Canada in 1909, as an adjunct to the office of the Secretary of State and subsequently the Prime Minister's office,[10] Canada's foreign relations continued to be administered by the United Kingdom. When Britain entered the First World War on August 4, 1914, Canada and the other self-governing states within the Empire automatically went to war as well. The indivisibility of the Sovereign precluded the attribution of an international personality necessary for the Sovereign in right of Canada to take political actions distinct from those of the Sovereign in right of the United Kingdom.

The issue of the potential for the legal and political divisibility of the Sovereign within the Empire came to the fore in the aftermath of the First World War, a war which saw Canada and the other self-governing states play a significant role. Despite their contributions to the war effort however, Canada and the other self-governing states, in what was now beginning to be described as the British Commonwealth, were perceived by the nations at the Versailles Peace Conference and by the world at large to be subject to the sovereignty of the United Kingdom and therefore lacking an independent international legal personality although it was recognized that each of the self-governing states within the British Empire enjoyed internal self-government. Canada, Australia, New Zealand, and South Africa were permitted to sign the Versailles Peace Treaty in an order that immediately followed the signatures made on behalf of the United Kingdom but only in the capacity of states which ultimately remained subordinate to the sovereignty of the United Kingdom.[11]

The war had brought a new stature to Canada while at the same time the United Kingdom's will to maintain the empire was diminished by the sheer political, financial, and human effort required to successfully prosecute four long years of war against the Central Powers. Those factors combined to present Canada with an opportunity for the Canadian realm to assert its divisibility from other realms within the British Commonwealth, and thus to establish a right to its own international legal personality.

The achievement of a divisible Sovereign in the international context (which we can equate with the recognition by the international community of the formal independence of the Canadian state) was evolutionary. The Supreme Court of Canada has said, in the *Reference Re Offshore Mineral Rights of British Columbia*, [1967] SCR 792 (Canada, SC) that; "There can be no doubt now that Canada has become a sovereign state. Its sovereignty was acquired in the period between its separate signature of the Treaty of Versailles in 1919 and the Statute of Westminster [in 1931]".[12] There was however, no clean break between Canada's subordination to the Sovereign of the United Kingdom and the establishment of an independent Sovereign of Canada. For instance, in 1923-24, Canada negotiated and signed its first international treaty with a foreign power without the assistance of the imperial power (the Halibut Fishing Treaty with the United States of America) although in the same year the United Kingdom concluded World War One hostilities with Turkey, the successor state to the Ottoman Empire, by signing the Treaty of Lausanne on behalf of itself and the constituent parts of the British Empire and Commonwealth, including Canada.

The evolutionary development of Canada's international personality reached a tipping point in the Imperial Conference of 1926 and resulted in the Balfour Declaration, which recognized the divisibility of the Sovereign in the international and intra-Commonwealth arenas, and allowed for the creation of international legal personalities in the self-governing states which remained in the Commonwealth. The conference recognized that the self-governing realms were:

> . . . autonomous Communities within the British Empire, equal in status, in no way subordinate one to another in any aspect of their domestic or external affairs, though united by a common allegiance to the Crown, and freely associated as members of the British Commonwealth of Nations.[13]

That conference also recognized that in the future the Governors General of Canada (as well as those of the other self-governing states) should report directly to the Sovereign rather than to the British Secretary of State for the Dominions. In effect, the Governors General ceased from that point onwards to be regarded as an officer of the Imperial Government.

The Balfour Declaration is particularly striking in one other respect; neither the Imperial Parliament nor the Parliaments of the self-governing states were consulted about it. Rather, it arose as a result of a Commonwealth constitutional convention. Yet it recognized the *de facto* political independence of the self-governing states within the Commonwealth and their evolution into international statehood. After the Balfour Declaration Canada became competent to enter into treaties with foreign states and to use its own royal seals for their authentication.

As the evolution of a divisible Sovereign occurred, Canada began to send its first ambassadors abroad, initially to Washington, Paris and Tokyo in 1926.[14] Diplomatic recognition of an international legal personality for the realm of Canada helped mark the evolution of Canada from a colony of Great Britain into an independent state, a status which was formally recognized in constitutional law in 1931, with the passage of the *Statute of Westminster, 1931.* That Act capped the independence of Canada by ending the jurisdiction of the British Parliament over Canada except in cases where Canada expressly requested and consented to the application to Canada of legislation enacted by the Parliament of the United Kingdom. Through the *Statute of Westminster, 1931* the Parliament of Canada obtained the power to enact laws having an extraterritorial effect, one of the basic characteristics of a state with an international legal personality.

Ironically, Canadians themselves were somewhat ambivalent about their new status. Thus, when the Second World War broke out in September 1939, many Canadians still seemed unsure about whether Canada automatically became a belligerent when the United Kingdom declared war on Germany on September 3, 1939. Unlike the situation in 1914 however, the British declaration of war on September 3, 1939, did not mean that Canada was also at war. One author has suggested that it was a personal act of President Franklin Roosevelt which may have spurred Canada's separate declaration of war on September 10, 1939.[15]

The most interesting example of the development of an international legal personality provided by the self-governing members of the British Commonwealth was that of Eire, the Irish Free State, which remained neutral during the Second World War. An Irish Charge d'affaires remained at his post in Berlin as his country's diplomatic representative throughout the war. His credentials to the German government continued to stand in the name of King George VI, who was then at war with Germany in each of his other sovereign capacities. These wartime distinctions, more than any other factors, illustrated the divisibility of the Sovereign in external relations.

2.4   Divisibility of the Sovereign and the Commonwealth

As a parallel development to the establishment of an international status for Canada and the other self-governing countries within the Commonwealth, the common law began to recognize distinctions in respect of the Crown within the British Commonwealth. Historically, the Sovereign was considered to be indivisible throughout the Empire.[16] However, in *Attorney General v Great Southern and Western Railway Company of Ireland*, [1925] AC 754 (England, HL) an issue arose concerning responsibility for a contractual obligation entered into by the Imperial Government during wartime. The House of Lords held that the creation of the Irish Free State as one of His Majesty's dominions transferred the liability of the Crown, with respect to a contract to restore rail facilities from the King in right of the United Kingdom to the King in right of the Irish Free State. Lord Phillimore stated:

> The property of the Crown in the Dominion is held for the purposes of that Dominion. Its benefits accrue to the Dominion Exchequer, and liabilities in connection with it must be discharged out of the same Exchequer. His Majesty has separate Attorney-Generals to sue and be sued in respect of each Dominion.[17]

The position advanced by the House of Lords in the *Great Southern and Western Railway Company of Ireland* case was subsequently echoed by the High Court of Australia in *Faithorn v The Territory of Papua* (1938), 60 CLR 772 (Australia, HC), which involved a wrongful dismissal suit by a public servant. The plaintiff had been employed by the government of the Territory of Papua, a state occupying the southeastern portion of the island of New Guinea, which was then a colonial dependency of Australia.

At issue was whether the Australian government or the government of the Territory of Papua was the proper defendant in the action. A majority of the Justices, led by Justice Dixon, found that the Territory of Papua rather than the

Commonwealth of Australia was the proper defendant in the action and applied the principle from *Great Southern and Western Railway Company of Ireland.*

Justice Dixon echoed his opinion respecting the divisibility of the Crown in the subsequent case of *The Federal Commissioner of Taxation v E.O. Farley Limited,* [1940] 63 CLR 278 (Australia, HC). His observations in that case concerned the application of the prerogative right of the Crown to priority in debt, over the debts due to a subject, following the liquidation of assets. According to Justice Dixon:

> It is not in accordance with the division of the Empire into separate polities that a prerogative of government affecting the treasury of one part of the Empire should be exercisable in another part and, moreover, exercisable to the prejudice of the citizens of that other part. The right of priority is one affecting the revenues and ingatherings of the Crown in right of the dominion. On the corresponding side of liabilities and expenditures there is no doubt that the strictest separation is necessary.18]

This approach to the question of the divisibility of the Sovereign within the Empire and Commonwealth has continued to be applied both in the United Kingdom and elsewhere in the Commonwealth. In *R v Secretary of State; Ex Parte Bhurosah,* [1967] 3 All ER 831 (England, CA) an issue arose concerning the citizenship of certain Mauritians as a result of a grant of passports to them by the Governor of Mauritius under an exercise of a Royal Prerogative power. The passports bore the Royal Arms of the United Kingdom and a request by the Governor, in the name of Her Majesty the Queen, that the bearers be allowed to pass freely. The Court of Appeal found that the issuance of the passports in Mauritius did not amount to a recognition of British citizenship in the bearer. The Court found that the passports were issued by the Queen of Mauritius, not by the Queen of the United Kingdom.

Finally, and in relation to Canada, the issue of the divisibility of the Crown within the Commonwealth arose in the early 1980s, in the context of the patriation of the *Constitution of Canada* from the United Kingdom. A number of aboriginal groups, concerned about the impact of patriation on their status in Canada, and mindful of the historic obligations of the Crown in relation to the aboriginal peoples, sought declarations that treaty obligations between the aboriginal peoples and the Crown remained obligations of Her Majesty in right of the United Kingdom. In *R v Secretary of State for Foreign and Commonwealth Affairs, ex parte Indian Association of Alberta,* [1982] 2 All ER 118 (England, CA) Lord Denning M.R. stated:

> Hitherto I have said that in constitutional law the Crown was single and indivisible. But that law was changed in the first half of this century, not by statute, but by constitutional usage and practice. The Crown became separate and divisible, according to the particular territory in which it was sovereign. This was recognized by the Imperial Conference of 1926.[19]

Lord Denning's judgment relied upon the *Bhurosah* and *Mellenger*[20] cases in concluding that ". . . obligations which were previously binding on the Crown simpliciter are now to be treated as divided. They are to be applied to the dominion or province or territory to which they relate: and confined to it". In denying leave to appeal from that judgement the House of Lords, per Lord Diplock, confirmed the view expressed by the Court of Appeal, stating: ". . . any obligations of the Crown in respect of the Indian peoples of Canada are . . . the responsibility of Her Majesty's Government in Canada, and it is the Canadian courts . . . that alone have jurisdiction to determine what those obligations are."[21] The law throughout the Commonwealth on this point is now clear; the Sovereign is divisible within the various national territories over which she exercises sovereign rights.[22]

2.5   Divisibility of the Sovereign Within Canada

As we have seen, convention recognized the external divisibility of the Sovereign for the purposes of international relations. The common law also came to recognize the divisibility of the Sovereign within the Commonwealth, between those several countries for whom the Sovereign is head of state. However, within the Canadian federation the divisibility of the Crown has not received an identical constitutional recognition.

For instance, cases involving Crown rights in respect of real property have shown that while the legal title to public lands is always vested in Her Majesty the Queen, the beneficial interest in those lands will depend upon the application of the *Constitution Act 1867*, or, more commonly, on administrative arrangements entered into between the federal and provincial governments by statute or order-in-council; *St. Catherine's Milling and Lumber Company v The Queen*, [1888] 14 AC 46 (Canada, JC); *Ontario Mining Company et al v Seybold et al*, [1903] AC 73 (Canada, JC); *Burrard Power Company v The King*, [1911] AC 87 (Canada, JC); *Attorney General of Canada v Western Higbie and Albion Investments Ltd.*, [1945] SCR 385 (Canada, SC).

The case of *In Re Silver Brothers Limited*, [1932] AC 514 (Canada, JC) provides an instructive example of the indivisibility of the Sovereign in her domestic capacity. That case concerned Crown debts and the existence of both federal and provincial legislation, each providing for a privileged ranking of Crown debts before the debts of other creditors in bankruptcy. His Majesty in right of Canada and His Majesty in right of Quebec claimed priority in debt but there were insufficient funds available to satisfy both claims. Much turned on the provisions of the *Interpretation Act*,[23] which did not differentiate between the Crown in right of Canada and the Crown in right of a Province. However the Judicial Committee of the Privy Council, in ruling that the priority of the two Crown debts must run *pari passu*, made this observation about the divisibility of the Crown within Canada:

> It is true that there is only one Crown, but as regards Crown revenues and Crown property by legislation assented to by the Crown there is a distinction made between the revenues and property in the Province and the revenues and property in the Dominion. There are two separate statutory purses. In each the ingathering and expending authority is different.[24]

Although the Judicial Committee appeared to be taking a view similar to the view espoused by the House of Lords in the case of *AG v Great Southern and Western Railway Co. of Ireland*, in actual fact the Judicial Committee was careful to maintain the lack of legal distinctiveness between the Crown in right of Canada and the Crown in right of a province. Although the reader might consider that a division of the Sovereign for legal purposes within Canada would be a natural outgrowth and constitutional effect of federalism, the concept of an indivisible Crown within Canada has been largely maintained in Canadian jurisprudence.

In *The Queen v Canadian Transport Commission*, [1978] 1 SCR 61 (Canada SC) the Supreme Court wrestled with the question of whether Her Majesty in Right of the Province of Alberta was bound by the provisions of the *Aeronautics Act*,[25] and the *Air Carrier Regulations*[26] promulgated thereunder, which required that notice be given to a regulatory commission upon any change in control of a licensed air carrier. The Act was not binding upon the Sovereign and at common law the Sovereign could not be bound except by an express provision, or where it was clear by necessary implication from the statute that the intention of the legislature was to bind the Sovereign to the provisions of the statute. The province relied on the common law principle while the Federal Government took the view that the definition of "Her Majesty" in the *Interpretation Act*[27] was confined to Her Majesty in right of Canada, to the exclusion of Her Majesty in right of a Province.

The Court found that the *Interpretation Act*, did not define "Her Majesty" in such a way as to restrict the term to Her Majesty in right of Canada, essentially because the definition in the *Interpretation Act* was substantially the same as that contained in the *Royal Style and Titles Act*[28]. Under both statutory and common law authority, the Sovereign was not bound by that legislation. The case is important for its discussion of the degree to which a broad concept of the divisibility of the Sovereign in domestic law has not developed in Canadian jurisprudence. Chief Justice Laskin said:

> There may be something to be said for the view that, having regard to the nature of Canada's federal system, the notion of the indivisibility of the Crown should be abandoned. The Constitution of Canada distributes legislative power between a central Parliament and provincial Legislatures and prerogative or executive power (which is formally vested in the Queen) is similarly distributed to accord with the distribution of legislative power, thus pointing to different executive authorities. Decisions of the Courts, including decisions of the Privy Council, have, however,

treated a general reference to the Crown in provincial legislation and in federal legislation as referring to the Crown indivisible.[29]

Subsequent case law has continued to maintain the traditional indivisibility of the Crown within Canada. In *Mitchell v Sandy Bay Indian Band*, [1986] 2 WWR 477 (Manitoba CA) Justice O'Sullivan of the Manitoba Court of Appeal stated: ". . . the very fabric of our legal system depends on accepting that we have one Sovereign over both Canada and each province.[30]

Nevertheless, the practical aspect of governing a federation such as Canada, with jurisdiction and responsibilities divided between a federal government and multiple provincial governments, requires that some distinction be made for identification purposes between the Sovereign acting in a federal capacity and the Sovereign acting in a provincial capacity. This is necessary because under the principles of responsible government the Sovereign and her representatives must act in their executive and legislative roles on the advice of those ministers appointed by the Crown who have jurisdiction to deal with the specific subject-matters assigned to them by the constitution. Otherwise, without some means of distinguishing the capacity in which the Sovereign and her representatives are purporting to act, confusion may result concerning which level of government the expressions "Her Majesty" or "the Crown" refers to in a legal instrument or document.

Where it is necessary to distinguish between a federal crown and a provincial crown, the practice is to add the words "in right of Canada" or, for example, in the case of a province, "in right of Saskatchewan" to the expression "Her Majesty" or "the Crown". References in legislation or legal instruments to Her Majesty in right of Canada or to Her Majesty in right of a province are references to the Sovereign acting pursuant to federal constitutional powers, or provincial constitutional powers, as the case may be.[31]

It is sometimes thought that these expressions are synonymous with, and can be replaced by another reference, such as reference to the "Government of Canada" or to the government of a province[32] but these alternative formulations suffer from even more imprecision than references to the Sovereign acting in a particular capacity. A reference to a government may be interpreted as a restrictive reference to the executive branch and, in the case of a reference to the Government of Canada the northern territories, which have their own legislative bodies but otherwise form part of the Crown in Right of Canada, would likely be excluded from the scope of such a formulation. Thus, for domestic legal purposes it remains necessary to use the formulation of the Queen in right of Canada, or the Queen in right of a province, in order to effectively distinguish between the different emanations of the indivisible national Crown. A general reference to the Crown in legislation is ordinarily interpreted to include the political ministry currently holding office nationally or in a province.[33]

Where the Sovereign acts in a legislative capacity, one must distinguish, for the purposes of applicability, between legislation enacted by the Sovereign in the federal capacity, and legislation enacted by the Sovereign in a provincial capacity. In legislation generally, the federal Parliament can bind the Sovereign in right of a province where the subject-matter of the legislation falls squarely within one of the federal heads of power pursuant to the *Constitution Act, 1867*; *Attorney General for Quebec v Nippissing Central Railway Company*, [1926] AC 715 (Canada, JC).

However, a statute enacted by a Provincial legislature may only bind the Sovereign in Right of Canada where the provincial enactment falls within one of the provincial heads of power pursuant to the *Constitution Act, 1867* and the Sovereign in Right of Canada subsequently seeks to take the benefit of that provincial statute; *Toronto Transportation Commission v The King*, [1949] SCR 510 (Canada, SC). In such cases the federal crown must accept the burdens of a statute where it seeks to take the benefit of a statute. Where the Sovereign in right of Canada does not choose to take the benefit of a provincial statute, the provincial legislation cannot bind the Crown in right of Canada.

However, despite a continuing adherence to the indivisibility of the Crown for domestic legal purposes it is considered by the courts that the office of a provincial Crown Attorney is divisible, and thus a decision by a Crown Attorney in one province not to prosecute a person will not necessarily prevent a prosecution of that person from being commenced by a Crown Attorney in another province.

2.6   Federal and Provincial Disputes

While the indivisibility of the Crown has historically placed limitations on the access to the courts by different levels of Canadian government to resolve intergovernmental disputes, it has never been impossible to seek judicial resolution of such intergovernmental disputes through the courts. Legislation has provided a means for the judicial resolution of disputes between the Crown in right of the federation and the Crown in right of a province. Thus, where an Ontario statute provided for actions for a declaration with respect to the constitutional validity of a statute it was possible for the Crown in right of Canada to commence an action against the Crown in right of Ontario; *Canada (Attorney General) v Ontario (Attorney General)* (1894), 23 SCR 458 (Canada, SC).

Furthermore, Section 19 of the *Federal Courts Act* has long provided a mechanism for the judicial arbitration of disputes between the dual emanations of the Crown. That provision states [RSC 1985, c. F-7, s.19]:

If the legislature of a province has passed an Act agreeing that the Federal Court, the Federal Court of Canada or the Exchequer Court of Canada has jurisdiction in cases of controversies between Canada and that province, or between that province and any other province or provinces that have passed a like Act, the Federal Court has jurisdiction to determine the controversies.

The purpose of this provision was considered in *Quebec (Attorney General) v Canada (Attorney General)* (2008) FCA 201 (Canada, FCA) where Justice Letourneau held:

The parties correctly pointed out that the Act is silent on the nature of the remedy provided by section 19 and the applicable proceeding to resolve their dispute. The appellant argued that the remedy was in the nature of a judicial review, and thus it was governed by the rules applicable to judicial reviews, in particular, those relating to the standard of review for administrative decisions and the deference owed to the administrative decision maker. I hasten to point out, and I shall restrict myself to this, that section 19 does not involve administrative disputes between the government and an individual. Instead, it concerns disputes ("controversies") between two political entities under the same indivisible Crown.

The principle to be applied under this section of the *Federal Courts Act* was considered by Chief Justice Jackett of the Federal Court of Appeal in an earlier case, *Canada (The Queen) v Prince Edward Island (The Queen)* (1978) 83 DLR (3d) 492 at 513 (Canada, FCA) where he stated:

In my view, this legislation (section 19 and the provincial Act) creates a jurisdiction differing in kind from the ordinary jurisdiction of municipal courts to decide disputes between ordinary persons or between the Sovereign and an ordinary person. It is a jurisdiction to decide disputes between political entities and not as between persons recognized as legal persons in the ordinary municipal courts. Similarly, in my view, this legislation creates a jurisdiction differing in kind from international courts or tribunals. It is a jurisdiction to decide a dispute in accordance with some "recognized legal principle . . .

It is a unique feature of this provision that the court is clothed with jurisdiction to decide the dispute only when the parties have consented to submit the dispute to the court under section 19 of the *Federal Courts Act*.

More generally however, the courts have increasingly been willing to entertain disputes between the Crown in right of Canada and the Crown in right of a province where the subject matter of the dispute is capable of legal cognizance, and it is justiciable. Thus, the courts have been willing to examine disputes between the levels of government that contains a political aspect where constitutional conventions have been at issue; see *Manitoba (Attorney General) v Canada (Attorney General) (Patriation Reference)*, [1981] 1 SCR 753 (Canada, SC); *Reference re: Amendment to the Canadian Constitution*, [1982] 2 SCR 791 (Canada, SC). The courts have also found a basis to consider a dispute with political overtones between the levels of government where they are able to find a sufficient legal component to ground the jurisdiction of the courts over matters of law; see *Reference Re Canada Assistance Plan (BC)*, [1991] 2 SCR 525 (Canada, SC).[34]

From the perspective of constitutional law, the domestic indivisibility of the Sovereign has thus been maintained in Canadian jurisprudence, although there is a recognition by the courts of the practical difference between the Crown in right of the federation and the Crown in right of its constituent provinces, for the purposes of litigation and dispute resolution.

2.7   Federal – Provincial Agreements

Given that the Sovereign in her legal capacity is indivisible within Canada, ordinary legal relations between the Sovereign in right of Canada and the Sovereign in right of a province cannot be governed by the ordinary law of contracts because at common law a person cannot contract with themselves.[35] To regulate joint arrangements between the Sovereign in her federal and provincial capacities, an instrument described as a Memorandum of Understanding (often abbreviated in bureaucratic documents as an "MOU") is employed. Although an MOU may appear on its face to be a document in the form of a contract it does not create, nor is it intended to create, a contractual legal relationship between the two parties because of the indivisibility of the Crown. Nevertheless, MOUs are regarded as binding upon the governments that make them, and upon the public servants who administer them. In effect, MOUs, are backed by the full faith and honour of the Crown in right of Canada and the Crown in right of a province with respect to their dealings with each other. As a practical expedient they are necessary instruments where federal and provincial joint arrangements are required, or where joint arrangements are made between two or more federal departments, or agencies, or between two or more provincial departments, or agencies.

There is no prescribed form for an MOU and they may be executed on behalf of the federal or provincial governments by ministers or by subordinate officials without reference to the Sovereign's representatives. The latter are, of course, entitled to be informed of the contents of an MOU, or to examine the document if they wish to do so, particularly if it represents a significant policy or administrative initiative.

2.8   Divisibility Within a Single Level of Government

There is yet another element of the divisibility question that merits attention. From time to time the question has arisen as to whether one part of a single layer of the government of Her Majesty can be internally divisible from another part of the same government. Generally, the answer is no.[36] This issue often arises where there is need for cooperation in some endeavour by two or more government departments within the same level of government and a binding arrangement between them is sought. However, two or more departments of the Crown acting within their own spheres of legislative and administrative competence under the constitution may not enter into binding arrangements with one another. The indivisibility of the Crown principle will prevent one department of the Crown from binding another department of the Crown within the same level of government. Such a situation would be very much like a natural person attempting to bind themselves, to themselves, through contract law – a clear legal impossibility.

Nevertheless, cooperative agreements or arrangements by two components of the Crown exercising their legislative or administrative competencies within the same level of government and predicated on the full faith and honour of the officials entering into them offers no substantive legal objections, provided that such agreements, or arrangements, do not purport to be legally binding. For such purposes the instrumentality of the MOU is often used.

Finally, although the northern territories are not separate from Her Majesty in Right of Canada under the *Constitution of Canada,* they are nevertheless, for practical purposes, treated as separate and the northern territories may commence legal proceedings on their own behalf.[37]

2.9   *The Separation of Powers Doctrine*

The separation of powers is a principle that maintains a strict non-interference between branches of government, particularly in the relations between the Crown and its ministry on the one hand, and the judiciary on the other. The concept arose out of the early conflicts between the Crown and the Parliament in the United Kingdom that was eventually resolved by constitutional conventions which developed over the course of the eighteenth and early nineteenth centuries. Those tensions between the Crown and Parliament were still operative in the late eighteenth century when the United States won its independence from Great Britain and developed its own constitutional framework. In the United States constitution the strict separation of powers became an organizing principle of its constitutional structure, and Canada's proximity to the United States has probably resulted in the increasing emphasis placed on this concept in the evolution of Canadian constitutional law.

Unlike the United States however, Canada does not possess a strict separation of powers doctrine like the constitutional principle of the separation of powers in the United States. In Canada the Sovereign is the head of state of Canada and, as such, the government of the country is carried on in the name of the Sovereign. The Sovereign, through her representatives is the head of the executive government of the federal state and of each province. Each of those governments may be characterized as Her Majesty's Government, although that is not the Canadian practice. The Ministers who control the executive are appointed by the Crown in the exercise of the Royal Prerogative and they hold office at the pleasure of the Crown (and are also responsible and accountable to the legislature). All ministers are appointed to the Queen's Privy Council for Canada, or a provincial Executive Council, where they serve as the formal advisors to the Sovereign and to the Sovereign's representatives. Thus, in Canada, there is no formal distinction between the executive and the Crown.

The Sovereign is also one of the three components of the Federal Parliament, which consists of the Queen, the Senate, and the House of Commons. New legislation can only be enacted by the combined approvals of all three components of Parliament. Similarly, in the provincial legislatures the Crown forms one of the two components of the legislative body. No provincial enactment can be lawfully made without the combined approvals of the Legislative Assembly and the Queen.

The guiding force in Parliament or the provincial legislatures is the Cabinet chosen by the Prime Minister or the Premier. The members of the Cabinet (including the Prime Minister or the Premiers) are all Ministers of the Crown. All persons appointed to be a minister must either hold office as a Member of Parliament, or a Member of the Legislative Assembly of a province, or must seek election to the House of Commons, or obtain an appointment to the Senate, at the first available opportunity in the case of the federal government, or must seek election to a provincial legislature at the first available opportunity in the case of a provincial government. Thus, there is no formal separation between the officials of the Crown and the members of the legislative bodies in Canada. The Crown and its ministers are part of both the executive and the legislature, and to retain office the Prime Minister or Premier at the head of a ministry must always command a majority of the seats in the legislative body, either directly through their own political party, or through a cooperative arrangement with other political parties. In Canada, the executive put into office by the Crown must directly control the legislature. There is no real separation between them.

Finally, the Sovereign is the titular head of the judiciary. The courts of law are Her Majesty's Courts, and all justice is provided in the name of the Sovereign. Members of the judiciary occasionally serve in the executive branch as Administrators of Canada, or as Administrators of a province, when the Sovereign's representative is absent from the jurisdiction, or unable to fulfill their duties as the Sovereign's representative. In such capacity the judges, as Administrators, may exercise the Royal Prerogative powers of the Crown. At a formal level therefore, constitutional linkages exist between the judiciary and the Crown.

Nevertheless, there is a functional separation of powers in Canada in relation to the courts notwithstanding that there is no formal separation between the Crown and the judiciary. The Sovereign no longer participates in the direct administration of justice, nor can ministers or public officials forming part of the executive have any role in the application of justice, other than with respect to advising the Crown concerning the exercise of the prerogative power of mercy. Nor can Parliament or a provincial legislature purport to exercise judicial powers except in relation to their own proceedings, a matter concerning which the courts are careful not to intrude.

Thus, in Canada there is actually a formal unity of government under the Crown, but a functional separation of powers that is based on a mutual respect for the differing spheres of activity of the branches of government. The principle was articulated in *New Brunswick Broadcasting Co. V Nova Scotia (Speaker of the House of Assembly)*, [1993] 1 SCR 319 (Canada, SC) at 389 where Justice McLachlin (as she then was) stated:

> Our democratic government consists of several branches: the Crown, as represented by the Governor General and the provincial counterparts of that office; the legislative body; the executive; and the courts. It is fundamental to the working of government as a whole that all these parts play their proper role. It is equally fundamental that no one of them oversteps its bounds, that each show proper deference for the legitimate sphere of activity of the other.

In practical terms, the separation of powers doctrine in a government system characterized by the Westminster model tends to focus on the relationship between the judiciary and Parliament, given that there is a formal integration between the Crown, the executive, and the legislative bodies. This was emphasized in a Commonwealth case, *DPP v Mollinson (No. 2)*, [2003] 1 LRC 756 (Jamaica, JC) where Lord Bingham stated:

> Whatever overlap there may be under Constitutions on the Westminster model between the exercise of executive and legislative powers, the separation between the exercise of judicial powers on the one hand and legislative and executive powers on the other is total or effectively so. Such separation, based on the rule of law, [is] 'a characteristic feature of democracies'.[38]

The Supreme Court of Canada further addressed this subject in *Canada (House of Commons) v Vaid*, [2005] 1 SCR 667 (Canada, SC) where Justice Binnie stated: "It is a wise principle that the courts and Parliament strive to respect each other's role in the conduct of public affairs. Parliament, for its part, refrains from commenting on matters before the courts under the *sub judice* rule. The courts, for their part, are careful not to interfere with the workings of Parliament".[39]

[1] See *The Queen in Right of Canada v The Queen in Right of Prince Edward Island*, [1978] 1 FC 533 (Canada, FC) Appendix B, at page 569

[2] at p. 9b

[3] at p. 1082

[4] ". . . a sovereign in his political capacity is regarded as 'immortal'. The person who is sovereign may change but the sovereign is always present" per Tan Lee Meng J. in *State of Johor v Abdul Rahman et al*, [2006] 3 LRC 187 (Singapore, HC) at page 202.

[5] at page 47. See also *Northwest Territories v Public Service Alliance of Canada*, [2001] 3 FC 566; (Canada, FCA)

[6] at page 117

[7] at page 148

[8] at page 147

[9] The explanation of this fiction that is most compatible with modern values is that the Sovereign herself cannot countenance an unlawful act – not that she is beyond the reach of the law. She is subject to the common law, as are all of her subjects.

[10] Ollivier, at page 484. Originally this department was under the management of the Secretary of State but from 1912 responsibility for the department became a responsibility of the Prime Minister. In 1946 the departmental legislation was amended to permit a Minister of the Crown other than the Prime Minister to be given responsibility for external affairs. In the 1990's the legislation was amended to change the ministerial title to Minister of Foreign Affairs from Minister of External Affairs.

[11] Newfoundland was content to allow the signature of the United Kingdom to stand for its adherence to the Peace Treaty.

[12] at page 816

[13] Quoted in *R v Secretary of State; ex parte Indian Association of Alberta*, [1982] 2 All ER 118 (England, CA) at page 128

[14] Ollivier, at page 484

[15] Shortly after the outbreak of the war a Presidential Proclamation was placed before President Roosevelt pursuant to the American *Neutrality Act*. The President, with a fine understanding of the constitutional stature brought about by the *Statute of Westminster, 1931*, is said to have struck out the application of the *Neutrality Act* Proclamation to Canada, South Africa and Ireland pending

THE MONARCHY IN LEGAL THEORY 43

decisions by those countries concerning their status as belligerents. However, the *Neutrality Act* Proclamation retained its references to New Zealand and Australia, which had not yet taken advantage of the powers conferred by the *Statute of Westminster, 1931* and which therefore remained *de jure* dependencies of the United Kingdom. See *Essays on the Constitution, Aspects of Canadian Law and Government* Frank R. Scott, University of Toronto Press, Toronto, 1977, at page 168 (afterwards "*Scott*").

[16] *Theodore v Duncan*, [1919] AC 696 (Australia, JC) per Viscount Haldane at 706. In the 1880's, the Imperial Government initially objected to the creation by Canada of the quasi-diplomatic post of High Commissioner for Canada in London on the grounds that " . . . the Queen could not appoint an ambassador to herself." (Nancy Gelber, *Canada in London: An Unofficial Glimpse of Canada's Sixteen High Commissioners 1880-1980*, Canada House, London, 1980, at page 11.)

[17] at page 779

[18] at page 302

[19] at page 127

[20] See Chapter 6

[21] [1982] 1 QB 937

[22] For a more recent example of the application of this principle see *R v Secretary of State for Foreign and Commonwealth Affairs, Ex.p. Quark Fishing Limited*, [2006] 1 AC 529 (England, HL) which was concerned with whether an allocation of fishing licences was an act of Her Majesty in right of the United Kingdom or Her Majesty in right of the South Georgia and South Sandwich Islands Territory, an overseas dependency of the United Kingdom. The House of Lords upheld the principle of the divisibility of the Crown.

[23] RSC 1906, c. 1, s. 16

[24] at page 524

[25] RSC 1970 c. A-3

[26] CRC 1978, c. 3 (rep.)

[27] RSC 1970, c. I-23

[28] RSC 1970, c. R-12

[29] at page 71

[30] at page 479

[31] *Mai v. Mississauga*, [1990] 72 OR (2d) 97 (Ontario, HC)

[32] See the *obiter dicta* comment of Lord Bingham in *R (Quark Fishing Ltd.) v Secretary of State*, [2006] 3 LRC 577 (England, HL) at 586: "From *R in Right of Alberta v Canadian Transport Commission* is derived the proposition, which cannot I think be doubted, that the Crown in right of Alberta may be equated with the Government of Alberta".

[33] *The Queen v Canadian Transport Commission*, [1978] 1 SCR 61 (Canada SC)

[34] at page 545

[35] Thus where the Crown is indivisible legal relations between its various emanations cannot be governed by the law of contracts. Such arrangements depend for their performance on the constitutional relationship between the two governments and their good faith toward each other; *John Cooke & Co. v Commonwealth of Australia*, [1922] 31 CLR 394 (Australia, HC).

[36] Despite the fact that Canadian constitutional law does not admit the possibility of a divisibility of the Crown within a single layer of government it is nevertheless possible for some purposes relating to the disclosure of information in the course of a prosecution to differentiate between the investigating police and the office of a Crown Attorney.

[37] *Northwest Territories v. Public Service Alliance of Canada*, [2001] 3 FC 566 (Canada, FCA)

[38] at page 767. Lord Bingham quoted from the judgment of Lord Steyn in *R(Anderson) v Secretary of State for the Home Department*, [2003] 2 LRC 703 at para. 50

[39] at para. 20

THE TITLE TO THE CANADIAN THRONE

3.1   The Throne of Canada

The Sovereign of Canada is *sui generis,* and represents the sole political office under the Canadian constitution which passes to each successor pursuant to hereditary rules. Under the Canadian constitution the laws establishing the title to the throne are based on both the written text of the Canadian constitution as well as unwritten principles derived from the constitutional laws and conventions of England.

The Throne of Canada is established by the *Constitution of Canada* and more particularly by the *Constitution Act, 1867.* The existence of the Canadian Throne, the identification of its rightful occupant, and the descent of the Throne according to the rules of succession are based on Canadian constitutional rules and principles that emanate from a variety of sources including:

1. The written text of the *Constitution Acts 1867 – 1982,* as amended;

2. Written and unwritten principles of the *Constitution of Canada* recognized in the preamble of the *Constitution Act, 1867;*

3. Unentrenched constitutional statutes that have been received from England under the reception doctrine which inform the principles of the *Constitution of Canada* through the preamble to the *Constitution Act, 1867;* and

4. The English common law, including feudal laws relating to the descent of property.

How is the Canadian Sovereign determined? In a nutshell, a constitutional rule of recognition flowing from the *Constitution Act, 1867,* provides for the recognition of the Sovereign of the United Kingdom as the Sovereign of Canada. The actual right to the Throne is ultimately founded upon the parliamentary grant of an English Convention Parliament, sitting in the waning years of the 17th century, and preserved in Canadian constitutional law by the *Constitution of Canada.* Furthermore, a constitutional principle of symmetry, acknowledged in the preamble to the *Constitution Act, 1867,* and embodied in a Commonwealth convention that received legislative recital in the *Statute of Westminster, 1931,* mandates that a common personal Sovereign will be maintained by the separate realms of the United Kingdom of Great Britain and

Northern Ireland, Canada, and the other realms that recognize the Sovereign of the United Kingdom as their own national sovereign.

3.2 The Constitutional Rule of Recognition

The constitutional rule of recognition provides a mechanism for identifying the person who is entitled to possess the Throne of Canada. Under this constitutional rule the rightful Sovereign of the United Kingdom automatically becomes the rightful Sovereign of Canada through the operation of law. The components of this rule of recognition are found in the express entrenched provisions of the *Constitution Act, 1867*, as well as the unentrenched constitutional statutes of England, or the United Kingdom, that entered Canadian law either through their direct application to Canada by the Imperial Parliament during the colonial era, or via the principles relating to the reception of English law in those settled or conquered colonies of the empire that eventually became Canada. The constitutional rules contained in the unentrenched statutes received by Canada, or applied to it by the United Kingdom, articulate principles that have been imported into Canada's constitution through the preamble of the *Constitution Act, 1867*. It is therefore to the *Constitution Act, 1867*, that we must first turn.

3.3 The Preamble to the Constitution Act, 1867

The preamble of the *Constitution Act, 1867*, is crucial to understanding the existence of the constitutional rule of recognition which provides for the identification of the rightful occupant of the Canadian throne. The preamble to the *Constitution Act 1867* Act states:

Whereas the Provinces of Canada, Nova Scotia, and New Brunswick have expressed their Desire to be federally united into *One Dominion under the Crown of the United Kingdom of Great Britain and Ireland, with a Constitution similar in Principle to that of the United Kingdom*: And whereas such a Union would conduce to the Welfare of the Provinces and promote the Interests of the British Empire:

And whereas on the Establishment of the Union by Authority of Parliament it is expedient, not only that the Constitution of the Legislative Authority in the Dominion be provided for, but also that *the Nature of the Executive Government therein be declared*:

And whereas it is expedient that Provision be made for the eventual Admission into the Union of other Parts of British North America... (author's emphasis)

The preamble expresses a clear intention that the new country of Canada was to be formed "under the Crown of the United Kingdom" and that it was to have "a constitution similar in principle to that of the United Kingdom". Since the United Kingdom was (and is) a constitutional monarchy, one can easily see from the content of the first paragraph of the preamble to the *Constitution Act 1867* that the new country was to maintain the existing constitutional monarchy in the newly federated Dominion of Canada.

Furthermore, the third paragraph of the preamble specifically states the desirability of setting out the "nature of the executive government" of the new state which took, and continues to take, a monarchical form.

In the constitutional world that resulted from the patriation of the *Constitution Acts 1867-1982* from the United Kingdom in 1982 the preamble has obtained a renewed importance in Canada's constitutional law. The decision by parliamentarians to exclude older English constitutional statutes from the entrenched and supreme written *Constitution of Canada* has compelled the Supreme Court to interpret the underlying constitutional principles from those statutes, and to incorporate them into Canadian domestic constitutional principles through the instrumentality of the preamble to the *Constitution Act, 1867*, which provides that Canada will have a constitution similar in principle to that of the United Kingdom.

The leading case for this approach to constitutional interpretation is *New Brunswick Broadcasting Co. v. Nova Scotia (Speaker of the House of Assembly)*, [1993] 1 SCR 319 (Canada, SC). In *New Brunswick Broadcasting* the Speaker of the Nova Scotia legislature had banned television cameras from the legislature and the broadcasting company objected to that arguing that under the *Canadian Charter of Rights and Freedoms* the broadcasting company was entitled to record the proceedings of the legislature under the *Charter* rubric of freedom of expression, including the freedom of the press and other media of communication. Writing for the majority of the Supreme Court of Canada Justice McLachlin (as she then was) opined that the underlying principles of section 9 of the *Bill of Rights 1689*, which established parliamentary privilege, were incorporated into the *Constitution of Canada* through the preamble to the *Constitution Act, 1867*, and that it was a trite rule of constitutional law "that one part of the Constitution cannot be abrogated or diminished by another part of the Constitution" and thus the provisions of the *Canadian Charter of Rights and Freedoms* could not be used to strike down constitutional rules that appeared to offend provisions of the *Charter* itself. Thus, the courts had no power to review the Speaker's ruling in the matter of parliamentary privileges.

The key feature of this case for the present discussion is its treatment of the English *Bill of Rights, 1689*, which forms part of the public law of England received by Canada under the reception doctrine but which was not incorporated into the schedule of the *Constitution Act, 1982*, and therefore now lacks supremacy in terms of actual Canadian constitutional law. By extracting underlying constitutional principles from the provisions of the English *Bill of Rights, 1689*, and then applying those principles through the preamble to the *Constitution Act, 1867* the Supreme Court of Canada was able to establish a foundation for the important principle of parliamentary privilege notwithstanding the omission of the *Bill of Rights, 1689* from the supremacy clause of the written constitution. In doing so, the preamble obtained an expanded importance in recognizing for Canadian purposes the ancient but still relevant principles of English constitutional law in the modern Canadian constitutional context.

Nevertheless, while constitutional principles derived from English constitutional statutes can thus serve to fill in certain gaps in the *Constitution Acts 1867-1982* the primacy of the written constitutional text must always be emphasized. Constitutional principles can never oust the primacy of the written constitutional texts; *Reference Re Secession of Quebec,* [1998] 2 SCR 17 (Canada, SC).[1]

3.4   The Ninth Section of the Constitution Act 1867

Section 9 of the *Constitution Act, 1867,* confers the executive government of Canada upon the Sovereign in the following terms:

> The Executive Government and Authority of and over Canada is hereby declared to continue and be vested in the Queen.

The importance of this provision is clear. The Sovereign (at the time of confederation in 1867 the Sovereign was Queen Victoria) is authorized and empowered to continue the executive government of the country, and thus the future acts of the government of the new Dominion of Canada were to be undertaken as acts of the existing Sovereign's Canadian government. This substantive provision reinforced the desire expressed in the preamble to the *Constitution Act, 1867,* that Canada be formed under the Crown of Great Britain.

The combined effect of the preamble and section 9 of the *Constitution Act 1867* is to provide for a unity of identity with the respect to the person who occupies the separate thrones of the United Kingdom and Canada. This is constitutional symmetry; Canada and the United Kingdom have preserved a common personal monarch although both countries are now separate realms, each with their own constitutionally separate Sovereign operating within their own respective constitutional frameworks.

3.5   The Commonwealth Convention of Symmetry

There is an additional element to the concept of symmetry between the identity of the Sovereign of the United Kingdom and the Sovereign of Canada. In addition to the constitutional symmetry provided for in the *Constitution Act, 1867,* there is also a political convention of symmetry that governs relations between those state members of the Commonwealth of Nations that recognize the Sovereign of the United Kingdom as the Sovereign of their own nation. Under the Commonwealth convention of symmetry no change to the order of the succession or to the essential elements of the royal style and titles may be made by one country without the concurrence of all of the other countries that share the person of the Sovereign as their head of state.

When the Imperial Conference of 1930 determined that the political divisibility of the Crown described and defined by the Balfour Declaration of 1926 ought to be made manifest in the constitutional law of the Commonwealth it was decided that legislation to effect and confirm the change that had taken place should be established by a statute of the Imperial Parliament. The *Statute of Westminster, 1931*, recognized that in each of the dominions beyond the seas the King now occupied separate thrones, and exercised his powers on the advice of the legitimate constitutional actors in each jurisdiction. Consequently, the hierarchy of laws by which imperial laws prevailed over dominion laws was terminated (with an exception, for Canada preserving imperial legislative competency over the *British North America Act, 1867* until Canadians could agree on a constitutional amending formula). The independent realms were empowered to change any imperial laws that had been made applicable to them prior to the enactment of the *Statute of Westminster, 1931*.

However, a personal monarchical union of the various states of the Commonwealth continued to be desirable as a symbol of unity within the Commonwealth, with the Sovereign of the United Kingdom serving as the Sovereign of each independent realm. Now that each realm was separate some mechanism was required to ensure that each of them would maintain the personal union with the occupant of the British Throne. The mechanism that was devised to accomplish that was the creation of political convention requiring each Commonwealth realm to retain an essential commonality with the other realms within the Commonwealth with respect to the identity and titles of the Sovereign, and to obtain the consent of every other realm to any changes in the succession to the Throne, or to the royal style and titles. The preamble of the *Statute of Westminster, 1931* states, in part:

> And whereas it is meet and proper to set out by way of preamble to this Act that, inasmuch as the Crown is they symbol of the free association of the members of the British Commonwealth of Nations, and as they are united by a common allegiance to the Crown, it would be in accord with the established constitutional position of all the members of the Commonwealth in relation to one another that any alteration in the law touching the Succession to the Throne or the Royal Style and Titles shall hereafter require the assent as well of the Parliaments of all the Dominions as of the Parliament of the United Kingdom.

The *Statute of Westminster, 1931* (with the exception of section 4 of that statute) has since been made an explicit part of the *Constitution of Canada*, as a scheduled statute under section 52 of the *Constitution Act, 1982*. As a consequence, the preamble to the *Statute of Westminster 1931*, now forms part of the *Constitution of Canada* and for the purpose of changing the succession to the Throne of Canada, or the common elements of the royal style and titles, Canada would require the assent of the Parliament of the United Kingdom, as well as the assent of the parliaments of each of the other fourteen realms within the Commonwealth that recognize the British Sovereign as their own Sovereign in order for Canada to obtain recognition for such changes.

3.6   Summary of Recognition and Symmetry

Since the creation of Canada as a political entity in 1867, the Throne has been held by the reigning Sovereign of the United Kingdom of Great Britain and [Northern] Ireland, who remains the personal Sovereign of Canadians. Under the current version of the Canadian constitution, a divergence in the thrones of Canada and the United Kingdom could not result from any monarchial act by the reigning Sovereign, such as an abdication, or an abandonment, of the Canadian Throne, or from any legislative act by Canada, such as a different method of regulating the descent of the title to the Canadian Throne other than that provided for under the laws of the United Kingdom, unless there is an amendment to the *Constitution of Canada*. This symmetry between the separate thrones is derived from the written text of the preamble which incorporates the unwritten principles of the English and British constitutions and the effect of section 9 of the *Constitution Act, 1867*. Today, any divergence in the thrones would not only require constitutional change in Canada but would also require compliance with the Commonwealth convention of symmetry flowing from the *Statute of Westminster, 1931*, which requires the assent of the Parliaments of the other realms within the Commonwealth for any such change. As a result, the prospect of any change to the succession to the Throne in Canada, as a result of a Canadian initiative, is likely to be theoretical at best.

In essence, the practical issue from a Canadian perspective is to correctly identify the Sovereign of the United Kingdom. Once that is determined, the identity of the Canadian Sovereign is clear. Thus, the laws of the United Kingdom concerning the succession to the Throne of that realm are essential to determining the occupant of the Throne of Canada.

3.7   The Title to the Throne in the United Kingdom

In the United Kingdom, the title to the Throne is determined by common law and statute. It has rested for more than three centuries on the revolutionary act of the Convention Parliament of England taken in 1688 without the consent of the Sovereign, following the flight of King James II from England. From that original English grant, the title to the throne in the United Kingdom devolves upon each succeeding Sovereign in accordance with hereditary rules that find their origin in the ancient common law relating to the descent of property.

The Convention Parliament convened to declare the throne vacant and to then offer it to Prince William of Orange and Princess Mary, the daughter of King James II. The grant to William and Mary was confirmed by an enactment of the Parliament of England, the *Bill of Rights 1689*[2], and has been preserved in Canada as an unentrenched Canadian constitutional statute law received by Canada under the reception doctrine as part of the public laws of England. While not part of the *Constitution of Canada*, the *Bill of Rights, 1689*, does inform the underlying principles of the Canadian constitution that are applicable through the preamble to the *Constitution Act, 1867*.

3.8   Male-Preference Primogeniture

In the law concerning the succession to the Throne of the United Kingdom before March 26, 2015, the Throne passed by lineal descent under the feudal legal doctrine of male-preference primogeniture,[3] with the legitimate male offspring of the reigning Sovereign preferred over the Sovereign's legitimate female offspring. Thus, the legitimate male offspring of the Sovereign inherited the Throne in their birth order. Where the Sovereign had no legitimate male offspring the Throne passed to the Sovereign's legitimate female offspring in their birth order. Where a Sovereign had no legitimate offspring, the Throne passed to the Sovereign's legitimate male siblings, or to their legitimate descendants, or, where the Sovereign did not have a legitimate male sibling, to the Sovereign's legitimate female siblings, or to their legitimate descendants. For succession purposes legitimate half-blood siblings were treated the same as legitimate full-blood siblings with respect to inheriting the Throne.

3.9   The Protestant Title to the Throne Before 2015

The monarchial history of England and Scotland in the late middle ages was rife with religious disputes and schisms[4]. Eventually, the Protestant faith came to dominate in both England and Scotland (but not Ireland) and the Sovereigns of both England and Scotland (joined in one personal monarch after the death of Queen Elizabeth I) followed Protestant religious doctrines. However, in 1685, the Duke of York came to the throne of England as King James II upon the death of King Charles II. James had been raised as a Protestant but he had converted to Roman Catholicism as an adult and so he came to the Throne as a Roman Catholic. There were tensions and conflicts with Parliament over religion during the reign of James II, and the birth of a Catholic prince to King James and his wife Queen Mary brought those tensions to a head, leading to a rebellion and an invitation by leading Protestant politicians to James' eldest daughter from his first marriage, Princess Mary, and her husband Prince William of Orange, to come to England and to assume the Throne as joint monarchs. Rather than face open conflict King James II decided to flee the realm, dropping the Great Seal of the Realm into the Thames river during the haste of his departure from London. Although the King was captured before making good his escape, Prince William of Orange, who had landed with a Protestant army in England, and who had no wish to harm his father-in-law, permitted him to escape to France. The parliaments of England and Scotland did not officially depose James but declared the Throne to have been abandoned, or forfeited, by King James II, and recognized his daughter Mary, and her husband William, as the succeeding Queen and King of England and Scotland.

The *Bill of Rights 1689* was enacted to confer the Throne (essentially by a parliamentary grant) on William and Mary and their offspring, provided that no heir could subsequently inherit the Throne if he or she were a Roman Catholic, or married to a Roman Catholic. The effect of this legislation was to ensure that the thrones of England and Scotland, (which subsequently became the Throne of the United Kingdom following the union of England and Scotland) would always be secured to the members of the reigning royal house who followed the Protestant reformed religion established by law within each of those two kingdoms.

The *Bill of Rights 1689* is part of the public law of Canada, having been received into Canada as part of the inheritance of English law through the reception doctrine. The Supreme Court of Canada has stated that the statute is "undoubtedly in force as part of the law of Canada,"[5] although the Supreme Court has also subsequently ruled that, following the patriation of the *Constitution Acts, 1867-1982*, the statute itself is not part of the *Constitution of Canada* for the purposes of applying the supremacy clause of the *Constitution Act, 1982*. The *Bill of Rights 1689* is therefore a constitutional statute outside of the *Constitution of Canada* but its principles inform the principles of the *Constitution of Canada* through the preamble of the *Constitution Act, 1867*, which confers upon Canada "a Constitution similar in Principle to that of the United Kingdom".[6]

In subsequent years, and in consideration of the possibility that neither King William III or his successor, Queen Anne (the younger daughter of James II by his first wife) would be survived by legitimate children, the Parliament of England enacted the *Act of Settlement 1701*[7] which determined the future descent of the Throne, and it is from that statute today that the current line of succession to the Canadian Throne can be identified.

The *Act of Settlement, 1701*, contained restrictions on the succession to the Throne intended to prevent a person who professes the Roman Catholic faith from succeeding to the Throne or marrying into the line of succession. It is notable that the bar against persons in the line of succession marrying outside of the Protestant faith only captured marriages to Roman Catholics but did not capture the members of other faiths. In this, the *Act of Settlement, 1701,* reflected the complex issues of religion and politics which were current in the seventeenth and eighteenth centuries. The statute was enacted in relation to the kingdoms of England, France and Ireland, as the Crown of England in 1701 still asserted claims to the Throne of France and in view of the fact that Ireland was a separate kingdom, held in a personal union with the Sovereigns of England. In addition, the Act was made applicable to all dominions held by those kingdoms, which made the *Act of Settlement, 1701* applicable to overseas colonies, including those parts of Canada which were then, and subsequently, subject to the sovereignty of England, or Great Britain. While the *Act of Settlement, 1701,* continues to form part of the public law of Canada under the reception doctrine it is not a part of the *Constitution of Canada* because it is not within the list of constitutional statutes included in the *Constitution of Canada* under section 52(1) of the *Constitution Act, 1982.* However, as with the *Bill of Rights 1689,* the Supreme Court of Canada has found the *Act of Settlement, 1701,* is a source for the principles of the unwritten constitution transferred from the United Kingdom through the preamble to the *Constitution Act, 1867.* In *Reference re Remuneration of Judges of the Provincial Court (P.E.I.),* [1997] 3 SCR 3 (Canada, SC) Chief Justice Lamer stated that "... judicial independence in the United Kingdom, and thus in the Canadian Constitution, can be traced to the *Act of Settlement* of 1701 ... [and] ... is an unwritten norm, recognized and affirmed by the preamble to the *Constitution Act, 1867*".

The *Act of Settlement, 1701,* established the basic rules of succession, stating that in the event that King William (who was predeceased by his wife Queen Mary) died without legitimate offspring and if Princess Anne, Queen Mary's sister, to whom the Throne would next pass, also died without legitimate offspring the Throne would then pass to Princess Sophia, the Electress of Hanover, in Germany, who was the granddaughter of King James I, and subsequently to her legitimate offspring. Ultimately, King William III died without legitimate offspring as did Queen Anne (despite giving birth in her lifetime to five children) and so the Throne passed to the heirs of the Electress Sophia of Hanover (who herself had predeceased Queen Anne by only a few months). King George I of Hanover thus became the first Sovereign of the new royal house of the United Kingdom of Great Britain. The current Sovereign of the United Kingdom can trace direct descent from King George I.

3.10   Religious Disqualifications and Canada

The legal rules in the United Kingdom relating to the succession to the Throne under the *Act of Settlement, 1701* provides for discrimination on the basis of religious affiliation by rendering Roman Catholics ineligible to ascend to the

Throne. Given the entrenchment of fundamental freedoms and equality rights in the Canadian constitution under the *Constitution Act, 1982*, questions have naturally arisen concerning the constitutional validity of the rules for the succession to the Throne in relation to Canada.

In particular, questions have arisen concerning the extent to which the vesting of the title to the Throne in the adherents of one particular religious denomination, or the bar on marriage to Roman Catholics by persons in the line of succession to the Throne, could be supported under the *Canadian Charter of Rights and Freedoms*, which is part of the *Constitution Act, 1982*. Although the preamble to the *Charter* states: "Whereas Canada is founded upon principles that recognize the supremacy of God and the rule of law," section 2(a) enacts that: Everyone has the following fundamental freedoms: "(a) freedom of conscience and religion;" and subsection 15 (1) of the *Charter* provides:

> Every individual is equal before and under the law and has the right to the equal protection and equal benefit of the law without discrimination and, in particular, without discrimination based on race, national or ethnic origin, colour, religion, sex, age or mental or physical disability.

Therefore, on its face, the religious bar against Roman Catholics becoming the Sovereign of the United Kingdom, and thus the Sovereign of Canada, or a person in the line of succession to the Throne marrying a Roman Catholic, conflicted with the constitutional prohibition against discrimination based on religion that is prescribed by subsection 15 (1) of the *Charter*. However, a constitutional principle has also been articulated by the Supreme Court of Canada which establishes that the *Canadian Charter of Rights and Freedoms* cannot be used to strike down other parts of the *Constitution of Canada*. That principle was articulated in the jurisprudence litigating the issue of sectarian schools (see *Re An Act to Amend the Education Act*, [1987] SCR 1148 (Canada, SC).[8] Therefore, the rules of succession and their relationship to the *Charter* remained uncertain, and provided a basis for a *Charter* challenge.

This issue came before the courts in the case of *O'Donohue v. Canada* (2003) 109 CRR (2d) 1 (Ontario, Sup. Ct.); affd. *O'Donohue v. Canada* (2005), CanLII 6369 (Ontario, CA). In *O'Donohue* the Applicant sought a declaration that the provisions of the *Act of Settlement, 1701*, that barred Roman Catholics from ascending the Throne, and which disqualified persons in the established line of succession who chose to marry a Roman Catholic from inheriting the Throne, were of no force or effect as they offended the provisions of the *Charter* that protect against religious-based discrimination. The Attorneys General of Canada and Ontario contested the claim made in *O'Donohue* and required the Applicant to prove his entitlement to legal standing (a determination that an applicant has a substantive legal interest that would support his engagement of the courts of law with respect to the issue that has been raised).

Claims arising under the *Charter* may be brought by a person in one of two ways. Firstly, a person whose direct substantive interests are at issue can assert a personal interest standing as of right. Alternatively where a person does not have a direct interest in the subject matter of the dispute, and therefore cannot assert a personal interest standing, they may still seek public interest standing if they can show that they are raising a serious issue concerning the validity of legislation and that they have a citizen's genuine interest in the subject matter of the proposed litigation, and that there is no other reasonable or effective method that would allow the issue to come before the courts of law.

In *O'Donohue*, the Applicant had no personal relationship to the Royal Family and therefore he lacked a personal interest sufficient to support a personal interest standing. However, he was a member of the Roman Catholic faith and maintained a genuine citizen's interest in the validity of the succession rules because of his faith. Therefore the Applicant sought public interest standing to maintain the application, contending that in the absence of a grant of public interest standing to the Applicant the issue was unlikely to come before the courts for resolution.

In the Superior Court of Ontario, Justice Rouleau, before whom the application was presented, determined that the court should first analyze whether the issue presented by the Applicant was justiciable, or capable of cognizance, by the courts of law in Canada before determining the issue of public interest standing.

After first noting the central place of the monarchy in the Canadian constitutional structure, Justice Rouleau found that the rules of succession to the Throne were integral to the framework of the Canadian constitution and embodied the principle of unity between the Crown of Canada and the Crown of the United Kingdom. The rules of succession are constitutionalized as part of the unwritten constitutional rules that enter the *Constitution of Canada* through the preamble to the *Constitution Act 1867*, which mandates that Canada shall possess a constitution similar in principle to the United Kingdom. As Justice Rouleau noted, the Supreme Court of Canada had previously decided in the case of *New Brunswick Broadcasting Company v Nova Scotia* that unwritten constitutional rules inherited from Great Britain could be recognized as constitutional principles within the *Constitution of Canada* through the preamble to the *Constitution Act 1867*. As Justice Rouleau stated:

> . . . it is clear that Canada's structure as a constitutional monarchy and the principle of sharing the British monarch are fundamental to our constitutional framework. In light of the preamble's clear statement that we are to share the Crown with the United Kingdom, it is axiomatic that the rules of succession for the monarchy must be shared and be in symmetry with those of the United Kingdom and other Commonwealth countries. One cannot accept the monarch but reject the legitimacy or legality of the rules by which this monarch is selected.[9]

Justice Rouleau noted that the *Act of Settlement, 1701* was part of the constitutional statutes of Canada, and referred to its inclusion within the constitutional statutes in the published statutes of Ontario but he refrained from going so far as to hold that the *Act of Settlement, 1701* was itself an entrenched part of the *Constitution of Canada,* holding that: "The impugned provisions of the *Act of Settlement* are an integral part of the rules of succession that govern the selection of the monarch in Great Britain. By virtue of our constitutional structure whereby Canada is united under the Crown of Great Britain, the same rules of succession must apply for the selection of the King or Queen of Canada and the King or Queen of Great Britain".[10] Justice Rouleau found that the rules of succession were constitutionalized through the preamble to the *Constitution Act 1867* as unwritten constitutional principles, and therefore, as part of the *Constitution of Canada,* they could not be altered or struck down by the operation of the *Canadian Charter of Rights and Freedoms* based on earlier jurisprudence which forbade using the *Charter* to strike down other portions of the *Constitution of Canada.* In the result, the rules of succession were immune from a challenge based on the *Charter.* Thus, the issues raised by the Applicant were non-justiciable issues and public interest standing could not be granted to the Applicant. Accordingly, the application for a declaratory judgement was dismissed. The judgement of Justice Rouleau in *O'Donohue* was subsequently upheld without substantive reasons by the Ontario Court of Appeal [(2005), CanLII 6369 per: Doherty, Laskin, Macfarland, JJ.A.]

3.11   Absence of a State Religion in Canada

The fact that the title to the Throne of the United Kingdom is vested in a particular religious denomination and the fact that the Sovereign of that state becomes the Sovereign of Canada does not mean that Canada possesses an established state religion. A state-established religion would be a clear violation of the *Charter* expression of freedom of conscience. In *Attorney General of Quebec v Quebec Association of Protestant School Boards,* [1984] 2 SCR 66 (Canada, SC), the Supreme Court said:

> An Act of Parliament or of a legislature which, for example, purported to impose the beliefs of a State religion would be in direct conflict with s. 2(a) of the *Charter,* which guarantees freedom of conscience and religion, and would have to be ruled of no force or effect without the necessity of even considering whether such legislation could be legitimized by s.1 [of the *Charter*].

3.12   The Royal Marriages Act 1772

The *Royal Marriages Act 1772*[11] prohibited any descendant of King George II under the age of twenty-five from entering into matrimony without the prior permission of the Sovereign, whose permission had to be expressed in an instrument made under the Great Seal of the Realm and declared in the Imperial

Privy Council. Once granted, the permission was entered in the records of the Imperial Privy Council. An exception from the provisions of the Act existed for the issue of princesses who married into foreign families, and for whom no permission to marry was required to be obtained. Any marriage otherwise contracted without permission of the Sovereign, as required by the Act, was void. Furthermore, it was made an offence to solemnize a marriage entered into contrary to the *Royal Marriages Act 1772*.

Nevertheless, descendants of King George II who were above the age of twenty-five could contract a valid marriage with or without the consent of the Sovereign. If the marriage was to be entered into without the Sovereign's consent the intending member of the Royal Family was required to give one years notice to the Privy Council, and that notice had to be entered into the records of the Imperial Privy Council. At the expiration of twelve months following the giving of notice, the member of the Royal Family intending to marry could validly contract a marriage with the person to whom they were betrothed. However, during the one year notice period Parliament could expressly disapprove of the marriage, in which case the marriage could not be solemnized.

The Committee for Privileges of the House of Lords considered the effect of this Act in the *Sussex Peerage Case*, [1844] All ER Rep 55 (United Kingdom, HL). That case concerned a claim by the natural son of the Duke of Sussex, sixth son of King George III, to inherit his father's peerage following the decease of his father. The claimant's parents were married in an Anglican ceremony in Rome in 1793, apparently in an attempt to avoid the *Royal Marriages Act 1772*, on the basis that the Act did not apply to the King's subjects when they were abroad.

However, the House of Lords held that the marriage of the Duke of Sussex was invalid according to the law of the United Kingdom because it violated the *Royal Marriages Act 1772*. The Lords found that Parliament had jurisdiction to enact legislation applicable to a subject of the Crown outside of the realm, and therefore a marriage contracted abroad, even though valid by the laws of another state, could not be recognized under United Kingdom law. Thus, the claim to the peerage of the Duke of Sussex failed.

Over the passage of years the number of descendants of King George II grew quite large and many of them were far removed from the Royal Family though remaining (distantly) in the line of succession. In modern times there was a considerable body of opinion in the United Kingdom that suggested that the antiquated drafting methods used in the eighteenth century resulted in the *Royal Marriages Act 1772* no longer applying to very many members, and possibly to none of the Royal Family, particularly due to the exemption for "the issue of princesses who have married, or may hereafter marry into foreign families." Although some authorities did suggest that the Act was spent members of the

Royal Family in the line of succession continued to seek the consent of the Sovereign for their marriages. But it was not at all clear that all descendants had continued to obtain permission under the Act before contracting their marriages, and thus there was a possibility that some marriages were void even though the marriage partners fully intended for their marriage to be legally valid.

3.13   Royal Marriages and Canada

The *Royal Marriages Act 1772* is not legislation that was either enacted with reference to British colonies nor was it likely to have been received as part of Canada's inheritance of English law through the reception doctrine. For instance, there was no Canadian Privy Council until 1867 and therefore it would have been impossible to apply the legislation as received English law. Therefore, it is properly viewed as local law enacted with reference to the United Kingdom and not as imperial legislation, or received English statute and common law. However, as the *Sussex Peerage* case showed, from the time of its enactment it would have bound members of the Royal Family wherever they were situated in the world and therefore members of the Royal Family could not have contracted a valid marriage in Canada without the Sovereign's approval.

The consent of the Sovereign of the United Kingdom to a royal marriage is a decision that is made on the advice of the Privy Council of the United Kingdom, in accordance with the principles of responsible government. Essentially, British Ministers provide the formal advice to the Sovereign concerning the proposed marriage.

Subsequent to the divisibility of the Crown brought about by the Balfour Declaration and the *Statute of Westminster, 1931*, a constitutional practice arose whereby Canada has been consulted by the United Kingdom with respect to a class of royal marriages that engage Canadian interests. Such interests would not only include the impact of an unsuitable match on public respect for the institution of the monarchy but could also engage foreign relations if the person to whom a member of the Royal Family becomes betrothed is a member of a foreign dynasty.

Under United Kingdom constitutional practice Canada may nominate a person to represent it at a meeting of the Privy Council of the United Kingdom where the approval of a marriage of a person in the line of succession to the Throne is being considered. However, the evolution of constitutional practice since the divisibility of the Crown was established by convention in 1926, as well as the legislative break between the two countries as a result of the *Canada Act, 1982*, has precluded Canada from sending a representative to formally participate in the deliberations of a British constitutional body, even in circumstances where Canadian interests with respect to the monarchy may be engaged. This precedent was set in 1947 when the Canadian Ministry chose not to send a Canadian member to a meeting of the United Kingdom Privy Council to approve the marriage of Princess Elizabeth to Prince Philip of Greece and Denmark, though invited to do so by King George VI. Formal consultation between the governments of the United Kingdom and Canada has since been the preferred method for Canada to advance its own interests with respect to a royal marriage. Where formal consents have been required the Canadian practice has been to convene the Queen's Privy Council for Canada in a non-partisan way to provide any necessary consents to a royal marriage.

The class of marriages that directly engages Canadian interests concerns those marriages involving the Sovereign, or the direct heir to the Throne. Although the *Royal Marriages Act 1772* never bound the Sovereign, the marriage of a reigning Sovereign is a matter affecting the interests of Canada, as well as the other realms, and there is an expectation that Canada will be consulted and provided with an opportunity to submit advice on the subject where advice is deemed to be necessary by the Government of Canada. Thus, Prime Minister Mackenzie King was among those Commonwealth leaders who were consulted in 1936 with respect to the proposed marriage of King Edward VIII and an American divorcee, Mrs Simpson. Prime Minister Mackenzie King, on behalf of the Government of Canada, ultimately supported the British Prime Minister, Stanley Baldwin, in his advice to King Edward VIII, that the marriage would be unsuitable and that formal advice from the British Prime Minister precipitated the 1936 abdication crisis.

In 1947 when the heir apparent to the throne, Princess Elizabeth, sought permission from her father King George VI to marry Prince Philip of Greece and Denmark, and again in 1981 when Prince Charles, the Prince of Wales, sought permission from his mother Queen Elizabeth II, to marry Lady Diana Spenser, meetings of the Privy Council for Canada were convened in Ottawa to signify Canadian assent to the marriages. The Canadian approvals were passed under the seals of the Canadian Privy Council.

However, the Queen's Privy Council for Canada was not convened to approve the marriage of Prince Charles, the Prince of Wales, and Ms. Camilla Parker Bowles early in the twenty-first century. Canadian officials publicly stated as reasons for not convening the Canadian Privy Council that upon the accession of Prince Charles to the Throne, his second spouse would not become Queen Consort. Furthermore, there would be no impact on the line of succession, as the heir's second marriage to a spouse aged 57 would not result in offspring due to the age of Ms. Bowles.[12]

As a matter of constitutional law, Canada is not strictly required to offer formal advice to the Sovereign on the question of the marriage of the Sovereign or the Sovereign's heir but may do so where Canadian interests are engaged. However, in the past, the Queen's Privy Council for Canada has offered formal advice on the suitability of the first marriage of the royal heir in response to a request from the Sovereign and would doubtless do so again in the future if a future request is made by a Sovereign. While there is no Commonwealth convention with respect to royal marriages there is at least evidence of a Commonwealth practice whereby the Canadian government will be informed by the Sovereign, or by the British Government of a proposed marriage of the Sovereign, the heir apparent, or the heir presumptive, and that Canada will be afforded an opportunity to express its views on the matter should it desire to do so.

3.14   Proposals to Modernize the Rules of Succession to the Throne

In the latter part of the twentieth century and the beginning of the twenty-first century there were concerns in the United Kingdom, Canada, and in the other realms with respect to the rules of succession to the Throne. Male-preference primogeniture was increasingly viewed as an anachronism that did not reflect the views of society in the United Kingdom, Canada, or in any of the other realms concerning the equality of males and females. At the same time, it was also recognized that the restrictions on the Sovereign and members of the Royal Family in the line of succession from marrying persons of the Roman Catholic faith were antiquated, and were no longer relevant to twenty-first century political governance in the United Kingdom, Canada, or the other realms.

Accordingly a major reform effort began in the early years of the twenty-first century involving consultations between the Government of the United Kingdom and the governments of the other realms within the Commonwealth to bring about equality between male and female members of the Royal Family with respect to the succession to the Throne. It was also considered to be past time for the reform of the laws disqualifying persons within the line of succession who marry a Roman Catholic from inheriting the Throne. Therefore, in September, 2011, the Prime Minister of the United Kingdom, David Cameron, wrote to his counterparts in the other Commonwealth realms to consult with them on proposals to modernize the succession to the Throne and, in particular, the need to provide for equality between males and females.

Those consultations bore fruit and culminated in an agreement at the 2011 meeting of the Commonwealth Heads of Government at Perth, Australia, between the United Kingdom and the other fifteen realms that are joined in a personal union with the Sovereign of the United Kingdom to change the laws of succession to reflect the modern equality between males and females, and to remove unnecessary discriminatory restrictions concerning the succession to the Throne that were based on marriages to a Roman Catholic.

3.15   The Perth Agreement and the United Kingdom Legislation

The *Agreement in Principle among the Realms* dated October 28, 2011, ("the *Perth Agreement*") called for an orderly change to the succession laws applicable to all of the realms and established a working group of officials chaired by New Zealand to oversee recommendations for implementing the proposed changes. The working group recommended that the introduction of British legislation should precede a formal agreement by the other realms to the changes and that the in-force date for the subsequent British legislation ought to be deferred until all of the other realms completed their own internal processes for altering the laws of succession to their Throne.

That procedure was deemed acceptable by all of the realms and the British legislation was introduced into Parliament in the latter part of 2012, culminating with the passage of the *Succession to the Crown Act 2013*.[13] Section 1 of that Act states:

> In determining the succession to the Crown, the gender of a person born after 28 October 2011 does not give that person, or that person's descendants, precedence over any other person (whenever born).

As a consequence of this proposed legislation the descent of the Throne in the United Kingdom (and in the other Commonwealth realms) would now be based upon absolute primogeniture, rather than on male-preference primogeniture, and thus both male and female offspring could inherit the throne equally if they were otherwise eligible by virtue of their birth order. However, male-preference primogeniture would continue to apply to those persons born on or before October 28, 2011, thus grandfathering the places in the line of succession achieved before the proposed changes were announced.

3.16   Reforms to Royal Marriages

The Parliament of the United Kingdom took advantage of the opportunity presented by the reform to the succession rules to repeal the *Royal Marriages Act, 1772*, and to modify the restrictions on marriage applicable to the members of the Royal Family. Under the new rules, only the persons standing among the first six persons in the line of succession to the Throne are required to obtain the permission of the Sovereign to marry. In abolishing the *Royal Marriages Act, 1772*, the Parliament of the United Kingdom enacted provisions that retroactively validated any void marriages under the former *Royal Marriages Act, 1772*, for all persons beyond the first six persons in the line of succession where they had no intent to avoid the statute, and where no person involved in the marriage treated it as void at any time after it was entered into.

Under the *Succession to the Crown Act, 2013*, a failure by any one of the first six person in the line of succession to obtain the Sovereign's consent to marry disqualifies that person and their descendants from inheriting the Throne but their non-compliance with the statute will not invalidate their marriage.

Section 2 of the Act retrospectively removed the disqualification of those persons in the line of succession who married a Roman Catholic from inheriting the Throne. That section stated:

> (1) A person is not disqualified from succeeding to the Crown or from possessing it as a result of marrying a person of the Roman Catholic faith.

> (2) Subsection (1) applies in relation to marriages occurring before the time of the coming into force of this section where the person concerned is alive at that time (as well as in relation to marriages occurring after that time).

As a result of this change it is now possible for the Sovereign to marry a Roman Catholic and for all persons in the line of succession to the Throne in the United Kingdom to also marry a Roman Catholic (or to have married a Roman Catholic) without disqualification of their place in the line of succession. The sole remaining religious qualification in relation to the succession to the Throne that was retained is the requirement that the Sovereign be a Protestant in communion with the Church of England. That requirement was maintained because of the historical and current position of the Sovereign of the United Kingdom as the Head of the Church of England.

3.17   The New Rules of Succession and the Commonwealth

The proposed legislative changes were acceptable to the other realms and a final concurrence was given to the United Kingdom's government in December, 2012. Accordingly, British legislation to modernize the succession rules was enacted by the Parliament of the United Kingdom on April 25, 2013. However, consistent with the Perth Agreement, the coming into force of the British legislation was deferred until all of the other realms could bring their laws in relation to the succession to the Throne in line with the changes mandated by the British legislation.

Following the enactment of legislation by the Parliament of the United Kingdom the other realms took the necessary actions required to implement this constitutional change within their own realm. In nine of the realms the governments determined that assenting legislation would not be required. Those realms included Antigua and Barbuda, The Bahamas, Belize, Grenada, St. Lucia, Jamaica, Papua New Guinea, Solomon Islands and Tuvalu. Six realms enacted legislation in their national parliaments and of those, four of the realms, St. Christopher and Nevis, Barbados, St. Vincent and the Grenadines, and Canada only enacted assenting legislation in their national parliaments. A fifth realm, New Zealand, enacted legislation in the national parliament that not only assented to the changes made by the United Kingdom but also enacted amendments to both the *Act of Settlement, 1701,* and the *Bill of Rights, 1689,* and, as well, New Zealand repealed the *Royal Marriages Act, 1772,* in so far as it applied to New Zealand.

In Australia, the Commonwealth government determined that it should enact assenting legislation only following the enactment of legislation by each of the six states of Australia requesting that the Commonwealth Government enact such legislation. As Canadians well know, coordinating two-tiered legislation within a federation is a time consuming process and therefore it was not until March, 2015, that the final Australian state, Western Australia, enacted its own legislation requesting legislative action at the federal level in Australia. Following the legislative requests by the legislatures of the six Australian states, the national parliament of Australia enacted its assenting legislation on March 19, 2015.

On March 26, 2015, The *Succession to the Crown Act, 2013* (U.K.) and all of the legislation in the other realms came into force simultaneously across all of the sixteen realms within the Commonwealth of Nations (albeit at different local times) by commencement orders in the United Kingdom, Canada, Australia, New Zealand, Barbados, St. Christopher and Nevis, and St. Vincent and the Grenadines. The remaining realms took the view that the changes were automatic in their jurisdictions when the changes came into force in the United Kingdom.

3.18   The New Rules of Succession in Canada

In Canada, the Federal Government introduced a bill to assent to the changes in the laws concerning the succession to the Throne that were proposed to be made by the Parliament of the United Kingdom in the *Succession to the Crown Act, 2013.* The Federal Government was of the view that assenting legislation was required by the preamble of the *Statute of Westminster, 1931,* which codified the Commonwealth convention of symmetry in regards to the monarchy in the various realms. In reaching this conclusion the Federal Government had to consider whether the changes to the succession laws would involve the governments of the ten provinces of Canada because a) the Sovereign was the head of state in each of the provinces, as well as head of state of the federation as a whole; b) the laws of succession contained in the common law, and in such statutes as the *Bill of Rights, 1689,* and the *Act of Settlement, 1701,* formed part of the laws received by the various provinces as their legal inheritance from England; and, c) whether the changes to the laws of succession constituted a change to the office of the Queen of Canada, which would require a constitutional amendment pursuant to section 41(a) of the *Constitution Act 1982.*

The Federal Government concluded that a role for the provinces in this matter was not required. Firstly, the Crown is indivisible in domestic law and therefore the Sovereign of Canada is automatically the Sovereign in each of the several provinces. Secondly, as the court in *O'Donohue* had concluded, the rules of succession are constitutionalized through the preamble to the *Constitution Act, 1867* but the specific provisions of the imperial statutes in which those rules are contained are not part of the formal *Constitution of Canada* defined by section 52 of the *Constitution Act, 1982*, thus eliminating any requirement for a constitutional amendment pursuant to section 41(a) of the *Constitution Act, 1982* in order to implement the proposed changes[14]. Thirdly, the plenary power of the Federal government under the Peace, Order and Good Government clause in section 91 of the *Constitution Act, 1867*, clothed Parliament alone with the authority to enact an expression of assent by Canada to the changes proposed to be made in the Parliament of the United Kingdom, the assent required by Commonwealth convention in conformity with the preamble to the *Statute of Westminster, 1931*.

The Federal Government stated in its backgrounder to the *Succession the Throne Act, 2013*[15] that:

> The changes to the laws of succession do not require a constitutional amendment. The laws governing succession are UK law and are not part of Canada's constitution. Specifically, they are not enumerated in the schedule to our *Constitution Act, 1982* as part of the *Constitution of Canada*. Furthermore, the changes to the laws of succession do not constitute a change to the "office of The Queen", as contemplated in the *Constitution Act, 1982*. The "office of The Queen" includes the Sovereign's constitutional status, powers and rights in Canada. Neither the ban on the marriages of heirs to Roman Catholics, nor the common law governing male preference primogeniture, can properly be said to be royal powers or prerogatives in Canada. As the line of succession is therefore determined by UK law and not by the Sovereign, The Queen's powers and rights have not been altered by the changes to the laws governing succession in Canada.

The *Succession the Throne Act, 2013*, provided in section 2 that:

> The alteration in the law touching the Succession to the Throne set out in the bill laid before the Parliament of the United Kingdom and entitled *A Bill to Make succession to the Crown not depend on gender; to make provision about Royal Marriages; and for connected purposes* is assented to.

The Canadian legislation was subsequently challenged in both the province of Ontario and in the province of Quebec. In Ontario an application was brought to the Superior Court that essentially re-litigated the issues that had been dealt with earlier by the courts in *O'Donohue v Canada*. In *Teskey v. Canada (Attorney General)* (2013), ONSC 5046 (Ontario, Sup. Ct.) affd. *Teskey v. Canada (Attorney General)* (2014), ONCA 612 (Ontario, CA) the Applicant challenged the federal legislation assenting to the changes in the succession laws enacted in the United Kingdom upon the ground that the *Canadian Charter of Rights and Freedoms* precludes the Parliament of Canada from agreeing to a change in the succession laws that leaves in place the requirement that the Sovereign of Canada be a member of the Protestant faith in communion with the Church of England. As in the *O'Donohue* case, the issues turned on justiciability and public interest standing, with the court eventually concluding that the Applicant lacked any interest other than an adherence to the Roman Catholic faith to support his request for public interest standing. Furthermore, as in *O'Donohue*, the court held that the constitutionalized rules of succession, and the requirement for symmetry between the United Kingdom and Canada, could not be the subject of a *Charter* challenge and therefore the issues raised by the Applicant were not justiciable. Accordingly, public interest standing to bring an application for a declaration was denied for lack of justiciability.

A more serious challenge emerged in the province of Quebec. There, two law professors sought a declaration that the *Succession to the Throne Act* was invalid because it was not enacted in compliance with the mechanism for amending the *Constitution of Canada* set out in section 41(a) of the *Constitution Act 1982*, as well as the incompatibility of the succession rules with section 15(1) of the *Canadian Charter of Rights and Freedoms*, which prohibits religious discrimination. That application was supported by the provincial government of Quebec, in so far as the issues involved the alleged non-compliance with the mechanism for amending the *Constitution of Canada*.

The matter came before Justice Bouchard in the Superior Court of Quebec who held in the case of *Motard et al v Canada (Attorney General)* (2016), QCCS 588 (Quebec, Sup. Ct.) that the constitutional rule of recognition by which Canada recognizes and identifies the Sovereign of the United Kingdom as the Sovereign of Canada exists in the *Constitution of Canada* by virtue of the preamble and section 9 of the *Constitution Act, 1867* and that:

> As such, the rule of automatic recognition means that the Queen or King of the United Kingdom is also the Queen or King of Canada, with no need to amend Canadian law for it to be so.[16]

Thus the only requirement that pertained to Canada in relation to a change to the rules of succession in the United Kingdom is to grant or withhold Canada's assent to those proposed changes in accordance with the conventional requirements of the preamble of the *Statute of Westminster, 1931*. On this interpretation, the act of the Parliament of Canada in providing its assent to the proposed changes to the rules of succession embodied in the legislation enacted by the Parliament of the United Kingdom did not engage the provisions of the *Constitution Act, 1982*, concerning amendments to the office of the Queen, and therefore no constitutional amendment was required in order to effect the changes in the rules of succession. In arriving at this conclusion the Quebec court determined that the change to the rules of succession proposed by the Parliament of the United Kingdom and to which the Parliament of Canada assented pursuant to a Commonwealth convention did not amount to a change to the office of the Queen within the meaning of section 41(a) of the *Constitution Act, 1982*. In order to engage the unanimous amending formula in relation to the office of the Queen a proposed change would have to affect the "powers, status and constitutional role of the monarch", which was clearly not the case where the rules of succession were being modernized. Justice Bouchard concluded that:

> . . . the constitutional protection granted to the "office of the Queen" through the application of the amendment procedure set out in section 41(a) of the 1982 Act seeks primarily to ensure that the powers, status and role conferred on the Crown as an institution cannot be amended without the agreement of those listed therein, regardless of who is designated to occupy the function of King or Queen of the United Kingdom.

> That being the case, since the rules succession to the throne enacted by the United Kingdom have no effect on the "office of the Queen" and do not form an integral part of the Canadian constitution, they are not subject to the amendment procedure in the 1982 Act.[17]

On the secondary issue as to whether the rules of succession offended section 15(1) of the *Charter,* the Quebec court found, as did the Ontario courts, that the rules of succession had been constitutionalized through the preamble to the *Constitution Act 1867* and the *Charter* itself could not be used to challenge and strike down other components of the *Constitution of Canada*.[18] In any case, the legislative changes in the Parliament of the United Kingdom were beyond the purview of the *Charter*.[19]

3.19   The New Rules for Royal Marriages in Canada

The Canadian jurisprudence did not specifically address the subject of royal marriages. However, by enacting the *Succession to the Throne Act, 2013*, the Parliament of Canada assented to the changes in the law of succession to the Throne that were brought about in the United Kingdom through the *Succession to the Crown Act, 2013*. The Parliament of Canada thus assented to all of the changes to the rules of succession made by the United Kingdom, including changes to the requirements for members of the Royal Family to obtain the Sovereign's permission to marry.

3.7.6   The Continuing Importance of the Parliament at Westminster

The modernization of the title to the Canadian Throne in the early part of the twenty-first century has highlighted the continuing role played by the

Parliament at Westminster in the Canadian constitution. Because of the fact that Canada shares the Throne with the United Kingdom and the other Commonwealth realms any substantive changes in the title to the Throne can only be effected through substantive legislation passed by the Parliament of the United Kingdom, with Canada enacting legislation assenting to the British legislation in order to satisfy the conventions of the Commonwealth. At the time of the patriation of the constitution in 1982 it was thought that Canada's last constitutional links with the Parliament at Westminster had been sundered by the *Canada Act, 1982*, but as the modernization of the title to the Throne shows, at least with respect to the Commonwealth's multi-jurisdictional constitutional monarchy, a significant constitutional link to the United Kingdom Parliament still remains.

3.20   The Modern Title to the Throne of Canada

As a result of the reforms brought about by the Perth Agreement, and by the *Succession to the Crown Act, 2013*, and the related legislation of the Commonwealth realms, the modern rule of primogeniture applicable to the succession to the Throne for any person born after October 28, 2011, is now based on absolute primogeniture. This means that in the future the Throne will be inherited by the offspring of the Sovereign in their birth order regardless of their gender and, in the absence of any living offspring of a Sovereign, the Throne will pass to the next eldest sibling of the Sovereign regardless of their gender in their birth order or to the descendants of a deceased eldest sibling in their birth order, regardless of their gender. However, the order of the succession that prevailed on or before October 28, 2011, which was based on male-preference primogeniture, will continue to apply to the class of persons whose claim to the Throne was fixed by male-preference primogeniture before that date until their decease.

There remains a discriminatory requirement that the Sovereign herself or himself be a member of the Protestant faith in communion with the Church of England because of the fact that the Sovereign of the United Kingdom remains the Head of the Church of England, which is an established state church. Despite that obvious discriminatory requirement in relation to the Sovereign, which exists as a result of historical developments, the marriage of a Sovereign or any other person in the line of succession to the Throne to a person who professes the Roman Catholic faith will no longer disqualify any person from keeping or succeeding to the Throne.

As regards royal marriages, the modern requirement is that the first six persons in the line of succession must seek and obtain the permission of the Sovereign to wed, failing which they and their descendants will be disqualified from succeeding to the Throne in the United Kingdom and in Canada. However, the failure to obtain the Sovereign's permission will not invalidate such a marriage under the laws of the United Kingdom, and presumably the marriage would also be recognized in Canada.

As a result of the reformulation of the rules of succession there is no longer any discrimination based on gender in the selection of the person who can become the Sovereign of Canada, subject to the preservation of the rights of those members in the line of succession who were born on or before October 28, 2011, and there is no longer any disqualification from the succession to the Throne of any member of the Royal Family who marries, or who has married, a member of the Roman Catholic faith.

[1] at para. 53. In the *Secession Reference* the Supreme Court of Canada identified a number of other important constitutional principles including the rule of law, democracy, constitutionalism, federalism and the protection of minorities (see para. 49)

[2] 1 William & Mary Sess. 2 c. 2

[3] Male primogeniture was also the basis for the rules of succession for the Sovereign of Canada before 1763, when the French House of Bourbon constituted the Royal Family of Canada. The French law was also stricter than the English law in this respect: females could not inherit the Throne under the succession laws of France, although they could serve as a Regent.

[4] Religion was also a factor under the French monarchy in Canada. The first Sovereign of settled Canada, King Henri IV, was required to convert from Protestantism, his professed faith while King of Navarre, to Roman Catholicism, in order to ascend the Throne of France. The title to the Throne of France, and hence of Canada before 1763, was always in the Roman Catholic faith.

[5] *Re: Resolution to amend the Constitution*, [1981] 1 SCR 753 (Canada, SC) at 785.

[6] *New Brunswick Broadcasting Co. v. Nova Scotia (Speaker of the House of Assembly)*, [1993] 1 SCR 319 (Canada, SC). See, in particular the judgement of Chief Justice Lamer at p. 354 where he states: "To incorporate by way of the preamble the broad principle of of the fostering of the independence of the legislative process through the exercise of parliamentary privileges is much more palatable than incorporating a specific article of the *Bill of Rights* of 1689." Justice McLachlin (as she then was) held the same view stating at p. 374: "... absent specific reference, the wording of the preamble should not be understood to refer to a specific article of the English *Bill of Rights*. This is not to say that the principles underlying art. 9 of the English *Bill of Rights* of 1689 do not form part of our law".

[7] 12 & 13 Will. c. 3 (Eng.)

[8] "The Charter cannot be applied so as to abrogate or derogate from rights or privileges guaranteed by or under the Constitution" per Justice Wilson at para. 60.

[9] at para. 27

[10] at para. 36.

[11] 12 Geo 3 c. 11

[12] "Scholars scurry to find implications of royal wedding" Michael Valpy, *Globe and Mail*, February 11, 2005. Similarly, it does not appear that the Queen's Privy Council for Canada was convened to pass upon the marriage of Prince William, the Duke of Cambridge, to Ms. Catherine Middleton, although it is likely that the Government of Canada was informed of the engagement.

[13] 2013, c. 20 (UK)

[14]An amendment pursuant to section 41(a) of the *Constitution Act, 1982* would only have been necessary if the office of the Queen was being affected by the British legislation. However, the rules for selecting the monarch in the United Kingdom were not integral to the office of the Queen in Canada, and therefore a constitutional amendment was not required. If Canada were to unilaterally change the laws of succession so that the constitutional rule of recognition were breached it would engage section 41(a) of the *Constitution Act, 1982* and thus require a unanimous amendment to the constitution.

[15] S.C. 2013, c. 6 (in force March 26, 2015). The backgrounder is entitled: *Introduction of Line of Succession Legislation*, Department of Canadian Heritage, Ottawa, January, 2013.

[16] at para. 109 (translation)

[17] at paras. 139-140 (translation)

[18] at para. 154

[19] There was also an issue as to whether the official language provisions contained in section 133 of the *Constitution Act 1867* were complied with during the enactment process, as the Canadian legislation refers to a British enactment that was not enacted in both English and French. However, as the British statute was held not to have been incorporated into Canadian law there was no breach of any constitutional provisions relating to official languages.

THE SOVEREIGN AND THE ROYAL FAMILY

4.1   The Dynasty

The current Royal Family of Canada is the Royal Family of the United Kingdom. The dynasty is styled the House of Windsor and is the third dynasty to reign over Canada, although the distinction among the second and third dynasties can be viewed as nominal.

The first dynasty to reign over Canada was the House of Bourbon which ruled Canada from the founding of Quebec in 1608, under the reign of King Henri IV, until the cession of Canada by France to Great Britain in the Treaty of Paris in 1763. The House of Hanover, which was the reigning Royal Family in the United Kingdom then became the royal house of Canada until the death of Queen Victoria in 1901, following which the House of Saxe-Coburg and Gotha became the royal house of Canada. The House of Saxe-Coburg and Gotha was subsequently renamed the House of Windsor due to anti-German sentiment during World War One.

Although the royal house changed after the death of Queen Victoria from Hanover to Saxe-Coburg and Gotha that event reflected the paternal line of Prince Albert, the Prince Consort of Queen Victoria and the father of her children. No such change occurred in the style of the royal house during the reign of Queen Elizabeth II, who decreed that her descendants would continue to be known as the House of Windsor. Thus, members of the Royal Family of Canada can trace their descent through male and female ancestors directly to Princess Sophia, the Electress of Hanover, upon whom the Throne of England was conferred by the parliamentary grant of the Parliament of England contained in the *Act of Settlement, 1701*. Hence, the distinction between the House of Hanover and the House of Saxe-Coburg and Gotha (later Windsor) is essentially a nominal distinction.

4.2   The Sovereign's Accession to the Throne

The Sovereign accedes to the Throne upon one of two events, the death or abdication of their predecessor, and such transfers are known in law as a demise of the Crown. A third possibility, involving a revolutionary event such as transpired in 1688, is now regarded as an impossibility in the modern era.

The Throne passes from one Sovereign to another immediately upon the death of the preceding Sovereign, or upon the ratification by the Parliament of the United Kingdom of the previous Sovereign's signature on an Instrument of Abdication, without the requirement of any particular ceremony. Thus there is no interregnum between two reigns, and the new Sovereign immediately succeeds to the powers, rights, and dignities of the office of the Sovereign. However, under British constitutional law and practice there are prescribed procedures that a new Sovereign must follow upon acceding to the throne. The first such obligation placed upon the new Sovereign is to appear before the Accession Council at the earliest opportunity.

4.3   The Accession Council

The Accession Council is a body which exists by constitutional custom and usage, rather than by statute, and its purpose is to acclaim the new Sovereign. It is composed of all members of the Privy Council of the United Kingdom and all members of the House of Lords, as well as the Lord Mayor, Aldermen, and leading subjects of the City of London, and the High Commissioners of the Commonwealth realms residing in London.

The convening of the Accession Council follows shortly after the demise of the Crown. The Accession Council meets at St. James Palace in London, England. Following the meeting of the Accession Council, heralds from the English College of Heralds will publicly proclaim the accession of the new Sovereign under the new Sovereign's chosen regnal name to the City of London. The accession of the Sovereign can then be proclaimed in all of the Sovereign's other realms, including Canada.

4.4   The Regnal Name

Prior to, or no later than the new Sovereign's appearance before the Accession Council, the Sovereign must choose the name by which they will be known during their reign. The choice of a name is necessary because the proceedings of the Accession Council will result in the issuance of a royal proclamation of the ascension to the Throne of the new Sovereign. In choosing a regnal name the new Sovereign may choose the name that they are known by, or they may choose a different name. Various Sovereigns of the United Kingdom have taken names different from the name they were commonly known by, including Queen Victoria (Alexandrina), King Edward VII (Albert), and King George VI (Albert). Others have chosen their own personal names as their regnal names, including King George V and Queen Elizabeth II.

4.5   The Accession Declarations

Upon appearing before the Accession Council, it is customary for the new Sovereign to read the declaration prescribed by the Act Ratifying and Approving [a] Treaty of the Two Kingdoms of Scotland and England of the Scottish Parliament in 1707 in which the Sovereign swears to uphold the Protestant religion established by law in Scotland.

There is a second accession declaration that is prescribed by the *Accession Declaration Act 1910*.[1] That legislation modified the original declaration which the Sovereign was enjoined to make subscribe, and audibly repeat pursuant to Section 1 of the *Bill of Rights 1689* and section 2 of the *Act of Settlement 1701*. In the accession declaration, the Sovereign states:

> I [here insert the name of the Sovereign] do solemnly and sincerely in the presence of God profess, testify, and declare that I am a faithful Protestant, and that I will, according to the true intent of the enactments which secure the Protestant succession to the Throne of my Realm, uphold and maintain the said enactments to the best of my powers, according to law.

This accession declaration, however, is not made in the presence of the Accession Council but rather is normally made by the Sovereign in the House of Lords at the first meeting of the Sovereign and the Parliament of the United Kingdom following the accession. If it is impossible for the new Sovereign to meet with the Parliament of the United Kingdom before the coronation of the Sovereign this accession declaration will be made at the coronation.

4.6   Canada and the Accession

In Canada, the heir to the Throne immediately ascends the throne following the death or abdication of the previous Sovereign. However, the operation of the constitutional machinery in the United Kingdom is a necessary prerequisite for the acclamation of the new Sovereign in Canada.

Under the current practice in the United Kingdom (i.e., the practice that prevailed at the last meeting of an Accession Council, in 1952), the High Commissioners of the Commonwealth countries are invited to attend the meeting of the Council. In 1952 the outgoing Canadian High Commissioner to the United Kingdom, Vincent Massey (who had just been appointed as the next Governor General of Canada as the final act of King George VI in regards to Canada) was invited to attend the Accession Council to acclaim Queen Elizabeth II as the Sovereign.

It is a constitutional custom for a Canadian representative to attend the Accession Council in London because the Accession Council is the body that formally recognizes and proclaims the new Sovereign of the United Kingdom, following which the Sovereign will be proclaimed in Canada. The operation of the Canadian constitutional rule of recognition requires that Canada take official cognizance of the rightful heir to the Throne under the established succession laws of the United Kingdom.

Within Canada, the constitutional practice is to summon a meeting of the Queen's [or King's] Privy Council for Canada to acclaim the new Sovereign following the acclamation of the new Sovereign in the United Kingdom. The meeting of the Canadian Privy Council should occur after the Accession Council of the United Kingdom has proclaimed the new Sovereign, in order to properly implement the constitutional rule of recognition whereby Canada identifies its rightful Sovereign based on their succession to the Throne of the United Kingdom. It is also desirable for the Accession Council in London to formally proclaim the new Sovereign under their chosen regnal name of before the acclamation of the new Sovereign by the Canadian Privy Council, lest the wrong regnal name be used in the Canadian proclamation.

A meeting of the Canadian Privy Council was summoned in 1952, upon the accession of Queen Elizabeth II by the Administrator of Canada rather than the Governor General because the outgoing Governor General, Viscount Alexander, had departed Canada but the incoming Governor General, Vincent Massey, was still in London wrapping up his term as the Canadian High Commissioner to the United Kingdom.

Following the meeting of the Queen's Privy Council for Canada, the following proclamation was issued to the public:

> WHEREAS it hath pleased Almighty God to call to His Mercy Our Late Sovereign Lord King George the Sixth of blessed and glorious memory by whose decease the Crown of Great Britain, Ireland and all other His late Majesty's dominions is solely and rightfully come to the High and Mighty Princess Elizabeth Alexandra Mary, Now Know Ye that I, the said Right Honourable Thibaudeau Rinfret, Administrator of Canada as aforesaid, assisted by Her Majesty's Privy Council for Canada do now hereby with one voice and consent of tongue and heart, publish and proclaim that the High and Mighty Princess Elizabeth Alexandra Mary is now by the death of Our late Sovereign of happy and glorious memory become our only lawful and rightful Liege Lady Elizabeth the Second by the Grace of God, of Great Britain, Ireland and the British Dominions beyond the Seas Queen, Defender of the Faith, Supreme Liege Lady in and over Canada, to whom we acknowledge all faith and constant obedience with all hearty and humble affection, beseeching God by whom all Kings and Queens do reign to bless the Royal Princess Elizabeth the Second with long and happy years to reign over us.

> Given under my Hand and Seal and arms at Ottawa, this Sixth day of February, in the year of Our Lord one thousand nine hundred and fifty-two, and in the first year of Her Majesty's reign".[2]

4.7   The Coronation

The Coronation of the Sovereign is held some months after the accession. The ceremony is one which is undertaken in the grandest style, befitting its symbolic significance. However, there is no constitutional requirement for a Sovereign to be crowned and enthroned in a formal coronation ceremony in order for the Sovereign to exercise the powers of their office. That principle was established as long ago as 1608, in *Calvin's Case* (1608), 7 Co Rep 1a at 10b; ". . . for coronation is but a Royal ornament and solemnization of the Royal descent, but no part of the title." As a contemporary example of the application of this principle, no coronation ceremony was held for King Edward VIII, who nonetheless exercised all of the prerogatives of his office during his reign.

Nevertheless, it is the custom for the Sovereign to be crowned and enthroned at a coronation ceremony. The effect of the ceremony, in historical terms, has been to quiet all controversies with respect to the accession of the new Sovereign.[3] In modern times that purpose is no longer as important as it once was but the coronation continues as pageantry, and as the opportunity for the new Sovereign to commit their reign to the rule of law.

The content of the coronation ceremony is not fixed by law but is determined upon each occasion by the Sovereign, who is advised by the Privy Council of the United Kingdom. Thus, no two coronations will be exactly alike. Nevertheless, the procedures for a coronation do not markedly depart from custom and precedent, and the essential elements today can still be seen in the surviving records of an earliest recorded coronation of an English monarch, that of King Edgar in 973.[4] Coronation practices in European monarchies, including England, were generally influenced by biblical references, particularly those from the Old Testament, such as the investiture of Solomon as the King of Israel.[5]

The modern practice is for a committee of the Privy Council of the United Kingdom to be appointed by the Sovereign to prepare for the coronation ceremony. This Coronation Committee principally acts through a subcommittee known as the Executive Committee. In addition, a Coronation Joint Committee is established by the Coronation Committee, which consists of representatives of those Commonwealth countries whose citizens owe allegiance to the Sovereign. A court of claims is also established to adjudicate upon the hereditary rights of the Sovereign's subjects in the United Kingdom to perform certain ancient ceremonial offices in connection with the coronation.

The coronation ceremony is both a religious[6] and a political event of symbolic significance and is presided over by the Archbishop of Canterbury, the senior prelate of the Church of England, who is assisted by the Archbishop of York. The ceremonials evolve over time but an ancient record of past coronations has been kept in the form of an illuminated manuscript, known as the *Liber Regalis* dating from approximately 1390, which is used as a manual of precedents in respect of coronation ceremonies. The manuscript is kept in the custody of the Dean and Chapter of Westminster Abbey (formally, that church is known as The Abbey Church of St. Peter, Westminster) where all coronations of English or British monarchs since King William I in 1066 have been conducted.[7] The coronation involves the great officers of state, the Earl Marshal of the Realm, the Lord Great Chamberlain, the Lord High Steward, the Lord High Constable, the Lord Privy Seal and the Lord Chancellor. Some of those great officials occupy offices that are only of historical significance and are therefore appointed only for the purposes of the coronation (e.g., the Lord High Constable).

4.8   The Ceremonial Procession[8]

The Coronation Ceremony itself may be conveniently divided into two parts, the Ceremonial and the Service, the whole of which is under the administration of the Earl Marshal of the Realm, the Duke of Norfolk, who is the senior peer of the realm in the United Kingdom in the British order of precedence. During the Ceremonial there is a formal procession into the Abbey led by royalty, the great officers of state, peers directed to bear the royal regalia, and the Archbishops of Canterbury and York, all of whom wear their robes of state.

The procession is divided into separate and distinct groups who are preceded into the Abbey by heralds. The procession begins with the members of the Royal Family other than the princes and princesses who are entitled to be addressed as a Royal Highness. They are followed by the royal and non-royal representatives of foreign states, and then by the rulers of states under the protection of the British Crown.[9] These are then followed by the Dean and Prebendaries of Westminster Abbey and then by the Princes and Princesses of royal blood who are entitled to be addressed as a Royal Highness. If the Sovereign has a surviving parent (other than one who has abdicated the Throne) they will proceed next in the procession, along with surviving siblings of the Sovereign.

At this point in the Ceremonial a break in the procession occurs with the delivery of the regalia, which is delivered first to the Lord High Constable by the officials representing the Lord Chamberlain and then by the Lord High Constable, or his representative, to the Lord Great Chamberlain who delivers them to the designated lords who will carry the regalia in the abbey. The regalia that is delivered into the hands of the Lords attending the Sovereign at the Coronation ceremony consists of the following:

-St. Edward's staff

-The Sceptre with the Cross

-The Golden Spurs

-The Pointed Sword of Justice to the Temporality, or Third Sword

-The Pointed Sword of Justice to the Spirituality, or Second Sword

-The Curtana or Sword of Mercy

-The Sword of State

-The Rod with the Dove

-The Orb

-St. Edward's Crown

-The Paten

-The Chalice

-The Bible

By this time, the procession of the Sovereign, which begins from Buckingham Palace, will have now reached the Abbey and the entrance procession of the Sovereign commences led by the Abbey Beadle, and followed by the chaplains, the domestic chaplains, the representatives of the free churches, the representatives of the Church of Scotland, the Dean and Prebendaries of Westminster, and subsequently by the heralds.

Following the procession of the religious leaders, the representatives of the orders of knighthood will proceed into the abbey led by the representatives of the Order of the British Empire and they are followed by the representatives of the Royal Victorian Order, the Order of St. Michael and St. George, the Order of the Bath, the Order of the Thistle, and finally the Order of the Garter.

Following the knights come the standards of all the realms that owe allegiance to the Sovereign, including the Canadian national standard, which is borne by the High Commissioner of Canada to the United Kingdom according to custom and precedent. The standards of the United Kingdom and the royal standards will follow the national standards of the realms. Knights bearing the canopy that will shield the Sovereign during the anointment come next in the procession, and the canopy is carried by knights of the Garter. The Prime Ministers or other representatives of the Commonwealth of Nations follow in the procession, and then comes the Archbishop of York, the Lord Chancellor, and the Archbishop of Canterbury.

The Sovereign's spouse then precedes the regalia in the procession and following the regalia comes the Sovereign, dressed in a royal robe of crimson velvet trimmed with ermine (in 1953 it was Canadian ermine), bordered by gold lace, and wearing the collar of the Order of the Garter and (if the Sovereign is a female) a diadem of precious jewels. The Sovereign is supported on each side by a Bishop of the Church of England and following her or his train are the various officials of the Royal household. The Sovereign, after making Adoration and private devotions at a faldstool, takes their seat in the Chair of Estate as the Ceremonial concludes and the Service begins.

4.9   The Coronation Service

The Coronation Service, which is the substantive content of the ritual, commences with the laying of the regalia upon the altar. The Bishops bearing the Bible, Chalice, and Paten present them to the Archbishop of Canterbury at the altar. The Lords bearing regalia also present each item of the regalia at the altar except the swords, which remain with the Lords bearing them.

4.10   The Recognition

The Recognition of the Sovereign then takes place. This is an ancient relic of the service from the time when the community had the right to express their approval or disapproval of a prospective Sovereign's candidacy for the Throne. In more modern times it provides an opportunity for the representatives of the community to identify and acclaim the new Sovereign. In the Recognition, the Archbishop of Canterbury comes down from the altar and stands together with the highest officers of state, the Lord High Chancellor, the Lord Great Chamberlain, the Lord High Constable, and the Earl Marshal of the Realm while the Sovereign arises from the Chair of Estate and stands next to King Edward's Chair.[10] The Archbishop, together with the great officers of state, and preceded by the Garter King of Arms (a heraldic official), then formally presents the Sovereign to the people while facing east and then does the same while accompanied by the great officers of state to the south, the west and finally to the north.[11] The Sovereign faces the people in each direction in which the Archbishop makes his presentation. After each presentation the people acclaim the Sovereign with the statement "God Save Queen [or King] . . . ". Trumpets are sounded after each acclamation. The Sovereign, the Archbishop, and the great officers of state then return to their original positions.

4.11   The Coronation Oath

At the last coronation in 1953 the administration of the Coronation Oath was restored to its medieval position immediately after the Recognition in the order of the Service. From a legal perspective, the most important part of the coronation ceremony is the swearing of the Coronation Oath by the Sovereign.

A Coronation Oath has always been an important part of coronations held in Europe. In France the Coronation Oath was seen as a recognition by the Sovereign of his moral and religious obligations to do right but it was unconnected to law.[12] That reflected the French emphasis on the sacredness of the connection between the Sovereign and God as a foundation for monarchical absolutism.[13] However, the governing political philosophy in England was different. There, the Coronation Oath has always reflected the view that the Sovereign's conduct of their office is circumscribed by their oath. A sacred oath has always been administered to the Sovereigns of England and Great Britain by the priesthood in the presence of the most senior nobles of the realm, and it had a marked effect on the development of the medieval constitution in England.[14]

Originally, the English Coronation Oath required the Sovereign to preserve peace, to abjure rapacity and iniquity, and to enjoin equity and mercy in judgement. In 1308, a notable change occurred to the structure of the oath when, following the *Magna Carta* of 1215, and its subsequent reissues, the Coronation Oath was amended to require the Sovereign to follow the laws made during the Sovereign's reign by the national community.[15] That change was significant because for the first time the Sovereign was placed under an obligation to follow not only the laws that existed when the Coronation Oath was taken but also future laws made according to the accepted procedures of the realm. As such, that development was important for the evolving concept of the rule of law. Although in continental European monarchies the Coronation Oath gradually came to signify a moral obligation, in England it gradually came to signify a legal obligation willingly taken by a new Sovereign.

In the Coronation Oath the Sovereign swears to provide good governance to all their subjects by upholding the rule of law and it is subject to that obligation that all government in the Commonwealth realms, including Canada, is carried on in the Sovereign's name by ministers and officials. The Coronation Oath should therefore be viewed as a solemn affirmation by the highest authority in the state of the obligation of all state actors to submit to the rule of law.[16]

The Coronation Oath forms an important part of the social compact between the Sovereign and subjects, and an indication of its early importance can be seen in *Proceedings against Hugh and Hugh Le Despencer*, (1320), 1 State Tr. 23 at 29, which attributes the following obligation to the Sovereign:

> And we are bound by the oath we made at our coronation, and obliged to do right to all our subjects, and to redress and cause to be amended all wrongs done to them when we are required, according to the Great Charter, by which we are not to sell or delay right and justice to any one;

Although originally part of the *Coronation Ordo* (the original Roman Catholic directions for the Coronation Service), the Coronation Oath was subsumed into statute following the revolution that brought William and Mary to the throne of England in 1689. The basic form of the modern oath was established by the *Coronation Oath Act, 1689* [1 Will. & Mary, c. 6]. The oath, to be administered by the Archbishop of Canterbury is established by section 3 of the Act in the following terms:

> Will you solemnly promise and swear to govern the people of this kingdom of England, and the dominions thereto belonging according to the statutes in parliament agreed on, and the laws and customs of the same?
>
> **The King and Queen shall say,**
>
> I solemnly promise so to do.
>
> Will you to your power cause law and justice in mercy to be executed in all your judgments?
>
> **King and Queen**
>
> I will.
>
> Will you to the utmost of your power maintain the laws of God, the true profession of the gospel and the protestant reformed religion established by law? and will you preserve unto the bishops and clergy of this realm, and to the churches committed to their charge, all such rights and privileges as by law do or shall appertain unto them, or any of them?
>
> **King and Queen**
>
> All this I promise to do
>
> After this, the King and Queen laying his and her hand and on the holy gospels, shall say,
>
> **King and Queen**
>
> The things which I have here before promised, I will perform and keep: So help me God.
>
> **Then the King and Queen shall kiss the book.**

Section 4 of the Act stipulates that the same oath shall be administered to every King or Queen who shall succeed to the crown of the realm. That requirement was subsequently reinforced by the *Act of Settlement 1701*. The *Act of Settlement 1701* provides that every person who comes into possession of the throne must swear the coronation oath. Section 2 of that Act states, in part:

> . . . and that every King and Queen of this realm, who shall come to and succeed in the imperial crown of this kingdom, by virtue of this act, shall have the coronation oath administered to him or her or them, at their respective coronations, according

to the act of parliament made in the first year of the reign of his Majesty, and the said late Queen Mary intituled, An act for establishing the coronation oath, and shall make, subscribe, and repeat the declaration in the act first above recited mentioned or referred to, in the manner and form thereby prescribed.

In fact, the form, but not the substance of the Coronation Oath, has been modified by circumstances in the years since the enactment of those statutes.

In modern times, the various realms over which the Sovereign exercises regal authority are now specifically described in the oath. That flows from the development of the Commonwealth realms into distinct sovereignties within a divisible monarchy. In the Coronation Oath taken by King George VI in 1937 the independent dominions were mentioned by name within the oath for the first time. In 1953 when the coronation oath was administered to Queen Elizabeth II, she pledged as follows:

> I promise and swear to govern the Peoples of the United Kingdom of Great Britain and Northern Ireland, Canada, Australia, New Zealand and the Union of South Africa, Pakistan and Ceylon, and of my Possessions and the other Territories to any of them belonging or pertaining, according to their respective laws and customs.
>
> I will to my power cause Law and Justice, in Mercy, to be executed in all my judgements.
>
> I will to the utmost of my power maintain the Laws of God and the true profession of the Gospel. I will to the utmost of my power maintain in the United Kingdom the Protestant Reformed Religion established by law.
>
> And I will maintain and preserve inviolably the settlement of the Church of England, and the doctrine, worship, discipline, and government thereof, as by law established in England. And I will preserve unto the Bishops and Clergy of England, and to the Churches there committed to their charge, all such rights and privileges as by law do or shall appertain to them or any of them.
>
> These things which I have here before promised I will perform and keep. So help me God.

There are four elements to the coronation oath but only the first two elements have application to the governance of Canada, the last two being elements relating to the maintenance of the Protestant state religion in the United Kingdom. The essential elements of the oath as it applies to the governance of Canada are:

1) to govern the peoples of the Sovereign's realms (including Canada) according to their respective laws and customs; and

2) within the power of the Sovereign, to require law and justice tempered by mercy to be executed in all judgments.

Essentially, the obligations of the coronation oath confirm the rule of law and the subordination of royal authority to the rule of law. Justice Rooney quoted the following passage from Halsbury's Laws of England on this point with approval, in the Supreme Court of Fiji in *Bavadra V Attorney General (Fiji)*, [1988] LRC (Const) 13 (Fiji, SC): "Constitutional law clothes the person of the Sovereign with supreme sovereignty and pre-eminence. She is, however, bound by the terms of her coronation oath and the maxims of the common law, to observe and obey the law (Halsbury, Vol. 8, para. 894)."

Nevertheless, a breach of the Coronation Oath, should it occur, would not be justiciable against the Sovereign personally in a court of law since the royal prerogative provides that the Sovereign is immune from legal process in a personal capacity. Furthermore, the oath only binds the conscience of the Sovereign, and support for that view can be gleaned from case law in another monarchy within the Commonwealth; *Mokotso v HM King Moshoeshoe II*, [1989] LRC (Const.) 24 (Lesotho, HC), where Chief Justice Cullinan addressed the legal consequences which flowed from the taking of an oath for the due execution of the office of the King of Lesotho. He stated:

> In the absence of statutory sanction an oath but binds the conscience. As I see it therefore, compliance with an oath as such, rather than with the underlying obligations involved, is an act in one's private capacity. I do not see therefore that suit would lie against the King in respect of the oath of office, even if such a suit were well-founded.

As a matter of conscience, the obligations of the Sovereign expressed in the Coronation Oath bind and colour all of the actions of the Sovereign, and of the public officers and officials who advise the Sovereign in the conduct of government in her or his realms, including Canada. Thus, constitutional advice must not be given to the Sovereign by Canadian constitutional actors that would have the effect of precipitating a breach of the Sovereign's Coronation Oath.

In the Coronation Service, the Coronation Oath is administered by the Archbishop of Canterbury, or by another bishop to whom the task is delegated by the Sovereign if circumstances require. The Archbishop poses the prescribed questions to the Sovereign who must answer affirmatively. The Sovereign then rises from the Chair of Estate and, preceded by the Sword of State, proceeds to the altar and kneels, placing their right hand on the Bible and articulates the Coronation Oath, afterwards kissing the Bible following which the Sovereign returns to the Chair of Estate. The Sovereign later signs a written copy of the Coronation Oath.

4.12   The Presentation of the Holy Bible

The presentation of the Holy Bible to the Sovereign is intended to represent the tendering of the most valuable object on Earth (in the tradition of the Christian civilization) to the Sovereign. The Archbishop and the Moderator of the Church of Scotland receive the Holy Bible from the Dean of Westminster at the altar and they jointly present it to the Sovereign with an appropriate presentation statement, following which the Holy Bible is returned to the altar.

4.13   The Anointing

The Anointing of the Sovereign is the most heavily endowed religious element of the Service. In ancient theological terms the anointment arose from a desire to transform the natural person of the Sovereign into a man or woman of majesty through divine grace.[17] The anointing of a Sovereign was the most important component of any European coronation until (in the case of England and then Great Britain) the Coronation Oath gained political significance. For example, in France, whose Sovereigns reigned over Canada from 1608 until 1763, the holy oil used in the coronation ceremony was held to have been a gift from heaven to Clovis, the first Christian Sovereign of France, and the sacredness of the anointment with this holy oil was the foundation for the King's honorific title of His Most Christian Majesty.[18] In England, from the earliest coronations, the Roman Catholic Church authorized the use of the holy oil of chrism (a combination of olive oil and balsam) for the anointment of a new Sovereign at a coronation. Into the twentieth century the anointment continued to be viewed as a significant transformative element of the Coronation Service.

The procedure for the anointment begins after the conclusion of the Creed with the singing of a hymn[19] followed by the Archbishop of Canterbury reciting the prayer of Consecration. Next the assembly sings the hymn Zadok the Priest[20] while the Sovereign, leaving the Chair of Estate, is assisted in the removal of their crimson robe, diadem (if the Sovereign is female), and Garter collar. A plain white anointing gown is donned for the anointing procedure. The Sovereign then proceeds to King Edward's Chair preceded by the Sword of State and is seated upon it. A party of four Knights from the Order of the Garter carries a canopy of gold cloth over the chair to shield the Sovereign during the anointing. Although the Anointing is regarded as the most important element from a religious perspective, this part of the ceremony is shielded somewhat from public view, in all probability to accentuate the mystery of the proceeding and in conformity with royal conceptions of personal modesty.

The Dean of Westminster then proceeds from the altar carrying the Ampulla containing the Holy Oil and the Anointing Spoon and pours some of the Holy Oil into the Spoon. The Archbishop of Canterbury then takes the oil and anoints the Sovereign by drawing a cross in oil on firstly on their hands, then on their breast, and finally on their forehead.[21] The Dean of Westminster then withdraws with the Ampulla and Anointing Spoon to the altar and the Knights of the Garter withdraw the canopy. The Sovereign then arises and goes to the faldstool where they kneel and receive the blessing of the Archbishop of Canterbury before arising and retaking their seat on King Edward's Chair.

4.14   The Colobium Sindonis, the Supertunica, and the Girdle

The next procedure during the Coronation Service involves the investiture of the Sovereign with special apparel that is placed over the clothes that the Sovereign wears to the Service. Depending on the Sovereign's sex, they will be assisted by the Groom of the Robes, or by the Mistress of the Robes. At their coronation a male Sovereign would wear a uniform but for a female Sovereign, or Consort, a dress will be specially designed for the occasion. It is the modern practice for the dress of a female Sovereign, or Consort, to incorporate design elements from each of the Sovereign's realms. Thus, in 1953, the dress worn by Queen Elizabeth II to her coronation included botanical references to her various realms such as oak leaves (England), thistle (Scotland), leeks (Wales) and shamrocks (Northern Ireland) for the countries of the United Kingdom, and, for her other realms maple leaves (Canada), a mimosa or wattle flower (Australia), silver fern (New Zealand), lotus (Ceylon), protea (South Africa), and wheat cotton and jute (Pakistan).

The first item to be put on by the Sovereign is a simple sleeveless garment of white linen cambric known as the *Colobium Sindonis*. This apparel represents royal authority as a gift of the people, since this type of garment was once commonly worn by all people in society and is derived from the clothing worn in the ancient Roman Empire. A *Colobium Sindonis*, is made for each Sovereign for their coronation.

Next, the Sovereign will don the *Supertunica*, a rich garment of cloth of gold modelled on an ancient costume of the Byzantine Court which was itself derived from priestly origins, and thus denotes the connection of the Sovereign to the sacred. The *Supertunica* is an ankle length garment and is secured with a garment known as the Girdle but which can be more properly understood as a belt. After the Sovereign has been assisted in the donning of these garments, the Sovereign will once again take their seat on King Edward's Chair.

4.15   The Presentation of the Spurs

Following the investiture of the royal garments the Dean of Westminster delivers the Golden Spurs to the Lord Great Chamberlain who then presents them to the Sovereign. The Sovereign will then touch the Golden Spurs as a sign of her or his acceptance of them and the Lord Great Chamberlain will deliver them back to the Dean of Westminster who will return them to the altar.

4.16   The Presentation of the Sword of State

The peer who has custody of the Sword of State at the Service then delivers it to the Lord Chamberlain of the Household, and receives from him the Sword for the Offering, which has been brought out of the St. Edward's Chapel by the Keeper of the Jewel House. The Sword of State is then taken into St. Edward's Chapel and the Sword for the Offering is presented to the Archbishop of Canterbury who places it upon the altar. The Archbishop will say a prayer over the sword after which, in the company of the Archbishop of York and other prelates he will deliver the sword to the Sovereign who will rise from King Edward's Chair and return the Sword for the Offering to the altar, giving it to the Dean of Westminster before returning to King Edward's Chair.

The peer who originally had custody of the sword of state then proceeds to the altar where he will redeem the sword of state from the Dean of Westminster for 100 shillings and will give the jewelled scabbard to the Keeper of the Jewel House while keeping the sword for the remainder of the ceremony.

4.17   The Presentation of the Armills

The Armills are a type of bracelet that the Dean of Westminster brings down from the altar and gives to the Archbishop of Canterbury who them places them on the Sovereign's wrists with a statement regarding their presentation. In the 1953 coronation new Armills were cast for the occasion and paid for by the Commonwealth realms.[22]

4.18   The Stole Royal and the Pallium

Next in the coronation procedures comes the investiture of the Sovereign with the Stole Royal and the *Pallium,* or Cloth of Gold. The Stole Royal is a type of scarf made of gold cloth and the *Pallium* or Mantle is also made of gold cloth bordered by crimson-coloured silk and bearing silver coronets and eagles. Both robes are delivered to the Dean of Westminster by the Groom of Robes and the Dean, assisted by the Groom or (if the Sovereign is female) by the Mistress of Robes, will assist the Sovereign in their donning, following which the Lord Great Chamberlain fastens the clasps of the *Pallium* while the Archbishop intones words of presentation. While Coronation robes are invariably created anew for each coronation, the practice has been to continue to use the *Pallium* that was created for the coronation of King George IV in 1820.

4.19   The Presentation of the Orb

The Sovereign's Orb, a small globe-shaped object topped by a cross, is an ancient Christian symbol reflecting God's dominion over the Earth. Originally, it was held by the Roman and Byzantine Emperors as symbolic of their rule on God's behalf. In a more modern context in the United Kingdom it symbolizes the protection of the Christian Church by the Crown. In the coronation ceremony the Dean of Westminster will convey the Orb to the Archbishop who them presents it to the Sovereign who takes the Orb in their right hand. After the presentation the Sovereign gives the Orb back to the Dean of Westminster who returns it to the altar.

4.20   The Presentation of the Ring and the Glove

Following the presentation of the Orb, the Dean of Westminster delivers the Sovereign's ring from the altar to the Keeper of the Jewel House who brings it to the Archbishop who then places the royal ring on the Sovereign's fourth 'finger of the right hand. A peer designated for the purpose then emerges, kneels before the Sovereign and presents a glove to the Sovereign which they will assist the Sovereign in placing on their right hand, now bearing the royal ring.

4.21   The Presentation of the Sceptre and the Rod

The Dean of Westminster will next bring forth the Sceptre topped by a cross, and the Rod topped by a dove from the altar and give them to the Archbishop who will place the Sceptre into the Sovereign's right hand and the Rod into their left hand. The Sceptre is emblematic of royal authority while the Rod topped by a dove (sometimes referred to as the Rod of Equity and Mercy) represents the Sovereign's spiritual jurisdiction as the head of the Church of England.

4.22   The Crowning

The Archbishop of Canterbury then proceeds to the altar where, after taking St. Edward's Crown in his hands he performs a prayer of benediction, and then leaves the altar in procession with the Archbishop of York and other bishops and proceeds to the foot of King Edward's Chair where the Sovereign is seated. The Dean of Westminster then takes St. Edward's Crown from the altar and delivers it to the Archbishop of Canterbury who then raises the Crown and places it on the head of the Sovereign. At this point in the Service all those present will shout out "God Save the Queen [or King]" and the Princes, Princesses, and Peers or Peeresses all put their coronets on their heads, as does the heraldic Kings of Arms (who, like peers, are entitled to wear a type of crown), while trumpets blast forth and artillery outside the abbey at the Tower of London will fire a twenty-one-gun salute. The Archbishop of Canterbury then intones a prayer over the Sovereign, following which the abbey choir will sing a hymn.[23]

4.23   The Benediction

Following the Anointing, the Investiture of the royal regalia, and symbols, and the crowning of the Sovereign, the Archbishop of Canterbury then offers a benediction, a blessing upon the Sovereign.

4.24   The Enthronement

Now, having been crowned, the Sovereign arises from King Edward's chair and accompanied by the Archbishop, bishops, officers of state and peers who bore the regalia and preceded by the Sword of State proceeds to the Throne Chair which is on an elevated platform. Assisted by the prelates and peers the Sovereign is then assisted, or lifted up and into the Throne. The prelates and peers retreat to the foot of the elevated platform where the Archbishop performs an Exhortation.[24]

4.25 The Homage

With the crowning and the enthronement now completed, the Sovereign divests themselves of the Sceptre, the Rod, and the Glove, these being given into the custody of the peers who delivered the Sceptre and the Rod, and who remain with those objects at the side of the Sovereign. The Archbishop comes forward to the Throne and kneeling before the Sovereign pronounces his fealty to the Sovereign while holding his hands between the Sovereign's hands. The other prelates likewise pledge homage to the Sovereign from their positions at the foot of the Throne.

Following the fealty of the spiritual lords the peers and peeresses render homage beginning with the royal consort (if any) and continuing with the royal dukes who will also kneel before the Sovereign and pledge their fealty. The senior peer in each degree of nobility will then follow and pledge fealty while those in the same degree of nobility do likewise from their place in the abbey. After the completion of the Homage the Sovereign will recover the Sceptre and the Rod and the people will shout out "God Save Queen [or King] . . . " and "Long Live Queen [or King] . . . " and "May the Queen [or King] live for ever."

4.26 The Communion

The Sovereign arises from the Throne and proceeds to the altar preceded by the Sword of State where the Sovereign lays down the Sceptre and the Rod and takes off the Crown and kneels for the Communion. Bishops will provide the Paten and the Chalice to the Sovereign who gives them to the Archbishop who will place them on the altar and say a prayer. The Sovereign then makes an oblation (an offering to God) of an altar cloth which the Sovereign receives from the Lord Great Chamberlain, and an ingot of gold, and the Archbishop will place both offerings on the altar. The Sovereign then arises and proceeds to their own faldstool for the religious act of communion. After the completion of communion and the reciting of the Lord's Prayer, the Sovereign obtains the Crown and the Sceptre and Rod and returns to the Throne while the choir sings a hymn[25] and then the *Te Deum*.

4.27 The Recessional

Following the communion service the Sovereign, now wearing the crown of St. Edward, and bearing the Sceptre and the Rod and preceded by the four Swords descends from the Throne and enters St. Edward's Chapel within the Abbey where the Sovereign will deliver the Crown, the Sceptre, and the Rod to the Archbishop of Canterbury who will place them on the altar before entering a private traverse where, assisted by the Groom of Robes, or the Mistress of Robes, depending upon the Sovereign's sex, will divest themselves of the royal robes used in the coronation and don the Royal Robe of Purple Velvet. Upon emerging, the recessional procession will form with the four swords preceding the Sovereign wearing the purple robe, and the Imperial State Crown, and bearing the Sceptre in their right hand, and the Orb in their left hand. When the procession is ready, the Earl Marshal will signify that the recessional procession should begin and the royal anthem "God Save the Queen [or King] will ring out as the Sovereign departs the abbey in state.

4.28   The Coronation Parade

Upon the departure from Westminster Abbey the Sovereign is escorted back to Buckingham Palace through the streets of London in a great parade of military and civil officials, diplomats, and guests. It is customary for Canada to dispatch a Canadian Coronation Contingent to the United Kingdom consisting of personnel from the Canadian Armed Forces and the Royal Canadian Mounted Police to participate in this Coronation Parade. The parade concludes the Coronation Ceremonial and Coronation Service.

4.29   Infirmity, Illness and Tender Years

Although the Sovereign, in their capacity as a corporation sole, knows no minority in law some provision must be made for the appointment of a Regent where a Sovereign in their natural capacity is under the age of eighteen years at the date of the Sovereign's accession to the Throne. Until parliamentary supremacy was established, such matters fell within the purview of the Sovereign or closely related members of the Royal Family but since the establishment of parliamentary supremacy the constitutional practice requires that Parliament enact legislation to provide for a regency. A regency vests authority in a person to act in the place of the Sovereign for most purposes, although certain functions, such as the power to grant Royal Assent to legislation that would have the effect of altering the succession to the Throne, are typically withheld from a Regent by Parliament. Before 1937 the constitutional practice in the United Kingdom was for a regency statute to be enacted when particular circumstances required that a regency be established. Thus, regency statutes were enacted during the infancy and youth of a direct heir to the throne as and when required.

However, in 1937 the United Kingdom Parliament enacted a broad statute that was intended to provide for the circumstances of a regency in all future cases. The *Regency Act, 1937*,[26] provided that where a Sovereign is under the age of eighteen, all royal functions may be performed by a Regent, who will have guardianship over the Sovereign until the Sovereign has reached his or her eighteenth birthday. The Regent is entitled to exercise all powers of the Sovereign whether those powers arise by statute or Royal Prerogative, and the Regent may receive the homage due to the Sovereign. The only power denied to the Regent is the power to grant Royal Assent to a bill which would change the order of succession to the Throne.

A regency can also be established where a Sovereign who is of the age of eighteen is incapable of performing the functions of their office because of an infirmity of body or mind. In such cases, a regency will be established upon the making of a declaration of infirmity by at least three of the following persons; the Royal Consort, the Lord Chancellor, the Speaker of the House of Commons in the Parliament at Westminster, the Lord Chief Justice of England, and the Master of the Rolls.

A declaration of infirmity must be made to the Privy Council of the United Kingdom and must be communicated to all of the Sovereign's other realms, pursuant to section 2(2) of the Act. As a matter of protocol, if not of law, a declaration of infirmity would presumably also be communicated to all of the members of the Commonwealth of Nations whenever the Sovereign occupies the office of Head of the Commonwealth.

The *Regency Act, 1937*, makes additional provision for the establishment of a regency in circumstances where the Sovereign is not available to perform their royal functions. Presumably, this would include circumstances where the Sovereign is missing or has been prevented from executing their office by capture during war or rebellion. The same declarations are required as in the case of infirmity, and the same communications of the declaration to the Sovereign's other realms must be made.

The Act provides that the person next in line to the Throne following the Sovereign becomes the Regent unless that person is not a British Subject aged eighteen or older, is not domiciled in some part of the United Kingdom, or is incapable of inheriting, possessing and enjoying the Crown under section 2 of the Act of *Settlement, 1701*, or section 3(3) of the *Succession to the Crown Act, 2013*.

A person who would otherwise qualify for the office of Regent except for the fact that they were not of the age of eighteen years will accede to the Regency upon reaching that age if a Regent continues to be required under the terms and provisions of the *Regency Act, 1937*. If the Regent dies, or becomes disqualified, the office passes to the person who would have become Regent if the necessity for a regency had arisen immediately after the death of the Regent.

Before entering into the office of Regent, the person acceding to that office must swear an oath of office before the Privy Council of the United Kingdom. The office of Regent terminates by operation of law upon the anniversary of the Sovereign's eighteenth birthday, by rescission of a declaration of infirmity, or by the renewal of the Sovereign's ability to carry out the duties of office where the Sovereign had been previously prevented from executing the office of Sovereign by some cause such as war, insurrection etc.

4.30   Canada and a Regency

The *Regency Act, 1937,* does not form part of the law of Canada, as it was enacted subsequent to the date of the *Statute of Westminster, 1931,* and it does not contain the necessary recital that the United Kingdom statute was requested and consented to by Canada. Absent that recital, no United Kingdom statute enacted in 1937 could extend to Canada as part of its law between 1931 and 1982 (when the *Canada Act, 1982,* came into force and all formal legislative connections between Canada and the Parliament at Westminster were sundered).

Canada took the view that it was unnecessary for it to accept the *Regency Act 1937* as part of its law because the Governor General of Canada could perform the functions of an infirm or infant Sovereign. However, that view is not entirely correct because certain functions relating to the administration of the Canadian government continue to be exercised by the Sovereign personally (e.g., the appointment of a new Governor General, or the exercise of power to add Senators pursuant to section 26 of the *Constitution Act, 1867*). Furthermore, the Sovereign is traditionally consulted on some matters of public administration (e.g., the creation of new honours). Therefore, it would still appear desirable for Canada to make some provision for the exercise of the powers of the Sovereign upon the creation of a regency in the United Kingdom.

The Parliament of Canada could enact its own legislation to recognize the authority of the Regent appointed pursuant to the *Regency Act, 1937,* by the United Kingdom, or Parliament could appoint another person to be the regent of Canada. The Governor-General or Administrator of Canada would have constitutional power, pursuant to the *Letters Patent Constituting the Office of Governor General of Canada, 1947,* to grant Royal Assent to such a statute in the name of the Sovereign for whose benefit the regency was to be established.

It may also be possible for the Crown in Right of Canada to simply issue a royal proclamation by the Governor General under the Great Seal of Canada in reliance on the constitutional rule of recognition concerning the identity of the Sovereign in order to recognize the existence of a state of constitutional facts concerning the Sovereign, including the need for the establishment of a regency in the United Kingdom and hence in Canada. The Regent appointed under the United Kingdom statute could therefore become the Regent of Canada for Canadian constitutional purposes.

Equally, of course, Canada could decline to take any action, if it thought that the reasons for the establishment of a regency in the United Kingdom were unjustified. In the result, the Sovereign would continue to exercise royal powers in relation to Canada despite the existence of a regency within the United Kingdom.

4.31   Counsellors of State

The *Regency Act, 1937,* also provides for the office of a Counsellor of State. Where the Sovereign is absent from the United Kingdom for a limited period of time, or where illness or infirmity of a temporary duration has occurred, the Sovereign can appoint, by letters patent officers known as Counsellors of State who may exercise some of the royal functions of the Sovereign during the latter's temporary absence or infirmity. The functions which are delegated to the Counsellors of State are always specified in the appointing instrument. Delegated functions must be exercised jointly by the Counsellors of State, or by such number of them as is indicated in the instrument of appointment. Certain functions such as the dissolution of the Parliament of the United Kingdom, or the appointment of peers, are generally withheld from a Counsellor of State. The mandate of a Counsellor of State ceases automatically upon the demise of the Crown, or upon an event which requires a regency, or the appointment of a new Regent.

Historically, it appears that Counsellors of State were appointed without statutory authority where circumstances required that such officials be appointed.[27] At common law there was no impediment to the exercise of monarchical powers by the Sovereign when the Sovereign was outside of the realm and that is the modern rule as well. However, Counsellors of State were appointed for the sake of convenience so that public business would be not impeded during a brief absence out of the realm by the Sovereign of the United Kingdom.

It is unlikely that Canada would need to recognize Counsellors of State appointed in the United Kingdom for the purposes of the discharge of the Sovereign's functions in relation to Canada. In the modern era, with virtually instantaneous communications, a temporary absence of the Sovereign from the United Kingdom would be irrelevant to the discharge of any necessary royal functions in relation to Canada by the Sovereign.[28] Furthermore, the Governor General can exercise virtually all of the Sovereign's functions in relation to Canada. However, as in the case of a Regent, the Parliament of

Canada would have authority to enact a statute for the appointment of Counsellors of State if for any reason it was deemed necessary to do so.

Under the United Kingdom's 1937 legislation the qualifications of a Counsellor of State are the same as those for a Regent and therefore any person who is not eligible for appointment as Regent is also disqualified from being appointed a Counsellor of State. The instrument of appointment may exclude any person who although qualified for the appointment, would be absent from the United Kingdom during all or part of the period for which Counsellors of State would be required.

A Regent may also appoint Counsellors of State pursuant to the Act in the same manner as a Sovereign.

4.32   Vacancy of the Throne

The common law does not recognize a vacancy in the Throne. Where there is a demise of the Crown, the Throne passes immediately to the lawful heir and from that point in time the new Sovereign may exercise all of the royal powers, and enjoy all of the royal privileges and prerogatives, of his or her predecessor.

4.33   Abdication

A Sovereign may abdicate the throne by a formal instrument of abdication. However, since the supremacy of Parliament was established by the Convention Parliament in 1689, a Sovereign's act of abdication must be ratified by an Act of Parliament. Thus, when King Edward VIII abdicated the throne in 1936 for himself and any future children of his, the Parliament of the United Kingdom enacted *His Majesty's Declaration of Abdication Act*,[29] which ratified the King's instrument of abdication and provided for an immediate demise of the Crown upon King Edward VIII's Royal Assent to that Act.

On December 10, 1936, King Edward VIII despatched a message to the House of Commons in the United Kingdom advising Parliament that he had decided, in the exercise of his royal will, to abdicate the Throne as King. The King's instrument of abdication which he had signed, and which had been witnessed by his three royal brothers, accompanied the message. A bill entitled *His Majesty's Declaration of Abdication* was then introduced into the House of Commons and received first reading.

In Canada, the Federal Government had been kept abreast of the developing crisis[30] and on December 10, 1936, the date of the King's abdication, the Governor General in Council passed Order in Council P.C. 3144 of 1936 which noted that the preamble to the *Statute of Westminster, 1931*, required the assent of Canada to any alteration in the laws of succession in the United Kingdom and that under section 4 of that Act Canada must expressly request and consent to the application to Canada of any legislation enacted by the Parliament of the United Kingdom. Order in Council PC 1936-3144 went on to invoke the request and consent procedure for both the ratification of the King's instrument of abdication and the change to the law of succession as well as to acknowledge that the Parliament of Canada would have to express its own consent to the change in the law of succession when it next met.[31] Section 4 of the Order in Council stated:

> That, in order to insure that the requirements of the fourth section of the Statute are satisfied, it is necessary to provide for the request and consent of Canada to the enactment of the proposed legislation; and, in order to insure compliance with the constitutional convention expressed in the second recital of the preamble, hereinbefore set forth, it is necessary to make provision for securing the assent of the Parliament of Canada thereto;

The Order in Council then went on to state:

> (a) That the enactment of legislation by the Parliament at Westminster, following upon the voluntary abdication of His Majesty the King, providing for the validation thereof, the consequential demise of the Crown, succession of the heir presumptive and revision of the laws relating to the succession to the Throne, and declaring that Canada has requested and consented to such enactment be hereby approved.

The Order in Council also went on to state in paragraph c) that the United Kingdom legislation would be laid before the Parliament of Canada at its next sittings " . . . so as to enable the Parliament of Canada to take appropriate action pursuant to the provisions of the *Statute of Westminster*;" a reference to the need for Parliament to express its assent to the changes to the law of succession to the Throne.

In accordance with section 4 of the *Statute of Westminster Act, 1931*, the United Kingdom legislation ratifying the abdication was expressly recited to have been enacted at the request and with the consent of Canada. The UK statute amended the *Act of Settlement, 1701*, to exclude King Edward VIII's issue from the succession, and from the provisions of *The Royal Marriages Act, 1772*.

The abdication bill proceeded through the British Parliament and was enacted on December 11, 1936, receiving Royal Assent from King Edward VIII as his last royal act as Sovereign. Prince Albert immediately succeeded his brother as King George VI of both the United Kingdom and of Canada. Subsequently, Canada enacted *His Majesty's Declaration of Abdication Act*[32] to express the assent of the Parliament of Canada to the alteration to the succession to the Throne as described in the United Kingdom statute. Royal Assent to the Canadian Act was given by the Governor General of Canada, in the name of the then reigning Sovereign, King George VI.

The procedure followed in 1936 must be viewed in its own context. Canada had only recently emerged into *de jure* independence and the Federal Government was both anxious to assert Canadian independence from the United Kingdom and to ensure that no legal vulnerability would exist with respect to Canada's endorsement of King Edward VIII's abdication. In hindsight, the invoking of the section 4 procedure in the *Statute of Westminster, 1931*, the requirement that Canada request and consent to the application of a statute enacted by the United Kingdom Parliament to Canada, was not required in order for the King's abdication to take effect in Canada. The constitutional rule of recognition would have applied to recognize both the demise of the Crown upon the King's abdication, and the immediate accession of his successor.

In 1936 however, the constitutional actors in Canada desired to assert Canadian independence by ensuring that the abdication became effective in Canada through the use of the section 4 process in the *Statute of Westminster, 1931*, to accomplish that end. As a result of the enactment of the *Constitution Act, 1982*, the procedure set out in section 4 of the *Statute of Westminster, 1931*, no longer forms part of Canadian constitutional law and thus those procedures would not be available should another abdication occur. Nor, as a matter of constitutional law, would they be required.

What was legally required of the Parliament of Canada in 1936, and would still be required today, is an expression of Canadian assent to any change in the laws of succession to the Throne made by the Parliament of the United Kingdom. That requirement flows from the preamble to the *Statute of Westminster, 1931*, which continues to form part of the *Constitution of Canada* because it is included in the schedule to the *Constitution Act, 1982*.

4.34 Abandonment of the Throne

A declaration of the abandonment of the Throne can only occur as part of a revolution against the Crown and therefore it is not considered to be possible in modern circumstances. Historically, however, there is one example of an abandonment of the Throne. In England in the 1680s a battle for supremacy between the King and Parliament resulted in the flight from England to France of King James II. In consequence, the English Parliament met as a Convention Parliament (i.e., a Parliament that is irregular because of the absence of the Sovereign) and held that the King had breached the social contract between the King and his subjects. The Convention Parliament declared the Throne vacant and appointed successors to the King by an invitation to the daughter of the King, and to her husband, to accede to the Throne as joint Sovereigns.

4.635 Demise of the Crown

A demise of the Crown occurs when the Throne is transferred from one natural person to another. In such circumstances the Throne passes immediately to the heir. Ordinarily, a demise occurs when the reigning Sovereign has died but a demise can also occur where the Sovereign has abdicated the throne.

Formerly, a demise of the Crown carried significance in law because it affected appointments to public offices, legal processes, and even the continuation of Parliament itself. However, statute law has long since ameliorated the undesirable legal effects of a demise, both on appointments and on the life of Parliament. In Canada, the *Interpretation Act*[33] provides, in respect of a demise of the Crown as follows:

46 (1) Where there is a demise of the Crown,

(a) the demise does not affect the holding of any office under the Crown in right of Canada; and

(b) it is not necessary by reason of the demise that the holder of any such office again be appointed thereto or, having taken an oath of office or allegiance before the demise, again take that oath.

(2) No writ, action or other process or proceeding, civil or criminal, in or issuing out of any court established by an Act is, by reason of a demise of the Crown, determined, abated, discontinued or affected, but every such writ, action, process or proceeding remains in full force and may be enforced, carried on or otherwise proceeded with or completed as though there had been no such demise.

In respect of the Parliament of Canada, the *Parliament of Canada Act* [RSC 1985, c. P-1] in section 2 stipulates that on a demise of the Crown:

Parliament shall not determine or be dissolved by the demise of the Crown and, notwithstanding the demise, shall continue, and may meet, convene and sit, proceed and act, in the same manner as if that demise had not happened.

Section 3 of the same Act preserves the Royal Prerogative to nonetheless prorogue or dissolve Parliament.

Similar provisions have been made in provincial legislation, usually in the public officers or public departments statutes of a province or occasionally in legislation specifically directed at a demise, or in interpretation or constitutional statutes. Thus, while the demise of the Crown is a significant historical event, it does not impede the continuance of the legislative, judicial, and administrative functions of government.

Upon the death of a Sovereign it is customary for legislative bodies such as Parliament, and the provincial or territorial legislatures, to pass resolutions expressing sympathies to the Royal Family, and confirming the loyalty of the legislative body to the new Sovereign. It is also customary for a national day of mourning to be proclaimed.

In the United Kingdom, the appointment of a Regent or of Counsellors of State pursuant to the *Regency Act, 1937,* as amended, does not result in a demise of the Crown. But a demise of the Crown will terminate the appointment of a Regent, or the appointment of Counsellors of State.

4.36   The Royal Style and Titles

When Queen Elizabeth II acceded to the throne in 1952, the Canadian proclamation which announced her accession proclaimed her to be:

> Our only lawful and rightful Liege Lady Elizabeth the Second by the Grace of God, of Great Britain, Ireland and the British Dominions beyond the Seas.

Even in 1952 it soon became obvious that the description of the title of new Sovereign did not reflect the evolution of the Commonwealth and the independence of Canada. Therefore, in December 1952, at a meeting of the Heads of Government of the Commonwealth it was resolved that:

> . . . in the present stage of development of the Commonwealth relationship, it would be in accord with the established constitutional position that each member country should use for its own purposes a form [of the royal title] suitable to its own particular circumstances but retaining a substantial element common to all . . .

In Canada the description of the Sovereign's monarchial title is now regulated by the *Royal Style and Titles Act.*[34] In that Act, the Parliament of Canada assented to the issue by Her Majesty of a royal proclamation, under the Great Seal of Canada, establishing her royal style and titles for Canada in the following form:

> Elizabeth the Second, by the Grace of God of the United Kingdom, Canada and Her other Realms and Territories Queen, Head of the Commonwealth, Defender of the Faith.

At the present day, each member of the Commonwealth of Nations remaining one of the Sovereign's realms is free to adopt a royal style and title suitable for that particular realm. However, it is a convention of the Commonwealth that the various royal styles and titles of each member of Her Majesty's realms should retain a common element.

The common elements that remain in royal titles within the Commonwealth include the description of the Sovereign as "Queen" or "King," rather than by some other royal title such as "Empress" or "Prince," a reference to the Sovereign's "other realms," and a reference to the Sovereign's position as "Head of the Commonwealth". Subject to those common elements, the various realms of Her Majesty may adopt a title that is suitable to their own particular needs. Thus, for example, the royal style and titles for the Queen of New Zealand, describe the Sovereign as:

> ELIZABETH THE SECOND, by the Grace of God Queen of New Zealand and Her Other Realms and Territories, Head of the Commonwealth, Defender of the Faith

while in Australia the Sovereign is described as:

> ELIZABETH THE SECOND, by the Grace of God Queen of Australia and Her Other Realms and Territories, Head of the Commonwealth.

Other states within Her Majesty's realms generally use the same style as the Australian model, with the substitution of the name of each particular realm.

The Canadian royal style and titles continue to give equal prominence to the role of the Sovereign as the Monarch of both the United Kingdom and Canada, although that in itself may only reflect the fact that the Canadian royal styles and titles have not been revised since the beginning of the present reign.

The title *Defensor Fideii* or Defender of the Faith was a religious title originally conferred on King Henry VIII of England by Pope Leo X in the sixteenth century to acknowledge the contributions King Henry VIII made to refuting the teachings of Martin Luther. However, King Henry VIII had his own subsequent falling out with the Vatican and the title of *Defensor Fideii* was stripped from him by a papal bull of Pope Clement VII. Nevertheless, *Defensor Fideii* was restored to the Sovereign's titles by an Act of the Parliament of England; *King's Style Act*[35], enacted in 1543-44. The title now exists by virtue of statutory provisions in the United Kingdom, Canada, and New Zealand. It has been discontinued in other Commonwealth realms.

The expression "by the Grace of God" reflects the perspective of medieval society that the Sovereign was God's chosen governor of the realm. The expression appears in the royal style and titles in fifteen of the realms that recognize the British monarch as their own Sovereign. Only Papua New Guinea omits the phrase from its own royal style and titles.

Although the current Federal legislation was lawfully enacted by Parliament pursuant to Section 91(1) of the *British North America Act*, that provision was repealed by the *Constitution Act, 1982*, and replaced in part by section 41(a) of the *Constitution Act, 1982*. Nevertheless, in the view of the author, the Parliament of Canada may continue to enact legislation respecting the royal style and titles pursuant to the residual peace, order and good government power contained in the preamble of the *Constitution Act, 1867*, in particular in relation to the capacity of Parliament to enact legislation with respect to matters having a national dimension, or aspect, provided however, that the office of the Queen is only incidentally affected. Thus, upon the demise of the Crown, new legislation enacting a royal style and title for the new Sovereign that provides for substantial commonality with other Commonwealth realms would be within the jurisdiction of the Parliament of Canada to enact.

However, should Parliament desire to change the royal style and titles in a substantial way as, for example, removing the reference to Queen or King and replacing it with a different title that would suggest a change to the office of the Queen. Section 41(a) of the *Constitution Act, 1982,* provides that no change to the office of the Queen can be perfected without the consent of both Houses of Parliament as well as the consent of the legislatures of each Province. This unanimity rule would prevent any substantial unilateral action by Parliament to affect the office of the Sovereign. In addition, a substantial change to the royal style and title would engage the Commonwealth convention addressed in the preamble to the *Statute of Westminster Act, 1931,* requiring assent by the other realms in the Commonwealth to any such Canadian initiative.

The Sovereign is the symbol of the free association of the nation states which are members of the Commonwealth of Nations. As such, the present Sovereign has been given the title of Head of the Commonwealth, a title which is also recognized in the royal style and title of Canada, and in the other Commonwealth realms, although the Sovereign's office of Commonwealth Head has no constitutional significance in Canada.

Both Parliament and the legislatures of the provinces may, by legislation, provide for suits against the Sovereign to be taken in a name other than that of Her Majesty the Queen; *Perepelytz v The Department of Highways for the Province of Ontario,* [1958] SCR 161 (Canada, SC).

4.37   The Royal Family

Until the Treaty of Paris in 1763, the royal house and family of Canada consisted of the House of Bourbon which originated with the accession of King Henry IV, the King of Navarre, who ascended the throne of France in 1589, and became Sovereign of Canada (then officially described as New France) with the establishment and settlement of Quebec in 1608. The House of Bourbon continued to rule over Canada until the final transfer of sovereignty over Canada from France to Great Britain following the Treaty of Paris in 1763.

From 1763, the Royal Family of Canada consisted of the House of Hanover, the ruling house of Great Britain which came to the British Throne in 1714, following the death of the last British monarch from the House of Stuart, Queen Anne, who died without an heir. Under the terms of the *Act of Settlement, 1701,* the Throne then passed to the heirs of Princess Sophia, the Electress of

Hanover, which brought her son Prince Georg Ludwig of the German Electorate of Hanover, to the Throne of Great Britain as King George I. The House of Hanover continued as the reigning family of the British Empire and supplied all of its monarchs from King George I to and including Queen Victoria.

The marriage of Queen Victoria to Prince Albert created a new royal house, the House of Saxe-Coburg and Gotha which provided two subsequent monarchs, King Edward VII and King George V. However, during World War One public anti-German sentiment caused King George V to re-found the royal house and family of the United Kingdom as the House of Windsor by letters patent and proclamation in 1917. Between 1917 and 1919 some members of the former House of Saxe-Coburg and Gotha who had allied themselves with the Crown of Imperial Germany during World War One were stripped of their British titles as part of the process of re-founding the royal house in Great Britain. The House of Windsor has supplied the reigning monarchs of the United Kingdom of Great Britain and Northern Ireland, and of Canada and the other Commonwealth realms, since the accession of King Edward VIII in 1936. When Queen Elizabeth II ascended the throne in 1952, the Queen issued a proclamation declaring her wish that her descendants would continue to be known as members of the House of Windsor and that there would be no reestablishment of the royal house following her marriage to Prince Philip of Greece and Denmark.

However, in 1960 the Queen announced that members of her family that did not bear a royal title could bear the surname Mountbatten-Windsor, thus acknowledging the surname that her husband had adopted as his own. At the present time, all of the members of the House of Windsor are the descendants of three sons of King George V. Some of the members of the royal house bear royal titles and some do not. There does not appear to be legal criteria to determine who obtains a title and who does not, and such titles are in the discretion of the Sovereign (who doubtless takes into account the wishes of a child's parents).

The Sovereign possesses certain prerogative rights with respect to the members of the Royal Family. Apart from the statutory right to approve of some of their marriages, pursuant to the *Succession to the Crown Act, 2013*, the Sovereign has the right to direct the care and education of the Sovereign's children, grandchildren, and the heir presumptive.

A consort of a King may be styled as a Queen Consort[36], and is entitled to her own royal court and officers. She can be represented in a court of law by her own Attorney-General and Solicitor General. Otherwise, she is an ordinary subject of the Sovereign. It is the practice for a Queen Consort to be crowned during the coronation ceremony but she is not constitutionally entitled to a coronation. In *Queen Caroline's Claim to the Crowned* (1821), 1 State Tr (NS) 949 (United Kingdom, PC) the estranged wife of King George IV asserted a claim to be crowned Queen Consort during the King's coronation at Westminster. After hearing argument on this question, the Privy Council decided:

> That as it appears to them that the Queens-Consort of this realm are not entitled as of right to be crowned at any time, Her Majesty is not entitled as of right to be crowned at the time specified in Her Majesty's Memorials.

Queen Caroline remained to the end of her life an uncrowned Queen of the United Kingdom of Great Britain and Ireland.

A male consort of a Queen regnant is an ordinary subject of the Sovereign. Unlike a Queen Consort, he does not take the title of King Consort, nor does he possess any of the special privileges of a Queen Consort, such as the right to his own royal court and officers, or to be represented in the courts of law by his own Attorney General, or Solicitor General. There is no special recognition of a male consort during the coronation ceremony for a Queen regnant and he is not crowned. In addition to whatever title he may possess in his own right he may be created a Prince or a Duke of the Realm by the Queen. It is customary for the consort of the Sovereign, male or female, to be appointed to the Sovereign's Privy Councils. Prince Philip, the Duke of Edinburgh, is a member of the Queen's Privy Council for Canada, having been appointed to that office on October 14, 1957.

In accordance with the *Act of Settlement, 1701,* the *Succession to the Crown Act, 2013,* and the law of absolute primogeniture, the eldest child of the reigning Sovereign is the Heir Apparent to the throne. The children of the Sovereign are styled a Royal Highness. All except the Heir Apparent are otherwise ordinary subjects of the Sovereign.

The living mother of a reigning Monarch is a Queen dowager and may bear the style of Queen Mother.

4.38   The Canadian Royal Family and Nationality Law

From time to time the question is raised concerning the status of members of the Royal Family under Canadian nationality law. As it concerns the Sovereign, this issue is relatively clear-cut. Any question of citizenship or nationality in relation to the Sovereign is irrelevant in Canadian law. The Sovereign is the embodiment of constitutional and national sovereignty in each of the realms in which she is the Monarch.

Members of the Royal Family other than the Sovereign do acquire nationality under domestic laws. Undoubtedly, members of the Royal Family owe allegiance to the Sovereign in respect of each realm over which the Sovereign reigns, and members of the Royal Family do carry out royal duties in each of the Sovereign's realms with the consent or at the direction of the Sovereign, and at the request and upon the advice of the governments of those countries. Thus, with respect to Canada, the members of the Royal Family owe allegiance to the Sovereign in her capacity as the Sovereign of Canada. The allegiance of the Royal Family to the Sovereign of Canada is reinforced by the assumption of both civil and military offices in Canada by members of the Royal Family, such as appointments to the Queen's Privy Council for Canada, and appointments as Captain General or Colonel-in-Chief of Army Regiments, and Honorary appointments to naval and air ranks. Members of the Royal Family, particularly those holding civil and military appointments may therefore be regarded as subjects of the Sovereign of Canada.[37]

The members of the Royal Family are, however, not citizens of Canada under the *Citizenship Act* (unless they bear or have obtained Canadian citizenship in their individual capacity.[38]) They are however, recognized as Commonwealth citizens under the *Citizenship Act*.[39] In accordance with the established relationships between Commonwealth states, a non-Canadian Commonwealth citizen is not considered to be a foreign person, or an alien, under Canadian domestic law.

At the behest of Prince Phillip, the Duke of Edinburgh, who refused to accept an Honorary award of the Order of Canada because such awards are made to foreign persons and he considered himself Canadian, as the consort of Queen Elizabeth II, the Government of Canada created a separate division of the Order of Canada to accommodate awards to members of the Royal Family, as well as Governors General. That act was a recognition by the Federal Government that the position of the members of the Royal Family was *sui generis*, occupying a position in Canadian society that was neither foreign nor domestic.

Members of the Royal Family are entitled to Canadian consular assistance, and to the protection of the Sovereign's armed forces of Canada, when they are outside of the Sovereign's realms and in need of protection or assistance.

4.39   The Royal Household

The Royal household consists of officers providing the necessary administrative support services to the Sovereign and the members of the Royal Family. The Lord Chamberlain has responsibility for the general supervision of the Royal household. Other officials include the Lord Steward and the Master of the Horse who have mostly nominal responsibilities, and the Master of the Household, who does have significant administrative responsibilities. The most important official from a Canadian constitutional perspective is the Private Secretary to the Sovereign. The Private Secretary is appointed by the Sovereign in the exercise of a personal discretion. The incumbent acts in the same capacity with respect to all of the realms which recognize the Sovereign as Head of State. Thus, the incumbent is Private Secretary to the Queen of Canada, New Zealand etc., in addition to being the Private Secretary to the Queen of the United Kingdom.

The duties of the Private Secretary are to keep the Sovereign informed on current events, issues, and topics in her realms so that she may exercise her right to be consulted, to encourage, and to warn. However, the Private Secretary is not a constitutional advisor and the Sovereign is under no obligation to accept any advice that they may receive from the secretary. The Private Secretary may obtain information from any source, including members of opposition parties but must at all times maintain a strict political neutrality.

With respect to Canadian affairs, the Private Secretary works closely with the Secretary to the Governor General and with the Canadian Secretary to the Sovereign when that office has been filled.

4.40   Canadian Royal Household Officials

Certain officials have been appointed in Canada to assist the Sovereign in the execution of royal duties in relation to Canada. Since 1959 there has been an official known as the Canadian Secretary to the Queen who advises and coordinates royal visits to Canada, assists with royal correspondence, advises government on matters of royal ceremony, or protocol, and more recently, has chaired the Advisory Committee on Vice-Regal Appointments, which recommends candidates to the Prime Minister for appointments as Governor General, Lieutenant Governors, or territorial Commissioners. However, at the time that this work is being completed (2017) the Federal Government has announced that the position of Canadian Secretary to the Queen is vacant and its future is under review. Officials of the Department of Canadian Heritage have assumed some of the duties of the Canadian Secretary. It has been announced by the Federal Government that the Advisory Committee on Vice-Regal Appointments, a recently created body, has now become dormant and it appears unlikely that it will be revived in the foreseeable future.

Other Canadian royal household officials may include Ladies-in-Waiting, and Equerries, as well Official Police Officers, the Honorary Physician, the Honorary Dental Surgeon, the Honorary Nursing Officer and military aides de camp. Some of these household officials are appointed only in connection with royal visits.

4.41   Royal Visits

Members of the Royal Family began to visit Canada and develop a substantive connection with the country during the colonial period. Queen Victoria's father, Prince Edward, the Duke of Kent and Strathearn, resided in Canada while he served as Commander-in-Chief of the imperial forces stationed in North

America between 1799 and 1802. Prince Albert, the Prince of Wales (later King Edward VII) memorably visited Canada in 1860, and his grandson, Prince Edward, the Prince of Wales (subsequently King Edward VIII) owned a ranch in the Province of Alberta. However, it was not until 1939, on the eve of the world war, that a reigning Sovereign in the person of King George VI, and his consort, Queen Elizabeth, made the first royal visit by a reigning Sovereign to Canada. During the reign of Queen Elizabeth II there have been a great number of royal visits by the Sovereign, and by other members of the Royal Family.

While in Canada, the Sovereign may exercise royal powers if requested to do so by the government but for the most part the visits are ceremonial in nature. Where the Sovereign is present in the country the powers exercised on her behalf by the Governor General of Canada, or by a Lieutenant Governor of a province, are not impaired and unless the Sovereign chooses to personally exercise a power at the request of a government, the Sovereign's representatives may continue to exercise royal powers in a representative capacity despite the presence of the Sovereign in the country, or in a particular province.

4.42   Linguistic Duality

There is no stated requirement for a Sovereign or any other member of the Royal Family to have the capability of expressing themselves in both of Canada's official languages, English and French. Nevertheless, like other senior positions in the hierarchy of the federal state, such as the Governor General of Canada, or the Prime Minister, there is an expectation that the Sovereign will be able to communicate with Canadians in both official languages. Fortunately, the Royal Family has included French within the subjects that are taught to members of the Royal Family in childhood. The present Sovereign at the time of this writing, Queen Elizabeth II, is well-known in Canada for her ability to communicate in French as well as in English. Queen Elizabeth has spoken in French on public occasions, and she has received official briefings from her Canadian ministers in French.[40]

4.43   Protection of the Sovereign's Person

In Canada, the Sovereign's person is protected under the *Criminal Code*.[41] Section 46 of the *Criminal Code* creates the offence of high treason for attacks on the Sovereign's person. It states:

(1) Every one commits high treason who, in Canada,

(a) kills or attempts to kill Her Majesty, or does her any bodily harm tending to death or destruction, maims or wounds her, or imprisons or restrains her;

...

(2) Every one commits treason who, in Canada,

...

(c) conspires with any person to commit high treason . . .

(d) forms an intention to do anything that is high treason . . . and manifests that intention by an overt act;

...

(3) Notwithstanding subsection (1) or (2), a Canadian citizen or a person who owes allegiance to Her Majesty in right of Canada,

(a) commits high treason if, while in or out of Canada, he does anything mentioned in subsection (1); or

(b) commits treason if, while in or out of Canada, he does anything mentioned in subsection (2).

Section 47 of the *Criminal Code* provides that offences under subsection (1) or (2) are indictable offences, punishable by imprisonment for life. Section 49 of the *Criminal Code* also creates the offence of alarming Her Majesty:

Every one who willfully, in the presence of Her Majesty,

(a) does an act with intent to alarm Her Majesty or to break the public peace, or

(b) does an act that is intended or is likely to cause bodily harm to Her Majesty, is guilty of an indictable offence and liable to imprisonment for a term not exceeding fourteen years.

Offences against the Queen's person require proof beyond a reasonable doubt of both a criminal intent, as well as proof of a wrongful act. It does not appear that a prosecution of a person has yet occurred in Canada for an offence in relation to the Sovereign's person.

[1] 10 Edw, 7 & 1 Geo. V, c. 29) (Imp.)

[2] *Documents on Canadian External Relations,* Department of Foreign Affairs and International Trade (1952), Queen's Printer for Canada, Ottawa, 1952, at page 18.

[3] Not all monarchies provide for a coronation of their monarch. For example, the investiture of a monarch in Spain does not involve the crowning of the monarch. However, it has always been a feature of both the French and British monarchies, and hence of Canada.

[4] *Coronation: A History of Kingship and the British Monarchy*, Roy Strong, Harper Collins, London, 2005 at page 8 (afterwards *"Strong"*)

[5] *Strong*, page 9

[6] The religious elements draw from the pre-reformation *Coronation Ordo* of the Roman Catholic Church updated to represent the theological understanding of the Protestant reformation. It is therefore a Christian religious ceremony and while the coronation is part of the British constitution there are references to Canada in the ceremony as well as Canadian participation. The participation of Canadian officials in a state ceremony with a strong religious foundation does not offend the prohibition against religious discrimination in Canada contained in the *Canadian Charter of Rights and Freedoms*, nor is it incongruent with the *Constitution of Canada*, which states in the preamble to the *Constitution Act 1982* that " . . . Canada is founded upon principles that recognize the supremacy of God and the rule of law."

[7] Prior to the cession of Canada by France to Great Britain in 1763, all coronations of the French Sovereigns of Canada occurred at the Cathedral of Notre-Dame de Reims, in Reims, France. The last Sovereign of Canada to be crowned at Reims was King Louis XV in 1722. The first Sovereign of Canada to be crowned at Westminster Abbey was King George IV in 1821.

[8] For the description of the coronation ceremonial and the coronation service the author has drawn from *The Ceremonies to be Observed at the Royal Coronation of Her Most Excellent Majesty Queen Elizabeth II in the Abbey Church of St Peter Westminster on Tuesday the Second Day of June 1953*, author unknown, presumably published under the authority of the Earl Marshal of the Realm, London, 1953 and *Strong, Coronation: A History of Kingship and the British Monarchy*. Great attention to detail in involved in the planning for the coronation even including, in 1953, the creation of particular shade of lipstick (red with a blue cast) to be worn by Queen Elizabeth II so that it would match the colour of her robes of velvet (*At Her Majesty's Service*, Peter Russell and Paul James, Fontana/Collins, Glasgow, 1986, at pages 176-77).

[9] At present there are no states under the protection of the British Crown but at the time of the last coronation in 1953 the monarchs of the Malay states, and Brunei, Zanzibar, Maldives and Tonga all fell into this category. Brunei, which regained its formal sovereignty from the United Kingdom in 1984, was the last protected state under British suzerainty. Presumably, this category will no longer form part of future coronation ceremonials.

[10] In the Coronation Ceremony the Sovereign uses three different chairs. The Chair of Estate in which the Sovereign sits during the first part of the Coronation Ceremony, the ancient King Edward's Chair in which the Sovereign is crowned,

and the Throne Chair in which the Sovereign is seated after the crowning to receive homage and fealty from the attending nobility

[11] At the 1937 coronation of King George VI a slight change was made in the Archbishop's presentation. Instead of referring to "the undoubted King of this realm" he was referred to as "your undoubted King". The change was made to accommodate the divisibility of the Crown, which had only been recently codified in law by the *Statute of Westminster,1931*; *Strong*, at page 444.

[12] *Strong*, at page 281

[13] *Strong*, at page 80

[14] *Strong*, at page 61

[15] *Strong*, at page 92

[16] Section 4 of the *Act of Settlement, 1701,* further states that the laws of the realm are the birthright of the people and that the Sovereign should administer the government according to those laws. As a matter of law, of course, the Sovereign is bound to obey the rule of law regardless of the Coronation Oath but the oath is a public affirmation of her or his duty, and the duty of those who are employed by the Sovereign.

[17] *Strong*, at page 10

[18] *Strong*, at page 80

[19] In 1953 this hymn was *Come Holy Ghost, Our Souls Inspire.*

[20] This hymn is invariably sung at British coronations

[21] *Strong*, at page 481

[22] *Strong*, at page 444

[23] In 1953 the hymn was *Be Strong and of a Good Courage.*

[24] In 1953 thematically the Exhortation called upon the Sovereign to "Stand firm and hold fast."

[25] In 1953 it was the *Gloria.*

[26] 1 Edw. 8 & 1 Geo. 6, c. 16 (UK). This Act was amended by the *Regency Act, 1943*, 6 &7 Geo. 6 c. 42 and the *Regency Act, 1953*, 2 & 3 Eliz. 2 c. 1

[27] L S Amery PC *Memorandum* in *Despatch No. 3 to the Irish Free State* dated February 6, 1929, LAC File No: RG 25, D1, Vol. 740, File No: 132, 1929: "The appointment by the King of the Royal and other personages to perform certain functions on His Majesty's behalf was made in accordance with the only constitutional forms which in the circumstances were available for the purpose, and in accordance with tradition." The issue addressed by that memorandum concerned the objections raised by the Irish Free State to the fact that British politicians, acting as Counsellors of State on behalf of King George V, ratified a treaty on behalf of the Irish Free State. At that point in history the Irish Free State was a separate dominion and, following the divisibility of the Crown that had been agreed upon in the Balfour Declaration of 1926, Ireland expected the Sovereign alone to discharge ratification functions concerning foreign treaties binding upon the Irish Free State, acting on the advice of Irish ministers. However, King George V had suddenly become ill and he was temporarily unable to discharge his constitutional responsibilities and hence the need to appoint Counsellors of State. The troubled history between Britain and Ireland made the appointment of British political figures as counsellors a flashpoint in the relations between the two realms.

[28]. Counsellors of State did act for on behalf of Canada in limited circumstances where the Sovereign was unable to act in the period before the enactment of the *Statute of Westminster, 1931*.

[29] 1 Edw. 8, c. 3 (UK)

[30] Apparently, an open telephone line had been maintained between London and Ottawa to ensure that Ottawa would be informed as soon as the House of Lords approved the British legislation accepting the abdication (Nancy Gelber, *Canada in London: An Unofficial Glimpse of Canada's Sixteen High Commissioners 1880-1980*, Canada House, London, 1980, at page 53.)

[31] The Parliament of Canada was not currently sitting at the time of King Edward VIII's abdication.

[32] SC 1937, c. 16

[33] RSC 1985, c. I-21, s. 46. See also the *Parliament of Canada Act* RSC 1985, c. P-1, s. 2.

[34] RSC 1985, c. R-2

[35] (35 Hen 8 c.3 (Eng)

[36] This is not an invariable rule. The current Prince of Wales has announced that his wife, Camilla, will retain her title as Duchess of Cornwall should the Prince of Wales accede to the Throne.

[37] Admittedly, the boundaries of who constitutes a Canadian subject are an unrefined and inchoate concept of Canadian law.

[38] RSC 1985, c. C-29. Several members of the Royal Family do hold Canadian citizenship, by birth or descent.

[39] RSC 1985, c. C-29, s. 32(1). All citizens of Canada hold Commonwealth citizenship under the *Citizenship Act*. The concept of a Commonwealth citizen appeared in the first Canadian *Citizenship Act* in 1950.

[40] Author's private communication with a former Prime Minister of Canada.

[41] RSC 1985, c. C-46. At the time of writing a bill has been introduced into the House of Commons (Bill C-51) that if enacted will repeal section 49 of the *Criminal Code*.

THE SOVEREIGN AND THE PEOPLE

The relationship of the Sovereign to his or her people in Canada has both a historical and a contemporary importance. This chapter examines the relationship between the Sovereign and the people of Canada who owe allegiance to the Sovereign, as well as the special relationship between the Crown and the aboriginal peoples of Canada

5.1   Subjects of the Sovereign of Canada

The subjects of the Sovereign of Canada comprise all persons who owe allegiance to the Sovereign in Right of Canada. Allegiance is the principle legal relationship between Canadians and their Sovereign. *Calvin's Case* (1608) 7 Co Rep 1a, defines allegiance to be "a true and faithful obedience of the Subject due to his Sovereign. This ligeance and obedience is an incident inseparable to every subject: for as soon as he is born he oweth by birth-right ligeance and obedience to his Sovereign".

Feudal law attributed to the Sovereign the position of a liege lord, i.e., a person to whom allegiance was due, and who was in turn required to provide protection and good governance to their people. A liege was therefore a subject bound in allegiance to their Sovereign lord or lady. Although feudal principles are but a faint echo in the modern common law, it is still correct to state that the citizens of Canada are subjects of the Sovereign, and are therefore the Sovereign's lieges. Allegiance is due to the Sovereign in both the Sovereign's natural capacity and in their capacity as a body corporate.

Allegiance arises in one of three circumstances. The first kind of allegiance is that which results from birth in Canada, or birth abroad to citizens of Canada. In such cases, the infant owes allegiance as a natural-born subject of the Canadian Sovereign immediately from the time of their birth.

The second kind of allegiance arises from the act of accepting Canadian citizenship. Everyone who obtains the citizenship of Canada immediately owes allegiance to the Sovereign of Canada. Their allegiance is not dependent upon any particular form of citizenship or other oath, although currently the oath of citizenship does require new citizens to swear allegiance to the Sovereign and to her heirs and successors.

The third kind of allegiance is local allegiance, which every alien who enters into Canada owes to the Sovereign of Canada while they remain under her protection. This allegiance is owed by those aliens who have been granted a right of abode in Canada as permanent residents.

Where a person owing allegiance to the Sovereign violates their allegiance, they are punishable under sections 46 to 48 and section 50 of the *Criminal Code*[1] in relation to treason, or under sections 59 to 62 in relation to sedition.

As a result of the divisibility of the Crown, allegiance is owed by Canadians and others under the protection of the Sovereign only to the Sovereign in their capacity as the Sovereign of Canada. No allegiance is owed to the Sovereign in any other capacity, such as the capacity of Sovereign as the Sovereign of another realm. Modern authority for this view can be found in *obiter dicta* in an Australian case; *Bradley v Commonwealth of Australia* (1973) 1 ALR 241 (Australia, HC). In that case a person owing local allegiance to the Queen of Australia was employed by the government of Southern Rhodesia, which was then in rebellion against the Queen of the United Kingdom. The Postmaster General terminated postal services to that person at his place of occupation, causing the Appellant to seek a declaration and an injunction against the Crown. In the judgment of the Court granting the relief requested by the plaintiff, the Court found that the fact that the plaintiff was supporting an illegal regime in another of Her Majesty's realms was not a sufficient reason to deny him relief against the Australian Crown. In effect, the plaintiff owed no duty to the Sovereign in her capacity as Sovereign of another realm.

A concomitant principle to the obligation of allegiance is the duty of the Crown to protect a subject. This obligation is generally of most importance to a subject when they are outside of the realm, and therefore potentially subject to the actions of foreign states, or foreign non-state actors. The extent of the duty to protect mainly involves a request by the Crown to a foreign state for the protection of the Crown's subject and therefore the ability to protect does not necessarily lie within the power of the Crown. Thus, the duty to protect is characterized by the jurisprudence as an imperfect obligation, and one that is not necessarily enforceable against the Crown in its conduct of the Royal Prerogative over foreign affairs, although it may possibly be asserted to prevent the Crown from taking into account irrelevant considerations in deciding whether to assist a subject; *Hicks v Ruddock*, [2007] 2 LRC 560 (Australia, FC). In regards to the Crown's duty to protect Canadians abroad the Supreme Court of Canada has found that the courts in Canada have "a narrow power to review and intervene on matters of foreign affairs to ensure the constitutionality of executive action"; *Canada (Prime Minister) v Khadr*, [2010] 1 SCR 44 (Canada, SC).

For the most part, the duty of allegiance owed to the Sovereign by her subjects is a passive duty amounting generally to obedience to the laws of the realm and thus overt displays of loyalty are not generally required. Nevertheless, it is customary for the government to declare a public holiday to mark the anniversary of the Sovereign's birth in order for subjects to express their allegiance. In Canada, the Sovereign's birthday is celebrated on Victoria Day, which was originally the birthday of Queen Victoria, the second longest reigning monarch (after King Louis XIV) in Canadian history. A proclamation was issued in 1957 to permanently fix the celebration of the Sovereign's birthday on the first Monday preceding the twenty-fifth day of May (*Proclamation Queen's Birthday*).[2] This occasion is often accompanied by both public and private displays of fireworks.

In some circumstances, however, there may be an obligation placed upon some subjects to express overt respect to the monarchy, and to publicly display their allegiance to the Sovereign. Such circumstances arise particularly with respect to the members of Her Majesty's Canadian Forces, where it is obligatory to salute the Sovereign, the Sovereign's Representatives, the National flag, the Union flag (in circumstances where it is used as a symbol of allegiance to the Sovereign, or to Canada's membership in the Commonwealth of Nations), the Royal Anthem (*God Save the Queen*), and to participate in the Loyal Toast to the Sovereign at formal military mess dinners. In *Giolla Chainnigh v Canada (Attorney General)*, [2008] FC 69 (Canada, FC) Justice Barnes of the Federal Court held that those requirements did not infringe upon an Applicant's freedom of expression under the *Canadian Charter of Rights and Freedoms* and, to the extent they did, they were a reasonable and demonstrably justified limitation in a free and democratic society. Justice Barnes stated: "I cannot think of any Canadian institution where an expectation of loyalty and respect for the Queen would be more important than the Canadian Forces".[3]

5.2   Natural Allegiance

Natural allegiance is the most common form of allegiance owed by Canadians to the Sovereign, simply because it arises through birth within Canadian citizenship. Natural allegiance requires loyalty to the Sovereign from all of her natural-born subjects, and that loyalty cannot be divested by them except through a formal renunciation of their Canadian citizenship pursuant to the *Citizenship Act* and by their acquisition of foreign citizenship.[4]

At common law natural allegiance could not be voided by committing acts of treachery or mutiny against the Sovereign. This point has been recently made in the case of *Christian and Others v R*, [2004] 5 LRC 706 (Pitcairn Islands, CA) a case originating from the Pitcairn Islands of the Pacific Ocean which were originally settled by mutinous seamen from the Royal Navy vessel HMAV Bounty. The Court of Appeal addressed the question of whether the

Bounty mutineers had sundered their natural allegiance by their act of mutiny, by stating:

> It was first submitted that the mutineers ceased to be British subjects following the commission by them of what were described as acts of treason and piracy, particularly the seizure and later burning of HMAV Bounty. Therefore it was said the settlement of the island in 1790 was by individuals who were not then British subjects. We do not find the submission sustainable. The duty of allegiance owed by the mutineers was never broken, either by their own acts or any act of the King.[5]

Today the subject of renunciation of Canadian citizenship, and therefore allegiance to the Canadian Sovereign, is addressed by statute law. A person owing a natural allegiance to the Sovereign of Canada may renounce their Canadian citizenship, and thus their allegiance, pursuant to the procedures set out in section 9 of the *Citizenship Act*.[6]

Where a Canadian performs an act that is incompatible with the duty of allegiance to the Sovereign they may be punished under the provisions of the *Criminal Code* concerning high treason, or treason *simpliciter*. A person owing natural allegiance to the Sovereign cannot plead the receipt of superior orders as a defence to a charge of treason based on facts that occurred within the Sovereign's realm; *Axtell's Case* (1660), 5 State Tr 1146 at 1157 (plea of superior orders in respect of the regicide of King Charles I rejected).

Nor will it be possible for a person owing natural allegiance to the Sovereign to raise as a defence that the offence of treason cannot be established for actions that occurred outside of the realm. The case of *R v Casement*, [1917] 1 KB 98 (England, KB and Court of Criminal Appeal) concerned the prosecution for treason of Sir Roger Casement, a subject of the King in right of the United Kingdom who, during the First World War, attempted to recruit Irish prisoners of war held in Germany to take up arms against the King to fight for Irish independence. Casement was naturally aided and abetted in his endeavours by the Imperial German authorities, who were anxious to cause difficulty and disruption to the war-making capacity of the British Empire. Casement was captured and charged with treason. His defence argued that the statutes relating to treason only applied to a treason committed within the realm, and did not apply to treason committed outside of the realm. The Court of Criminal Appeal rejected that defence, stating:

> . . . we think that if a man be adherent to the King's enemies in his realm by giving to them aid or comfort in his realm, or if he be adherent to the King's enemies elsewhere, that is by giving them aid or comfort elsewhere, he is equally adherent to the King's enemies, and if he is adherent to the King's enemies, then he commits [treason]. Reasons may be given for that, but we think a very good reason is to be found in this, that the subjects of the King owe him allegiance, and the allegiance follows the person of the subject. He is the King's liege wherever he may be, and

he may violate his allegiance in a foreign country just as well as he may violate it in this country.[7]

The Second World War produced the case of *R v Inouye Kanao* (1947, unreported) (Hong Kong, SC) which involved the prosecution of a man born in British Columbia. Inouye Kanao had lived in Canada with his parents until he emigrated to Japan with them at the age of ten years. Kanao harboured grievances against Canada, based on his understanding of the discriminatory laws in force in British Columbia that applied to persons of oriental ancestry in the years prior to the war. After coming of age in 1937, however, Kanao did not divest himself of his status as both a British Subject and a Canadian National by making a declaration of alienage, which the applicable law in Canada at the time permitted him to do.

During the Second World War Kanao enlisted in the Japanese Army and after completing his army service he volunteered for the Japanese gendarmerie in Hong Kong. His efforts in Hong Kong were directed against the King and involved the mistreatment of Canadian prisoners of war, as well as counter-espionage against the British.[8]

After the war Kanao was arrested, but he successfully evaded a conviction under a war crimes statute on the basis that he was a Canadian, and therefore a subject of the King, and not Japanese. The Crown Attorney in Hong Kong then laid a charge of high treason against Kanao. The accused put forward a defence based on dual citizenship, and stated that at all material times he regarded himself as a subject of the Emperor of Japan. However, Chief Justice Blackall advised the jury that dual citizenship was no defence to a charge of high treason stating: ". . . I have to direct you that joining the forces of any State does not have the affect of changing the nationality of a British Subject" and later:

> In deciding whether or not a man is a British Subject, you have to go by what the law is and not what the particular individual believes it to be. So, even if he believed himself to be a Japanese subject, that would not operate to make him one and I have directed you that he was a natural born British subject and that he remained so at all material times.

As a result, Inouye Kanao was convicted of treason by the jury, sentenced to death by the Chief Justice, and hanged shortly afterwards in Hong Kong.[9]

5.3   Acquired Allegiance

Allegiance to the Sovereign of Canada will be acquired by the acquisition of Canadian citizenship. Prior to 1947 there was no concept of Canadian citizenship, owing to the common status of a British Subject throughout the British Empire and Commonwealth. However, the logical result of the acquisition of *de jure* independence by the self-governing states in the

Commonwealth, as a result of the *Statute of Westminster, 1931*, was that common citizenship could no longer suffice for all purposes. Therefore, in the immediate postwar period the United Kingdom, Canada, and other independent members of the Commonwealth enacted domestic citizenship laws to differentiate the citizenship of their state from other states within the Commonwealth.[10]

Currently, the acquisition of Canadian citizenship is regulated by the provisions of the *Citizenship Act*. Immediately upon acquiring Canadian citizenship, a new citizen owes allegiance to the Sovereign of Canada. Although allegiance to the Sovereign is reflected in the oath of citizenship, which includes of a pledge of allegiance to the Sovereign, allegiance to the Sovereign arises irrespective of any form of the citizenship oath. A Canadian who has acquired the citizenship of this country is in exactly the same position with respect to their allegiance to the Canadian Sovereign as is a natural-born subject of the Canadian Sovereign.

Where citizenship has been acquired, the Crown retains the right, under certain circumstances, to divest the acquirer of their Canadian citizenship. For example, divestiture may occur where the acquirer has obtained citizenship through false pretenses. Action has been taken by the Crown to divest citizenship from naturalized Canadians who acquired their citizenship after the Second World War by misleading the authorities with respect to their participation in Nazi atrocities during the hostilities.

As with natural-born citizens, any person who acquires Canadian citizenship may renounce their citizenship pursuant to the procedures set out in section 9 of the *Citizenship Act*.

5.4   Local Allegiance

Aliens who come within the domain of the Sovereign owe to the Sovereign a temporary allegiance while they remain under the Sovereign's protection. In return, the Sovereign owes protection to that alien while the alien is subject to Sovereign's jurisdiction. The temporary allegiance owed to the Sovereign by an alien is described as local allegiance, reflecting the fact that it ceases upon the alien's departure from the Sovereign's protection, usually (but not always) when the alien departs the country.

The principle of local allegiance has been the subject matter of litigation a number of times in the common law over the course of the past three hundred years. *R v De la Motte* (1781) 21 State Tr. 688 (England, CP) concerned a subject of the King of France who resided in Great Britain during a war with France. De la Motte was found to have collected and supplied intelligence to France during his sojourn in Great Britain. He was charged with treason and convicted upon the ground that he owed a local allegiance to the King of Great Britain. In sentencing him, Justice Buller stated:

> During your residence in this country, as well as during the course of your trial, you have received the protection of the laws of the land. As such, you owed a duty to those laws, and an allegiance to the king whose laws they are . . . [11]

The same issues arose during the Boer War at the turn of the twentieth century. *De Jager v Attorney General of Natal*, [1907] AC 326 (Natal, JC) concerned a citizen of the South African Republic who resided in Natal prior to and after the outbreak of war between Great Britain and the South African Republic. Although the alien resident took no action against the Sovereign's interests subsequent to the outbreak of the war, he accepted public office and responsibilities from the authorities of the South African Republic when the armed forces of that nation occupied Natal. Later, after the defeat of the South African Republic and the restoration of British administration over Natal, De Jager was called to account for his actions during the occupation. De Jager argued that his local allegiance to the British Sovereign ended when his own countrymen occupied the portion of British territory in which he resided. The Judicial Committee rejected that argument, holding:

> The protection of a State does not cease merely because the State forces, for strategical or other reasons, are temporarily withdrawn, so that the enemy for the time exercises the rights of an army in occupation. On the contrary, when such territory reverts to the control of its rightful Sovereign, wrongs done during the foreign occupation are cognizable by the ordinary Courts. The protection of the Sovereign has not ceased. It is continuous, though the actual redress of what has been done amiss may be necessarily postponed until the enemy forces have been expelled. Their Lordships consider that the duty of a resident alien is so to act that the Crown shall not be harmed by reason of its having admitted him as a resident. He is not to take advantage of the hospitality extended to him against the Sovereign who extended it.[12]

A corollary to an alien's local allegiance is the Sovereign's duty to protect those aliens who owe the Sovereign their local allegiance. Hence, aliens who owe a local allegiance have as much right to expect the Crown to act according to the rule of law as do natural born subjects, or alien-born subjects who have acquired a permanent allegiance to the Sovereign through the acquisition of citizenship.

In *Johnstone v Pedlar*, [1921] 2 AC 262 (Ireland, HL) a man born in Ireland (at that time under British rule) but at the relevant point in time a naturalized citizen of the United States of America, took part in the 1916 Easter Rebellion in Dublin and was interned. Upon his release from internment he was arrested for illegal activities and a sum of money in his possession was seized. That seizure was the subject of an action in which the House of Lords ruled that a friendly alien owing a local allegiance to the Crown was in turn owed the protection of the Sovereign. Since there was no basis in law for the seizure and detention of his money, the sums that were taken from him had to be returned to him. Lord Atkinson's judgement aptly summed up the nature of the relationship:

> It is true that the respondent flagrantly violated his allegiance. It is true that he abused the rights which the protection of the King secured for him. It is true that he might presumably have been tried for high treason. It is certain that he might have been expelled from the country. But none of those things have been done. The protection to a resident alien is given by the Crown. The Crown alone can withdraw it. The appellant is still the subject of a State at amity with Great Britain. He does not come within the definition of an alien enemy, and the Crown has given no indication whatever that it has withdrawn his implied licence to reside within this realm. The fact that he has shown himself unworthy of the Sovereign's protection, has abused his privileges and violated his allegiance, cannot, in my view, *ipso facto* terminate the protection with all the rights which flowed from it which the Sovereign extended to him, or *ipso facto* withdraw the implied licence which the Sovereign gave to him to reside in this country.[13]

Thus, the protection of the Sovereign which accompanies local allegiance is established even where an alien, residing in the Sovereign's domain, has committed acts which might have provided a basis for a charge of treason. It is also apparent from the case law that local allegiance may continue where an alien has travelled abroad under the protection of Sovereign, as for instance with a passport issued in the name of the Sovereign, even though the alien may have obtained that passport without having a valid right to it.

In *Joyce v DPP*, [1946] AC 347 (England, HL) the prosecution alleged that Joyce, a natural born citizen of the United States of America who had long resided in the United Kingdom, travelled abroad on a British passport at the outbreak of the Second World War and reached Germany, where he accepted employment as a government radio announcer. He retained that employment (under which he was known as Lord Haw Haw) throughout the war, disseminating German propaganda in English to the United Kingdom and allied forces. After the war, he was prosecuted for treason. In the House of Lords, Lord Jowitt, the Lord Chancellor, held that an alien who owes a local allegiance to the Sovereign, and who obtains a passport to travel abroad, continues to claim the Sovereign's protection. Thus:

> By the possession of that document [i.e., a passport] he is enabled to obtain in a foreign country the protection extended to British subjects. By his own act he has maintained the bond which while he was within the realm bound him to his sovereign. The question is not whether he obtained British citizenship by obtaining the passport, but whether by its receipt he extended his duty of allegiance beyond the moment when he left the shores of this country. As one owing allegiance to the King he sought and obtained the protection of the King for himself while abroad . .

.

In these circumstances I am clearly of opinion that so long as he holds the passport he is within the meaning of the statute a man who, if he is adherent to the King's enemies in the realm or elsewhere commits an act of treason.[14]

In the case of *Joyce*, the House of Lords acknowledged that an alien who claimed the protection of the British Sovereign while abroad could divest himself of that protection. But on the facts of that case there was no evidence that Joyce had done so and, accordingly, he was convicted of treason, sentenced to death and hanged.[15]

Aliens who avail themselves of the protection of the Canadian Sovereign owe allegiance to the Sovereign whether they are within this country or, though outside of it, nevertheless maintain their right to the protection of the Canadian Sovereign. Failure to adhere to this local allegiance may make them criminally liable for actions they take which are incompatible with their local allegiance.

5.5   The Oath of Allegiance

An oath of allegiance to the Sovereign may be voluntarily made by a subject but the taking of an oath of allegiance does not add to the obligations which are owed to the Sovereign by a natural born, or naturalized, subject. As such, oaths of allegiance often serve the purpose of binding the moral conscience of the oath-taker, impressing upon them the duty of loyalty owed to the Sovereign.For those who must or who wish to take an oath of allegiance the Parliament has provided a legal form of the oath in the *Oath of Allegiance Act*.[16]

Thus, while an oath of allegiance to the Sovereign is not necessary in order to establish the fact of allegiance to the Sovereign, in many situations the taking of an oath of allegiance is required by statutes as a prerequisite to entering upon or performing the duties of a public office. In this latter sense the oath of allegiance acts as an oath of office. The jurisprudence surrounding the taking an oath of allegiance as an oath of office has often revolved around the question of whether the swearing or affirming of an oath, or declaration of allegiance, was mandatory or directory. If the former, a failure to take the oath of allegiance could have the effect of disqualifying a person from entering upon, or lawfully performing, the duties of a public office to which they have been appointed. However, where the provision requiring the making of an oath of allegiance is found to be directory only, a failure to swear, or affirm, the oath will not deprive a person from the entering upon an office, or from performing the functions of an office to which they have been appointed.

Formerly, federal public servants were required to make an oath of allegiance upon their appointment to the public service of Canada. Under the 1952 version of the *Civil Service Act* a failure on the part of a public servant to make the oath of allegiance would deprive them of their salary.[17] However, subsequent versions of the *Public Service Employment Act* removed the consequences imposed on public servants by their failure to take the oath of allegiance and thus the administration of the oath of allegiance to public servants came to be viewed as a directory requirement, rather than a mandatory requirement. At the same time, developments in the common law relating to public service labour relations increasingly assimilated the position of public servants to that of an ordinary employment relationship with the Crown, rather than as the entry of a person into a public office. As a result, the oath of allegiance came to be viewed as unnecessary and it was abolished in 2005.[18] The use of an oath of allegiance is still often used as an oath of office in the provinces however.

The federal *Oaths of Allegiance Act,* provides the form of the oath or solemn affirmation of allegiance to the Canadian Sovereign. Section 2 is quite broad and permits any person to take the oath. It states in subsections (1) and (2) as follows:

> (1) Every person who, either of his own accord or in compliance with any lawful requirement made of the person, or in obedience to the directions of any Act or law in force in Canada, except the Constitution Act, 1867 and the Citizenship Act, desires to take an oath of allegiance shall have administered and take the oath in the following form, and no other:

> I, . . . , do swear that I will be faithful and bear true allegiance to Her Majesty Queen Elizabeth the Second, Queen of Canada, Her Heirs and Successors. So help me God.

> (2) Where there is a demise of the Crown, there shall be substituted in the oath of allegiance the name of the Sovereign for the time being.

Section 3 provides for the taking of a solemn affirmation in lieu of an oath. No oath, other than the oath or affirmation prescribed by the Act, is required to be taken in order to display allegiance. Pursuant to the Act, the Governor in Council may make regulations imposing the requirement to take the oath of allegiance, or a more general oath of office, on the holders of federal public offices. The making of the oath or affirmation prescribed by the statute by a natural born citizen, or by a person who has acquired Canadian citizenship, does not alter or affect the allegiance that they already owe to the Sovereign.

In addition to the general oath of allegiance there is a special oath of allegiance to the Sovereign that is made by all new Canadians under the provisions of the *Citizenship Act.* That oath has sparked controversy, particularly among some immigrants who have come to Canada from countries that had a history of difficult colonial relations with the United Kingdom. In *McAteer et al. v Attorney General of Canada,* [2013] 117 OR (3d) 353 (Ontario, SC) the applicants sought to show that the oath of Canadian citizenship[19] violated their constitutionally protected rights to expression, religion, and equality under the *Canadian Charter of Rights and Freedoms.* The court, per Justice Morgan, held that a *prima facie* case was established to show that the *Charter* rights of the Applicants were infringed by the form of the oath requiring an expression of allegiance to the Sovereign but he held that the infringement was justified under the *Charter*, as a reasonable and demonstrably justified limitation in a free and democratic society. The oath of allegiance to the Sovereign within the oath of citizenship reflected the constitutional principles under which the Canadian realm was organized. Justice Morgan stated:

> In requiring a vow of commitment to national values at the moment of citizenship, the Act, as indicated earlier in these reasons, places a limit on free speech; but it does so in a way that is appropriate to the free and democratic society that is Canada. Indeed, the Act, with its mandatory oath, restricts a Charter right in a way "that reflects the very purpose for which rights were entrenched," Lorraine E. Weinrib, "The Supreme Court of Canada and Section 1 of the Charter" (1988), 10 Sup Ct L Rev 469, at 494. As a statement that embraces constitutional values, it is a rights-enhancing measure that is justified under section 1 of the Charter.[20]

Accordingly, the Charter-based challenge to the citizenship law was dismissed.

5.6   A Special Relationship: The Crown and the Aboriginal Peoples

The earliest years of Canada's existence were precarious for the European settler community and required that the Crown enter into arrangements with the original inhabitants of the country to secure the safety of settler populations, and to create a framework for relations between the expanding European population and the aboriginal inhabitants of Canada. That relationship was established by both the Crown in Right of France and subsequently by the Crown in Right of the United Kingdom, and entailed the negotiation of treaties between the Crown and the aboriginal peoples on a nation to nation basis. Initially, the treaties were primarily treaties of alliance but over time they evolved to provide for the acquisition of land rights by the Crown, and established the rights and obligations of both the Crown and the aboriginal first nations. Thus the Sovereign's representatives became the interlocutors between the settler communities that were becoming established in Canada and the original inhabitants of the country. The aboriginal peoples naturally looked to the Crown as the guarantor of the rights that the Crown had recognized in the treaties that it had made with them. However, it is a sad fact of history that many of the treaties were breached, or their obligations overlooked, whenever it was convenient for the colonial, federal, or provincial governments to do so.

Nevertheless, the treaties remained in force and they are now often the source of claims by the aboriginal peoples of Canada for recognition of their special rights as the first inhabitants of the country. Toward the latter part of the twentieth century, and on into the twenty-first century, a number of important legal cases were brought before the Supreme Court of Canada that breathed new life into the treaty obligations that the Crown accepted in the treaties with the aboriginal first nations. The Federal Government began to rectify the unjust application of the treaties, and to recognize and restore the rights of the aboriginal peoples under the pressure of the evolving jurisprudence relating to aboriginal law. Those judicial developments underscored the special relationship between the Crown and the aboriginal peoples that is expressed by the legal concept of the Honour of the Crown.

5.7   The Pre-1763 Period

When Canada was under the sovereignty of France, the Crown did not recognize that the aboriginal peoples residing within the territory of Canada held any particular rights vis-a-vis the government or the setter community. The Crown was unwilling to consider that the aboriginal peoples formed separate sovereign nations but as a practical matter it did recognize that they inhabited particular territories. The Crown, during the Bourbon monarchy, entered into political and military alliances with the aboriginal first nations that it encountered but without conferring any particular rights on the aboriginal peoples. In fact, to acquire recognized rights at that time it was necessary for an aboriginal person to acquire the legal status of a French Subject which, in turn, required the aboriginal person to convert to Roman Catholicism. During this period of constitutional development relations between the Crown and the aboriginal population were regarded as an external relationship, except for those individual circumstances where aboriginal persons converted to Catholicism and obtained the status of a French Subject.

5.8   The Royal Proclamation of 1763

Following the acquisition of sovereignty over Canada by Great Britain in 1763, a shift in relations between the Crown and the aboriginal first nations occurred. The British Crown did recognize that the aboriginal first nations were separate nations, and that they held possession of their traditional territories. The Crown undertook to obtain title to aboriginal lands through treaties before the Crown could dispose of aboriginal traditional lands to others, such as European settlers. From the time of the conquest of Canada, therefore, the concept of aboriginal title became germane to the efforts of colonial authorities to solidify and expand the territory under the sovereignty of the Crown.

The foundation for the concept of the honour of the Crown as a legal principle in Canadian law is the *Royal Proclamation, 1763*, issued on October 7, 1763, by King George III following the Treaty of Paris that ended hostilities between Great Britain and France during the Seven Years War, and which implemented the transfer of *de jure* sovereignty over Canada from France to Great Britain. The purpose of the *Royal Proclamation, 1763*, was to order the establishment of governments in the colonies that were newly acquired from France but it also addressed the issue of how settler communities could interact with the aboriginal first nations present in Canada. Chief among the requirements of the *Royal Proclamation, 1763*, was the protection of aboriginal title to the lands possessed by the aboriginal people. The proclamation forbade private subjects of the Crown from making direct purchases of lands from the aboriginal people and required that any transfer of lands must first occur on a nation to nation basis through arrangements entered into directly by the Crown with the aboriginal first nations.

Thus, the Crown became an intermediary between the aboriginal and settler communities within Canada, and the arbiter of their respective rights, especially in connection with land rights. From the time of the establishment of British sovereignty it was not possible for aboriginal lands to be transferred to anyone other than the Crown. Regulations concerning the acquisition by the Crown of aboriginal lands were subsequently issued in 1764 and relations with the aboriginal peoples of Canada remained a responsibility of the Imperial Government until 1850, as the authorities in London primarily viewed the aboriginal peoples as military allies in the defence of the colonies. After 1850 the responsibility for aboriginal affairs was transferred to the Colonial Government, consistent with the progression of responsible government in Canada.

Local control of aboriginal affairs in the nineteenth century led to abuses, with many of the rights of the aboriginal peoples of Canada that derived from the *Royal Proclamation, 1763*, and preceding, or subsequent treaties, becoming honoured more in the breach than in the norm in the relations between the Crown and the aboriginal first nations. Nevertheless, the formal legal obligations remained in force and in the latter part of the twentieth century the courts, particularly the Supreme Court of Canada, have acted to restore the balance between aboriginal rights and the rights of the Crown.

5.9   The Honour of the Crown

As the Supreme Court explained in *Manitoba Metis Federation Inc. v Canada (Attorney General)*, [2013] 1 SCR 623 (Canada, SC) the Crown is under an obligation to act with honour in all of its dealings with the aboriginal peoples of Canada. This constitutional principle has been captured by the phrase the honour of the Crown, which "refers to the principle that servants of the Crown must conduct themselves with honour when acting on behalf of the sovereign". The principle of the honour of the Crown arose from the assertion of the Crown's sovereignty over Canada and the aboriginal peoples that resided in Canada at the time of the assertion of the sovereignty of the Crown. Thus, "the ultimate purpose of the honour of the Crown is the reconciliation of pre-existing Aboriginal societies with the assertion of Crown sovereignty" (para. 66).

Earlier cases such as *Guerin v The Queen*, [1984] 2 SCR 335 (Canada, SC) and *R v Sparrow*, [1990] 1 SCR 1075 (Canada, SC) established the principle that the Crown in Right of Canada is subject to a *sui generis* constitutional obligation to act toward the aboriginal peoples of Canada in the capacity of a fiduciary. As a fiduciary, the Crown must act in a trust-like manner toward the aboriginal peoples. The scope and extent of the fiduciary obligations owed by the Crown to the aboriginal societies are often fact-specific and may be framed by the particular obligations that the Crown accepted as a result of historic treaty negotiations. As a result, the Crown must consult with aboriginal first nations even when it exercises the Crown's rights under a treaty, if the exercise of that right could have an effect on an aboriginal first nation (see *Mikisew Cree First Nation v Canada*, [2005] 3 SCR 388 (Canada, SC)).

The nature of the engagement of the honour of the Crown will vary according to the factual and other circumstances that exist in each unique situation where the relations between the Crown and aboriginal peoples intersect. In the *Manitoba Metis Federation* case, the Supreme Court summarized four circumstances where the concept has applied in previous jurisprudence:

(1) The honour of the Crown gives rise to a fiduciary duty when the Crown assumes discretionary control over a specific Aboriginal interest;

(2) The honour of the Crown informs the purposive interpretation of s. 35 of the *Constitution Act, 1982*, and gives rise to a duty to consult when the Crown contemplates an action that will affect a claimed but as of yet unproven Aboriginal interest;

(3) The honour of the Crown governs treaty-making and implementation leading to requirements such as honourable negotiation and the avoidance of the appearance of sharp dealing; and

(4) The honour of the Crown requires the Crown to act in a way that accomplishes the intended purposes of treaty and statutory grants to Aboriginal peoples.[21]

In implementing the honour of the Crown as a principle in dealings with the aboriginal peoples the Crown must not take a narrow approach to the interpretation of its constitutional obligations to aboriginal peoples, and it must act purposefully to discharge its obligations to aboriginal peoples. The principle of the honour of the Crown underscores the important relationship between the Sovereign, in whose name the government is carried on, and the aboriginal peoples of Canada. Where there has been a deficiency by government actors in discharging the Crown's obligations to the aboriginal peoples of Canada the honour of the Crown provides a doctrinal basis for the rectification of the deficiency.

An important element of this principle is the duty to consult with aboriginal first nations on developments within their traditional territories that can affect them. This principle has been developed in a series of important precedents from the Supreme Court of Canada, among them, *Haida Nation v British Columbia (Minister of Forests)*, [2004] 3 SCR 511 (Canada, SC); *Rio Tinto Alcan Inc. v Carrier Sekani Tribal Council*, [2010] 2 SCR 650 (Canada, SC); and *Clyde River (Hamlet) v Petroleum Geo-Services Inc.* (2017), SCC 40 (Canada, SC). The principle of the honour of the Crown remains a developing principle of constitutional law, and may evolve further in the future as a result of judicial pronouncements. There have been some efforts to extend this principle beyond the context of the relationship between aboriginal peoples of Canada and the Crown but to date such attempts have not been accepted by the courts.

The honour of the Crown reflects the special relationship between the Crown and the aboriginal peoples of Canada. Despite that special relationship however, the aboriginal peoples of Canada remain ordinary subjects of the Crown and possess the same civil rights and obligations of other Canadian citizens, including the obligations of allegiance. Ultimately, the principle of the honour of the Crown serves to protect the integrity of the Crown with respect to its historic commitments, and thus it reinforces the obligations of the Sovereign toward the rule of law that is expressed by the Sovereign in the Coronation Oath.

[1] RSC 1985, c. C-46

[2] *Proclamation Queen's Birthday* SOR/57-55

[3] at para. 50. A secondary argument alleging a violation of the Applicant's religious rights failed to establish a *prima facie* case.

[4] It is not the policy of the Government of Canada to permit the creation of stateless persons by their renunciation of Canadian citizenship.

[5] at page 720.

[6] RSC 1985, c. C-29, s. 9; 1992, c. 21, s. 8; 2014, c. 22, s. 7

[7] at page 137

[8] *Rex v Inouye Kanao* Public Records Office, Hong Kong (HKRS 163, D 7 S 1/2/216 War Criminals – Inouye)

[9] Ibid, and *Desperate Siege, The Battle of Hong Kong*, Ted Ferguson, Doubleday Canada Limited, Toronto, 1980, at pages 223-224

[10] For Canada this was done by the *Citizenship Act* SC 1946, C. 15 (in force January 1, 1947).

[11] at page 814

[12] at page 328

[13] at page 285

[14] at pages 370-371

[15] In Canadian criminal law, this situation is now covered by subsection 46(3) of the *Criminal Code* RSC 1985, c. C-46.

[16] RSC 1985, c. O-1

[17] *Civil Service Act* RSC 1952, c. 48, ss. 42(1).

[18] However, newly appointed public servants are still required to swear or affirm an oath of confidentiality with respect to the information that they become privy to in the course of their employment.

[19] The oath of citizenship states: I swear (or affirm) that I will be faithful and bear true allegiance to Her Majesty Queen Elizabeth the Second, Queen of Canada, Her Heirs and Successors, and that I will faithfully observe the laws of Canada and fulfill my duties as a Canadian citizen.

[20] at para 81

[21] at paragraph 73

POWERS, PREROGATIVES AND OBLIGATIONS

6.1   The Symbolic Functions of the Monarchy

The Sovereign of Canada is the personification of the Canadian state following upon the constitutional traditions inherited by Canada from France and Great Britain. To this day, all of the great offices of state are held by a grant from the Sovereign and the governance of the country is carried on in the Sovereign's name, and in accordance with the Sovereign's Coronation Oath. Public acts are performed in the name of the Sovereign who reigns and acts according to the rule of law.

As the personification of the State, various words are used to describe the Monarch. The *Interpretation Act* provides the following definition in section 35:

> Her Majesty", "His Majesty", "the Queen", "the King" or "the Crown" means the Sovereign of the United Kingdom, Canada and Her other Realms and Territories and Head of the Commonwealth.

The definition includes the natural person of the Sovereign and the Sovereign in their body politic capacity or, more accurately, the state. Today, many of words used to describe the monarchy in the *Interpretation Act* are synonymous with "Government" or "the State".[1]

It has been held that the definition of "Her Majesty" in the *Interpretation Act* is not restricted to Her Majesty in right of Canada, but may also include Her Majesty in right of a province, on the ground that the *Interpretation Act* provision is largely a recital of her title as prescribed by the *Royal Styles and Titles Act*; *The Queen v Canadian Transport Commission*, [1978] 1 SCR 61 at 70 (Canada, SC).

The Sovereign is an essential component of Parliament, and the sovereignty of the nation is vested in the Queen (or King) in Parliament together with the Queen (or King) in the legislatures of the provinces. All laws of Parliament, or of the provincial legislatures, are made by the Sovereign acting with the advice and consent of the Senate and House of Commons in Parliament, or with the advice and consent of the legislatures of the provinces.

The Sovereign is the fount of all justice and the courts of law are the Sovereign's courts. By a legal fiction, the Sovereign is always deemed to be present in the courts of law[2] and the Sovereign is required by their Coronation Oath to ensure that law and justice is available through the courts. All justice is dispensed in the Sovereign's name.

The Sovereign is the fount of all honours and dignities in Canada and all honours and titles, orders of state, decorations, medals, and heraldic emblems, are conferred in the name of the Sovereign. Some honorary offices of state are also conferred on individuals by a grant from the Sovereign.

Essentially, the Sovereign personifies the legitimacy of the state and its various organs of government and administration. As the personification of the legitimacy of the state, and the personal Monarch of Canadians, the Sovereign is one constitutional symbol of the unity of Canada.

Thus, in a strictly constitutional sense, the Sovereign continues to provide a high symbolic degree of constitutional unification as the apex of public governance in Canada. It is in the Sovereign's name that both the federal and provincial components of the State are governed, public offices held, the military commanded, and the coin and currency circulated, all of which serves to bind the country together in a constitutional union. This unity of governance is symbolized by the Sovereign not only in the representational sense but also in a personal sense, through periodic visits throughout the country, and by the presence of the Sovereign or other members of the royal family at important state ceremonies and events.

6.2   The Rule of Law

The rule of law is a central feature of a Westminster-style constitution and the concept has been inherited by all countries which now possess a Westminster-style constitution. In Canada, the Supreme Court has determined that the rule of law forms an essential component of the framework of Canadian law. It arises implicitly, in the preamble to the *Constitution Act, 1867*, which expresses the desire of Canada to possess "a Constitution similar in principle to that of the United Kingdom", and explicitly, in the preamble of the *Constitution Act, 1982*, which recognizes that Canada is founded upon the rule of law; *Reference Re: Manitoba Language Rights*, [1985] 1 SCR 750 (Canada, SC). The Supreme Court of Canada has stated that "the exercise of all public power [must] find its ultimate source in a legal rule.[3]

A notable British Professor of law and constitutional theorist, Albert Venn Dicey, described the rule of law as consisting of three parts. Firstly, no one may be punished except by the regular courts of law for a breach of established law. Thus, the reach of personal discretion or arbitrary behaviour by authoritarian figures is excluded.[4] Secondly, all persons are equally subject to the law and within the jurisdiction of the regular courts of law.[5] Thirdly, there is no special law for government but rather constitutional law has evolved from the principles of the ordinary private law in a Westminster parliamentary system.[6]

As a basic constitutional principle the rule of law is synonymous with the early struggles to contain the tendency toward absolute monarchy in England. The seminal development of this principle was the *Magna Carta*, issued by King John in 1215, and reissued several times in the centuries which followed.[7] The *Magna Carta* resulted from the tensions between the monarchy and the nobility in England during the early medieval ages. During the reign of King Richard I (1189-99) opposition to taxation and the administration of government began to grow. Following the accession of his brother King John (1199-1216), the English nobility exacted the concessions of the *Magna Carta* from the King under the threat of rebellion.

The most important clauses of the *Magna Carta* from the modern perspective concern the administration of justice. Article 39 states:

> No freeman shall be arrested, or imprisoned, or dispossessed, or outlawed, or banished, or in any way molested; nor will we set forth against him, nor send against him, unless by the lawful judgment of his peers and by the law of the land.

Other provisions banned the sale of justice, or its refusal, or delay, and promised the establishment of fixed courts of law to adjudicate disputes. The *Magna Carta* also banned new forms of exactions (scutage and aid) which were forerunners of taxation, "save by the common council of our kingdom". Knights were protected against exactions, and peasants against the compulsory taking of their carts and horses for transport.

The *Magna Carta* had an influence on English constitutional law far beyond that which was intended by King John and his barons, owing to the fact that much was read into the instrument by succeeding generations. The charter was reissued by King John's successors on various occasions, the most significant being the *Magna Carta (1297)* which formed (and still forms) part of English statute law. The *Magna Carta* is part of the legal inheritance that all of the Commonwealth realms received, as did the wider Commonwealth of Nations. This aspect was addressed by Lord Justice Laws in *R (Bancoult) v Secretary of State*, [2001] 3 LRC 249 (England, QB (Administrative Court) at 275:

> It is clear that the *Magna Carta* is not applied to any colony by express words; it may only be so, therefore, by 'necessary intendment'. There was much argument at the Bar as to the extent to which the *Magna Carta* 'followed the flag'. That expression appeared in a judgment in the Canadian Supreme Court in *Calder v A-G of British Columbia* (1973) 34 DLR (3d) 145 at 203, where it was said that *Magna Carta*: "had always been considered to be law throughout the Empire. It was a law which followed the flag as England assumed jurisdiction over newly discovered or

acquired lands or territories. That statement . . . was approved by Lord Denning MR in *R v FCO, ex p Indian Association of Alberta*, [1992] 2 All ER 118 at 124.

Later in his judgment Lord Justice Laws confirmed the principle, stating that: "So far as it [*Magna Carta*] is a proclamation of the rule of law, it may indeed be said to follow the flag . . . ".[8]

In Canada, the *Magna Carta* is not part of the *Constitution of Canada*, as defined by the *Constitution Act, 1982*, but it is nevertheless part of Canada's constitutional inheritance from England under the reception doctrine, and it has informed the overall development of Canadian constitutional law.[9]

As a constitutional document relating to the monarchy, the *Magna Carta* can be viewed as an important early legal instrument which subordinated plenary monarchial power to the common law. From this starting point, constitutional monarchy would later evolve in England and subsequently in Canada.

In the seventeenth century the principle that the Sovereign was subordinate to the rule of law became established in English constitutional law. That the Sovereign could be restrained by the judiciary from an uninhibited exercise of royal power is apparent from the judgement in *Prohibitions Del Roy* (1607), 12 Co Rep 64, (England, KB) which contained a judicial riposte to the royal view that the King could exercise a personal judicial discretion in the exercise of his prerogative powers. Sir Edward [later Lord] Coke took a dim judicial view of the King's assertions regarding the extent of monarchical powers by stating:

> . . . that the King in his own person cannot adjudge any case, either criminal, as treason, felony or betwixt party and party, concerning his inheritance, chattels or goods but this ought to be determined and adjudged in some Court of Justice, according to the law and custom of England.[10]

Therefore, Coke stated, "the King cannot take any cause out of any of his Courts, and give judgment upon it himself.[11]

In 1628 the *Petition of Right*[12] restrained the Sovereign from requiring gifts from subjects and punishing those who refused to provide such gifts, imprisoning subjects without cause, or applying martial law within the realm in peacetime. The practice of billeting servicemen in private houses was also prohibited.

In the aftermath of the Glorious Revolution of 1688, the English *Bill of Rights, 1689*, ended the power of the Sovereign to suspend or dispense with the laws of the realm, and the monarch's prerogative power to raise monies through taxation without recourse to Parliament. It also confirmed the right of free speech in Parliamentary proceedings.[13]

Subsequently, the *Act of Settlement, 1701,* more firmly enshrined the rule of law by declaring that:

> ... the laws of England are the birthright of the people thereof, and all the Kings and Queens, who shall ascend the throne of this realm, ought to administer the government of the same according to the said laws, and all their officers and ministers ought to serve them respectively according to the same ... [14]

That Act also established the tenure of judges and provided for their removal only upon an address to the Throne by both houses of Parliament.[15] Thus the *Act of Settlement, 1701,* by crystallizing the principle that the Sovereign ruled according to law, and by establishing the independence of the judiciary, completed the process of removing aspects of arbitrary monarchial power from the English constitution. At confederation in 1867, this principle also became fully operative within the Canadian constitution.[16]

The foundational principle of the rule of law was reinforced in Canadian law by the judgment of the Judicial Committee in *Eastern Trust Company v McKenzie, Mann & Co. Limited,* [1915] AC 750 (Canada, JC). The facts in that case involved subsidy payments made by the Province of Nova Scotia to a contractor, notwithstanding the fact that the Executive Council of the Province knew that the contractor had been judicially restrained from receiving those funds by an order of the Nova Scotian courts. The actions of the government of Nova Scotia were greatly deprecated by the Judicial Committee and a very forceful passage from the judgment of Sir George Farwell has been cited in Commonwealth jurisprudence to explain the obligation of the Sovereign to govern in accordance with the rule of law. The Judicial Committee said:

> ... It is the duty of the Crown and of every branch of the Executive to abide by and obey the law. If there is any difficulty in ascertaining it the Courts are open to the Crown to sue, and it is the duty of the Executive in cases of doubt to ascertain the law, in order to obey it, not to disregard it.[17]

This principle runs deeply throughout the jurisprudence of Canada and of the Commonwealth. In ruling on a motion to strike a statement of claim on the grounds that it did not disclose a cause of action known to law in *Bavadra v Attorney General,* [1988] LRC (Const) (Fiji, HC), Justice Rooney followed the judgment of the Judicial Committee in the *Eastern Trust Co.* case in construing the modern powers of the Sovereign:

> Constitutional law clothes the person of the Sovereign with supreme sovereignty and preeminence. She is, however, bound by the terms of her coronation oath and the maxims of the common law, to observe and obey the law. The Queen may not suspend laws or the execution of laws without the consent of Parliament. That means, in the case of Fiji, the Parliament established by the Constitution. The Queen

may not dispense with laws. She cannot therefore, alter or repeal the Constitution of Fiji which is the supreme law or any part of it . . .

The Queen reigns but does not rule over her subjects. The claim in the ninth paragraph of the summons appears to be based upon a misconception as to the nature and purpose of royal authority. Whatever may have been the power of ancient Kings to rule over their subjects and enact measures which had to be obeyed, no vestige of such authority remains in the hands of the Monarch to-day.[18]

In *Reference Re: Manitoba Language Rights*, [1985] 1 SCR 721 (Canada, SC) the Supreme Court of Canada defined the rule of law to possess two separate but related components, by stating:

The rule of law, a fundamental principle of our Constitution, must mean at least two things. First, that the law is supreme over officials of the government as well as private individuals, and thereby preclusive of the influence of arbitrary power . . . Second, the rule of law requires the creation and maintenance of an actual order of positive laws which preserves and embodies the more general principle of normative order. Law and order are indispensable elements of civilized life.[19]

As a result, the defence of an act of state as an exemption to the rule of law is unavailable to the Crown and its officers under the common law; *Walker v Baird*, [1892] AC 491 (Newfoundland, JC). *Walker v Baird* concerned an incident in which a British naval commander on the Newfoundland fisheries station entered upon a messuage (a dwelling and its outbuildings) and prevented its use as a lobster fishery, ostensibly in compliance with obligations that the Sovereign had entered into with France, which at that time had fisheries interests on the Newfoundland coast pursuant to the Treaty of Paris, 1763.

In a suit in trespass, the naval commander pled an act of state as a defence, stipulating that his actions had been in conformity with the instructions of Her Majesty's Government as a matter of state and public policy. On a motion by the plaintiff to strike out the defence as one which did not disclose a defence known to the common law, both the Supreme Court of Newfoundland and the Judicial Committee of the Privy Council sided with the plaintiff. Lord Herschell in the Judicial Committee wrote that it was "wholly untenable" to suggest that the actions of the naval officer, obeying instructions from the Crown which resulted in a trespass, could be justified as an act of State.[20]

Just as the authority of Sovereign cannot be exercised in violation of law, so too it cannot be used to excuse a breach of the law, other than by way of a pardon. In *Yip Chiu-cheung v R*, [1994] 2 LRC 795 (Hong Kong, JC) the Judicial Committee considered an appeal from an appellant who was convicted of conspiracy to traffic in heroin. The basis of the appeal was that the appellant had dealings with a person who was actually an undercover American law enforcement agent working with the Royal Hong Kong Police Force, and, as such, the American undercover agent could not have formed the necessary mens rea, or criminal intent, to constitute the offence. The defence asserted that if one of the two parties to the transaction was incapable of forming criminal intent in conjunction with an offence of trafficking in heroin that required criminal intent, there could be no conspiracy to traffic in heroin. However, the Judicial Committee rejected that defence, holding that the American undercover agent could formulate a criminal intent to commit the offence. Although the authorities had discretion not to prosecute the American, the Crown could not alter the law which made the transaction an offence.

The High Court of Australia in *A v Hayden* (1984), 156 CLR 532 (Australia, HC) declared that there was no place for a general defence of superior orders, or of Crown, or Executive fiat in Australian criminal law. Gibbs CJ said: "It is fundamental to our legal system that the executive has no power to authorize a breach of the law and that it is no excuse for an offender to say that he acted under the orders of a superior officer."[21]

Neither the Sovereign nor the Sovereign's ministers may suspend laws in the exercise of royal authority. In *Fitzgerald v Muldoon*, [1976] NZLR 615 (New Zealand, SC) the Prime Minister of New Zealand had purported to suspend the operation of a superannuation scheme established by an Act of the Parliament of New Zealand. It was alleged in court that the action of the Prime Minister violated section 1 of the *Bill of Rights, 1689* which stated; "That the pretended power of suspending of laws or the execution of laws by regall authority without consent of Parlyament is illegal." The Court found that the Prime Minister derived his authority from the Crown and therefore his announcement of the suspension of the superannuation scheme was an act of royal authority that contravened the *Bill of Rights 1689*. The Court stated:

> He is the Prime Minister, the leader of the government elected to office, the chief of the executive government. He had lately received his commission by royal authority, taken the oaths of office, and entered on his duties. In my opinion his public announcement of 15 December, made as it was in the course of his official duties as Prime Minister, must therefore be regarded as made "by regall authority" within the meaning of section 1 . . . [22]

and further:

> . . . in so doing he [the Prime Minister] was purporting to suspend the law without consent of Parliament. Parliament had made the law. Therefore the law could be amended or suspended only by Parliament or with the authority of Parliament.[23]

A more recent description of the rule of law as it applies to the monarchy is provided by the judgement of the Carribean Court of Justice in *Attorney General et al v Joseph et al*, [2007] 4 LRC 199 (Barbados, CCJ) where Wit J. stated:

> The multi-layered concept of the rule of law establishes, first and foremost, that no person, not even the Queen or her Governor General, is above the law. It further imbues the Constitution [of Barbados] with other fundamental requirements such as rationality, reasonableness, fundamental fairness and the duty and ability to refrain from and effectively protect against abuse and the arbitrary exercise of power.[24]

Such cases illustrate the principle that the rule of law is one of the great principles of the common law, which resounds in the constitutional obligations of the Crown in Canada as it does in other realms which have inherited the legal norms of England and Great Britain as part of their own constitutional law.

6.3   The Sovereign and Executive Powers

The Executive powers constitute the power over the Government of Canada and reflect the fact that all government operations in Canada trace the source of their authority to the Sovereign. It is in the name of the Sovereign that the work of the government proceeds.

6.4   Executive Government

The most solemn constitutional power possessed by the Sovereign is the power over the executive government of Canada. Section 9 of the *Constitution Act, 1867*, states: "The Executive Government and Authority of and over Canada is hereby declared to continue and be vested in the Queen".

As companions to this provision, sections 12, 64, and 65 provide for the Sovereign's representatives to discharge the executive functions, in relation to Canada, or the provinces, that were formerly vested in the Governor General or Lieutenant Governors of the colonial provinces, immediately prior to confederation. As a matter of law those provisions confer the whole responsibility of government upon the Sovereign and her representatives.

However, as explained elsewhere in this text, the Sovereign exercises her powers in relation to Canada in accordance with the principles of responsible government, which means that the Sovereign and her representatives act only by and with the advice of the Sovereign's constitutional advisors in almost all matters of state. Public acts in relation to Canada, or one of its provinces on the Sovereign's own initiative are exceedingly rare events, and by and large the acts of the Sovereign are executed through departments or agencies of the state and by ministers and civil servants who are appointed for those purposes.

Thus it is the Sovereign's constitutional advisors, the members of the Queen's Privy Council for Canada, and the members of the Executive Council in each province, who must accept responsibility for the public acts of the Sovereign. If holding ministerial office they may be impeached by Parliament, or be made subject to civil and criminal liability in their individual capacity in respect of torts or criminal acts committed by them in office. They cannot plead in their defence that they acted pursuant to the orders of the Sovereign, and they remain accountable in law to the Sovereign, and to the Sovereign's constitutional representatives who possesses the legal power to dismiss them from their posts.

6.5 Commander in Chief of the Armed Forces

Section 15 of the *Constitution Act, 1867*, declares the continuation of the command of the military forces of Canada to be in the Sovereign. This provision of the Act is declaratory of the common law, which vests the supreme command of the armed forces in the Sovereign by prerogative right. The Canadian Forces are the royal forces of Canada by virtue of section 14 of the *National Defence Act*[25] which states: "The Canadian Forces are the armed forces of Her Majesty raised by Canada and consist of one Service called the Canadian Armed Forces".

A notable constitutional principle arose in England in the 17th century when King James II sought to intimidate the English Parliament by maintaining a standing army near the capital, one of the actions that led to the revolution of 1688. In the aftermath of that revolution the English Parliament prohibited the Sovereign from maintaining a standing army in peacetime without the consent of Parliament. That principle was embodied in the *Bill of Rights 1689*, and was subsequently inherited by Canada as an organizing principle of the Canadian constitution through the preamble to the *Constitution Act. 1867*. To give effect in law to this historic principle of the constitution, section 14 of the *National Defence Act* has been enacted by Parliament to provide parliamentary authority for the continuation of the Canadian Forces as a standing permanent force.

The powers accruing to the Sovereign as commander in chief are Royal Prerogative powers and include the appointment of the officers to whom command is delegated, the disposition of units of the armed forces at home or abroad during peace or war, and, in general, the entire conduct of military affairs. Despite those constitutional powers of the Sovereign royal acts in relation to the military are now captured by the principle of responsible government and the Sovereign's public acts in respect of the military forces are undertaken by and with the advice of constitutional advisors. The Sovereign's prerogative role as commander in chief is represented by the Governor General, who also enjoys the status of commander in chief in and over Canada by virtue of clause 1 of the *Letters Patent Constituting the Office of Governor General of Canada, 1947*.[26] However, the managerial control of the military is for all practical purposes, vested in the Minister of National Defence under the provisions of the *National Defence Act* and the operational control falls to the Chief of the Defence Staff and the commanders of the land, air and naval services.

6.6 Senate Appointments

Section 26 of the *Constitution Act, 1867*, is an important constitutional provision that permits the appointment of additional members to the Senate, the upper house of the Parliament of Canada, beyond the maximum number of senators specified by section 21 of the *Constitution Act, 1867*. The original purpose of section 26 was to break any legislative deadlock that may emerge between the lower, elected, House of Commons, and the appointed upper chamber. Section 26 was originally proposed by the Imperial Government during the political conferences that occurred in Charlottetown, Quebec City, and in London that resulted in the crafting of the *British North America Act, 1867*. Canadian delegates initially resisted the proposal but eventually succumbed to imperial pressure and agreed to a provision in the new constitutional statute that would break any legislative deadlock between the two houses of Parliament. The power to summon additional senators was vested in the Sovereign because the Canadian delegates realized that a power vested in the Governor General would result in constitutional advice to summon additional senators being given by the Canadian Ministry that was in office, which the Governor General would be expected to follow. There was a fear among the delegates that a government could use this provision to disrupt the carefully negotiated regional balance of the Senate through a misuse of this power. Thus, the delegates proposed to place the appointment power in the hands of the Sovereign upon a recommendation to the Sovereign by the Governor General. In that way, an independent constitutional actor would determine whether the request should be granted. Under the constitutional structure that existed at confederation the Canadian delegates were well aware of the fact that the Sovereign would act on advice of British ministers rather than Canadian ministers.[27] However, all of that changed in 1926 when the divisibility of the Crown was established between the United Kingdom and the other realms of the Commonwealth. Today, this provision is one upon which the Sovereign of Canada would act only on the recommendation of the Governor General of Canada, who in turn would act only on the advice of their Canadian federal ministers.

Section 26 is the only provision in the *Constitution Act, 1867*, which requires that a recommendation be made by the Governor General to the Sovereign as a condition precedent to the exercise of a power by the Sovereign. Section 26 states:

> If at any Time on the Recommendation of the Governor General the Queen thinks fit to direct that Four or Eight Members be added to the Senate, the Governor General may by Summons to Four or Eight qualified Persons (as the Case may be), representing equally the Four Divisions of Canada, add to the Senate accordingly.

In order that any such additional senators should not form a permanent increase in the membership of the Senate, section 27 further provides:

In case of such Addition being at any Time made, the Governor General shall not summon any Person to the Senate, except upon a further like Direction by the Queen on the like Recommendation, to represent one of the Four Divisions until such Division is represented by Twenty-four Senators and no more.

In the course of Canadian history two ministries have sought to rely on section 26 in order to increase the size of the Senate in order to secure the passage of legislation.

The first attempt was made in the 1873 by the Liberal government of Prime Minister Alexander Mackenzie. A Liberal ministry had been formed in November of that year following the resignation of Sir John A. Macdonald's Conservative ministry. Mackenzie was concerned that Macdonald had appointed a large number of Conservative supporters to the Senate and he wanted to make the partisan balance in the Senate more equitable. Therefore, in December 1873, Mackenzie recommended to the Governor General, Lord Dufferin, that Queen Victoria be advised to permit additional members be summoned to the senate pursuant to the power contained in section 26 of the *Constitution Act, 1867.*

It is noteworthy that at the time that Prime Minister Mackenzie made his recommendation to the Governor General there was no dispute or deadlock between the two houses of Parliament. Indeed, Parliament had been prorogued at the request of Mackenzie and thus his government had not met the House of Commons since taking office. Subsequently, at Mackenzie's request, the Governor General dissolved the House and a general election was held which prompted the Governor General to defer consideration of Prime Minister Mackenzie's request for additional senators. In the election Mackenzie's Liberal Party was returned with a solid majority and the Governor General was then compelled to forward Mackenzie's request for additional senators to Queen Victoria, via the Colonial Secretary, Lord Kimberley.

The Colonial Secretary took the view that the conditions necessary for the Queen to exercise her powers under section 26 had not been met, as there was no deadlock between the two chambers of Parliament. In Kimberly's view the provision to appoint additional Senators was not designed to provide for a more equitable balance of power in the Senate when one Canadian Ministry succeeded another, as Mackenzie wished, but rather to break a true legislative deadlock between the two houses of Parliament when deadlock threatened to prevent a ministry from discharging its responsibility to govern the country. In refusing to place Mackenzie's request before the Queen, Lord Kimberley stated that he would only do so if "a difference had arisen between the two Houses of so serious and permanent a character, that the Government could not be carried on without Her intervention, and when it could be shown that the limited creation of Senators allowed by the Act would apply an adequate remedy".[28]

In denying Prime Minister Mackenzie's request, Lord Kimberley emphasized the need for a parliamentary deadlock as a prerequisite to the exercise of the Queen's powers under section 26 of the *Constitution Act, 1867*.

The second attempt to use section 26 occurred in 1989, when the Progressive Conservative government of Prime Minister Brian Mulroney faced an attempt in the Senate by the opposition Liberal party to obstruct the passage of a goods and services tax as a replacement for a manufacturer sales tax. When a legislative deadlock occurred, the Canadian Ministry advised the Governor General to recommend to Queen Elizabeth II, that eight additional members should be summoned to the Senate pursuant to the power contained in section 26 of the *Constitution Act, 1867*. In that instance Queen Elizabeth II, carefully letting it be known that she was being advised by her Canadian ministers, accepted the recommendation of the Governor General that eight additional Senators should be summoned to the Senate pursuant to Section 26 of the *Constitution Act, 1867*. By Letters Patent under the Great Seal of Canada the additional eight Senators were summoned to the Senate and assisted in securing the passage of the legislation through the upper chamber.

The decision of Queen Elizabeth II in this matter spawned two separate constitutional cases in the provincial superior courts.[29] In *Reference Re Constitutional Question Act* (B.C.) (1991), 78 DLR (4th) 245 (British Columbia, CA) the British Columbia provincial government challenged both the continuing validity of section 26, as well as the exercise of that power by the Queen.

In its opinion on the reference, the British Columbia Court of Appeal was careful to distinguish between matters of law, which are within the purview of the courts, and matters of constitutional convention, which are not. The Province had argued that section 26 was inoperative because it required the Queen to act on the advice of the Privy Council of the United Kingdom, an action incompatible with the status of Canada as an independent state.

However, the Court found that as a matter of law section 26 had not been rendered inoperative by the constitutional development of Canada and that the Queen, advised by the Queen's Privy Council for Canada, was empowered by the *Constitution Act, 1867*, to exercise the powers conferred by section 26. Justice Hollingrake described the Sovereign's power as "an independent discretion," which is restricted only by the necessity of obtaining the recommendation of the Governor General. He further stated that the provision was "a model of clarity" and that attempts to read into the power a legal duty imposed upon the Sovereign to consult with the Privy Council of the United Kingdom were without foundation.[30] In the result, the Court found that section 26 was a power that was constitutionally exercised by the Queen. The Court also advised that, as a matter of law there was no legal requirement imposed upon the Sovereign or the Governor General to follow the advice of the Queen's Privy Council for Canada in exercising the section 26 power, although the Queen and the Governor General could be (and were) constrained by constitutional convention in the exercise of that power.[31] The Court therefore declined to answer questions posed to it concerning the criteria that should apply to the exercise of the section 26 power, viewing that as a matter of constitutional convention, rather than a matter of constitutional law.

Similar issues were raised before the Ontario Court of Appeal in *Leblanc v Canada* (1991), 80 DLR (4th) 641 (Ontario, CA). In that case, the Ontario Court declined to issue an opinion on the question of whether section 26 of the *Constitution Act, 1867*, required the Queen to act on the advice of her British ministers, or at least independently of her Canadian ministers. The Court considered those questions to be matters of constitutional convention, rather than of constitutional law.

However, the Ontario court noted that of the several drafts of the original *British North America Act, 1867*, a single draft called for the Queen to be advised on the exercise of this power by her Privy Councillors in the United Kingdom but that particular draft was not the draft which was ultimately enacted by the Imperial Parliament. There was no inference, according to the Court, that the Queen must be advised by imperial, rather than Canadian Privy Councillors with respect to the exercise of the section 26 power. The Ontario Court of Appeal restricted its ruling to a judgment stating that section 26 does not limit the Queen's powers by preventing her from relying upon the advice of the members of the Queen's Privy Council for Canada.

Additionally, the Ontario Court agreed with the British Columbia Court that the question of whether section 26 required a parliamentary deadlock as a prerequisite to the exercise of the section 26 power was not a matter of law but rather was a matter of constitutional convention, and hence was not justiciable. The Ontario Court also agreed with the British Columbia courts that section 26 had not been rendered inoperative by the constitutional evolution of Canada into an independent state.

The Ontario Court of Appeal was presented with an assertion that the Sovereign had delegated away the powers under section 26 to the Governor General by the terms of the *Letters Patent Constituting the Office of Governor General of Canada, 1947*, which conferred executive powers over Canada on the Governor General of Canada, and thus the Queen could not exercise power under section 26 of the *Constitution Act, 1867*. Here the Court was able to draw on general principles of law for its ruling, stating that as a general principle of law a delegation of power does not, by implication, result in the delegator parting with that power. Absent words of transfer, or release, in the *Letters Patent Constituting the Office of Governor General of Canada, 1947*, this principle applied to the exercise of authority by the Queen under section 26 of the *Constitution Act, 1867,* and therefore the Queen could exercise concurrent authority even assuming that in law she could actually delegate her powers under section 26 to the Governor General, given the distinct powers and functions separately conferred on both the Sovereign and the Governor General by that provision.[32] In the circumstances, the Ontario court declined to go any further to embark upon an analysis of whether such a delegation was permissible under the *Constitution Act, 1867.*[33]

Notwithstanding the fact that the Sovereign, in exercising power under section 26 of the *Constitution Act, 1867,* must act in accordance with constitutional convention on the advice of her Canadian ministers, section 26 remains one of the very few instances in Canadian constitutional law where the Sovereign's personal exercise of formal power involves significant political consequences. Surprisingly, Section 26 appears to have largely escaped the perennial Canadian penchant for generating proposals for constitutional reform.

6.7   Summoning and Prorogation of Parliament or a Legislature

The power to summon a legislative body to meet, and the corollary power to prorogue a legislative body (which is to dismiss it from sitting without dissolving it) are essential functions of the Sovereign and the Sovereign's representatives in Canada. Although the power to summon Parliament to meet is stated expressly in section 38 of the *Constitution Act, 1867* that provision is only declaratory of a Royal Prerogative power which is not otherwise limited or supplanted by section 38. Thus, the power to summon Parliament can be viewed as both an executive power, arising out of the terms of the *Constitution Act, 1867,* and a power of the Royal Prerogative.

Closely associated with the power to summon Parliament is the power to prorogue Parliament but the power to prorogue is not mentioned at all in the written constitution. It is grounded only in the Royal Prerogative and that power was transferred to Canada at confederation through the words of the preamble to the *Constitution Act, 1867,* which mandate that Canada shall have a form of government similar in principle to the government of the United Kingdom.

The summoning of Parliament, or a provincial legislature, has been a relatively uncontroversial subject in Canada but circumstances may arise where it could become controversial. For example, where Parliament is not sitting and a by-election result leads to a change in the majority in the House of Commons, or a provincial legislature, there would undoubtedly be concerns raised as to whether a governing ministry could still command the confidence of the legislative body. In such circumstances, the Sovereign's representative may have to consider whether the ministry should be requested to meet Parliament, or a provincial legislature, in order to test the confidence of the legislative body in the ministry.

In any event Parliament or a provincial legislature must meet once every year as provided for by section 5 of the *Constitution Act, 1982*, and it is a duty of the Sovereign's representatives to insist that this requirement of constitutional law be adhered to by a ministry.

One aspect of this particular constitutional power that has proved to be controversial in Canada has been the power to prorogue Parliament, which results in the termination of a Parliamentary session and places the Parliament or the provincial legislature in a hiatus until a date fixed by royal proclamation for the legislative body to meet again.[34] The general purpose of prorogation is to allow a government to reset its agenda by sweeping away the bills and proceedings currently before Parliament, or a provincial legislature, and allow the ministry to commence an entirely new legislative session, with a new Speech from the Throne. Under normal circumstances, prorogation is uncontroversial, and the Sovereign's representative will grant the request in accordance with the principles of responsible government without looking behind the request to examine the motivations of a first minister in making the request for prorogation. However, where the circumstances are unusual, and there is a real question of whether a particular ministry continues to hold the confidence of the House of Commons or a provincial legislature, it may be necessary for the Sovereign's representative to play a more robust role.

Such a situation occurred in 1873, when Prime Minister Sir John A. Macdonald requested prorogation in the face of a potential non-confidence motion arising over the building of the transcontinental railway. Macdonald's political opponents urged the Governor General, Lord Dufferin, to deny the prorogation request but the Governor General demurred. Instead, he granted prorogation after coming to an agreement with Prime Minister Macdonald that the period in which Parliament would not sit would be limited to ten weeks and that a royal commission would be appointed to investigate the controversies surrounding the building of the transcontinental railway.[35] When Parliament eventually resumed the non-confidence motion was carried and the Macdonald Ministry collapsed.

In 2008, the power to prorogue Parliament again became the source of political controversy. A general election held on October 14, 2008, returned a second minority Conservative government under Prime Minister Stephen Harper. Holdover partisan rancour from the general election, as well as concerns by the opposition parties that the governing Conservative ministry was failing to address the ramifications of an unfolding global economic crisis, led the opposition parties in the House of Commons to attempt to oust the Conservative ministry with a motion of non-confidence.[36] A formal coalition agreement between the Liberal Party and the New Democratic Party was established with each party to hold a proportional number of ministerial positions in any government that would be formed by the coalition. In order to secure the confidence of the House of Commons the regional Bloc Québécois Party was admitted to the coalition under conditions that deprived it of ministerial posts but which allowed that party to continue to vote independently on any votes in the House of Commons that did not constitute a vote of confidence in the coalition government. Under the agreement, the leader of the Liberal party in the House of Commons would have taken on the role of Prime Minister but only for a short period of time, as he had previously indicated a personal intention to step down as party leader. A letter outlining the prospective formation of a new ministry that could obtain the confidence of the House of Commons was despatched to the Governor General by the leader of the Liberal party.

To forestall the immediate defeat of his ministry and to buy time to rebuild his political support in the House of Commons Prime Minister Harper sought prorogation of Parliament from Governor General, Michaëlle Jean. A series of parliamentary and other political manoeuvres took place preceding a formal meeting between the Prime Minister and the Governor General on December 4, 2008. The political manoeuvring had delayed the date that the Prime Minister and his ministry would have been forced to meet the House of Commons and face a non-confidence motion until December 8, 2008. At the meeting between the Prime Minister and the Governor General, Prime Minister Harper formally requested prorogation of Parliament to avoid the non-confidence vote. The Governor General, who had retained constitutional scholars to offer her assistance, took some time after receiving the Prime Minister to consult with her advisers, and to reflect on her decision, before granting the Prime Minister's request.

The two-hour delay in providing the Prime Minister with an answer has been viewed as not only necessary for the Governor General's personal decision-making process but also as confirmation to the country that, in extraordinary circumstances, such as those that prevailed in 2008, the Governor General may legitimately extract conditions to the grant of prorogation requested by a Prime Minister without offending the principles of responsible government. The Governor General may extract agreement to conditions to prevent a ministry from abusing its position in order to remain in office after its political support in the House of Commons had collapsed.

In 2008, the Governor General decided to grant Prime Minister Harper's request but like Lord Dufferin in 1873 she made her approval subject to certain conditions. The conditions that were agreed-to in 2008 were that the prorogation period would be a short one, and that no extension of the prorogation period would be subsequently sought. The Governor General and the Prime Minister also agreed that upon the reconvening of Parliament the Harper Ministry would meet the House of Commons and test the confidence of the House of Commons through the presentation of a budget. In the result, Parliament was prorogued until January 26, 2009, and a new budget presented the next day after the House of Commons resumed. The budget went some way to address the concerns of the Liberal Party concerning the Conservative government's response to the economic crisis and, accordingly, the Liberal Party agreed to support the government's budget, thus ending the political crisis.

The actions of the Governor General on this occasion were the subject of varying expert opinions. While it was true that the Prime Minister sought a way out of facing a non-confidence motion in the House of Commons the electorate had only very recently expressed its preferences in a general election and in such circumstances a Parliament should generally be given time to determine if a stable government could be established. Although there was an alternative government available, it consisted of a coalition of three opposition parties headed by a prospective Prime Minister who would only serve for an interim period before giving way to someone else.[37] Governor General Jean could be forgiven for considering this alternative to the existing Canadian Ministry to be inherently unstable. Therefore granting the Harper Ministry a brief respite in which to formulate policies that would satisfy the House of Commons and rebuild confidence was the right course for the Governor General to take. However, as in 1873, it was both wise and necessary for the Governor General to put conditions on her grant of prorogation. She required that, given the circumstances, the period of prorogation be brief and that the Harper Ministry obtain the confidence of the House of Commons soon after the return of Parliament, both of which were necessary conditions for maintaining a stable government.

6.8   Reservation and Disallowance of Legislation

The Sovereign is empowered by the *Constitution Act, 1867,* to exercise a right of disallowance over legislation passed by the House of Commons and the Senate of Canada. Section 56 of the Act states:

> Where the Governor General assents to a Bill in the Queen's Name, he shall by the first convenient Opportunity send an authentic Copy of the Act to one of Her Majesty's Principal Secretaries of State, and if the Queen in Council within Two Years after Receipt thereof by the Secretary of State thinks fit to disallow the Act, such Disallowance (with a Certificate of the Secretary of State of the Day on which the Act was received by him) being signified by the Governor General, by Speech or Message to each of the Houses of Parliament or by Proclamation, shall annul the Act from and after the Day of such Signification.

Also of significance, is the companion power to, in effect, veto legislation which has been reserved for the Sovereign's pleasure. Section 57 of the Act of 1867 says:

> A Bill reserved for the Signification of the Queen's Pleasure shall not have any Force unless and until, within Two Years from the Day on which it was presented

to the Governor General for the Queen's Assent, the Governor General signifies, by Speech or Message to each of the Houses of the Parliament or by Proclamation, that it has received the Assent of the Queen in Council.

An Entry of every such Speech, Message, or Proclamation shall be made in the Journal of each House, and a Duplicate thereof duly attested shall be delivered to the proper Officer to be kept among the Records of Canada.

In the first decade following confederation frequent resort to these powers was made by the Governors General of Canada, owing to the requirements of the early Royal Instructions issued to the Governors General by the Imperial Government, which set out certain classes of parliamentary bills that were to be sent to London for review by the Imperial Government. Several times in the very early years following confederation in 1867, the reservation and disallowance powers were exercised by the Imperial Government in London in relation to Canadian federal legislation.[38] The early Royal Instructions reflected a continued will to the exercise of sovereignty over Canada by the United Kingdom following confederation in 1867. However, in 1878, the Royal Instructions were revised to omit the requirement that the Governor General remit mandatory categories of Bills to London for review and approval by the Imperial Government.

As a matter of law, these provisions vest a discretionary power in the Queen acting on the advice of her Privy Council in London. This is readily apparent by the references to the "Queen in Council" and "Her Majesty's Principal Secretaries of State", both of which refer to offices and officers of state in the government of the United Kingdom. As a result of Canada's evolution into an independent State, those provisions are now constitutionally obsolete and the exercise of those powers by the government of the United Kingdom has been precluded by convention at least since the Imperial Conference of 1930. There is no longer any doubt that these provisions have fallen into desuetude, and they are no longer operative components of the Canadian constitution, despite the evident failure to repeal those provisions.

The probable reason for the retention of those provisions in the *Constitution Act, 1867*, relates to the fact that sections 56 and 57 are adopted by reference in section 90 of the *Constitution Act, 1867*, which permits the Federal Government to exercise the same powers of reservation and disallowance in relation to legislation enacted by the provincial legislatures as the Imperial Government was originally entitled to do in relation to federal legislation. Here again, the power of the Federal Government to reserve or disallow provincial legislation has long fallen into practical disuse but it cannot be said with certainty that future circumstances might not warrant a need to reassert this constitutional power in relation to provincial legislation. Therefore, the powers in section 56 and 57 remain part of the constitution in order to give legislative substance to section 90, which remains an operative element of constitutional law. It is likely that section 90 of the *Constitution Act, 1867*, would only be resorted to the political or territorial integrity of the state was at issue as, for example, in the case of a unilateral declaration of independence by a province of Canada.

6.9   The Royal Prerogative

Writing long ago, the English legal scholar and jurist Sir William Blackstone regarded the Royal Prerogative as the unique powers, privileges, rights and immunities which the Sovereign enjoyed at common law separate and distinct from ordinary subjects. In the nineteenth century Professor Albert Venn Dicey considered the royal prerogative to consist of the residue of legal rights and discretionary powers vested in the Sovereign which has not been transformed into statute law. The Royal Prerogative can also be viewed as a series of exceptions from common law rules, rather than as substantive legal rights and privileges vested in the Sovereign.[39] Regardless, it does not appear that the differing theoretical approach of legal scholars as to the origins of the Royal Prerogative has had any significant substantive consequences in law.[40] Although it was historically separate from the common law the Royal Prerogative, in the modern context, is defined by the common law courts in their application of the common law and it is now limited by the courts through the application of the *Constitution of Canada* as the supreme law of the land and by evolving common law principles.

The Royal Prerogative entered Canadian law through the reception doctrine and it has remained an important component of the powers of government in Canada at both the federal and provincial levels of administration. In *R v McLeod*, [1883] 8 SCR 1 (Canada, SC) Justice Ritchie characterized the Royal Prerogative as constitutional law, stating that it consisted of " . . . great constitutional rights, conferred on the sovereign, upon principles of public policy, for the benefit of the people, and not, as it is said, "for the private gratification of the sovereign – they form part of and are generally speaking "as ancient as the law itself".[41]

More recently, in *Ross River Dene Council Band v Canada* [2002] 2 SCR 816 (Canada, SC) Justice Lebel, writing for a majority of the Supreme Court of Canada held that:

> Generally speaking, in my view, the royal prerogative means "the powers and privileges accorded by the common law to the Crown". The royal prerogative is confined to executive governmental powers, whether federal or provincial. The extent of its authority can be abolished or limited by statute: "once a statute has occupied the ground formerly occupied by the prerogative, the Crown [has to] comply with the terms of the statute".

The Royal Prerogative is part of the law of Canada and is as extensive in this country as the Royal Prerogative powers that were historically exercised in England by the Sovereigns of England, except for those prerogatives that are clearly of a local nature and therefore practically confined to England.

Thus the Royal Prerogative in Canada includes the following important categories:

1 Prerogatives which deal with the Sovereign's regal status, including their supremacy, inviolability, perfection and perpetual nature;

2 Prerogatives of governance including the power to summon and prorogue Parliament and the enactment of legislation in the Parliament of Canada, or in the legislature of a province, the conduct of foreign affairs and the power to enter into and ratify treaties[42] with foreign sovereigns, or to withdraw from a treaty,[43] and the power to declare war,[44] the command of the armed forces; issuance of passports and grants of titles and honours; the appointment of the Governor General or the Lieutenant Governors of a province and the appointments of some civil servants,[45] and the power to appoint royal commissions of inquiry;[46]

3 Judicial prerogatives, including the position of the Sovereign as the head of the judiciary,[47] the prerogative power to issue writs; *parens patriae*;[48] mercy and clemency (including pardons and remissions);

4 Immunities and privileges,[49] including priority as a creditor, and immunities from arrest, distress, suit,[50] execution, taxation, and especially immunity from the application of statute law[51] (or more accurately, the Sovereign's immunity from the burdens imposed by statutes, since the Sovereign may always take the benefit of a statute[52]);

5 Miscellaneous prerogatives, such as the right to create monopolies,[53] including the power to confer exclusive patents of invention; rights in respect of property[54] (e.g., precious metals, treasure trove, wrecks, escheat or *bona vacantia*[55]); the power to create Indian reserves;[56]

6 Power to legislate with respect to the powers remaining to the Sovereign under the Royal Prerogative but without depriving any subject of any rights they possess at common law, or by statute, or under the *Constitution of Canada*, or to impose new obligations upon them, or to grant immunities from the operation of law;[57] and

7 Reserve Powers exercised as a personal discretion by the Sovereign, the Governor General, or a Lieutenant Governor, including the power to dissolve Parliament or a provincial legislature; the appointment or dismissal of a Prime

Minister or Premier; the discretion to decline advice from a ministry that has lost the confidence of Parliament, or a provincial legislature, or that has been defeated in an election; the right to be consulted on government activities, the right to encourage and to warn; the power to preserve constitutional order where constitutional government has ceased to function.[58]

This list is by no means exhaustive and a full treatment of the Royal Prerogative would require a lengthy textbook in itself.[59]

As Canada is a federal state, the Royal Prerogative powers were divided between the Federal Government and the provincial governments at confederation in 1867.[60] In *The Queen v Mar-Dive Corporation et al* (1997), 141 DLR (4th) 577 (Ontario, GD) an Ontario court stated:

> At the time of Confederation in 1867, the Royal Prerogatives of the English Crown were recognized and granted to the Crown in Right of the Provinces by virtue of s. 109 of the *Constitution Act, 1867*. All Royal Prerogatives associated with provincial lands, including the right to escheats, *bona vacantia*, treasure trove, etc., vest in the provincial, rather than the federal Crown.[61]

At a very early period in the development of English law, the Royal Prerogative was extensive, and encompassed many activities of public government. Over time, as parliaments asserted themselves against the Crown, the scope of the Royal Prerogative became restricted. As a result of the firm establishment of the rule of law, the supremacy of Parliament, and the independence of the judiciary, Royal Prerogative powers can no longer be created, or extended, but they can be abolished or placed into abeyance by statute.

The historical process by which the Royal Prerogative was increasingly constrained by the developing supremacy of Parliament and by the rule of law enforceable by the paramount courts of law was described by the Supreme Court of the United Kingdom in *R (on the application of Miller and Dos Santos) v Secretary of State for Exiting the European Union* [2017] UKSC 5 (United Kingdom, SC) as follows:

> Originally, sovereignty was concentrated in the Crown, subject to limitations which were ill-defined and which changed with practical exigencies. Accordingly, the Crown largely exercised all the powers of the state (although it appears that even in the 11th century the King rarely attended meetings of his Council, albeit that its membership was at his discretion). However, over the centuries, those prerogative powers, collectively known as the Royal prerogative, were progressively reduced as Parliamentary democracy and the rule of law developed. By the end of the 20th century, the great majority of what had previously been prerogative powers, at least in relation to domestic matters, had become vested in the three principal organs of the state, the legislature (the two Houses of Parliament), the executive (ministers and the government more generally) and the judiciary (the judges). It is possible to identify a number of seminal events in this history, but a series of statutes enacted in

the twenty years between 1688 and 1707 were of particular legal importance. Those statutes were the *Bill of Rights 1688/9* and the *Act of Settlement 1701* in England and Wales ... [62]

The abolition of a Royal Prerogative power is within the power of Parliament or a provincial legislature where the subject matter of the prerogative falls to one body or the other pursuant to the division of powers in the *Constitution Act, 1867,* but the legislative body should clearly enact the extinguishment of the prerogative power if that is its intention. For example, the *Bill of Rights 1689* clearly expressed the intention to abolish the Royal Prerogative power in relation to the levying of taxes upon the subjects of the Crown. Explicitness is required because there has been a past reluctance on the part of the courts to find that a particular Royal Prerogative power has been abolished or affected by a statute through the doctrine of necessary implication, and thus the application of that doctrine to the extinguishment of the royal prerogative remains unclear.[63] [64]

An abeyance of a Royal Prerogative power occurs where the prerogative matter is regulated by statute without the express abolition of the prerogative right; *AG v De Keyser's Royal Hotel,* [1920] AC 508 (England, HL).[65] In *R v Secretary of State for the Home Department, ex parte Fire Brigades Union,* [1995] 1 All E.R. 888 (England, CA) it was asserted that the Home Secretary of the United Kingdom had abused his powers by supplanting an existing scheme of criminal injuries compensation that was established pursuant to the Royal Prerogative with a new prerogative scheme that differed substantially with both the former scheme as well as with a statutory scheme that had been enacted by Parliament but which had not yet been brought into force. The Court of Appeal for England and Wales held that the Home Secretary possessed a discretion to delay the coming into force of the statutory scheme and to continue the former prerogative scheme but he did not have the authority to create a new scheme under the Royal Prerogative in the face of an enactment of the statutory scheme by Parliament. Consequently, the appeal was allowed and declaratory relief provided. The vitality of the Royal Prerogative to create a new prerogative scheme was thus placed in abeyance by the enactment of the statute, although the previous prerogative scheme, created before the enactment of the statute remained in effect pending the coming into force of the statutory scheme.[66]

The modern approach to determine whether a Royal Prerogative power may be relied upon by the Crown involves a three-part test. Firstly, it must be determined what historical prerogatives the Sovereign possessed with respect to a particular subject. Secondly, an inquiry must be made as to whether those historical prerogatives of the Sovereign have been abolished, placed into abeyance, or limited by a statutory enactment. Thirdly, an examination is required with respect to how that prerogative power has been exercised in recent times – in other words has it been limited in practice by custom or usage.

Following this analysis the modern scope of a Royal Prerogative power may be determined.

The power of the Crown to legislate under the Royal Prerogative is now confined solely to administrative rules such as the *Constitution of the Order of Canada*. There is no remaining power in the Sovereign to legislate under the Royal Prerogative in a way that would bind the subjects of the Crown; *Reference re Anti-Inflation Act, 1975* (Canada), [1976] 2 SCR 373 (Canada, SC) per Chief Justice Laskin at 433:

> There is no principle in this country, as there is not in Great Britain, that the Crown may legislate by proclamation or order in council to bind citizens where it so acts without the support of a statute of the legislature.[67]

The Crown may delegate a Royal Prerogative power but it may not entirely divest itself of a prerogative power; *Attorney General (Canada) v Attorney General (Ontario)*, [1894] 23 SCR 458 (Canada, SC).

6.10   The Exercise of the Royal Prerogative

Most of the remaining Royal Prerogative powers are now exercised by the Sovereign, or the Sovereign's representatives, upon the advice of ministers in accordance with the conventions of responsible government.[68] And yet the importance of the Royal Prerogative to the Canadian constitution cannot be underestimated. It is a singular feature of executive government in Canada, permitting a wide range of government activity which otherwise would require the sanction of legislation.

While the Sovereign can exercise the powers of the Royal Prerogative in relation to Canada, for the most part those powers have been delegated to the Governor General with respect to the subject matter that falls to the Federal Government under the *Constitution Act, 1867*, or to the Lieutenant Governors of the provinces where provincial jurisdiction exists under the *Constitution Act, 1867*. In the *Ross River* case the Supreme Court (per Lebel J.) stated:

> The royal prerogative in Canada is exercised by the Governor General under the letters patent granted by His Majesty King George VI in 1947 (see the Letters Patent constituting the office of Governor General of Canada). In the usual course of things, the Governor General exercises these powers for the Queen in right of Canada, acting on the advice of a Committee of the Privy Council (which consists of the Prime Minister and Cabinet of the government of the day).[69]

In the modern era in Canada the exercise of the Royal Prerogative, with the exception of the reserve powers, has been increasingly concentrated in the hands of the ministry holding office, and particularly in the Prime Minister, or the Premier at the provincial level, directly or through the constitutional conventions of responsible government in Canada. In fact the practical concentration of power has now occurred to such a degree that it may no longer be accurate to describe many of these powers as the Royal Prerogative, except perhaps as a reference to its historical origins.

In the exercise of the Royal Prerogative constitutional actors must remain aware that the Royal Prerogative today is a residual category of law the exercise of which must remain consistent with the rule of law. Furthermore, the exercise of a Royal Prerogative may be regarded as unusual, and therefore its use must be plainly adverted to by constitutional actors. In *Scarborough (City) v Ontario (Attorney General)* (1997), 32 OR (3d) 526 (Ontario, GD) the failure of provincial orders-in-council to explicitly state that they were issued under the Royal Prerogative compelled the court to find that they were not made under the prerogative power.

6.11   The Powers of the Sovereign as a Natural Person

Another source of the Sovereign's formal power in Canada consists of the legal powers of a natural person. As a natural person the Sovereign can do anything that any other natural person can undertake to do. As a result, officials acting in the name of the Sovereign may rely on the Sovereign's natural legal capacity in carrying out certain public acts. Thus the power of government to enter into a contract does not need specific constitutional authority because the Sovereign, as a natural person, has the capacity to enter into contracts subject to the ordinary requirements of contract law.[70] Similarly, the power of government to hold title to property, and to enter into conveyances and other transactions in relation to real or personal property, does not flow from the Royal Prerogative but rather flows from the powers and abilities of the Sovereign as a natural person.

6.12   Liability of the Sovereign in Tort

It is now possible for the Sovereign to be sued in tort law for alleged civil wrongs. The immunity of the Crown and other legal impediments to the ability of the subjects of the Sovereign to commence tort litigation against the Crown has been dispensed with by statute in Canada.[71] However there are still some unique features of the Crown's activities that can affect recovery in torts, especially where policy decisions are at issue. A fuller description is beyond the scope of this book.

6.13   Statutory Powers and Judicial Review of Crown Decisions

It is a common Canadian practice of statecraft to vest discretionary powers by statute in the Governor General, acting by and with the advice of the Queen's Privy Council for Canada, or a Lieutenant Governor acting by and with the advice of their Executive Council at the provincial level. The Canadian practice in this regard is significantly different from the practice in some of the other Commonwealth realms, where statutory powers are often devolved by legislation upon specific Ministers of the Crown.

The nature of a discretionary power exercised by the Governor General in Council can most often be characterized as administrative or legislative in nature, often involving matters of public policy. In such cases the courts are reluctant to interfere with that discretion. Thus, the Governor General in Council cannot be held liable in damages for a refusal to exercise a discretionary power in a manner that would be favourable to a petitioner; *Lake Champlain and St. Lawrence Ship Canal Co. v The King* (1946), 35 DLR 670 (Canada, SC).

Since the inception of the modern state in 1867, judicial review of legislative action has been a principal pillar of the judiciary's ability to enforce the application of the Canadian constitution. For more than a century the basis of judicial review of Canadian legislation was the division of powers between Parliament and the provincial legislatures. Historically, however, the courts remained hostile to expanding the scope and ambit of judicial review where the Crown was concerned, and they often found that even ministerial decisions grounded in the exercise of a statutory discretion were immune from judicial review, particularly where it could be inferred from the facts of a particular matter that the Governor in Council or a minister was implementing political policy when exercising of a statutory discretion. Thus, in *The King v Imperial Bank of Canada* (1923), 3 DLR 345 (Canada, Ex. Ct.) the Court refused to go behind a ministerial decision to expropriate lands, stating:

> The Minister having deemed it advisable to expropriate, as provided by the *Expropriation Act*, has exercised his statutory discretion, and the Court has no jurisdiction to sit on appeal or in review of such decision. These questions are political in their nature and not judicial. The Courts cannot enquire into the motives which actuate the executive or governmental authorities or into the propriety of their decision.

Although historically, equitable remedies such as an injunction or mandamus could not be applied against the Sovereign, the Sovereign's representatives, or Ministers of the Crown in ordinary circumstances, it was possible for such remedies to lie against a Minister of the Crown where the facts showed that a Minister had failed to exercise a statutory duty, or was acting in an illegal manner.[72] In former times, judicial review could also lie against a ministerial decision where it could be shown that a minister acted as an agent of Parliament or of a legislature in exercising a statutory duty for the benefit of third parties, and was not acting as an agent of the Sovereign; *Minister of Finance of British Columbia v The King*, [1935] SCR 278 (Canada, SC).

By and large however, the courts remained averse to permitting judicial review of the statutory decisions of the Governor in Council where the subject matter involved economic policy and politics rather than questions of law. In *Re Kingston Enterprises and Minister of Municipal Affairs* (1970), 12 DLR 516 (Ontario, HC) the Ontario Minister of Municipal Affairs had changed the conditions of land planning approvals to impose more onerous obligations upon a land developer. In examining the Minister's power to change the conditions of a land planning approval the Ontario High Court characterized the Minister's function as one of policy, and therefore as a function which emanated from the Crown, rather than a matter of statutory discretion. As such, the Minister's role was sufficient to render the Minister immune from judicial review.[73] Of like effect was the judgement of the Supreme Court of Canada in *Thorne's Hardware v The Queen* (1983), 143 DLR (3d) 577 (Canada, SC) where the Court characterized the issue in that case as one of "economic policy and politics and not one of jurisdiction or jurisprudence" and noted that the "Governor in Council quite obviously believed that he had reasonable grounds" to extend the limits of the port of St. Johns Newfoundland and, as such, the court "cannot inquire into the validity of those beliefs in order to determine the validity of the order-in-council".[74]

This traditional reluctance to contemplate judicial review of actions by the Crown under prerogative and statutory powers began to come under renewed judicial scrutiny in the 1970's. In *Re Doctors Hospital and Minister of Health* (1976), 68 DLR (3d) 220 (Ontario, DC) the Ontario Divisional Court permitted judicial review of an exercise of a statutory discretion by the Lieutenant Governor in Council, finding that the statutory discretion had to be exercised by the Lieutenant-Governor in Council according to the objects of the statute and that the courts could review the decision to ensure that it conformed to statutory objectives. However, in *Doctors Hospital*, the judiciary continued to maintain that it could not supply judicial review remedies for acts undertaken pursuant to the Royal Prerogative.

It remained for the Supreme Court of Canada to ultimately establish a general concept of judicial review for the actions of the Crown when the Crown exercises a statutory power. In *Attorney General of Canada v Inuit Tapirisat of Canada* (1980), 115 DLR (3d) 1 (Canada, SC) the Governor in Council had exercised a statutory power of review with respect to the decision of a federal telecommunications tribunal. The Supreme Court had to consider whether the exercise of a statutory power of review by the Governor in Council was amenable to judicial review on the grounds of procedural fairness. In finding that the Governor General in Council was subject to judicial review on administrative law grounds Justice Estey stated on behalf of the Court that:

... the essence of the principle of law here operating is simply that in the exercise of a statutory power the Governor in Council, like any other person or group of persons, must keep within the law as laid down by Parliament or the Legislature. Failure to do so will call into action the supervising function of the Superior Court whose responsibility is to enforce the law, that is to ensure that such actions as may be authorized by statute shall be carried out in accordance with its terms, or that a public authority shall not fail to respond to a duty assigned to it by statute.[75]

The *Inuit Tapirisat* case thus established the principle that the execution by the Crown of powers based on a statutory provision, exercised on the advice of responsible ministers, could be made the subject of judicial review on general administrative law principles, such as procedural fairness. While the actions of the Governor in Council in exercising a statutory discretion will attract procedural fairness obligations, the content of the fairness obligation where broad public policy concerns are at issue may be less onerous and thus, for example, an oral hearing may not be a requirement necessary to discharge the procedural fairness functions of the Governor in Council, although the Governor in Council does have the right to convene an oral hearing before making a decision; *Canada (Attorney General) v Inuit Tapirisat of Canada*. However, the procedural obligations owed to individuals whose specific individual rights or interests are affected by a statutory decision of the Governor in Council can attract substantial procedural fairness obligations. This will be most evident where the Governor in Council has taken action to remove a person from a public office; *Weatherhill v Canada (Attorney General)*, [1999] 4 FC 107 (Canada, FC); *Vennat v Canada (Attorney General)*, [2007] 2 FCR 647 (Canada, FC).

In exercising statutory powers of decision, the Governor in Council normally operates by way of a written process. However, oral hearings have been held in the past with respect to the exercise of review powers under the *Railway Act*.[76] Oral hearings were also contemplated (but never held) with respect to the Manitoba school question under section 93(3) of the *Constitution Act, 1867*, in 1895.[77]

In succeeding years the courts continued to take an expanding view of the availability of judicial review where Crown actors exercised statutory powers.[78] The cases of *Doctors Hospital* and *Inuit Tapirisat* marked a significant departure from the former conception of administrative law that had excepted from judicial review actions taken by the Crown pursuant to statute law. It remained to be seen, however, whether that departure would be extended to actions that were taken by the Crown in the exercise of the Royal Prerogative.

6.14 The Test for Judicial Review

In Canada, the basis for the judicial review of actions by governing authorities has been the subject of evolutionary legal change throughout the last half of the twentieth century and into the twenty-first century. As a result, the exposition by the judiciary of the test for judicial review of administrative may be anticipated to continue to evolve over time. Currently, the relevant tests are set out in *Dunsmuir v New Brunswick*, [2008] 1 SCR 190 (Canada, SC) where the Supreme Court of Canada decided that the standard for judicial review would be correctness where the constitution, statutory jurisdiction, and pure questions of law outside the scope of the decision-makers expertise were at issue but in all other cases the appropriate standard would be reasonableness. A fuller discussion of the principles of judicial review in Canada is however, beyond the scope of this book.

6.15 Judicial Review and the Royal Prerogative

Although it was perhaps not immediately apparent at confederation that the Royal Prerogative would be divided between the federal and provincial aspects of the Crown in Canada, the Judicial Committee of the Privy Council made it clear that this was so in its judgment in *Bonanza Creek Gold Mining Co. v The King*, [1916] 1 AC 566 (Canada, JC). There, the Judicial Committee determined that the distribution of Royal Prerogative powers flowed along the same channels as the distribution of legislative powers, primarily under sections 91 and 92 of the *Constitution Act, 1867*.

Logically it flowed from that judgment that judicial review of the exercise of prerogative powers would be available to review an exercise of the Royal Prerogative upon the grounds of a division of powers. The Royal Prerogative thus became amenable to judicial review on the same division of powers basis as legislation enacted by Parliament, or the provincial legislatures. However, the Crown remained immune from injunctive relief, although, exceptionally, injunctive relief could lie against the Crown if it was necessary to ensure that unconstitutional legislation would not be implemented by public authorities.[79]

Judicial review was available in the case of an exercise of a Royal Prerogative power but only for the purposes of determining (a) whether a particular power existed under the Royal Prerogative in Canada; (b) determining the scope and extent of the Royal Prerogative power; and [c] which level of government in Canada, federal or provincial had the jurisdiction to exercise that prerogative power.

Thus the Supreme Court of Canada held in *British Columbia Power Corporation v British Columbia Electric Company et al*, [1962] SCR 642 (Canada, SC), that the Crown in right of the province of British Columbia could not rely upon principles of Crown immunity to prevent the attachment of a receivership order to property that was expropriated under legislation of dubious constitutional validity. The Court held that the Royal Prerogative could not be relied upon to assert rights under legislation that was beyond the competence of a provincial legislature. To have permitted the Crown to assert such rights would have been tantamount to allowing the Crown to obtain a result through an exercise of the prerogative that it could not have obtained under legislation that the province was incapable of constitutionally enacting.

Despite those early inroads into the traditional exception of the Crown from judicial review beyond the basis of the division of powers it remained uncertain whether there could be any other basis for judicial review of actions taken by the Crown pursuant to the Royal Prerogative.

Ultimately, change came about in the *Charter* era, in the Supreme Court's landmark judgment in *Operation Dismantle Inc. v The Queen*, [1985] 1 SCR 441 (Canada, SC). That judgment ushered into Canadian constitutional law a new approach to the judicial review of Crown actions, including actions that were taken in the exercise of the Royal Prerogative as a consequence of the entrenchment within the *Constitution Acts 1867-1982* of the *Canadian Charter of Rights and Freedoms.*

Section 32(1) of the *Charter* is particularly important in this context because it stipulates that:

32. (1) This Charter applies

(a) to the Parliament and government of Canada in respect of all matters within the authority of Parliament . . . and

(b) to the legislature and government of each province in respect of all matters within the authority of the legislature of each province.

The issue for the Supreme Court of Canada in *Operation Dismantle* involved the judicial review of a decision by the Government of Canada to permit the United States of America to conduct flight tests of a cruise missile weapon over Canadian territory. The government's decision was grounded in the constitutional head of power relating to national defence, in sections 15 and 19 of the *Constitution Act, 1867*, as well as in the Royal Prerogative relating to foreign relations.

In discussing the extent to which a collective decision of the Sovereign's ministers could be reviewed, Chief Justice Dickson, with whom four other Justices concurred stated: "I have no doubt that the executive branch of the Canadian Government is duty bound to act in accordance with the dictates of the *Charter*".[80]

Justice Wilson was the only member of the Court to address the issue from the perspective of the Royal Prerogative. In argument it was asserted that the Crown's power to enter into a treaty, and its power to make decisions with respect to matters of national defence emanated from the Royal Prerogative.

Further, it was argued that the words in section 32(1) of the *Charter*, which makes the *Charter* applicable "to the Parliament and government of Canada in respect of all matters within the authority of Parliament", were words of limitation which operated to exclude any law, other than statutory law, from the purview of the *Charter*. On that point Justice Wilson stated:

> The answer to this argument seems to me to be that those words of limitation, like the corresponding words "within the authority of the legislature of each province" in s. 32(1)(b), are merely a reference to the division of powers in ss. 91 and 92 of the Constitution Act, 1867. They describe the subject-matters in relation to which the Parliament of Canada may legislate or the Government of Canada may take executive action . . . the royal prerogative is "within the authority of Parliament" in the sense that Parliament is competent to legislate with respect to matters falling within its scope. Since there is no reason in principle to distinguish between Cabinet decisions made pursuant to statutory authority and those made in the exercise of the royal prerogative, and since the former clearly fall within the ambit of the Charter, I conclude that the latter do so also.[81]

In the *Operation Dismantle* case, the Supreme Court was unable to find proof of a causal link between the executive action of the (Pierre)Trudeau Ministry, in permitting the United States to test the missile, with the harm claimed by the Appellants (the heightened risk of a nuclear war) and consequently the application for judicial review of the government's action failed. Difficulties of proof can often prevent the full exposure of actions taken pursuant to the Royal Prerogative from the glare of *Charter* scrutiny, particularly where the prerogative actions are encompassed within the foreign relations or national defence policy spheres.

Further elaborations of the principle that decisions made under the Royal Prerogative are subject to judicial review arose in a case involving royal honours; *Black v Canada (Prime Minister)*, [2001] 54 OR (3d) 215 (Ontario, CA) where the courts went beyond *Charter* questions to embrace a broad concept of judicial review of actions undertaken pursuant to the Royal Prerogative. Writing for the Court of Appeal, Justice Laskin stated:

> . . . the expanding scope of judicial review and of Crown liability make it no longer tenable to hold that the exercise of a prerogative power is insulated from judicial review merely because it is a prerogative and not a statutory power. The preferable approach is that adopted by the House of Lords in [*Council of Civil Service Unions v Minister for the Civil Service*, [1985] AC 374 (England, HL)]. There, the House of Lords emphasized that the controlling consideration in determining whether the exercise of a prerogative power is judicially reviewable is its subject matter, not its source. If, in the words of Lord Roskill, the subject matter of the prerogative power is "amenable to the judicial process", it is reviewable; if not, it is not reviewable. Lord Roskill provided content to this subject matter test of reviewability by explaining that the exercise of the prerogative will be amenable to the judicial process if it affects the rights of individuals.[82]

The proper exercise of a power under the Royal Prerogative however, may operate as a limitation prescribed by law for the purposes of applying the *Canadian Charter of Rights and Freedoms*.[83]

In *Khadr v Canada (Attorney General)*, [2007] 2 FC 218, (Canada, FC) the Federal Court held that denial of a passport through an exercise of the Royal Prerogative was amenable to judicial review. The principles of procedural fairness and natural justice, including the concept of legitimate expectations with respect to procedural fairness, applied to the exercise of a prerogative power to deny a passport to the Applicant. In that case national security considerations relating to the issuance of passports were not contained in the version of the *Canadian Passport Order* that was issued and in force under the Royal Prerogative at the time that the Applicant's passport application was denied by the Minister of Foreign Affairs. Furthermore, the Applicant was not informed that the Minister of Foreign Affairs would personally be the decision-maker with respect to his application. The public information available to the Applicant merely stated that the l Passport Office would make the decision. Consequently, the Applicant had a legitimate expectation that the Passport Office would rule on his application, and the failure to advise him that the Minister would be exercising the power personally, and that national security considerations would be germane to the decision, rendered the decision reviewable.

The modern cases have now expanded the scope of judicial review to include the exercise of almost any power by the Sovereign. *Operation Dismantle* in particular stands for the proposition that decisions taken by a ministry will be subject to the *Charter* regardless of whether the Crown derives powers from statute, common law, or the Royal Prerogative. The *Inuit Tapirisat, Black,* and *Khadr* cases confirm that an exercise of the Royal Prerogative is also reviewable on the general grounds of natural justice and procedural fairness. Thus, the exercise of all actions taken by the Sovereign or her agents, whether pursuant to a statute or the Royal Prerogative, must now be evaluated in the light of the remedies of judicial review available to aggrieved subjects of the Crown.[84] Those remedies can control the exercise of a power under the Royal Prerogative to ensure that, as a matter of principle, it is within the constitutional competence of the level of government which has purported to exercise that power, and that the exercise of the Royal Prerogative is compatible with the *Canadian Charter of Rights and Freedoms,* and the general principles of public law.

6.16   Justiciability of the Royal Prerogative

Despite the new willingness of the courts to review actions taken by the Crown pursuant to a Royal Prerogative power, in assessing whether a particular action taken by the Crown pursuant to the Royal Prerogative will be amenable to judicial review the question of establishing a causal link between alleged harm and government action under the Royal Prerogative will inevitably raise the issue of the justiciability of an alleged wrongful act. Justiciability is a conceptual tool employed by the courts of law to distinguish issues that are appropriate for a court of law to entertain from those issues that are more appropriately the concern of Parliament, or the executive. In short, justiciability goes to the question of whether a particular issue is a judicial issue or a political issue. Following its decision in the *Operation Dismantle* case, the Supreme Court of Canada addressed the subject of justiciability more specifically in *Canada (Auditor General) v Canada (Minister of Energy, Mines and Resources,* [1989] 2 SCR 49 (Canada, SC) where the Chief Justice, on behalf of the Court described the principle of justiciability in the following terms:

> ... As I noted in *Operation Dismantle Inc. v The Queen,* [1985] 1 SCR 441 at p. 459, justiciability is a "doctrine . . . founded upon a concern with the appropriate role of the courts as the forum for the resolution of different types of disputes", endorsing for the majority the discussion of Wilson J. beginning at page 460. Wilson J. took the view that an issue is non-justiciable if it involves "moral and political considerations which it is not within the province of the courts to assess" (p. 465). An inquiry into justiciability is, first and foremost, a normative inquiry into the appropriateness as a matter of constitutional judicial policy of the courts deciding a given issue or, instead, deferring to other decision-making institutions of the polity.[85]

Thus, a decision by the Chretien Ministry to participate in a NATO action in the Balkans involving the aerial bombardment of the former state of Yugoslavia was held to be a matter of high public policy that did not give rise to justiciable issues over and above claims made under the *Charter; Aleksic v Attorney General (Canada) (2002), 215 DLR (4th) 720 (Ontario, DC)* at paras 31-35.

In *Copello v Canada (Minister of Foreign Affairs)* (2003), 308 NR 175 (Canada, FCA) a foreign diplomat recalled by his country sought to dispute the decision of the Minister of Foreign Affairs to seek his recall. The court found that the Crown's request to a foreign state to recall a diplomat accredited to Canada, and whom Canada had declared to be *persona non grata,* was an act of the Royal Prerogative relating to foreign relations and on the spectrum of activities subject to judicial review it was a political matter that was not justiciable.

In *Black v Canada (Prime Minister),* [2001] 54 OR (3d) 215 (Ontario, CA) the question for the court was whether an exercise of the Royal Prerogative in relation to the grant of royal honours was justiciable. The facts of that case involved formal advice given to Queen Elizabeth II by the Prime Minister of Canada concerning the grant of a dignity to a dual Canadian-British citizen in which the Prime Minister had advised the Queen not to make the appointment. The court in that case decided that the issues raised were not justiciable because the grant of an honour " . . . engages no liberty, no property, no economic interests. It enjoys no procedural protection. It does not have a sufficient legal component to warrant the court's intervention . . . It [the conferral of honours] involves moral and political considerations which it is not within the province of the courts to assess."[86]

In *Smith v Canada (Attorney General)*, [2009] FC 234 (Canada, FC) however, the Government of Canada undertook a policy change whereby it ceased to make active representations for clemency to certain foreign governments that held incarcerated Canadian citizens subject to the death penalty under the laws of the foreign state. The Federal Government argued that the policy change fell within the Royal Prerogative relating to foreign affairs, and was thus a matter of high public policy that was not justiciable. The Federal Court disagreed, holding that the policy change was subject to a duty of procedural fairness that was owed to Canadian citizens incarcerated abroad under a penalty of death, and therefore the question was justiciable.

In summary, the courts have moved away from an assumption that the exercise of a power under the Royal Prerogative is, *ipso facto*, immune from judicial review toward a modern approach whereby the exercise of the Royal Prerogative will be subject to judicial review on the grounds of *Charter* infringement, or upon other grounds depending where an analysis of whether the rights or legitimate expectations of an individual have been engaged, and where there is a sufficient legal content with respect to the impugned prerogative action.

Thus, there will be a spectrum of activities undertaken pursuant to the Royal Prerogative ranging from those activities that are inherently subject to judicial review because the rights and legitimate expectations of the Crown's subjects are impacted by the Crown's exercise of its prerogative powers, to those activities that are inherently not subject to judicial review because of an absence, or near-absence, of an essential legal content in respect of that activity, rendering the matter subject only to political, as opposed to legal, remedies.

[1] see the expression "Crown" in the *Crown Liability and Proceedings Act* RSC 1985, c. C-50, s. 2 where the Crown is defined in the French version of the statute to mean "state" and *Formea Chemicals Ltd. v Polymer Corporation* (1968), 69 DLR (2d) 114 (Canada, SC) where "Her Majesty" was equated with "Government of Canada". Further, the expression "government" has now been given an independent meaning for the purposes of the *Canadian Charter of Rights and Freedoms*; see section 32(1).

[2] *R v Sayward Trading and Ranching Co.*, [1924] Ex CR 15 (Canada, Ex.Ct.)

[3] *Reference Re Remuneration of Judges of the Provincial Court (Prince Edward Island)* (1994), 125 Nfld & PEIR 335 (Prince Edward Island, AD)

[4] *Dicey,* at page 110

[5] Ibid, page 114

[6] Ibid, page 121

[7] The current version is the *Magna Carta* of Edward 1 (25 Edw. 1, c. 29) (1297).

[8] at page 277

[9] Justice Hall in *Calder v Attorney General of British Columbia* (1973), 34 DLR (3d) 145 (Canada, SC) at p. 203 in discussing the *Royal Proclamation, 1763* states; "Its [the *Royal Proclamation, 1763*] force as a statute is analogous to the status of *Magna Carta* which has always been considered to be the law throughout the Empire." In addition, consider the judgement of Justice Gale (as he then was) in *Re Toronto Newspaper Guild, Local 87, American Newspaper Guild (C.I.O.) and Globe Printing Company,* [1951] OR 435 (Ontario, HC) who stated: "...while this is not frequently mentioned, *Magna Carta* is the law of this Province by virtue of R.S.O. 1897, c. 322, which is *"An Act respecting certain rights and liberties of the people"*: see R.S.O. 1950, vol. 5, Appendix "A". That Act provides that the King shall not "deny or defer to any man, either justice or right" and gives force to the contention that any act of a tribunal which disallows to any person who comes before it his privilege of justice is ultra vires of that tribunal . . . "

[10] at page 64

[11] at page 65. This case established one of the most important principles of a Westminster-style constitution, namely, the principle of the separation of powers between the executive and the judiciary.

[12] 3 Cha. 1, c. 1 (1628)

[13] The power to suspend the laws of Parliament allowed the Sovereign to render the laws enacted by Parliament to be inapplicable to everyone. The power to dispense with the laws enacted by Parliament allowed the Sovereign to specify that the laws would not apply to particular groups or individuals. The prohibition against suspension and dispensation contained in the *Bill of Rights, 1689,* has been applied in Canada; *R. v Catagas* (1977), 81 DLR (3d) 396; [1978] 1 WWR 282 (Manitoba, CA).

[14] at section 4

[15] Justice Locke stated in *Boucher v The King,* [1951] SCR 265 at 319 (Canada, SC), that the commissions granted to English judges from the

commencement of the reigns of King William III and Queen Mary II endured during good behaviour, rather than at the pleasure of the Sovereign, as had previously been the case.

[16] Laskin, at pages 39-40

[17] at page 759

[18] at page 104

[19] at page 748

[20] at page 497

[21] at paragraph 2

[22] at page 622

[23] Ibid

[24] at page 314

[25] RSC 1985, c. N-5

[26] RSC 1985, App. II, No. 31

[27] It is interesting to note that in the third draft of the *British North American Act ,1867* this provision stated that the decision whether to approve the summoning of additional senators would be made by Her Majesty in Council which is a clear reference to the Crown acting on the advice of the Imperial Privy Council but in the fourth draft and the legislation as passed the reference to the Imperial Privy Council was removed.

[28] Senate, *Journals*, 1877, at page 77

[29] There was a third case in New Brunswick that is not relevant to the present discussion.

[30] Justice Hollingrake stated: "On the face of s. 26, the Queen is given an independent discretion to decide whether to appoint four or eight additional members to the Senate, the only limitation on the exercise of this discretion being that she must receive the recommendation of the Governor-General to make such a direction. To read in a limitation on Her Majesty's power that she must, as a matter of law, act by and with the advice of Her Privy Council in London when making a direction under s. 26 would be to add words to a provision which can fairly be described as a model of clarity. In my view s. 26 contains a clear and express procedure for increasing the membership of the

Senate in the manner contemplated therein and I cannot see any reason as a matter of law or construction to import into s. 26 any additional limitations on Her Majesty's power."

[31] As a matter of constitutional convention however, the Sovereign and the Governor General would be constrained to follow the formal advice of the Queen's Privy Council for Canada.

[32] The court stated: "It will be noted that s. 26 confers separate and distinct functions upon the Queen and upon the Governor General in connection with the appointment of additional senators. Assuming that it is possible for the Queen, upon whom such statutory authority is specifically conferred, to delegate that authority, the general rule is that a delegation of power does not imply parting with authority and the delegating body retains the power to act concurrently within the area of delegated authority. The 1947 Letters Patent do not contain words of transfer or release which would negate the application of this general principle".

[33] In the view of this author the separation of functions between the Governor General and the Queen prevent the power from being delegated to the Governor General. Were it otherwise the Governor General would be in the position of making a recommendation to himself or herself. Therefore, in my view, the procedures followed in 1989 were the correct procedures under the *Constitution Act, 1867*.

[34] In some jurisdictions the date for the legislative body to meet may be set forth in the prorogation proclamation but in others a separate instrument will be issued at a later date.

[35] D Michael Jackson, *The Crown and Canadian Federalism*, Dundurn, Toronto, 2013, at pages 70-71 (afterwards, *"Jackson"*).

[36] A proposed austerity measure that would have affected the financing of political parties also played an important role in motivating the opposition parties to attempt to topple the ministry.

[37] The leader of the Liberal party stepped down after the prorogation request was granted by the Governor General.

[38] *Dicey*, pages 58-59

[39] *Crown Law*, Paul Lordon Q.C., Butterworths, Markham (Ont.) 1991, page 63 (afterwards *"Lordon"*).

[40] Professor Dicey's approach might subject some Crown actions to judicial review that might otherwise be excluded by Blackstone's approach.

Consequently, the courts in Canada have tended to favour the approach of Professor Dicey; see *Khadr v Canada (Attorney General)*, [2007] 2 FCR 218, (Canada, FC).

[41] at page 26

[42] "The right to enter into treaties is one of the prerogative powers of the Crown. No one other than the Queen can conclude a treaty. In practice, . . . this prerogative power is exercisable on behalf of Her Majesty by the Governor General or by a minister acting under the Governor General's authority." per Lord Hope in *Roberts v Minister of Foreign Affairs*, [2007] 3 LRC 261 (The Bahamas, JC) at page 267. In Canada, the question of treaty implementation is affected by the federal nature of the state. While the Federal Government may exercise the Royal Prerogative for the purpose of entering into a treaty with a foreign state, the implementation of a treaty with another state may require legislative action by both the Federal Government and provincial governments, or exclusively by one level or another. The Royal Prerogative of Her Majesty in right of Canada therefore only extends to the making of a treaty and does not extend to its implementation, which must be done by the Queen in Parliament or the Queen in the provincial legislature(s), or both.

[43] In the absence of a challenge under the *Canadian Charter of Rights and Freedoms* a court will incline to the view that the exercise of the Royal Prerogative to withdraw from or terminate an international treaty is not justiciable; *Turp v Canada (Minister of Justice)*, [2014] 1 FC 439; (Canada, FC) at para. 18.

[44] A treaty with a foreign state is not, in and of itself, justiciable in Canadian courts unless the treaty has been implemented in domestic legislation; *Re Arrow River & Tributaries Slide & Boom Co. Ltd.* (1932), 39 CRC 161 (Canada, SC). See also *The Republic of Italy v Hambros Bank*, [1950] 1 All ER 430 (England, ChD).

[45] Originally, the appointment of civil servants was an act under the Royal Prerogative but it has been increasingly assimilated to employment contract law by legislation; *Thomson v Canada (Deputy Minister of Agriculture)*, [1992] 1 SCR 385 (Canada, SC) per Cory J.: " Originally, it was the monarch that appointed and managed the public service. The power of appointment was historically a royal prerogative." Nevertheless, the Royal Prerogative of appointments in respect to civil services has not been abolished and would be effective again if the applicable legislation was repealed. Further, in the case of the most senior public servants (e.g., Deputy Ministers) appointments to office are still made by an order-in-council in the federal administration, which is itself an exercise of the Royal Prerogative of appointment.

[46] Royal commissions are invariably constituted as a statutory commission of inquiry under the *Inquiries Act* or similar legislation because a royal commission created under the Royal Prerogative lacks the ability to compel testimony from witnesses. Creating a commission of inquiry as a royal commission is therefore essentially symbolic and in recent years has fallen somewhat into disuse.

[47] The Sovereign is deemed to be always present in court and therefore at common law, a non-suit will not lie against the Crown (*Scott*, at page 134).

[48]As *parens patriae*, the Sovereign is the legal guardian of infants and persons suffering from mental incompetency (*Scott*, at page 134).

[49] The salient cases involving immunities tend to arise in factual situations involving Crown agents. For discussion of how servants of the Crown can claim Crown immunity see *R v Stradiotto* (1973), CCC (2d) 257 (Ontario, CA) per Evans J.A. and the treatment of that case by Dickson J in *R v Eldorado Nuclear Ltd. et al*, [1983] 2 SCR 551 at 568 (Canada, SC).

[50] Under the historic common law principles the Sovereign was immune from a lawsuit in torts (delict in Quebec) but this immunity has now been extinguished by statute in all Canadian jurisdictions. Some residual immunities in the context of litigation still exist such as the
Crown's immunity from discovery in cases in which the Crown is not a party. In order for Parliament to extinguish a Crown immunity there must be a "clear and unequivocal expression of legislative intent"; *Canada (Attorney General) v. Thouin*, 2017 SCC 46 (Canada, SC) and that is a principle that finds legislative expression in section 17 of the *Interpretation Act* RSC 1985, c. I-21.

[51] *Madras Electric Supply Corporation LD. v Boarland*, [1955] AC 667 (England, HL)

[52] It should be noted that the traditional immunity of the Sovereign from statute law has been reversed in British Columbia, pursuant to the *Interpretation Act* RSBC 1979, c. 206, s. 14(1) and in Prince Edward Island by the *Interpretation Act* SPEI 1981, c. 18, s. 14.

[53] *East India Company v Thomas Sandys* (1684), St. Tr. 519 (England, KB)

[54] The Sovereign has a prerogative to permit both the use of and the disposition of Crown property; see *Fitzherbert v Williams* (1818), Nfld LR 115 (Newfoundland, SC) where the issue related to the disposition of pews in a church, which had been subscribed by the Governor.

[55] *Bona vacantia* relates to things that cannot be the subject of a property claim.

[56] *Ross River Dene Council Band v Canada* [2002] 2 SCR 816 (Canada, SC)

[57] *R v Criminal Injuries Compensation Board, ex p. Lain*, [1967] 2 QB 864, (England, QB). A royal proclamation " . . . cannot deprive any subject of any rights to which he is entitled at common law or by statute, or grant to him any immunities . . . ".

[58] The power to act to preserve constitutional order is based on both the Royal Prerogative and the doctrine of necessity.

[59] The most comprehensive historical compendium is entitled *A Treatise on the Law of the Prerogatives of the Crown: And the Relative Duties and Rights of the Subject*, Joseph Chitty, London, Butterworths, 1820. In the Canadian context reference may also usefully be taken to Paul Lordon QC, *Crown Law*, Butterworths, Toronto (Markham), 1991; *Halsbury's Laws of Canada, 1st Edition(Crown 2017 Reissue)* Lexis-Nexis, Toronto, 2017; *Canadian Encyclopaedic Digest, 4th Edition (Crown)* Carswell, Toronto.

[60] Prerogative royalties are assigned to the provinces by the *Constitution Act, 1867*, s. 109; see also *Attorney General of Ontario v Mercer*, [1883] 8 AC 767 (Canada, JC), *Attorney General of British Columbia v Attorney General of Canada*, [1889] 14 AC 295 (Canada, JC); *The King v Attorney General of British Columbia*, [1924] AC 213 (Canada, JC).

[61] At page 588. Section 109 of the *Constitution Act, 1867*, states:

"All Lands, Mines, Minerals, and Royalties belonging to the several Provinces of Canada, Nova Scotia, and New Brunswick at the Union, and all Sums then due or payable for such Lands, Mines, Minerals, or Royalties, shall belong to the several Provinces of Ontario, Quebec, Nova Scotia, and New Brunswick in which the same are situate or arise, subject to any Trusts existing in respect thereof, and to any Interest other than that of the Province in the same."

[62] at paragraph 41

[63] In *Ross River Dene Council Band v Canada* Bastarache J. stated: "There is no doubt that a royal prerogative can be abolished or limited by clear and express statutory provision: see *R. v. Operation Dismantle Inc.*, [1983] 1 FC 745, at p. 780, affd. [1985] 1 S.C.R. 441, at p. 464. It is less certain whether in Canada the prerogative may be abolished or limited by necessary implication. Although this doctrine seems well established in the English courts (see *Attorney-General v De Keyser's Royal Hotel, Ltd.*, [1920] AC 508 (H.L.)), this Court has questioned its application as an exception to Crown immunity (see *R. v Eldorado Nuclear Ltd.*, [1983] 2 S.C.R. 551, at p. 558; *Sparling v*

Quebec (Caisse de dépôt et placement du Québec), [1988] 2 SCR 1015, at pages 1022-1023)."

[64] *Lordon*, at page 66; see also *Sabally et al v Attorney General*, [1964] 3 All ER 377 (England, CA)

[65] The question of whether an abeyance of a federal prerogative power in Canada is possible in light of the provisions of section 43 of the *Interpretation Act*, has not been conclusively determined. Section 43 of the *Interpretation Act* states that the repeal of an enactment does not revive a thing that was not in force at the time of the repeal. Older case law suggests that the provision of the *Interpretation Act* may not apply to the Royal Prerogative; *Re D Moore Co.*, [1928] 1 DLR 383 (Ontario, CA). However, the application of newer approaches to statutory construction may give a different result.

[66] See also *R (Miller) v Secretary of State for Exiting the European Union* where the majority acknowledged (para. 112) that: "If prerogative powers are curtailed by legislation, they may sometimes be reinstated by the repeal of that legislation, depending on the construction of the statutes in question."

[67] See also *Scarborough (City) v Ontario (Attorney General)*, [1997] 32 OR (3d) 526 (Ontario, GD) and *R v Criminal Injuries Compensation Board, ex p. Lain*, [1967] 2 QB 864, (England, QB).

[68] Except for the reserve powers which continue to be exercised without formal constitutional advice.

[69] at paragraph 63

[70] *Canada (Attorney General) v. Newfield Seeds Ltd.*, (1989) 63 DLR (4th) 644 (Saskatchewan, CA). Furthermore, the fact that Parliament has failed to appropriate funds to support a contract made by the agents of the Sovereign will not render the contract void, and the Crown will be liable for a failure to perform it.

[71] See the *Crown Liability and Proceedings Act* RSC 1985, c. C-50.

[72] at page 346

[73] Justice Grant stated: "His [ie. the Minister's] decision is to be based on the policy which he determines proper, having regard to the rights and interests of the parties interested as well as those of the public. In doing so he, as one of the Executive Council, formulates the Crown policy of his department in the particular matter. Therefore he acts in the matter on behalf of the Crown and not as a statutory officer. The Minister may have to defend his decision in the Legislature but not in legal proceedings brought to challenge his authority."

[74] at page 115

[75] at page 752

[76] *Canadian Transportation Economics*, A W Currie, University of Toronto Press, Toronto, 1967, at page 403; *The Politics of Freight Rates: The Railway Freight Issue in Canada*, Howard Darling, McClelland and Stewart, Toronto, 1980 at pages 62, 80 and 156

[77] *Smith*, at page 99

[78] See *Gestion Complexe Cousineau v Canada (Minister of Public Works and Government Services)*, [1995] 2 FC 694 (Canada, FCA)

[79] In appropriate circumstances, the courts may also now make an interim preservation order against the Crown to preserve the *status quo* in ongoing litigation where a court has jurisdiction over a dispute that involves the Crown; *Couchiching First Nation et al v Canada (Attorney General)*, [2010] 103 OR (3d) (Ontario, Sup.Ct.).

[80] at paragraph 28

[81] at page 497

[82] at paragraph 47

[83] *Kamel v Canada (Attorney General)*, [2009] 4 FCR 449; 388 NR 4 (Canada, FCA)

[84] The immunity of the Royal Prerogative from judicial review has also eroded in Australia; *Minister for Arts Heritage and Environment v Peko-Wallsend Ltd.* (1987), 75 ALR 218 (Australia, FC).

[85] at pages 90-91

[86] at paragraph 62

THE RESERVE POWERS AND THE DOCTRINE OF NECESSITY

7.1   The Reserve Powers

The reserve powers are a special class of the Royal Prerogative. They consist of that remaining portion of the Royal Prerogative which permits the Sovereign, or the Sovereign's representatives, to take independent action without recourse to the constitutional convention that the Sovereign must act only on the advice of her constitutional advisors.

Primarily, the reserve powers fall into two fields, the selection and dismissal of a ministry, and the dissolution of Parliament or a provincial legislature. Within these fields the monarchy retains its historic independent prerogative because any advice from a ministry in such circumstances would carry with it a high risk of self-serving advice. Without an umpire, the principles of democracy which underlies the Canadian constitution could be placed in jeopardy. For that reason, the monarchy's reserve powers remain both extant and vital.

Historically, the reserve powers have been regarded as non-justiciable although within our system of constitutional government they are as important as legal rules for determining the validity of actions undertaken by the Sovereign, and the Sovereign's representatives. The exercise of the reserve powers has been excepted from the traditional bases of judicial review because they are bounded by rules of convention, rather than by legal rules, and the courts have forborne from entering the field of constitutional convention for the purposes of judicial review.

However, the *Charter* now provides a new basis for judicial review of constitutional powers, including the exercise of the Royal Prerogative. To what extent can the exercise of the reserve powers be constrained by judicial review under the *Charter*? It appears that even after *Operation Dismantle* and subsequent cases, and the increased willingness of the courts to entertain disputes over the exercise of the Royal Prerogative for the purposes of judicial review, the reserve powers are still considered to fall on the very far end of the spectrum of prerogative powers, and therefore beyond the reach of judicial review.

Should the courts decide in a proper case that the exercise of a reserve power is theoretically subject to judicial review any judicial scrutiny would likely founder on questions of justiciability, as in the *Operation Dismantle* and *Black* cases. Thus, the reserve powers are likely to remain beyond the scrutiny of judicial review even though the *Charter* now provides a basis for judicial inquiry into the exercise of the Royal Prerogative, and despite the fact that the courts have increasingly articulated a broad theory for judicial review of all forms of governmental action.

In the context of the reserve powers it is important that responsible government under the Sovereign be continued without interruption but that in maintaining the continuance of government the Sovereign, or the Sovereign's representatives in Canada, ought not be drawn into political controversies by those political figures who seek an office in the gift of the Crown.[1]

Much of the United Kingdom constitutional practice is reflected in the scope and extent of the reserve powers as they are exercised in Canada at the present time. But there are some important differences in the Canadian practices, most importantly the fact that the reserve powers in Canada are not exercised directly by the Sovereign for the most part but rather by her representatives, the Governor General of Canada, and the Lieutenant Governors of the provinces.

7.2   Formal Advice and the Exercise of the Reserve Powers

In situations where the Sovereign or the Sovereign's representative, is called upon to exercise the reserve powers inherent in their office there will naturally arise the potential for a conflict between the Crown and the Canadian Ministry. For this reason, the Sovereign and the Sovereign's representatives are not bound by constitutional convention, custom, or practice, to accept any formal advice offered to them by a Canadian Ministry. The exercise of the reserve powers constitutes a personal discretion that the *Constitution of Canada* vests in the Sovereign and the Sovereign's representatives.

Therefore, in the exercise of the reserve powers the Sovereign and the Sovereign's representative may consult and seek advice privately from those persons whom they wish to consult, or they may simply act on their own best judgement without consulting anyone. In Canada both former Governor General Michaëlle Jean and former Ontario Lieutenant Governor David Onley were known to have consulted privately with constitutional experts in preparation for their exercise or potential exercise of the reserve powers.[2]

Within the Commonwealth realms there have been occasions when a representative of the Sovereign has consulted with the Chief Justice of their jurisdiction. This has occurred, for example, in Australia at the state level. Consultation by the Governor General of Australia with the Chief Justice of

Australia also occurred during the 1975 constitutional crisis that resulted in the dismissal of the Australian Ministry headed by Prime Minister Gough Whitlam.[3] In Fiji during the 1987 military uprising that eventually led to the abolition of the monarchy, the Governor General was advised during the crisis by the Chief Justice of Fiji.[4]

7.3   Walter Bagehot's Trilogy of Rights

Though not a true constitutional reserve power but perhaps the most substantial and yet least controversial of the powers possessed by the monarchy of Canada consists of the British essayist Walter Bagehot's famous nineteenth century trilogy of monarchial rights: "the right to be consulted, the right to encourage, the right to warn".[5] The obligation to respect these rights is one imposed on all governments in Canada. In governing, a Canadian Ministry is required to keep the representative of the Sovereign fully informed about the conduct of public policies and the objectives of the government, and to consider whatever encouragement or warnings they may receive from the Sovereign's representatives.

As part of this responsibility, the Sovereign's representatives possess the right to request additional information from Ministers of the Crown and to ask the government to reconsider a particular public policy. Ultimately however, the Sovereign's representative must follow the formal constitutional advice of responsible ministers and it is a clearly understood constitutional convention that any encouragement or warning from the Sovereign's representative will not constrain the discretionary judgment of a ministry.

First ministers(e.g., Prime Ministers or Premiers) have often found the Sovereign or the Sovereign's representatives to be useful to them as a counsellor. In his memoirs, former Prime Minister Pierre Trudeau said that the Sovereign always impressed him by her wise perspectives during their private audiences.[6] Similarly, he also spoke favourably of the counsel he received from former Governor General Roland Michener.[7] A first minister may accept or reject whatever counsel they hear from the Sovereign, or the Sovereign's representative with perfect equanimity, as the monarchy lacks the constitutional competence to pass final judgment upon the political wisdom of the policies endorsed by a ministry. That power is reserved for the members of Parliament, or the provincial legislatures, and, ultimately, for the electorate.

In Canada, at the present day, there is clearly an obligation to keep the Governor General and the Lieutenant Governors apprised of the business on the public agenda but whether they receive more than a very general overview of the work of the government is often unclear.[8] In some respects this reflects the quasi-partisan nature of some of the appointments, particularly with respect to the Lieutenant Governors, which may hamper effective relations between a

Sovereign's representative and a first minister. However, the effectiveness of the relationship will most often depend upon the personal qualities and character of the constitutional actors themselves, regardless of any past partisan affiliations. Perhaps the most that can be said is that Bagehot's trilogy of monarchial rights continues to form part of the conventions of the Canadian constitution but the degree to which they are implemented depends upon the assertiveness of the Sovereign's representative, the respect afforded to constitutional principles by first ministers, and the personal relations between the individuals concerned.

7.4   Particular Reserve Powers

There is no elaborate list or description of the reserve powers that accrue to Canada's constitutional monarchy. The vagueness attaching to the reserve powers is deliberate because the exercise of a reserve power is fitted to the circumstances, and to the times. However, the principle reserve powers are generally known, and the following is a discussion of the most important reserve powers that are applicable in the Canadian context.

7.5   The Dissolution of a Legislative Body

In Canada, as in the United Kingdom, only the Sovereign, or the Sovereign's representative, may formally dissolve Parliament, or a provincial legislature. At the federal level there is a practice that was first confirmed by Order-in-Council P.C. 1853, 1 May 1896, and subsequently reconfirmed from time to time by further orders-in-council, which provides that it is the sole responsibility of the Prime Minister to advise the Governor General when Parliament should be dissolved and a general election held.

A Prime Minister may request a dissolution of Parliament but may not demand one. When such advice is given, it becomes the responsibility of the Sovereign's representative to accept or reject that advice. The constitutional convention which requires that the Sovereign's representative must act upon the advice of responsible ministers does not apply to the advice of a first minister that Parliament or a provincial legislature be dissolved. The Sovereign's representative has a personal discretion under the reserve powers to act according to the dictates of their own judgment. In Conacher v Canada (Prime Minister), [2011] 4 FCR 22 (Canada, FCA) Justice Stratas, writing for the Federal Court of Appeal on this subject stated:

> But under our constitutional framework and as a matter of law, the Governor General may consider a wide variety of factors in deciding whether to dissolve Parliament and call an election. In this particular case, this may include any matters of constitutional law, any conventions that, in the Governor General's opinion, may bear upon or determine the matter, Parliament's will . . . advice from the Prime Minister, and any other appropriate matters.[9]

Nevertheless, the exercise of this reserve power is a passive, rather than an active power. The Sovereign's representative may grant or deny the request but does not have an independent power to force a dissolution of Parliament. Furthermore, the constitutional practice relating to a dissolution requires the use of the Great Seal which is held in the custody of a minister (and an order-in-council authorized by a quorum of the Queen's Privy Council for Canada to permit its use). The employment of a royal seal, such as the Great Seal of Canada, requires that the minister who has actual custody of the seal accept political responsibility for its use. Therefore, the agreement of several ministers (i.e., the Prime Minister or Premier, the minister having custody of the Great Seal and the Ministers of the Crown who will form a quorum of the Privy Council) is required simply for the mechanics of dissolving Parliament to be carried out. The necessity of obtaining the concurrence of the Privy Council to implement the dissolution of Parliament or a provincial legislature prevents a Sovereign's representative from forcing the dissolution of Parliament in the absence of an acceptance of political responsibility for that act by responsible ministers.

Quite commonly in the past a government nearing the end of its traditional four or five-year mandate would choose an appropriate time to seek another mandate from the electorate. In those circumstances dissolution became a routine matter, which the Governor General would ratify upon the advice of the Prime Minister. Since the turn of the twenty-first century however most political jurisdictions in Canada, including the federal level of government, have moved to adopt election dates fixed by law to improve the fairness of the election process by removing the advantage of sitting governments to determine the date of an election. At the time of writing all provinces have four-year fixed election cycles except Nova Scotia. The prescribed four year electoral cycle does not, however, unduly constrain a sitting government with respect to the timing of an election. The legislation establishing fixed four-year electoral cycles has been careful to preserve the prerogative powers of the Governor General or the Lieutenant Governor to grant or withhold a dissolution. In the northern territories there is a fixed election date in the Northwest Territories but both Nunavut and Yukon have maintained the older procedure which leaves election timing to the government of the day.

The *Constitution Act, 1982*, provides in section 4(1) that no Parliament or provincial legislature may extend beyond five years from the date of the return of election writs in respect of a general election and thus regardless of whether fixed legislative terms have been implemented in a particular jurisdiction there will be an upper limit to the longevity of legislative bodies in Canada.

If, after being granted a dissolution, the general election which follows does not produce a clear winner the Sovereign's representative will be called upon to act if the incumbent ministry resigns before meeting Parliament, or upon losing the confidence of the House of Commons after meeting it. If a Prime Minster resigns for one of the foregoing reasons, the Sovereign's representative ought to offer the chance to form a new ministry to the leader of a party possessing the largest number of seats in the House of Commons.

The reserve power of a Sovereign's representative to grant an early dissolution is important in Canada in situations involving minority governments, which has been a common enough occurrence in Canadian political history. Where a minority government loses the confidence of a legislative body it must either resign in favour of the opposition party, or parties, or its leader must seek from the Sovereign's representative an early dissolution of the legislative body, and a general election.

In the United Kingdom it is considered that the Sovereign may be justified in refusing a dissolution where the existing Parliament remained capable of discharging public business, or where an alternative government could govern for a reasonable length of time.[10] This remains the general principle in Canada as well. However, the historic conventions in relation to a dissolution in Canada have been affected by the constitutional crisis of 1926, at least at the federal level of government. The discretion of the Sovereign's representative to grant or deny a dissolution formed the basis of that famous constitutional crisis.[11]

The 1926 crisis began with a dissolution of Parliament granted to Prime Minister William Lyon Mackenzie King in 1925. Mr. King's government had enjoyed a four-year term with a Liberal majority. However, in the election which followed, Mackenzie King's Liberal government suffered badly at the polls. The makeup of the Parliament which met after the 1925 election consisted of 101 Liberals, 116 Conservatives, and 28 Progressives, Labour, and independent members.

Prime Minister Mackenzie King chose not to resign, relying instead on a natural political affinity for Liberal policies amongst the members of the Progressive Party to sustain his government. A situation thereupon developed in which a party which was not the largest party in the House of Commons formed a minority government. In this unstable political atmosphere it was perhaps inevitable that the Parliament would not serve out a normal five year term.

By June of 1926 the ability of the Liberal ministry to control the House of Commons was breaking down. In part that was due to a political scandal, which resulted in what was tantamount to a motion of censure being brought against the government in the House of Commons. Over a critical weekend, Prime Minister Mackenzie King sought a dissolution from the Governor General, Viscount Byng of Vimy. Lord Byng refused the dissolution whereupon the Prime Minster and his ministers resigned and immediately vacated their offices. When the House met on the following Monday, the country was without a government. The Governor General sent for the opposition leader, Arthur Meighen, who accepted the Governor General's request that he form a government and he became Prime Minister.

At that time, the *Senate and House of Commons Act* required that members of Parliament who accepted a salaried office from the Crown, a so-called "office of profit", including the office of a Minister of the Crown, had to vacate their seats in the House of Commons and stand for reelection in a by-election. In order to forestall the absence of many of his politically experienced associates while the House of Commons remained unsettled, Prime Minister Meighen resigned his own seat to stand in a by-election but secured the appointment of some of his colleagues as acting ministers in order to avoid having them stand down to run in their own by-elections. Acting ministers were not required to vacate their seats in the House of Commons under the parliamentary rules that prevailed at that time. Thus Meighen thought he had circumvented a rule which potentially jeopardized his government.

However, Meighen's strategy created its own controversy, and Prime Minister Meighen's government was able to control the House of Commons for only a few days before it too fell on a question of confidence. Governor General Lord Byng granted a dissolution of Parliament to Meighen at Meighen's request, as there was clearly no alternative government waiting in the wings that the Governor General could call upon. The resulting 1926 election restored the Liberals to office with a majority government.

The 1926 constitutional crisis focused much attention and controversy on the role of the Governor General in denying a dissolution of Parliament to Prime Minister Mackenzie King while granting a dissolution to Prime Minister Meighen. Prime Minister Mackenzie King took the view that he had been entitled to a dissolution as a matter of constitutional convention because he had not been defeated on a question of confidence when he advised the Governor General to dissolve Parliament. However, in taking that position Mr. King was clearly incorrect, as the Governor General possessed a broad reserve power to deny a dissolution.

In addition, Prime Minister Mackenzie King sought a dissolution when his government faced a pending motion of censure in the House of Commons and it was unprecedented for a government to seek a dissolution before such a motion had been decided upon by the House of Commons. On the other side of the ledger however, the Governor General appears to have had a poor appreciation of the unsettled conditions in the House of Commons and the likelihood that Arthur Meighen's Conservatives would be able to secure the confidence of the House of Commons for any reasonable length of time. As it was, Lord Byng's refusal of Prime Minister King's request for a dissolution and King's subsequent resignation placed Meighen in the awkward position of taking office in circumstances where the exercise of the reserve powers was extremely controversial, and where he had to defend their use to the electorate in short order. The lustre of the Sovereign's representative was seemingly diminished by the electorate's subsequent rejection of the Meighen government.

As a result, in each instance subsequent to 1926 when a minority government has sought a dissolution (1958, 1963, 1965, 1974, 1979, 2005, 2008, and 2011) the request has been granted even though, as in 1974 and 2011, the Prime Minister who sought the dissolution had also received the prior dissolution. No subsequent representative of the Sovereign has chosen to refuse a dissolution in the exercise their reserve power, as did Lord Byng. Thus, the outcome of the 1926 crisis has been to impose a greater degree of caution on the representatives of the Sovereign in the exercise of the reserve powers in relation to dissolutions in Canada.

While constitutional convention suggests that the Sovereign's representative should consult with the leader of the opposition to determine whether an alternative government is possible before deciding upon a request for a dissolution where a ministry has been defeated on a confidence vote, there is little doubt today that considerable attention must be given by the Sovereign's representative to the sustainability of any alternative government over an extended period of time before a dissolution is refused. Canadian constitutional history may now have rendered the refusal of a requested dissolution to be a very unlikely prospect. Nevertheless, the Sovereign's representatives are careful to preserve the independence of their decision in such situations by taking time to deliberate before rendering their decision. Thus, when the Clark Ministry was defeated on a confidence vote in 1979, Governor General Edward Schreyer reserved his decision on Prime Minister Clark's request for a dissolution after meeting with him, and subsequently telephoned him with a decision granting his request after the Governor General had taken time to consider the matter.[12]

Whenever, the Sovereign, or the Sovereign's representatives, are faced with these circumstances sound judgment and common sense is the best guide. Since convention rather than law is involved there are no legal precedents by which a Sovereign's representative can judge the merits of a dissolution request. However, minority governments often reflect a passing mood of uncertainty on the part of the electorate, which may be resolved after only a short elapse of time following an inconclusive general election. For instance, the inconclusive 1925 election was followed by the 1926 election, which restored the Liberals to office with a majority government.

More recent examples include the inconclusive 1972 result, in which the majority Liberal government was reduced to a minority, barely ahead of the opposition Progressive Conservatives in numbers. However in the subsequent 1974 election, which followed the defeat of the Liberal government on a question of confidence, the Liberals were restored to office with a majority government. In 1979 that Liberal government was defeated in a general election and a minority Progressive Conservative government took office but it was defeated on a question of confidence later in 1979. In the subsequent 1980 election, the electorate returned the Liberals to office with a comfortable majority. Thus, early elections in minority government situations should not necessarily be avoided out of a desire to sustain a sitting Parliament. Rather, it may be necessary to permit the electorate to have a further opportunity to make a democratic choice.

The true importance of the reserve power of dissolution is that it exists to prevent a government from unfairly taking advantage of its position in order to sustain itself in office, a possibility that has now been considerably constrained by the move to fixed election dates. Nevertheless no representative of the Sovereign should consider granting a dissolution immediately after a general election to any government which has not been as successful as it wished at the polls. In 1971, in the province of Newfoundland and Labrador an inconclusive general election severely jeopardized the chances of the governing Liberal party to remain in office and the Lieutenant Governor of Newfoundland and Labrador had to refuse multiple requests by the Premier for a second dissolution prior to the Legislature being summoned.

In the aftermath of a general election, where it is clear that an alternative government has a reasonable chance of sustaining itself in the House of Commons, or a provincial legislature, the Sovereign's representative should consider calling upon the leader of the opposition party to form a government. In 2017 an inconclusive provincial election in the province of British Columbia returned a minority Liberal ministry to office under Premier Christy Clark. However, the opposition New Democratic Party and the Green Party entered into a formal agreement under which they pledged to cooperate with each other to defeat the Clark Ministry in the British Columbia Legislative Assembly. When the legislature met a few weeks after the election the Clark Ministry was defeated on a vote of confidence and Premier Clark, in tendering her resignation to Lieutenant Governor Judith Guichon, asked the Lieutenant Governor to grant another dissolution of the legislature. The Lieutenant Governor declined to grant a further dissolution and instead called upon the leader of the opposition to form a government, after receiving assurances that he could form a stable British Columbia Ministry.

Finally, any attempt to restrict or limit the powers of the Crown with respect to a dissolution of Parliament or a provincial legislature would require a constitutional amendment. That flows from Section 41(a) of the *Constitution Act, 1982*, which prevents changes to the offices of the Queen, the Governor General, or the Lieutenant Governors, without the assent of both houses of Parliament and the legislatures of each province. This principle was highlighted by Justice Shore in the Federal Court of Canada in the case of *Conacher and Democracy Watch v Canada*, [2009] FC 920 (Canada, FC) affd. *Conacher v Canada (Prime Minister)*, [2011] 4 FC 22 (Canada, FCA) who stated:

> . . . the Governor General has discretion to dissolve Parliament pursuant to Crown prerogative and Section 50 of the *Constitution Act 1867*. Any tampering with this discretion may not be done via an ordinary statute, but requires a constitutional amendment under Section 41 of the *Constitution Act 1982*, which requires unanimous consent of all provincial governments as well as of the federal government before a change can be made to the "office of the Governor General.[13]

7.6 The Appointment of a First Minister

One of the most important remaining reserve powers is the power to appoint a Prime Minister at the federal level, or a Premier at the provincial level of government. It is a fundamental obligation of the Sovereign's representative to take the initiative to ensure the formation of a responsible ministry to govern the nation or a province.

However, the importance of this reserve power has waned with the development of established political parties. Invariably, modern political parties choose their own leaders through a democratic process and it is those leaders to whom the Sovereign's representative will look to in selecting the head of a government. In fact, it would be inconceivable in the modern context for a Sovereign's representative to select as Prime Minister, or Premier, someone other than the leader of the political party that controls Parliament, or a provincial legislature.

After an election where a political party has secured the majority of the seats in the House of Commons, or provincial legislature, the Sovereign's representative will call upon the leader of that party to form a ministry and to seek the confidence of Parliament, or a provincial legislature, through a Speech from the Throne. Ordinarily, this will be a fairly straightforward process. However, where the general election has returned a minority government, that is, one that commands less than half of the elected members of the House of Commons, or of a provincial legislature, the Sovereign's representative will be faced with a choice of whom to summon to form a ministry. The constitutional practice that has evolved in Canada since the 1950's, when minority governments became more common, is for the Sovereign's representative to recognize that the leader of the political party with the largest number of seats following a general election (though still less than a majority of the seats) has the predominant claim to attempt the formation of a ministry that can command the confidence of the House of Commons, or of a provincial legislature.[14] Thus, it has been the invariable practice of the Sovereign's representatives since the middle of the twentieth century to call upon the leader of the party with the greatest number of seats to occupy the post of first minister – at least until the confidence of the House of Commons or of the provincial legislature can be tested.

At times the opposition parties in a minority situation that do not have the most seats in Parliament or a provincial legislature may resolve to cooperate in forming a sustainable ministry with combined numbers that would exceed the number of seats required to sustain legislative confidence in a ministry. Under that scenario, a commitment in writing by the leaders of the opposition parties proposing to collaborate for a defined period of time may be received by the Sovereign's representative as evidence of a sustainable ministry. The Sovereign's representative may call upon the leader of such a formal or informal coalition but only after the leader of the party with the largest number of seats has declined a mandate to attempt to form a ministry, or has formed a ministry but has not succeeded in obtaining the confidence of the House of Commons, or of a provincial legislature. That situation occurred in Ontario, in 1985, when an informal coalition was formed between the Liberals and the New Democratic Party in the Ontario Legislature that allowed Lieutenant Governor John Black Aird to call upon the leader of the Liberals, David Petersen, to form a government with the support of New Democratic Party leader Bob Rae after the Conservative ministry of Premier Frank Miller was unable to secure a vote of confidence in the Ontario Legislature.[15] The same process occurred in 2017 in British Columbia when a general election returned a legislature in which the Liberal party under Premier Christy Clark held the most seats but was just shy of a majority. The opposition New Democratic Party under John Horgan entered into a formal agreement with the small Green Party led by Andrew Weaver in which they agreed to form a sustainable ministry. Under the written agreement the Green Party committed to support the NDP Ministry on confidence matters for the expected term of the legislature, and the New Democratic Party ministry committed to consult the Green Party on policy development, and on certain specific initiatives.[16] When the Liberal ministry was subsequently defeated following the Speech from the Throne in the British Columbia Legislative Assembly Lieutenant Governor Judith Guichon called upon John Horgan to form a new ministry after receiving the resignation of Premier Clark.

Where there has been a loss of confidence by Parliament or a provincial legislature, a Prime Minister or Premier must tender their resignation to the Sovereign's representative under the constitutional conventions of responsible government. The resignation of a Prime Minister or Premier in circumstances where confidence in the government they head has been lost automatically results in the resignation of all of the members of the ministry. Where a resignation results from a loss of the confidence of the House of Commons, or of a provincial legislature, and a dissolution of the legislative body is not advised by the first minister, or is not granted by the Sovereign's representative, the constitutional practice is for the Sovereign's representative to call upon the leader of the opposition party to form a government. Where there is no leader of the opposition, the person who moved the successful non-confidence motion against the government may be summoned.[17]

If there is a refusal by the leader of the opposition, or the member who successfully moved a non-confidence motion, to form a new government the Sovereign's representative must consider whether some other person in Parliament or in a provincial legislature could form a sustainable government. In doing so the Sovereign's representative may enter into consultations with other political leaders or, in the case of the Federal Government, with any Privy Councillor including those who are out of office, or out of Parliament. None of the persons with whom the Sovereign's representative consults need be under consideration as a potential first minister.

In discharging this duty, the Sovereign's representative should be guided by a knowledge of the political situation in the country or the province. He or she must choose someone who can obtain the confidence of the House of Commons or of a provincial legislature, and thereby form a strong and durable administration. Ultimately, if no one will accept responsibility for undertaking the formation of a new ministry, the Sovereign's representative should recall the former first minister, and grant to him or her a dissolution of Parliament or of the provincial legislature.

Alternatively, a Sovereign's representative may refuse to accept a resignation and ask the first minister who has lost the confidence of the legislative body to carry on as the head of a caretaker ministry for a temporary period. In 1922, in the Province of Manitoba, Lieutenant Governor Sir James Aikins refused to accept the resignation of the Premier of Manitoba on the grounds that the opposition was fractured and unlikely to cooperate in the formation of a new ministry that could obtain the confidence of the Manitoba legislature. Aikins directed the ministry to stay in office to obtain supply, following which the legislature was dissolved and an election was held.[18]

7.7   The Death, Incapacity, or Disappearance of a First Minister

Where this particular reserve power may still have a practical application is in circumstances where the first minister has become incapable of carrying out his or her duties, or has died, or disappeared. In those circumstances, the Sovereign's representative must act to ensure that a ministry capable of carrying on the government exists. Even here however, the Sovereign's representative should allow scope for the members of the political party in office to express their views on whom their leader should be, at least in circumstances where the first minister has died, or disappeared while in office.

In 1891, when Prime Minister Sir John A. Macdonald died in office the Governor General, Lord Stanley, engaged in consultations with members of the Conservative party for several days before calling upon Senator J C Abbott to succeed Macdonald as Prime Minister. The death in 1894 at Balmoral Castle in Scotland of Prime Minister Thompson, who had succeeded Abbott upon Abbott's retirement, required the Governor General, Lord Aberdeen, to spend several days in consultation with members of the Conservative party before he called upon Sir Mackenzie Bowell to form a ministry.

Closer to the contemporary era, the deaths in 1959 and 1960 of Premiers Maurice Duplessis and Paul Sauve of Quebec resulted in the Union Nationale party caucus submitting a petition to the Lieutenant Governor requesting that he call upon the leader selected by the caucus to become the new Premier. In both instances the Lieutenant Governor agreed to the petition and called upon the individual selected by the caucus to form a ministry. The same procedure was followed in 1968 when Premier Daniel Johnson of Quebec also died in office, although his successor submitted himself to a party leadership convention after taking office to ensure that the rank and file of his party supported his selection as their leader.

Although the death of a Prime Minister or a provincial Premier has not subsequently occurred to the date of this writing, the Quebec precedents will serve as precedents in other provinces, or nationally, should the death of a first minister occur in one of those jurisdictions.

The disappearance of a Prime Minister or Premier will obviously be a very rare event. In such cases however, it becomes the immediate duty of the Sovereign's representative to make inquiries and, if necessary, to terminate the appointment of a vanished Prime Minister or Premier and to call upon someone else to form a new ministry. At all times the principle is that the Sovereign's government must be carried on and it cannot be left in a paralysed condition. In 1873, at the height of a political crisis involving the proposed Pacific Railway, Prime Minister Macdonald suddenly disappeared for a week. Neither his family nor his close associates knew what had happened to him. The Governor General, Lord Dufferin, made the necessary inquiries and finally tracked him down to a location where he had sought escape from the political pressures which surrounded him, and pressed him to return.

In Australia, in December 1967, Prime Minister Harold Holt disappeared while swimming in the Pacific Ocean. Friends saw him carried out by the current where they lost sight of him. Although a widespread search was undertaken, the Prime Minister could not be found and the government was temporarily rudderless. The Governor General summoned the Deputy Prime Minister (the leader of the Country Party, the junior party in a Liberal-Country party coalition government) to office as Prime Minister, thus terminating the appointment of Prime Minister Holt. The Liberal Party subsequently held a leadership convention in January 1968, at which time they elected a permanent successor to Holt as party leader, and that person was then able to reassemble the former coalition, and take office as Prime Minister of Australia.

Instances of first minister incapacity have also been rare in Canadian history. However, in 1891 Prime Minister Macdonald, facing his final illness, was unable to speak for several days and signified his consent to public business by a slight squeezing of his hand. Governor General Lord Stanley advised his ministers to proceed with the public business before Parliament which Macdonald had previously authorized but he forbade them from introducing any new measures. In effect, Lord Stanley insisted upon the creation of a caretaker ministry during the Prime Minster's incapacity. Where the incapacity lasts for a longer period, the responsibility of removing the incapacitated Prime Minister will rest with the Sovereign's representative. In such circumstances the Sovereign's representative will wish to obtain access to the best available medical expertise with respect to the nature of the incapacity before making a decision.

7.8   The Personal Retirement of a First Minister

On occasion, the Sovereign's representative will be faced with a resignation of a first minister that is a personal retirement. In those circumstances no question arises concerning the ability of the government to continue, or to enjoy the confidence of the House of Commons, or the provincial legislature. The personal resignation of a first minister does not automatically result in the resignation of the other members of the ministry (although a succeeding first minister may well choose to reconstitute the ministry, which would involve changes in personnel). Thus, there is no need for the Sovereign's representative to consult with the leader of the opposition in such circumstances.

Where a personal retirement occurs, the Canadian practice is for the outgoing Prime Minister, or Premier, to advise the Sovereign's representative with respect to the selection of a successor. However, such advice is regarded as informal, or non-constitutional advice which the Sovereign's representative is free to accept or reject. In the United Kingdom, it appears that upon a personal retirement, the outgoing Prime Minister is only entitled to provide personal advice concerning his or her replacement if the Sovereign specifically asks for such advice. The discretion to call upon any particular individual to form a ministry always remains with the Sovereign or the Sovereign's representatives, notwithstanding any personal advice from a departing first minister.

Despite the fact that the advice given by the outgoing Prime Minister or Premier is in the nature of personal advice the modern reality of defined political parties means that the discretion of the Sovereign's representatives in such circumstances is severely constrained. While the discretionary reserve power remains the necessity of appointing a sustainable ministry means that the Sovereign's representative should generally, as a practical matter, take the outgoing first minister's advice and appoint the person that the political party in office has selected as the successor to their leader to be the new Prime Minister, or Premier.[19]

7.9   The Dismissal of a First Minister

The Sovereign's representatives possess an undoubted reserve power to dismiss first ministers. However, resort to that power cannot be taken arbitrarily, such as where the Sovereign's representative disagrees with the policies of the government, or thinks that the policies of the government may be illegal.

As in the case of the death of a first minister, or a resignation following a loss of confidence by Parliament, or a provincial legislature, the dismissal of a first minister results in the Cabinet ceasing to exist as a collective entity, and the offices of the entire ministry are immediately placed at the disposal of the succeeding first minister. In dismissing a first minister the Sovereign's representatives place themselves in the position of having to find a replacement to accept constitutional responsibility for the dismissal of their predecessor. Should the Sovereign's representative be unable to find anyone in Parliament, or a provincial legislature, who is willing to accept that responsibility the Sovereign's representative will have no choice but to recall to office as first minister the person they had previously dismissed from office.

Dismissal has never occurred at the federal level of the Canadian state but it has occurred in two of the provinces of Canada. In the nineteenth and early twentieth centuries two Quebec governments (in 1878 and 1891) and three governments in British Columbia (in 1897, 1900, and 1903) were dismissed by the Lieutenant Governors of those provinces. In Quebec, Lieutenant Governor Letellier dismissed his Premier ostensibly because he did not approve of his policies. In Letellier's view, the ministry supported an arbitrary measure which affected vested rights, did not heed his admonitions, and spent too much public money on railways.[20] In British Columbia, the absence of strong party politics and the presence in Lieutenant Governor MacInnes of a forceful representative of the Sovereign led to a series of dismissals.

Both Letellier and MacInnes were themselves subsequently dismissed by the Federal Government, underscoring the sensitivity of the monarchy's intervention into responsible government through resort to this reserve power. In dismissing Lieutenant Governor MacInnes of British Columbia, the ministry of Prime Minister Laurier used language such as "extraordinary" and "improper" to describe the Lieutenant Governor's dismissals of his Premiers. Although only one of the Premiers selected by MacInnes was subsequently repudiated by the electorate, the fact that the Lieutenant Governor had dismissed one Premier and selected another who could not obtain a mandate from the electorate essentially sealed his political fate.

The exercise by the Sovereign's representatives in Quebec and British Columbia of the power to dismiss their Premiers occurred fairly early in the constitutional history of modern Canada and reflected the political conditions of that era. Those dismissals must be viewed in their own historical context and are no longer considered to be acceptable constitutional precedents for the exercise of the reserve power of dismissal in the politically sophisticated landscape of present-day government in Canada.

The controversies engendered by dismissals carry with them the potential to destroy the restraint and impartiality which are essential for the effective conduct of their office by a Sovereign's representative. Elsewhere in the Commonwealth realms, the depths of such controversies were plumbed on November 11, 1975, when the Governor General of Australia, Sir John Kerr, dismissed Australian Prime Minister Gough Whitlam. Whitlam's party controlled the House of Representatives, the lower house of the Australian Parliament but not the Senate, the elected upper house of the Parliament. The Whitlam Ministry found itself in the predicament of having its supply bills blocked in the Senate and was faced with the prospect of great difficulties in maintaining the operations of the Australian government. The Prime Minister declined to advise the Governor General to dissolve Parliament, presumably because he thought that the Senate would give way at the last moment. However, the Governor General presumed the existence of a parliamentary deadlock, dismissed Whitlam, and then called on the leader of the opposition to form a caretaker government. The new Prime Minister was instructed to pass supply and to refrain from making any new appointments, or initiating new policies prior to a general election.

Queen Elizabeth II refused to intervene in the crisis, although she was requested to do so by some Australian political actors, on the grounds that the Australian constitution prevented her from interfering in matters constitutionally vested in the Governor General of Australia. Nor would she consider dismissing Governor General Kerr unless formal advice was received by her from the new Prime Minister of Australia, Malcolm Fraser.[21] In the subsequent general election Prime Minister Fraser was returned to office, resolving the constitutional crisis, although much bitterness lingered thereafter in Australian politics.

In Canada it appears that there are few circumstances where a Sovereign's representative would consider the exercise of the reserve power to dismiss a first minister. In all likelihood, dismissal would be considered only where a ministry has lost the support of the House of Commons, or of a provincial legislature, and the Prime Minister or Premier refused to resign, or to advise a dissolution, or, having advised a dissolution and been refused, then refuses to resign to make way for an alternative government. Additionally, where a first minister refuses to summon Parliament, or a provincial legislature, for a sitting once every twelve months and thereby contravenes section 5 of the *Constitution Act, 1982*, dismissal is an option for the Sovereign's representative in order to ensure that the principle of accountable government is maintained. Lastly, in the very unlikely event that a first minister actually attempts to unconstitutionally usurp power the Sovereign's representative may have no choice but to dismiss the first minister in order to preserve the integrity of the constitution.

7.10   The Power to Decline Advice from a Defeated Ministry

Another reserve power that merits discussion is the power of the Sovereign's representative to refuse advice where the ministry has been rejected by the electorate but has not yet left office or, where, following an inconclusive election, it is not clear whether the ministry will continue to enjoy the confidence of the House of Commons, or of a provincial legislature. This principle was clearly established in 1896, following the defeat of Sir Charles Tupper's Conservative government in the federal general election of that year but prior to its departure from office. On that occasion, the Governor General, Lord Aberdeen, refused to make several appointments to the Senate which Prime Minister Tupper advised him to make after Tupper's defeat in the election.

Today, following the dissolution of Parliament or a provincial legislature, or the defeat of a ministry, or during its continuance in office pending the grant or denial of the confidence of the House of Commons or of a provincial legislature, the Sovereign's representative can exercise a discretion to defer, or even to reject advice, from a ministry until the political uncertainty has been resolved. Historically, at least since 1896, both ministers and permanent officials of government have displayed sufficient responsibility in the exercise of power to respect this discretion, and have thus avoided placing the Sovereign's representative in a position where a constitutional issue concerning advice from a ministry that actually, or potentially, suffers from a lack of parliamentary confidence could arise.

7.11   The Dismissal of a Governor General

An evolving reserve power in the Commonwealth realms concerns formal advice to the Sovereign to dismiss a Governor General. As the Sovereign's sole, or senior representative, in each of the Commonwealth realms the Governor General occupies an essential position in the maintenance of the principles of responsible government in each realm. During the reign of Queen Elizabeth II the Sovereign has supported her Governors General whenever political stress has enveloped their realm. As always, the Sovereign is concerned that the principles of responsible government are maintained. Thus, her refusal to become embroiled in the Australian political crisis of 1975, and the support for her Governor General of Fiji during the 1987 coup d' etat in Fiji (even to the point of refusing to meet with her ousted Fijian Prime Minister in order to avoid disrupting the Governor General's attempts to restore constitutional government) illustrate the Queen's primary focus on supporting her Governors General.

In the Australian political crisis of 1975 there were clear calls for the dismissal of Governor General Kerr from several political quarters but no formal advice to dismiss was provided to the Sovereign by either the Whitlam Ministry (before its dismissal) or the succeeding Fraser Ministry. In Canada, during the 2008 prorogation crisis there were whispers (at least among the political chattering class) of the possibility of formal advice being given to the Sovereign to dismiss Governor General Jean, as a possible last ditch effort by the Harper Ministry to prevent a denial of prorogation and an opposition ministry being formed in the minority Parliament. Nothing came of it, of course, and the prorogation request was subsequently granted by the Governor General (with conditions). It does, however, raise the question of whether formal advice may be tendered by a beleaguered Prime Minister to the Sovereign to obtain the dismissal of a Governor General where the Prime Minister thinks that the Governor General may not provide them with the political relief that he or she seeks from the Governor General in order to maintain a falling ministry in office.

There is one existing Commonwealth precedent concerning the judicious exercise of the royal discretion in such matters that comes from the smallest of the realms of Queen Elizabeth II, the Pacific island nation of Tuvalu. The impetus for the crisis in 2013 was the prospect that the Tuvaluan Ministry would be defeated in the legislature by a vote of non-confidence. To prevent the vote the ministry had attempted to force an adjournment of the legislature by arranging for the resignation of one of its members (which the ministry thought would have required an adjournment under the constitution of Tuvalu) but the Attorney General advised that the non-confidence motion could go ahead notwithstanding a vacancy in a constituency. The opposition then sought the assistance of the Governor General to ensure that the legislature would meet, and that the legislature's confidence in the ministry could be tested in accordance with the principles of responsible government.

To prevent the Governor General from compelling a meeting of the legislature to test the confidence of the assembly in the Tuvaluan Ministry, the Prime Minister of Tuvalu advised Queen Elizabeth II to dismiss the Governor General. The Queen, however, did not act on the formal advice she received from her Prime Minister, and subsequently the Governor General of Tuvalu dismissed the Prime Minister and called upon the opposition leader to be Acting Prime

Minister pending the holding of a formal non-confidence vote which resulted in the removal of the Tuvaluan Ministry that had lost its majority in the legislature. A new Tuvaluan Ministry was formed from the opposition majority. The Queen's deferral of action with respect to the formal advice received by her from her Prime Minister allowed the resolution of the crisis to occur through the application of the principles of responsible government in the constitutional context of Tuvalu.

The Tuvaluan precedent illustrates an important constitutional principle – that the Sovereign is not a mere cipher in such circumstances. She has a discretion to exercise and she is entitled, at the very least, to take whatever time is required in order to fully consider the matter. Further, in the view of the author, the Sovereign may exercise a reserve power to decline formal advice seeking the removal of a Governor General where a government that actually or potentially does not possess the confidence of its legislative body is seeking to prolong its tenure in office by using the threat of dismissal to pressure a Governor General for prorogation, or seeks to politically punish a Governor General who has refused prorogation in circumstances where parliamentary confidence is at issue. Formal advice need not be accepted by the Sovereign from a ministry that is unwilling to acknowledge and abide by the conventions of responsible government. The uncertainty of whether a ministry in such a situation retains the confidence of its legislature allows the Sovereign the latitude to decline a formal recommendation to dismiss a Governor General.

Whether such formal advice is explicitly declined by the Sovereign or whether, as happened in the Tuvalu scenario, the Sovereign simply fails to act immediately on the advice from the Prime Minister of the realm, the effect will be the same.[22] The Governor General will not be dismissed, and he or she will continue to have the necessary freedom of action to insist that the conventions of responsible government be sustained. Should the Sovereign exercise the power to defer or decline consideration of formal advice to remove a Governor General the ministry must then either face the legislative body and the application of the conventions of responsible government, or resign from office, or possibly accept a subsequent dismissal by a Governor General.

In other circumstances where, for example, dismissal of a Governor General is sought for reasons such as personal criminality, or issues of moral turpitude, or lack of capacity, or competence, the Sovereign should act on the formal advice of a Prime Minister by removing a Governor General pursuant to the conventions of responsible government.

7.12   Summary of the Reserve Powers

Of the reserve powers generally, it has been said that they remain undefined in scope, potentially controversial and difficult to employ again following a significant controversy. There is even reluctance to publicly discuss the circumstances under which the remaining reserve powers may be used precisely because of the controversy they may engender. Perhaps the last word on the controversial nature of the reserve powers should go to former Prime Minister Mackenzie King, who played such a major role in the one great constitutional crisis in Canada brought about by the exercise of the reserve powers. He has been quoted as saying " . . . it is always important to remember the significance of the things the Governor General did not do",[23] which is sage advice for any representative of the Sovereign who contemplates the exercise of the reserve powers.

7.13   The Doctrine of Necessity and Preserving Political Order

The Crown has an important responsibility, arising from Royal Prerogative and the doctrine of necessity, for the protection of the realm. In times of great constitutional or public crisis, the Sovereign and her representatives may have to act to ensure the preservation of the state, the continuance of constitutional government, or the maintenance of public order in circumstances where there may be no other constitutional actors capable of taking the requisite actions that are required.[24] At such times the doctrine of necessity will permit the exercise of extraordinary powers by the Sovereign, and by the Sovereign's representatives.

These extraordinary powers are incapable of precise enumeration due to the rarity of their exercise but the fact of their existence in the common law is indisputable. The Supreme Court of Canada relied on the doctrine of necessity in order to prevent legal chaos in the Province of Manitoba where it was determined that laws of Manitoba were invalid because they had been enacted in English, rather than in both English and French, as the constitution required. In reviewing Commonwealth jurisprudence on the subject of necessity the Supreme Court noted that:

> . . . under conditions of emergency, when it is impossible to comply with the
> Constitution, the Court may allow the government a temporary reprieve from such
> compliance in order to preserve society and maintain, as nearly as possible, normal
> conditions. The overriding concern is the protection of the rule of law.[25]

Some references to examples emanating from other Commonwealth realms will also serve to illustrate the principle.

When an unlawful usurpation of authority occurred in the colony of Southern Rhodesia in 1965,the issue of the applicability of the doctrine of necessity came to the forefront of judicial consideration. In *Madzimbamuto v Lardner-Burke*, [1969] 1 AC 645 (Southern Rhodesia, JC) the Judicial Committee of the Privy Council was concerned with the issue of whether a usurping colonial government in the colony of Southern Rhodesia could be regarded as the lawful government and whether the Rhodesian courts could give effect to the actions of that government. At the time, the lawful sovereign (the Queen in right of the United Kingdom) was attempting by constitutional means to reassert her control over the rebel territory. That attempted assertion of authority persuaded the Judicial Committee that the purported acts of the usurpers were unlawful and could not be validated by the doctrine of necessity.

Nevertheless, the Judicial Committee did not foreclose the application of the principle in an appropriate case stating; "It may be that there is a general principle, depending on implied mandate from the lawful Sovereign, which recognizes the need to preserve law and order in territory controlled by a usurper". In dissent, Lord Pearce would have accepted the validity of the actions of the usurpers, since the lawful Sovereign was unable, as a practical matter, to reassert authority. In reviewing the doctrine of necessity he stated:

> I accept the existence of the principle that acts done by those actually in control without lawful validity may be recognized as valid or acted upon by the courts, with certain limitations namely (a) so far as they are directed to and reasonably required for ordinary orderly running of the State, and (b) so far as they do not impair the rights of the citizen under the lawful . . . Constitution, and (c) so far as they are not intended to and do not in fact directly help the usurpation and do not run contrary to the policy of the lawful Sovereign. This last . . . is tantamount to a test of public policy.[26]

Another application of the doctrine of necessity in a Commonwealth constitutional context occurred in *Mitchell v Director of Public Prosecutions*, [1985] LRC 127 (Grenada, HC), which arose in the aftermath of an extraordinary series of events in the realm of Grenada during the 1970s and 1980s. The parliamentary opposition had unlawfully usurped power but some time later was itself violently overthrown. Immediately following that event the country was invaded and occupied by military forces from the United States of America and other Caribbean nations.

Through of all this constitutional and political turmoil Queen Elizabeth II and her Governor General remained in their respective positions as head of state and the Sovereign's representative. After the success of the invasion, they constituted the only officials of the civil government of Grenada. In the absence of authority, and in consideration of the emergency situation, Governor General Sir Paul Scoon issued proclamations to restore constitutional and lawful order in Grenada.

The actions of the Governor General became the subject of examination in the High Court of Grenada. Chief Justice Nedd found that when one of the territories of which Queen Elizabeth II is Queen is in dire danger of ceasing to be free she has, through her representative the Governor General, a reserve power capable of being used to avoid the extinction of that territory as a civilized state. Chief Justice Nedd based his judicial conclusion on the doctrine of necessity although recognizing that there are inherent limitations to the application of the doctrine of necessity in such situations and those limitations include " requirements of absoluteness, extremeness, imminence" but that such criteria were met with respect to the actions taken by the Governor General of Grenada.

Subsequently, in the Court of Appeal, the judgment of Chief Justice Nedd was affirmed on the basis of the doctrine of necessity. President Haynes of the Court of Appeal pointed out the circumstances under which the Governor General was able to exercise extraordinary powers beyond those which he was ordinarily entitled to exercise under the constitution of Grenada. The President of the court stated that in circumstances of chaos and the breakdown of law and order where neither the Parliament of Grenada nor its ministry was capable of functioning, the Governor General represented the executive power and the shared legislative sovereignty of the state. In such circumstances, the actions of the Governor General, motivated by a desire to preserve the state, were justified under the doctrine of necessity.

Thus, the actions of the Governor General in legislating by emergency proclamations to restore constitutional order and government in Grenada were valid. The courts of Grenada upheld the right of the Sovereign's representative in a situation of a constitutional emergency to legislate, and to exercise the powers of the Royal Prerogative without the presence of Parliament, or the assistance of constitutional advisors, pursuant to the doctrine of necessity.

Another extraordinary situation arose in the realm of Fiji in 1987. On May 14 of that year the Royal Fiji Defence Forces stormed Parliament while it was in session and abducted the Prime Minister and his government. When informed of the apparent coup d'etat, the Governor General, Ratu Sir Penaia Ganilau, informed the coup leader that his actions were unconstitutional and, advised by the Chief Justice, he declared a state of emergency and assumed control of the government.

The root of the disorder in Fiji was communalism, with the indigenous Melanesian population fearful of their possible loss of political control of the state to the descendants of nineteenth century immigrants from the Indian subcontinent. Between the first Fijian coup in May, and a second one in September, the Governor General attempted to mediate the differences between the coup leaders and the ousted Prime Minister. In doing so the Governor General performed a number of acts such as pardoning the coup leaders, dismissing the lawful government, and dissolving Parliament, without the assistance of responsible constitutional advisors who could assume political responsibility for his actions. His actions however, could be justified by the doctrine of necessity in the circumstances of a military rebellion.

Subsequently, after some four months of administration by the Governor General the deposed Prime Minister was invited by the Governor General to form an interim caretaker administration while a committee, chaired by a non-Fijian, explored alternative forms of democracy for Fiji. Although the ousted Prime Minister accepted the task a second coup d'etat occurred, which swept away the monarchy a few days later.[27]

Queen Elizabeth II, as the Sovereign of Fiji, acted throughout the crisis in support of efforts by the Governor General to restore constitutional government to Fiji. Initially she called upon the Governor General to stand firm as the "guardian of the Constitution".[28] Later, acting on advice from the Governor General of Fiji, she went so far as to decline to meet with her deposed Prime Minister, Mr. Bavadra, when he visited London seeking the Queen's support, in order to allow the Governor General the necessary latitude to attempt a restoration of constitutional authority. Instead, she referred her ousted Prime Minister to her private secretary for discussions of the Fijian political situation.

The Governor General of Fiji attempted to restore constitutional government to Fiji, even after the second coup in September of 1987, by refusing to surrender his authority to the army or to accept the presidency of a proposed Fijian republic. However, following the military proclamation of a republic the Governor General resigned his office and the Fijian monarchy was swept away.

The role and motives of the Queen and the Governor General during the crisis have been questioned[29] but in the view of this author both the Queen of Fiji and the Governor General of Fiji acted as prudently as possible, with the intention throughout the crisis of restoring constitutional government. This was an extraordinary circumstance in which there was open mutiny and rebellion by the military forces of the Crown. That the Queen and the Governor General were unable to succeed only reflects the risks and challenges faced by constitutional authorities in situations where constitutional authority is violently disrupted.

7.14 Summary of the Doctrine of Necessity

These examples show the nature of the extraordinary powers possessed by the Sovereign and the Sovereign's representatives in circumstances of great constitutional or national stress. These principles do have application in Canada, although their definition and scope, and the circumstances in which they might be applied, are incapable of precise legal description. It could be ventured to state however, that these principles might find application in circumstances where a Canadian Ministry had ceased to function as a result of , a foreign invasion, a civil insurrection, a mutiny by the armed forces of the Crown, or possibly an unconstitutional secession of a province or territory from Canada.

[1] "The Monarchy, The throne behind the power", Peter Hennessy, in *The Economist*, Dec 24, 1994, London, at page 78 (afterwards *"Hennessy"*)

[2] "Ontario Lieutenant-Governor David Onley shares insights on his seven year term,"Adrian Morrow, in *The Globe and Mail*, Monday, Sep. 22, 2014;"Jean feared 'dreadful crisis' when Harper sought prorogation," Steven Chase, in *The Globe and Mail*, Monday, Jun. 25, 2012; "Inside a crisis that shook the nation; Secret meetings, shocking alliances, faulty strategies—and one wonky video camera," John Geddes and Aaron Wherry, in *Macleans Magazine*, December 11, 2008.

[3] *The Governor General and the Prime Ministers*, Edward McWhinney, Ronsdale Press, Vancouver, 2005, pp. 66-67 (afterwards *"McWhinney"*)

[4] *Fiji, Coups in Paradise, Race, Politics and Military Intervention*, Victor Lal, Zed Books Ltd., London, 1990, at pages 202-203 (afterwards *"Lal"*)

[5] *Hennessy*, page 77

[6] *Memoirs*, Pierre E. Trudeau, McClelland and Stewart, Toronto, 1993, at page 313

[7] *The Crown in Canada*, Frank Mackinnon, Glenbow – Alberta Institute, Calgary, 1976, at page 103 (afterwards *"MacKinnon"*)

[8] *The Office of Lieutenant Governor*, John T. Saywell, University of Toronto Press, Toronto, 1957, at page 34 (afterwards *"Saywell"*)

[9] at para. 6

[10] *Hennessy*, page 78

[11] This subject has been exhaustively discussed by a number of authors, notably Eugene A Forsey in *The Royal Power of Dissolution in the British Commonwealth*, Eugene A Forsey, Oxford University Press, Toronto, 1943 (afterwards *"Forsey"*)

[12] *McWhinney*, at page 99

[13] at paragraph 53

[14] *McWhinney*, at pages 77, 98

[15] *McWhinney*, at pages 108-09

[16] The specific provisions of the agreement relating to the support of the Green Party on matters of confidence stated:

1. Should the Lieutenant Governor invite the Leader of the BC New Democrats to form anew government, this agreement will continue until the next scheduled election.

2. The Leader of the New Democrats will not request a dissolution of the Legislature during the term of this agreement, except following the defeat of a motion of confidence.

3. The BC Green MLAs will neither move, nor vote non-confidence during the term of this agreement, so long as the principle of good faith and no surprises has been observed.

4. Both parties will ensure that they have all their elected members at all sittings of the House as reasonable, and will vote in favour of the government on confidence motions.

5. While individual bills, including budget bills, will not be treated or designated as matters of confidence, the overall budgetary policy of the Government, including moving to the committee of supply, will be treated as matters of confidence.

6. BC Green support for policy and legislation which does not relate to confidence or supply is not subject to this agreement and will be decided on an issue by issue basis. (Source: *2017 Confidence and Supply Agreement between the BC Green Caucus and the BC New Democrat Caucus,* May, 2017.)

[17] A possibility in the nineteenth century but no longer likely to occur in Canada due to the development of formal political parties.

[18] *Saywell,* at page 158

[19] In the United Kingdom the Sovereign has not faced the prospect of exercising a personal discretion to appoint a succeeding Prime Minister since the appointment of Lord Home in 1963.

[20] *Memorandum on the Office of Lieutenant Governor of a Province: Its Constitutional Character and Functions,* Department of Justice, Queen's Printer and Controller of Stationary, Ottawa, 1955, at page 3 (afterwards *"Dept. of Justice 1955"*)

[21] *O Hood Phillips,* at page 763

[22] Here one may think of the traditional statement from the Norman French that was used in centuries past by Sovereign's of the United Kingdom or of England to veto legislation: "La Reyne s'avisera" (The Queen will think about it). In *The Queen's Other Realms: The Crown and Its Legacy in Australia, Canada and New Zealand*, Peter Boyce, The Federation Press, Sydney, 2008, the author, in discussing the sudden dismissal of the Prime Minister of Australia in 1975 notes that the Governor General hesitated to give a direct warning of the possibility of a dismissal to his Prime Minister because he feared the Prime Minister would seek the Governor General's dismissal by Queen Elizabeth II but the author goes on to say that ". . . in the years since the 1975 dismissal there has been some acknowledgement that the monarch would be unlikely to give instant effect to a prime minister's request . . ."

[23] Quoted in *Smith*, at page 59.

[24] An example of a Sovereign's representative assuming a political role in the governance of a realm beyond that provided for by the principles of responsible government occurred in India after the partition of the Indian subcontinent in 1947. Partition was accompanied by independence for two new realms, India and Pakistan which resulted in significant communal strife in both countries. The Governor General of India, Lord Mountbatten, chaired a government security committee during this emergency period in which the Indian Prime Minister, Ministers of the Crown, and Indian officials all played a subordinate role. In that example however, the Governor General was invited to assume his extraordinary role by the Indian Ministry, and therefore the outward facade of responsible government was maintained. Nevertheless, the actions of the Governor General of India on this occasion can be viewed as the adoption of extraordinary powers by a Sovereign's representative which was justified under the doctrine of necessity during a period of public disorder and national crisis. See *Mountbatten*, Philip Ziegler, Alfred A. Knopf, New York, 1985 at pages 432-433; *Freedom at Midnight*, Larry Collins and Dominique Lapierre, Avon Books, New York, 1976, at pages 364-366.

[25] at page 763

[26] at page 732

[27] *Lal*, at pages 200-208

[28] Quoted in *Lal*, at page 203.

[29] *Lal*, pages 210-212.

THE FEDERAL - PROVINCIAL MONARCHY

8.1   The Equality of the Federal and Provincial Sovereign

Canada is a federal state, a form of state organization that presented unique considerations for Crown law following confederation in 1867. The founders of the modern Canadian state preferred a centralist model for state governance, with a powerful Federal Government retaining links to the Crown and the Imperial Government in London, while Canada's provincial governments were intended to be local governments, devoting their attention to matters of purely local significance, and thus remaining subordinate to the Federal Government.

That view underwent a wholesale revision by the courts in a series of cases in the late nineteenth and early twentieth centuries. The result was a constitution which was not quasi-federal, as the founders undoubtedly intended, but one that was overtly federal. To a considerable degree, it was the monarchy which provided a basis for the courts, and particularly the Judicial Committee of the Privy Council in London, to interpret the Canadian constitution from this perspective. Ultimately, it was equality between the Crown in right of Canada and the Crown in right of the provinces that contributed to the achievement of a truly federal constitutional structure for Canada.

The seminal case concerning the equality of the Sovereign in her federal and provincial capacities was *The Queen v The Bank of Nova Scotia,* [1885] 11 SCR 1 (Canada, SC). The issue in that case was whether or not the Crown in right of Canada could assert a priority on recovery in relation to debts owed to the Crown under the Royal Prerogative, following the insolvency of a private bank. The Supreme Court of Canada held that the Crown in right of Canada possessed a prerogative right to assert priority in as full a measure as the Crown in right of a province on the basis of the indivisibility of the Crown within Canada.

However, the major development in the concept of the equality of the Crown in both its federal and in its provincial aspects had to await the judgment of the Judicial Committee in *The Liquidators of the Maritime Bank of Canada v The Receiver-General of New Brunswick,* [1892] AC 437 (Canada JC). In that case, the Maritime Bank had failed and at the time of its failure the Province of New Brunswick had funds on deposit with it. Although the *Bank of Nova Scotia* case had decided that the Federal Government could assert the Royal Prerogative of priority in respect of creditors claims, the issue in this case was whether the provinces possessed a like prerogative of priority in respect of debts owed to a province. The Judicial Committee, in affirming decisions of the Courts below, held that the Province of New Brunswick also possessed the Royal Prerogative of priority in respect of debts. But much what is more important, the Committee went further to explain the true character of the Lieutenant Governor as the Sovereign's Representative, stating:

> The act of the Governor-General and his Council in making the appointment [i.e., of a Lieutenant Governor] is, within the meaning of the statute, the act of the Crown; and a Lieutenant-Governor, when appointed, is as much the representative of Her Majesty for all purposes of provincial government as the Governor-General himself is for all purposes of Dominion government.[1]

With that judgment, the Judicial Committee of the Privy Council elevated the Lieutenant Governors to a status within the provinces as a representative of the Sovereign in Canada that was equal to that of the Governor General's status as the representative of the Sovereign in respect of the country as a whole. The *Maritime Bank* judgment affected the very nature of the constitutional framework of Canada as it had been understood up to that time. Henceforth, the provinces were to enjoy a coordinate status with the Federal Government in the system of constitutional monarchy established by the *Constitution Act, 1867*.

The final assault on early constitutional conceptions of the Governor General as the sole representative of the Sovereign in Canada came with the Judicial Committee's judgment in *Bonanza Creek Gold Mining Co. v The King* (1916), 26 DLR 273 (Canada JC). In that case it was held that the *Constitution Act, 1867*, distributed the grant of executive powers, including the Royal Prerogative, in the same way as the legislative powers were distributed under the 1867 constitution. Therefore, the Lieutenant Governors of the provinces were entitled to exercise the Royal Prerogative whenever the prerogative involved matters that fell under the exclusive grant of legislative authority to the provinces under the *Constitution Act, 1867*.

The equality of the Crown in Canada in both its federal and provincial aspects has been noted elsewhere in Commonwealth jurisprudence. In *Re Fedele*, [1988] LRC (Const) 879 (Cayman Islands, G.Ct.) Chief Justice Collett said in relation to the status of a Canadian Lieutenant Governor, or an Australian state Governor:

> In such self-governing but federated entities the respective governors or lieutenant-governors are the executive heads of their respective states or provinces and thus the sovereign's representative therein in relation to state or provincial matters, as contrasted with federal affairs: see *Liquidators of the Maritime Bank of Canada v Receiver General of New Brunswick*, [1892] AC 437.[2]

The effect of this equality of the Crown in both the federal and provincial levels of Canadian government can readily be seen in *Mellenger v New Brunswick Development Corporation*, [1971] 2 All ER 593 (England CA). There, the English Court of Appeal considered a claim of sovereign immunity asserted on behalf of the Province of New Brunswick in a suit brought against it in the United Kingdom. The judgment of Lord Denning relied on the *Maritime Bank* case in reaffirming the status of the provincial Crown as a sovereign entity stating:

> It was suggested by counsel for the plaintiffs that the Province of New Brunswick does not qualify as a sovereign state so as to invoke the doctrine of sovereign immunity. But the authorities show decisively to the contrary. The *British North America Act 1867* gave Canada a federal constitution. Under it the powers of government were divided between the dominion government and the provincial governments. Some of those powers were vested in the dominion government. The rest remained with the provincial governments. Each provincial government, within its own sphere, retained its independence and autonomy, directly under the Crown. The Crown is sovereign in New Brunswick for provincial powers, just as it is sovereign in Canada for dominion powers . . . It follows that the Province of New Brunswick is a sovereign state in its own right, and entitled, if it so wishes, to claim sovereign immunity.[3]

The *Mellenger* case is clear authority for the proposition that provincial sovereign immunity applies when the Crown in right of a province is impleaded in a foreign court. Domestically, the *Mellenger* case was applied by the Supreme Court of British Columbia in *Western Surety Co. v Elk Valley Logging Ltd.* (1985), 23 DLR (4th) 464 (British Columbia, SC), which held that the province of Alberta could assert a claim of sovereign immunity in the Courts of British Columbia.[4] Nevertheless, there is an alternative line of cases that suggests that sovereign immunity should not be applied in Canada domestically, as between the Crown in right of the provinces, and that only the principle of Crown immunity should be applied.[5] There has also been academic criticism of the concept of sovereign immunity being applied domestically, although the principle of the *Mellenger* case appears sound with respect to the position of the Crown in right of a province in the courts of foreign jurisdiction.[6]

The elevation of the provincial Lieutenant Governors to the status of equal representatives of the Sovereign distinguished them from the status of a quasi-federal governor in the new post-confederation constitutional structure. Thus, unique to federal states such as Canada, the Sovereign and her federal and provincial representatives fulfill the role of the executive head of government for each level of government, and give to each level of government an equality of status within the federation concomitant with the distribution of constitutional powers under the *Constitution Act, 1867*. By judicial interpretation, the status of the provinces was thus elevated to that of partners in confederation, rather than being relegated to a sub-sovereign element as the founders may have originally intended. In elevating the status of the provinces, the courts reinforced the regional, cultural, and linguistic distinctiveness of the Canadian provinces, and prevented the homogenizing effects of an all-powerful federal authority.[7]

The equality of the Sovereign in right of Canada and the Sovereign in right of a province was achieved over time through the evolution of constitutional case law. The equality of the Crown in both the federal and provincial spheres of constitutional jurisdiction did not, however, void the principle that in domestic law Canada's sovereign remains indivisible. The juristic person of the Sovereign is singular throughout the federation, even though the Sovereign acts in different federal and provincial capacities through her representatives, the Governor General of Canada, or the Lieutenant Governor of a province.

8.2   Provincial Communications with the Sovereign

Despite the equality in constitutional law between the Governor General and the Lieutenant Governors direct relations between the Sovereign and the provincial Lieutenant Governors are conducted through the Governor General of Canada via a federal Minister of the Crown. That procedure reflects the fact that under the *Constitution Act, 1867*, Canadian Lieutenant Governors are appointed not by the Sovereign, as in Australia, but rather are appointed by the Governor General of Canada acting on the advice of the Canadian Ministry. Therefore, a provincial Lieutenant Governor does not have the constitutional authority to communicate directly with the Sovereign except through a federal Minister of the Crown and the Governor General of Canada.

Whenever it is necessary for communications to occur between a provincial government and the Sovereign, those representations are transmitted from the Lieutenant Governor of the province via the responsible federal minister to the Governor General, who then transmits the provincial communication to the Sovereign via the Sovereign's Private Secretary. In this respect, the formal Canadian structures differ from that of Australia, which is the other major federation in Her Majesty's realms. In Australia, a state Governor is appointed by the Sovereign and direct communications between a state ministry and the Sovereign is possible, in certain circumstances.[8]

8.3   The First Ministers Conferences

Canadian federalism works best when there is cooperation between the Federal government and the governments of the various provinces. To facilitate cooperation at the highest levels of the federal and provincial governments Canadian federalism has invented the mechanism of First Ministers Conferences. The purpose of First Ministers Conferences is to allow the Prime Minister and the provincial and territorial Premiers to engage with one another on public issues that concern the federation. All of the meetings are held in private to enhance the prospects for cooperation and consensus among the first ministers.

Provincial first ministers initially met together in 1887 and 1892, while the first federal-provincial meeting of first ministers (then called dominion-provincial conferences) began in 1906. There has been a total of about 80 such meetings between 1906 and 2016. From 1927 until 1964 the meetings of first ministers were largely *ad hoc* meetings, with little or no systematic preparation but beginning in 1968 they have become much more planned affairs.

The Prime Minister of Canada chairs the meetings of first ministers, although that was not necessarily the case in the early days of such conferences, when it was usual for a provincial Premier to chair the conference where it was held in their province. The leaders of the government in the territories initially began to participate in first ministers conferences in the 1960's as members of the federal delegation but in the early 1970's they began to participate on their own as observers. In 1978, they were invited as participants and, from 1992, they have held the same status as the provincial Premiers.

The first ministers conferences are supported by an agency known as the Canadian Intergovernmental Conference Secretariat (CICS) which was established in 1973, and designated as a federal department in November of that year. Despite its organizational home as a constituent part of the federal public administration the CICS is actually an intergovernmental agency with its staff and budget coming from the federal, provincial and territorial governments. The CICS reports to Parliament through the President of the Queen's Privy Council for Canada. It has an appointed Secretary who serves as the deputy head of the agency and who has charge of the organization and its staff.

[1] at page 443

[2] at page 881

[3] at pages 595-596

[4] The cases of *Phillips (Guardian ad litem of) v Beary* (1994), 29 CPC (3d) 258 (British Columbia, SC); *Kaman v British Columbia* (1999), 242 AR 336 (Alberta, QB); and *Bouchard v J. L. Le Saux Ltée* (1984), 45 OR (2d) 792 (Ontario, SC Master) revd. [1984] 48 OR (2d) 799 (Ontario, HC), revd. and affd. (1986), 58 OR (2d) 124 (Ontario, CA) are of like effect.

[5] See *Weir v Lohr* (1967), 65 DLR (2d) 717 (Manitoba, QB) involving the issue of the recovery in Manitoba of hospital expenses that were incurred by Her Majesty in right of Saskatchewan pursuant to a public health scheme with respect to a Saskatchewan resident injured in Manitoba, who had contributed

to the Saskatchewan scheme through his provincial income taxes. Objection was taken to recovery by Her Majesty in right of Saskatchewan through the Manitoba Court of Queen's Bench upon the grounds that the revenue laws in a sovereign jurisdiction are not recognized by the courts of another sovereign jurisdiction. However, the Manitoba Queen's Bench held that the Crown in right of a Province is not a foreign sovereign in the courts of law within another province. Though *Weir v Lohr* preceded *Mellenger*, it was followed in *Commission Hydroélectrique de Quebec v Churchill Falls (Labrador) Corp.*, [1980] CA 203 (Quebec, CA) where Justice Monet stated at page 209 (translation): ". . . I am of the view that the rules of international law on immunity – which the jurisprudence of our tribunals recognizes – must not be confused with the principle of the sovereignty of Canadian provinces within their own jurisdiction". Of similar effect is *Athabasca Chipewyan First Nation v British Columbia* (2001) 199 DLR (4th) 452 (Alberta, CA). But see *Unifund Assurance Co. v Insurance Corporation of British Columbia*, [2003] 2 SCR 63 (Canada, SC) where the majority of the court, per Binnie, J. held that a " . . . territorial restriction is fundamental to our system of federalism in which each province is obliged to respect the sovereignty of the other provinces within their respective legislative spheres, and expects the same respect in return."

[6] Walker, Janet, "Interprovincial Sovereign Immunity Revisited", *Osgoode Hall Law Journal* 35.2 (1997) at pages 379-397.

[7] Despite the constitutional equality of the Crown in right of Canada and the Crown in right of a province the latter remain unable to legislatively bind the Crown in right of Canada, although the Crown in right of Canada may bind the Crown in right of a province through legislation.

[8] For a discussion of the Australian situation see "Responsible Government and the Divisibility of the Crown" Anne Twomey, *Legal Studies Research Paper No. 08/137*, November 2008, The University of Sydney Law School.

THE GOVERNOR GENERAL OF CANADA

The Sovereign of Canada is not a resident Sovereign, and in respect of most state business exercises powers in and for Canada through appointed representatives, the Governor General of Canada, and the Lieutenant Governors of the provinces. This chapter explores the role of the Governor General of Canada.

9.1   The Office of the Governor General of Canada

Although the office of the Governor General is referred to in several sections of the *Constitution Act, 1867*, it was not created as an office by that Act. Rather, the office was created by an exercise of the Royal Prerogative and although the office has now received constitutional protection in the Canadian constitution under section 41(a) of the *Constitution Act, 1982*, it continues to be founded upon those prerogative powers today. The current foundation of the office of the Governor General of Canada is contained in the *Letters Patent Constituting the Office of Governor General and Commander-in-Chief of Canada, September 8, 1947*, issued by King George VI.[1]

The Sovereign's power to create a high office of this nature through the exercise of the Royal Prerogative was confirmed by the High Court of New Zealand in *Burt v Governor General of New Zealand*, [1989] LRC 187 (New Zealand, HC) where Justice Grieg stated:

> The letters patent themselves are an exercise of the Sovereign's prerogative power in constituting on her behalf a Governor General and Commander-in-Chief in New Zealand and delegating to him such powers and authorities as Her Majesty thinks fit. That certainly is a power which only the Sovereign and no subject may exercise.[2]

Article 1 of the 1947 *Letters Patent* establishes the office of the Governor General of Canada, stating:

> We do hereby constitute, order, and declare that there shall be a Governor General and Commander-in-Chief in and over Canada, and appointments to the office of Governor General and Commander-in-Chief in and over Canada shall be made by Commission under Our Great Seal of Canada.

There follows a series of powers and provisions to clothe the office with its authority and responsibilities of which the most important is the second article, which confers broad powers upon the Governor General to act in name of the Sovereign:

> And We do hereby authorise and empower Our Governor General, with the advice of Our Privy Council for Canada or of any members thereof or individually, as the case requires, to exercise all powers and authorities lawfully belonging to Us in respect of Canada, and for greater certainty but not so as to restrict the generality of the foregoing to do and execute, in the manner aforesaid, all things that may belong to his office and to the trust that We have reposed in him according to the several powers and authorities granted or appointed him by virtue of *The British North America Acts 1867 to 1946* and the powers and authorities hereinafter conferred in these Letters Patent and in such Commission as may be issued to him under Our Great Seal of Canada and under such laws as are or may hereinafter be in force in Canada.

In addition to the broad conferral of power under Article II, the *Letters Patent, 1947* confer a series of specific powers on the Governor General including:

a) Power to keep and use the Great Seal of Canada (Article III);

b) Power to appoint ministers, other public officers (including diplomatic and consular officers) judges, justices, and commissioners (Article IV);

c) Power to suspend or remove any officer appointed by commission or warrant (Article V);

d) Power to summon, prorogue, and dissolve Parliament (Article VI);

e) Power to appoint deputies and delegate powers, functions and authorities of the Governor General to the deputies so appointed (Article VII);

f) Power to grant pardons to accomplices in an offence where they cooperate with the Crown authorities, to grant free pardons to offenders who have been convicted, to commute sentences of death in capital cases[3] and to remit any fine, penalty, or forfeiture imposed upon a person (Article XII); and

g) Power to issue *exequaturs*[4] to foreign consuls.

9.2   The Legal Effect of the Letters Patent, 1947

The effect of the *Letters Patent, 1947,* was to make it legally possible for the Governor General to exercise most of the Sovereign's powers in respect of Canada.[5] Under the *Letters Patent, 1947,* the Governor General is the Sovereign's representative for Canada as a whole, and as such acts as the representative in Canada of the Sovereign, who is the head of state of Canada.

Initially, following the *Letters Patent, 1947*, no changes were made to the class of executive matters which were submitted directly to the Sovereign for approval. Those matters involved many of the senior appointments in respect of the Federal Government. In fact, it was only in 1976 that the expanded powers conferred by the *Letters Patent, 1947*, began to be fully utilized by the Governor General.[6]

After the 1976 transfer of responsibilities from the Sovereign to the Governor General, new procedures were put in place to ensure that there would be consultations between the Prime Minister and the Governor General with respect to the most sensitive public appointments, such as the Chief and Puisne Justices of the Supreme and Federal Courts of Canada, the Chief of the Defence Staff, the Secretary to the Cabinet, Lieutenant Governors of the provinces and certain senior diplomatic appointments, as well as any patronage appointments of former cabinet ministers. For other appointments such as senators, deputy ministers and the heads of government agencies and the like, the Governor General would generally be informed in advance, although there would not necessarily be any formal consultation.[7]

The Sovereign of Canada possesses an international legal personality and it is through the Canadian Sovereign that Canada conducts its relations with foreign states. The new powers conferred by the *Letters Patent* of 1947 included the power to exercise full royal powers in respect of signing treaties and issuing letters of credence to ambassadors. It was a key objective of the Canadian Ministry in office in the late 1970s to enhance Canada's international profile by transferring certain diplomatic appointments from the Sovereign to the Governor General.

However, diplomatic appointments have always been a sensitive issue, since they may involve communications between one Sovereign and another. For this reason authority in respect of diplomatic appointments has long been retained by the Sovereign. When a consensus was reached between the Sovereign and her Canadian Ministry in 1977 on the transfer of functions to the Governor General, it was decided that Queen Elizabeth II would retain the power to issue Letters of Credence to Canadian Ambassadors, at least initially.[8] It was also decided that the Governor General would obtain responsibility for the appointments of High Commissioners to other Commonwealth countries.[9] As well, it was determined that the Governor General would approve the establishment, or severance, of diplomatic relations between Canada and foreign states, the appointment and recall of Canadian Ambassadors accredited to foreign states, and the Governor General would accept the Letters of Recall tendered by foreign ambassadors.[10]

9.3   Is the Governor General a Viceroy?

A question that sometimes arises is whether the effect of the *Letters Patent, 1947*, was to constitute the Governor General as the Queen's Viceroy for Canada. In the hierarchy of the British constitutional structure a Viceroy is a constitutional alter ego of the Sovereign, a perfect substitute for the monarch. As such, a Viceroy would stand in the place of the Sovereign in respect of a realm and would exercise all royal powers on behalf of the office of the Viceroy, rather than on behalf of the office of the Sovereign. In effect this type of appointment would mean that the fullest extent of the royal powers would be transferred to the Viceroy, who would thereafter exercise original jurisdiction, and not merely exercise power as the Queen's delegate.

Conversely, where a Sovereign's representative cannot be considered to be a Viceroy, the representative may only exercise the powers that are given to them by the Sovereign, either expressly or by necessary implication. Hence, they are considered to be an agent of the Sovereign. In *Musgrave v Pulido*, [1879] 5 AC 102 (Jamaica, JC) the Judicial Committee distinguished between a Viceroy as one "having the delegation of the whole of the royal power", and a Governor, whose "authority is derived from his commission, and limited to the powers thereby expressly or impliedly entrusted to him".[11] The same principle animates any analysis of the constitutional role of the Governor General of Canada today.

The appointment of a Viceroy is rare in British constitutional practice and the only two officials who are considered to have fulfilled that role are the Viceroy of India, prior to the independence of India and Pakistan, and the Lord Lieutenant of Ireland, before the establishment of the Irish Free State. Only the Viceroy of India actually bore the title of Viceroy. In India the title was granted by the Sovereign's commission and was also reflected in warrants of precedence, both of which constituted acts emanating from the Royal Prerogative.

The legal distinction between a Sovereign's representative who is constituted as a Viceroy and one who is not is that where the prerogative acts of a Sovereign's representative are challenged in a court of law a representative who is an agent of the Sovereign must show to the court that his or her actions are actions that the Sovereign's representative was permitted to undertake by the terms of the authority conferred upon them by the Sovereign. Where a Viceroy is concerned however, it would only be necessary to show to a court that the Sovereign herself had the authority to undertake the action that was impugned in a court of law.

In Canada, notwithstanding the fact that no Governor General has received the title of Viceroy in their commission, arguments have been presented both in favour and in opposition to the concept that the Governor General of Canada nevertheless possesses the status of a Viceroy. Much turns on the interpretation to be given to the words of the *Letters Patent, 1947,* and in particular Article II. While Article II does confer a very broad authority on the Governor General by the use of the words " . . . to exercise all powers and authorities lawfully belonging to Us in respect of Canada . . . " which seemingly implies a transfer of power, the article proceeds to state that notwithstanding the generality of those words the grant of power includes the powers conferred on the office of Governor General by the *Constitution Act, 1867* together with the powers conferred by these Letters Patent " . . . and in such Commission as may be issued to him under Our Great Seal of Canada . . . ". The inclusion of the Governor General's commission as a potential source of his or her authority is an indication that the *Letters Patent, 1947,* was not intended to be a complete transfer of royal powers to the Governor General because additional grants of royal authority could be made in the commission that is issued to the Governor General by the Sovereign.

Furthermore, there are restrictions in the *Letters Patent, 1947* on the Governor General that are incompatible with a true transfer of royal authority from the Sovereign to the Governor General. Article XIV provides that the Governor General is not to depart from the realm without the Sovereign's permission, although that permission is to be obtained through the office of the Prime Minister of Canada. Additionally, a proviso to Article VIII stipulates that the Governor General may not exercise their powers in and over Canada where they are absent from the realm for a period of time longer than thirty days, even with the Sovereign's permission to be absent. These limitations on the office of the Governor General are consistent with the grant of limited authority from the Sovereign to the Governor General, rather than a full transfer of royal authority.

Finally, the behaviour of constitutional actors is of some importance in determining whether the effect of the *Letters Patent, 1947,* was to constitute the Governor General of Canada a Viceroy. At the time of the issuance of the *Letters Patent, 1947,* Prime Minister Mackenzie King did not present them to the country as a significant break with established Canadian constitutional traditions. In fact, for many years after the issuance of the *Letters Patent, 1947,* the Sovereign continued to exercise some of the powers that were conferred on the Governor General of Canada by the *Letters Patent, 1947.*[12] The behaviour of the constitutional actors is relevant to this question. It seems on the basis of understandings and practices during the reigns of both King George VI and Queen Elizabeth II that the full powers of the Sovereign were not intended to be transferred to the Governor General but only those powers which both Sovereigns decided should be transferred within the framework of the *Letters Patent, 1947.* Thus, the intentions of the Sovereign can colour the actual words of the *Letters Patent, 1947,* and the powers of the Governor General must therefore be defined within the context of the relations between the Sovereign and their representative, as disclosed by the customs and practice associated with the exercise of the royal powers in Canada.[13]

A further indication that the Letters Patent, 1947, was not intended to transfer all of the royal powers to the Governor General is presented by the transfer, in 1988, of the Sovereign's power to grant heraldic armorial bearings to Canadians from the Sovereign acting through the College of Arms in England, to the Governor General of Canada. If the full powers of the Sovereign had indeed been transferred from the Sovereign to the Governor General by the Letters Patent, 1947, it would not have been necessary for the Sovereign to pass further letters patent in 1988 to transfer the power to grant heraldic arms to the office of the Governor General of Canada.

A true construction of the Letters Patent, 1947, leads to a conclusion that they were not sufficient to transfer the full royal authority of the Sovereign to the Governor General, and to thereby constitute the Governor General of Canada as a Viceroy. Rather, the effect of the Letters Patent, 1947, was to establish the office of the Governor General as an agent of the Sovereign, with the powers of the Sovereign that are necessary for the Governor General to faithfully discharge their office as the national representative of the Sovereign. This result is consistent with the view expressed by the Judicial Committee in the period prior to the de jure independence of Canada, in the case of Bonanza Creek Gold Mining Co. v The King, [1916] 1 AC 566 (Canada, JC) which held that on a proper construction:

> These and other provisions of the British North America Act appear to preserve prerogative rights of the Crown . . . and to negative the theory that the Governor General is made a viceroy in the full sense, and they point to the different conclusion that for the measure of his powers the words of his commission and of the statute itself must be looked to.[14]

Both section 10 of the Constitution Act, 1867, and section 2 of the Governor General's Act[15] also reinforce the view that the Governor General is not a Viceroy as in both provisions the role of the Governor General is essentially equated with the role of a "chief executive officer . . . carrying on the Government of Canada on behalf and in the name of the Sovereign. . . ".

What are the legal implications of the status of the Governor General as a delegate of the Sovereign? Firstly, as has been noted above, the Governor General, in the exercise of royal powers, including the powers of the prerogative, must be able to show that such powers adhere to him or her by reason of an express or implied grant in the Letters Patent, 1947, or by statute.

Secondly, as the delegate of the Sovereign, the Governor General may not further delegate the powers that have been devolved upon the Governor General by the Sovereign without offending the rule against the sub-delegation of powers which is expressed in the legal maxim *delagatus non potest delegare*. Thus, the Governor General may not delegate the powers of their office to another individual but must personally exercise the royal powers, unless delegation has been expressly permitted by the terms of the *Letters Patent, 1947*, or the Governor General's Commission. In *Lenoir v Ritchie*, [1879] 3 SCR 575 (Canada, SC) the Supreme Court held that: "The Governor General, alone, exercises the prerogative of the Queen in Her name in all cases in which such prerogatives can be exercised in the Dominion by any one else than Her Majesty herself".[16] This principle is also consistent with Article VII of the *Letters Patent, 1947*, which specifically empowered the Governor General to appoint deputies, and to delegate power to them. Under the interpretative principle of *expressio unius est exclusio alterius* the existence of a specific power to delegate powers to a third party negatives the existence of a general power to sub-delegate.

Finally, as the Governor General of Canada is not a Viceroy but rather remains an ordinary subject of the Sovereign who represents the Sovereign in Canada, and acts as her agent in respect of her constitutional obligations, the Governor General remains responsible under tort or criminal law for his or her personal actions which fall outside the scope of his or her commission from the Sovereign.

Although the Governor General is not constituted as a Viceroy in law, it is nevertheless customary in Canada to refer to the Governor General of Canada as a vice-regal representative. The use of the adjectival form of viceroy is a custom in Canada (and in other Commonwealth realms) and does not alter the law with respect to the legal status of the Governor General.

9.4   The Commander-in-Chief in and over Canada

After confederation in 1867 Imperial troops continued to garrison Canada until 1871, when they were withdrawn from Canada except for local garrisons at the major naval bases at Halifax, Nova Scotia, and Esquimalt, British Columbia. At Halifax a general officer continued to be appointed by the Imperial Government whose responsibilities reflected the continuing security obligations of the Imperial Government toward Canada. However, technological change and geopolitical developments, especially the British rapprochement with the United States around the turn of the twentieth century, and the growing challenge presented by the rise of Imperial Germany, prompted the Imperial Government to review the deployment of its forces. That review resulted in a decision to withdraw the remaining garrison forces in Halifax and Esquimalt, and turn the bases over to the Federal Government. As a consequence, a British general officer would no longer be present in Canada. The Governor General, however, continued to be drawn from the British nobility and at that time the Governor

General continued to exercise a dual function as both an officer of the Imperial Government and an officer of the Federal Government. It was natural, therefore, for the Imperial Government to assign military commander-in-chief responsibilities to the Governor General when the senior British general was withdrawn in 1904, in order to reassure the Canadian public that the Imperial Government was not wholly withdrawing from its responsibilities with respect to Canada and its defences.

Thus, the Governor General's title of Commander-in-Chief in and over Canada began to date from the *Militia Act* of 1904 which declared that "the Command-in-Chief of the Militia is declared to continue and be vested in the King, *and shall be administered by His Majesty or by the Governor General as his representative*". That was followed in 1905 by a revision to the *Letters Patent, 1905*, constituting the office of Governor General to describe the office as the "Governor General and Commander-in-Chief". The title went through a number of iterations with specific reference to the militia as well as the naval and air forces. In the *Letters Patent, 1931*, it became "Governor General and Commander-in-Chief in and over Our Dominion of Canada" and then finally in the *Letters Patent, 1947*, the title took on its current form of "Governor General and Commander-in-Chief in and over Canada".[17] The words "in and over Canada" are taken from the original commissions issued to the Governors General following confederation but are merely descriptive, and are not considered to be words of limitation.

The title of Commander-in-Chief is intended to better represent the function of the Crown in relation to the military forces and thus to emphasize the control of the military forces of the Crown by the civil government. The title of Commander-in-Chief is not a source of power for the Governor General. The actual power over the armed forces flows from the Royal Prerogative which is delegated to the Governor General under the broad powers conferred by Article II of the *Letters Patent, 1947*. Through the prerogative control of the armed forces the Sovereign, and hence the Governor General under the authority conferred by the Sovereign in the *Letters Patent, 1947*, may issue orders, including operational orders, to the personnel of the Canadian Forces. However, such orders that are given are based on constitutional advice from the Canadian Ministry appointed to govern the realm in accordance with the principles of responsible government, and represent political decisions made in relation to the use of the armed forces. That advice invariably incorporates professional military advice from military leaders where actual deployment decisions are involved. The Governor General is almost always a civilian appointee and does not take personal command of any part of the Canadian Forces. All purely military questions are left to the professional military staffs to implement as the military alone has the knowledge and skill to execute military missions.

As a practical matter, the duties of the Governor General of Canada in relation to the armed forces include the appointment of the Chief of Defence Staff, who is the senior military officer in the Canadian Forces, the issuance of commissions to officers, the awarding of military honours, the approval of new military heraldic badges and symbolism, and the presentation of colours to units of the armed forces. The Governor General also approves recommendations from the Minister of National Defence for the appointment of members of the Royal Family (other than the Sovereign) as colonel-in-chief of Canadian regiments. The Governor General undertakes visits to military personnel stationed at home and abroad and represents the Crown at annual Remembrance Day ceremonies in Ottawa on November 11th of each year. To better reflect the Governor General's role with respect to the military a special form of military dress has been created for the Governors General, denoting their special rank of Commander-in-Chief.

9.5   The Governor General as a Corporation Sole

By section 2 of the *Governor General's Act,* the Governor General is constituted a corporation sole. In this respect, the Governor General possesses a like capacity as the Sovereign, who is a corporation sole by virtue of the common law. The effect of this characterization is to ensure that the office of the Governor General is perpetual notwithstanding that the incumbent, as a natural person, holds office only for a limited term of years. The *Governor General's Act* also provides that any bond, recognizance or other instrument of a public nature shall be taken to and sued upon by the Governor General's name of office and will not vest in the personal representatives of either the Governor General or the Administrator of Canada, in whose name they were taken.

9.6   The Evolution of the Office of Governor General

Following Confederation in 1867 a commission was issued by the Sovereign, in the form of letters patent, to both establish the office of Governor General post-confederation,[18] and to appoint a person to that office. Each of the first two succeeding Governors General had their office and appointment defined and confirmed by a commission in the form of letters patent. This proved to be inconvenient because each time a new appointment was made the former letters patent had to be revoked and new letters patent issued to reestablish the office of the Governor General and to make the new appointment.

The first three commissions also incorporated within the documents the *Royal Instructions* to the Governor General.[19] *Royal Instructions* told the Governor General how to conduct his office and defined those matters that the Imperial Government considered to go beyond the affairs of the federation and to affect wider imperial interests. For those matters the Governor General was required to reserve for the signification of the Queen's pleasure eight classes of bills enacted by the Canadian Parliament.[20] In the early years following confederation even such mundane matters as bills of divorce were considered to exceed the concerns of the federation, and were reserved for the consideration of Queen Victoria and the Imperial Privy Council in London.

A solution was needed to avoid the inconvenience of issuing a new commission reestablishing the office of the Governor General each time there was a new appointment. The solution adopted by the Imperial Government was to discontinue the practice of reconstituting the office of Governor General in each commission issued for an appointment to that office. Instead, by letters patent dated October 5, 1878,[21] the Sovereign permanently constituted the post-confederation office of Governor General and subsequent appointments to that office were made by a separate commission.[22] The *Letters Patent, 1878*, provided for the constitution of the office of Governor General of Canada and the conferral of its powers. The major features of the *Letters Patent, 1878*, included the following:

a) Constitution of the office of Governor General of Canada;

b) Provision for appointments to the office by commission;

c) Conferral of authority upon the Governor General to act pursuant to statutory authority, and by way of the prerogative powers;

d) Grant of the custody of the Great Seal of Canada to the Governor General;

e) Conferral of authority to appoint judges and other officers necessary for the administration of justice;

f) Provision for the Governor General to remove anyone appointed to an office by the Crown;

g) Authorization for the Governor General to summon, prorogue, or dissolve Parliament;

h) Empowerment of the Governor General to appoint deputies;

i) Provision for the absence, incapacity, removal, or death of the Governor General by vesting the executive authority in an official styled the Lieutenant Governor of Canada, or failing any appointment to that office, to an Administrator of the government or, failing an appointment to that office, for the government to be administered by the senior officer in command of the imperial troops in the country;

j) A charge to all public officers to obey and assist the Governor General; and

k) Reservation to the Sovereign of the power to alter or vary the letters patent.[23]

Furthermore, the constraints imposed by the early *Royal Instructions* had caused a great deal of frustration for the first two Canadian ministries, leading Edward Blake, the Minister of Justice in Prime Minister Alexander Mackenzie's cabinet, to persuade the Imperial Government to alter the arrangements contained in the *Royal Instructions*. Blake used the argument that the breadth of the Governor General's instructions to reserve federal bills for review and approval by the Queen exceeded the powers of the Sovereign in the United Kingdom under the principles of responsible government, and thus implied that there was a difference in character between responsible government in Canada and responsible government in the United Kingdom.[24] The Imperial Government acceded to the views advanced by Edward Blake and separate *Royal Instructions* began to be issued in 1878. The new *Royal Instructions* omitted the requirement that classes of legislation be reserved for the signification of the Queen's pleasure, thus eliminating a significant aspect of colonial status.[25]

The new *Royal Instructions*, dated October 5, 1878, authorized or instructed the Governor General to perform the following duties in connection with their office:

a) The publication of the Governor General's Commission,

b) The oaths to be taken by the Governor General upon the assumption of office,

c) The oaths which may be administered by the Governor General,

d) Requirements that the Governor General communicate any imperial instructions to the Canadian Government,

e) Requirements that laws reserved for the signification of Her Majesty's pleasure be abstracted in the margins with notes concerning the reasons why the laws were proposed in the first place, and any other explanations, together with the pertinent journals and minutes of Parliament,

f) Matters concerning the grant of pardons and the circumstances under which banishment from the realm was permissible, and

g) Instructing the Governor General not to leave the country without the Queen's permission, as evidenced by a document under her sign manual or signet, or through the permission of an imperial minister.

Blake's action in seeking changes to the *Royal Instructions* greatly enhanced the legislative power of the Canadian Parliament and afterwards only a few specific bills became the subject of imperial scrutiny. Whenever imperial concerns subsequently developed with respect to Canadian legislation, it was often possible for negotiations to reconcile the imperial and national positions without the draconian remedy of reservation and disallowance. One example concerned a dispute over the Canadian *Copyright Act* of 1889, which was given Royal Assent but never proclaimed as a result of negotiations with the Imperial Government.[26] After 1878, only one bill was reserved by a Governor General for consideration by the government in London.[27]

Although the *Letters Patent, 1878,* were subsequently revoked and reissued on June 15, 1905, these rules remained, in substance, the constitutional exposition of the role and responsibilities of the Governor General of Canada throughout the late nineteenth and early twentieth centuries. The only change which occurred between the 1878 version and the 1905 version was the deletion in the 1905 version of references to the commander of the imperial forces assuming the role of the Administrator of Canada in the event that the Governor General was unavailable and no other person had been appointed as Administrator.[28] Although the imperial troops were largely withdrawn from Canada by 1871, imperial garrisons had remained at Halifax and Esquimalt until 1905 to provide security for the imperial naval bases. The senior imperial army officer was always located at Halifax. The imperial troops were withdrawn from the naval bases in 1905,[29] and shortly afterwards responsibility for the fortresses at Halifax and Esquimalt were transferred from the Imperial Government to the Federal Government, necessitating the change to the letters patent.

Significant changes to the office of the Governor General came about only in 1926, following the constitutional crisis of that year. Prime Minister Mackenzie King desired that the role and responsibilities of the Governors General be reassessed at the Commonwealth Conference. That conference resulted in the Balfour Declaration, which formalized the modernization of the office of Governor General throughout the Commonwealth, by abolishing the functions of the Governor General as an imperial officer, and by confirming that each realm's Governor General was the personal representative of the Sovereign in the realm, and was not a representative of the Imperial Government.

Perhaps out of a lingering concern that a loss of internal prestige would result from the abolition of the Governor General's functions as an imperial officer, the conference suggested that a Governor General should receive important documents and be kept fully informed of Cabinet affairs in their realm, in the same manner as would the King in respect of the affairs of the Government of the United Kingdom.[30]

The Balfour Declaration itself did not lead to any immediate change to the *Letters Patent, 1905*. New Letters Patent were not issued until March 23, 1931. One significant change between the 1905 version and the 1931 version was that, in the latter version, the Governor General could only leave Canada with the permission of the Sovereign, or the Canadian Prime Minister, rather than by leave of the Sovereign, or a Minister of the Crown in the Imperial Government. That change, predating the *Statute of Westminster, 1931*, reflected the new constitutional position of the Governor General following the Balfour Declaration and the results of the Imperial Conference of 1930.

Amending letters patent to the constitution of the office of the Governor General dated September 25, 1935, provided that the Governor General could continue to exercise the powers of their office while lawfully outside of Canada during visits to foreign states, provided that the Governor General's absence did not exceed one month in duration.

On September 8, 1947, a new *Letters Patent Constituting the Office of Governor General of Canada* was issued by King George VI, with effect from October 1, 1947. The new letters patent consolidated the changes that had taken place over time in previous letters patent, and included the relevant portions of the former *Royal Instructions*. After the promulgation of the *Letters Patent, 1947*, *Royal Instructions* ceased to be issued to Canadian Governors General and that constitutional instrument thus became obsolete at the federal level of government in Canada.

The powers previously exercised by the Governor General were confirmed in the 1947 version and were further expanded by the conferral of authority on the Governor General to enter into treaties in head of state form, obviating the necessity of having a treaty in head of state form approved by the Sovereign in London. The *Letters Patent, 1947*, have not undergone any further substantive changes. However, in 1952, the *Letters Patent, 1947*, were reissued because the 1947 version did not provide a means for a voluntary resignation from office by Lord Alexander of Tunis, who desired to do so.[31] The powers of the Governor General of Canada have been augmented by a subsequent delegation of authority from the Sovereign to the Governor General with respect to heraldry that was made through the issuance of separate *Letters Patent, 1988*, by Queen Elizabeth II.[32]

Neither the *Letters Patent, 1947*, nor the heraldic *Letters Patent, 1988*, have been formally entrenched in the *Constitution of Canada* by inclusion in the schedule to the *Constitution Act, 1982*, which defines the *Constitution of Canada* but the effect of section 41(a) of the *Constitution Act, 1982*, nevertheless affords constitutional protection to the office of the Governor General equivalent to entrenching the letters patent within the constitution. Section 41(a) provides that no change can be made to the office of the Governor General without the consent of the Senate and the House of Commons, as well as the consent of each of the provincial legislatures. Thus, an attempt by a Canadian Ministry to advise the Sovereign to issue new letters patent that would reduce or constrain the powers of the Governor General of Canada would constitute a change to the office of Governor General within the meaning of section 41(a) of the *Constitution Act, 1982*. As such, a change or reduction in the powers of the office of the Governor General would trigger the application of the unanimity amending formula provided for within section 41(a) of the *Constitution Act, 1982*, requiring the consent of both houses of Parliament and the legislature of each province.

9.7   The Governor General as an Imperial Officer

In historical terms, the Governor General possessed two functions, those of an imperial officer, and those of the Sovereign's representative. The powers of the office were divided between those two functions. In the first capacity the Governor General was charged with the responsibility of ensuring that no actions taken by Canadian authorities infringed upon the prerogatives or obligations of the Imperial Government in London. From 1867 until the end of the first quarter of the twentieth century, the Governor General was primarily perceived by Canadian statesman to act in the capacity of an imperial officer.

Increasingly however, Canadian governments sought to tender advice to the Sovereign without the intermediary of the Imperial Government. With the more prominent international role played by Canada as a result of its efforts in the First World War, and at the subsequent Versailles treaty negotiations, that effort was accelerated. Thus, the stage was set for the most significant change in the history of constitutional relations in the Empire. At the Imperial conference of 1926, which was convened in the aftermath of the 1926 Canadian constitutional crisis, the self-governing dominions obtained the Balfour Declaration, in which the Imperial Government pledged to respect the self-governing dominions as:

> . . . autonomous Communities within the British Empire, equal in status, in no way subordinate one to another in any aspect of their domestic or external affairs, though united by a common allegiance to the Crown, and freely associated as members of the British Commonwealth.[46]

As a consequence, it was decided that the Governors General would act solely as the representative of the Sovereign and would no longer act as the representatives of the Imperial Government.[47] From that point in time the Governor General of Canada ceased to be an imperial officer. The Imperial conference was clear about the change in status of the Governor General, stating:

> . . . it is an essential consequence of the equality of status existing among members of the British Commonwealth of Nations that the Governor-General of a Dominion is the representative of the Crown, holding in all essential respects, the same position in relation to the administration of public affairs in the Dominion as is held by His Majesty the King in Great Britain and that he is not the representative

or agent of His Majesty's Government in Great Britain or any department of that Government.[48]

In Canada, this change in status was not reflected in changes to the text of the *Constitution Act, 1867*. Even today, certain powers exercised by the Governor General under the *Constitution Act, 1867*, primarily relate to the duties of the Governor General as an imperial officer. Included within those powers is the power to disallow bills or reserve them for the signification of Her Majesty's pleasure. Section 55 of the statute states:

> Where a Bill passed by the Houses of Parliament is presented to the Governor-General for the Queen's Assent, he shall declare, according to his discretion, but subject to the Provisions of this Act and to Her Majesty's Instructions, either that he assents thereto in the Queen's Name, or that he withholds the Queen's Assent, or that he reserves the Bill for the Signification of the Queen's Pleasure.

Section 57 of the constitution was enacted in relation to reservations and it stipulates as follows:

> A bill reserved for the Signification of the Queen's Pleasure shall not have any Force unless and until within Two Years from the day on which it was presented to the Governor-General for the Queen's Assent, the Governor-General signifies, by Speech or Message to each of the Houses of Parliament or by Proclamation, that it has received the assent of the Queen in Council.
>
> An entry of every such Speech, Message or Proclamation shall be made in the Journal of each House, and a Duplicate thereof duly attested shall be delivered to the proper officer to be kept among the Records of Canada.

Those powers are now obsolete but have been retained in the *Constitution Act, 1867*, because they constitute, with minor adjustments made pursuant to Section 90 of the Act, the powers by which the Governor General may disallow, or by which a Lieutenant Governor of a province may reserve, any measure enacted by the legislatures of the provinces. As such, they constitute an emergency legal check on the powers of the provinces, which no federal ministry appears anxious to surrender.

With respect to the power of reservation of federal bills for the signification of the Queen's pleasure, it should be recalled that although that power continues to exist as a matter of law, the provision itself indicates that the power to grant assent is vested in the British government, through the use of the phrase "the Queen in Council". Since 1926, the process which commenced with the Balfour Declaration and continued with the Imperial conference of 1930, and the subsequent enactments of the *Statute of Westminster, 1931*, and the *Canada Act, 1982*, has severed the former constitutional links between the parliaments of Canada and of the United Kingdom. As a result, the reservation power with respect to federal bills is now obsolete and, by constitutional convention, neither the Governor General nor the Sovereign in Right of the United Kingdom may exercise any of the reservation powers remaining in Section 57 of the *Constitution Act, 1867*, with respect to enactments of the Parliament of Canada.

9.8   *The Governor General as the Sovereign's Representative*

The Governor General's primary constitutional duty in the modern context is to act as the Sovereign's representative in Canada, by exercising the powers conferred upon the office of the Governor General by the *Constitution of Canada*, federal statutes, and the Royal Prerogative. In addition, the Governor General is responsible for keeping the Sovereign informed of Canadian affairs by means of private letters.[49]

The Governor General performs many symbolic functions on behalf of the Sovereign. Efforts have been made in the contemporary period to rid the office of much of its former imperial pomp and circumstance, by retiring the vice-regal civil uniform formerly worn by all Governors General and the Governor General's private rail cars.[63] This process was part of a wide-ranging effort to "Canadianize" the monarchy and to recast it into a mould more consistent with the contemporary Canadian national image. Today, public ceremonies surrounding the office of the Governor General are more reserved than similar ceremonies in many other monarchical states.

The most important public ceremonies at which the Governor General participates involve Parliament, where the Governor General is the representative of the Sovereign. The Governor General appears in Parliament for the opening of Parliament, and the reading of the Speech from the Throne, which sets out the policy and legislative objectives of the government in the ensuing session of Parliament. The speech is written for the Governor General by the Canadian Ministry, and the Governor General plays no part in its actual creation. In addition, the Governor General, usually acting through a deputy but sometimes in person, occasionally appears in Parliament to grant Royal Assent to bills passed by the House of Commons and the Senate.

In recognition of Canadian sovereignty, the Governor General receives foreign heads of state and diplomatic representatives, and makes state visits to foreign countries.[64] The Governor General participates in military ceremonies in his or her capacity as Commander-in-Chief in and over Canada.

Recognition of excellence is an important modern function of the Governor General. As the representative of the Sovereign, who is the fount of honour, the Governor General makes awards of orders of state, decorations, medals, and commendations to deserving Canadians and others. The Governor General also provides trophies and prizes for various aspects of academic, literary, volunteering and sporting life in Canada.[65]

National unity is promoted by the Governor General's attendance and participation at important public ceremonies such as Canada Day, Remembrance Day, and important regional holidays, as well as by travel throughout Canada. National identity is closely related to national unity and involves the exercise of the Crown's heraldic functions, and the Governor General's patronage of social, artistic, cultural, and aboriginal events.

9.9   The Governor General and the Executive

The powers of the Governor General may be said to arise by virtue of the office in accordance with the written constitution (the *Constitution Acts 1867-1982*) as well as other constitutional legislation, the Balfour Declaration, the *Statute of Westminster, 1931*, the *Seals Act*, and the *Letters Patent Constituting the Office of Governor General of Canada, 1947*, and the *Letters Patent, 1988* (Heraldry).[50] In Canadian statecraft many powers are delegated in legislation enacted by Parliament to the Governor General acting by and with the advice of the Queen's Privy Council for Canada, which for all practical purposes will be a committee of Ministers of the Crown constituted from among the Canadian Ministry currently holding office. The Governor General will validate the policy actions of the executive that are implemented through regulations and other statutory instruments. In addition, the Governor General will also implement executive actions taken by the Canadian Ministry through the Royal Prerogative.

In exercising any of these powers the Governor General must, by constitutional convention, act in accordance with the advice the Governor General receives from his or her constitutional advisors, the members of the Queen's Privy Council for Canada. Any exercise of the Governor General's powers, with the exception of the reserve powers, without such advice would be a violation of constitutional convention and would be unconstitutional even if, as a matter of law alone, the actions of the Governor General could be upheld as actions that were within the legal powers of the Governor General. Thus, the participation of the Governor General in the executive government of the country is both a necessary function but only formal requirement under the principles of responsible government.

The Governor General is entitled to request information from ministers to enable the Governor General to understand actions that they are being advised to take by the Canadian Ministry, and to enable the Governor General to exercise his or her constitutional right to be consulted by the Canadian Ministry, to encourage the ministry, and to warn the ministry.

9.10   The Governor General and Royal Assent in Parliament

The Parliament of Canada consists of the Sovereign, the Senate, and the House of Commons and thus the Sovereign is an essential component of Parliament. No legislation can be enacted without the positive action of all three components of the Parliament. The function of the Crown is to formally approve the legislation that has been passed by the two houses of Parliament, the House of Commons and the Senate of Canada, according to the rules of those bodies. The granting by the Governor General of the Sovereign's approval to legislation that has been passed by the House of Commons and the Senate of Canada is known as Royal Assent. It is the most important royal function that is exercised in Parliament by the Governor General.

In Canada, at the federal level, the ceremony of Royal Assent for legislation passed by the House of Commons and the Senate is held in the Senate Chamber of the Parliament of Canada in respect of federal bills. At the federal level the ceremony is arranged under the authority of a Minister of the Crown, formerly the President of the Privy Council but now a responsibility of the Government House Leader. The ceremony is held before adjournment, prorogation, or the dissolution of Parliament, but it may also be held on other occasions if the enactment of a statute is urgently required or if a public assent to a bill would be symbolically important. At the ceremony itself, a clerk reads out the name of a Bill to the Governor General, or his or her deputy, who then indicates Royal Assent to the Bill by a nod of their head. On very rare occasions during royal visits to Canada the Sovereign has participated in the Royal Assent ceremony but normally the Royal Assent ceremony has been conducted by the Governor General or, more frequently, by a Deputy of the Governor General, usually one of the Puisne Justices of the Supreme Court of Canada.[51]

Owing to the inconvenience of preparing and conducting the Royal Assent ceremony, a new procedure has been created for the expression of Royal Assent. Under the *Royal Assent Act*[52] Royal Assent to legislation may be expressed in the traditional manner or by means of a written declaration of the Governor General.[53] Where the written declaration method is used, the written declaration may be witnessed by one or more members of a house of Parliament[54]. The declaration of the Governor General must be expressed separately to the Speaker of each house of Parliament.[55] The practice in the Senate is for the Speaker of the Senate to read the Governor General's declaration to the assembled Senators. Royal Assent is deemed to have been given on the date that both houses of Parliament are notified of the written declaration by the Governor General.[56]

The *Royal Assent Act* does seek to preserve tradition however, by specifying in section 3 that the traditional ceremony for Royal Assent is to continue to be used twice in each calendar year, the first occasion being for the approval of "the first bill of the session appropriating sums for the public service of Canada based upon main or supplementary estimates".[57] However, where the traditional method is not used no act of Royal Assent is invalidated by reason of that failure.[58] The purpose of the *Royal Assent Act* was to increase the efficiency of the law-making process, reduce inconveniences, and modernize the legislative process while maintaining the traditional method of Royal Assent for limited purposes. This legislation has brought Canada's legislative procedures in line with the practices generally followed in other Commonwealth realms.

Royal Assent for legislation passed by the House of Commons and Senate should be granted before a dissolution of Parliament. The normal constitutional procedure is to seek Royal Assent to bills passed by the current Parliament, which includes the House of Commons, the Senate, and the Sovereign. Where that procedure is not followed, and the House of Commons has been dissolved, or a new House has been constituted by election and it is then sought to grant Royal Assent to legislation passed in a previous Parliament, the views of the new House of Commons will not have been made known, and therefore the Sovereign may not be constitutionally empowered to enact legislation "by and with the advice and consent of the House of Commons and Senate of Canada", as every federal statute asserts in every enacting clause.

The powers of the Sovereign and of the Governor General to veto a bill in the exercise of the Royal Prerogative are now purely nominal. By convention, the Sovereign has ceased to exercise a personal veto over legislation. No British Sovereign has attempted to disallow a bill passed by Parliament since the reign of Queen Anne, who vetoed a bill in the British Parliament in the early years of the eighteenth century. Conventional limitations on the exercise of the Sovereign's powers to veto legislation entered into the Canadian constitution through the preamble to the *Constitution Act, 1867*. In Canada, the Sovereign and the Governor General are now considered to be restricted by constitutional convention from withholding Royal Assent to bills passed by both houses of Parliament.

Nevertheless, purely as a matter of law, and ignoring for the moment the question of constitutional convention, it remains lawful for the Governor General to withhold Royal Assent from bills passed by Parliament in the exercise of the Royal Prerogative. However, when the subject is examined from the perspective of constitutional convention it is clear that that the Crown has no discretion to withhold Royal Assent to a bill that has been passed by the House of Commons and the Senate of Canada except in one narrow circumstance. The only circumstance where constitutional convention would permit the Governor General to exercise their legal power to withhold Royal Assent is in respect of a situation where formal constitutional advice to veto legislation is received by the Governor General from the Queen's Privy Council for Canada. Although it is difficult to imagine the circumstances in which that might occur, one possibility could be if a Canadian Ministry was suddenly replaced as a result of the loss of confidence of the House of Commons. In that event there might arise a situation where legislation has passed both the Commons and the Senate but in respect of which a new Canadian Ministry, formed from the opposition, is unable to accept the legislation for political reasons. The new ministry, acting through the Privy Council, could then advise the Governor General to deny Royal Assent. A veto under those circumstances would represent a constitutional action on the part of the Governor General because it would be consistent with the principles of responsible government. It is more likely however, that a newly-formed government in that situation would allow the bill to be given Royal Assent and then seek to repeal the legislation, rather than to use the formal procedures of a veto by the Crown.

The question of whether the Governor General can be restrained from granting Royal Assent by prerogative remedies such as an injunction has not been conclusively determined under Canadian law. Nevertheless, judicial authority exists in Australia to support the view that injunction may lie against officers whose responsibility it is to present bills to a State Governor for Royal Assent, where it is alleged that manner and form requirements respecting the enactment of ordinary legislation have not been complied with; *Eastgate v Rozzoli* (1990), 20 NSWLR 188 (New South Wales, CA).[59] A manner and form requirement is a procedural restriction applied to proposals to change existing legislation. An example would be a requirement in a statute that any repeal of the statute must be passed by a two-thirds majority of the legislative body instead of a simple majority. Manner and form requirements in legislation operate as a gloss on the doctrine of parliamentary sovereignty, which maintains that a sovereign Parliament can never be bound by a law enacted in a previously constituted Parliament. A manner and form requirement is in effect a method of entrenching legislation. In Canadian legislative practice a manner and form requirements in legislation are rare.[60] In practice, manner and form requirements have been more prominent in the context of legislative bodies that have limited sovereignty, such as a colonial legislature; see *Rediffusion (Hong Kong) Ltd. v Attorney General of Hong Kong*, [1970] AC 1136 (Hong Kong, JC).[61] Clarification of the ability of the courts to restrain Royal Assent in Canada must await further judicial scrutiny.

Parliament cannot remove the power of the Governor General to exercise the Royal Prerogative to grant (or in the very limited circumstances described above, to deny) Royal Assent to legislation as that would involve a change to the offices of the Queen, the Governor General, or the Lieutenant Governor of a province, and thereby engage the amending formula in section 41(a) of the *Constitution Act 1982*, which requires the unanimous consent of the Senate, the

House of Commons, and the legislature of each province in order to perfect such a change.[62]

9.11   Appointment, Installation and Dismissal

The Governor General is the only representative of the Sovereign in Canada who holds a commission issued under the personal authority of the Sovereign.[33] Since the 1890's, the Imperial Government began to consult with local governments concerning the choice of a governor.[34] When Eire (the Irish Free State established as a dominion in 1922) obtained the right to reverse this process, that is, to submit its own candidate to London for approval, it was only a matter of time before that right was extended to the other realms of the Commonwealth.[35] In 1930, Canada engaged in the process of selecting Lord Bessborough as Governor General, and the appointment of Lord Tweedsmuir, in 1935, was made solely on the recommendation of the Canadian Ministry.[36]

Thus, from 1935, all persons appointed to the office of Governor General of Canada have been appointed on the direct recommendation of the Canadian Prime Minister to the Sovereign. The modern practice does not require that other ministers or the leader of the opposition be consulted on the appointment.[37] In 2012 the Harper Ministry established an Advisory Committee on Vice-Regal Appointments to provide advice to the Prime Minister of Canada on the appointments of the Governor General, the Lieutenant Governors of the provinces and the Commissioners of the northern territories.[38] The Advisory Committee on Vice-Regal Appointments consists of the Canadian Secretary to the Queen as the Chair of the committee together with two permanent appointees representing the two linguistic components of the country, Anglophones and Francophones, who serve for a term of six years. In addition, where the pending appointment is of a Lieutenant Governor, or a territorial Commissioner, two appointments of up to six months in duration may be made from among the residents of the jurisdiction where the appointment is to be made. The recommendations of the committee are made to the Prime Minister who makes the selection decision and recommends the appointment (to the Sovereign, in the case of the appointment of a Governor General, and to the Governor General with respect to the other appointments).

Historically, appointments to the office of the Governor General of Canada were made from amongst noblemen of first France and later Britain. During the long colonial period the only Canadian to serve in the office of Governor General, was Pierre de Rigaud, Marquis de Vaudreuil, who was the Governor General during the period which saw the military invasion and conquest of Canada by the British in the Seven Years War. In the modern period, Canadians began to be appointed to the office of the Governor General beginning with the appointment of Vincent Massey in 1952. Since then, only Canadian citizens have been appointed to the office, and it has become a constitutional custom to alternately appoint Anglophones and Francophones to the office of the Governor General in order to foster national unity. There are no statutory qualifications for the office of Governor General.

As in other Commonwealth realms, the validity of a Governor General's appointment, and the nature of the powers of the appointee must be determined under the constitution and the general laws of each particular realm; *Re Nori's Application*, [1989] LRC (Const) 10 (Solomon Islands, HC). In Canada, this means that one must look to the *Letters Patent, 1947*, the Governor General's Commission of Appointment issued by authority of the Sovereign, and the powers vested in the Governor General under the *Constitution Acts 1867 – 1982*, as well as the applicable common law principles in order to determine whether particular acts of the Governor General are valid in law.

The installation of a Governor General takes place in the Senate of the Parliament of Canada and is broadcast to the nation. Important dignitaries invited to attend the ceremony include members of the Senate and House of Commons, the Chief Justice of Canada, the Puisne Justices of the Supreme Court, military officers, the diplomatic corps, and other notables.

There is no specific form of ceremony for the installation that is fixed by law but normally a dignified ceremony is conducted in the Senate Chamber of the Parliament building in Ottawa and it may include special flourishes, especially musical performances, requested by the incoming Governor General. Under the former traditional practice, the departing Governor General did not attend the installation ceremony for their successor and therefore, by longstanding constitutional custom, the Chief Justice of Canada has always represented the Sovereign in the capacity of a Deputy of the Governor General at the installation ceremony.[39] Elements that are common to the ceremony as it has been performed in recent years include a ceremonial entry into the Senate Chamber of the Parliament, a welcome on behalf of the aboriginal peoples of Canada, the playing of the Royal Anthem and the National Anthem, the reading of the Sovereign's Commission and the swearing by the Governor General-Designate of three oaths, the oath of allegiance to the Sovereign, the oath of office as Governor General and Commander in Chief in and over Canada, and the oath of the Keeper of the Great Seal of Canada. The incoming Governor General is also presented with those orders of state for which the Governor General serves as Chancellor of the order.

The oath of allegiance taken by the Governor General-Designate is prescribed in the fifth schedule of the *Constitution Act, 1867*, and is administered by the Chief Justice of the Supreme Court of Canada in the following form;

> I A.B. do swear [or affirm], That I will be faithful and bear true allegiance to Her Majesty Queen Elizabeth the Second, Queen of Canada, Her heirs and successors.

[So help me God] [Note: the name of the currently reigning Sovereign is to be substituted].

The oath of office, is then administered in the following form:

I do swear [or affirm] that I will well and truly serve Her Majesty Queen Elizabeth the Second in the office of Governor General and Commander in Chief of Canada, and duly and impartially administer justice therein. [So help me God.] [Note: the name of the currently reigning Sovereign is to be substituted].

Finally, the oath of office as Keeper of the Great Seal of Canada is administered in the following form:

I do swear [or affirm] that I will well and truly serve Her Majesty Queen Elizabeth the Second in the office of Keeper of the Great Seal of Canada. [So help me God.] [Note: the name of the currently reigning Sovereign is to be substituted].

The new Governor General is then presented with the Chancellor's collars of the Canadian orders of state, the Order of Canada, the Order of Military Merit and the Order of Merit of the Police Forces. (On some occasions in the past the Canadian Forces Decoration has also been presented). The chain of the Canadian Heraldic Authority is also presented to the Governor General.

Following the presentation of the honours, the Prime Minister of Canada makes a public address and then the new Governor General of Canada makes an installation address. The Governor General then signs a proclamation advising the country of his or her installation as Governor General of Canada.

There is no fixed term of office for a Governor General. However, by constitutional custom the term is considered to be five years in length, although an incumbent may serve for a longer period and many have served six years or even longer.[40] The term of office may be shortened by death, incapacity, or removal from office. In cases of incapacity, or removal, the Sovereign will receive formal advice from the Prime Minister of Canada concerning the appropriate action to be taken.

Although varying degrees of incapacity have occurred, there has been a reluctance to remove a Governor General while he or she is still capable of performing at least some of the functions of the office. Innovations in constitutional practices may be employed in such circumstances. Thus, after Governor General Jules Leger suffered a stroke during his term of office, his wife[41] performed some public acts on his behalf, such as reading the Speech from the Throne to open Parliament in 1976 and 1978.[42]

No Governor General has been dismissed in Canadian history, not even Lord Byng following the political tempest of 1926.[43] While it has been suggested

222 Crown and Constitutional Law

that a Governor General essentially serves at the pleasure of the Prime Minister,[44] by convention the Governor General is not considered to be a politically partisan figure and so far as is known no Prime Minister has ever attempted the removal of a Governor General.

However, if it could be shown that a Governor General violated a constitutional convention, for instance, by attempting to exercise the powers of the office in a politically partisan manner, or if there was a personal failing involving a violation of the law, or a breach of public morals, it would be possible for a Prime Minister to advise the Sovereign to dismiss the Governor General. In that event, the Sovereign could be expected to act on the formal advice of the Prime Minister, according to constitutional convention, and dismiss the Governor General.[45] Clearly however, the particular fact situation must be conclusive for the removal of a Governor General to receive the assent of the Sovereign, and the support of the population.

9.12   The Governor General and Linguistic Duality

As the representative of the Sovereign in Canada the Governor General stands at the apex of the federal administration. In that position he or she is called upon to interact with a wide variety of Canadians across the country. It is essential in such a position that the incumbents are able to communicate with a high degree of fluency in both of Canada's official languages, English and French. Since the appointment of native-born Canadians to the post in the modern era beginning with the appointment of Vincent Massey in 1952, great care has been taken by successive Canadian Ministries to ensure that appointees to the position of Governor General are bilingual. Fluency in both official languages has become a superordinate national value and it is seen to be necessary that the senior Canadian appointee in the hierarchy of Canadian government should reflect that value. As Governor General of Canada, the incumbent promotes respect for bilingualism throughout Canada.

9.13   Salary and Emoluments

Section 4 of the *Governor General's Act*[66] provides for a salary to be paid to the Governor General and by subsection 4(2) the Act stipulates that the Governor General's salary forms the second charge against the Consolidated Revenue Fund. Part II of the Act provides for a retiring annuity to be paid to a retired Governor General and to his or her survivor(s). Section 81(1)(n) of the *Income Tax Act* (RSC. 1985, c. 1 (5th Supp.)) provides that only that portion of the income from the office of the Governor General that is received as salary under the *Governor General's Act* is taxable. Expenses incurred by a former Governor General after they cease to hold office that are in relation to their tenure of office as Governor General may be recovered by the former Governor General from the Federal Government.

In addition, the Governor General has the use of Rideau Hall in Ottawa as an official residence during the Governor General's term of office, and the use of apartments set aside in the Citadel in Quebec City, as a second official residence. There is a large establishment of officials to support the work of the Governor General, the most important of which is the Secretary to the Governor General who exercises managerial control over the public servants who support the office of the Governor General.

9.14   The Deputy of the Governor General of Canada

The Governor General may appoint one or more deputies to assist the Governor General in carrying out the functions of their office. Section 14 of the *Constitution Act, 1867*, states:

> It shall be lawful for the Queen, if Her Majesty thinks fit, to authorize the Governor General from time to time to appoint any Person or Persons jointly or severally to be his Deputy or Deputies within any Part of Parts of Canada, and in that Capacity to exercise during the Pleasure of the Governor General such of the Powers, Authorities, and Functions of the Governor General as the Governor General deems it necessary or expedient to assign to him or them, subject to any Limitations or Directions expressed or given by the Queen; but the Appointment of such a Deputy or Deputies shall not affect the Exercise by the Governor General himself of any Power, Authority, or Function.

By Article VII of the *Letters Patent, 1947*, the Sovereign has empowered the Governor General to appoint deputies in accordance with section 14 of the *Constitution Act, 1867*.

The practice in Canada has been that each incoming Governor General will appoint two classes of deputies to assist him with the duties of the office. The first class typically consists of the Chief Justice and the Puisne Justices of the Supreme Court of Canada, who are appointed as deputies to act whenever the Governor General is precluded from exercising the powers of office by absence or illness. However, the power to dissolve Parliament is expressly excluded from the powers delegated to the deputies. In the past, particularly before the enactment of the *Royal Assent Act*, it was quite common for deputies to represent the Governor General in Parliament for the purposes of granting Royal Assent to bills passed by both Houses of Parliament. Deputies may also appear in Parliament in order to prorogue Parliament although that is rare because the normal practice is to prorogue when the House of Commons has been adjourned, in which case prorogation occurs by proclamation.

The second class of deputies appointed by a Governor General includes the Secretary to the Governor General (and potentially other members of the Governor General's staff) who are appointed for the limited purposes of signing letters patent, such as those for land grants, and warrants, such as those with respect to heraldry. In practice it is the Secretary to the Governor General who generally exercises these powers. As of 2011 the Secretary to the Governor General is empowered to exercise all of the Governor General's powers with the exception of the powers relating to the summoning, proroguing or dissolving Parliament, appointing Ministers, or granting Royal Assent in Parliament (but the Secretary may grant Royal Assent when it is done by way of a written declaration pursuant to the *Royal Assent Act*).[67] Since 1940 it has apparently not been the custom to administer an oath to any of the deputies of the Governor General.[68] The power to appoint a Deputy of the Governor General can only be exercised where there is an incumbent Governor General. If the office of Governor General is vacant there is no authority to appoint a deputy or to continue the appointment of a previously appointed deputy.

In a case challenging both the appointments of Supreme Court Justices to be deputies of the Governor General, and for such deputies to grant Royal Assent to legislation, it was held that nothing in the *Constitution Act, 1867*, or the *Judges Act*,[69] precluded the appointment of a Supreme Court Justice to be a Deputy of the Governor General. Nor is there any limitation in the *Letters Patent, 1947*, that limits the number of Supreme Court Justices who may be appointed as deputies of the Governor General. Furthermore, the duties of a Justice of the Supreme Court of Canada acting as a Deputy of the Governor General do not offend the principle of the independence of the judiciary. In granting Royal Assent to legislation a Deputy of the Governor General is subject to the same constitutional conventions as the Governor General; *Tunda v Canada (Citizenship and Immigration)* (1999), 190 FTR 1 (Canada, FC).

9.15   The Administrator of Canada

Constitutional law and practice have made provision for situations where a Governor General is absent from Canada for an extended period of time, or dies, becomes incapacitated, or is removed from office. The commissions issued to the first three Governors General, as well as the letters patent issued in 1878, 1905, and 1935, constituting the office of Governor General of Canada, all made provision for the appointment of an official styled the Lieutenant Governor of Canada. However, no commission was ever issued for or in respect of that office, and the office of the Lieutenant Governor of Canada has subsequently disappeared from Canadian constitutional law and practice.

The *Constitution Act, 1867*, makes provision for an officer styled the Administrator of Canada, and it is that office which is called upon when it is necessary to ensure the continuation of government in situations where the Governor General is absent, incapacitated, or has died. Section 10 of the *Constitution Act, 1867*, states:

The Provisions of this Act referring to the Governor General extend and apply to the Governor General for the time being of Canada, or other Chief Executive Officer or Administrator for the time being carrying on the Government of Canada on behalf and in the name of the Queen, by whatever title he is designated.

In the early years following confederation, the senior officer in command of the imperial forces at Halifax acted as Administrator in the absence of the Governor General,[70] and it was not until 1904, upon the departure of the last British garrison at Halifax, that the senior imperial military officer ceased to be called upon to exercise the office of Administrator. Under the *Letters Patent, 1947*, the office of the Administrator of Canada was vested in the Chief Justice of Canada or, in the absence of the Chief Justice, in the senior Puisne Justice of the Supreme Court of Canada.[71]

Pursuant to the *Letters Patent, 1947*, the powers of the Administrator arises *ex officio*, and no commission is required to be issued to the Administrator before he or she assumes the duties of that office. However, as required by the *Letters Patent, 1947*, the Administrator must take the oath of allegiance, the oath of office, and the oath as Keeper of the Great Seal of Canada in like manner as does the Governor General before entering upon the office of Administrator. Upon assuming their office the Administrator must also issue a proclamation announcing their assumption of office in the same manner as does the Governor General.[72] The term of office of the Administrator is indefinite, and depends upon the length of time required to appoint a new Governor General where the incumbent has died in office, or until the return of an absent Governor General, or the cessation of an incumbent Governor General's incapacity. Unlike the Deputy of the Governor General, the Administrator possesses all of the powers of the Sovereign's representative, including the power to dissolve Parliament.

[1] RSC 1985, Appendix II, No.31

[2] at page 194

[3] Capital punishment has now been abolished in Canada, in 1976 as a criminal punishment and in 1998 for military offences.

[4] In diplomatic relations, *exequaturs* are a form of letters patent issued to a consul appointed by the commission of a foreign state whereby the consul is recognized by the receiving state and their rights and privileges as a foreign consul are confirmed.

[5] *The Parliament of Canada*, George Hambleton, Ryerson, Toronto, 1961, at page 51 (afterwards "*Hambleton*")

[6] *Smith*, at page 61

[7] Ibid. The Australian author Peter Boyce has questioned whether the substance of these reforms survived past the term of Jules Leger as Governor General; *The Queen's Other Realms: The Crown and Its Legacy in Australia, Canada and New Zealand*, Peter Boyce, The Federation Press, Sydney, 2008, at page 79.

[8] *The Structure of Canadian Government*, James R Mallory, Toronto, Gage, 1984, at page 38 (afterwards *"Mallory"*)

[9] From their inception prior to formal *de jure* independence, the appointments of High Commissioners to other parts of the Empire or Commonwealth were made by the Governor General, on the basis that relations between the constituent parts of the Empire or the Commonwealth did not involve relations between two separate sovereigns. The historical practice has continued despite the alterations in the law concerning the divisibility of the Crown.

[10] *Mallory*, at page 38

[11] at page 111

[12] For example, the approval of letters of credence for Canadian High Commissioners and Ambassadors which both King George VI and Queen Elizabeth II continued to sign on behalf of Canada until the 1970's when this function was transferred to the Governor General of Canada.

[13] *Mallory*, at page 37

[14] At page 586. See also *Cameron v Kyte* (1835), 12 ER 678 (Malta, JC) where the committee stated: "If a Governor had, by virtue of that appointment, the whole sovereignty of the Colony delegated to him as a Viceroy, and represented the King in the government of that Colony, there would be good reason to contend that an act of sovereignty done by him would be valid and obligatory upon the subjects living within his government, provided the act would be valid if done by the Sovereign himself . . . But if the Governor be an officer, merely with a limited authority from the Crown, his assumption of an act of sovereign power, out of the limits of the authority so given to him, would be purely void, and the Courts of the Colony over which he presided could not give it any legal effect. We think the office of the Governor is of the latter description, for no authority or dictum has been cited before us to show that a Governor can be considered as having the delegation of the whole Royal power, in any colony, as between him and the subject, when it is not expressly given by his commission. And we are not aware that any commission to colonial governors conveys such an extensive authority . . .".

[15] RSC 1985, c. G-9

[16] At page 624, per Taschereau J. A different view was expressed by the Ontario Court of Appeal in *Black v Canada (Attorney General)* where the court stated: ". . . nothing in the Letters Patent [of 1947, establishing the powers of the office of the Governor General] or the case law requires that all prerogative powers be exercised exclusively by the Governor General. As members of the Privy Council the Prime Minister and other Ministers of the Crown may also exercise the Crown prerogative. The reasons of Wilson J in *Operation Dismantle* affirm that prerogative power may be exercised by cabinet ministers and therefore does not lie exclusively with the Governor General." Although the Supreme Court has held that the Royal Prerogative may not be sub-delegated at least some aspects of the royal prerogative are exercised by ministers as a practical matter, such as claims for Crown immunity advanced by the Attorney General in lawsuits.

[17] Curiously, the *Letters Patent, 1935* (which made one amendment to the *Letters Patent, 1931*) referred in the preamble to the "Governor General in and over Our Dominion of Canada" without referring to the companion title of commander-in-chief.

[18] Historically, the office of the Governor General of Canada has existed since the founding of Canada in 1608, when Samuel de Champlain became the first Governor of New France.

[19] *Ollivier*, at page 626

[20] *Frank R Scott*, at page 33

[21] Formally described as *Letters Patent passed under the Great Seal of the United Kingdom, constituting the Office of Governor General of the Dominion of Canada*, October 5 and 7, 1878.

[22] *Ollivier*, at page 638

[23] *Ollivier*, at pages 638-640

[24] *The Prime Minister and the Cabinet*, W A Matheson, Meuthen, Toronto, 1976, at page 9 (afterwards *"Matheson"*)

[25] *Frank R Scott*, at page 33

[26] *Ollivier*, at page 623

[27] *Smith*, at page 43

[28] *Smith*, at page 145

[29] *Frank R Scott*, at page 30

[30] *Dawson's The Government of Canada, sixth edition*, Robert MacGregor Dawson and Norman Ward, University of Toronto Press, Toronto, 1987, at page 188 (afterwards *"Dawson"*).

[31] *Mallory*, at page 46

[32] *Letters Patent authorizing the granting of armorial bearings in Canada*, dated June 4, 1988.

[33] *Memorandum on the Office of a Lieutenant Governor*, Department of Justice, 1955, at page19 (afterwards *"Lieutenant Governor, 1955"*)

[34] *Ollivier*, at page 624

[35] Ibid

[36] *Smith*, at page 45

[37] Ibid, at page 129

[38] It remains to be seen whether this newly established committee will become a permanent addition to Canadian constitutional practice. It was not used by Prime Minister Justin Trudeau with respect to the appointment of astronaut Julie Payette as Governor General of Canada in 2017.

[39] In recent years the tradition of non-attendance has been amended and outgoing Governors General now attend the installation of their successor, although the Chief Justice is still considered to be the representative of the Sovereign at the ceremony, in their capacity as a Deputy of the Governor General.

[40] In 2017, Governor General David Johnston completed a seven-year term as Governor General of Canada.

[41] The wife of a Governor General is sometimes referred to by the honorific title of Chatelaine but that is not an official title for a vice-regal spouse.

[42] *Smith*, at page 124

[43] In the colonial period Lord Durham resigned as Governor General in the aftermath of the 1837 Rebellions when the Imperial Government refused to endorse Durham's summary exile of Patriote leaders because the procedural rights of the rebels were violated. He was effectively recalled by the Imperial Government as a fallout from that matter.

[44] *Mallory*, at page 46

[45] See the discussion in chapter 7 concerning the reserve power of the Sovereign to delay, defer or decline formal advice to dismiss a Governor General in certain circumstances.

[46] Quoted in *R v Secretary of State; ex parte Indian Association of Alberta*, [1982] 2 All ER 118 (England, CA) at page 128.

[47] *O Hood Phillips*, at page 748

[48] Quoted in *Hambleton*, at page 37

[49] *Mallory*, at page 41

[50] *Lieutenant Governor, 1955*, at page 36

[51] In 1939, King George VI personally granted Royal Assent to several bills in the Parliament of Canada.

[52] SC 2002, c. 15

[53] Section 2

[54] Section 3(3)

[55] Section 4

[56] Section 5

[57] Section 3(2)

[58] Section 7

[59] President Kirby of the court summarized the Australian practice as follows:

1. "In relation to the compliance by the Parliaments of the Commonwealth of Australia, Federal and State, with constitutional or other lawful requirements concerning their internal procedures, Australian courts have powers different from those conventionally accepted by the courts of the United Kingdom in respect of the Parliament of that country.

2. The power to issue injunctions and to make declarations in relation to the deliberative stages of proceedings in Parliament will virtually always be refused out of the necessity to permit Parliament to conclude its deliberations.

3. After the passage of legislation through the House or Houses of

Parliament and before presentation of the resulting Bill to the Governor for the Royal Assent, the courts have asserted the power to issue an injunction to restrain the officers responsible for presenting the Bill to the Governor for the Royal Assent. *A fortiori* they have asserted a power to make a declaration as to the validity of the legislation at that stage.

4. Nevertheless, it is now settled practice in Australia that such an injunction will virtually never be issued, nor a declaration made, at that stage. It will be left to the applicant to seek relief after the Royal Assent has been given and the Bill has become law.

5. Such relief will be available virtually immediately and may be directed to the officials who would otherwise have the responsibility of enforcing the allegedly invalid law."

The joint judgment of Justices Priestly and Handley stated:

". . . the plaintiff sought to have the Court intervene in the law making processes of Parliament by granting an injunction to restrain the presentation of the Bill to the Governor for the Royal Assent. In our opinion it would be essential for the plaintiff to prove, before the Court would begin to consider such an exercise of jurisdiction, that the plaintiff's basis of legal challenge to the Bill would cease to be available once the law-making process had been completed by the Bill being enacted into law."

[60] Such requirements do, however, appear in the *Constitution of Canada*, notably in the amending formulas such as the requirement in section 41(a) of the *Constitution Act, 1982*, that any change to the office of the Governor General of Canada can only be made by and with the consent of the House of Commons and Senate of Canada, and the legislative assemblies of each of the provinces.

[61] In *Rediffusion* the Appellants sought to restrain the enactment of an ordinance of Hong Kong that would have seriously affected their legal right to engage in the business of the rediffusion of television signals. The powers of the Hong Kong legislature were derived from the Governor's Commission and the *Royal Instructions*, and the appellants contended that the proposed ordinance was not within the legislative powers of the Hong Kong legislature. Furthermore, the *Colonial Laws Validity Act, 1865* (28 & 29 Vic. c. 63) (Imp.) contained, in section 4, a provision that would have precluded the Appellants from seeking to overturn the ordinance in court after its enactment. Thus, by waiting until the enactment of the legislation the Appellant would have been deprived of a legal remedy. The Judicial Committee allowed the appeal, and found that in the circumstances where there would be no remedy after completion of the legislative process, there must be a remedy available from the courts before that legislative process was completed The Judicial Committee stated:"The immunity from control by the courts, which is enjoyed by members

of a legislative assembly while exercising their deliberative functions is founded on necessity. The question of the extent of the immunity which is necessary raises a conflict of public policy between the desirability of freedom of deliberation in the legislature and the observance by its members of the rule of law of which the courts are the guardians. If there will be no remedy when the legislative process is complete and the unlawful conduct in the course of the legislative process will by then have achieved its object, the argument founded on necessity in their Lordships' view leads to the conclusion that there must be a remedy available in a court of justice before the result has been achieved which was intended to be prevented by the law from which a legislature which is not fully sovereign derives its powers."

[62] Even prior to the *Constitution Act, 1982*, there were limitations on the ability of a legislative body in Canada to effect changes to the powers of the Crown to grant or deny Royal Assent. In *Re Initiative and Referendum Act*, [1919] AC 935 (Canada, JC) the Manitoba legislature had enacted a scheme of binding referenda whereby legislation could be enacted through a popular initiative and referendum process. The Judicial Committee struck down that legislation on the grounds that it abrogated the discretion of the Lieutenant Governor to grant or withhold Royal Assent, and such a change in the powers of the Lieutenant Governor was beyond the jurisdiction of the Manitoba legislature to implement.

[63] However, air transportation for both the Sovereign and the Governor General continues to be provided by a special VIP squadron of the Royal Canadian Air Force.

[64] Official foreign visits by the Governor General are, however made on the formal advice of the Canadian Ministry.

[65] Prominent in Canadian sports is the Stanley Cup, for professional hockey, and the Grey Cup for professional football, both of which were originally donated to sporting associations by former Governors General. Other Governors General have provided trophies for amateur sports.

[66] RSC 1985, c. G-9

[67] *Senate Procedure in Practice*, Senate of Canada, Ottawa, June 2015, at page 52

[68] *Mallory*, at page 65

[69] RSC 1985, c. J-1

[70] *Bourinot*, at page 51

[71] Article VIII of the *Letters Patent, 1947*, stipulates

"And We do hereby declare Our pleasure to be that, in the event of the death, incapacity, removal, or absence of Our Governor General out of Canada, all and every, the powers and authorities herein granted to him shall until Our further pleasure is signified therein, be vested in Our Chief Justice for the time being of Canada (hereinafter called Our Chief Justice) or, in the case of the death, incapacity, removal or absence out of Canada of Our Chief Justice, then in the Senior Judge for the time being of the Supreme Court of Canada, then residing in Canada and not being under incapacity; such Chief Justice or Senior Judge of the Supreme Court of Canada, while the said powers and authorities are vested in him to be known as Our Administrator.

Provided always, that the said Senior Judge shall act in the administration of the Government only if and when Our Chief Justice shall not be present within Canada and capable of administering the Government.

Provided further that no such powers or authorities shall vest in such Chief Justice, or other judge of the Supreme Court of Canada, until he shall have taken the Oaths appointed to be taken by Our Governor General.

Provided further that whenever and so often as Our Governor General shall be temporarily absent from Canada, with Our permission, for a period not exceeding one month, then and in every such case Our Governor General may continue to exercise all and every the powers vested in him as fully as if he were residing within Canada, including the power to appoint a Deputy or Deputies as provided in the Eighth Clause of these Our Letters Patent."

[72] *Mallory*, at page 63

THE LIEUTENANT GOVERNOR OF A PROVINCE

10.1   The Office of a Lieutenant Governor of a Province

The office of the Lieutenant Governor of a Province is provided for each province by section 58 of the *Constitution Act, 1867*, although the powers of the Lieutenant Governors are not set out in the *Constitution Act, 1867*. Like the office of Governor General, the powers of the Lieutenant Governors are derived from a series of constitutional instruments, including the *Constitution Act, 1867* and the provincial constitutions, which consist variously of provincial statutes, instruments created by the Crown under Royal Prerogative, or both. Additionally, both the commissions granted to a Lieutenant Governor by the Governor General in Council, and the *Governor General's Instructions* issued to each newly appointed Lieutenant Governor by the Governor General in Council, are also sources for the powers of a Lieutenant Governor of a province.[1]

At confederation in 1867 the nations' founders did not really intend for the Lieutenant Governors to be much more than a pale reflection of the Governor General. The Lieutenant Governors were primarily intended to fulfill a role as a federal officer in the provinces, in much the same way that the early Governors General were perceived to be imperial officers with respect to the dominion.[2] Nevertheless, the office of Lieutenant Governor has evolved over time through judicial pronouncements and today the office of a Lieutenant Governor is as much a representative of the Sovereign within each province as is the Governor General in respect of the country as a whole.[3] Consequently, much of the following discussion of the powers of the Lieutenant Governors mirrors the earlier discussion of the office of the Governor General.

Although at confederation the provinces were perceived to be subordinate levels of government within the constitutional framework of the federation, judicial decisions by the Supreme Court in *The Queen v The Bank of Nova Scotia*, and more substantially by the Judicial Committee in *The Liquidators of the Maritime Bank of Canada v The Receiver-General of New Brunswick*, established parity between the Crown in its federal and provincial aspects subject to the restrictions resulting from their allotted fields of constitutional jurisdiction under sections 91 and 92 of the *Constitution Act, 1867*. The effect of those judgments was revisionary, and they converted Canada from the quasi-federal state intended by the framers of the *Constitution Act, 1867*, into a true federal state with coordinate jurisdictions at both the federal and provincial levels. As a result, a Lieutenant Governor today exercises the sovereign powers of the Crown within the territory of each province.

10.2   The Role of the Government of Canada

The Federal Government retains a paramount position with respect to the appointment of the Lieutenant Governors as it the prerogative of the Governor General in Council to appoint a Lieutenant Governor for each province. A Lieutenant Governor is appointed by the issuance of a Lieutenant Governors' commission of appointment and is accompanied by the formal *Governor General's Instructions* to the Lieutenant Governor. Modern commissions appoint the Lieutenant Governor and authorize and empower him or her to exercise all of the powers conferred upon their office by the provincial constitution. The abiding restriction on a Lieutenant Governor, as with the Governor General, and the Sovereign, is to act within the scope of the constitutional powers adhering to their office.

In the contemporary era, standing *Governor General's Instructions* are issued by the Governor in Council to supplement the commissions issued to provincial Lieutenant Governors. The *Governor General's Instructions* provide for the publication of the Lieutenant Governor's commission, the oaths of office to be taken by the Lieutenant Governor (which are similar to the oaths which a Governor General must take) and administrative provisions with respect to the reservation or disallowance of provincial bills by the Governor General in Council.

In addition, the Governor General in Council retains authority to issue specific instructions to the Lieutenant Governors in addition to the generic *Governor General's Instructions* as political circumstances warrant. Instructions from the Governor General in Council can potentially have a significant impact on the freedom of Lieutenant Governors to exercise some of the Royal Prerogative powers, particularly in connection with the granting of Royal Assent to legislation although the likelihood of specific instructions being issued to a Lieutenant Governor by a Canadian Ministry today is considered to be remote.

10.3   Is the Lieutenant Governor a Viceroy?

Much like the Governor General, the Lieutenant Governors of the Canadian provinces are not Viceroys in the legal sense of the word but are the delegates of the Sovereign with respect to the exercise of the Sovereign's powers as the head of state of a province, and they are also officers of the Federal Government in the same way that a Governor General was once an officer of the Imperial Government. As a delegate of the Sovereign, the Lieutenant Governor must act within the limits of the provincial constitution, their commission of appointment and the formal *Governor General's Instructions* that are received by them.

In *Commercial Cable Company v Government of Newfoundland*, [1916] AC 620 (Newfoundland, JC) the Judicial Committee stated that the effect of the Governor's commission was to subject him to constitutional restrictions since: ". . . he is not a viceroy in the sense of being a person to whom the full prerogative power of the Crown has been delegated. His capacity is defined and limited by his commission and instructions".

In a more recent case, a former Lieutenant Governor of Quebec was prosecuted by the Crown for a series of criminal acts committed during her term of office, including breach of trust, forgery, and fraud relating to the expenditures incurred by her office which were unrelated to her functions on behalf of the Government of Quebec, or the Government of Canada. After being committed for trial the former Lieutenant Governor moved for an order of *certiorari* upon the grounds that, as the Sovereign's representative in Quebec, a Lieutenant Governor enjoyed absolute immunity from the criminal justice system essentially on the legal theory that a Lieutenant Governor was a Viceroy and stood in the place of the Sovereign and thus enjoyed immunity from criminal process. That theory was rejected by the Superior Court of Quebec and on appeal in *R v Thibault* (2012), QCCA 2212 (Quebec, CA) the Court of Appeal rejected the application of the principle of absolute immunity to a Lieutenant Governor. The Court, endorsing the view of legal authorities with respect to the question of immunities,[4] stated that ". . .they [the Governor General and the Lieutenant Governors] do not enjoy the same immunities as the Queen" and:

> The Governor General and the Lieutenant Governors are not viceroys and do not benefit from the same immunities as the Queen. They may be sued for their civil and criminal wrongs, but not for acts committed in the performance of their duties. See Musgrave v Pulido, (1879) 5 AC 102 and Bonanza Creek Gold Mining Co. v R, [1916] 1 AC 566-587.

> The Court shares this point of view: the appellant does not enjoy absolute immunity.[5]

Thus, the Lieutenant Governor acts in the dual capacities of the representative of the Sovereign in the province and as an officer of the Federal Government, and is not a provincial Viceroy. The practical legal effect of this result is that a Lieutenant Governor is an agent of the Sovereign and in the determination of the true scope and ambit of the prerogative powers of a Lieutenant Governor attention must be given to the Lieutenant Governor's commission and the *Governor General's Instructions*, in addition to the legislative grant of powers to the provinces contained in the *Constitution Act, 1867*, and the powers granted by the provincial constitution.

Finally, as the representative of the Sovereign, the Lieutenant Governor must exercise prudence in all of their public and private actions. Where their actions depart from accepted norms, or expected standards of conduct, they may be subject to the liabilities or penalties imposed by law. As the sentencing court stated in *R v Thibault* (2015), QCCQ 8910 (Quebec, QC) per St. Cyr, JCQ [translation] ". . . the Lieutenant Governor is responsible for any action or behaviour that may be considered inappropriate or illegal and that are not justified by the office."[6]

10.4   The Lieutenant Governor as a Federal Officer

A Canadian Lieutenant Governor is both a federal officer and the representative of the Sovereign. The office was originally designed to parallel the relationship between the Governor General and the Imperial Government in London. Just as the Governor General was an imperial officer, in addition to being the Sovereign's representative, so too the Lieutenant Governor was to be both a federal officer and the representative of the Sovereign in the province in respect of matters lying within provincial jurisdiction. Under this scheme, it was decided that the Lieutenant Governor would be appointed by the Governor General upon the advice of the Canadian Ministry, and they would be bound by the *Governor General's Instructions* in like manner as the Governor General was bound by the Imperial Government's *Royal Instructions*.

The provinces were accordingly forbidden by the constitution from altering the constitutional position of the Lieutenant Governor. The constitutional prohibition in section 92(1) of the *Constitution Act, 1867* [rep. and repl. by s. 41(a) of the *Constitution Act, 1982*] reinforced the constitutional position of the Lieutenant Governor as a federal officer throughout the early period of the constitutional evolution of the modern Canadian state. In *Attorney General for Canada v Attorney General for Ontario (the Pardoning Power Case)* (1891), 20 OR 222; (1893), OAR 31; (1894) 23 SCR 458 Chancellor Boyd said in the Ontario Court ((1891), 20 OR 222 at 247:

> That veto is manifestly intended to keep intact the headship of the Provincial Government, forming, as it does, the link of federal power; no essential change is possible in the constitutional position or functions of this chief officer, but that does not inhibit a statutory increase of duties germane to the office.

Chancellor Boyd's view that the provinces could expand the powers of a Lieutenant Governor in ways that did not attempt to effect a substantial change to the office in the absence of federal consent was subsequently confirmed by the Judicial Committee in *Shannon v Lower Mainland Dairy Products Board*, [1938] AC 708 (Canada, JC).[7]

At confederation a short-lived department styled the Department of the Secretary of State for the Provinces was created to handle official correspondence between the Federal Government and the Lieutenant Governors. Today, formal communications may still pass between the Federal

Government and the provinces through the Lieutenant Governors, but the role of the Lieutenant Governor as an intermediary in relations between the Federal Government and the provinces has been supplanted by direct communications between first ministers and between other ministers at each level of government, as well as by the rise of periodic federal-provincial conferences.

One area where the Lieutenant Governor continues to play a potential constitutional role as a federal officer concerns the reservation of bills passed by a provincial legislature. Section 90 of the *Constitution Act, 1867*, states:

> The following Provisions of this Act respecting the Parliament of Canada, namely, – the Provisions relating to Appropriation and Tax Bills, the Recommendation of Money Votes, the Assent to Bills, the Disallowance of Acts, and the Signification of Pleasure on Bills reserved, – shall extend and apply to the Legislatures of the several Provinces as if those Provisions were here re-enacted and made applicable in Terms to the respective Provinces and the Legislatures thereof, with the Substitution of the Lieutenant Governor of the Province for the Governor General, of the Governor General for the Queen and for a Secretary of State, of One Year for Two Years, and of the Province for Canada.

This provision makes sections 55 through 57 of the *Constitution Act, 1867*, applicable to the provinces, with the Federal Government of Canada standing in place of the Imperial Government with respect to all bills passed by the provincial legislatures, and thus allows the Federal Government to disallow provincial legislation and for the Lieutenant Governor of a province to reserve a provincial bill for the signification of the pleasure of the Governor General of Canada.

In the early years of confederation controversy erupted over the question of whether the Lieutenant Governor could exercise an independent discretion to reserve a bill for the signification of the Governor General's pleasure. Prime Minister Macdonald was firmly of the view that a Lieutenant Governor did not possess an independent discretion in this matter. A minute drafted by the Prime Minister and approved by the Privy Council was sent to all of the Lieutenant Governors of the time stating that:

> The Lieutenant-Governor is not warranted in reserving any measures for the assent of the Governor General on the advice of his Ministers. He should do so only in his capacity as a Dominion officer and only on instructions from the Governor General. It is only in a case of extreme necessity that a Lieutenant-Governor should without such instructions exercise his discretion as a Dominion officer in reserving a Bill. In fact, with the facility of communication between the Dominion and Provincial Governments such a necessity can seldom if ever arise.[8]

Thus, the Federal Government moved decisively to discourage the provinces from passing any politically dangerous legislation upwards to the federal level.

In addition, the federal authorities deprecated any independent action by Lieutenant Governors to reserve bills.[9] As the country developed, and the provinces became more and more sophisticated in their governance, the continued justification of a power of reservation vested in the Governor General in Council has increasingly been questioned.

The last significant reservations took place in 1937, in respect of Alberta bills which clearly violated the division of powers between Parliament and the Alberta Legislature. The Lieutenant Governor of Alberta did not receive formal instructions to reserve the bills but he may have received tacit instructions from the Federal Government to use the reservation power. The Government of Alberta subsequently challenged in the courts the power of the Lieutenant Governor to reserve the bills .

In *Reference Re Power of Disallowance and Power of Reservation,* [1938] 2 DLR 8 (Canada, SC) the Supreme Court of Canada ruled that the powers of reservation and disallowance in the *Constitution Act, 1867,* were valid and subsisting powers, restricted only by the constitutional requirement for the Governor General in Council to disallow provincial bills within one year after the receipt by the Governor General of an authentic copy of the provincial statute, and by the limitations on the reservation of bills imposed by any *Governor General's Instructions* issued to the Lieutenant Governor. Thus, the 1937 reservations which resulted in the *Reference Re Reservation and Disallowance Power* case confirmed the continuing constitutional vitality of the reservation and disallowance powers in connection with provincial legislation.

The latest reservation of a provincial bill by a Lieutenant Governor occurred in Saskatchewan in 1961. On his own initiative, and without any federal instructions to do so, the Lieutenant Governor of Saskatchewan reserved a bill that would have empowered the Government of Saskatchewan to vary mineral contracts by an order-in-council. The Lieutenant Governor was apparently concerned about the legal and policy principles underlying the province's legislative action. Prime Minister Diefenbaker (who represented a Saskatchewan riding as a Member of Parliament) responded to the reservation by stating that no instructions to reserve the bill had been given by the Governor in Council and that a province's competent legislation should not be reserved, except in extraordinary circumstances and then in accordance with the constitution (i.e., upon receipt of instructions from the Governor General).[10] The Governor General in Council granted Royal Assent to the Saskatchewan bill by a subsequent order-in-council which specifically noted that the bill was within provincial legislative competence and that, to justify a reservation, any purported conflict with national policy must involve a "practical or physical effect".[11]

Thus, it is unlikely that the power of reservation will be employed in the future by a Lieutenant Governor except in an extraordinary circumstance. Where it is employed however, reservation is an act of the Lieutenant Governor in his capacity as a federal officer and the act of reservation should not be construed as an expression of a lack of confidence by the Sovereign's representative in the ministry.[12] Thus, there is no constitutional obligation on a provincial Premier to tender the resignation of the provincial ministry if a provincial bill has been reserved.

With respect to the companion power to disallow provincial legislation, the Lieutenant Governor plays only a minor role pursuant to Section 56 of the *Constitution Act, 1867.* Under that provision, the disallowance of a provincial statute becomes effective only when the Lieutenant Governor communicates official knowledge of the fact of a disallowance to a provincial legislature by a Speech, Message, or by the issuance of a Proclamation. (The *Governor General's Instructions* require that a proclamation be issued.)

10.5   The Lieutenant Governor as the Sovereign's Representative

At the time of confederation in 1867, Prime Minister Macdonald took the view that the Lieutenant Governors were merely the representatives of the Governor General and it was the Governor General who was the only true representative of the Sovereign. MacDonald's view was echoed by Canada's first post-confederation Governor General, Viscount Monck, who clearly perceived the Lieutenant Governors to be subordinate officials.[13] The Supreme Court of Canada did not agree. In *Mercer v Attorney General of Ontario,* [1883] 5 SCR 637 (Canada, SC) Justice Ritchie described the role of a Lieutenant Governor as follows:

> . . . they represent the Queen as lieutenant governors did before confederation, in the performance of all executive or administrative acts now left to be performed by lieutenant governors in the name of the Queen.[14]

Chief Justice Duff further explained how the appointment of a Lieutenant Governor was linked to the Sovereign, in the following passage from the *Disallowance Reference*:

> . . . in the appointment of a Provincial Governor, the Governor General in Council under section 58 is acting as the Executive Government of the Dominion which, by section 9 of the statute, is declared to be vested in the Queen.[15]

Nevertheless, there is a distinction between the constitutional position of the Governor General and the Lieutenant Governors vis-a-vis the Sovereign, and the practical effects of that distinction are that the Lieutenant Governors remain subordinate to the Governor General with respect to their mutual relations with the Sovereign. Thus, a Lieutenant Governor does not communicate directly with the Sovereign on matters of state. Any discussion of state business between a Lieutenant Governor and the Sovereign must be transmitted to the Sovereign through the Governor General, or the Governor General in Council. That restriction does not however, detract in any way from the legal status of the Lieutenant Governor as an equal representative of the Sovereign within a province.

Although as late as the 1950s there was still confusion at the royal court in London concerning whether a Lieutenant Governor was a representative of the Sovereign, and therefore entitled to be formally received in an audience by the Sovereign, the position of the Lieutenant Governor as true representatives of the Sovereign within their province is now well established. They are customarily granted one audience with the Sovereign during their term of office.[16] Additionally, the Lieutenant Governor is the host of the Sovereign, or other members of the Royal Family, when the Sovereign and the members of the Royal Family visit a province. As a matter of protocol, the Lieutenant Governor is accorded precedence on such occasions, even over the Governor General if the latter is present.

As the Sovereign's representative, the Lieutenant Governor is the chief executive of a province and may exercise all of the Royal Prerogatives that are within the legislative competence of a province, on the advice of responsible provincial ministers (except for the reserve powers which the Lieutenant Governor personally exercises). That principle was settled in the judgment of the Judicial Committee in the cases of *Liquidators of the Maritime Bank of Canada* and *Bonanza Creek Gold Mining Co. v The King*, where, in the latter case, the ability of the Lieutenant Governor of Ontario to authorize the incorporation of a company with the capacity to exercise powers outside of Ontario was upheld by the Judicial Committee based upon the broad grant of power conferred on the Lieutenant Governor in his commission of appointment.

As a corollary to the position of the Lieutenant Governor as the Sovereign's representative, the provinces have been prevented from enacting any radical change to their constitutions at the provincial level of the state. The principle was expressed in *Re The Initiative and Referendum Act*, [1919] AC 935 (Canada, JC) where the Judicial Committee considered the constitutionality of an Act of the Manitoba Legislature that purported to adopt *referenda*, by means of a direct vote of provincial electors, as a valid method of enacting laws. The Manitoba bill would have required the Lieutenant Governor to submit a proposed law to a body other than the Manitoba Legislature, and would have rendered the Lieutenant Governor powerless to prevent a proposal from becoming law. The Lieutenant Governor would have also lost the legal right to prevent the repeal of legislation, as any repeal would have become automatic thirty days after a referendum result showed that a majority of the electors favoured a repeal. The Judicial Committee noted that the Lieutenant Governor was the Sovereign's representative in the Province of Manitoba and formed an essential part of the provincial legislature. Since the proposed bill purported to alter the position of the Lieutenant Governor as the constitutional representative of the Sovereign, it was held to be beyond the powers of the Manitoba Legislature to enact under section 92(1) of the *Constitution Act, 1867*.

10.6   The Commission and the Governor General's Instructions

Prior to Confederation, colonial Governors, or Lieutenant Governors, were appointed by the Sovereign upon the advice of an imperial minister by way of letters patent under the Great Seal of the Realm of the United Kingdom. The jurisdiction of a colonial Governor or Lieutenant Governor was defined by the commission granted to him by the Sovereign, and by any *Royal Instructions*.[17] That regime was retained after confederation, except for the fact that the appointments were now made by a commission issued by the Governor General upon the advice of his or her Canadian federal ministers. The *Governor General's Instructions* which accompanied a Lieutenant Governor's commission were likewise issued by the Governor General upon the advice of Canadian ministers.

The commission issued in the contemporary period to a Lieutenant Governor appoints an individual to serve in the office during pleasure. It empowers the incumbent to exercise the powers conferred by the *Constitution Act, 1867*, and the powers of the Royal Prerogative in accordance with the formal *Governor General's Instructions*. It also provides that upon taking office the commission will supersede the commission issued to the previous Lieutenant Governor.

The modern form of a commission to a Lieutenant Governor is as follows:

> Elizabeth the Second, by the Grace of God of the United Kingdom, Canada and Her other Realms and Territories QUEEN, Head of the Commonwealth, Defender of the Faith.
>
> TO: ...
>
> Greeting:
>
> Be advised that, placing special trust and confidence in your prudence, courage, loyalty, integrity and ability, we, by and with the advice of Our Privy Council for Canada, pursuant to section 58 and 59 of the *Constitution Act, 1867*, do hereby appoint you, . . . during the pleasure of Our Governor General of Canada, effective on the day on which you make and subscribe the Oaths of Allegiance and Office required by section 61 of the *Constitution Act, 1867*.
>
> And we do hereby direct you to carry out your duties in accordance with the powers granted to you by the *Constitution Act, 1867* and any other statutes, Our present

Commission and the annexed instructions, or instructions that may from time to time be given to you by Our Governor General of Canada or by Our Privy Council for Canada, and in accordance with such laws as are in force in the Province of . . .

And we do hereby direct that as soon as you have made and subscribed the Oaths, Our present Commission supersedes Our Commission issued under the Great Seal of Canada on . . . appointing the Honourable . . . to be Lieutenant Governor of the Province of . . .

In testimony whereof, We have caused these Our Letters to be made Patent and the Great Seal of Canada to be hereunto affixed.

Witness:

By Command,

Registrar General of Canada

The standing *Governor General's Instructions* are contained in order-in-council P.C. 1976-2593, dated October 21, 1976. Article I requires the Lieutenant Governor to cause the Royal Commission to be read and published in the presence of the Chief Justice, or other Judge of the Supreme Court of the province, and the members of the provincial Executive Council. Article II requires the Lieutenant Governor to take the oath of allegiance and the oath of office. Article III instructs the Lieutenant Governor to administer oaths to persons as may be required. Article IV requires that all laws assented to by the Lieutenant Governor, or reserved for the signification of the Governor General's pleasure, be abstracted in the margins, and be accompanied by explanatory observations on the reasons why the law was proposed. Article V requires the Lieutenant Governor to transmit to the Minister of Canadian Heritage, within six months of the date of prorogation of the legislature, a copy of all laws assented to by the Lieutenant Governor during that legislative session. Article VI requires the Lieutenant Governor to issue a proclamation of the fact of a disallowance of any provincial statute by the Governor General, and the certificate of the Governor General attesting to the receipt date of that [disallowed] provincial law. Finally, article VII provides that the Lieutenant Governor must not leave the province without permission from the Minister of Canadian Heritage and must not leave Canada in an official capacity without obtaining leave from the Minister of Canadian Heritage. The Governor General in Council retains the power to issue supplementary instructions to a Lieutenant Governor where circumstances warrant doing so.

A failure by a Lieutenant Governor to obey the *Governor General's Instructions* only results in a possibility of a personal sanction, such as a dismissal from office. It does not vitiate the enactment; *Currie v MacDonald* (1948), 29 Nfld & PEIR 314 at 324 (Newfoundland, SC) per Dunfield J., affd. (1949), Nfld & PEIR 294 (Newfoundland, CA).

A Lieutenant Governor may not request formal advice from a Governor General about matters concerning the execution of the office of the Lieutenant Governor, except by way of communications addressed to the federal minister charged with the responsibility for official relations between the Federal Government and the Lieutenant Governors.[18] In recent years the designated federal minister has been the Minister of Canadian Heritage. Those procedures for formal communications have, however, not prevented successive Governors General from holding seminars at Rideau Hall in Ottawa for the Lieutenant Governors to assist then in discharging their functions on behalf of the Crown.[19]

10.7   Royal Assent in the Legislative Assembly

Like the Governor General, the Lieutenant Governor is vested with constitutional authority pursuant to section 55 of the *Constitution Act, 1867*, to grant or withhold Royal Assent to a bill passed by the provincial legislature. The existence of this discretion is tempered by constitutional convention but as a matter of law there is no doubt that it is a discretion that can be employed by a Lieutenant Governor. Thus, in *Rex ex. rel. Tolfree v Clark* (1943), OR 319 (Ontario, HC) Hope J., in considering the circumstances during wartime under which a legislature could prolong its lawful existence stated: ". . . there always exists as a safeguard against unwarranted prolongation, the right of the Lieutenant Governor, in the exercise of the Royal Prerogative, to refuse assent to an enactment". More recently the Supreme Court of Canada recognized that the legal power of a Lieutenant Governor to withhold Royal Assent to a bill continues to exist as a matter of law, and that a decision by a Lieutenant Governor to withhold Royal Assent is not reviewable by the courts; *Reference Re: Manitoba Language Rights*, [1985] 1 SCR 721 at 753 (Canada, SC). However, as a matter of constitutional convention, a Lieutenant Governor should not refuse Royal Assent to a bill on their own initiative; *Babineau v Ontario (Lieutenant Governor)* (2009), (unreported) CanLII 55370 (Ontario, DC).

At the federal level the withholding of Royal Assent is a constitutional measure that has long fallen into obsolescence. However, at the provincial level, some 28 bills have been denied Royal Assent since 1867. Of that total, 27 bills were vetoed on the advice of the Executive Council of the Province. The remaining bill spawned the case of *Gallant v The King* (1949), 2 DLR 425 (Prince Edward Island, SC).

Gallant dealt with alcohol prohibition legislation and Lieutenant Governor LePage of the province of Prince Edward Island chose to withhold Royal Assent when an amendment to the *Prohibition Act*[20] was presented to him for assent by the Prince Edward Island Legislature. The Lieutenant Governor withheld Royal Assent without receiving the advice of the Prince Edward Island Ministry

244 Crown and Constitutional Law

shortly before the expiration of his appointment as Lieutenant Governor. His successor, on the advice of the Executive Council, issued letters patent purporting to grant Royal Assent during a period in which the Legislature was not in session.

Perhaps inevitably, (since the *Prohibition Act* was criminal legislation), an attack was made on the validity of the amendment. The Supreme Court of Prince Edward Island did not comment upon the constitutional propriety of withholding Royal Assent, as it was clear that Lieutenant Governor LePage had the legal power to do that under the provincial constitution. However, the Court found that the bill to which Royal Assent was purportedly given by his successor, by letters patent, had not been properly enacted by the Legislature because the bill had not been re-presented by the Assembly to the new Lieutenant Governor following the initial withholding of Royal Assent. Chief Justice Campbell stated:

> It would perhaps, be stating the case too strongly to say that the withholding of the Sovereign's assent is equivalent to a veto, or that it kills the Bill, as conceivably the Legislature might re-present the same Bill, and it might thereupon receive assent but no provision being made for subsequent action on a withheld assent, the Lieutenant Governor would appear to be *functus officio*, at least until the Bill is re-presented to him by the House.

The Chief Justice further stated:

> The precision with which the B.N.A. Act set forth the procedure for later considerations of Bills assented to or reserved seems to me to indicate an intention to cover the whole field of Royal Assent, and to exclude the possibility of a withheld assent being later conferred by a method similar to (or, *a fortiori*, less precise than) the methods prescribed for later proceedings on assents granted or reserved.[21]

The failure of the Prince Edward Island Legislature to re-present the Bill to the new Lieutenant Governor, subsequent to the withholding of Royal Assent by the outgoing Lieutenant Governor resulted in the nullification of the purported subsequent Royal Assent, and consequently of the statute. The *Gallant* case is thus authority for the proposition that Royal Assent may be considered only upon presentation of a bill to a Lieutenant Governor and the decision of a Lieutenant Governor to withhold Royal Assent may only be cured by a new vote and subsequent re-presentation of the bill by the provincial legislature to the Lieutenant Governor.

The *Gallant* case is also interesting because it illustrates an important principle of constitutional law in Canada. A lawful action (i.e., withholding Royal Assent) can also be an unconstitutional action (violation of a constitutional convention). Lieutenant Governor LePage was well within his legal rights under the *Constitution Act, 1867,* and the provincial constitution to withhold Royal

Assent, as that power is clearly conferred upon his office by the Royal Prerogative and declared in section 56 of the *Constitution Act, 1867*. However, by withholding Royal Assent without being advised to do so by his ministers, Lieutenant Governor LePage violated the constitutional convention that the Sovereign's representatives must act only in accordance with constitutional advice received from ministers who are responsible to the provincial legislature. Had his appointment not naturally expired shortly after his action in withholding Royal Assent, the Governor General in Council would have been well within its constitutional rights to dismiss Lieutenant Governor LePage for this breach of constitutional convention.

Where *Royal Instructions* are contained or appended to the commission issued to a colonial Governor, the Judicial Committee has held that the Courts of Law can inquire into whether or not it is lawful under the commission for a Governor to enact a proposed bill; *Rediffusion (Hong Kong) Ltd. v Attorney General of Hong Kong*, [1970] AC 1136 (Hong Kong, JC). While the *Rediffusion* case was decided in the context of a less than sovereign entity, the principle may be applicable in Canada in relation to the Lieutenant Governors if a Lieutenant Governor's Commission and/or the *Governor General's Instructions* required them to reserve bills passed by their provincial legislatures.

The question of whether the Governor General can be restrained from granting Royal Assent by prerogative remedies such as an injunction has not been conclusively determined under Canadian law. Nevertheless, judicial authority exists in Australia to support the view that injunction may lie against officers whose responsibility it is to present bills to a State Governor for Royal Assent, where it is alleged that manner and form requirements respecting the enactment of ordinary legislation have not been complied with; *Eastgate v Rozzoli* (1990), 20 NSWLR 188 (New South Wales, CA).

10.8   The Symbolic Functions of the Lieutenant Governor

Like the Governor General, the Lieutenant Governor of a Province has several symbolic roles to fulfill in relation to the constitutional monarchy of Canada.

Each new session of the Legislature is opened by the Lieutenant Governor in the name of the Sovereign and, in all provinces but Quebec, the Lieutenant Governor reads the Speech from the Throne, which articulates the government's legislative policies and programs. The Speech is written by the members of the Executive Council and the Lieutenant Governor plays no part in its development. In Quebec, the Lieutenant Governor continues to fulfill the constitutional function of opening the Quebec National Assembly. However, since 1976, the Speech from the Throne has been replaced by an Inaugural Speech which is read to the legislature by the Premier of Quebec.[22]

The Lieutenant Governor grants Royal Assent to legislation passed by a provincial legislature. The provincial practices in granting Royal Assent have not been uniform in Canadian history. Although the *Constitution Act, 1867*, in section 90, implies that Royal Assent is to be given in the name of the Governor General, no province has adopted that practice. Royal Assent has always been given in Ontario and Quebec in the name of the Sovereign and, in some of the Maritime Provinces, in the name of the Lieutenant Governor.[23] The Supreme Court of Canada has indicated that the grant of Royal Assent in a manner more August than that which was contemplated by the Constitution is not a defect in assent; *Reference Re Power of Disallowance and Power of Reservation* (1938), 2 DLR 8 at 12, per Sir Lyman P. Duff, Chief Justice of Canada.

Perhaps the most important symbolic function of the Lieutenant Governor is that, merely by their presence as the representative of the Sovereign, the legislatures of the provinces are equated in sovereign status with the Parliament of Canada. The Sovereign thus forms part of both legislative bodies and the Sovereign's representatives in the legislatures of the provinces, the Lieutenant Governors, together with the Governor General in Parliament, symbolically represent the sovereign power of the realm.

10.9   Appointment, Installation and Term of Office

Appointees to the office of Lieutenant Governor often have close links to the political party forming the Federal Government which has appointed them. As with the position of Governor General, there are no particular constitutional or other requirements for the position, although Prime Minister Laurier once suggested that candidates should have "knowledge of constitutional law and a fair mind". During the very early years after confederation many of the Lieutenant Governors had much greater political experience than did their Premiers, which perhaps gave some stability to early provincial governance. Today however, the converse is most often true, as many Premiers have wide political experience and many Lieutenant Governors do not.[24]

Although in the early years of modern Canada there were several Lieutenant Governors who had few ties with the province over which they presided, it is now the invariable practice to appoint as Lieutenant Governor only those individuals who have a close connection to a particular province. Given the extensive social commitments imposed on a Lieutenant Governor, appointments have sometimes been made of persons who have access to private means to supplement the official budget available for social purposes.

In 2012 the Federal Government established an Advisory Committee on Vice-Regal Appointments to provide advice to the Prime Minister of Canada on the appointments of the Governor General, the Lieutenant Governors of the provinces, and the Commissioners of the northern territories. The Advisory

Committee on Vice-Regal Appointments consists of the Canadian Secretary to the Queen, as the Chair of the committee, together with two permanent appointees representing the two linguistic components of the country, Anglophone and Francophone, who serve for a term of six years. In addition, where the pending appointment is of a Lieutenant Governor or a territorial Commissioner two temporary appointments of up to six months may be made of persons who are residents of the jurisdiction where the appointment is to be made. The recommendations of the committee are made to the Prime Minister, who makes the final selection decision. [Currently, as of 2017, the Advisory Committee is moribund pending a review of its functions.]

As with the case of the Governor General, there is no ceremony fixed by law for the installation of a Lieutenant Governor. However, the installation ceremony is similar to that of a Governor General's installation, with some differences. The outgoing Lieutenant Governor may preside at the ceremony. After the reading of the Royal Commission, the Lieutenant Governor designate takes the same oath of allegiance prescribed by the *Constitution Act, 1867,* for the Governor General. It is administered in the following form:

> I . . . do swear that I will be faithful and bear true allegiance to Her Majesty Queen Elizabeth the Second, Queen of Canada, Her Heirs and Successors. So help me God.

The oath of office as Lieutenant Governor and as Keeper of the Great Seal of the Province has been administered jointly, in the recent era, in the following form:

> I . . . shall well and truly execute the office and trust of Lieutenant Governor of the Province of . . . and duly and impartially administer justice therein. I shall well and truly execute the office and trust of Keeper of the Great Seal of Her Majesty's Province of . . . according to the best of my knowledge and ability. So help me God.

The new Lieutenant Governor then signs the oaths following which the Great Seal of the Province is presented and custody remitted to the appropriate provincial official. The Premier of the Province delivers an address, as does a Minister of the Crown representing the federal government, following which an address is made by the new Lieutenant Governor.

The instrument of appointment of a Lieutenant Governor is a commission under the Great Seal of Canada authorized by a federal order-in-council. No term of office is stipulated for Lieutenant Governors but section 59 of the *Constitution Act, 1867* provides that during the first five years of a Lieutenant Governor's term they shall not be terminated by the Governor in Council except for cause. Beyond the anniversary of their fifth year in office a Lieutenant Governor's continued service is at the pleasure of the Governor in Council. During World War II, Prime Minister Mackenzie King asked all of the then serving Lieutenant Governors to continue in their office for the duration of the war. No new commissions were issued to those Lieutenant Governors whose terms subsequently exceeded five years.[25]

The Governor in Council has the constitutional authority to dismiss a Lieutenant Governor and during the nineteenth century two Lieutenant Governors, Letellier of Quebec, and MacInnes of British Columbia, were dismissed for cause. At the time of the dismissal of Lieutenant Governor Letellier a question arose concerning the powers of the Governor General in relation to his dismissal. The matter was referred to the Imperial Government and the Law Officers of the Crown took the view that a Governor General had the legal power to dismiss a Lieutenant Governor. However, in a dispatch to Governor General Lord Lorne that was approved by Queen Victoria, the Governor General was advised by the Colonial Office that while he should act on the advice of his ministers in exercising his power to dismiss a Lieutenant Governor, he also had a personal responsibility in such situations.[26] In the end, Lord Lorne approved the dismissal of Lieutenant Governor Letellier but required the order-in-council to clearly state that the Governor General had dismissed Letellier on the advice of the Canadian Ministry.[27]

The dismissal of Lieutenant Governor MacInnes in 1900 was a consequence of his multiple dismissals of his own governments. Although politicians in British Columbia, during the period in question, were relatively unsophisticated by the standards of today, MacInnes' multiple dismissals alarmed the Federal Government. In the summary which preceded the advice to remove him, the federal Minister of Justice stated that Lieutenant Governor MacInnes dismissals were "extraordinary", and "improper". After his chosen Premier was repudiated at the polls, the federal government removed him, noting that the electorate had not endorsed his choice for Premier of the province.

Section 59 of the *Constitution Act, 1867,* requires that any removal of a Lieutenant Governor for cause must be communicated to him or her within one month after the order-in-council of dismissal is made. If Parliament is sitting when the dismissal occurs, the Governor General must send a Message to both the House of Commons and the Senate within one week after the order-in-council relating to the dismissal is made.

Where a dismissal of a Lieutenant Governor occurs beyond the fifth anniversary of the incumbent's appointment there is no requirement that the dismissal be for cause, as the Lieutenant Governor holds office at pleasure for any period beyond the fifth anniversary of the date of the original appointment.

10.10   Linguistic Duality

Given that Canada has two official languages it is highly desirable for a Lieutenant Governor to be able to communicate in both English and French.

However, that is not necessarily viewed as an essential skill at the provincial level of government in the same way as it is for individuals who have national duties to perform, such as the Sovereign and the Governor General. Consequently, it is not uncommon for appointees to the office of a Lieutenant Governor of a province to be fluent in only one of the official languages of Canada. Fluency in both official languages will be of proportionally greater importance in provinces where the minority language groups are of a substantial size, such as New Brunswick, Quebec, and Ontario. Fluency in French is, of course, essential in the province of Quebec.

10.11   Salary and Emoluments

As the constitution provides that a Lieutenant Governor will be appointed by the Governor in Council, the salary and other emoluments of office paid to a Lieutenant Governor are the responsibility of Parliament. The salary of a Lieutenant Governor is fixed pursuant to section 3 of the *Salaries Act*,[28] and superannuation and death benefits are paid upon retirement, death, or disability, pursuant to the *Lieutenant Governors Superannuation Act*[29].

Although the salary and other employment benefits are paid to a Lieutenant Governor by the Federal government, it has been held by the Exchequer Court of Canada that an employer and employee relationship does not exist between the Queen in right of Canada and a Lieutenant Governor; *Carroll v The King*, [1947] Ex CR 410 (Canada, Exch. Ct.) affirmed *sub. nom. His Majesty The King v Dame Juliette Carroll, et al*, [1950] SCR 73 (Canada, SC). In the Supreme Court, Justice Taschereau, applying the Quebec *Civil Code* to the facts of the case, stated:

> By a fiction of the law, the Lieutenant-Governor stands in a unique position, fulfilling in the Province for which he is appointed the duties fulfilled by the King himself in England, and which no one else can exercise. And in acting in that capacity, he is not an employee of His Majesty in the right of the Dominion. I fail to see between the appellant and the respondent any of the essential contractual elements necessary to bring the claim within section 2260 [of the] *Civil Code*.[30]

Therefore, a Lieutenant Governor is an officer of Her Majesty in respect of a provincial office, despite the fact of their appointment by the Governor General in Council, and despite the payment of their salary, allowances and benefits by the federal treasury.

In addition to the standard federal benefits the Lieutenant Governors in some Provinces may be provided with an official residence by the province during their term of office. Where an official residence is not provided, a Lieutenant Governor is normally provided with apartments and a separate office for their use during their term as Lieutenant Governor.

10.12   The Administrator of a Province

A Lieutenant Governor may continue to exercise the functions of their office when they outside of the province and, unlike the Governor General, there is no prescribed maximum period of absence similar to Article VIII of the *Letters Patent, 1947*, which limits the ability of a Governor General to the exercise of their powers when outside of Canada to a maximum of thirty days. Although a Lieutenant Governor does not have a time restriction on the exercise their powers when they are outside of their province, a Lieutenant Governor cannot leave their province without formally notifying the Crown in Right of Canada, through the appropriate federal minister, of their forthcoming absence from the province. A Lieutenant Governor must also obtain the formal permission of the Crown in right of Canada, again through the appropriate federal minister, before departing Canada to visit another country in an official capacity.[31]

When a Lieutenant Governor is absent from their province, or ill, it may become necessary, or practical, to provide for an Administrator of the Province to carry on the government. Section 67 of the *Constitution Act, 1867*, empowers the Governor General in Council to appoint an Administrator of a Province whenever a Lieutenant Governor is unable to execute their office because of an absence, illness, or some other inability. Absence, in this context, can be an absence within the province, such as a vacation, or it can also be a physical absence from the province. It would not however, include a situation where the Lieutenant Governor is absent from the province for reasons of official travel because a Lieutenant Governor can continue to exercise the functions of their office while travelling abroad.

Formerly, appointments of an Administrator were made each time a Lieutenant Governor was absent. However, in 1953, permanent Administrators were appointed, and in most instances consist of the Chief Justice of the Province.[32] The Administrator acts only in the event of the illness, absence, or inability of the Lieutenant Governor to act in office but does not act upon the death or resignation of an incumbent Lieutenant Governor because section 67 of the *Constitution Act, 1867*, is silent with respect to those events, and they are not otherwise addressed.[33] In the case of death or resignation from office it becomes necessary for the Governor General in Council to appoint a new Lieutenant Governor with due despatch lest the vacancy in the office of the Lieutenant Governor compromise the ability of the provincial government to govern the province.

Where the permanent Administrator is not available to act, it is the practice for the Governor in Council to appoint another judge to act as the Administrator from amongst the Puisne Judges of the Court of Appeal for that Province.

10.13   The Deputy of the Lieutenant Governor

Provincial constitutions may provide that the Lieutenant Governor may appoint a deputy on the advice of the Executive Council of the Province for the purpose of executing licences, commissions, or other documents. The powers of the deputy may be limited by the Lieutenant Governor to certain parts of a province. The role and powers of a deputy so appointed will be terminated by the death, or resignation of the deputy, or by the death, resignation, or retirement of the Lieutenant Governor.

10.14   The Territorial Commissioners

In the northern territories, which have yet to attain the status of a province, the Sovereign remains the Sovereign in Right of Canada, rather than the Sovereign in Right of the territory (see *Commissioner of the Northwest Territories v Canada*, [2001] 3 FCR 641, (Canada, FCA) per Decary, J.A.: "Constitutionally, the Territories do not have the same status as provinces. They remain a creature of the federal government, subject in principle to the good will of the Government of Canada. Her Majesty the Queen, in the Territories, is Her Majesty the Queen in right of Canada".[34]

In the three northern territories the government is administered by an officer with the title of Commissioner. In the nineteenth century when all of the current territories formed part of one large Northwest Territories the officer administering the government from the territorial capital in Regina was styled as the Lieutenant Governor of the Northwest Territories but that officer only represented Her Majesty the Queen in right of Canada. When Yukon was made a separate district of the Northwest Territories in 1895 an officer was appointed to administer the district and was given the title of Commissioner, as the district still formed part of the Northwest Territories which was then under the administration of the Lieutenant Governor of the Northwest Territories. When Yukon was made a separate territory in 1897 the title of Commissioner was continued, and it was subsequently applied to the remainder of the Northwest Territories when the creation of the provinces of Saskatchewan and Alberta in 1905, and the extension northwards of Manitoba to Hudson Bay, removed the settled parts of the territory.[35]

A territorial Commissioner is appointed by the Governor General in Council by a commission under the Great Seal of Canada with the same signatures and countersignatures as is required in the case of the appointment of a Lieutenant Governor of a Province.[36] However, formal instructions with respect to the conduct of their offices are not issued to the Commissioners by the Governor General in Council but rather are issued to them by the federal Minister of the Crown responsible for northern affairs.

Traditionally, the territorial Commissioners have been viewed as officers of the Federal Government and not as independent representatives of the Sovereign.

To the extent that territorial commissioners represent the Sovereign at all they represent the Queen in Right of Canada, and thus they lack the dual capacity of the provincial Lieutenant Governors, who represent both the Queen in right of Canada in their capacity as a federal officer, and the Queen in right of the Province with respect to provincial sovereignty.[37] The role of the territorial commissioners as exclusively federal officers is congruent with the executive role that they historically fulfilled in the Yukon territory and in the Northwest Territories, and reflects the constitutional fact that territories remain subordinate to the Federal Government.

Nevertheless, with the evolution of responsible government in the northern territories, the role of the territorial commissioner has undergone a substantial change. In Yukon, the Northwest Territories, and in Nunavut, the Commissioner now acts in a role which is very similar to that of a Lieutenant Governor in southern Canada. Like the Governor General at the federal level, and the Lieutenant Governors at the provincial level, the primary duty of the Commissioners is to ensure that a ministry is in place in each territory to conduct territorial governance. There are, however, significant differences in the implementation of that duty in two of the northern territories, Nunavut, and the Northwest Territories, both of which have adopted a consensus form of responsible government in which there are no recognized political parties in the legislature, and no clear division between the government and an official opposition in the legislature. The ministers and legislators in a consensus government seek to forge a consensus before implementing new policies through legislation. The consensus government model is considered to be more suited to the cultural frame of the northern territories, which have substantial aboriginal populations. The demographics of the Yukon Territory render it more like one of the southern provinces and it therefore follows the Westminster model of government with both a traditional governing party and an opposition party in the Yukon Legislative Assembly.

In terms of symbolic functions the Commissioners of the northern territories operate in the same manner as the Lieutenant Governors of the provinces, and represent the Canadian constitutional monarchy within the northern territories.

In 2012 the Federal Government established an Advisory Committee on Vice-Regal Appointments to provide advice to the Prime Minister of Canada on the appointments of the Governor General, the Lieutenant Governors of the provinces, and the Commissioners of the northern territories.

The Advisory Committee on Vice-Regal Appointments consists of the Canadian Secretary to the Queen as the Chair of the committee together with two permanent appointees representing the two linguistic components of the country, English and French, who serve for a term of six years. In addition, where the pending appointment is of a Lieutenant Governor or a Commissioner up to two appointments of up to six months may be made from the jurisdiction where the appointment is to be made. The recommendations of the committee are made to the Prime Minister who makes the final selection decision. [Currently, as of 2017, the Advisory Committee is moribund pending a review of its functions.]

Provision has been made in the territorial constitutions for the appointment of an officer to act in the place of a Commissioner where a Commissioner is unable to act, or where the office of the Commissioner is vacant. In Nunavut and the Northwest Territories that officer is styled the Deputy Commissioner and in Yukon as the Administrator. If neither the Commissioner nor the Deputy Commissioner/Administrator is able to act a judge of the Supreme Court of the territory is empowered to fulfill the role of the Commissioner.

As with the Lieutenant Governors, it is desirable but not essential that Commissioners of the territories possess a fluency in both of Canada's official languages. However, due to the unique demography of the northern territories it may be more desirable, at least in the Northwest Territories and in Nunavut, for the Commissioner to maintain some capability to speak in one of Canada's aboriginal languages. That is particularly important in Nunavut where the majority of the population is Inuit, and the Inuit Language (Inuktitut and Inuinnaqtun) is widely used by more than 80% of the population.

[1] *Lieutenant Governor*, 1955, at page 32

[2] *Saywell*, at page 163

[3] Even in the early years following confederation the provinces passed legislation to confer the status of a corporation sole on their Lieutenant Governors (*Walter S Scott*, at page 142). Modern provincial constitutions typically declare that the Lieutenant Governor of a province is a corporation sole.

[4] Henri Brun, Guy Tremblay and Eugénie Brouillet, *Droit constitutionnel, 5th ed.*, Yvon Blais, Cowansville, Que, 2008, at pages 358-359

[5] The defendant also asserted a claim for relative immunity based on the argument that a Lieutenant Governor, as the chief executive of the province, is not an official within the meaning of sections 118 and 122 of the *Criminal Code*. That argument was also rejected by the trial judge who ruled that the meaning of "official" in both sections 118 and 122 was a broad one, and it was sufficient to capture the alleged misdeeds of a Lieutenant Governor: *R v Thibault* (2014), QCCQ 6474 (Quebec, QC)

[6] at paragraph 15

[7] at page 722

[8] Quoted in *Saywell*, at page 203. Between 1867 and 1961 there were 71 reservations of bills for the consideration of the Governor General in Council (Boyce, in *The Queen's Other Realms*, at page 102, citing *The Canadian Crown*, Jacques Monet, Clarke, Irwin & Co. Toronto & Vancouver, 1979 at pages 63-64).

[9] *Saywell*, at page 210

[10] Ibid, at page 267

[11] Ibid

[12] Ibid, at page 114

[13] Ibid, at page 15

[14] at page 643

[15] at page 76

[16] *Smith*, at page 55

[17] *Ollivier*, at page 658. In addition, see the judgment of the Judicial Committee in *Rediffusion (Hong Kong) Ltd. v Attorney General of Hong Kong*, [1970] AC 1136 (Hong Kong, JC)

[18] *Smith*, at page 167

[19] Ibid, at page 54

[20] 1937 (PEI) c. 27

[21] at page 430

[22] *Smith*, at page 52

[23] *Saywell*, at pages 8-9

[24] Ibid, at page 39. Although appointments of Lieutenant Governors are not ordinarily controversial, Lieutenant Governor Jean-Louis Roux of Quebec resigned his office shortly after his appointment in 1996, as a result of media reports concerning his participation in a 1942 anti-conscription rally, held during wartime.

[25] *Saywell*, at page 232

[26] Ibid, at page 246

[27] Ibid at page 248

[28] RSC 1985, c. S-3

[29] RSC 1985, c. L-8

[30] at page 79

[31] Currently, the Minister of Canadian Heritage is the designated minister for these purposes. This requirement flows from the formal *Governor General's Instructions* issued to the Lieutenant Governors.

[32] Section 67 of the *Constitution Act, 1867* does not limit appointments of an Administrator to periods in which the Lieutenant Governor is ill, absent, or unable to act. Only the powers of the Administrator are limited to those events. However, it is doubtful if section 67 would permit the appointment of multiple Administrators.

[33] *Saywell*, at page 231

[34] At paragraph 39. The constitutional history and evolution of responsible government in the three northern territories is briefly summarized by Johnson J. in *NTI v Canada (Attorney General)*, 2008 NUCJ 11, [2008] NJ No 13 (QL); 58 CPC (6th) 46 (Nunavut, CJ) at paragraphs 68-85.

[35] J H Aitchison, *The Political Process in Canada: Essays in Honour of R. MacGregor Dawson*, University of Toronto Press, Toronto, 1963, at page 138.

[36] *Formal Documents Regulations*, CRC 1978, s. 4(14), (15)

[37] As to whether the office of a territorial commissioner could evolve into a representative of the Sovereign there are no precedents but see *Re Tooley; ex part Northern Land Council* (1981) 38 ALR 439 (Australia, HC) where, in a minority view, two judges of the Australian High Court held that the Administrator of the Northern Territory had achieved the status of representative of the Sovereign subsequent to the enactment of legislation conferring self-government on the Northern Territory and constituting the territorial government as a body politic within the Australian constitutional framework.

CROWN COUNCILS, THE MINISTRY, AND CABINET

11.1   Introduction

The constitutional principle of responsible government requires that the Sovereign and the Sovereign's representatives accept formal advice on the exercise of the Crown's powers from constitutional actors whose political legitimacy is derived from democratic principles.

There are three components in any discussion of the Crown's constitutional advisors in Canada.[1] Firstly, there are the formal councils which exist to advise the Sovereign and her representatives in Canada. At the federal level, the formal advisory council is styled The Queen's Privy Council for Canada, and it consists of a permanent body of constitutional advisors whose continuance in office is independent of the existence of particular governments. Appointments to the Queen's Privy Council for Canada are for the lifetime of the appointee. The membership of the Privy Council includes both former and current ministers of the Crown, as well as a sprinkling of distinguished citizens from other fields.

At the provincial level, there is no permanent council of advisors. Rather, there is a body which is styled the Executive Council and which consists of those individuals who currently hold office as a provincial Minister of the Crown. When an individual minister ceases to hold office as a provincial minister they also cease to hold office as a member of the Executive Council of a province. Thus, the Executive Council of a province is synonymous with the Provincial Ministry that currently holds office within a province. The situation in the northern territories is the same as in a province. There is an Executive Council but its membership only consists of the current complement of territorial ministers.[2]

In addition to the Privy or Executive councils, there is also the ministry, which consists of those members of the Council who have been sworn into office as Ministers of the Crown, and who are accountable to the Crown and Parliament for the governance of Canada or one of its provinces, in accordance with the principles of responsible government. The concept of the ministry is identical at both the federal and provincial levels of government.[3]

Finally, there is the cabinet, which is a committee of ministers who are sworn into the Privy or Executive Councils and who are responsible to Parliament or a legislature for the development of the public policies which will guide the fortunes of the nation or of a province or territory between general elections. Although the cabinet may be viewed as an institution of Parliament, rather than of the monarchy, its evolution from monarchial institutions, and its paramount importance in Canadian government at the present day, requires an appreciation of its role in executive government in Canada. As with the ministry, the concept of the cabinet is identical at the federal and provincial levels of government in Canada.

11.2   The Queen's Privy Council for Canada

Within the Commonwealth realms, the office of Privy Councillor exists in the United Kingdom and in Canada.[4] In the United Kingdom and Canada the purpose of the Privy Council is to provide constitutional advice (i.e., formal advice which constitutional convention requires the Sovereign, or the Sovereign's representatives, to accept and act upon). In Canada, the Governor General generally stands in the place of the Sovereign for the purpose of receiving formal advice from the Privy Council.

The origins of the Privy Council are found in the history of government in England. The Privy Council emerged from the *Curia Regis*, which was the King's private council and which advised him on matters of policy. The *Curia Regis* consisted of a small body of administrators and the tenants in chief of the realm.[5] Eventually, the *Curia Regis* divided into two parts, the Star Chamber, which possessed judicial functions, and a small body of advisors who travelled with the King throughout his realm advising him on matters of politics and policy.[6] The smaller body was known as the *Concilium Regis*, and consisted of the chancellor, justiciar, and the great officers of the royal household.[7] This small body of advisors evolved into the Imperial Privy Council, which became the model for the Queen's Privy Council for Canada.

In Canada the Privy Council has a statutory basis within the written constitution. Section 11 of the *Constitution Act, 1867*, states:

> There shall be a Council to aid and advise in the Government of Canada, to be styled the Queen's Privy Council for Canada; and the Persons who are to be Members of that Council shall be from time to time chosen and summoned by the Governor General and sworn in as Privy Councillors, and Members thereof may be from time to time removed by the Governor General.

Thus the members of the Canadian Privy Council are the constitutional advisors to the Crown and, by constitutional convention, no matter involving the exercise of a power conferred by statute upon the Sovereign, or the Sovereign's representatives, or the exercise of a Royal Prerogative power, may be performed without the tendering of advice to the Sovereign or the Sovereign's representative by at least one member of the Privy Council. The only exceptions to this constitutional convention involve the exercise of the reserve powers, which are exercisable by the Sovereign or their representatives without any advice from the Crown's constitutional advisors. Thus, the Privy Council occupies a unique and powerful place in the constitutional structure of Canadian government although that may not always clear to the citizenry because of the close connection between the Privy Council, the Canadian Ministry, and the Cabinet, which tends to shroud the formal distinctions between those several bodies.

By constitutional convention and practice no one may be sworn into the Canadian Ministry without first being sworn into the office of a Privy Councillor. That is because section 11 of the *Constitution Act, 1867,* provides that it is the members of the Queen's Privy Council for Canada that "aid and advise" the Governor General in the discharge of the executive functions of the Government of Canada. The first members of the Queen's Privy Council for Canada were sworn into office by Governor General Viscount Monck at confederation on July 1, 1867. Each member sworn into office on that occasion took the oath of office as a Privy Councillor and immediately thereafter an oath as a Minister of the Crown. At that point in Canadian history, the membership of the Privy Council and the complement of the Canadian Ministry was identical.

In the subsequent federal election of 1867 however, the Honourable A. Archibald P.C., a Minister of the Crown in the Macdonald Ministry, was defeated at the polls and he submitted his resignation as both a Minister and as a Privy Councillor. Viscount Monck thought it would be desirable for the Canadian Privy Council to possess some of the institutional prestige which attached to the Privy Council in the United Kingdom and therefore he accepted Archibald's resignation as a Minister of the Crown but he refused Archibald's resignation as a Privy Councillor. From that point onwards the membership of the Canadian Ministry and the Privy Council has never coincided in Canada.[8] The precedent established by Viscount Monck has been maintained and therefore a Minister of the Crown does not cease to be a Privy Councillor when he or she loses their position in the Canadian Ministry. Their appointment as a Privy Councillor continues at the pleasure of the Governor General for the duration of the appointee's life.

11.3   Appointments to the Queen's Privy Council for Canada

The appointment of a Privy Councillor is effective from the date that they take the oath of office and continues at the pleasure of the Governor General for the duration of the Privy Councillor's life. After first swearing, or affirming, the oath of allegiance to the Sovereign,[9] the Privy Council oath is administered in the following form:

> I, ..., do solemnly and sincerely swear (affirm) that I shall be a true and faithful servant to Her Majesty Queen Elizabeth II, [or the name of the reigning Sovereign] as a member of Her [His] Majesty's Privy Council for Canada. I shall keep secret all matters committed and revealed to me in this capacity, or that shall be secretly treated of in Council. Generally, in all things I shall do as a faithful and true servant ought to do for Her [His] Majesty. (So help me God.)[10]

The newly sworn Privy Councillor is required to sign the Privy Council Oath Book, and the Governor General and the Clerk of the Privy Council will sign the book as well.[11] If a large number of new Privy Councillors are summoned, the oath of allegiance and the Privy Council oath may be administered once to the group, rather than separately to each member.[12] That particular procedure however, has been avoided since the ceremony began to be televised.

While the membership of the Privy Council at any point in time often reads like a list of prominent personages in Canadian politics over the preceding quarter century, occasional appointments are also made of distinguished persons who are not politicians. For instance, the Chief Justice of Canada is sworn into the Privy Council and it is customary to appoint the Consort of the Sovereign to be a member of the Privy Council. Occasionally, other royalty, distinguished Premiers of the provinces, and sometimes the federal Leader of the Opposition, are also appointed to the Privy Council.[13] Former Speakers of the House of Commons and the Senate are also sometimes appointed. Since 1960, as a result of a decision of the Privy Council, a Governor General may not be sworn as a member of the Privy Council until they have retired as Governor General. However, a Governor General who was previously sworn into the office of Privy Councillor remains a member of the Privy Council during their tenure of office as the Governor General.[14]

Members of the Queen's Privy Council for Canada are granted the use of the title Honourable for the duration of their life and they may also use the post-nominal letters P.C. (for "Privy Councillor") after their name. The title of Honourable was conferred upon Canadian Privy Councillors by Queen Victoria in 1868 in the initial *Table of Titles to be used in Canada*.

11.4   Retirement or Dismissal from the Queen's Privy Council for Canada

Appointments as a Privy Councillor are a lifetime appointment but they can be terminated. While no specific provision is made for the retirement of a Privy Councillor the Governor General, acting on advice from the Prime Minister, has permitted a member of the Privy Council to resign so that the member could stand for election in a municipal election process.[15]

Although a Privy Councillor may be dismissed that is a rare event. The power to dismiss is contained in section 11 of the *Constitution Act, 1867*. However, since the appointee holds a public office under the constitution, the decision to remove a person from the Privy Council is impressed with a duty of procedural fairness. The Privy Councillor must be given a formal notice of the Governor General's consideration of their removal as well as an opportunity to respond to that notice by presenting submissions as to why they should not be removed. However, the requirements of procedural fairness do not require the Governor General to provide an oral hearing, or audience, to the Privy Councillor facing removal. An opportunity to provide written submissions will be sufficient to discharge the procedural fairness obligations imposed by law.[16]

The title of Honourable borne by Privy Councillors for life is an honour that is separately granted by the Crown apart from the office itself, and therefore removal from the Privy Council will not automatically remove the honorific title.

11.5   *Meetings of the Privy Council and the Committee of Council*

As a result of the extensive membership of the Privy Council, it never meets as a complete body. Most business which requires that advice be tendered to the Crown is conducted at a meeting to which only currently serving Ministers of the Crown are summoned. Such meetings are styled a meeting of the Committee of the Privy Council, rather than a meeting of the Privy Council itself, because no meeting of the Privy Council can occur unless the Sovereign or the Sovereign's representative is physically present.[17]

Although there is no statutory quorum required for a meeting of the Queens Privy Council for Canada, or for a Committee of the Privy Council, constitutional practice stipulates that the normal quorum for a meeting of the Privy Council (including a Committee of the Privy Council) consists of four Privy Councillors. The quorum of four first appeared in the original *Royal Instructions* issued to the Governor General of Canada after confederation in 1867. Although the quorum of four was not contained in the *Royal Instructions* issued in 1878, or subsequently, it has remained the constitutional practice to summon four ministers. The four member quorum has also been mentioned in orders-in-council addressing the scope of the Prime Minister's power to give formal advice on the use of Royal Prerogative powers in some circumstances.[18]

A Privy Councillor does not have the right to attend a meeting of the Privy Council or a committee thereof, but attends only upon the invitation of the Sovereign, the Sovereign's representative, or the chair of the Committee of the Privy Council.[19]

During the reconstruction of a ministry, following the death of the first minister, or a withdrawal of confidence by the House of Commons, the Sovereign's representative has the right to consult with any member of the Privy Council on the formation of a new ministry. Nevertheless, constitutional practice has limited the exercise of that right to those members of the Privy Council who are responsible Ministers of the Crown.[20] An exception to this constitutional practice exists where a national emergency occurs.[21] In those circumstances, the Sovereign, or the Sovereign's representative, may summon Privy Councillors other than those who then currently hold ministerial office for consultations.

When public business has been considered at a meeting of the Committee of the Privy Council advice may subsequently be tendered to the Governor General in the form of a recommendation which, after approval by the Governor General, creates the legal fiction of a meeting of the Privy Council and constitutes, in law, the legal action of the Governor General in Council.

Barring exceptional circumstances, the Committee of the Privy Council can, in practical terms, be considered to consist of the Canadian Ministry (or that part of the Canadian Ministry which constitutes the Federal Cabinet) acting in its capacity as the constitutional advisor to the Sovereign in right of Canada. That is true whether it is the full Canadian Ministry which meets as a Committee of the Privy Council or a meeting of a smaller group of ministers.

Meetings of all committees of the Privy Council, as well as meetings of the Privy Council itself, are confidential, and the public is not admitted, although civil servants may be permitted to attend to provide explanations, or to provide information concerning matters before the committee, or council. In addition, those civil servants whose duties involve record-keeping also attend the committee and council meetings.

Meetings of the full Privy Council, with the Sovereign, or the Sovereign's representative physically present, are rare compared to the number of committee meetings. Only one Sovereign of Canada, Queen Elizabeth II has formally met with the Canadian Privy Council. The Queen met with her Privy Council in Ottawa in 1957 upon the occasion of the administration to her Royal Consort Prince Phillip, the Duke of Edinburgh, of the oaths of a Canadian Privy Councillor.[22] In 1959, Queen Elizabeth II met again with the Privy Council in Halifax, Nova Scotia, to approve the appointment of George Vanier as Governor General of Canada. Formal meetings of the Privy Council with the Sovereign's representative present also occur following a demise of the Crown in order to approve an Accession Proclamation, and on occasions when it has been deemed necessary to express a formal approval for a royal marriage. A meeting of the Privy Council under the presidency of a Deputy of the Governor General was convened in 1947, upon the betrothal of Princess Elizabeth to Prince Philip, and again in 1981, upon the betrothal of Prince Charles, the Prince of Wales, to Lady Diana Spencer.[23]

On such occasions when the Privy Council formally convenes in the presence of the monarch or the Governor General, or Administrator, the custom is to summon Privy Councillors from all political parties who have membership on the Privy Council so that the occasion is seen to be a state occasion, rather than a political meeting. The last such formal meeting occurred on March 27, 1981, to approve the marriage of Prince Charles, the Prince of Wales, to Lady Diana Spencer.

The Privy Council is also sometimes convened informally in the presence of the Sovereign. For example, all members of the Privy Council were invited to attend a luncheon for King George VI and his consort, Queen Elizabeth, at Quebec City on May 17, 1939, to mark the first occasion that a reigning Sovereign visited their realm of Canada. A luncheon for Queen Elizabeth II and all members of the Privy Council was also held in Ottawa, on April 17, 1982, to mark the proclamation of the *Constitution Act, 1982,* and the patriation of the Canadian constitution.

In contrast, meetings of the Committee of the Privy Council with membership drawn from the Canadian Ministry in power have been a routine occurrence in Canadian government. In practice the Committee of the Privy Council meets as the formal mirror image of the political Cabinet to formally approve government actions. In the early years following Confederation it appears that meetings of a Sovereign's representative with the Committee of the Privy Council also sometimes occurred. Governor General the Earl of Dufferin apparently attended meetings of the Committee of the Privy Council at which public business was debated during his term of office.[24] Since Dufferin's day, however, a constitutional practice has become established which precludes the Sovereign's representative from attending any meeting of Privy Councillors at which public policies may be debated.[25] In the contemporary period most of the work of the Canadian Ministry is undertaken in Cabinet or, more accurately, the committees of the Federal Cabinet and when a meeting of the Committee of the Privy Council is required to formalize decisions taken by the Federal Cabinet it is the Treasury Board, a statutory committee of the Privy Council, which often fulfills that function although whenever necessary the Canadian Ministry can convene as a Committee of the Privy Council to grant formal approval to actions that have been approved by the cabinet or a cabinet committee.

Section 11 of the *Supreme Court Act*[26] requires that the administration of the oath of office to the Chief Justice of Canada must be performed before the Governor General in Council and thus a meeting of a Committee of the Privy Council is expressly required for that purpose.

11.6   Specialized Committees of the Privy Council

In addition to the Committee of the Privy Council, which is for practical purposes the Canadian Ministry acting as a formal constitutional advisor to the Crown on all matters of governance, certain specialized committees of Privy Councillors have been established for more limited administrative purposes.

One such special committee of the Privy Council has been established by statute. The Treasury Board is a statutory committee of the Privy Council established by section 5(1) of the *Financial Administration Act*.[27] It was originally created by an exercise of the Royal Prerogative at confederation in 1867, and received its statutory powers in 1869. The Treasury Board is responsible for the management of the financial, administrative, and personnel resources of the Federal Government as well as the approval of the bulk of federal regulations and federal orders-in-council.[28] In this latter capacity, the Treasury Board advises the Governor General with respect to the passage of orders-in-council under legislation conferring statutory powers upon the Governor in Council, or in the exercise of the Royal Prerogative. In this respect, Treasury Board has an important role to play in relation in supervising the various regulatory approvals that are required to be made pursuant to federal statutes.

The Treasury Board consists of a minister styled as the President of the Treasury Board as the chair, with the Minister of Finance and four other members of the Privy Council, nominated by the Governor in Council, as members. While the members of the Treasury Board must be Privy Councillors they do not have to be Ministers of the Crown in order to be appointed to the Board (other than the President and the Minister of Finance, both of whom automatically become members of the Canadian Ministry upon their appointment as Ministers of the Crown). Further, where other Ministers of the Crown are appointed to the Treasury Board they are not required to be cabinet ministers.

The President, pursuant to section 6(1) of the Act, presides at meetings of the Board and between meetings exercises such powers, duties, and functions of the Board as the Board, in conjunction with Governor in Council, determines to be appropriate. The Treasury Board Secretariat has been established to support the work of the Board and it consists of officers and employees appointed pursuant to the *Public Service Employment Act*.[29] Provision is also made for the appointment of a senior public servant as Secretary of the Treasury Board and of a Comptroller General of Canada, both of whom hold the rank of a deputy head in the Public Service of Canada.

Although it is not formally created as a committee of the Privy Council, the members of the Security and Intelligence Review Committee established pursuant to the *Canadian Security Intelligence Service Act*[30] must be drawn from amongst those members of the Privy Council who are not members of the Senate or the House of Commons. Appointees to that Committee are therefore summoned and sworn into the Privy Council.

Formerly, there was a Special Committee of Council that dealt with routine orders-in-council and appointments but its duties have now been subsumed into the Treasury Board.

11.7 Confidences of the Queen's Privy Council for Canada

Matters discussed within the Privy Council, or within a Committee of the Privy Council, are confidential, and members of the Privy Council are sworn to keep confidential the matters deliberated upon in council or in one of its committees. In order to further protect the confidences of the Privy Council, section 69 of the *Access to Information Act* provides that the *Access to Information Act* does not apply to confidences of the Queen's Privy Council for Canada. Similarly, section 39(1) of the *Canada Evidence Act* states that:

> Where a minister of the Crown or the Clerk of the Privy Council objects to the disclosure of information before a court, person or body with jurisdiction to compel the production of information by certifying in writing that the information constitutes a confidence of the Queen's Privy Council for Canada, disclosure of the information shall be refused without examination of the information by the court, person or body.

Subsection (2) of Section 39 provides a statutory definition of what constitutes a "confidence" for the purposes of the *Canada Evidence Act*. The statutory definition includes, without restricting the generality of the phrase "confidence of the Queen's Privy Council for Canada," the following:

> (a) a memorandum the purpose of which is to present proposals or recommendations to Council;

> (b) a discussion paper the purpose of which is to present background explanations, analyses of problems or policy options to Council for consideration by Council in making decisions;

> (c) an agendum of Council or a record recording deliberations or decisions of Council;

> (d) a record used for or reflecting communications or discussions between ministers of the Crown on matters relating to the making of government decisions or the formulation of government policy;

> (e) a record the purpose of which is to brief Ministers of the Crown in relation to matters that are brought before, or are proposed to be brought before, Council or that are the subject of communications or discussions referred to in paragraph (d); and

(f) draft legislation.

The substance of the definition of "confidences" in section 69(2) of the *Access to Information Act* and section 70(1) of the *Privacy Act* are substantially the same as that contained in the *Canada Evidence Act*, with the addition of an exclusion in the *Access to Information Act* for any records containing information about the contents of any record described in the class of records mentioned in categories (a) through (f).

11.8   The Executive Council of the Provinces

For each Province of Canada there is an Executive Council. The Executive Councils of the Atlantic provinces are established under an exercise of the Royal Prerogative, in the commissions originally issued to the colonial governors. The *Constitution Act, 1867*, established Executive Councils for Ontario and Quebec.[31] For the provinces which entered confederation subsequent to 1867, the Executive Councils are established by legislation, usually in the act which created the province or territory.[32] The Executive Council functions as the Crown's advisory council in each province of Canada. All formal advice to the Crown in right of a province must be tendered to the Sovereign's representative in that province by the Executive Council, which thus acts as the formal constitutional advisor to the Crown in provincial matters.

The Executive Council in the Provinces consists of the members of the Provincial Ministry who hold currently hold ministerial office. The Premier of the province is generally designated as the President of the Executive Council while in office. Members of the Executive Council obtain their appointments upon being sworn into office as a Minister of the Crown for their province. The members of an Executive Council may use the title of Honourable preceding their name while they are in office but they do not have the right to append post-nominal letters to their name to denote their membership on an Executive Council. Unlike the Canadian Privy Council a provincial Executive Council does not contain a permanent membership, and the resignation or dismissal of a person from a Provincial Ministry will also terminate their membership on the provincial Executive Council. As a result, there is no permanent body of Executive Councillors similar to that of the Canadian Privy Council. In this respect, a provincial Executive Council is more similar to the Executive Councils of other Commonwealth realms, such as those of Australia, or New Zealand, than to the Queen's Privy Council for Canada.

The exercise of a Royal Prerogative power, or a statutory power, vested in the Lieutenant Governor in Council requires that a submission to the Lieutenant Governor be adopted by the members of the Executive Council. Formal advice to the Lieutenant Governor must be accepted by the Lieutenant Governor pursuant to constitutional convention in the same way that such advice is accepted by the Governor General at the federal level. Meetings at which advice is formulated for submission to the Lieutenant Governor are no longer personally attended by the Lieutenant Governor. In the past however, it is unclear to what extent Lieutenant Governors met with their Executive Councils, although there is little doubt that in the early years following confederation some Lieutenant Governors did attend meetings of their Executive Councils at which public business was conducted. At the present day, the constitutional practice is that Lieutenant Governors do not meet with their Executive Councils unless the occasion is purely formal and does not involve a discussion of public business.

11.9   The Executive Councils of the Northern Territories

In the northern territories the Executive Councils in some territories function differently than their provincial counterparts. While the Executive Council of the Yukon Territory operates in the same fashion as the provincial Executive Councils, the Executive Councils of the Northwest Territories and Nunavut function in a very different manner. Influenced by the aboriginal traditions the legislative assemblies of the Northwest Territories and Nunavut are not organized along partisan political lines.[33] Instead, a form of responsible government known as consensus government is practiced, which is based on the election of independent members of the legislature. The result has been a more cooperative approach to responsible government, which continues to evolve.

Consensus governments have a markedly different method for selecting an Executive Council subsequent to a general election. After each general election, the members of the territorial legislature will meet to select a Speaker, Premier, and the Territorial Ministry.[34] By convention, the Commissioners of the Northwest Territories and Nunavut call upon the persons selected by the assembly to become the Premier, ministers and members of the Executive Council of the Territorial Government.

The Executive Councils of the northern territories are not advisory councils in the same sense as a provincial Executive Council because the Commissioners of the northern territories are essentially federal officers and do not directly represent the Sovereign in their territories. Rather, the Commissioners represent the Sovereign in right of Canada within the territory, as the northern territories remain constitutionally subordinate to the Federal Government until such time as they are transformed into provinces.

11.10   The Ministry

The discussion which follows is largely focused on the ministry at the federal level of the state. However, the same concepts apply to the conduct of a ministry at the provincial level, and the same or similar legislative provisions can be found in counterpart provincial legislation.

11.11   Definition and Membership

At the federal level, a person who has been sworn into the Queen's Privy Council for Canada may subsequently be sworn into office as a Minister of the Crown. Once sworn into office as a Minister of the Crown he or she forms part of the Canadian Ministry, which consists of those Privy Councillors who are assigned to preside as Ministers of the Crown over the established departments of government, or who serve as Ministers of State. The Canadian Ministry does not include Parliamentary Secretaries, who are appointed to assist Ministers in the House of Commons and who may speak on behalf of a Minister in the House of Commons when a Minister is absent.

Executive power in the Government of Canada flows from the Sovereign through the Sovereign's representative to the Canadian Ministry. Occasionally Ministers of the Crown have felt compelled to remind Parliament of this constitutional fact. For example, the Honourable J C Isley, Minister of Finance, stated in the House of Commons in 1945:

> The authority of the government is not delegated by the House. His Majesty's advisors are sworn in as advisors to the Crown. The government is responsible to Parliament but that is a different thing from the doctrine that the Government is a committee of the House of Commons or that it exercises authority delegated by the House of Commons.[35]

Members of the Canadian Ministry constitute Her Majesty's Government and may refer to themselves as such, although within the Commonwealth that expression is not commonly used by governments outside of the United Kingdom.

All members of the Canadian Ministry must be Privy Councillors. Beyond that requirement there are no immutable rules with respect to membership in the Canadian Ministry. By constitutional convention, members of the Canadian Ministry must obtain a seat in the House of Commons, or in the Senate, but membership in one of the Houses of Parliament is not a prerequisite to appointment to the Canadian Ministry. Thus, General A L MacNaughten served as Minister of Defence for nine and one-half months in 1944-45 without holding a seat in Parliament. He resigned from the ministry after twice failing to be elected to the House of Commons. Since that time there have been other examples of appointments to the Canadian Ministry of persons who did not initially hold a seat in one of the two houses of Parliament. The Canadian Ministry will necessarily include all members of the Federal Cabinet but membership in the Canadian Ministry does not, *ex officio*, entitle anyone to membership in the Federal Cabinet, other than the Prime Minister, who is always the head of the cabinet.

11.12   Appointment to Office

After an election, or the defeat of a previous ministry in the House of Commons, the Governor General will summon the person who the Governor General thinks is most likely to be able to form a new ministry that can secure the confidence of the House of Commons. After accepting a mandate to govern from the Governor General, that person becomes the Prime Minister-Designate and he or she will then proceed to offer a position in the incoming Canadian Ministry to those persons who, in the judgement of the Prime Minister-Designate, are deserving of office. Once the selections are made and accepted, the Prime Minister Designate will submit an Instrument of Advice to the Governor General. That instrument constitutes formal advice concerning the identity of those persons who the Governor General should summon to hold office as members of the Canadian Ministry. The Governor General accepts the advice of the Prime Minister-Designate by countersigning the Instrument of Advice.

By convention, the previously defeated Canadian Ministry is obligated to continue in office after its defeat in a general election, in a caretaker role until a successor ministry can be formed in its place.[36] Once the Governor General has accepted the Instrument of Advice submitted by the Prime Minister-Designate, a transition between ministries can take place. The date and time of the swearing-in of the new Canadian Ministry are fixed in discussions between the Prime Minister-Designate and the Governor General, and the outgoing Prime Minister is advised of the date and time.

At the appointed time, the transition between the incoming and outgoing Canadian Ministry takes place. The outgoing Prime Minister submits his formal resignation, which includes the resignations of all the members of the outgoing Canadian Ministry to the Governor General at Rideau Hall and then departs from office. The outgoing Minister of the Crown who occupies the office of the Registrar General of Canada presents the Great Seal of Canada to the Governor General and departs from office.

Shortly afterwards, the Prime Minister-Designate, together with the members of his or her incoming Canadian Ministry, is summoned into the presence of the Governor General at Rideau Hall to be sworn into office. The oaths are administered by the Clerk of the Privy Council in the presence of the Governor General.

The process begins with the administration of the required oaths to the Prime Minister-Designate. The oath of allegiance to the Sovereign, the oath of a Privy Councillor (if the Prime Minister is not already a member of the Privy Council) and the oath of office is administered to the Prime Minister-Designate. Next, those persons who were previously sworn into the office of a Privy Councillor will swear the oath of allegiance and the oath of office but the Privy Council oath will not be taken by them. They are then formally presented by the Prime Minister to the Governor General.

Ministers-Designate who are not Privy Councillors are then administered the oath of allegiance, the Privy Council oath and the oath of office before their formal presentation to the Governor General by the Prime Minister. Finally, Ministers of State who are not members of the Privy Council are administered the oath of allegiance, the Privy Council oath, and the oath of office, following which they are presented to the Governor General by the Prime Minister.[37]

The oath of office for the new members of the Canadian Ministry is administered in the following form:

> I, ..., do solemnly and sincerely promise and swear [or affirm] that I will truly and faithfully, and to the best of my skill and knowledge, execute the powers and trusts reposed in me as [Minister of ....]. (So help me God) [omitted if the individual is affirming rather than swearing].

Members of the Canadian Ministry are individually presented or sworn in chronological order dating from the date of their first election to the House of Commons, or from the date of their appointment to the Senate of Canada.

11.13   Ministerial Commissions

All Ministers receive a commission that is issued under the Great Seal of Canada, appointing them to their ministerial office. The commission issued to Ministers is based on the Instrument of Advice tendered to the Governor General by the Prime Minister-Designate. Commissions are provided to the new Ministers at some point in time following the formal swearing-in ceremony.

11.14   Confirmation By-elections

In former times a member of the House of Commons who was appointed to an office in the gift of the Sovereign, including a ministerial office, that carried a salary (a so-called "office of profit") was obliged to surrender their seat in the House of Commons and to seek reelection in a by-election. However, that rule is now abrogated insofar as ministerial offices are concerned by section 33(2) of the *Parliament of Canada Act*.[38]

11.15   Size of the Ministry

There is no limitation on the size of the Canadian Ministry. At times the membership in the ministry has reached forty persons. Although the Sovereign can create ministerial offices, only Parliament can provide a salary for an office, and the necessary funding to support the work of a Minister of the Crown. Thus, there is a practical limitation on the size of the Canadian Ministry, although given the parliamentary control exercised by a modern Canadian Ministry, the latter may be an effectual limitation only in periods of minority governments.

11.16   Classification of Ministers

At the Federal level there are four types of ministers that can be distinguished by the legal foundations of their ministerial offices. Although most ministerial offices are constituted by a form of statutory authorization, it ought to be noted that all of the appointments of a person to a ministerial office, regardless of whether the office is created by statute, or otherwise, constitutes an exercise of the Royal Prerogative by the Sovereign's representative.

11.17   Ministerial Offices Created by the Royal Prerogative

The first category of federal Ministers of the Crown are those ministers occupying a permanent office of government that has been created by an exercise of the Royal Prerogative. There are two current examples of such ministerial offices, the office of the Prime Minister, and the office of the President of the Queen's Privy Council for Canada. Both of those ministerial offices were created under the Royal Prerogative at the time of confederation in 1867.

The position of Prime Minister is wide-ranging since he or she has control over the entire expanse of government through their ability to chair the Federal Cabinet, and to control the work of all ministers. The political power of the Prime Minister derives from their position as the leader of the political party, or a coalition of political parties, that can muster a majority of the votes in the House of Commons.

The relationship of the Prime Minister with the Crown is defined by constitutional convention rather than by law, and is primarily based on the convention that the Governor General will call upon the leader of the party, or coalition of parties, that commands a majority in the House of Commons to become the head of the Sovereign's government for the country.

As head of the Government of Canada the Prime Minister has the primary responsibility of advising the Sovereign, or the Sovereign's representatives on the exercise of the Crown's Royal Prerogative powers. He or she will also provide direction to those persons forming the Canadian Ministry, and oversee the entirety of the work of the Cabinet. An incoming Prime Minister normally issues general guidelines to incoming Ministers emphasizing their role and responsibilities as Ministers.[39]

Despite the importance of the position of Prime Minister in the constitutional framework of Canadian government the office of Prime Minister is scarcely mentioned in either the *Constitution of Canada*, or federal statutes. There is a passing reference to the Prime Minister in section 35 of the *Constitution Act, 1982*, and a brief reference to the Prime Minister in the *Salaries Act*.[40] Otherwise, no mention is made of the office in federal legislation.

The President of the Queen's Privy Council for Canada is the Canadian equivalent of the Lord President of the Council in the Ministry of the United Kingdom. As President of the Privy Council the incumbent presides at meetings of the Canadian Privy Council, when the council meets as a whole, which is admittedly a very rare event. Effectively, the Presidency is a senior position that can be given discrete responsibilities by the Prime Minister whenever convenient. Since the position does not carry any onerous responsibilities, it has often been combined with other ministerial positions.

In the nineteenth and twentieth centuries the Presidency of the Queen's Privy Council for Canada was considered a great office of state and a senior minister often held the position. For lengthy periods in the twentieth century the Presidency of the Privy Council was actually held by the Prime Ministers. From the early twenty-first century, however, it has been held by very junior ministers and is now often combined with the ministerial office responsible for intergovernmental relations, or democratic reforms. A statutory reference to the office of the President of the Queen's Privy Council for Canada is contained in the *Salaries Act*.[41]

There is a third type of ministerial office that can be created by an exercise of the Royal Prerogative and that is the office of a Minister without Portfolio. A Minister without Portfolio is a Minister of the Crown who does not have any departmental responsibilities. The purpose of such an appointment may be political, as in the need to provide for a linguistic, regional, ethnic, or gender balance within the Canadian Ministry, or it may be that the Prime Minister would like to give a special assignment at a ministerial level. There are statutory references in passing to the office of a Minister without Portfolio in the *Parliament of Canada Act*[42] but there is no current reference to Ministers without Portfolio in the *Salaries Act*. No appointment of a Minister without Portfolio has been made at the federal level since the 1970's.

The individual and collective responsibilities of the President of the Queen's Privy Council for Canada and a Minister without Portfolio are essentially the same as the responsibilities and accountabilities of a Minister of the Crown who is responsible for a department of government, with due allowance made for the fact that this class of ministerial appointments lacks an assignment to a specific department of government.

11.18   Ministers of Departments (or Portfolios)

Departmental (or Portfolio) Ministers consist of those Ministers of the Crown who have been given charge over an operating department of government. Their offices are permanent and they derive their authority from the statute which establishes their office. Invariably, these positions are occupied by the leading members of the political party in power, and are therefore also Cabinet Ministers. The responsibilities of a Minister of the Crown responsible for a department of government can be divided into two broad streams, firstly their individual responsibility and accountability, and secondly their collective responsibility.

The individual responsibilities of a Minister of the Crown are three-fold. Firstly, they are individually responsible to the Sovereign and the Governor General for the actions undertaken by them in the discharge of their ministerial office. In consistency with the Sovereign's Coronation Oath, and the installation oath of the Governor General, the actions of a Minister of the Crown responsible for a department of government must follow the rule of law, and must not bring disrepute upon the Crown. Secondly, Ministers of the Crown responsible for departments are accountable to the Prime Minister for the competent discharge within their department of the political and policy goals established by the Prime Minister, and for their ethical conduct while in office. Thirdly, Ministers of the Crown responsible for a department are individually responsible to the House of Commons for the operations of the department of government with which they have been entrusted. That includes responsibility for the activities of public servants within their departments who have carried out duties on the authority of the departmental minister.

As for the second broad stream of ministerial responsibilities, collective responsibility, a Minister of the Crown responsible for a department will invariably be included within the Cabinet. As Cabinet Ministers they will be collectively responsible to the House of Commons for the honest, efficient, and competent administration of the Government of Canada and, by constitutional convention, they must retain the confidence of the House of Commons at all times.

11.19   Associate Ministers

Some statutes establishing departments specify that an Associate Minister may be appointed under the Great Seal to carry out such functions of the departmental minister as the Governor in Council may specify. The purpose of appointing an Associate Minister is to relieve the burdens placed upon the departmental minister in departments that carry heavy responsibilities.[43] Associate Ministers carry the same rank and status as a departmental or portfolio minister.

11.20   Ministers of State

The final two categories of a minister arise under the *Ministries and Ministers of State Act.*[44] Pursuant to the statute, two types of non-departmental Minister may be appointed, Ministers of State Responsible for a Ministry of State, and Ministers of State Assigned to Assist a Minister. Generally, a reference to a minister in federal legislation will include both a Minister of the Crown in charge of a department of government and a Minister of State but on rare occasions a distinction between the two offices may be drawn and so a careful examination of relevant legislation may be required.

Ministers of State may be either inside or outside of the Cabinet.

11.21   Ministers of State Responsible for a Ministry of State

Section 2 of the Act provides for the appointment of a Minister of State charged with the responsibility of formulating and developing new and comprehensive policies in areas under federal jurisdiction. The Governor General in Council may, by proclamation, establish a Ministry of State containing a portion of the public service to support the work of a Minister of State. Although this particular type of minister does have operating responsibilities, those responsibilities are generally temporary, or of lesser importance, than the responsibilities associated with a Minister of the Crown assigned to a permanent department of the government. The intention of Parliament in providing for Ministers of State and Ministries of State is to create temporary ministerial organizations which can study particular issues without the distractions of major operating responsibilities. Currently, no such appointments have been made since the 1980's.

11.22   Ministers of State Assigned to Assist a Minister

The final category of minster is a Minister of State appointed to assist departmental Ministers in the discharge of their duties. Provision is made for such appointments in section 11 of the *Ministries and Ministers of State Act*. The main intention of these appointments is to reduce the workload of departmental ministers in very complex departments, or to enhance a particular subsection of policy that exists within the larger policy framework of a major department. Thus, special responsibilities can be assigned to such ministers by a departmental minister. The Minister of State assigned to assist a departmental minister is responsible to Parliament for the execution of the special responsibilities assigned to them by the departmental Minister.

Where a Minister of State Assigned to Assist a Minister is not a Cabinet Minister, the Carltona doctrine will have application to the relationship between the two ministers so that the Minister Assigned to Assist a Minister may exercise the powers and authorities vested by statute in the minister of a department; *R v Secretary of State for the Home Department ex. p. Doody*, [1993] 3 WLR 154; [1994] 1 AC 531 (United Kingdom, HL).[45] The Carltona Doctrine will have application to this relationship where it is shown that a senior and junior relationship exists between the ministers. A Minister of State Assigned to Assist a Minister does not act in their own name when exercising the powers of the departmental Minister under the Carltona doctrine. Rather they will explicitly state in any executive or Crown instrument that their action is taken on behalf of the minister responsible for the department. However, where a Minister of State Assigned to Assist a Minister is also a Cabinet Minister their relationship to the portfolio minister is that of a peer, and they are not then regarded as a subordinate of the portfolio minister.[46] In such cases the common law Carltona Doctrine would not have application to the relationship between the ministers.

The appointment of Ministers of State to assist other ministers continues to be a relatively common practice at the present time. Sometimes the title of this class of ministers has been changed to Secretary of State (by an exercise of the Royal Prerogative) without amending the Act to change the statutory title, and without any change in the powers or responsibilities of the position.[47]

11.23   Parliamentary Secretaries

Section 46 of the *Parliament of Canada Act*[48] provides for the appointment by the Governor in Council of Parliamentary Secretaries from among the members of the House of Commons to assist ministers. Parliamentary Secretaries hold office for a term of one year and assist their minister in such manner as the minister directs. The Parliamentary Secretaries are not members of the Canadian Ministry, and their duties are mostly confined to parliamentary duties, sometimes including speaking on behalf of an absent minister but mostly acting as liaison between the minister and other members of the House caucus or the Senate. Parliamentary Secretaries may occasionally be given specific policy-related duties although that is not their usual function.[49] Parliamentary Secretaries are not sworn into the Privy Council. They are however, entitled to an additional salary under the *Salaries Act*[50] for their work as a Parliamentary Secretary.

11.24   Acting Ministers

When a minister is absent or incapacitated, an Acting Minister may be appointed and the Acting Minister may exercise all of the powers vested in the minister, by virtue of paragraph 24(2)(a) of the *Interpretation Act*.[51] That provision states:

(2) Words directing or empowering a minister of the Crown to do an act or thing, regardless of whether the act or thing is administrative, legislative or judicial, or otherwise applying to that minister as the holder of the office, include

(a) a minister acting for that minister or, if the office is vacant, a minister designated to act in the office by or under the authority of an order-in-council;

Acting ministers at the federal level may exercise authority in one of two ways. Firstly, an informal assignment of a minister to act in the place of another minister, without a formal appointment to office by the Governor General, may occur. Typically, the practice at the federal level is for the Governor General in Council to periodically issue a Minute of the Privy Council with an attached schedule appointing ministers as acting ministers in another minister's department to take account of absences, or temporary incapacities.

In instances where a minister has acted for another minister, and there is no minute or other indicium of a designation to act, the courts may nevertheless apply the legal maxim *omnia praesumuntur rita ese acta* (the actions of public officials are presumed to be regular) to warrant the authority of the Acting Minister. This was the approach taken by the Supreme Court of Alberta in *R. v Thompson* (1913), 14 DLR 175 (Alberta, SC) where the right of a Minister acting on behalf of the Attorney General was upheld, despite the lack of evidence that he had been appointed to act in the place of the Attorney General by the Lieutenant Governor.

An Acting Minister may also be formally appointed by an order-in-council and, at the federal level, a formal appointment by an order-in-council is required where the permanent ministerial office is vacant. It is noteworthy that although the Prime Minister is the head of the government, and has the general superintendence of the work of all members of the ministry, the Prime Minister has no special authority to exercise the functions of any other member of the Canadian Ministry. The Prime Minister can only exercise such functions if the Prime Minister is named as an Acting Minister in the minute–of-council concerning acting ministerial appointments.

The Canadian approach to acting ministerial appointments reflects a more rigorous approach to the implementation of the principles of responsible government, perhaps due to a greater emphasis on the personal responsibility, and accountability, borne by individual ministers. Therefore, Acting Ministers must be established through a formal instrument (a minute-of-council) and acting appointments in the event of a vacancy in an office are made by a formal order-in-council, or instrument of appointment.

However, in other Commonwealth realms there appears to be a greater degree of flexibility around the capacity of members of a ministry to act in place of one another. For example, the office of Secretary of State in the ministries of the United Kingdom, the most senior level of the British ministerial offices, is effectively generic, and one Secretary of State is able to execute the functions of another Secretary of State unless the empowering legislation, or instrument, has very specifically confined the exercise of that power to one named Secretary of State. In Australia, the courts have upheld the ability of Her Majesty in right of Australia to appoint two ministers to oversee the work of one department, with each able to exercise the authority of the other minister; *Attorney General v Foster* (1999), 161 ALR 232 (Australia, FCA). Finally, the *Acts Interpretation Act*[52] of Australia now permits a Minister of the Crown to authorize another Minister to act in their place.[53]

11.25   Ministers Posted Abroad

A Minister is not deemed to be absent where they are permanently posted outside of Canada. Although it is rare for Canadian ministers to be posted abroad there have been two such examples in Canadian constitutional history. In the late nineteenth century Sir Charles Tupper remained a Minister of the Crown while serving as Canada's High Commissioner to the United Kingdom.[54]

In 1914, Lord Strathcona, a long-serving High Commissioner of Canada to the United Kingdom, died at the age of 93 and during his final months the communications between the government in Ottawa and the High Commission were interrupted. Consequently, upon Lord Strathcona's death, Prime Minister Borden dispatched Minister without Portfolio Sir George Perley to London to investigate the current circumstances surrounding the operations of the High Commission. While he was in London the World War One broke out and Borden asked Perley to remain in London as Acting High Commissioner while also retaining his seat in the Canadian Ministry, as a Minister without Portfolio. Later, to ensure that he could effectively support the army in Europe, Perley was created Minister of Overseas Military Forces by a 1916 order-in-council. The purpose of the Minister of Overseas Military Forces was to oversee the interests of the Canadian armed forces positioned in the European theatre of military operations. However, Perley chose not to stand for election in the 1917 general election and thereafter retired from the Borden Ministry, although he continued in London as High Commissioner until 1921.[55]

Temporary absences of Ministers from Canada for short durations are quite common and acting ministers will assume responsibilities at home while a Minister is abroad. Occasionally, in extraordinary situations, such absences can become lengthy. For example, Prime Minister Robert Borden spent a considerable amount of time in the United Kingdom in the latter stages of the World War One, when he served as a member of the Imperial War Cabinet.

11.26   Delegation and Succession

The workload of a Minister is often extremely heavy and it is not possible for each Minister to make every decision that he or she is empowered by law to make. Under the Carltona doctrine, which emerged from *Carltona Ltd. v Commissioner of Works*, [1943] 2 All ER 560 (England, CA), the exercise of a ministerial discretion by a subordinate official is constitutionally permissible and does not offend the common law presumption of statutory interpretation described by the Latin phrase as *delegatus non potest delegare* that powers conferred by statute on a decision-maker must be exercised by that person and cannot be sub-delegated.[56]

In *Carltona*, Lord Greene stated:

> In the administration of government in this country the functions which are assigned to ministers (and constitutionally properly given to ministers because they are constitutionally responsible) are functions so multifarious that no minister could ever personally attend to them . . . The duties imposed upon ministers and the powers given to ministers are normally exercised under the authority of the ministers by responsible officials of the department. Public business could not be carried on if that were not the case. Constitutionally, the decision of such an official is, of course, the decision of the minister. The minister is responsible. It is he who must answer before Parliament for anything that his officials have done under his authority . . . [57]

Essentially, under the *Carltona* doctrine, a departmental official may act as the alter ego of the minister for the purposes of exercising a ministerial discretion. When doing so the decision made by the official becomes in law the decision of the person who has been given the lawful power, i.e., the minister. Thus, the exercise of the statutory powers of a minister by a subordinate official will nevertheless constitute the act of the minister and not of the official. That distinguishes the power under the *Carltona* doctrine from a delegation of power because where a delegation of power is provided for a decision by a delegate is in law the decision of the delegate, and is not the decision of the person on whom the statutory authority has been conferred by a statute.

Carltona has been described as a "common law constitutional power"[58] and has been accepted in Canadian law by the judgment of the Supreme Court of Canada in *R v Harrison* (1976), 66 DLR (3d) 660 (Canada, SC). The *Carltona* principle is applicable to administrative acts executed by an official on behalf of a minister even where an official act in the form of a notice relating to conscription had the effect of curtailing the liberties of the subject.[59]

The *Carltona* doctrine is applicable to officials who serve in the department which is under the administration of a minister as well as to officials who serve in agencies that are separate from a department but are within the portfolio assigned to a particular minister. However, the doctrine is inapplicable to other members of a Canadian Ministry, or to officials in another department unrelated to the minister upon whom the decision-making authority is conferred. Essentially, the minister upon whom the power has been conferred must be able to take political responsibility for the actions of the official who has exercised the power. Where that official is inside the minister's department, or overall portfolio, the application of the doctrine will be appropriate but where the official is not within the department, or within the minister's overall portfolio, then the *Carltona* doctrine cannot apply.

In examining the applicability of the *Carltona* doctrine to particular factual circumstances the courts will stress the factors of ministerial control over the officials and the degree to which the minister is accountable and answerable to Parliament for the actions of those officials. The courts will also examine the appropriateness of the exercise of a particular power by subordinate officials and the language conferring the power will be an essential determinant of whether the power is capable of being exercised by a subordinate official rather than by a minister personally.

Nevertheless, certain statutory exceptions exist in relation to the application of the *Carltona* doctrine. Firstly, reliance on *Carltona* may be ousted by express legislation which contemplates a personal exercise of discretion by a minister; *Re Golden Chemical Products Ltd.*, [1976] Ch 300 (England, Ch). In *Attorney General of Quebec v Carriéres Ste.-Thérèse Ltée* (1985), 59 NR 391 (Canada, SC) Carltona was excluded by a statutory provision which conferred power on the Minister "himself". The codified version of the Carltona doctrine in subsection 24(2) of the *Interpretation Act* (see below) was held to be excluded where applicable regulations stated that ". . . the Minister may, in his sole discretion. . ." make the required decision: *Edgar v Canada (Attorney General)*, [1999] 46 OR (3d) 294 (Ontario, CA).

The *Carltona* doctrine will also be excluded where the statute itself encompasses the category of persons who may act in the name of a minister. Thus, in *Harrison*, a statutory scheme provided that the Attorney General or the "lawful deputy" of the Attorney General could perform the function. The Court held that the phrase "lawful deputy", "comprehended all persons appointed to act on behalf of the Attorney General, when acting within the scope of their authority".

Where a particular statute distinguishes between powers vested in a Minister and powers vested in subordinate officials, those officials may not act on behalf of the minister pursuant to the *Carltona* principle. Thus in *Campbell v Unitow Services* (1983), 43 BCLR 231 (British Columbia, SC) it was held that a statutory scheme which conferred specific powers on a minister, as well as specific powers on fisheries inspection officers, precluded the latter from exercising ministerial powers in reliance on *Carltona*.

Further, where a specific person has been appointed to act on behalf of a minister under a statutory scheme, other persons cannot purport to act for the minister pursuant to the *Carltona* doctrine; *Commissioners of Customs and Excise v Cure and Deeley Ltd.*, [1962] 1 QB 340 (England, QB). Where the overall statutory scheme divided authority between the minister and officials there was a presumption that the minister must exercise the power himself; *Ramawad v Minister of Manpower and Immigration*, [1978] 2 SCR 375 (Canada, SC).[60] Nevertheless, the mere existence of a statutory scheme which expressly permits delegation will not necessarily exclude the application of the *Carltona* doctrine where the power to delegate has not been exercised; *Minister for Aboriginal Affairs v Peko – Wallsend Ltd.*, [1987] LRC (Const) 822 (Australia, HC)

A minister can determine which level of officials of the department may act on his or her behalf, although the case law contemplates that officials of suitable rank and experience should be selected; *Re Golden Chemical Products Ltd.* [1976] Ch 300 (England, Ch). Only the officials of a minister's own department may exercise ministerial functions under the doctrine; *Mancuso Estate v The Queen*, [1980] 1 FC 269, affd. 35 NR 344 (Canada, FC). The *Carltona* doctrine will apply where the function of the minister is administrative in nature but not necessarily where the function is quasi-judicial or legislative; *Canadian Bronze Co. v Deputy Minister of National Revenue* (1985), 57 NR 338 (Canada, FCA). It should be noted that where a ministerial power has been properly exercised by a subordinate official a minister may not subsequently purport to exercise that power personally in order to obtain a different result. In such cases the proper exercise of a power by the subordinate official exhausts the power under the *functus officio* doctrine.

The principles of the *Carltona* doctrine have been codified at the federal level in the *Interpretation Act*,[61] which provides in subsection 24(2)(c)and (d) that:

(2) Words directing or empowering a minister of the Crown to do an act or thing, regardless of whether the act or thing is administrative, legislative or judicial, or otherwise applying to that minister as the holder of the office, include . . .

(c) his or their deputy; and

(d) notwithstanding paragraph (c), a person appointed to serve, in the department or ministry of state over which the minister presides, in a capacity appropriate to the doing of the act or thing, or to the words so applying.

Generally, a liberal interpretation should be given to the word "deputy", in subsection 24(2)(c). It clearly applies to a "deputy minister", the senior permanent civil servant in each department but it can be construed according to its normal meaning to also refer to a person authorized to act in place of another; *Canadian Bronze Co. v Deputy Minister of National Revenue* (1985),

57 NR 388 (Canada, FCA). Subsection 24(2)(d) provides for further flexibility by empowering other public servants of suitable rank and appropriate position in a department of government to also exercise ministerial powers.

The codified power under the *Interpretation Act* offers additional flexibility in that subsection (2) provides that the powers of the office holder can be exercised by an appropriate subordinate regardless of whether the power is administrative, legislative, or quasi-judicial in nature. This expands the categories of powers that can be exercised by a subordinate under the common law *Carltona* doctrine. However, note should be taken of subsection 24(3) which excludes from the devolution of power to a subordinate official the enactment of a regulation to which the *Statutory Instruments Act*[62] applies.

The *Carltona* doctrine and its codification in the *Interpretation Act* is intended to provide flexibility in governance by permitting officials to exercise discretionary ministerial powers in the interests of efficiency, while preserving the obligations of a minister to act in person where the nature of the power, or the statutory expression of the power, clearly contemplates the exercise of the minister's personal discretion. A decision rendered by a subordinate official pursuant to subsection 24(2)(d) of the *Interpretation Act* is a valid ministerial act and cannot be construed as mere advice to a minister.[63] Further, the powers of subsection 24(2) apply to statutory decision-making regardless of whether the substantive powers existed before the enactment of subsection 24(2) of the *Interpretation Act*, or were created afterwards.[64]

Apart from discretionary powers however, a minister is often invested with duties or particular responsibilities that are non-discretionary, and thus require the minister to act in a specific way. With respect to non-discretionary functions any public servant within the minister's department, or a Minister of State Assigned to Assist the Minister, may discharge that function on behalf of, or in the name of, the departmental minister.

Any power or function that is imposed upon a minister by statute may be exercised by their successors in office.[65] In addition, Section 24(5) of the *Interpretation Act* stipulates that the powers of an office may be exercised by the person who is executing the responsibilities of that office for the time being. Thus, an acting minister has the authority to exercise the powers and functions of the ministerial office in which they are acting.

Any power, duty, or function of a minister, or the control or supervision of a portion of the federal public administration that is vested in a minister, may be transferred from that minister to another Minister of the Crown, or to a Minister of State pursuant to the *Public Service Rearrangement and Transfer of Duties Act*.[66] That Act also provides, in section 4, that where a transfer of powers, duties or functions has been made to a minister by name, and that minister subsequently dies in office the powers, duties, and functions of that minister may be transferred to another minister.

11.27   Deputy Ministers Distinguished

In Canadian constitutional practice a Deputy Minister is a public official who is appointed by order-in-council to preside over a department or agency of government in a managerial capacity. They act under the direction and supervision of a Minister of the Crown and are not part of the Canadian Ministry. Deputy Ministers are considered to be the senior level of public servants in Canada, and they are normally drawn from the senior ranks of the civil services. As such, they are considered to be nonpartisan appointments and they usually continue to serve the Canadian Ministry even after the composition of the ministry has changed following a general election, or the replacement of a government following a defeat on a matter of confidence in the House of Commons.

A Deputy Minister may exercise some of the powers of the Minister of the Crown under whose supervision and direction they perform their duties pursuant to the *Carltona* doctrine, and they may also be given specific powers by legislation. However, when acting for a Minster of the Crown they may not exercise the power of a Minister to promulgate regulations.[67] Policy restrictions at the federal level of government may also prevent Deputy Ministers from signing Treasury Board submissions that request new monies, or that seek the approval of new policies. In addition, Deputy Ministers do not sign Memoranda to Cabinet, as it is considered that such memoranda ought to be personally signed by a minister.[68]

Deputy Ministers are accounting officers under Federal accountability legislation.[69] They are responsible for the work of all of the public servants who work in the department in which the Deputy Minister serves, except for a category of employee described as exempt staff who are generally political appointees of the minister, and who assist the minister with his or her partisan political duties.[70] Deputy Ministers are personally accountable to the ministers whom they serve, and, through the Clerk of the Privy Council (who is the Head of the Public Service of Canada) they are accountable to the Prime Minister.[71]

Some departmental statutes provide that Associate Deputy Ministers may also be appointed to carry out departmental duties assigned by the Minister under the overall direction of the Deputy Minister of the department.[72]

11.28   Resignation and Retirement

The Prime Minister is entitled to request the resignation of any minister from the Canadian Ministry and ministers are also entitled to retire from the Canadian Ministry by resigning from their office. Notwithstanding that all ministers serve the Sovereign, the constitutional practice is for ministerial letters of resignation to be addressed to the Prime Minister.[73] Resignation or retirement terminates the minister's position in the Canadian Ministry. However, a resigning or retiring minister is not required to resign or retire from the Queen's Privy Council for Canada and without doing so they will remain a Privy Councillor for life. As members of the Privy Council, they will also continue to be permitted to use the title Honourable as a prefix to their name and to append the post-nominal letters P.C.

The decision to remove a minister from the Canadian Ministry constitutes the exercise of a power under the Royal Prerogative that is exercisable by the Prime Minister. The decision is one that is at the far end of the spectrum of decisions involving the Royal Prerogatives that are capable of being reviewed by the courts. Thus, in *Guergis v Novak*, [2012] 112 OR (3d) 118 (Ontario, Sup. Ct.) it was held that the dismissal of a minister was a matter of Crown prerogative, and allegations of tortious conduct made against the Prime Minister by a member of the Canadian Ministry who had been removed from office were insufficient to warrant the court reviewing the removal of the minister. Justice Hackland stated:

> ... the plaintiff's contentions are wrong and, if sustained, would render meaningless this important privilege. The prime minister would be required to answer, in court, for the political decisions he makes as to the membership of his cabinet ... There is no authority that would support the proposition that Crown prerogative is waived or is inapplicable if the otherwise-protected decisions are alleged to be tortious ... In this case, I find that it is plain and obvious that the actions of the prime minister, in relation to the removal of the plaintiff from cabinet, fall within Crown prerogative ... [74]

11.29   Access of Ministers to the Sovereign's Representative

The Canadian Ministry exists to make decisions of governance. However the Sovereign's representative must be kept informed of the decisions taken by the Canadian Ministry so that the Crown can exercise its constitutional rights to be informed, to encourage, and to warn. It is the role of the Prime Minister to act as the communication link between the Canadian Ministry and the Sovereign, or the Sovereign's representative. Thus, the Prime Minister has a constitutional obligation, arising from convention, to advise the Sovereign's representative of the proposed actions of the Canadian Ministry. This does not mean that the Sovereign or the Sovereign's representatives are entitled to know the opinion of particular ministers in the Federal Cabinet on policy issues but rather it means that the Sovereign's representative is entitled to know the conclusions reached by the Federal Cabinet and the proposed actions of the Canadian Ministry.

Individual ministers have a right of access to the Sovereign's representative with respect to matters affecting their own departments or responsibilities. In exercising that right, ministers should inform the Prime Minister of the subject-matter of the meeting before it occurs, or immediately thereafter.[75]

Where the power to do something has been conferred by statute upon the Governor in Council it is necessary for a Committee of the Privy Council to convene in order to render advice to the Governor General prior to the exercise of the power. Formal acts by the Canadian Ministry which requires the exercise of the Royal Prerogative, or of a statutory discretion vested in the Governor in Council, must be submitted to a meeting of a committee of the Privy Council. For most Orders-in-Council this function is currently discharged by the Treasury Board. According to constitutional convention, only a minister may submit a matter to the Committee of the Privy Council for its consideration.[76] When the usual quorum of four Privy Councillors has considered the matter and agreed to a proposal the matter is submitted to the Governor General for approval. The subsequent acceptance of that advice by the Governor General constitutes the lawful act of the Governor General in Council.

It is customary at the federal level for each incoming Canadian Ministry to pass an order-in-council to enable the Prime Minister alone to make recommendations to the Sovereign's representative on behalf of the Privy Council with respect to the dissolution and convening of Parliament, the calling of meetings of the Privy Council, the appointments of the Governor General, Lieutenant Governors, Privy Councillors, Ministers, Administrators of a Province, Speakers of the Senate, Senators, Crown appointments to both Houses of Parliament, the Governor General's Secretary's staff, Chief Justices of all Courts, Deputy Heads of departments, Librarians of Parliament, and membership on subcommittees of the Privy Council and the Treasury Board. The first such Order-in-Council appears in the public records of Canada as P.C. 1853 dated 1 May 1896.[77]

In addition, constitutional convention prescribes one instance in which the Prime Minister-Designate alone must advise the Governor General. That circumstance involves the tendering of advice to the Governor General upon a change in government concerning the identity of the persons who the Governor General should summon to become members of the Privy Council, and subsequently to be sworn into the Canadian Ministry. As the new Canadian Ministry does not yet exist at the time the advice is given, the Prime Minister-Designate must, out of constitutional necessity, act alone for the purpose of providing formal advice to the Governor General on the appointment of new Privy Councillors, and the composition of the new Canadian Ministry.

11.30   Obligations of Ministers to the Crown

Members of the Canadian Ministry are subject to certain legal obligations to the Crown during their tenure of office. For instance, they are under an obligation to render formal advice to the Sovereign and the Sovereign's representatives where necessary in order for executive action to be effected.[78] Ministers are required by their oath as Privy Councillors to keep confidential all of their advice, both oral and written, that is tendered to the Sovereign, or to the Sovereign's representatives. Private conversations concerning matters of state held between Ministers and the Sovereign, or the Sovereign's representatives, are privileged communications, and a claim for an absolute privilege in regards to such conversations may be asserted, if necessary, in proceedings in a court of law.

When a government has been defeated in a general election, it loses its right to give constitutional advice which the Crown must follow by constitutional convention.[79] Commonwealth realm precedent suggests that the same result would apply where a ministry publicly concedes that it has lost its majority in the legislature; *Hilly v Governor-General of the Solomon Islands*, [1994] 2 LRC 27 at 33 (Solomon Islands, CA).

Formal advice tendered by Ministers to the Crown must be advice that can be supported by the Constitution. In *Air Canada v Attorney General of British Columbia*, [1988] LRC (Const) 38 (Canada, SC) a petition of right was issued seeking a declaration that the Applicant was entitled to a refund of monies paid to the Province under a taxation statue that was alleged to be unconstitutional. The Lieutenant Governor of British Columbia refused to issue a fiat on the advice of the Executive Council, which in turn relied upon a recommendation from the Attorney General of the Province. The refusal to issue a fiat was upheld by the Supreme Court of British Columbia and by the British Columbia Court of Appeal. However, on appeal to the Supreme Court of Canada the judgments of the lower courts were reversed.

The Supreme Court held that the Attorney General was under an imperative duty to advise the Lieutenant Governor to issue a fiat.[80] The Executive Council, to the extent that it was consulted by the Attorney General preparatory to the provision of advice to the Lieutenant Governor, was likewise subject to the same duty. To countenance the Executive Council, or the British Columbia Ministry, acting otherwise would violate the constitution. The Supreme Court relied on *The Cheng Poh v Public Prosecutor, Malaysia*, [1980] AC 458 (Malaysia, JC) for the proposition that mandamus would lie against a Minister to compel the provision of proper advice where a constitutional abuse of power by the Crown has occurred. *Ten Cheng Po* involved the powers of the Malaysian monarch, the Yang di-Pertuan Agong, and the revocation of a security proclamation. After noting that the courts themselves were powerless to revoke the security proclamation, the Judicial Committee stated that mandamus could issue against the Malaysian Cabinet to require them to advise the Monarch to revoke the proclamation.[81]

A similar view was expressed in *Wari v Ramoi*, [1987] LRC (Const) 152 at 160 (Papua New Guinea, SC) by Kapi DCJ, who held that advice given to the Governor General of Papua New Guinea was non-justiciable unless the advice was inconsistent with, or *ultra vires* of a statute, or inconsistent with the Constitution of Papua New Guinea.

Formal advice tendered by a ministry to the Crown need not be the result of personal judgment alone. Ministers are entitled to rely on sources of information other than their own personal investigations when formulating their advice. Thus, where a Chief Minister of a colony advised a Governor to dismiss a minister following the receipt of a report of a Commission of Inquiry, it was held that the dismissal of the Minister was in accordance with the constitution of the territory. In *Hodge v Herdman*, [1991] LRC (Const) 111 (British Virgin Islands, CA) Byron J.A. speaking for the Court held that the decision to advise the Governor to dismiss was properly made by the Chief Minister even if the Chief Minister's views were shaped or influenced by the report which the Chief Minister had received.[82]

Where a minister indicates to a subject that a recommendation will be made to a Lieutenant Governor in Council respecting the exercise of a prerogative power in favour of that subject, the minister's intimation that a favourable recommendation will be made does not bind the Lieutenant Governor in Council. Thus, where there was discretion to issue a crown patent in respect of lands, it was held that a minister's decision to recommend a patent could be reversed. In *Fitzpatrick v The King* (1926), 4 DLR 239 (Ontario, AD) the Court stated:

> The decision of the minister in favour of the issuing of a patent to Crown Lands is merely an intimation that he will recommend such issue, but it does not bind the Crown. If, in the meantime, it should appear to the minister to be in the public interest to withhold his recommendation, it is his duty to do so: thus his decision is a qualified one.[83]

In a federal state such as Canada, the obligations of a Minister of the Crown are complicated by the very nature of the federal structure. Thus, a purported undertaking by a provincial Minister of the Crown to the Sovereign in right of Canada, to pay the costs of maintaining troops in a province out of the revenues of the Sovereign in right of the province, was determined to be unenforceable where the expenditure was not authorized by the provincial legislature; *Reference Re Troops in Cape Breton*, [1930] SCR 554 (Canada, SC).

11.31   The Royal Recommendation

Bills introduced into the Parliament of Canada for the appropriation of monies out of the Consolidated Revenue Fund of the Federal Government, or new and distinct charges that were not previously addressed in the budgetary estimates submitted to Parliament, must be introduced into the House of Commons and dealt with there before they can be sent to the Senate of Canada. This constitutional requirement flows from section 54 of the *Constitution Act, 1867*.

A Royal Recommendation, which is a recommendation by the Governor General that the funds requested be appropriated, must be presented to the House of Commons in the parliamentary session in which the bill is proposed to be debated. The form of a Royal Recommendation is as follows;

> His/Her Excellency the Governor General recommends to the House of Commons the appropriation of public revenue under the circumstances, in the manner and for the purposes set out in a measure entitled (insert here the long title of the bill).

The custom is to provide the Royal Recommendation at the time that the appropriations bill is introduced into the House of Commons but under the rules of procedure governing the House of Commons the Royal Recommendation may be submitted to the House at any time up to the third reading of the bill. If the Royal Recommendation is not provided to the House of Commons by the time of the third reading of the bill, the bill cannot be passed by the House of Commons.

Without a Royal Recommendation, the House of Commons cannot pass a money bill. The Senate cannot act on such a measure before the House of Commons votes. Without legislation to appropriate funds the business of government cannot be carried on. Appropriations of funds by Parliament are an essential component of a Westminster model constitution, as the Judicial Committee held in *Auckland Harbour Board v The King*, [1924] AC 318 (New Zealand, JC) where Viscount Haldane stated:

> [I]t has been a principle of the British Constitution now for more than two centuries, a principle which their Lordships understand to have been inherited in the Constitution of New Zealand with the same stringency, that no money can be taken out of the consolidated Fund into which the revenues of the State have been paid, excepting under a distinct authorization from Parliament itself.[84]

There is legislative provision for funds to be appropriated by the Governor General by Special Warrant but only in situations where the House of Commons has been dissolved and a general election is being held. Where Special Warrants have been issued, the funds appropriated through that measure must be appropriated by Parliament after it convenes following the general election.

A Royal Recommendation must be presented by a Minister of the Crown because the Canadian Ministry has responsibility for the expenditure of funds necessary for good governance. Despite that requirement, it is possible under the Canadian parliamentary law applicable to the House of Commons for a private member to introduce a private members bill that calls for the expenditure of public funds. In such situations, the Canadian Ministry must present a Royal Recommendation before the private member's bill can be read a third time. In the absence of such a Royal Recommendation the private member's public bill cannot be passed by the House of Commons.

11.32   Royal Consent

Royal Consent is a parliamentary mechanism to protect the interests of the Crown, including the powers of the Royal Prerogative. It is part of the customary law of Parliament rather than a part of the common law, or of the written constitution. It is the duty of a Minister of the Crown having responsibility for a parliamentary bill which affects the Royal Prerogatives, hereditary revenues, personal property, or interests of the Sovereign, including legislative actions that would compromise, surrender, postpone or waive the rights of Royal Prerogatives attaching to the Crown, to obtain Royal Consent to the bill, and thereafter to formally advise Parliament of the granting of Royal Consent. Examples include measures that would affect property liens held by the Crown, or matters relating to property in which the Crown holds legal title. Where the legislative body consists of two houses (as does the Canadian Parliament) Royal Consent must be expressed separately in each house of Parliament.

The responsible minister must obtain the authorization of the Governor General before expressing Royal Consent in the House of Commons. Royal Consent in the House of Commons is normally stated by the responsible minister rising in the House of Commons and declaring that:

> His [or Her] Excellency the Governor General has been informed of the purport of this bill and has given his [or her] consent, as far as His [or Her] Majesty's prerogatives are affected, to the consideration by Parliament of the bill, that Parliament may do therein as it thinks fit.[85]

Since this is a matter concerning the Crown only a member of the Canadian Ministry, as a Privy Councillor, can perform this function in Parliament and thus it cannot be delegated to Parliamentary Secretaries or other members of the government caucus. Royal Consent can also be provided to Parliament in the form of a Message from the Governor General. Royal Consent may be provided at any point in the legislative process up to third reading of a bill but in Canada it most often occurs upon second reading of a bill.

If a minister is unable to signify Royal Consent to the bill to Parliament, the bill must be withdrawn.[86] If a bill is passed in one of the Houses of Parliament without the necessary Royal Consent being expressed the bill's passage is a nullity.

Where a private member who is introducing a private members bill into Parliament or a provincial legislature requires Royal Consent the normal practice is for the private member to seek leave for an Address to the Sovereign's representative to seek Royal Consent before the bill can be enacted.

Since the Governor General would act on the advice of the Canadian Ministry in deciding whether to grant Royal Consent there is little prospect of a denial of Royal Consent with respect to government bills. However, Royal Consent could be denied in the case of a private member's public bill, particularly in cases where the ministry is a minority government in the House of Commons if a private members bill was in danger of passing over the objections of the Canadian Ministry. Where the government commands a majority in the House of Commons however, the practice is not to withhold Royal Consent, as to do so could prevent parliamentary debate. Rather, Royal Consent is commonly granted, the bill is debated, and if the government still feels that its passage would be unwise it may vote the bill down on third reading by using its majority.

Royal Consent does not mean that the Crown approves of the contents of a bill, and the legal power (which now can only be exercised according to constitutional convention) to withhold Royal Assent upon passage of the bill is not waived by the granting of Royal Consent to a proposed bill. Similarly, approval of a measure cannot be imputed to the Federal Cabinet because a cabinet minister has arisen in the House or Senate and expressed Royal Consent to a proposed bill.

11.33   Obligations of Ministers to Parliament

The concept of individual accountability of ministers to Parliament is a constitutional convention that has a long, if somewhat chequered history. Essentially, the individual responsibility of ministers means that as the head of a political department of the government a Minister of the Crown is responsible for everything that department does, and must explain the actions of the department to Parliament, and answer all of Parliament's questions concerning departmental actions.

There are two aspects of this obligation: responsibility and answerability. Responsibility means that a serious error of policy or administration by a department may require a particular minister to resign his or her office.[87] This aspect of responsibility distinguishes a parliamentary form of government from an executive form of government. In the latter, responsibility tends to become focused on the failings of subordinate officials, who are often political appointees of the current administration.

In contrast, under the parliamentary form of government, as it is practised in Canada, the failings of subordinate officials are exactly the type of error which attracts ministerial responsibility. Nevertheless, with the growth of modern government in size and complexity, and the greater emphasis on cabinets' collegial responsibility, it is now axiomatic that a minister whose department has committed some administrative error will not be required to resign from the Canadian Ministry.[88]

Even where an individual minister is prepared to accept full responsibility resignation can depend upon such variable factors as the political popularity of the minister, his or her personal relations with the Prime Minister, and the political situation facing the government. In reality, the fate of the minister will be decided by the Prime Minister and his closest political advisors, as it is the Prime Minister who must select and dismiss members of the Canadian Ministry, miscreant or otherwise.

Thus, while the first aspect of ministerial accountability is now honoured more often in the breach than in practice, it is the second branch, answerability, which retains a continued vibrancy in constitutional convention in Canada. Ministers are required to answer questions posed in Parliament to both explain and defend departmental policies and decisions. However, this does not mean that ministers must answer every particular question put to them during Question Period in the House of Commons. Most attempt some form of an answer however, for the simple reason that failure to respond to a particular question may lead to an adverse inference being drawn by the opposition parties, or the media, and ultimately by the electorate.

By convention, neither responsibility, individual accountability, nor answerability will result in a minister being held to account for the actions of their predecessors in office. That is true in both those situations where a predecessor was a member of the same political party as well as those situations where a predecessor was a member of a different political party. Politically, ministers may also be held to account for their personal actions, since they are high public officials holding important offices. Ministers who engage in personal misconduct which is unlawful, immoral, or unethical, may feel obliged, or be obliged, to step down as a consequence.

Ministers enjoy the same parliamentary immunities as do all members of Parliament. Thus, their words expressed in Parliament cannot be made the subject of suits for libel or slander, and their parliamentary acts cannot be impugned in the courts of law. They are immune from examination for discovery in litigation with respect to their utterances in Parliament. In general, the proceedings of Parliament cannot be the subject of litigation in the courts of law.

11.34   Obligations of a Minister to the Judiciary

In general terms, the obligations of a minister to the judicial branch of government are identical to those of any subject of the Sovereign. However, there are some practical distinctions. Firstly, the public position of a minister often puts them in a position where they are invited to express comments upon matters that either are or may come before a court of law. In accordance with Canadian constitutional convention and constitutional custom a Minister should avoid any comments on matters that are pending before the courts because ministerial comments could prejudice the fairness of the legal process. Where a matter has been heard and decided by the courts, ministers must be circumspect in their comments on any judicial pronouncement. Unguarded outbursts may be perceived as scandalous and result in a conviction of a Minister for contempt of court. An example is afforded by the case of *Re Ouellet* (1976), 72 DLR (3d) 95 (Quebec, CA) where the reaction of a federal minister to a judgment appeared to question the sanity of the presiding Justice. The Minister was subsequently found guilty of contempt of court, and fined.

A Minister who acts outside of the scope of the powers entrusted to them for some improper purpose, or acts contrary to law, may be subject to criminal or civil penalties, or both, in their personal capacity. However, where a minister is challenged in the courts for acts that are within the scope of the minister's authority as a Minister of the Crown he or she will not be subject to criminal or civil penalties in their personal capacity but the Crown may be liable to injured parties in its corporate capacity (i.e., as a department) or be subject to a prosecution.

Ministers, while they are members of Parliament, are exempt from a citizen's duty to participate on a jury, and while Parliament is in session they may not be made the subject of a civil arrest for a period beginning 40 days prior to a Parliamentary session and ending 40 days after the dissolution of Parliament. Nor may ministers, as members of Parliament, be made the subject of a subpoena to testify in court as a witness in a civil or a criminal proceeding. However, ministers may waive their exemption from testifying in a court of law. Like any other member of Parliament ministers may be arrested in a personal criminal matter, as their immunities do not extend to the non-application of criminal law.

As a consequence of the duties of a minister it will be quite common for legal proceedings to be commenced against ministers in connection with their official acts. Where a minister claims privilege or immunities arising from their position as a member of Parliament, the courts of law will defer to Parliament for the assessment of the necessity for a claim of privilege, or immunity, so as not to interfere with the discharge of their parliamentary duties.

A minister may file an objection with a court to the disclosure of information if that information would disclose a confidence of the Queen's Privy Council for Canada. The courts may examine the circumstances of the assertion of this privilege to ensure that it is a proper assertion on its face. The information for which privilege is asserted must be a confidence of the Privy Council that has not been previously divulged, and the minister must act in good faith in asserting the claim.

In *Minister of Employment and Immigration v Bhatnager* (1990), 71 DLR (4th) 84 (Canada, SC) it was held that where a minister has been named in a court order and that order has not been obeyed, the minister will not be found guilty of contempt of court unless there is at least a reasonable inference of personal knowledge of that order by the minister, or evidence to show that the minister has engaged in willful blindness in relation to the judicial proceedings.

11.35   The Law Officers of the Crown

There are two ministerial offices that occupy a special position, the Attorney General and the Solicitor General. Those ministers are the Law Officers of the Crown and as such have a responsibility to the Sovereign to uphold the rule of law and the correct administration of justice.

At the federal level the office of Attorney General of Canada is attached to the office of the Minister of Justice. The Minister of Justice is *ex officio* the Attorney General of Canada and has the powers and duties of the Attorney General of England and Wales. Section 4 of the *Department of Justice Act*[89] states that the Minister of Justice is "the official legal advisor of the Governor General and the legal member of the Queen's Privy Council for Canada . . . " Thus, by statute the Minister of Justice is the solicitor to the Governor General. In practice, departmental counsel in the Department of Justice would provide such legal advice as the Office of the Governor General requires. Nevertheless, the Governor General can call upon the Minister of Justice directly to provide legal advice pursuant to section 4 of the departmental statute.[90]

The office of the Attorney General of Canada is not a separate office but rather is an *ex officio* title added to the federal office of Minister of Justice, although the functions of the Minister of Justice and the Attorney General of Canada are separate. Unlike the situation in the United Kingdom and in other Commonwealth realms in Canada the Attorney General of Canada is a political officer who is a cabinet minister. That raises the issue of a potential conflict between the officeholder's collegial responsibility as a cabinet minister, and their responsibilities to the law. In the event of any conflict between their political duties and their duties in connection with the rule of law and the administration of justice, the latter must supersede any political considerations.

The constitutional principle of interjurisdictional immunity applies to the office of Attorney General of Canada so as to preclude the application of provincial laws regulating the admission to practice of persons as lawyers to the office of the Attorney General of Canada. As a result there is no enforceable requirement that the Attorney General of Canada be a lawyer, and thus any person may be named to the post of Minister of Justice and Attorney General of Canada. Invariably, however, a lawyer is appointed to this important senior ministerial post.

While the provinces have the constitutional jurisdiction to regulate the legal profession in Canada, the requirements for a person to be called to the bar of a province also do not apply to a person appointed as Attorney General of a province, and thus a layperson may be appointed as a provincial Attorney General; *Askin v Law Society of British Columbia* (2013), 363 DLR (4th) 706 (British Columbia, CA).

At the federal level, the *Department of Justice Act* sets out the responsibilities of the Minister of Justice of Canada in section 4 of the Act:

The Minister is the official legal adviser of the Governor General and the legal member of the Queen's Privy Council for Canada and shall

(a) see that the administration of public affairs is in accordance with law;

(b) have the superintendence of all matters connected with the administration of justice in Canada, not within the jurisdiction of the governments of the provinces;

(c) advise on the legislative Acts and proceedings of each of the legislatures of the provinces, and generally advise the Crown on all matters of law referred to the Minister by the Crown; and

(d) carry out such other duties as are assigned by the Governor in Council to the Minister.

Thus, the Minister of Justice is the legal adviser to the Crown and discharges the obligation upon the Crown to ensure that the public administration is conducted according to law.

The functions of the Attorney General of Canada are separate and are set out in section 5 of the Act:

The Attorney General of Canada

(a) is entrusted with the powers and charged with the duties that belong to the office of the Attorney General of England by law or usage, in so far as those powers and duties are applicable to Canada, and also with the powers and duties that, by the laws of the several provinces, belonged to the office of attorney general of each province up to the time when the Constitution Act, 1867, came into effect, in so far as those laws under the provisions of the said Act are to be administered and carried into effect by the Government of Canada;

(b) shall advise the heads of the several departments of the Government on all matters of law connected with such departments;

(c) is charged with the settlement and approval of all instruments issued under the Great Seal;

(d) shall have the regulation and conduct of all litigation for or against the Crown or any department, in respect of any subject within the authority or jurisdiction of Canada; and

(e) shall carry out such other duties as are assigned by the Governor in Council to the Attorney General of Canada.

In general, the duties of the Law Officers of the Crown encompass all matters relating to the administration of justice and include such variegated obligations as responsibility for the courts of law, and the appointments of judges to them, the exercise of the prosecutorial function, the enforcement of the law, including the police and correctional services, responsibility for the legal profession, the conduct of all Crown litigation before the courts and tribunals, the provision of legal advice to the Crown and government departments or agencies, and the drafting of government legislation. The Attorney General must approve the form of Crown instruments issued under the Great Seal of Canada.

Although the Attorney General of Canada is given the powers and duties of the Attorney General of England much of the powers and duties of the Attorney General of England are not applicable to the Attorney General of Canada because the administration of justice in Canada largely falls to the jurisdiction of the provinces under section 92 of the *Constitution Act, 1867*. Thus the provincial Attorneys General who are also law officers of the Crown with respect to their provinces will exercise many of the historical powers of the English Attorney General noted in the paragraph above pursuant to provincial legislation. Those responsibilities will also include advising the Crown in Right of a province, conducting provincial litigation, acting as a guardian of the public interest and exercising the Sovereign's *parens patriae* jurisdiction, appearing as *amicus curiae*, and exercising the Crown's public prosecutorial functions in relation to criminal law. At the provincial level the office of the Attorney General may also be combined with the office of Minister of Justice in some of the provinces.

Since 2006 the prosecutorial functions of the Attorney General of Canada have been fulfilled by the Director of Public Prosecutions, an official whose office reports to Parliament through the Attorney General but is otherwise operationally independent of the Attorney General. The purpose in creating the office of the Director of Public Prosecutions was, in part, to insulate prosecutorial discretion from political considerations.

The office of the Director of Public Prosecutions is a Commonwealth innovation that has been designed to separate the function of laying a charge from the political functions of a cabinet minister. The concern that is addressed by the creation of an independent Director of Public Prosecutions is that a Minister of the Crown with the responsibility for initiating a prosecution could be influenced by political considerations. However, the concern about political considerations influencing the judgment of an Attorney General is also broader than the prosecutorial function, and various models have been used by the Commonwealth realms to attempt to insulate the office of the Attorney General from all political considerations.

In some jurisdictions, where the Attorney General is a public servant rather than a Minister, the office of Director of Public Prosecutions and Attorney General have been combined.[91] A second model involves the appointment of the Attorney General as a minister but one that is excluded from the cabinet.[92] A third model, which is the model that is prevalent in Canada, is the appointment of an Attorney General as a Cabinet Minister but with internal insulation from prosecutorial decision-making through the appointment of a Director of Public Prosecutions, or an equivalent official.[93] A fourth model completely separates the functions of the Director of Public Prosecutions from any subordinated relationship with the Attorney General.[94] A final model entails functional independence from the Attorney General of the Director of Public Prosecutions but the latter may be subjected to direction where the Director refers a matter to the Attorney General or a Minister responsible for justice designates a class of cases which must be referred by the Director.[95]

The Solicitor General was historically a deputy of the Attorney General and fulfilled some of the litigation and other important functions of the chief law officers of the Crown, the Attorney General. In Canada, at the federal level, the position of Solicitor General was a ministerial appointment but in the early years following confederation is was a position that was excluded from the Cabinet. Later, in 1966, the position of Solicitor General was made responsible for public security and penitentiaries and the office was elevated to Cabinet rank, whereupon the office effectively ceased to act as a deputy to the Attorney General.

In the twenty-first century public security duties have become the responsibility of a minister of public security who also held the office of Solicitor General but who did not bear the operational responsibilities of a Law Officer of the Crown and thus, in 2005, the position of Solicitor General was abolished by statute at the federal level. Most provincial governments have subsequently followed suit and abolished the office by statute.

The Law Officers of the Crown do not normally provide legal advice to Parliament, or to the provincial legislatures in the modern era although this was a historical responsibility of the office. In the contemporary period, legal advice concerning parliamentary law may be provided to the Speaker of a House of Parliament or the Speaker of a provincial legislature, or by the clerk of a legislative body, or by counsel specifically retained for that purpose by a house of Parliament, or a provincial legislature.

Proceedings against the Sovereign in right of Canada may be taken in the name of the Attorney General of Canada,[96] and the Attorney General of Canada may commence actions on behalf of the Sovereign in right of Canada.[97] Similarly, actions by or against the Sovereign in right of a province may be brought in the name of a provincial Attorney General. Where the Attorney General is not properly named the style of cause, the style of cause may be amended on the application of counsel representing the Attorney General.

11.36   Relations with Quasi-Judicial Bodies

Most governments in Canada have adopted codes of conduct which regulate even more strictly contacts between ministers and the quasi-judicial bodies under their administration. Increasing concern has been focused on the impact of even inadvertent suasion on the deliberations of such bodies. At the federal level, restrictions have taken the form of guidelines issued to ministers. The guidelines establish, as a basic principle, that ministers and ministerial (i.e., political staff) must not intervene on behalf of anyone before a federal quasi-judicial agency, in matters requiring a quasi-judicial decision by that agency. Ministers with portfolio responsibilities for particular quasi-judicial agencies however, may establish mutually agreed upon procedures and limits for the exchange of information on such matters as financial accountability with the agencies for which the minister is responsible to Parliament.

These guidelines have upgraded the protection afforded to quasi-judicial processes of the federal government by banning all contact by ministers with quasi-judicial agencies on adjudicative matters. Previously, interventions did occur, although in practice ministers generally avoided taking a position in favour of or opposed to particular applications before tribunals.[98]

11.37   Obligations of a Minister to the Sovereign's Subjects

A minister owes obligations to the general public. Stripped to its essential form, those obligations require a minister to act in accordance with the rule of law. That, in turn, is a derivative of the Sovereign's own obligation, fortified by the Coronation Oath, to obey the rule of law and to avoid arbitrary measures.

Thus, a minister cannot claim any right of search and seizure in respect of the property of the subjects of the Crown merely by virtue of holding ministerial office, or membership in the Privy Council; *Entick v Carrington*, [1765] All ER

Rep 41 (England, Com. Pleas). Nor may a minister refuse to submit a petition of right from a subject addressed to the Sovereign's representative, where a statute requires the minister to submit the petition. The failure of a minister to obey such a statutory duty is compensable by damages; *Fulton v Norton*, [1908] AC 451 (Canada, JC).

Where a Minister acts wholly outside the purview of their responsibilities, such as by procuring a revocation of a licence held by a subject solely because of the subject's religious beliefs, the Minister may be found liable in damages for an abuse of power; *Roncarelli v Duplessis*, [1959] SCR 121 (Canada, SC). The *Roncarelli* case is an important case in Canadian jurisprudence because it established the basis for the tort of misfeasance in public office under which individuals may seek damages for the willfully illegal acts of ministers and other public officials.

In *Marin v Attorney General*, [2011] 5 LRC 209 (Belize, CCJ) the Caribbean Court of Justice extended the principle of the tort of misfeasance in public office to allow a suit to be brought against former ministers by the Attorney General of Belize to recover funds that were alleged to have been improperly obtained by the former ministers. The historical practice of the common law however, has been to treat allegations of corruption against a minister or other public official as a matter for prosecution under the criminal law, rather than as a suitable subject for civil proceedings.[99]

Where a minister gives a formal undertaking to a subject, that undertaking may bind the Crown. Thus, in *Beauchamp v Hockin* (1989), 30 FTR (Canada, FC) the facts disclosed that the Minister of State for Finance had provided a written undertaking to members of a tribunal which was being abolished committing the Crown to refer questions of compensation in respect of the early termination of their public offices to the Trial Division of the Federal Court for an assessment. There was a delay in making the reference to the court and, upon an application being made, the court enforced the undertaking by setting a fixed date for the referral of the matter, should further negotiations between the parties not result in a settlement by the date fixed by the court for the referral.

An undertaking given to subjects by a minister cannot fetter the ability of individual legislators in Parliament or a provincial legislature to vote in favour of proposed legislation; *Reclamation Systems v Rae*, [1996] 27 OR (3d) 419 at 448 (Ontario, GD).

Where a minister acting in good faith makes a statement concerning the policy of the ministry and its intention to seek legislation from Parliament, no action will lie against the Crown for interference with private rights as it the minister's duty to articulate government policy from time to time; *Roman Corp. Ltd. v Hudson's Bay Oil and Gas Co. Ltd.* (1973), 36 DLR (3d) 413 (Canada, SC).

Similarly, political undertakings uttered in Parliament are not binding upon the Crown. The accountability for such statements rests with the electorate; *Penikett v R*, [1988] 2 WWR 481 (Yukon, CA)

11.38   Consensus Government in the Northern Territories

In the northern territories of Nunavut and the Northwest Territories, responsible government has been modified by the principle of consensus government. In those territories, candidates for the territorial legislatures do not stand for election as representatives of political parties but rather as individuals. Following a general election, the members of the territorial ministry are individually selected by the members of the legislature. Executive power in the Northwest Territories and Nunavut is concentrated in the territorial ministry but all members of the legislature meet informally in caucus to discuss political issues, and agendas, with the intention of reaching a consensus with respect to public policy.[100] The members of the legislature who are not members of the territorial ministry do not operate as a formal opposition group thus differentiating the territorial legislatures from the legislatures in Yukon or southern Canada. These unique structures serve to distinguish consensus government from the form of responsible government practised elsewhere in Canada.

Members of the legislatures where consensus procedures are used do have the ability to pass a motion of non-confidence in the territorial ministry in accordance with the principles of responsible government. The ancient parliamentary remedy of impeachment is also available.[101]

11.39   The Cabinet

The cabinet is a body which one seeks in vain to find recorded in Canada's written constitution.[102] Actually, it is an institution that evolved in the constitution of England from the Privy Council and was received by Canada as part of the constitutional conventions of the United Kingdom. As the English Privy Council became too unwieldy for effective governance, the Sovereign began to rely on an inner group of advisors who became known as the Cabinet (or secret) Council as early as 1625. The Sovereign attended this Cabinet Council and exercised effective political control over it. By the era of Queen Anne, there was a Privy Council to execute the royal will, a Committee of Council heading operating departments (a ministry) and a cabinet.

For a variety of reasons (not least of which was the fact that, as a German, he could not understand English) Queen Anne's successor, King George I, stopped attending the English cabinet, then known as the Select Lords, by about 1720. The cabinet continued to meet in the King's absence to discuss and conclude matters of public policy and ultimately achieved a paramount position in English constitutional government. In Canada, the cabinet became established at the time of the grant of responsible government in the 1840's, during the colonial era.

The cabinet must be distinguished from the ministry. In an early Australian case, *R v Davenport* (1874) QSCR 99 (Queensland, SC), Justice Lutwyche stated: "The Cabinet, as it is called, is not a body recognized by the Constitution, but the Executive Council, which is composed of the Governor and the different members of the administration – the heads of the departments – is".[103]

The cabinet has also been judicially defined elsewhere in the Commonwealth. Thus, in *Williams Construction Ltd. v Blackburn and Another*, [1990] 2 LRC 70 (Barbados, SC) the expression "cabinet" was defined as follows:

> The Cabinet decides important questions of policy while the details of the executive administration and the ordinary routine work of the executive are left to the various government offices and departments, controlled in the case of political departments by individual ministers.[104]

Under typical circumstances, the Cabinet makes policy and the Ministry implements that policy – either directly, or through actions taken by the Privy or Executive Councils. The process was described by Chief Justice Bowen in an Australian case, *Minister For Arts Heritage and Environment v Peko-Wallsend Ltd.* (1987), 75 ALR 218:

> The Governor General, except in very limited instances, acts on the advice of his Minister or Ministers conveyed to him in Executive Council. Often the advice flows from a decision of Cabinet. However, Cabinet is not mentioned in the Constitution and is not in any formal sense the Executive.[105]

In Canada the function of the Federal Cabinet is to establish and direct the political objectives of the government. One further distinction between the Federal Cabinet and the Canadian Ministry is that the cabinet is central to the brokering of political concerns in a large federal state such as Canada. Accordingly, the members of the Federal Cabinet are selected as much for the geographic areas of Canada which they represent, and their linguistic and cultural competencies, and even their gender, as for their executive abilities in government.[106] Prime Ministers generally seek to include at least one member of parliament from each province in their cabinet although that is not always possible.

The Federal Cabinet possesses a fluid organization, and thus in addition to the full cabinet it may be organized along committee lines, with committees established to deal with particular functional areas such as economic or social policy. On other occasions, a Cabinet Committee may be established to serve a particular purpose, as in the case of a War Cabinet, which has the object of directing the fortunes of the realm during wartime.

11.40   The First Minister

When the King ceased to attend cabinet meetings in England, around 1720, the First Lord of the Treasury began to preside at cabinet meetings and his position was enhanced by the King's reliance on the Treasury Department to persuade Parliament to grant supply, which is the provision of funds to carry on the government of the realm.[107] Eventually the pre-eminent position of the First Lord of the Treasury resulted in the recognition of the holder of that office as the first, or Prime Minister.

In colonial Canada the governors were always advised by a council of appointed officials, at first, during the Bourbon Monarchy, consisting of the Conseil Souverain and Conseil Supériure and later, under the British, the legislative councils. With the grant of representative government the position of the elected members of the legislature became important, and the legislative councils began to operate like a cabinet. Under representative government it was the office of Attorney General that was the most important ministerial office in the colonies.

Later, with the establishment of responsible government, an Executive Council began to function and the position of a first minister, or Premier, became established as the recognized ministerial leader in the colonial government. It was these two streams of constitutional evolution, in Britain and in Canada, that together coalesced to create the pre-eminent position of Prime Minister, or Premier, in the scheme of responsible government that is practised today in Canada.

The position of the first minister in Canada at the federal level of government is known as the Prime Minister, and at the provincial level of government the first minister is described as the Premier (in Quebec, the French expression for prime minister is also used to describe the provincial office).[108] The federal and provincial first ministers occupy similar positions at different levels in the scheme of responsible government in Canada.

The Prime Minister, or Premier, is the chief executive officer of the government of Canada, or of a province, and is the link in responsible government between the ministry and the monarchy. The Prime Minister, or Premier, is singularly responsible to the Sovereign as the head of the Crown's ministry but he or she is also collectively responsible with the other members of their cabinet to Parliament, or a provincial legislature, for their conduct of the governance of the country or a province.

At the federal level, the Prime Minister must hold or obtain membership in one of the houses of Parliament. Invariably, the Prime Minister is a member of the House of Commons since it is practically impossible to answer to the lower house for the actions of the Canadian Ministry while occupying a seat in the Senate. Nevertheless, it is theoretically still possible for a Senator to hold the office of Prime Minister and, in the nineteenth century, two Prime Ministers, Sir John J C Abbott, and Sir Mackenzie Bowell, held the office of Prime Minister while serving in the Senate. Like the Prime Minister, the Premier of a province must hold or obtain a seat in the legislature of the province.

Informally, the Prime Minister, or Premier, has responsibilities to the other members of their cabinet, emanating from the collegial nature of cabinet decision-making. However since the right of cabinet ministers to their position is dependent upon the will of the Prime Minister, or Premier, the first minister is pre-eminent in the operation of constitutional government in Canada and their office is central to the operation of the cabinet. The Prime Minister, or Premier, has the sole discretion to determine the agenda of the cabinet.[109]

Since a ministry must at all times maintain the confidence of the legislative body to which its members belong, the Prime Minister, or Premier, has an important responsibility, together with the other members of his or her cabinet, to ensure that the confidence of Parliament or a provincial legislature is maintained. The primary responsibility of determining whether Parliament or a provincial legislature has lost confidence in a ministry rests with the Prime Minister, or Premier.[110]

The powers exercised by the Prime Minister, or provincial Premier, are large in scope but consistent with their origins in unwritten English constitutional law. Those powers are not defined in the written *Constitution Acts 1867-1982*, nor in the myriad of constitutional statutes that pertain to the governance of Canada and its provinces. Rather, the powers of the Prime Minister, or provincial Premier, are derived from the constitutional conventions and, in particular, the conventions of responsible government that defines the roles of the Sovereign, the Sovereign's representatives, and their constitutional advisors. As a result, the office of the Prime Minister and the office of the provincial Premiers are not described in the written constitution and are mentioned only in passing in the *Constitution Act, 1982*, with respect to constitutional conferences. At the federal level the Prime Minister is also mentioned briefly in the *Salaries Act*.

11.41   Definition and Membership in the Cabinet

Formally the Federal Cabinet consists of those members of the Queen's Privy Council who have been sworn to the Canadian Ministry and who have been invited by the Prime Minister of Canada to sit in the Federal Cabinet. In the Provinces, where there is no Privy Council, the Provincial Cabinet consists of those Members of the Executive Council who have been invited by the Premier to sit in the cabinet.

The key characteristic of the cabinet is its close connection with a first minister. The Prime Minister or provincial Premier chooses the people who will join him or her in the cabinet. Neither the Sovereign, nor the Sovereign's representative, has any part to play in the selection of which ministers will join the cabinet. Unlike the membership in the Privy Council, or a ministry, royal permission or appointment to the cabinet is not provided for in the Canadian constitution. Thus the inclusion of a Minister of the Crown in the cabinet, as opposed to their appointment to the ministry, is solely within the discretion of a Prime Minister or provincial Premier. A Prime Minister or provincial Premier can terminate any minister's membership in their cabinet without affecting that minister's position as a member of a ministry, although this appears never to have been done in Canada. The normal practice, whenever it is necessary for a minister to be removed is to remove them from both the cabinet and the Canadian or Provincial Ministry at the same time, by dismissal, or forced resignation.

The Federal Cabinet and the Canadian Ministry are not identical. It is possible for a person to be a minister without being a member of the cabinet. For example, during the late nineteenth and early twentieth centuries, it was quite common for the Solicitor General to be sworn into the Canadian Ministry but not to be invited into the Federal Cabinet.[111] At times, Ministers of State Assigned to Assist a Minister have joined the Canadian Ministry but have not been invited into the Federal Cabinet.

The cabinet as a collective body continues to exist until the first minister dies in office, or resigns. Upon the death of a first minister in office, the cabinet immediately ceases to exist, although individual ministers retain their ministerial offices until a new first minister is appointed, and a new Canadian Ministry (or a Provincial Ministry) and cabinet is assembled. The resignation of a Prime Minster, or Premier following a defeat on a vote of confidence, or a defeat in a general election automatically includes the resignations of all of the other members of the Canadian Ministry (or a Provincial Ministry), and thus dissolves the federal or provincial cabinet. However, a resignation of a Prime Minister or Premier which is a mere personal retirement does not automatically include the resignations of the other members of the Canadian, or Provincial, Ministry, and therefore the cabinet remains intact unless and until it is altered by the succeeding Prime Minister or Premier.

11.42   Responsibility of the Cabinet to Parliament or a Legislature

A federal or provincial cabinet is collectively responsible to the House of Commons, or to a provincial legislature, and thus the cabinet is sometimes described as a committee of the House of Commons, or of a provincial legislature. A cabinet must retain the confidence of the House of Commons or of a provincial legislature at all times. If a cabinet loses the confidence of the House of Commons or of a provincial legislature constitutional convention requires that the first minister must surrender their mandate to carry on the Sovereign's government.[112] If the Sovereign's representative accepts that resignation, the Sovereign's representative must then ask a member of one of the Houses of Parliament (or a member of the provincial legislature in the case of the provinces) to form a new ministry, which will result in the formation of a new cabinet. The new ministry, which is guided in the formation and development of its policies by the cabinet, must then seek the support of the House of Commons, or of the provincial legislature.[113]

Thus, by constitutional convention, a cabinet faces the perpetual threat of a dissolution should it lose the confidence of Parliament, or a provincial legislature. In practice however, there is little expectancy of a dissolution due to the invention of cohesive and disciplined political parties, which are now firmly under the control of a party leadership. Nevertheless, in moments of great crisis, Parliament, or a provincial legislature, may be able to force a cabinet to stand aside, notwithstanding political party cohesiveness.[114]

If Parliament or a provincial legislature is sitting during a cabinet crisis, parliamentary practice allows questions to be asked each day by the opposition, with respect to the pace of progress in the formation of a new ministry. The House of Commons or a provincial legislature adjourns from day to day while the cabinet crisis is resolved.[115]

Not every defeat on a parliamentary vote will result in a loss of confidence in the cabinet. To be a question of confidence, the matter must be one of substance. Some government measures are automatically a question of confidence, such as supply (i.e., requests relating to the revenues and expenditures of government contained in a Royal Recommendation from the Sovereign's representative). The defeat of the government on a vote of confidence is a clear repudiation of the cabinet and its political program. However, a defeat which results from a snap vote, or a vote on a minor matter, may not necessarily result in a withdrawal of confidence. Often such defeats can be recovered by a muster of the government's full legislative strength. If the House of Commons or a provincial legislature continues to deny its confidence however, the first minister must tender his or her resignation (and the resignation of the ministry) to the Sovereign's representative, which dissolves the cabinet.

11.43   Obligations of Cabinet Ministers to Each Other

The cabinet is a collective decision-making body that must take collective responsibility for all of its decisions.[116] Accordingly, cabinet ministers owe an obligation of solidarity to one another. As part of this obligation, cabinet ministers concede to one another the right to bring forward policy proposals for the consideration of the cabinet. Policies may be debated and vigorously argued in cabinet but once the cabinet has made a policy decision it is the duty of every member of the cabinet to abide by that decision, and to support it publicly in Parliament and elsewhere. Cabinet Ministers who cannot, in good conscience, publicly support a cabinet decision must resign from the cabinet and the ministry or face dismissal. Thus, early in the twentieth century when the Minister of Public Works in Prime Minister Sir Wilfrid Laurier's cabinet publicly differed with the Federal Cabinet's policy on customs tariffs, he was dismissed from office for breaching cabinet solidarity.[117] Although Ministers of State are sometimes not invited to join the Federal Cabinet they will nevertheless participate in Cabinet Committee processes involving their own area of operations, and therefore they too are also bound by collective responsibility for cabinet decisions.[118]

As a corollary to collective responsibility, ministers must obtain the approval of cabinet for all initiatives of policy, or principle. The cabinet is responsible for all of the actions of its members on issues of public policy and it has collective responsibility for all of the government's initiatives from the time they are announced until they are implemented or withdrawn. If the cabinet has been compromised by the actions of a cabinet minister that minister should offer to leave the cabinet. The collective responsibility of the cabinet to one of its members ends when that cabinet minister resigns his or her office.[119] When a minister resigns their office the consent of the Sovereign's representative is required before the ex-minister may make a statement of justification, or clarification, to the House of Commons, or to the provincial legislature, as their explanations might reveal Privy Council or Executive Council confidences.[120]

By constitutional practice, ministers avoid involving themselves in the affairs of departments placed in the charge of their colleagues. When it is necessary for a minister to obtain information from another department, the practice is for the minister to seek such information through the office of the minister in charge of that department and not to directly contact civil servants, or officials of another department, although exceptions are made in the case of routine constituency matters.

11.44   Mandate Letters

The first minister is the head of the Cabinet and will set the political priorities of the Cabinet upon assuming office. In Canada, the practice at the federal level is for the Prime Minister to issue a mandate letter to each Cabinet minister in which the Prime Minister reviews the broad direction of public policy that his or her political party wishes to implement, and then sets out specific policy goals for each portfolio minister. The mandate letter focuses the attention of

Cabinet ministers on specific policy initiatives within their control, and establishes benchmarks against which their performance in their roles can be assessed by the Prime Minister and his senior political staff. The mandate letter also reviews the legal and ethical obligations that must be adhered to by each Cabinet minister. The modern practice is to publicly disclose the mandate letter issued to each Cabinet minister so they now tend to be drafted with public disclosure in mind. By publicly communicating the contents of a mandate letter the Prime Minister seeks to solidify public support for the electoral policies of his or her political party.

11.45   Cabinet Information

Cabinet records are a subset of government records and are not generally accessible to the public. There are four categories of federal government records. Institutional records concern the department or agencies of the government and are accessible by the public under the *Access to Information Act*[121] or the *Privacy Act*,[122] subject to certain exemptions. Personal records relating to a minister personally, including their constituency and personal political records are not, in general, accessible through access legislation. Ministerial records relating to the conduct of a minister's office are, in general, not accessible through access legislation. Cabinet documents are formally styled as confidences of the Queen's Privy Council for Canada and are accessible under access legislation but are excluded from public access for various periods of time until they are only of historical interest.[123]

A minister who leaves office is entitled to take their personal records with them but other records must be sent to the Library and Archives of Canada, except for cabinet records which must be sent to the Privy Council Office. A former minister can arrange through the Library and Archives Canada to review material relating to their time in office concerning their own particular department. When a government leaves office, its cabinet records are not generally accessible to the succeeding government in the absence of special arrangements.[124] The former government's records are retained in the custody of the Clerk of the Privy Council but remain under the control of the former Prime Minister. Access to records by former ministers or by a succeeding government must be made by way of application to the Clerk of the Privy Council.[125]

[1] The distinction among the three bodies is briefly discussed in *A Guide for Ministers and Secretaries of State*, Privy Council Office, Ottawa, 2002 at pages 31-32

[2] The Executive Council in the northern territories does not have the same status as a provincial Executive Council. For constitutional purposes the northern territories are subject to the Sovereign in right of Canada and thus there is no Sovereign in right of a Territory. The Executive Councils in the territories advise the Commissioner of the Territory, who is solely a Federal officer under the Crown in right of Canada and who is ultimately subject to direction by the Federal Government.

[3] For practical purposes this is also true for the ministry in the northern territories.

[4] Privy Councils also exist in some other Commonwealth realms, such as Barbados, where its functions are limited to advising on the Royal Prerogative of mercy, and Jamaica, where it advises on the exercise of the Royal Prerogative of mercy and discipline in the civil service.

[5] *The Canadian Constitution Historically Explained*, Walter S Scott, Carswell, Toronto, 1918, at page 121 (afterwards, *"W S Scott"*)

[6] *The Prime Minister and the Cabinet*, W A Matheson, Meuthen, Toronto, 1976, at page 1 (afterwards, *"Matheson"*)

[7] *W S Scott*, a page 121

[8] *Matheson*, at page 6

[9] *Oaths of Allegiance Act* RSC 1985, c. O-1

[10] The words in brackets are omitted if the person is affirming.

[11] *The Swearing-In of Privy Councillors*, Public Information Directorate, Government House, Ottawa, circa 1993, at page 2 (afterwards, *"Privy Councillors"*). There has been a past practice of providing to each new Privy Councillor the Bible (or other holy book) upon which Privy Councillor swore the oath.

[12] *The Swearing-In of a New Ministry*, Public Information Directorate, Government House, Ottawa, 1993 (afterwards, New Ministry)

[13] *Privy Councillors*, at page 2

[14] Ibid

[15] Ibid, at page 1

[16] Only one person has been removed from the Queen's Privy Council for Canada since 1867 – Mr. Conrad Black who was removed on January 31, 2014; (Historical Alphabetical List since 1867 of Members of the Queen's Privy Council for Canada http: //www.pco-bcp.gc.ca/ index.asp?lang=eng&page=information &sub=council-conseil &doc=members-membres/hist-alphabet-eng.htm). [accessed February 1, 2017].

[17] *Nature of the Privy Council*, in *Canadian Legal Studies*, Henry F. Davis, Butterworths, Toronto, December, 1968. at page 300 (afterwards, *"Davis"*).

[18] *Mallory*, at page 73; Matheson, at page 48

[19] *Davis*, at pages 302-303

[20] *Bourinot*, at page 165

[21] *Bourinot*, at page 164

[22] The Queen herself could not do this. Section 11 of the *Constitution Act, 1867*, empowers the Governor General, but not the Sovereign, to administer the oath of office to a Privy Councillor.

[23] *Mallory*, at page 70

[24] *Matheson*, at page 9

[25] However, it appears that Governor General the Duke of Connaught attended some meetings of the Privy Council during the early weeks of World War I; see *Davis*, at page 304.

[26] RSC 1985, c. S-26

[27] RSC 1985, c. F-11

[28] The principal powers of the Treasury Board as a statutory committee of the Privy Council is set out in section 7 of the *Financial Administration Act*.

[29] SC 2003, c. 22,

[30] RSC 1985, c. C-23, s.34

[31] in section 63

[32] for example, *The Alberta Act*, SC 1905, c. 3, s. 8; *The Saskatchewan Act* SC 1905, c. 42, s. 8.

[33] *Northern Governments in Transition*, Kirk Cameron and Graham White, Institute for Research on Public Policy, Montreal, 1995, at page 56 (afterwards *"Cameron/White"*)

[34] *Cameron/White*, at page 54

[35] *Hansard*, November 12, 1945, p. 2022

[36] Exceptionally, in 1926, the ministry of Prime Minister W L Mackenzie King resigned and immediately vacated office when Lord Byng refused a dissolution to Mackenzie King.

[37] *New Ministry*, at page 1. *Programme for the swearing-in of Ministers and Secretaries of State at Government House, June 11, 1997*, Public Information Directorate, Government House, Ottawa, 1997

[38] RSC, 1985, c. P-1

[39] For example, see *Open and Accountable Government 2015* (http://pm.gc.ca/eng/news/2015/11/27/open-and-accountable-government, accessed July 10, 2017) published by Prime Minister Justin Trudeau upon the assumption of office of the Trudeau Ministry in 2015.

[40] In Sections 4(1) and 4.1(1)

[41] In sections 4(2)(f) and 4.1(3)(f).

[42] See Subsection 33(2)(b) of the *Parliament of Canada Act*.

[43] See, for example, the *National Defence Act* RSC 1985, c. –5, s. 6, which creates an Associate Minister of National Defence.

[44] RSC 1985, c. M-8

[45] See the speech of Lord Mustill " . . . That the question whether statutory discretion is capable of delegation, and if so to what degree, principally depends upon the interpretation of the statute is beyond question . . . it is obvious that if delegation is possible at all, the power to fix the penal element can properly be entrusted to a junior minister . . . "

[46] *A Guide for Ministers and Secretaries of State*, Privy Council Office, Ottawa, 2002, at page 6.

[47] In the Chretien Ministry (in office between November 4, 1993 and December 11, 2003) there were two categories of Minister of State Assigned to Assist a Minister. Those formally styled Minister of State were invited to join

the Cabinet as Cabinet Ministers, while other Ministers of State Assigned to Assist a Minister were formally styled as Secretaries of State and were members of the Ministry but were not invited into the Cabinet as Cabinet Ministers.

[48] RSC 1985, c. P-1

[49] *Accountable Government: A Guide for Ministers and Ministers of State*, Privy Council Office, Ottawa, 2011, page 7.

[50] RSC 1985, c. S-3

[51] RSC 1985, c. I-21

[52] No. 2, 1901

[53] *Acts Interpretation Act* s. 18c (1)-(4)

[54] , *Canada in London: An Unofficial Glimpse of Canada's Sixteen High Commissioners 1880 – 1980*, Nancy Gelber, Canada House, London, 1980, at page 16.

[55] Ibid at page 28.

[56] A seminal article about the principle of sub-delegation was written by a Canadian scholar, John Willis, *Delegatus Non Potest Delegare* (1943) 21 Can. Bar Rev. page 257.

[57] see also *Lewisham v Roberts*, [1949] 2 KB 608 (England, KB)

[58] *R v Secretary of State for the Home Department; ex parte Oladehinde and Alexander*, [1990] 2 WLR 195 (England, CA) affd. [1990] 3 WLR 797 (England, HL)

[59] *Marshall v Deputy Governor of Bermuda*, [2011] 1 LRC 178 (Bermuda, JC).

[60] In *Ramawad* there was a specific provision in the statute that permitted the minister to delegate functions to two specific officials and that was a factor in the court's finding that other officials could not act for the minister.

[61] RSC 1985, c. I-21

[62] RSC 1985, c. S-22

[63] *King v. Canada (Minister of Human Resources and Social Development)*, [2010] 2 FCR 294, 2009 FCA 105, 392 NR 227 (Canada, FCA) per Sexton J.A.

[64] Section 3(1) of the *Interpretation Act* states "Every provision of this Act applies, unless a contrary intention appears, to every enactment, whether enacted before or after the commencement of this Act."

[65] *Interpretation Act* s. 24 (2)(b).

[66] RSC 1985, c. P-34

[67] *Interpretation Act* RSC 1985, c. I-21, s. 24(3). Particular statutory powers vested in a minister must also be carefully examined to determine if they require that a Minster of the Crown exercise a particular power personally. In such cases the presumption that a Deputy Minister may act for a minister under the *Carltona* doctrine or the codified version contained in interpretative acts may be rebutted.

[68] *Guidance for Deputy Ministers*, Privy Council Office, Ottawa, 2003, page 7.

[69] *Financial Administration Act* RSC 1985, c. F-11, as amended, s. 16.1-16.5.

[70] *A Guide for Ministers and Secretaries of State*, Privy Council Office, Ottawa, 2002, page 23.

[71] *Guidance for Deputy Ministers*, Privy Council Office, Ottawa, 2003, pages 22-24.

[72] See the (*Department of Justice Act* RSC 1985, c. J-2, s. 3(3).

[73] *Matheson*, at page 49

[74] At page 125, (para. 15)

[75] A Parliamentary Secretary or a Deputy Minister has no right of access to the Sovereign's representative.

[76] Occasionally, there may be exceptions to this convention. For instance, the former Canadian Transport Commission was empowered to make recommendations directly to the Committee of the Privy Council pursuant to the *Railway Act*, RSC 1985, R-3, s. 95(4), rep. by SC 1996, c. C-10, s. 185(1).

[77] *Smith*, at page 34

[78] Greig J. in *Burt v Governor General of New Zealand* at p 194 states: "It is a constitutional convention . . . that the Governor General in any action should take advice from his Ministers."

[79] The best example in Canadian constitutional practice occurred in 1896 after the defeat of the Conservative Party at the polls. Prime Minister Sir Charles Tupper advised Governor General Lord Aberdeen to make several appointments to the Senate which the Governor General, in the exercise of his reserve powers, declined to do because the Tupper Ministry could only be a caretaker government following its defeat at the polls and its consequential inability to secure the confidence of the House of Commons when that body next convened after the general election.

[80] Justice La Forest stated: "In my view, if even a statute cannot permit the retention of monies obtained under an unconstitutional statute, that result cannot be achieved under a purported exercise of a discretion to refuse a fiat, whatever may be the legal foundation of that purported discretion. All executive powers, whether they derive from statute, common law or prerogative, must be adapted to conform with constitutional imperatives."

[81] "...since he [the Yang di-Pertuan Agong] is required in all executive functions to act in accordance with the advice of cabinet, mandamus could, in their Lordship's view, be sought against the members of cabinet requiring them to advise the Yang di-Pertuan Agong to revoke the proclamation."

[82] "I do not think that any reliance which a Chief Minister places on decisions, resolutions or findings and recommendations in any of the above situations is inconsistent with his duty to advise. The views expressed if adopted by the Chief Minister would not have replaced his opinion but may have shaped, influenced or reinforced it. The power to revoke the minister's appointment conferred by s. 16(4)(b) of the Constitution was exercised in the precise manner which the Constitution laid down."

[83] at page 246, per Mulock, C.J.

[84] at pages 326-327

[85] *House of Commons Procedure and Practice*, Robert Marl and Camille Montpetit, House of Commons, Ottawa, 2000, at page 643

[86] *Glossary of Parliamentary Procedure*, Office of the Clerk of the House of Commons, Ottawa, 1992

[87] Instances of resignation of ministers are now relatively rare. The usual result of a failure now is for the minister to pledge to the legislative body that corrective action will be taken. Nevertheless, in modern times there are examples of ministers accepting responsibility for a policy or operational failure and resigning as a minister. Perhaps the most prominent example in the Commonwealth in recent decades was the resignation of the United Kingdom's

Foreign Secretary, Lord Carrington, following the invasion of the Falkland Islands by Argentina in 1982. He took responsibility for the failure of his department to heed the warning signs of the potential for an invasion by Argentina.

[88] *Public Administration in Canada; second edition*, Kenneth Kernaghan and David Siegel, Nelson Canada, Scarborough (ON), 1991, at page 380 (afterwards, *Kernaghan & Siegel*). The civil servants responsible for the administrative error may be disciplined for that error. An example of this was afforded by the admission into Canada in 1991 of a former Iraqi diplomat accredited to the United States, which became known as the Al-Mashat affair. No minister resigned but senior officials in the Department of External Affairs were publicly blamed.

[89] RSC 1985, c. J-2

[90] The Governor General may also have recourse to private legal advisers, which is often essential in circumstances where the Governor General may be contemplating the exercise of a reserve power. Advice may also be received from the Chief Justice in circumstances where an exercise of a reserve power is contemplated.

[91] This model has been used in The Bahamas.

[92] This model has been used in the United Kingdom.

[93] Although the Director of Public Prosecutions of Canada is subordinate to the Attorney General of Canada, the office of the Director is functionally independent.

[94] This model has been used in Jamaica.

[95] This model has not been used in any of the Commonwealth realms but has been used in the Commonwealth republics of Zambia and Malawi.

[96] *Crown Liability and Proceedings Act* RSC 1985, c. C-50, s. 23(1) as amended

[97] Department of Justice Act RSC 1985, c. J-2 s. 5(d), as amended

[98] For example, in 1986 a federal Minister personally appeared before the Canadian Transport Commission at an oral public hearing to consider an application by a railway company to abandon a railway branch line. The decision states that the Minister took an active part in the proceedings; *Re CNR Porter Subdivision Abandonment* (Decision WDR1986-12, December 3, 1986)

(Canada, Canadian Transport Commission – Railway Transport Committee Western Division).

[99] *Marin v Attorney General*, [2011] 5 LRC 209 (Belize, CCJ) at page 225 (para. 32).

[100] *Cameron & White*, at page 55

[101] Ibid, at page 54

[102] There are however, some references to the Cabinet in federal legislation; *Canada Evidence Act* RSC 1985, c. C-5, s. 39(3).

[103] at page 100

[104] at page 82. It should be noted that the written constitution of the realm of Barbados does refer to the Cabinet which it describes as the "principle instrument of policy."

[105] at page 222

[106] The Prime Minister may designate some cabinet ministers to be the political minister for a particular region and those so designated will exercise political duties in connection with the implementation of the government's policies and programs within that region.

[107] *Matheson*, at page 3

[108] Some of the earlier federal legislation referred to the Prime Minister as the First Minister; see the *Senate and House of Commons Act*, RSC 1952, c. 249, s. 14.

[109] *Akinbobala v. Canada (Attorney General)* (1997),155 FTR 215 (Canada, FC) at paras. 15-16.

[110] See *Conacher v. Canada (Prime Minister)*, [2010] 3 FCR 411, 2009 FC 920, 311 DLR (4th) 678; [2009] FCJ No 1136 (QL); 352 FTR 162 (Canada, FC) per Shore J. at para. 59: "A government losing the confidence of the House of Commons is an event that does not have a strict definition and often requires the judgment of the Prime Minister".

[111] This was also the case for the early appointees to the office of Controller of Customs and Inland Revenue.

[112] The issue of whether a particular ministry continues to hold the confidence of a legislative body can be obscure at times. Without any doubt a loss of

a vote concerning the Speech from the Throne rendered at the beginning of a new legislative session, or the loss of a vote concerning the approval of a ministry's proposed budget would be regarded as a loss of confidence in that ministry. Similarly where the parliamentary opposition introduces a motion of non-confidence in a ministry and that motion is passed by the legislative body the ministry will be considered to have lost the confidence of the legislative body. However, the loss of a vote on other legislation, particularly if it resulted from the temporary absence of government members, would not necessarily be regarded as indicative of a loss of confidence in the ministry. In those circumstances, a prompt recovery by a vote of confidence moved by the ministry, or another vote on the measure that was previously lost can provide proof that the ministry continues to enjoy the confidence of the legislative body.

[113] At the federal level there is a bicameral Parliament. However, it is not necessary for the cabinet to seek and retain the confidence of the Senate, which is the unelected upper house.

[114] Thus the Parliament of the United Kingdom was able to force Prime Minister Neville Chamberlain and his cabinet to stand down in 1940 due to a collapse in the confidence of Parliament concerning the ability of Chamberlain's Ministry to successfully prosecute the war against Nazi Germany, notwithstanding that Chamberlain had won the previous general election and his party still commanded a majority in the House of Commons.

[115] *Bourinot*, at page 168

[116] *Accountable Government: A Guide for Ministers and Ministers of State 2011*, Privy Council Office, 2011, at page 2

[117] *Matheson*, at page 17

[118] *Accountable Government: A Guide for Ministers and Ministers of State 2011*, Privy Council Office, 2011, at page 6

[119] *Bourinot*, at page 168

[120] *Mallory*, at page 61

[121] RSC 1985, c. A-1

[122] RSC 1985, c. P-21

[123] *Access to Information Act* RSC 1985, c. A-1 s. 69(3); *Canada Evidence Act* RSC 1985, c. C-5, s. 39(4); *Privacy Act* RSC 1985, c. P-21, s. 70(3).

[124] Special arrangements can be made for access by a new government to material in the previous government's records relating to national security or national defence.

[125] *Accountable Government: A Guide for Ministers and Ministers of State 2011*, Privy Council Office, 2011, at page 31.

CROWN LEGAL INSTRUMENTS

This chapter examines the legal instruments most closely associated with the Canadian constitutional monarchy. The instruments used in Canadian constitutional practice vary depending upon particular circumstances. Since the Sovereign and the Sovereign's representatives must act on the advice of their respective constitutional advisors, it is necessary to maintain written instruments and records to ensure that responsibility for the public acts of the monarchy can always be ascertained. Many of the legal instruments used in the Canadian constitutional monarchy have been inherited from the constitutional law, customs, practices, and usages of the United Kingdom.

12.1   Crown and Executive Instruments Distinguished

For the purposes of this book Crown instruments are defined as those instruments that are made by or on behalf of the Crown. In contrast, executive instruments are documents used by and within government for the development and execution of policy initiatives. Executive instruments include policy papers, guidelines, letters of understanding, directives, memoranda, reports, written opinions, and letters of agreement. Executive instruments are outside of the scope of this text and will not be addressed further in this chapter.

12.2   Types of Crown Legal Instruments

Through historical evolution a wide variety of legal instruments have been created to support the formal decision-making of the Crown and its officials. The following is a summary of the types of Crown legal instruments that are most likely to be encountered in Canada.

12.3   Address

An **Address** is a formal message to the Sovereign, or the Sovereign's representative, from the Houses of Parliament expressing a wish, opinion, or congratulations to the Sovereign and the Royal Family.[1] An **Address to the Throne** is commonly issued upon the occasion of a Sovereign's coronation but can also be used as a formal communication between Parliament and the Throne.[2] An Address may also be used by the Houses of Parliament to request the production of documents in the possession of the Crown, or to request the removal of a public officer for cause.

12.4   Charter

A **Royal Charter** is an instrument issued by the Sovereign to an individual, a collective group of individuals, or a body corporate, which conveys or confirms powers, rights or liberties to that group in perpetuity. The most well-known charter is the *Magna Carta*, or *Great Charter*, that was issued by King John of England to barons and other noblemen of the English realm in the year 1215 to secure to them their rights and liberties vis-a-vis the Crown of England. The *Magna Carta* is the earliest step toward a constitutional monarchy in British legal history.

Charters have also been granted to individuals creating large commercial enterprises and in Canada the most noteworthy example is the Hudson's Bay Company which was established by a Royal Charter on May 2, 1670, issued by King Charles II of England, Scotland, and Ireland to "The Governor and Company of Adventurers of England trading into Hudson's Bay". Charters have also been granted to municipalities created as a body corporate through an exercise of the Royal Prerogative such as the City of St. John, New Brunswick, which was created by Royal Charter in 1785. Institutions of higher learning such as universities, as well as charitable institutions have also been created by a Charter.

12.5   Commission

A **Commission** is an instrument issued in the name of the Sovereign under the Great Seal, or the Privy Seal, to appoint a person to an office established either by statute or by the Royal Prerogative.

The *Public Officers Act*[3] provides in section 3 that the Governor in Council may make regulations to declare and determine which federal dignitaries, officers, or classes of officers are entitled to be issued a Commission under a royal seal and the fees, if any, that shall be paid upon the issuance of a Commission. Section 4 of that Act imposes an obligation on the Registrar General of Canada to record the issuance of Commissions and to insert a notice of issuance in the *Canada Gazette*. The Registrar General must lay a list of the Commissions issued in any year before Parliament within the first 15 days of the next ensuing session of Parliament in each year. A Commission which is defective in form may nevertheless be an effective exercise of the Royal Prerogative for the purpose of appointing an individual to an office in the gift of the Sovereign; *Barnes v Government of Newfoundland* (1875), Nfld LR 89 (Newfoundland, SC).[4]

12.6   Instrument of Abdication

An **Instrument of Abdication** is a document under the sign-manual that may be issued by the Sovereign to express a Sovereign's intention to resign the Throne. The Instrument of Abdication must be witnessed and for this purpose the senior members of the Royal Family will be called as witnesses to the Sovereign's act of abdication. A Sovereign without heirs may express their intention to abdicate both for themselves and for their descendants in an Instrument of Abdication but a Sovereign may not abdicate on behalf of his or her living descendants. An Instrument of Abdication is not effective in law merely upon the signature of the Sovereign but must also be enacted into the laws of the United Kingdom by the Parliament of that realm before it can take effect there and in the Commonwealth realms. The sole modern example of this instrument is the abdication instrument of King Edward VIII in 1936.

12.7   Instrument of Advice

Beginning in 1953, Canadian constitutional practice developed the **Instrument of Advice**, which was a document devised to reflect the constitutional role of the Prime Minister. An Instrument of Advice is used in those situations where the Prime Minister acts as a quorum of one of the Privy Council, or in respect of the formal advice of a Prime Minister-Designate. A Prime Minister-Designate (i.e., a party leader who has won a general election and received a mandate to form a government but who has not yet been sworn into office) uses an Instrument of Advice to provide the Governor General with his or her recommendations for the appointments to both the Privy Council and to the new Canadian Ministry upon a change in government. It is also used in instances in which a Prime Minister exercises authority pursuant to an order-in-council to provide advice to the Crown on behalf of the Privy Council, such as in the calling of a general election. An Instrument of Advice takes the form of a letter signed by the Prime Minister and is subsequently countersigned by the Governor General.[5]

12.8   Instrument of Appointment

An **Instrument of Appointment** is a document used to appoint a person to an honour such as a national order of merit (e.g., the Order of Canada, or the Order of Military Merit). It consists of a document appointing a person to a particular grade of an Order, commending them to enjoy the dignity so granted, and formally admitting them to membership in the order. It is signed by the Governor General and by the Secretary General of the Order.

12.9   Letters Patent and Letters Close

The **Letters Patent** is a formal document issued in the name of the Sovereign under the Great Seal of Canada and has been described as "an ancient form of law-making under the prerogative".[6] Letters Patent are most often employed to grant a privilege within the gift of the Sovereign, such as the creation or conferral of offices or heraldic emblems, the conferral of authority to perform particular functions such as at a coronation, or to convey the title in Crown lands to an individual.[7]

Traditionally, transfers of land to subjects of the Sovereign and to others have been made by Letters Patent under the Great Seal, and that remains a lawful mechanism to effect a transfer of real property from the Crown. In *Farwell v The Queen*, [1894] 22 SCR 54 (Canada, SC) the Supreme Court held that: "The rights of the crown, territorial or prerogative, are to be passed under the great seal of the Dominion or province (as the case may be) in which is vested the beneficial interest therein . . . ".[8]

Letters Patent may also be used to ratify treaties or to create corporate bodies pursuant to a statute.[9] Letters Patent are so-called because the face of the document is open and thus the Letters Patent display the Great Seal to the reader. This distinguishes Letters Patent in law from **Letters Close**, or **Close Rolls**, which consist of a document issued by the Sovereign, or the Sovereign's representative, under the Great Seal but which are sealed in order that the document does not openly display the Great Seal. The use of Letters Close is unusual but may be used when documents are directed to particular individuals for a specified purpose.

12.10   Messages

A **Message** is a formal communication that is exchanged between the constituent elements of Parliament (e.g., between the House of Commons and the Senate, and between the Sovereign, or the Sovereign's representative, and the House of Commons).[10] A Message normally accompanies a bill, or a request such as a Royal Recommendation.

12.11   Minute-of-Council

A **Minute-of-Council** is a document that is used to:

a) Record advice given to the Sovereign's representative,

b) Summarize the deliberations of a meeting of a Committee of the Privy Council, or

c) Record a decision taken by the Committee of the Privy Council that is not grounded in legislation (i.e., an exercise of a Royal Prerogative power).

When it is necessary to provide formal advice to the Crown, a Minute-of-Council will be prepared and adopted at a meeting of the Committee of the Privy Council. A Minute-of-Council can always be identified in government documents by its opening words: "The Committee of the Privy Council, on the

recommendation of the Minister of _____ advise that _____
. . . ". A Minute is signed and certified by the Clerk of the Privy Council but they can also be signed by the Governor General. However, a Minute-of-Council does not express the exercise of a positive legal power by the Governor in Council. Where the specific exercise of a statutory power, or a Royal Prerogative power is required, an order-in-council is normally used for that purpose.

In recent times, Minutes-of-Council have declined in utility, owing to the growth in record keeping of Cabinet decisions and by the innovative use of formal letters to the Sovereign's representative, which may be used whenever it is merely necessary merely to record political accountability for a particular action by the Crown.[11]

12.12   Order-in-Council

If a formal legal act is required to be made by the Crown, an **Order-in-Council** will be issued pursuant to a statute or the Royal Prerogative to execute the Crown's decision. In effect, an Order- in-Council is a resolution of the Sovereign or Governor in Council.[12] An Order-in-Council is the act of the Governor General in Council exercising its legal powers. Although it can constitute a legislative act, an Order-in-Council most often represents an administrative action. Where the Order-in-Council is legislative in nature, it ordinarily constitutes a form of secondary legislation but sometimes an Order-in-Council can have the character of primary legislation as, for instance, an Order-in-Council made in relation to royal honours, or which implements an exercise of the reserve powers of the Crown.

An Order-in-Council may be identified by its opening words: "His/Her Excellency the Governor General in Council, on the recommendation of (the Minister of etc.), hereby orders (approves etc.) . . . ". An Order-in-Council will also bear the signature and certification of the Clerk of the Privy Council.

The passage of an Order in Council is supported by a number of subsidiary documents. Generally speaking, a representative example of the documents required would include the following in the case of an exercise of a routine statutory discretion vested in the Governor General in Council:

a) **Letter of transmittal** of documents from departmental officials to a Minister;

b) An **Explanatory Memorandum** to the Minister containing an explanation of the approval which is sought from the Crown;

c) A **Submission** to the Governor in Council recommending the exercise of a discretion, which must be signed by the responsible Minister, and which must have appended to it any necessary supporting documents;

d) A **second letter of transmittal** from departmental officials to officials at the Privy Council Office; and

e) A **draft Order-in-Council**.

The Submission is a key document which is required whenever there are matters which require actions by the Sovereign or the Governor General to be formalized by the issuance of an Order in Council. A Submission generally appears in the following form:

TO HIS/HER EXCELLENCY THE GOVERNOR GENERAL IN COUNCIL:

THE UNDERSIGNED has the honour to report:

THAT . . .

THAT . . .

THEREFORE the undersigned has the honour to recommend that Your Excellency in Council may be pleased, pursuant to section __ of the _____ Act, to approve etc.

Respectfully Submitted

Minister of _____

Once the Submission is considered and approved by the Committee of the Privy Council (e.g., the Treasury Board) it will be forwarded to the Governor General, who considers the submission and, in accordance with the conventions relating to responsible government, signifies his or her approval to the Order-in-Council. The Order-in-Council is then issued by the Privy Council Office, under the seal of that office, in a form similar to the following:

HIS/HER EXCELLENCY THE GOVERNOR GENERAL IN COUNCIL, on the recommendation of the Minister of _____, pursuant to section ____ of the _____ Act, is pleased hereby to approve, etc.

Clerk of the Privy Council

For the purposes of approving Orders-in-Council, drafts are put together in batches and display on their face the names of the Privy Councillors who were present at the meeting of the Committee of the Privy Council. The Governor General's name is also listed, as the Governor General will be presumed to be present for the purposes of approving the Orders-in-Council. In actual constitutional practice however, the Governor General is never present. Instead, at a subsequent date, the Governor General will sign the face page of a batch of Orders-in-Council that were considered at a meeting of a committee of the Privy Council and it is that signature which will give royal sanction to the issuance of the Order-in-Council.

Each individual Order-in-Council is subsequently signed and sealed by the officials in the Privy Council Office on behalf of the Clerk of the Privy Council, and issued. An Order-in-Council is revocable; "An order in council is an Act of the Crown, on the advice of its responsible ministers, and can always be revoked"; *The King v Ottawa Electric Company* (1933), 40 CRC 295 (Ontario, SC).

On the authority of an Order- in-Council, a number of other instruments may be issued by the Crown, such as Commissions.

12.13   Pardon

A **Pardon** can be a document issued under the Governor General's Privy Seal, where the pardon is granted under the Royal Prerogative of Mercy. A pardon releases an individual from the consequences and the odious disfavour resulting from a conviction for a criminal offense. A person who has been issued a Pardon may be able to maintain an action in defamation against aspersions against them based on a prior conviction to which a Pardon applies.[13] The Crown has no authority to release a prisoner except by a pardon issued under a royal seal; *Mitchell v Harvie* (1852), PEIR 45 (Prince Edward Island, SC).

12.14   Petition

A **Petition** is a document addressed by a Canadian subject to the Sovereign, or the Sovereign's representative, seeking redress for a grievance.[14] In Canadian constitutional usage, Petitions may be addressed to the Sovereign, or the Sovereign's representative, from a subject seeking special relief, or redress, where the subject believes that they have been oppressed by the conduct of an official, or the sentence of a judge. The making of a Petition to the Sovereign is an ancient right possessed by all subjects and is a right that was protected by the *Bill of Rights 1689*, which forms part of the laws of Canada under the reception doctrine, and from which Canadian constitutional principles may be derived.[15]

In Canadian constitutional practice Petitions are tendered to the Governor in Council. However, there is no legal obligation on the part of the Crown to respond to a Petition. A Petition is a matter of confidence between the subject and the Sovereign, and therefore government officials do not have the right to publicize the contents of a Petition without the permission of the Sovereign's representative, and the subject.

In some cases statutory provision has been made for the exercise of the Crown's discretion, upon Petition, in respect of decisions of subordinate administrative bodies, such as the Canadian Radio-television and Telecommunications Commission, or the Canadian Transportation Agency. In those instances, the Petition is in the nature of a request for discretionary relief against an order or decision of those bodies. Because of the regulatory aspect of such petitions public notice has been given in the *Canada Gazette* of some Petitions (e.g., those filed under the *Telecommunications Act*[16]).

12.15   Proclamation

A **Proclamation** is an instrument issued in the name of the Sovereign under the Great Seal which is a formal announcement of royal action.[17] It is an official notice from the Crown and its purpose is to call to the attention of the Sovereign's subjects existing laws, or to the existence of a public state of affairs, such as a state of war or peace, or the accession of a new Sovereign, or Governor General. It can also be a form of subordinate legislation in some cases. Thus, a Proclamation can represent a declaratory act, a legislative act, or an advisory act. But it was held in the *Case of Proclamations* (1611), 12 Co. Rep. 74 (England, KB) that the King cannot, by the issuance of a Proclamation, alter the statutes, common law, or customs of the realm although he could warn his subjects of the dangers of committing an infraction of those laws.

Rarely, a Proclamation may also be used as a means of recommending a particular course of conduct to the subjects of the Crown. In *Haney v Gaden* (1823), Nfld LR 298 (Newfoundland, SC) a Proclamation was issued by the Governor recommending that Spanish dollars be accepted as legal tender in Newfoundland at the rate of five shillings per dollar, owing to the shortage of sterling-based currency caused by the financial disruptions of the Napoleonic wars. In *obiter dicta*, the Supreme Court of Newfoundland said of this Proclamation:

> The Governors proclamation respecting the value of the dollar is purely recommendatory, and does not in any shape assume to prescribe a positive rule in regard to it. The greatest force that could attach to this proclamation would be to sanction, by the concurrence of the Crown, an alteration in the value of the dollar, if the inhabitants would consent to make such an alteration . . . [18]

Proclamations are sometimes used in a law-making capacity pursuant to the Royal Prerogative. However, the scope for law-making under the Royal Prerogative is circumscribed and any prerogative legislation can no longer affect the rights or privileges of the subjects of the Crown. Nevertheless, the Sovereign retains the power to legislate by Proclamation for colonial territories which are not possessed of a legislature. A Canadian example is the *Royal*

Proclamation, 1763, which among other things protected title to aboriginal lands from impairment by settlers.

Proclamations are most often employed in a law-making capacity in Canada in matters relating to royal honours or national symbols (eg. *Proclamation Designating the Maple Tree as the National Arboreal Emblem of Canada* SI/ 96-36 dated 15 May 1996) or in relation to the national coinage. Important Proclamations may be approved by the Sovereign directly, as in the case of the *Proclamation concerning the National Flag of Canada* (SOR/65-62, January 28, 1965) but in general Proclamations are approved by the Sovereign's representatives. More rarely a Proclamation may also be issued by a subordinate Crown official, for example, a Herald proclaiming a grant of arms to an armiger at a public presentation of a grant of armorial bearings to a subject. Formerly, it was the practice to bring federal statutes into force by the issuance of a Proclamation but that procedure has now fallen into disuse. Federal statutes are now brought into force by the issuance of an Order-in-Council.

A reference in a federal statute to a Proclamation is by virtue of section 18(1) of the *Interpretation Act*[19] to be construed as a reference to a Proclamation of the Governor in Council. Section 18(2) of that Act also provides that a Proclamation shall be understood to have been issued pursuant to an Order-in-Council but that it is not necessary to recite the fact of the issuance of an Order-in-Council within the Proclamation itself.

No particular form for a Proclamation is specified by law.[20] Thus, where the Federal Government disallowed provincial legislation, and sections 56 and 90 of the *Constitution Act, 1867*, contemplated that the Lieutenant Governor of Manitoba would issue a Proclamation respecting the disallowance, the publication in the *Manitoba Gazette* by the Lieutenant Governor of the federal Order-in-Council disallowing the legislation, together with the certificate of receipt of the provincial statute by the Governor General, was held to be a Proclamation within the meaning of the *Constitution Act, 1867*; *Attorney General of Canada v Ryan*, [1888] 5 Man LR 81 at 92-93 (Manitoba, QB).

12.16   Royal Instructions

Royal Instructions may be issued by the Sovereign to the Governor General or Administrator of Canada, or by the Governor General, or Administrator of Canada, to a Lieutenant Governor or Administrator of a Province. They consist of a document approved by the Sovereign, or Governor General, under the sign manual. Normally they are issued with a commission of appointment to an office but they may be issued at any time. With the evolution of Canadian independence, Royal Instructions can now only be issued in respect of a Sovereign's representative in Canada on the advice of the Queen's Privy Council for Canada.

12.17 Warrants

Warrants under the sign manual are issued for the purpose of authorizing acts in pursuance of the Royal Prerogative.[21] For example, they are issued to authorize the grant of arms under the prerogative powers in respect of heraldry and they are also used for some appointments to honours, such as the Order of Merit. **Governor General's Special Warrants** (or **Lieutenant Governor's Special Warrants**) may be issued by the Sovereign's representative under the sign manual on the advice of the ministry to approve the expenditure of funds out of a consolidated revenue fund in the absence of a statutory appropriation when a legislature is not in session and the funds are urgently required. At the federal level these Warrants can now only during the period that Parliament is dissolved for a general election.[22]

Special Warrants are an unusual instrument in that their abuse by a ministry in power in a province may be the subject of critical comment by the opposition parties in the legislature. Their misuse may provide justification for the exercise of the reserve powers by the Sovereign's representative. However, the provisions of the *Financial Administration Act*[23] at the federal level appear to have rendered this scenario unlikely in respect of a Canadian Ministry.

12.18 Writs

A **Writ** is a document issued in the name of the Sovereign under the Great Seal in the form of a royal command, which requires someone to do something, or to refrain from doing something. A common example in Canadian practice is a **Writ of Summons** requiring the members of Parliament or a Legislature to come together on an appointed date for the opening of Parliament, or a provincial legislature.

Some Writs, particularly those used in judicial process such as a judicial **Writ of Fieri Facias** may be issued upon the application of an ordinary subject of the Sovereign. However, Writs which are intended to be used for some important purpose of state may not be issued on the application of a subject. In *Parsons v Burk*, [1971] NZLR 244 (New Zealand, SC) a subject of the Queen of New Zealand sought the issuance from the Supreme Court of New Zealand of the prerogative **Writ ne Exeat Regno**, which restricts the ability of a subject to travel outside of the realm. The judgment of Justice Hardie Boys refused the issuance of that Writ upon the grounds that the responsibility of advising the Sovereign to issue it rested on her responsible ministers, who had declined to recommend its issuance. The Court decided that it would be tantamount to a judicial usurpation of the role of the New Zealand Ministry if the Court were to permit the issuance of a Writ intended to be used in a matter of state upon the application of a subject.

12.19   Execution of Crown Instruments

Original documents should be signed and sealed with the appropriate seal by the official with authority to execute the instrument, or by subordinate officials acting under the authority of the official possessing the authority to execute the document. In most cases involving Crown instruments that person will be the Sovereign's representative. Where ministerial countersignatures are required, they should also be affixed to the original document. However, it is not always possible for countersignatures or ministerial signatures on a recommendation document to be original. The Sovereign's representatives may be discharging their office away from the capital city and thus documents may have to be transmitted by facsimile or by electronic means. A reasonable argument can be made that the Sovereign's representative may act on the basis of a facsimile or electronic copy of a document signed by Ministers provided that the original and the copy are retained as proof of validity, and for archival purposes.

12.20   Revisions to Crown Instruments

From time to time it becomes necessary to revise or correct a formal instrument. The *Public Documents Act*[24] provides, in section 3, that Letters Patent under the Great Seal or any document issued under the Privy Seal, except Letters Patent granting lands, which contain the wrong name of a person, a clerical error or misnomer, or an erroneous description of material facts, may be cancelled by the Registrar General of Canada provided that the authority of the Governor in Council is obtained. A minute of the act of cancellation is entered in the margin of the registry of the original instrument. Corrected Letters Patent or corrected documents under the Privy Seal are then issued. By subsection 3(2), the corrected versions are effective in law from the date of the original documents.

The Act also provides, in section 2, that no instrument is required to be written on parchment and is equally valid if it is written on paper. The Act further specifies that nothing in it shall be construed to require that any instrument issued prior to June 22, 1869, be issued on parchment.

An instrument is not defective solely by reason of the fact that it bears a date prior to the date of its actual issuance, if the instrument merely formalizes an act which was validly taken on the date named in the instrument, according to Commonwealth precedent; *Whitfield v Attorney General*, [1989] LRC (Const) 249 at 267 (Bahamas, SC).[25]

12.21   Registration and Publication of Crown Instruments

At both the federal and provincial levels of government provision is normally made in legislation for the registration of some Crown instruments and their publication in official gazettes. At the Federal level, the applicable legislation is the *Statutory Instruments Act*,[26] which provides for the registration and publication in the *Canada Gazette* of certain Crown instruments such as Orders-in-Council, Letters Patent, Commissions, Warrants, Proclamations etc., in addition to a variety of other legal instruments, that meet the statutory criteria for registration and publication. Where related instruments issued pursuant to the Royal Prerogative are inadvertently registered in the wrong order, there is Commonwealth precedent that the registration error does not vitiate the Crown instrument.[27]

12.22 Royal Seals

From the earliest days of monarchial government in Canada, official acts have been promulgated in documents sealed with royal seals. The use of seals in Canada can be traced back to the earliest period of European colonial rule. Initially a commercial seal was used for engrossing official acts of the government during the French colonial era when the government was in the charge of the Compagnie des Cent Associés. However, after 1663, when Canada was elevated to the status of a royal province, a government seal was struck. This first seal was known as the Council Seal and was a small one-sided seal engraved with the Royal Arms of France and the words "Nouvelle France".[28] Other seals were subsequently struck and used throughout both the French and British eras in the colonial period.

Royal seals have long been used to authenticate Crown instruments issued by the Sovereign and the Sovereign's Ministers. There are four types of authentication involving royal seals or the like that have been historically used in relation to Canada, the Great Seals, the Privy Seal, the Signets and the Sign Manual.

12.23 The Great Seal of Canada

At confederation in 1867 the Great Seal of Canada was created. The Great Seal of Canada signifies the power and authority of the Sovereign and its impression on public documents represents authenticity, royal authority, and the exercise of the royal will.[29] All formal public documents issued in the name of the Sovereign are passed under the Great Seal of Canada. The Governor General of Canada has formal custody of the Great Seal of Canada and at his or her investiture, the Governor General takes an oath as the Keeper of the Great Seal of Canada. However, the actual physical custody of the Great Seal resides with the Registrar General of Canada. Invariably, the Registrar General is a Minister of the Crown and he or she receives the Great Seal of Canada from the Governor General upon being sworn into the Canadian Ministry. The Registrar General must present the seal to the Governor General when the Registrar General leaves office.[30] The Great Seal of Canada is replaced at the end of each Sovereign's reign and the old seal is defaced. The matrices of the defaced seal are given into the custody of the Library and Archives of Canada.[31]

All new royal seals are struck by the Royal Canadian Mint pursuant to a Royal Warrant issued by the Sovereign authorizing the striking of a new seal.[32] Pending the striking of a new Great Seal by the Mint at the commencement of a new reign, it is customary for the new Sovereign to issue a Royal Warrant authorizing the continued use of the preceding Sovereign's Great Seal until a new Great Seal can be completed.[33]

Seven Great Seals of Canada have been struck since 1867. The first was a temporary seal issued in 1867 and retired in 1869. A second, permanent Great Seal was issued by authority of Queen Victoria in 1869. One seal was struck during the reign of King Edward VII, another during the reign of King George V, and two were struck for King George VI, one as King and Emperor, at the beginning of his reign, and a second Great Seal in 1949, which omitted the title of Emperor that the King had discarded upon the independence of India in 1947. One seal has been struck in the reign of Queen Elizabeth II. No seal was struck during the reign of King Edward VIII, who authorized the use of his father's Great Seal during his short reign.

In appearance all of the permanent Great Seals of Canada have displayed the Sovereign seated upon the Throne. For that reason the striking of a new Seal awaits the coronation of the new Sovereign. The Sovereign is usually depicted crowned and holding the orb, which signifies the dominion of Christ. An exception occurred in the Great Seals struck during the reign of King George VI. Perhaps influenced by the gathering clouds of war, his seals depict the King holding his sword and sceptre.[35]

The Coat of Arms of Canada are displayed on the seal and traditionally the Royal Style and Titles have also been displayed in Latin, in the same manner as on the national coinage. However when Queen Elizabeth II's Great Seal was struck, the Latin motto was dropped in favour of the inscription "Reine du Canada – Elizabeth II – Queen of Canada". This bilingual seal is likely to be a model for English and French inscriptions of the primary title in future reigns.[36]

The Great Seals of Canada have been made from various materials. Originally silver was used but it proved to be too soft a metal. Currently tempered steel is the material of choice for the Great Seal, with the counter-seal being constructed of a copper alloy. The adhesive used between the seal and counter-seal was originally wax, later glue, and is now a gummed wafer.[37]

Between 1867 and 1937, all of the Great Seals of Canada were deputed, meaning that they were supreme in Canada but subordinate to the Great Seal of the Realm of the United Kingdom. However, that changed with the grant of *de jure* independence by the *Statute of Westminster, 1931*. Since 1937, the Great Seal of Canada has not been deputed, and is therefore supreme in Canada and is an emblem of national sovereignty.

The use of the Great Seal of Canada is governed by constitutional convention and custom. Firstly, there must be authority under an Order-in-Council for its use in order to ensure that members of the Privy Council accept responsibility for the use of the Great Seal. Secondly, the royal instrument to which any royal seal is affixed must also have upon it a countersignature of a responsible Canadian minister. That ensures that political responsibility for the public acts of the monarchy in Canada is accepted by political actors in accordance with the principles of responsible government. Finally, the Great Seal does not have to be personally affixed to a document by a Sovereign's representative. Rather, it may be affixed by a subordinate official; *R v Lars* (1994), 33 NSWLR 301 (New South Wales, CA).

The Great Seal is kept in secure custody by the Registrar General, a Minister of the Crown.

12.24   The Privy Seal

The Privy Seal is created for use by the Governor General of Canada. It is defined in section 2 of the *Formal Documents Regulations* as follows:

> Privy Seal means the seal adopted by the Governor General or the Administrator for the sealing of official documents that are to be signed by him, or with his authority by his deputy, and that does not require sealing with the Great Seal;

The Privy Seal bears an impression of the Governor General's personal coat of arms. Under the regulations, the Privy Seal is to be used on Commissions issued to officers of the Canadian Armed Forces, the appointment of Deputies of the Governor General or Deputies of the Administrator, Proclamations of the Sovereign's death, the issue of Certificates of Authentication and the Proclamation of the appointment of the Governor General.

12.25   The Sign-Manual, Signets and Cachet

Sometimes, an instrument is endorsed by the Sovereign, or the Sovereign's representative, without the use of a royal seal. In those cases the document is described as a document under the sign-manual. Essentially, this means that the document has on it the signature of the Sovereign, or the Sovereign's representative but it does not bear the impression of a royal seal. Nevertheless, a document under the sign-manual must contain the appropriate countersignature of a responsible Canadian minister.

In United Kingdom constitutional practice a document may be approved under the sign-manual and Signet. The Signet is a seal delivered by the Sovereign to each of the principal Secretaries of State in the United Kingdom, and includes the Lesser Signet or Second Secretarial Seal and Cachet.[38]

12.26 The Seals Act

The use of the royal seals, including the Great Seal of Canada, is regulated by the provisions of the *Seals Act*.[39] Section 3 of that Act provides as follows:

> Notwithstanding any law in force in Canada, any royal instrument may be issued by and with the authority of Her Majesty the Queen and passed under the Great Seal of Canada, or under any other royal seal approved by Her Majesty the Queen for the purpose.

The original intent of this provision, first enacted prior to King George VI's visit to Canada in 1939, was to permit the use in Canada of the Great Seal of the Realm of the United Kingdom.[40] The intention was to allow the King to issue royal instruments in Canada under either the Great Seal of the Realm of the United Kingdom, or the signets used in the United Kingdom. As the common law did not permit this, the enactment of a statute was deemed to be necessary.

At the time the statute was enacted in 1939 there were a number of Canadian Crown instruments that continued to be issued under British royal seals, or signets, including diplomatic instruments such as the grant of powers to plenipotentiaries, treaty ratifications, *exequaturs* issued to foreign consuls and instruments relating directly to the Crown, such as the *Letters Patent Constituting the Office of the Governor General of Canada*, the Commission and *Royal Instructions* to a Governor General, permission for the Governor General to be absent from the realm, and the appointment of an Administrator of Canada.[41]

Under the *Seals Act* it is still possible for a royal instrument in respect of Canada to be passed under the Great Seal of the Realm of the United Kingdom, or under the sign manual and signet of a Secretary of State of the United Kingdom. Although the Great Seal of the Realm and the signets have remained in the possession of British Ministers there was a recognition by Canada and the United Kingdom of a convention by which the Great Seal of the Realm or the Signets could be applied to a Canadian Crown instrument at the request of Canadian Ministers who would accept responsibility for that act. For that purpose a definition of a royal instrument was provided in the statute to assist in defining the type of instruments upon which the British seals and signets could be used.[42]

However, it is no longer the constitutional practice of Canada to utilize the seals and signets of the United Kingdom and this practice, while still legal under the terms of the federal statute and regulations, has fallen into constitutional desuetude. Currently, in Canada, the *Formal Documents Regulations*[43] do not contemplate the use of either the United Kingdom's Great Seal of the Realm, or the signets of United Kingdom Secretaries of State in Canada, although the statute still permits it. The *Seals Act* provides in section 3 for the use of the Great Seal of Canada in all situations where a royal seal is required to be affixed to a royal instrument.

According to Commonwealth precedent (in the particular case the use of the Great Seal of Australia rather than the United Kingdom's Great Seal of the Realm) where a royal instrument was alleged to have been passed under a royal seal that was not the appropriate seal in the circumstances, the formal document issued by the Sovereign will not be invalid. The use of one royal seal rather than another was characterized as an issue of form only, where there was no question concerning the intention of the Sovereign in issuing a royal instrument.[44]

Section 4 of the *Seals Act* provides that the Governor in Council may, subject to the approval of the Queen, make orders and regulations relating to the following matters:

a) The classes of instruments which require the use of royal seals;

b) Authorization of royal seals;

c) The custody of royal seals;

d) The procedures for the use of royal seals, including countersignatures;

e) Procedures for the issuance of documents under the sign-manual;

f) Procedures for obtaining the Queen's approval; and,

g) The manner of authenticating royal instruments.

It should be observed that the Governor General must obtain the approval of the Sovereign before issuing any orders or regulations under this provision.

Pursuant to the *Seals Act* and the *Public Officers Act*, the *Formal Documents Regulations* have been promulgated. Those regulations prescribe in some detail the classes of officers who are to receive Commissions, the seals and signatures required on their Commissions and the seals and signatures to be affixed on other royal instruments.

12.27   Other Seals

There are certain other official seals that are kept by ministers for purposes of authentication, or for other purposes.

12.28   The Seal of the Registrar General

The Registrar General is a Minister of the Crown to which the office of Registrar General has been assigned and who possesses an official seal which is also used on some public documents. The *Formal Documents Regulations* provide that the Seal of the Registrar General shall be affixed to Commissions issued to consuls, vice-consuls, temporary members of permanent federal boards, commissions, and corporations, members of temporary federal boards, commissions, and corporations, and certain officials in the Public Service of Canada.

12.29   The Seal of the Prime Minister

The Office of the Prime Minister has an official seal which is used on some documents issued by the Prime Minister in his or her capacity as the head of the government. The seal of the Prime Minister contains a stylized version of the Royal Arms of Canada encircled by the words "PRIME MINISTER OF CANADA – LE PREMIER MINISTRE DU CANADA". Presumably, the creation of this seal and its use of the Royal Arms of Canada denotes an exercise of the Royal Prerogative for its creation, although the seal of the Prime Minister has not been used on formal documents. It is, however, affixed to celebratory, or congratulatory, announcements, or certificates such as the Certificate of Appreciation issued to retiring public servants.

12.30   Court Seals

Her Majesty's Courts also possess seals which are to be used when official process such as judgments are issued by a court of law.[45] Judicial seals are retained in the custody of the Registrars of the court. Documents sealed with the official seal of a court are judicially recognized by other courts of law in Canada. Some quasi-judicial bodies that are recognized as courts of record are also permitted by statute to possess an official seal that is to be judicially noted by the courts of law.[46]

The officials who administer orders of state such as the Order of Canada possess a seal for uses associated with the work of those orders. The Canadian Heraldic Authority, which issues armorial bearings to Canadians, also possesses its own seal for use on Letters Patent issued to persons granted heraldic emblems.

12.31   Provincial Seals

The Lieutenant Governors of the Provinces receive custody of a Great Seal of a Province upon their assumption of office and may use that seal to dissolve the provincial legislature, or with respect to other acts performed in the Sovereign's name in the province pursuant to the Royal Prerogative.[47] The *Constitution Act, 1867,* contemplated, in section 136, that the legislatures or the Lieutenant Governors in Council of the Provinces would approve the design of a provincial Great Seal from time to time.[48]

As with the Federal government, some provinces also provide for the enactment of regulations to determine which classes of public officers will receive commissions under the Great Seal of the Province, and which classes of public officers will receive a commission under the Lieutenant Governor's Privy Seal.[49]

[1] *Glossary of Parliamentary Procedure,* Clerk of the House of Commons, Ottawa, 1992 (afterwards *"Glossary"*)

[2] See, for example, an *Address presented to His Majesty the King [George VI] on the occasion of His Majesty's Coronation* in SC 1937, Prefix, page vii.

[3] RSC 1985, c P-31

[4] In *Barnes v Government of Newfoundland* Robinson J. stated at pages 91-92: The Commission issued to Mr. Barnes on 31st January, 1874, was in a form for which no precedent was cited; it was a document not under the seal of the colony, but under the private seal of His Excellency [Governor] Sir Stephen Hill; it did not even run in the Queen's name, and did not allege that the appointment was to be held "during pleasure," nor did it specify any tenure whatever. Although it was thus deficient in the usual requisites of a commission from the Crown, it was nevertheless an instrument signed by the Governor of the colony, certified by the Attorney General, and counter-signed by the Colonial Secretary, and as such, it amounted to an appointment of the plaintiff to the situation of Superintendent of Fisheries which was an office that had for many years existed here, for which the Legislature had annually made provision, and again made provision in April, 1874, after Mr. Barnes' appointment".

[5] Ibid, at page 67

[6] *Sabha v Attorney General,* [2009] 4 LRC 818 (Trinidad and Tobago, JC) per Lord Hope at 835.

[7] The *Federal Real Property and Federal Immovables Act* SC 1991, c. 50, s. 5(1)(b) provides that grants of federal real property in fee simple may now be made by an **Instrument of Grant**, or an **Act of Concession**, both of which are creations of that statute. The purpose of creating the Instrument of Grant and an Act of Concession by statute was to avoid the internal procedural complexities inherent in the drafting and sealing of Letters Patent under the Great Seal.

[8] However, the form of federal conveyances is now regulated by the *Federal Real Property and Federal Immovables Act* SC 1991, c. 50, which provides in section 5 that federal real property and federal immovables may be granted by either letters patent under the Great Seal of Canada or by an instrument of grant, or an act of concession, in a form satisfactory to the Minister of Justice stating that it has the same force and effect as if it were Letters Patent.

[9] For example, insurance companies pursuant to the *Insurance Companies Act* SC 1991, c. 47, s 22; banks under the *Bank Act* SC 1991, c. 46, s22(1); and trust companies under the *Trust and Loan Companies Act* SC 1991, c. 45, s 21.

[10] *Glossary*

[11] *Mallory*, at page 66

[12] *The Law and Custom of the Constitution*, Sir William Anson, Clarendon Press, Oxford, 1907, at page 50 (afterwards, *"Anson"*)

[13] There is also an administrative procedure for the suspension of a criminal record that is provided for in the *Criminal Records Act* RSC, 1985, c. C-47.

[14] *Jowitt's Dictionary of English Law*, Rt. Hon. Earl Jowitt and Clifford Walsh, 2nd ed. by John Burke, Sweet and Maxwell, London, 1977 (afterwards *"Jowitts"*)

[15] In *Currie v MacDonald* (1949), 29 Nfld & PEIR 294 at 314 Justice Winters stated; "Even the humblest subject has the right to request even Parliament to do, or abstain from doing any particular act, provided he does so by lawful means; and no court has power to forbid or restrict him." For a discussion of the role of constitutional principle in Canadian constitutional law see the text at chapter 1, section 1.5, infra.

[16] SC 1993, c. 38, s. 12(1)

[17] *Anson*, at page 52

[18] *W S Scott* gives a further example in the form of a proclamation exhorting the population of the United Kingdom to practice economy in the consumption of grain during World War I (*W S Scott*, at pages 126-27).

[19] RSC, 1985, c. I-21

[20] However, through constitutional usage a particular form has been adopted for federal proclamations.

[21] *Anson*, at page 50

[22] *An Act to Amend the Financial Administration Act* SC 1997, c. 5.

[23] RSC, 1985, c. F-11

[24] RSC 1985, c. P-28

[25] This issue is addressed in section 23 of the federal *Interpretation Act* RSC, 1985, c. I-21.

[26] RSC, 1985, c. S-22

[27] *Francois v Attorney General*, [2002] 5 LRC 696 (St. Lucia, HC) at page 719.

[28] *The Great Seal of Canada*, Minister of Supply and Services, Ottawa, 1988, p. 10 (afterwards *"Great Seal"*)

[29] *Great Seal*, at page 5

[30] *Privy Councillors*, at page 2

[31] *Great Seal*, at page 13

[32] Ibid

[33] Ibid, at page 21

[34] (6 Anne, c. 41, Imp.)

[35] *Great Seal*, at page 28

[36] Ibid, at page 32

[37] Ibid, at page 13

[38] The cachet is a stamp bearing a facsimile of the Sovereign's sign-manual.

[39] RSC 1985, c. S-6

[40] The Great Seal of the Realm is defined in section 2 of the Act by reference to Article XXIV of *An Act for an Union of the two Kingdoms of England and Scotland*, (5 Anne, 1706, chapter VIII, Imp.).

[41] *Ollivier*, 456. Only Letters of Credence for Canadian diplomatic ministers plenipotentiary were issued by the King under the sign manual.

[42] *Ollivier*, p. 457.

[43] CRC 1978 c. 1331, as am. by SOR/82-400, SOR/83-46, SOR/98-274, SOR/2000-79 and SOR/2005-187

[44] *Fitzgibbon v Attorney General*, [2005] EWHC 114 (England, Ch) at para. 14. The Chancery Court also found that according to the divisibility principle, it was for the courts of Australia to determine the propriety of the use of one royal seal versus another, and the consequences that flow from that result, and not a matter for an English court to decide.

[45] See the *Rules of the Supreme Court of Canada* (SOR/2002-156), s.79 "A judgment rendered by the Court shall be dated, signed by a judge and sealed with the Court seal."

[46] An example is the National Energy Board which is permitted an official seal pursuant to section 11(2) of the *National Energy Board Act* RSC 1985, c. N-7.

[47] For example, the *Lieutenant Governor and Great Seal Act* RSNS 1989, c. 256, s. 6.

[48] It has been suggested that despite that provision the Sovereign still retains a prerogative power to grant a Great Seal for a province; *Parliamentary Government in the British Colonies*, Alpheus Todd, Longmans, Green & Co., London, 1894 at page 344.

[49] For an illustrative example, see the *Public Officers Act* RSQ 1977, c. E-6, s. 5.

DIGNITIES, HONOURS AND AWARDS

13.1   The Fountain of Honour – An Overview

Dignities and honours form a part of the Royal Prerogative powers that are closely associated with the Sovereign, who has an exclusive right to grant official honours and dignities to her subjects. Thus, in *The Prince's Case* (1608), 8 Co. Rep. 1a at 18b (England, CP) the court stated: "The King is the fountain of all honour and dignity". A subject in Canada obtains a dignity or honour by the gift of the Sovereign, in the exercise of the Royal Prerogative, an Act of Parliament, or by a provincial legislature, by marriage, or by descent. The Sovereign has the ability to confer a dignity or honour upon any subject, or to create new dignities or honours.

Awards are a form of recognition that the Sovereign, or other members of the Royal Family can create in their capacity as natural persons. Awards are not an emanation of the Royal Prerogative, and anyone in society can create an award. The purpose of awards is to encourage effort and achievement and they can be a particularly useful tool for motivating youth toward higher performance in a field of endeavour.

In modern societies, honours and dignities are a means of recognizing distinction, or rewarding loyal service. In the recognition of exceptional achievement, or service, through dignities and honours the state creates an aspirational framework to encourage the emulation by others of the achievements of exceptional members of Canadian society. Dignities and honours may also serve to enhance the loyalty and commitment of subjects to the realm. Initially honours and dignities were conferred not only because of the exceptional achievements of an individual but also to reward a family for their fealty of service to the Throne. While merit was the criterion that drove recognition it was not just individual merit that attracted a recognition of worthiness but the merit of one's family.[1] Collective or familial merit was important in feudal times when kings and queens were not secure upon their thrones and looked to the great families of their realms to support a monarch's legitimate title to their Throne. With the passage of the centuries merit has become focused on the achievements of an individual alone, and the individual's family has generally receded into the background as an element to be considered in making the gift of an honour or dignity.[2]

13.2   Constitutional Jurisdiction Over Honours and Dignities

At confederation in 1867 the subject of honours and dignities was not explicitly addressed in the *Constitution Act, 1867*, and therefore the Royal Prerogative concerning dignities and honours finds its source within the constitutional division of powers in the *Constitution Act, 1867*, and particularly in the residual peace, order and good government clause in section 91, which provides Parliament with jurisdiction concerning those matters that are not specifically enumerated in the division of powers in sections 91 and 92 of the *Constitution Act, 1867*. Consequently, it is the Sovereign in right of Canada that exercises the Royal Prerogative with respect to the grant of dignities and honours; *Lenoir v Ritchie*, [1879] 3 SCR 575 (Canada, SC). However, the Supreme Court in that case also upheld the right of the provinces to confer a statutory dignity or honour by creating provincial offices pursuant to section 92(4) of the *Constitution Act, 1867*.

In the result, while the Federal Government has the constitutional authority to confer and recognize honours and dignities pursuant to the Royal Prerogative under the peace, order and good government clause in section 91 of the *Constitution Act, 1867*, the provinces have jurisdiction under section 92(4) of the *Constitution Act, 1867*, to create provincial offices in the nature of a dignity or honour and to appoint people to those statutory dignities and honours. Thus, a province can, through its legislature, create offices of dignity or honour with the same or similar titles as the honours or dignities created by the Crown in Right of Canada under the powers of the Royal Prerogative.

13.3   The History of Honours and Dignities in Canada

There is a long and complex history to the subject of honours in Canada and it would not be possible to deal with all aspects of the history and policy of this area in this text. However, a brief historical summary is warranted.

Under the Bourbon Monarchy a number of Canadians were ennobled in the seventeenth and eighteenth centuries. For the most part, ennoblements ceased after 1700 except for officials holding the most senior appointments in the government, such as the Governor General, or the Intendant. After 1763 a few Canadians were ennobled for services rendered to New France before the Bourbon monarchy fell in the French revolution.

During the Bourbon period, King Louis XIV created the Ordre Royal et Militaire de Saint-Louis in 1693 as an incentive to the French nobility but one that also had a salutary effect on the military rank and file as well.[3] The Order was only given to officers in the army who were Roman Catholic but a companion order, the Institution du Mérite militaire was created by King Louis XV in 1759 to recognize Protestant officers. These orders ceased to be Canadian orders after 1763 when sovereignty over Canada was transferred from France to Great Britain.

With the extinguishment of the sovereignty of France in Canada at the conclusion of the Seven Years War by the Treaty of Paris, 1763 all French titles in Canada were terminated, with one rather peculiar exception. The hereditary title of the Baron de Longueuil, Charles le Moyne de Longueuil, who was a municipal governor in Trois-Rivières and Montreal, and who was ennobled by King Louis XIV in 1700, was terminated by the conquest in 1763. However, in the nineteenth century his heirs successfully petitioned Queen Victoria to recognize the title and upon receiving the Queen's recognition the title of the Baron de Longueuil was restored to the list of titles recognized in Canada.

In the period after the end of French rule in Canada there are three key periods relating to the history of honours and dignities in Canada. The first period extends from the establishment of British sovereignty over Canada in 1763 until 1878. During that period the Sovereigns of the United Kingdom exercised a substantial personal discretion over the awarding of honours and dignities. There were a number of peerages held by, or given to, British officials who exercised public responsibilities in relation to Canada. The grant of peerages to Canadians was more limited in number, and they were usually granted to prominent businessmen engaged with the development of railways, or media businesses. They were less frequently conferred on Canadian politicians.

During the early British colonial era, the Imperial Government contemplated a system of hereditary peerages to support an upper house of the legislature in Canada. Section 6 of the *Constitutional Act, 1791,* made provision for annexing to any hereditary peerage created in Lower or Upper Canada a hereditary right to be summoned to sit in the Legislative Council of those provinces. However, no such peerages were created while that Act was in force.

Orders of state were given much more frequently, including the most senior levels of orders which conferred a knighthood on the recipient. Of the first ten Prime Ministers of Canada after confederation in 1867 seven received a knighthood and two of the remaining three refused the offer of a knighthood. During this period the Crown was considered to be indivisible within the British Empire and all awards were imperial awards, meaning that the head of the Canadian Government was not necessarily consulted about the awarding of specific honours and dignities. Recommendations for honours for Canadians were made by the Governor General in his capacity as an imperial officer. After confederation in 1867, the Prime Minister of Canada could also make recommendations to the Governor General but the Governor General remained the final authority with respect to the composition of the list of recommended honours to be submitted to the Imperial Government.[4] This process was amended in 1902 to allow the Prime Minister of Canada to make recommendations with respect to service in the administration of government, or parliamentary affairs, and to remark upon the selections proposed by the Governor General but that new power did not stop the Governor General, as an imperial officer, from making independent selections for honours or dignities, nor did it affect the ability of the Imperial Government to reward Canadians for services or achievements of an imperial character.[5]

A key change in imperial honours occurred in 1878, when the Prime Minister of the United Kingdom, Benjamin Disraeli, persuaded Queen Victoria to acquiesce to a proposal that all recommendations for awards of honours and dignities should be coordinated in the office of the Prime Minister of the United Kingdom. This essentially resulted in the transfer of the discretion to award honours from the Sovereign to the Prime Minister.[6] The result was that honours now became a source of government patronage. As time progressed, more and more of the appointments became openly partisan. As electorates expanded, and elections were organized along party lines, it became necessary for political parties to obtain funding for their electoral activities. As a reward for assisting in the financing of elections, some well-heeled supporters of political parties began to receive honours in return for their financial assistance. The practice of rewarding financiers of political parties came to a head during World War One when a scandal erupted over what was considered to be the sale of honours by the British Ministry headed by Prime Minister David Lloyd-George, and a Royal Commission was appointed to investigate the abuses.[7]

In Canada, growing unease with the conferral of titles erupted into controversy during the same period. There had always been some ambivalence toward titular honours in Canada. Royal honours or titles have never held mass appeal for Canadians. After Prime Minister Sir Wilfrid Laurier obtained the ability to recommend politicians and civil servants for honours and dignities in 1902 there was a large increase in knighthoods, which made the possession of a titular honour more public but that clashed with the egalitarian values of the Canadian public.

Furthermore, the terrible sacrifices during World War One eliminated the patience of the public with political chicanery and the eruption of the scandal over the sale of peerages during this period led to calls for the cessation of titular dignities and knighthood honours in Canada. The issue came to the fore of public opinion when the unpopular Minister of Militia and Defence, Sam Hughes, was knighted in 1915, upon the recommendation of Prime Minister Sir Robert Borden, and two Canadian media barons, Max Aitken, and Hugh Graham were subsequently elevated to the peerage as Lord Beaverbrook, and Lord Atholstan respectively, by the Imperial Government. The elevation of Hugh Graham was particularly controversial because it was made on the recommendation of the British Ministry and was done against the advice of both Prime Minister Borden and the Governor General of Canada, the Duke of Devonshire.

As a result of these controversies a resolution was introduced into the House of Commons of Canada in 1917 by William Nickle M.P., calling upon the King to cease granting hereditary titles to Canadians. After debate, the *Nickle Resolution* was passed by the House of Commons in 1918.[8] Nickle followed up his original resolution with a subsequent resolution in April 1919, calling upon the King to cease conferring upon Canadians any honour that carried a title. After examination of the resolution by a Special Committee of the House on Honours and Titles, the recommendation prohibiting honours that conveyed a title to the recipient was passed by the House of Commons (both resolutions are together referred to as the *Nickle Resolution*).[9] As a result of the *Nickle Resolution* peerages, baronetcies, and knighthoods ceased to be conferred upon Canadians as a means of recognizing their contributions to national life. The *Nickle Resolution* expressed the will of the House of Commons although the resolution itself had no legal force and it could not legally prevent the grant of titular and hereditary honours to Canadians. But it did express a policy position that subsequent Canadian governments, with the one exception in the early 1930's, have been loathe to depart from.

After the *Nickle Resolution* subsequent Conservative and Liberal governments ceased to present recommendations for hereditary dignities or knighthoods to the King, although existing honours and dignities continued to be recognized. A brief revival of the practice of conferring knighthoods occurred during 1934-35, at the request of the Bennett Ministry but the practice was again discontinued after 1935. (Exceptionally, Prime Minister R B Bennett was raised to the peerage as a Viscount after he retired to the United Kingdom). The revival of knighthoods during the premiership of Prime Minister Richard Bennett in the 1930's is now seen as an historical aberration.[10] Prime Minister Mackenzie King, who held office for almost twenty-two years during the middle years of the twentieth century, was adamantly opposed to honours and his successor Prime Minister Louis St. Laurent was quite indifferent to them. As a result, the *Nickle Resolution*, over time, became a constitutional custom preventing Canadians from receiving a titular honour or dignity from the Sovereign, although the Sovereign retained the legal right to confer a peerage or knighthood upon Canadians.

Canadians serving under arms in the military continued to receive British honours for valour and gallantry in World War One, World War Two, and the Korean War, notwithstanding the conventional prohibition against titular honours and dignities. As the country's centennial of confederation approached in 1967 however, there was a renewed interest in establishing a system of national honours separate from the British honours. Committees were struck and a considerable effort was made to create a national system of honours. That

344 Crown and Constitutional Law

effort bore fruit with the creation in 1967 of the Order of Canada, followed in 1972 by the creation of a series of bravery decorations. A series of military valour decorations was established in 1993. Over time additional orders of state, decorations and medals have been added so that by the beginning of the twenty-first century Canada possessed a comprehensive system of honours and dignities that addressed most situations where some form of state recognition is desirable.[11]

13.4   Administration of Honours and Dignities

Prior to 1969 the responsibility for honours and dignities rested with the Office of the Secretary of State, a department of government that was originally established in 1867 as a conduit for relations between the Government of Canada and the Government of the United Kingdom. After that role ceased with the establishment of the divisibility of the Crown through the Balfour Declaration in 1926, and the *Statute of Westminster, 1931*, the Secretary of State continued with responsibility for registration and ceremonial functions. Occasionally other duties were also devolved upon it, such as the responsibility for government policy concerning honours.

In 1969 internal responsibilities for Canadian honours were transferred from the office of the Secretary of State to the Governor General's office, thus placing the Sovereign's representative in a position of responsibility with respect to Canada's system of honours. An interdepartmental committee of the federal government known as the Honours Policy Committee was established to provide advice to the Crown on the creation of new Canadian honours. The Honours Policy Committee consists of a body of deputy ministers, the Secretary to the Governor General, and the Clerk of the Privy Council.[12] The Clerk of the Privy Council, the most senior federal public servant, is the chair of the committee.[13] The Honours Policy Committee advises the Governor General on all aspects of the Canadian honours system, including proposals for new honours, or changes to existing honours.

In 1988, responsibility for heraldry was transferred from the Sovereign, acting through her College of Arms in the United Kingdom, to the Sovereign acting through her Governor General of Canada. A new Canadian Heraldic Authority was established as part of the Governor General's office to administer the Crown's heraldic authority in Canada.

13.5   The Role of the Sovereign

In law, throughout the Commonwealth realms, the Sovereign remains the ultimate source of authority for the creation of honours and dignities. In reviewing the creation of the Order of Trinity in the Commonwealth realm of Trinidad and Tobago, the Judicial Committee of the Privy Council noted that:

It was by and with the advice of the Cabinet that the Order of Trinity was established by Her Majesty [Queen Elizabeth II]. Constitutional validity was given in this way to its creation by the executive. But the authority to create the order lay not with the Cabinet but with Her Majesty in the exercise of the prerogative. The sovereign is the fountain of all honours in territories of which she is Queen.[14]

In Canada, the Sovereign has remained directly engaged in the creation and amendment of letters patent issued to create new Canadian orders of state, decorations, and medals, and she personally approves all usages of the royal Crown and cypher, and of the Sovereign's effigy in the design of orders of state, decorations, and medals.

Although the Governor General has authority under the *Letters Patent Constituting the Office of the Governor General and Commander-in-Chief of Canada, 1947,* to act in the Sovereign's name with respect to the creation of new Canadian orders of state, decorations, or medals, it has been a longstanding constitutional custom that the Sovereign retains the final right of approval for the creation of all new Canadian honours. The creation of new honours requires formal advice by the Queen's Privy Council for Canada to the Governor General requesting that the Governor General advise the Sovereign to issue letters patent under the Great Seal of Canada to create a new Canadian honour. Under existing constitutional practice letters patent will be issued to establish the new honour which will be governed by regulations appended to the letters patent. Subsequent changes to the letters patent creating the new honour are reserved for alteration by the Sovereign, the Sovereign's heirs, or by the Governor General of Canada. The constitutional custom and practice in Canada is that any changes to the regulations governing a particular honour are promulgated by the Governor General, following his or her receipt of formal advice from the Canadian Ministry but any change to the letters patent that created the honour are to be made by the Sovereign, again acting on the formal advice of the Canadian Ministry.

13.6   The Role of the Governor General

The Governor General plays a key role in the administration of the Canadian honours system. He or she has primary oversight over the honours conferred by the Crown and provides the necessary link between the Canadian Ministry and the Sovereign with respect to the creation of new honours. The Governor General also promulgates changes to the regulations governing particular honours and presides over the ceremonies at which honours are conferred in Canada.

Administration of the system of Canadian honours and dignities resides with the Chancellery of Honours, a branch of the Office of the Governor General. The Chancellery of Honours is headed by the Deputy Secretary to the Governor

General and contains separate directorates for Honours and for Heraldry. The Chancellery reports to the Governor General through the Office of the Secretary to the Governor General.

13.7   Justiciability of Honours and Dignities

The grant of a dignity or honour is an exercise of the Royal Prerogative. Historically, the common law did not provide for the judicial review of the exercise by the Crown of a Royal Prerogative power. However, with the evolution of the common law in the late twentieth century that barrier was breached in *Council of Civil Service Unions v Minister for the Civil Service*, [1985] AC 374 (England, HL) where the House of Lords concluded that the exercise of the Royal Prerogative could be subjected to the scrutiny of judicial review. Nevertheless, the House of Lords suggested that some prerogative powers, and more particularly the grant of honours, would not be subject to judicial review. With respect to the grant of honours Lord Roskill stated that they would not be subject to judicial review "because their nature and subject matter is such as not to be amenable to the judicial process." Thus, the House of Lords considered that ordinary judicial review was precluded with respect to honours and dignities, and that remains the approach of the courts within the United Kingdom.

However, Canada and other Commonwealth realms differ from the United Kingdom in that many have entrenched declarations of fundamental rights within their written constitutions, in Canada, the *Canadian Charter of Rights and Freedoms*. Where a particular realm has an entrenched declaration of fundamental rights, a constitutional basis exists for the judicial review of the Crown's actions, including the creation of an honour or dignity, or the grant of an honour or dignity. In Canada, the breadth of this option for constitutional judicial review was established by the Supreme Court in the *Operation Dismantle* case.[15]

An example of how constitutional values expressed in an entrenched declaration of rights may impact upon the Crown's decision to create an honour can be seen in the Commonwealth realm case of *Sabha et al v Attorney General*, [2009] 4 LRC 818 (Trinidad and Tobago, JC). In *Sabha*, the Judicial Committee dealt with a case where the multi-cultural, and multi-racial realm of Trinidad and Tobago had created a public honour shortly after receiving its independence in 1962. The honour created by the Crown was in the form of an order of state bearing the name the Order of Trinity and for which the recipients received the Trinity Cross, as the highest honour of the realm of Trinidad and Tobago.

However, the country had a substantial minority of people who professed the Hindu and Muslim faiths and a number of them took exception to a national honour that was framed as a Christian symbol. The written constitution of

Trinidad and Tobago contained entrenched provisions that protected individual human rights and civil liberties, and those who were opposed to the Order of Trinity commenced litigation seeking to strike down the letters patent which created the honour, particularly with respect to the symbolism of the cross.[16] The creation of the Order of Trinity (which had been subsequently renamed, and the cross replaced with a medal as a result of public pressure) survived the challenge in the local courts but not in the Judicial Committee of the Privy Council. In finding that the letters patent that created the Order of Trinity was contrary to the constitution of the realm, Lord Hope stated:

> . . . one of the limits to any power to make law was set by the declaration in s 2(1) of the Constitution that no law was to authorize the abrogation, abridgement or infringement of any of the rights and freedoms declared in s 1. Full effect must be given to that declaration, and it applies as much to the use of the prerogative to create rules for the administration of a national awards system as it does to an enactment by the legislature. This means that it was not open to the monarch, whether by the issue of letters patent in the exercise of the royal prerogative or otherwise, to act in a manner that was incompatible with the existence of the right to equality, the right to equality of treatment from any public authority and the right to freedom of conscience and religious belief.[17]

In the result, the Privy Council determined that the creation of the Order of Trinity was an infringement of the rights and freedoms of the Hindu and Muslim minority in Trinidad and Tobago, and therefore was unconstitutional.

In Canada, there have been no *Charter* challenges to date with respect to either the creation of honours or their award but there has been a number of cases that have sought to impugn the exercise of the Royal Prerogative concerning honours from the perspective of the administrative law principles of procedural fairness and legitimate expectations.

The justiciability of the exercise of the Royal Prerogative to confer dignities and honours upon Canadians first went before the courts of law in the case of *Black v Canada (Prime Minister)*, [2001] 54 OR (3d) 215 (Ontario, CA). The facts of that matter disclosed that in February 1999 Prime Minister Tony Blair of the United Kingdom informed Mr. Conrad Black, a Canadian citizen, that the Prime Minister would advise Queen Elizabeth II to confer a life peerage in the United Kingdom upon Mr. Black, with the rank of baron. On May 10, 1999, the United Kingdom formally asked Canada to advise if there was any legal impediment to the conferral of a peerage upon Mr. Black. Canada advised the British government that there was no impediment provided that Mr. Black obtained British citizenship, and did not use his British title in Canada. This was acceptable to Mr. Black and he requested and obtained British citizenship on June 11, 1999, following which Mr. Blair advised him that the Queen would confer a peerage upon him on June 18, 1999.

However, before that day arrived Prime Minister Jean Chretien of Canada formally advised Queen Elizabeth II that a British peerage should not be conferred upon Mr. Black due to the impediment presented by the *Nickle Resolution*, and the resulting constitutional custom that Canadians should not be awarded titular honours. Prime Minister Blair was then forced to advise Mr. Black that his proposed peerage was in suspension.

Black contacted Prime Minister Chretien who declined to change his advice to the Queen which was based on the *Nickle Resolution*. According to the facts in the subsequent litigation: "During this conversation the P[rime] M[inister] made reference to Black's treatment of him in the National Post, a Canadian newspaper published by Black. Black says this was the third occasion in six months that the P[rime] M[inister] had mentioned to Black his dissatisfaction with comments in that newspaper".[18]

Black challenged Prime Minister Chretien's formal advice to the Queen in the Superior Court of Ontario, requesting a declaration that the Prime Minister "had no authority to advise Her Majesty the Queen in right of the United Kingdom not to confer an honour on Black as a Canadian citizen, or as a dual citizen of both Canada and the United Kingdom".[19] However, his application for judicial review was denied by Chief Justice Le Sage in the Superior Court of Ontario who held that the application was non-justiciable because the Prime Minister's actions came "within the political area of the prerogative that is not subject to review in the courts".[20]

On appeal to the Court of Appeal of Ontario, Justice Laskin, for the court, held that Prime Minister Chretien, in giving advice to the Queen concerning the Canadian Honours Policy was exercising a power under the Royal Prerogative. As to whether that advice was reviewable in a court of law Justice Laskin agreed with the judgement of Lord Roskill in *Council of Civil Service Unions v Minister for the Civil Service*,[21] who stated that while "the controlling consideration in determining whether the exercise of a prerogative power is judicially reviewable is its subject matter, not its source", the grant of honours was an exercise of the Royal Prerogative that was not justiciable, unlike certain other decisions made pursuant to the Royal Prerogative that can affect the rights, interests, or expectations of a subject of the Crown. Justice Laskin stated:

> Here, no important individual interests are at stake. Mr. Black's rights were not affected, however broadly "rights" are construed. No Canadian citizen has a right to an honour. And no Canadian citizen can have a legitimate expectation of receiving an honour . . . The receipt of an honour lies entirely within the discretion of the conferring body. The conferral of the honour at issue in this case, a British peerage, is a discretionary favour bestowed by the Queen. It engages no liberty, no property, no economic interests. It enjoys no procedural protection. It does not have a sufficient legal component to warrant the court's intervention. Instead, it involves

"moral and political considerations which it is not within the province of the courts to assess".[22]

The *Black* case is an important Canadian precedent for the proposition that the grant of a dignity or honour by the Crown is non-justiciable under the ordinary principles of judicial review and that formal advice given to the Sovereign or the Sovereign's representative concerning the grant of a dignity or honour is therefore beyond the purview of judicial review. Notably, however, *Black v Prime Minister* did not involve an assertion that the Applicant's *Charter* rights had been violated. If there had been such an allegation it is likely that the court would have found that judicial review under the *Charter* was available, and would have proceeded to analyse the factual matrix to determine if such a claim were valid in the circumstances of that case.

While *Black v Prime Minister* stands for the proposition that judicial review will not lie against a recommendation for or against the grant of an honour to a subject by the Crown on the grounds of justiciabilty, the subsequent case of *Black v Advisory Council for the Order of Canada*, [2012] FC 1234 (Canada, FC) establishes that procedural protections may, in some circumstances, be afforded to persons who are in jeopardy of having an honour withdrawn by the Crown.

In *Black v Advisory Council* the Federal Court was faced with an application for judicial review which sought to establish the Applicant's right to an oral hearing before the Advisory Council before it considered whether to recommend his removal from the Order of Canada. The Federal Court held that an applicant for judicial review in these circumstances could apply for judicial review notwithstanding that it was only an interlocutory decision of the Advisory Council, and not the final decision of the Governor General that was the subject of the litigation.

Furthermore, while the grant or termination of an honour was, in substance, not justiciable, the adherence by the Advisory Council to a set of detailed procedures governing a termination proceeding did create a legitimate expectation that those procedures would be followed. Thus, to that extent that the Applicant claimed that the detailed procedures were not being followed, the matter was potentially justiciable. In this particular case, however, by applying the factors established by the Supreme Court in *Baker v Canada (Minister of Citizenship and Immigration)*, [1999] 2 SCR 817 (Canada, SC) it was apparent that Black was unable to show that a failure to provide procedural fairness was present in the circumstances. The procedural fairness requirements were found to be quite limited in this fact situation, and they did not rise to a level that would warrant the imposition of oral hearing rights since personal credibility was not an issue. On appeal to the Federal Court of Appeal (*Black v The Advisory Council of the Order of Canada* (2013), FCA 267 (Canada, FCA) the Federal

Court of Appeal agreed with the lower court judge that the *Baker* factors placed the procedural fairness requirements applicable to the Advisory Council at the lower end of the spectrum of procedural rights because:

a) the Council's process does not resemble judicial decision-making and is non-adversarial;

b) the Council's function is recommendatory and the Governor General's decision is discretionary;

c) Mr. Black had no legal right to an appointment, nor a legitimate expectation that it would not be terminated, and

d) any damage to his reputation flowed from his conviction [for an offence in the United States];

Therefore the Court held that "the Council was entitled to deference in the exercise of its discretion as to whether Mr. Black should be given an opportunity to make representations orally or in writing".[23] Thus, the decision of the Advisory Council not to provide for an oral hearing before considering termination but rather to permit written representations to be lodged with the Advisory Council before it formulated its recommendations to the Governor General was acceptable in the circumstances. Despite the Applicant's lack of success in this case it does establish that procedural rights are potentially available whenever a person is facing the potential of being stripped of an honour.

The question of whether a person is entitled to be considered for the grant of an honour has also been the subject of judicial scrutiny in Canada. In *Canada v Chiasson* (2003), 226 DLR (4th) 351 (Canada, FCA) Justice Strayer of the Federal Court of Appeal dealt with an appeal from a motion to strike an application for judicial review concerning the award of a bravery decoration pursuant to the *Canadian Bravery Decorations Regulations, 1996.*[24] In that case, an advisory committee known as the Canadian Bravery Decorations Committee refused to consider a nomination by an Applicant on behalf of this father for the award of a bravery decoration with respect to events that had occurred in World War Two. The refusal of the committee was based on an administrative rule established by the committee itself whereby no consideration was to be given to acts of bravery that occurred more than two years before the date of the committee's consideration of the matter. The Plaintiff challenged the rule on the basis that the two-year rule did not appear in the *Canadian Bravery Decorations Regulations*. Motions to strike the Plaintiff's action were dismissed by the Prothonotary and by a judge of the trial court. In the Court of Appeal Justice Strayer found that the matter was justiciable and stated at paragraph 16:

> . . . it is in my view arguable that where a procedure has been established by one public authority, in this case by way of Regulations published in the Canada Gazette, as to how and on what basis a specific Committee, another public body, is to deal with nominations made by any citizen, then a legitimate expectation is thereby created that the prescribed procedure will be followed to screen such nominations prior to the submission of a list of nominees for the exercise by the Governor General of the royal prerogative . . .

Similarly, in a case which challenged the appointment to the Order of Canada of a physician widely known for his promotion of abortion rights, *Chauvin v The Queen*, [2009] FC 1202, 355 FTR 200 (Canada, FC) Federal Court Prothonotary Aalto distinguished the Black case in finding that the challenge to an appointment could be justiciable. The Prothonotary stated at paragraphs 36 and 37:

> The Court of Appeal for Ontario upheld the motions judge in striking the action on the basis that the actions of the Prime Minister were an exercise of a prerogative that was non-justiciable. However, on its facts, *Black* is distinguishable from the case at bar. In that case there was no written instrument governing or controlling the power being exercised by the Prime Minister. Here, there are clear criteria set out in sections 8, 9 and 18 of the Constitution: the person must have the greatest merit; have distinguished service in or to a particular community, group or field of activity, and be a Canadian Citizen. Thus, as Justice Strayer observed in *Chiasson*:

> Unlike the *Black* case where there were no written instruments controlling the power being exercised by the Prime Minister, it is certainly arguable in the present case that the Regulations, once adopted, constitute a set of rules which provide criteria for a Court to determine if the procedure prescribed therein has been followed, and if the Committee has exercised the jurisdiction assigned to it. That the Regulations themselves were promulgated under the royal prerogative does not render questions of compliance with the procedure they prescribe matters plainly beyond judicial review. (para. 8)

> Therefore, in applying this test to this motion to strike, it is arguable that it is not plain and obvious that the issues raised by Mr. Chauvin are not justiciable.

In Canada, therefore, the question of the justiciability with respect to dignities and honours can be answered this way. Where there is an allegation that rights under the *Canadian Charter of Rights and Freedoms* have been breached a judicial review of government action in the area of honours will be available (*Operation Dismantle*) but otherwise the grant or denial of an honour will generally be immune from judicial review on substantive grounds (*Black v Canada (Prime Minister)*). However, where the Crown establishes detailed rules for the consideration of nominations for an honour, or for the withdrawal of an honour, those detailed rules may establish a legitimate expectation on the part of a subject that such rules will be followed, and that may provide a justiciable basis for judicial intervention by way of a judicial review application (*Canada v Chiasson; Chauvin v The Queen*) despite the apparent immunity of honours cases from judicial review generally (*Council of Civil Service Unions v Minister for the Civil Service; Black v Canada (Prime Minister).*

13.8   Honours and Dignities Distinguished

The Royal Prerogative provides for two categories of distinction: dignities and honours. Historically, the grant of a dignity was intended to provide the recipient with a higher social status, either by the conferral of a hereditary grant of nobility, or the right to publicly display inheritable identifying emblems, such as a coat of arms. An honour is a non-hereditary mark of individual distinction relating to an individual's merit or worth as reflected in their individual contributions to society, or to their worthy behaviours, such as their courage, service, and devotion to duty.

Dignities include peerages, which are hereditary grants of a title of nobility.[25] In the days of the empire, some Canadians received peerages and their titles have continued to be recognized in Canada. However, since the *Nickle Resolution* in 1918-19, Canadians are no longer eligible to be granted peerages.

Honours include orders of state, decorations and medals. In a few cases, honours may include a title, normally, the prefix Sir or Dame. Since the *Nickle Resolution* in 1918-19 Canadians have no longer received honours that confer a prefix title of Sir or Dame, with two exceptions. A small number of such honours were conferred upon Canadians in the closing months of the Bennett Ministry in 1934-35, and in a few subsequent cases dual Canadian and British citizens have been permitted to receive such honours from the United Kingdom for services they have rendered to that country. Such appointments have often reflected service by Canadians in the armed forces of the United Kingdom, or services rendered to British industry.

13.9   Dignities

A dignity represents the conferral of a hereditary honour upon a person by the Crown. The Sovereign of Canada has an unrestricted ability founded upon the Royal Prerogative to create and confer dignities. Dignities include peerages, baronetcies, and the grant or armorial bearings but it is possible for other dignities to be created pursuant to the Royal Prerogative and the most common dignities in Canada are honorifics, especially the suffix U.E., standing for United Empire, that was granted by Lord Dorchester to Canadian loyalists. Dignities are inalienable incorporeal hereditaments that descend to heirs in accordance with the terms of the original grant and the underlying laws of descent.

13.10   Peerages

Canadian peers are hereditary nobles created by the Sovereign's grant. At least five such peerages conferred before the *Nickle Resolution* in 1918-19 can be regarded as Canadian peerages because the Canadian Ministry was consulted by the Crown on those appointments.[26] The Canadian peerages are hereditary and descend according to the rules of male-preference primogeniture, unless the grant specified otherwise.[27] A peerage can be extinguished by an Act of Parliament or by the failure of heirs. If a peerage is inherited by co-heirs the peerage is deemed to be in abeyance and will not vest in a specific heir unless the Sovereign ends the period of abeyance by the appointment of one of the co-heirs to the peerage. Disputed peerages may be the subject of a petition to the Sovereign.

There are five classes of peers that can be conferred pursuant to the Royal Prerogative. The five classes of peerage, in their order of precedence, are, duke, marquess, earl, viscount and baron (the female equivalents, which are rare but do exist, are duchess, marchioness, countess, viscountess and baroness).

Following the adoption of the *Nickle Resolution* successive Canadian ministries refused to recommend to the Sovereign that Canadians be granted peerages and a constitutional custom crystallized under which it became no longer possible for a Canadian Ministry to recommend the grant of a peerage to Canadians, and thus no longer possible for the Sovereign to confer a peerage upon a Canadian. The prohibition against Canadians receiving a peerage was, and remains, a matter of custom however, and does not represent a legal constraint on the powers of the Sovereign, who retains the legal power to create and confer a Canadian peerage.

Several Canadian peerages that were created before the *Nickle Resolution* are still extant. A list of Canadians who hold hereditary peerages can generally be found in general reference works.[28] Despite the effects of the *Nickle Resolution* a few Canadians received peerages or were elevated in the peerage after 1919. With the exception of former Prime Minister Richard Bennett, all of the Canadians who received a peerage subsequent to the *Nickle Resolution* were honoured for their contributions to the United Kingdom, rather than to Canada. In some cases, they were required to relinquish their Canadian citizenship in order to receive the peerage.[29]

The members of the peerage display no emblems of rank or distinction except at a coronation ceremony when they wear a coronet and robe consistent with their rank in the peerage.

13.11 Baronetcies

A baronetcy is the grant of a hereditary knighthood enabling the recipient and his male heirs under the rules of male-preference primogeniture to use the prefix of Sir before their names as well as the use of the post-nominal abbreviation Bart. or Bt.. Some baronetcies also pass through females. A female baronet is addressed with the prefix Dame.

A baronet ranks behind a baron in the order of precedence. Seven Canadians were created as baronets on the advice of a Canadian Ministry but following the implementation of the *Nickle Resolution* all such appointments ceased. Those baronetcies that were created before the cessations of hereditary appointments continue to be recognized in Canada. By custom Canadians are no longer created as baronets but, as with peerages, the Sovereign retains the power under the Royal Prerogative to create baronets.

13.12   Knighthoods

A knighthood is the grant of an individual title of honour entitling the recipient to use the prefix Sir, if a male, and Dame, if a female. Knights rank after baronets in precedence. There are three ways in which Canadian knights were formerly created. Firstly, those persons summoned to be members of a chivalric order such as the Order of the Garter, or the Order of the Thistle, will have a knighthood automatically conferred upon them. Secondly, those persons appointed to the higher levels of a royal order, such as the Royal Victorian Order, or the higher level of a British national order, such as the Order of the Bath, automatically obtained a knighthood. The third way in which a knighthood was conferred was by appointment as a Knight Bachelor, which is a knighthood that is not included within any chivalric, royal, or national order. In the period before the *Nickle Resolution* a number of the senior members of the Canadian judiciary were appointed as Knights Bachelor.

A substantial number of Canadians were created knights in the period before the adoption of the *Nickle Resolution* but after 1919 knighthoods were no longer conferred upon Canadians. There was, however, a brief resuscitation of knighthoods during the Bennett Ministry in the mid-1930's, and a few knighthoods were conferred at that time. After 1935, however, Canadian knighthoods once again ceased and it is now a firmly established custom based on the policy of the *Nickle Resolution* that knighthoods will not be conferred upon Canadians for services to Canada.

However, a few people with dual Canadian and other commonwealth citizenship have subsequently secured with the acquiescence, or consent, of the Canadian government. In those circumstances it seems that Canadians have been permitted to accept the knighthood where the services of the person being honoured were in relation to the other Commonwealth realm that was conferring the knighthood, and not Canada.

13.13   Titles of Estate or Gentry

At common law, titles or ranks of estate within the gentry, or lower nobility, reflected social class, or status, and was closely associated with dignities but such appellations are now largely of historical or academic interest. Among the appellations recognized in the common law, and subsequently incorporated into tables of rank, were esquires, and gentlemen, or gentlewomen. Although a peer or a knight possessed a title of dignity, which ranked them above those who held only a title of estate, all knights and peers nevertheless were held to possess the estate of a gentleman, or a gentlewoman.

An esquire, was a rank sometimes expressed as a title of dignity, or as one associated with an office, which was next below a knight in the landed gentry. An esquire fell into one of six categories; 1) younger sons of peers and their heirs perpetually, 2) the sons of baronets, 3) the eldest son of knights and their eldest son perpetually, 4) esquires *ex officio* such as heralds, sergeants at arms, officers of state, Judges, Justices of the Peace, judicial officers, barristers (and in the Empire and Commonwealth both barristers and solicitors), higher military officers, and the holders of doctoral degrees in some faculties, 5) foreign peers and 6) three appointees of Knights of the Bath appointed to serve the knight at his installation into the Order, and at the coronation of a Sovereign.[30] However, the title is now more often used as a very formal salutation when writing to any adult male, in which case the abbreviation Mr. is not used in the salutation and the word Esquire or its contraction Esq. is placed after the man's surname.

The distinction of an esquire has traditionally been applied as a courtesy title to officers of the courts, and to barristers and solicitors in the common law provinces of Canada. However, this use of the title has now become uncommon, possibly because of the large influx of female barristers and solicitors into the legal profession in recent decades. The Law Society of Upper Canada, for example, ceased to use this appellation with respect to male barristers and solicitors around 1990. It was never used in connection with female barristers and solicitors.[31] The appellation was never in common use in the legal professions in the province of Quebec which follows a civil law system. There, however, the honorific Maitre (Eng. "Master") continues to be applied as a prefix to the names of advocates or notaries practising in Quebec, both male and female.

Below an esquire was a gentleman or gentlewoman, who were men or women of birth in social status above a yeoman, and who could trace their legitimate descent as free men or free women, or who bore a coat of arms. Historically, it was very difficult to differentiate between a gentleman and an esquire. In the modern era in Canada egalitarianism has triumphed and everyone is considered to be a gentleman or a gentlewoman.

The distinction of yeoman was below the rank of a gentleman and therefore outside of the gentry, which represented the lower ranks of English nobility. Yeoman, in England, referred to a commoner who owned free land sufficient to establish an annual value of at least 40 shillings which enabled them to serve on juries and to participate in the election of representatives to the early English parliaments. They were essentially middle class commoners and ranked above a husbandman, which was a tenant farmer.

In Canada titles of estate were never commonly used and Canada developed as a much more egalitarian society than its European progenitors but the descriptions did occasionally appear in legal documents for identification purposes. Although the use of the suffix appellation of an esquire, as applied to court officials or barristers and solicitors, is still occasionally seen in formal documents and letters, the use of all other such titles of estate have now been abandoned in Canada.

13.14   Heraldry

Heraldry is "an emblematic form of individual identification" which first appeared in the 12th century.[32] It includes coats of arms, badges, and flags, which can be collectively described as armorial bearings. Heraldry has been closely associated with the monarchy for several centuries and the grant of armorial bearings is classified as a dignity emanating from the Royal Prerogative.[33] Grants of arms were originally made under the authority of the Sovereign to persons who had the status of a gentleman (or more rarely to a gentlewoman) and who had a good public reputation. Arms were given particularly to those who had rendered valued service and whose actions and character entitled them to be honoured by the Crown.

Formerly, Canadians who wished to obtain heraldic emblems were required to petition the College of Arms in England or, if they had a connection to Scotland, to the Court of the Lord Lyon in Scotland, for the grant of arms. However, on June 4, 1988, Prince Edward delivered to Governor General Jeanne Sauve, Letters Patent, issued by Queen Elizabeth II on the advice of the Queen's Privy Council for Canada, which authorized and empowered the Governor General of Canada "to exercise, or provide for the exercise of all powers and authorities lawfully belonging to Us as Queen of Canada in respect of the granting of armorial bearings in Canada".[34]

The Governor General thereupon authorized the creation of the Canadian Heraldic Authority, which administers the grant of armorial bearings to Canadians. The Canadian Heraldic Authority consists of the Governor General, the Herald Chancellor, (who is otherwise the Secretary to the Governor General), the Deputy Herald Chancellor (otherwise the Deputy Secretary of the Governor General) who is responsible for the Chancellery Branch of the

Office of the Governor General, and the Chief Herald of Canada (the Director of Heraldry, and principal advisor to the Crown on heraldic matters). There are also several Heralds under the Chief Herald,including the Saint Laurent Herald, who is the Registrar and custodian of the seal of the Canadian Heraldic Authority, the Saguenay Herald who serves as Assistant Registrar, the Miramichi Herald, the Coppermine Herald, the Assiniboine Herald, and the Fraser Herald, who is the chief heraldic artist.

The major activities of the Canadian Heraldic Authority include the granting of arms, or the registration of existing arms, flags, and badges; registration of the symbols used by the First Nations of Canada; registration of military symbols, the collection of genealogical information concerning the inheritance of arms, and the provision of information about heraldry in Canada.

13.15   The Law of Arms of Canada

The use of heraldry is governed by the law of arms, an old and curious branch of the law. It is a part of the law of England but historically it was not considered to be a part of the common law of England,[35] and therefore not part of Canadian common law, although it has nevertheless been inherited by Canada under the reception doctrine. The law of arms was the law pertaining to military matters that fell outside of the common law. The substance of the law of arms was to be found in the ancient Court of Chivalry, which was the court of the Earl Marshal of the realm of England and the Lord High Constable of England, sitting jointly, which existed at least from the time of King Edward III, from August 1348.[36] The court, so constituted, was active until the execution in 1521 of the Lord High Constable of England, the Duke of Buckingham, which put the court, as an institution, into a hiatus. During the subsequent years however, it appears that the Earl Marshall continued to make rulings in matters pertaining to the jurisdiction of the court, sitting as an *ad hoc* tribunal, until the Court of Chivalry was formally reactivated by King James I by the issuance of new letters patent issued to the Earl Marshall on August 1, 1622.

The Court of Chivalry was a peculiar institution in the law of England because it was a civil law court rather than a common law court. As a civil law court its practice and procedure was derived from Roman law. However, the principles of Roman civil law mandated that honours and dignities should be adjudicated according to the customs of each country. Thus, the substantive law actually applied in the Court of Chivalry was derived from English customary law, even though the procedural law of the court was based on civil law principles.[37] The Court of Chivalry and the English law of arms were recognized by the early common law courts but the common law courts would not adjudicate on matters that belonged within the jurisdiction of the Court of Chivalry.

The jurisdiction of the court covered a variety of martial matters of which the law of armorial bearings was only one component. The jurisdiction of the High Court of Chivalry at various times covered such diverse matters as prisoners of war, and the practice of ransoming, indentures of war, as well as extra-territorial criminal jurisdiction for treasons and murders committed abroad.[38] Over time Parliament encroached by statute on the jurisdiction of the Court of Chivalry by transferring important matters to the common law courts with the result that it was left with little more than the law pertaining to heraldry. Even that jurisdiction largely lapsed through disuse, and the Court of Chivalry has sat in England only once (in 1954) between 1737 and the present time. Nevertheless, it is from the admittedly sparse records of that court that the substantive law of arms is derived.

Heraldic causes in the Court of Chivalry concerning the bearing of arms usually concerned the issue of whether a person was entitled to bear lawful arms, or whether the lawful arms of one person had been improperly usurped by another person. A case of unlawful entitlement to bear arms could be brought before the court on the application of the King's Advocate, who occupied a position in the High Court of Chivalry that was analogous to the position of the Attorney General in the common law courts. The High Court of Chivalry also dealt with cases where titles of estate were at issue and thus causes were brought before the court alleging the improper assumption by a yeoman of the gentry titles of esquire or gentleman.

To prove an entitlement to bear arms one had to show the court that the defendant, or the ancestors of the defendant, had been granted arms by a lawful authority or that one's ancestors had borne a coat of arms from time immemorial. A grant of arms could be made by the Sovereign or by one of the officers of arms appointed by the Sovereign. The officers of arms were styled as the King of Arms, Herald, or a Pursuivant. A grant to a named individual was clear and it was only necessary to confirm the validity of the letters patent to recognize the grant of arms. A grant of arms is transmissible from generation to generation with all legitimate male issue entitled to bear the arms of their forefathers.[39] Where the male line failed the arms of a father could be transmitted through his legitimate daughters as quarterings.[40] Proof of the use of armorial bearings was more complicated. At common law time immemorial meant before the accession of King Richard the Lionheart in 1189 but in the Court of Chivalry a different rule was applied, and time immemorial meant the period before the Norman Conquest by King William the Conqueror in 1066; *Scrope v Grosvenor* (1385-90) PRO C. 47/6/2-3 (England, Ct. Chiv.).

Furthermore, to prove immemorial use the armorial bearings had to be publicly displayed, as a mere private use was insufficient to establish an incorporeal right.[41] In a dispute concerned the use of a gold bend on a shield of azure ("Azure, a bend or") by two families in *Carminow v Scrope*, the reports of which were deposed to in *Scrope v Grosvenor*, the evidence showed that there was public user by both families from time immemorial (i.e., before the conquest) and the resulting judgment upheld the right of both families to the use of the design. To assist families in determining the validity of their coats of arms the heralds occasionally made visitations to the outlying areas of England and Wales to record and determine the validity of armorial bearings borne by English families.

More rarely heard were cases concerning the improper display of arms by persons that were entitled to bear arms. In *Oldys v Fielding* (1702) Her. Cas. 102 (England, Ct. Chiv.) it was alleged that the defendant had improperly displayed his arms on an imperial eagle, and that he had improperly displayed the coronet of an English duke, displayed an improper quartering, and incorrectly blazoned another quartering. He was also alleged to have improperly displayed his wife's family's arms on an escutcheon of pretence.[42] There were also cases where arms lawfully borne by someone improperly displayed supporters.[43]

After 1737 the Court fell into desuetude and there were many people who thought that the court was obsolete. Certainly there were no court officers or practitioners after the mid-1700's but in principle a court cannot be extinguished by non-user. Beginning in the twentieth century some armorial bearings, and particularly those that belonged to the King, began to be protected under trade marks legislation and by mid-century that protection also began to be extended to municipal corporations.

However, it was a petition by the City of Manchester, England, that resulted in a revival of the court by the Earl Marshal in 1954; *Manchester Corporation v Manchester Palace of Varieties Ltd.* [1955] P. 133; 1 All ER 387 (England, Ct. Chiv.). The City complained that a business had displayed the City's arms without permission. The Earl Marshall appointed a learned common law judge, Lord Goddard, to sit as his Surrogate although the Earl Marshall, together with the Surrogate and the heralds of the College of Arms for England and Wales was present for the formal opening of the court. Although the procedures of the court remained those derived from civil law the Surrogate, as well as the practitioners who appeared before the court in 1954, were all trained in the common law because the English civil law bar had been extinguished during the nineteenth century.[44]

In the *Manchester* case, the Surrogate ruled that the jurisdiction of the court over heraldic causes within the law of arms was an extant jurisdiction that had not been displaced by statute law.[45] However, the principles of the law of arms as applied in England are subject to change over time by custom and usage. This was noted by the Surrogate in the Court of Chivalry in the *Manchester* case where Lord Goddard stated:

> I am by no means satisfied that nowadays it would be right for this court to be put in motion merely because some arms, whether of a corporation or a family, have been displayed by way of decoration or embellishment. Whatever may have been the case 250 years ago, one must, I think, take into account practices and usages which have for so many years prevailed without interference".[46]

Lord Goddard eventually found that the actions of the commercial enterprise which had displayed the Manchester Corporations' arms were unlawful and they were enjoined from continuing to display those arms.

Certain basic principles of the law of arms can be distilled from the practice in the Court of Chivalry. Some of the key principles are:

a) a right to bear arms is a dignity conferred by the Royal Prerogative in the name of the Sovereign,

b) a right to bear arms in a family can also be recognized by a usage prior to the Norman conquest in 1066,

c) arms are transmissible between generations to all males, with heraldic differences to all but the eldest male,

d) upon the failure of a male line a daughter may transmit the arms of her father to her sons,

e) enhancements to arms which exceed the original design of arms that were granted are unlawful,

f) the Court of Chivalry exercises jurisdiction in England over disputes concerning the use of arms,

g) the law of arms may evolve over time through custom and usage.

13.16   The Historical Jurisdiction of the College of Arms

In England and Wales the Sovereign began to appoint officials to oversee the grant of armorial bearings by the fifteenth century. During the reign of Queen Mary I, the College of Arms was formally constituted and began to adopt its modern role as the exclusive grantor of arms on behalf of the Sovereign. The Earl Marshal of England oversees the work of the college, which is a corporation created by a royal charter.

The officers appointed by the King to make grants of armorial bearings were styled Kings of Arms, and they were given divided territorial jurisdictions within England. These officers could grant arms to anyone ordinarily a resident within their heraldic province within England, both men and women, including persons who were not English subjects. They could also award arms to corporate bodies – what were called in early times livery companies. Although there are records of a few grants of arms to foreigners residing in England in the early seventeenth century there are no modern examples of actual grants to foreigners. Through custom and usage the exercise of the prerogative power to make an ordinary grant of arms by the territorial Kings of Arms was confined to those persons that were resident in England and who were British subjects.

An additional office, the Garter King of Arms was created as the Principal King of Arms for Englishmen and was given both a supervisory role with respect to the College of Arms, and was also answerable to the Earl Marshall. This official was given an extraterritorial jurisdiction to make grants of arms to persons outside of England who continued to be English subjects, or, if they were not an English subject, to those persons who could nevertheless trace their descent from an English ancestor. For this latter class of petitioners the Garter King of Arms granted honorary armorial bearings provided that the jurisdiction to which the petitioners owed their allegiance did not object to the grant. Many honorary grants of this nature were made by the College of Arms to American citizens following the independence of the United States. The Garter King of Arms could also grant armorial bearings to English corporate institutions that were located abroad. The grant of arms to the College of William and Mary in Virginia in 1694 is an example. Finally, the Sovereign had the power to command the Garter King of Arms to grant armorial bearings to any foreign person that the Sovereign wished to honour.

The armorial jurisdiction of the College of Arms was extended to Ireland but not to Scotland, which had its own heraldic authority as part of the Kingdom of Scotland, the Court of the Lord Lyon. The Scottish authority has both an executive component, which includes the granting of Scottish arms, as well as a criminal jurisdiction with respect to the use of heraldry in Scotland. Unlike its English counterpart, the High Court of Chivalry, the Court of the Lord Lyon never fell into disuse and has maintained a robust heraldic jurisdiction throughout the centuries that continues to this day. With respect to the granting of coats of arms, the Court of the Lord Lyon primarily serves persons who are residents of Scotland, or who can establish Scottish ancestry. Its heraldic jurisdiction is otherwise limited to the territory of Scotland.

13.17   The Reception of the Law of Arms in Canada

During the colonial period following the Treaty of Paris in 1763 Canada received the laws of England according to the applicable reception dates in each province. The English law of arms was not part of the common law but was part of English law and therefore it was received by the Canadian provinces at various times. The Canadian law of arms is the English law of arms as it existed on the various reception dates. That law was capable of being altered over time by custom and usage but as the Court of Chivalry did not sit for 230 years there was little opportunity for substantial change in this field of law before 1954, which is much past any of the Canadian reception dates. Neither in the United Kingdom nor in Canada has there been any effort to modernize the law of arms through statutory law, although Parliament has jurisdiction over heraldry through the residual clause of section 91 of the *Constitution Act, 1867*.

Historically, the common law courts would not adjudicate on matters relating to the law of arms in the United Kingdom, or in Canada, although they did take notice of the law of arms, and the common law courts would dispose of related matters that fell outside of the law of arms, and thus came within the jurisdiction of the common law courts.[47]

What then, were the aspects of the law of arms that were received into Canadian law? The grant of arms is part of the Royal Prerogative and consistent with other aspects of the Royal Prerogative the Canadian law consists of the prerogative rights held by the Crown in right of England, or the United Kingdom, except those that were peculiar to England itself. Although the English law of arms was received into Canadian law through the reception doctrine there was no national heraldic authority in Canada before 1988, and Canadians wishing to bear arms before that date were required to make application to the College of Arms in England.

As a result of representations made to the Federal Government by those who were concerned with the lack of a national heraldry in Canada, the Canadian Privy Council formally advised and requested of Queen Elizabeth II that she establish a national heraldic authority in Canada. By *Letters Patent (Armorial Jurisdiction) dated June 4, 1988*, made under the Great Seal of Canada, the Queen formally transferred the exercise of her powers and authorities to grant armorial bearings in Canada to the Governor General of Canada. Pursuant to that grant of power the Governor General established the Canadian Heraldic Authority to exercise, in the name of the Sovereign, the powers conferred upon the Governor General with respect to armorial bearings. The powers granted by the Sovereign's *Letters Patent, 1988*, are in relation to the royal grant of arms to applicants but do not extend to any judicial powers in respect of the same.

The powers transferred to the Governor General include the power to grant armorial bearings to Canadian citizens located in Canada or resident abroad. Honorary grants of arms may also be made to foreigners (including permanent residents), who reside in Canada but in the view of the author the prerogative power of the English College of Arms to grant armorial bearings to petitioners of English descent who are no longer subjects of the Sovereign in right of the United Kingdom has not been transferred to Canada under the reception doctrine, and therefore could not be included within the powers to grant arms transferred under the *Letters Patent, 1988*. The prerogative power of the

Crown in England to grant honorary arms to persons of English descent is based on the ethnicity of the English population, and is thus must be considered peculiar to England. Canada has from its very inception has had a mixture of cultures and ethnicities, including Aboriginal, French, English, Scottish, Irish and Metis cultures in the early era, which has subsequently been layered upon by immigration from all over the world. Therefore, it is doubtful if there is any definite Canadian ethnicity that could be the foundation of a power, similar to the prerogative English power, to grant arms to foreigners who are of Canadian descent but who are no longer subjects of the Sovereign in right of Canada.

However, the broader prerogative power of the Queen of the United Kingdom to command the Garter King of Arms to grant armorial bearings to any foreign person that the monarch should choose to honour, is not based on English ethnicity, and therefore is a prerogative power that appears to have been received as part of the laws of Canada. Therefore, the Governor General of Canada presumably has a prerogative power to command the Canadian Heraldic Authority to issue an honorary grant of a coat of arms to a foreign person.

As with the English College of Arms, the Canadian Heraldic Authority has jurisdiction to issue corporate armorial bearings to Canadian corporations, and to issue a devisal of arms to foreign registered corporations in or outside of Canada (the latter again at the command of the Governor General).

The law of arms of Canada is thus the law of arms of England that was received by Canada, subject to any subsequent alterations in the law.[48] To date, there have been no substantive changes to the law of arms received by Canada from England. Parliament has not legislated with respect to heraldry in any substantive manner and, as the Supreme Court has noted in connection with the law of the Crown, "there is a presumption that the common law remains unchanged absent a clear and unequivocal expression of legislative intent" (*Canada (Attorney General) v Thouin*, 2017 SCC 46, at para. 19 (Canada, SC). The same principle applies to the law of arms despite the law of arms being separate from the common law. Legislation under the Royal Prerogative is no longer available in circumstances where it would affect the rights of individuals, and thus only Parliament may legislate substantively with respect to the law of arms in Canada.

Although the executive functions concerning the grant of arms were transferred to Canada in 1988 to date there has been no conferral of judicial jurisdiction with respect to the law of arms. Thus the judicial jurisdiction exercised by the High Court of Chivalry in England, or the Court of the Lord Lyon in Scotland, has no counterpart in Canada, although the Federal Court of Canada has perhaps the best claim to receive a grant of jurisdiction over heraldry by Parliament.

While the grant of arms is a hereditary dignity, armorial bearings were never considered to fall within the scope of the *Nickle Resolution* and therefore Canadians have continued to receive grants of arms from the Crown without interruption throughout the colonial and post-confederation periods.

13.18   Canadian Heraldry

Although the technical rules of English heraldic design were also received into Canadian law under the reception doctrine, the developing custom and usage of heraldry design by the Canadian Heraldic Authority has promoted a uniquely Canadian version of heraldry. While remaining true to its English roots the practice of heraldry design has been broadened in the Canadian context to include many elements that originate in the rich tradition of Canadian aboriginal art and symbolism, as well as contributions from other cultures that have become established in Canada. Many of the creations of the Canadian Heraldic Authority incorporate uniquely Canadian flora, fauna, and legendary beasts. In addition to new designs, the Canadian Heraldic Authority has the power to augment coats of arms that have been previously granted by the authority.

Canadian citizens should apply to the Canadian Heraldic Authority for the grant of arms. Canadians are not precluded from continuing to apply to foreign heraldic authorities but, grants from foreign sources will not be recognized in Canada unless a petition is made to the Canadian Heraldic Authority to register foreign arms. The extent to which recognition may be granted will depend upon the application of the law of arms of Canada, and the practice and procedure of the Canadian Heraldic Authority.[49]

13.19   The Differentiation of Arms

Under the law of arms that has been applied in Canada both before and after the 1988 transfer of executive powers over heraldry, the arms borne by different recipients in the same family must show a difference between the primary holder of the grant of arms and the other grantees. In the English practice a mark of difference, described as a mark of cadence was applied to the shield of the male children while the arms of a female were placed on a lozenge since the traditional chivalric practice of heraldry considered that a helmeted crest was an undesirable symbol for a female. According to the heraldic lawyer G D Squibb, heraldic differences first appeared in the habendum clauses of Crown grants of arms in 1595.[50]

In Canada, after 1988, this rule has been followed and where a parent has been granted arms by the Governor General, the living children of that parent are granted the same arms with a visual difference between the shield of the parent and the shield of a child. However, the Canadian Heraldic Authority has made a significant change to the English rules by:

a) explicitly granting armorial bearings to both male and female children of a grantee,[51]

b) granting arms that contain marks of cadence or differences for both male and female children, thus dispensing with the practice of creating a lozenge for the arms of a female, and[52]

c) permitting Canadian female grantees to display their arms with a crest.

The expectation of the Canadian Heraldic Authority is that succeeding generations will create additional marks of cadence or differences so that the arms borne by a family will continue to be individualized within single generations.[53]

13.20   The Descent of Arms

Armorial bearings are an inheritable dignity and are therefore transmissible between generations. Lord Coke referred to them as being similar to gavelkind, a type of socage tenure of lands in late medieval England in which all sons or heirs of a title holder shared in the distribution of the lands upon the father's decease. However, armorial bearings do not pass under a testamentary bequest but rather descend through the law of arms, and have their own rules of descent and applicable procedures.[54]

The English law of arms of England received by Canada under the reception doctrine provided for the descent of arms to all males of the succeeding generation with the primary successor, the heir of arms, receiving the undifferentiated armorial bearings of the grantee, i.e., without a mark of cadence. Sibling males of the heir of arms displayed their arms with a mark of cadence, and their sons would further distinguish their arms from their father's arms. This rule was taken notice of by the Committee for Privileges in the House of Lords in the *Wiltes Peerage Case*, [1869] 4 LR 126 (England, HL, Comm. of Priv.):

> All that this case of armorial bearings amounts to is this, that when the privilege of using arms is granted in a family, all the males are entitled to them, to be borne by the eldest without a difference, and by the younger with differences.[55]

In England, unmarried women who were not in receipt of their own grant of arms were entitled to display the arms of their father, and married women could impale (combine) her father's arms with the arms of her husband's family. Where the male line of a family fails a surviving daughter became a heraldic heiress and may transmit her family's arms to her sons, with her eldest son taking the undifferentiated arms of her father.

These rules have been modified in Canada to the following extent:

a) grants of arms to a person with children will include the children within the grant with marks of cadence or differences to distinguish the shield of each child,

b) the senior child, whether male or female, will inherit the undifferentiated arms of the parent upon the decease of the parent,[56] unless a parent receiving arms from the Crown has designated a junior child to inherit the undifferentiated arms of the parent.[57] This discretion vested in the grantee could, for instance, allow the transmission of the original (undifferentiated) arms through the male line where a male child is not the eldest child,[58]

c) in the second and subsequent generations the descendants of the original armiger, male or female, will be entitled to bear the arms, with the undifferenced arms transmitted through the eldest of the male line and junior males and females bearing the arms with a difference. Should there be a failure of the male line the eldest female in a succeeding generation may pass the undifferenced arms to her eldest male child as a heraldic heiress,[59]

d) where a grantee has designated a junior child to inherit the undifferenced arms both the senior and the junior child will bear marks of difference on the shields of their own arms while their parent is alive. Following the decease of the parent however, the child inheriting the undifferenced arms will remove the mark of difference from their shields while the other children will continue to bear their marks of difference on their shields.

While the transmission of arms follows the law of arms rather than the common law of testamentary bequests there appears to be no legal objection to a precatory clause to express a testator's intentions or desires with respect to the transmission of arms, as guidance to family members. While the arms cannot pass through a testamentary bequest the physical letters patent granting the arms are capable of passing in a testamentary bequest in which case the holder of the patent must allow reasonable access to other family members for the purpose of inspection; *Stubbs v Stubbs*, [1862] Exch. Rep. 257 (England, Ex Ct).

The Canadian Heraldic Authority adheres to the principle of one person, one coat of arms. Therefore, separate versions of an original grant or registration of existing arms should be prepared to distinguish between separate members of a family within a single generation. All differenced arms in succeeding generations should be registered with the Canadian Heraldic Authority, although there is no legal sanction in Canada if that is not done. Furthermore, persons who are entitled to bear arms by descent are not precluded from applying to the Canadian Heraldic Authority for a new original grant of arms for themselves.

Continental European heraldic rules differ from the English, Scottish and Irish rules in that they can provide for the use of undifferenced arms by everyone within a family line. While this is contrary to the English practice that Canada has received under the English law of arms it is also not unknown in the English law of arms. The work of the British heraldic lawyer G D Squibb has shown that there are examples of the grant of armorial bearings in earlier centuries that did not require family members to display differences in their arms.[60] Such undifferentiated armorial bearings descend in England to all who are within a family line. Currently, however, the Canadian Heraldic Authority does not permit such grants in Canada.

13.21   Practice and Procedure of the Canadian Heraldic Authority

At common law arms are a dignity from the Sovereign conferred by the Royal Prerogative and therefore petitioners for armorial bearings must demonstrate their worthiness to bear arms, usually by individual contributions to the nation or to their community.[61] An application for armorial bearings is made by way of a Petition seeking lawful authority to bear arms addressed to: The Chief Herald of Canada, Canadian Heraldic Authority, Rideau Hall, Ottawa, Ontario, K1A 0A1.

A Petitioner should provide a biography (or a corporate profile if a corporate body is applying), including details of their community service or contributions to Canada. The application requires that the names of two persons who can attest to the character of the petitioner should accompany the application. Character is of importance with respect to the decision of the Heralds and other officers to grant arms to a petitioner. Petitioners should expect that the names of the references that they submitted will be contacted and they will be asked about the nature of the petitioner's contributions to the community and to the country. Publicly available information about a petitioner may also be considered. To a certain extent there is self-selection aspect amongst petitioners, and thus few petitions have been denied.

If the Petitioner is found to be a suitable recipient for the grant of armorial bearings, the Chief Herald of Canada will recommend to the Herald Chancellor, or the Deputy Herald Chancellor, that the petition be granted. If the petition is granted, a warrant is issued to the Chief Herald authorizing a grant of arms to the Petitioner. The procedural need for a warrant can be traced back in the law of arms to Duck v St. George (1638), Her. Cas. (England, Ct. Chiv.) where proceedings were taken against the Norroy King of Arms and the Somerset Herald for granting arms to a man who was not a gentleman.

Should information subsequently come to light that would call into question the suitability of a petitioner for the grant of armorial bearings, the warrant can be revoked, as it is in the nature of an interlocutory order. Although the issuance of a warrant is not a final order, and a Petitioner does not acquire a right to a coat of arms by the issuance of a warrant, the Petitioner has crossed a procedural threshold by the issuance of a warrant and has acquired a procedural right to proceed. The revocation of that right to proceed before the Heralds would likely attract at least some minimal procedural fairness obligations before a warrant could be revoked. That may well entail providing the Petitioner with at least a summary of the information that would lead the Canadian Heraldic Authority to contemplate a revocation of a warrant.

Where the creation of a coat of arms has been approved by warrant, the arms will subsequently be developed in liaison between a Herald and the Petitioner but the design concept must ultimately be acceptable to the Chief Herald of Canada. Certain fees and charges may be assessed to the Petitioner to defray artistic and other costs associated with the grant of arms. The armorial bearings may include a coat of arms, a badge, a standard, and differenced shields for other members of the petitioners family who will participate in the grant.

An approval sketch is sent to the Petitioner who indicates his or her acceptance, and the acceptance of other family members where necessary, by signing and returning the approval sketch. The painting of the arms is undertaken by a painter who is on an approved list maintained by the Canadian Heraldic Authority. The artist independently contracts with the Petitioner for the artwork. A calligrapher, also independently contracted by the Petitioner from an approved list will complete the necessary calligraphy. If the grantee is including children in the grant, they must select appropriate marks of cadence or difference. There is a standard mark of cadency for an eldest child who will inherit and separate unique marks for other siblings. A unique mark of cadence will also be used where a child other than the eldest child will be the heir of arms. However, subject to the approval of the Chief Herald the Petitioner and his children can make their own suggestions for the creation of marks of difference.

Petitioners have two choices with respect to the final form of the letters patent granting arms. For both choices the Petitioner must bear all of the direct costs (e.g., the painter's fee and the calligrapher's fee). A single large sheet with painted arms and hand-drawn calligraphy can be produced showing the arms, badge, standard, and children's shields. This is the most attractive option but is also the most expensive option. A second option is a two-page document one with the painting of the arms and the other with letters patent produced through word processing. The cost of this option is considerably less than the option that includes hand-drawn calligraphy.

Upon completion of the Letters Patent to the satisfaction of the Canadian Heraldic Authority the arms are issued to the Petitioner. The Letters Patent of Arms may be issued and sent to the Petitioner by post or a ceremony may be held at which they are proclaimed and issued to the Petitioner in person. Normally, the ceremonial issuance of the armorial bearings to an individual takes place at the Chancellery of Honours in Ottawa. The issued armorial bearings are thereafter registered in the Public Register of Arms, Flags and Badges of Canada, and a notice of the grant is given in the *Canada Gazette, Part 1*.

13.22   Protection, Enforcement, and Judicial Review

Parliament has provided a limited form of protection for coats of arms through the *Trade-marks Act*. Section 9 of the *Trade-marks Act* provides:

> (1) No person shall adopt in connection with a business, as a trade-mark or otherwise, any mark consisting of, or so nearly resembling as to be likely to be mistaken for,

> (n.1) any armorial bearings granted, recorded or approved for use by a recipient pursuant to the prerogative powers of Her Majesty as exercised by the Governor General in respect of the granting of armorial bearings, if the Registrar has, at the request of the Governor General, given public notice of the grant, recording or approval;

This provision prohibits a commercial enterprise from using the arms lawfully granted to a grantee by the Canadian Heraldic Authority but only where the Governor General has requested the Registrar of Trademarks to give public notice of the grant of arms in the Register of Trademarks, and where the Registrar has done so. As can be seen from this provision there is no protection afforded to a grantee where an individual has misappropriated the arms granted by the Crown otherwise than in connection with a business. A mere personal use of the armorial bearings belonging to someone else will not come within the terms of the statutory prohibition, although it is an unlawful act under the law of arms. The use of a coat of arms in a corporate or institutional context for non-commercial purposes is also probably not prohibited by section 9 of the Act but would be unlawful under the law of arms.

The Canadian Heraldic Authority does not provide a mechanism to enforce either the correct carriage of coats of arms by armigerous persons, or the usurpation of arms by those not entitled to them. The Authority is strictly an executive body that administers the Crown's prerogative power to grant coats of arms.

In Canada, there is no specialized counterpart to the High Court of Chivalry in England, or the Court of the Lord Lyon in Scotland. Although in its heyday the High Court of Chivalry did exercise an extraterritorial jurisdiction that extraterritorial jurisdiction only concerned criminal law causes such as murder or treason out of the realm and there was no exercise of heraldic jurisdiction by that court out of England. Perhaps judicial jurisdiction, if any, over heraldic claims beyond England or Scotland lies with the domestic courts of each Commonwealth realm.

Although the common law courts in England have taken the view that the law of arms is outside of the jurisdiction of a court exercising a common law jurisdiction, the circumstances may well be different in Canada where, unlike England (or Scotland) there is no specialized court for heraldry. The superior courts of the provinces exercise original jurisdiction as between subject and subject as the Canadian successors to the royal courts of justice at Westminster in England. Whether those courts would entertain a proceeding with respect to the law of arms remains to be seen.

In cases where a grantee of arms has obtained protection for their armorial bearings under the *Trade-marks Act*, the Federal Court has concurrent jurisdiction with the provincial superior courts to hear cases alleging an infringement of a registered mark.

The Federal Court of Canada also has jurisdiction for the purposes of judicial review where the Crown has exercised the Royal Prerogative, by order. However, the question of justiciability remains a potential hurdle for anyone seeking judicial review of a decision by the Canadian Heraldic Authority, as the grant of dignities and honours is at the far reach of the spectrum of Crown decisions under the Royal Prerogative that are potentially competent for the courts to entertain.

Proceedings by the Crown to vacate a grant of armorial bearings do not appear to exist in the judicial history of the High Court of Chivalry, or in the law of arms generally. Where there is a need or desire by the Crown to expunge letters patent it has been suggested in older authority that the procedure to do so would require a writ of *scire facias*; see *Lenoir v Ritchie*, [1879] 3 SCR 575 (Canada, SC).

13.23   Honours

An honour is an individual distinction that is conferred by royal authority on a person for individual merit. It is not a form of property and therefore the honour is not capable of descent, although the emblem of that honour (e.g., a medal) is, subject to some exceptions, forms part of the personal property of the recipient which is capable of descent. Generally, honours do not confer a title.

13.24   Classification of Honours

Royal orders and orders of state, sometimes also described as societies of merit, descend from the historical role of medieval knights and have an institutional structure. They are the most senior level of honours in Canada. They are intended to recognize merit over the course of a lifetime, or exceptional service over a shorter period, that has had a substantial positive impact on society or on humanity in general. Orders receive an internal constitution that provides them with an institutional basis and makes provision for administrative officers, a corporate structure, ordinances or bylaws, official ceremonies, and networking opportunities such as regular dinners etc.[62] Members of an order can be dismissed, although that is a rare event, and generally involves conduct which is considered to display moral turpitude. Dismissals have also occurred during wartime, such as the dismissal from British orders of foreign sovereigns and princes of the Central Powers in World War One – a decision that was also extended in World War Two to all honorary members of British orders who held enemy nationality.[63]

Decorations and medals are physically similar but serve different purposes. Decorations are devices in the form of a cross, star, or a medallion that represents military valour, bravery (civilian or military) and faithful service. Decorations are among the most significant honours conferred upon an individual and often represent great, heroic, or singular achievements.

Medals are conferred for meritorious, or for long and faithful service. They are also awarded to signify participation in defined military campaigns by military personnel and to commemorate significant events, national milestones, and royal jubilees.

13.25   Orders of State

An order of state is a society of merit that recognizes significant achievement and conspicuous service to the Sovereign, Canada, or to humanity. For Canadian purposes the various orders recognized by the Crown can be categorized into four types: royal orders conferred in the personal discretion of the Sovereign, a singular chivalric order with an ancient patrimony, national orders of merit, and a Commonwealth order that is sometimes conferred upon Canadians.

The royal orders are closely associated with the Sovereign and admission to them is generally in the personal discretion of the Sovereign, while admission to one of the national orders of merit is generally on the recommendation of the advisory council that is associated with each particular order. Admission to the one Commonwealth order for which Canadians are eligible is by appointment by the Sovereign in Right of the United Kingdom upon the advice of the Privy Council of the United Kingdom following consultations between the British and Canadian governments, and with the grant of an express permission by the Governor General in Council for the Canadian recipient to receive it.

13.26   Royal Orders

After 1878 when the conferral of honours and dignities became centred in the office of the Prime Minister in the United Kingdom there was a desire by the monarchs for the creation of other honours that monarchs would control in the exercise of their personal discretion. Monarchs desired that the Crown could continue to recognize merit without having to take into account political considerations. These royal orders and honours included the Royal Victorian Order, Royal Victorian Chain, Royal Victorian Medal and the Order of Merit all of which are now recognized as part of Canada's national system of honours.[64]

From the time of the *Nickle Resolution,* which established the constitutional custom that Canadians would not be offered titular honours, there was a lapse in the conferral of royal orders. This situation was remedied after Canada created its own system of national honours in 1972. In June of that year the Cabinet confirmed that: "Neither the Government nor the Governor General of Canada would recommend Canadians for the honours given by the Queen. However, Her Majesty could still give honours to Canadians if she chose".[65] Subsequently, the prohibition on the Governor General of Canada making recommendations to the Sovereign for the award of royal honours was also relaxed. Nevertheless, the policy prohibition against the Canadian Ministry from making such recommendations has been maintained.

13.27   Royal Family Order

Beginning with the reign of King George IV in 1820, the Sovereign began to present a special family order to the female members of the Royal Family. All Sovereigns have created such an order since King George IV, except King William IV and King Edward VIII. The purpose of the order is to provide a visible distinction for the female members of the Royal Family on formal or state occasions. Unlike the male members of the Royal Family, the female members do not normally wear distinctive uniforms or medals. Therefore, the Royal Family Order serves as a mark of distinction for the female members of the Royal Family. It is given to female members of the Royal Family in the exercise of a personal discretion by the Sovereign. Canadian women who marry into the Royal Family are eligible to receive the order, and although it might seem that the marriage of Canadians into the Royal Family would be a rather remote possibility more than one such marriage has actually occurred.

The order consists of a jewelled portrait of the Sovereign on a ribbon that is of a different colour for each Sovereign. The order is described by reference to the reigning monarch, and thus in the current reign it is described as the Royal Family Order of Queen Elizabeth II. The exception to this nomenclature occurred during the reign of Queen Victoria when the order was established more formally, and was described as The Royal Order of Victoria and Albert.[66] The Royal Family Order of Queen Elizabeth II shows the Queen as a young woman, and is placed on a ribbon of chartreuse yellow. More than one Royal Family Order may be worn by recipients. Unlike other orders, the Royal

Family Order does not have an institutional structure with a constitution and officers. It is considered to be a private order of the Royal Family.

13.28 The Royal Victorian Order

The Royal Victorian Order was instituted in April 1896 by Queen Victoria and contains five classes; Knight Grand Cross, Knight Commander, Commander, Lieutenants, and Members. The first two classes confer knighthoods upon the recipients and the right to append the post-nominal letters GCVO and KCVO to their names. Commanders, Lieutenants and Members have no prefix title but do carry the post-nominal letters CVO, LVO, or MVO.[67]

The grant of this honour is within the personal discretion of the Sovereign and is given to Canadians or other Commonwealth citizens who have rendered extraordinary, important, or personal services to the Sovereign.[68] Although the Sovereign does have a personal discretion under the constitution of the order to award a knighthood within the order if she desires Canadians are only granted membership in the order up to the rank of Commander because of the *Nickle Resolution* prohibiting the conferral of titles upon Canadians. Most Sovereigns, except King Edward VII, have awarded this Royal Order sparingly. There was a hiatus in the conferral of this honour upon Canadians following the *Nickle Resolution* but after the creation of Canada's national honours system in 1972 the Canadian Ministry stated that appointments to the order by the Queen could resume, and that all such appointments would be entirely within the gift of Her Majesty. No political or formal constitutional advice is given to the Sovereign by a Canadian Ministry with respect to the conferral of this order on Canadians. By constitutional custom however, the Sovereign will to inform the Prime Minister after the Sovereign has publicized the grant of an award to a Canadian.

13.29 Royal Victorian Medal

The Royal Victorian Medal was established by Queen Victoria in 1896 and is part of the Royal Victorian Order. It was intended as a form of recognition for junior personnel forming part of the Royal Household. In Canada it may be awarded to the staff of Rideau Hall or to the staff of the Governor General's apartments at the Citadel in Quebec, a provincial Government House or the Offices of the Lieutenant Governors, and to junior public servants, non-commissioned personnel of the Canadian Armed Forces, or police officers, who have rendered personal services to the Sovereign or to the members of the Royal Family. All awards of the medal, like the Royal Victorian Order itself, are at the personal discretion of the Sovereign. The Royal Victorian Medal may be awarded in one of three classes, a gold, silver, or bronze medal. Recipients are entitled to use the post-nominal letters RVM.

13.30   The Royal Victorian Chain

The Royal Victorian Chain was created by King Edward VII at the time of his coronation in August 1902, with limited membership as a special mark of the Sovereign's pre-eminent favour and esteem. The Royal Victorian Chain is not, strictly speaking, a part of the Royal Victorian Order although the badge of the order is contained within the chain. It is not accompanied by any title nor does it confer the right to use post-nominal letters.

It has often been given to foreign monarchs, members of the Royal Family, and senior prelates. The chain must be returned to the Sovereign upon the death of the recipient. Rarely conferred, it has been held by five former Governors General of Canada, two of whom were Canadians, Vincent Massey and Roland Michener.[69]

13.31   Order of Merit[70]

The Order of Merit was established by King Edward VII on June 23, 1902, shortly before his planned coronation.[71] It is a highly exclusive non-titular honour, limited to 24 living members. It is awarded for exceptionally meritorious service by a citizen of the Commonwealth in the personal discretion of the Sovereign. The insignia of the order must be returned to the Sovereign following the death of the recipient. It is a rare honour and of the four Canadians who have received it three were former Prime Ministers (William Lyon Mackenzie King, Lester B. Pearson, and Jean Chretien). It was also awarded to the noted Montreal neurosurgeon, Dr. Wilder Penfield. The Order of Merit was formally reintegrated into the national honours system of Canada by Order-in-Council PC 2010-1499, dated November 26, 2010.[72]

13.32   Order of Chivalry

Orders of chivalry originated as a fraternity of medieval knights who displayed the social and moral virtues established in knighthood codes of conduct. These virtues were closely aligned with the virtues of Christianity, and Orders of Chivalry embody a strong religious component. In the Canadian honours system there is one such chivalric order.

13.33   Most Venerable Order of the Hospital of St. John of Jerusalem

The Most Venerable Order of the Hospital of St. John of Jerusalem is a charitable organization with historical antecedents to medieval orders of chivalry. It was established as a chivalric order in Great Britain by a Royal Charter granted by Queen Victoria in 1888. The Order of St. John supports health and humanitarian efforts in peace and war. Membership in the order is separate from membership in the more well known St. John Ambulance Brigade and Association with which the Order of St. John is linked.

The reigning Sovereign is the Sovereign of the Order and a Royal Duke or Prince serves as the Grand Prior. Priories have been established in several of the Sovereign's realms to administer the Order of St. John. In Canada, the Governor General is the Prior of the Order of St. John for Canada and the Lieutenant Governors and territorial Commissioners serve as Sub-Priors of the Order. There is also a Chancellor of the Order who serves in an executive capacity. Membership in the Order is by invitation of the Order of St. John and the appointments are made by the Governor General on behalf of the Sovereign from a list of recommended appointments prepared by the Order of St. John.

The Order of St. John confers both prefix titles and post-nominal letters but the titles and the post-nominal letters are only used only within the Order itself, or in biographical data. The titles and letters are Bailiff or Dame Grand Cross (GCStJ) Knight or Dame of Justice and Grace (KStJ or DStJ), Commander (CStJ), Officer (OStJ) and Serving Brother or Sister (SBStJ or SSStJ). The insignia consists of a breast star and members of the order also wear a mantle on ceremonial occasions.

The Most Venerable Order of the Hospital of St. John of Jerusalem has a peculiar history. It traces its origins to the same hospital in Jerusalem that provided the foundation for the Sovereign and Military Hospitaller Order of St. John of Jerusalem, of Rhodes, and of Malta, which is usually referred to as the Order of Malta. That Order existed in England but it was suppressed during the reigns of King Henry VIII and Queen Elizabeth I. The Order of Malta controlled the island of Malta until that island country was seized by Napoleon Bonaparte in 1798. After the defeat of the Napoleonic Empire an effort to revive the order was undertaken by a Capitular Commission, and the principals concerned wished to reestablish the order in Great Britain so as to obtain British influence for the restoration of the Order of Malta, and perhaps to obtain the grant of a sovereign island for the order. However, the principals who exercised control through the Commission ceased to function as the guiding body of the Order of Malta and its control reverted to the Holy See, which then enforced the rule that the Order of Malta was a Roman Catholic order to which Protestants were debarred from membership. That led to a severance between the Order of Malta and its fledgling British priory, which then developed informally on separate lines as a Protestant-dominated order. In 1888, Queen Victoria granted the Order of St. John a Royal Charter which gave it an established status as a British Empire Order of Chivalry with the Sovereign of the United Kingdom as the Sovereign of the Order.[73] Subsequently, the Order became active throughout the British Empire, including Canada, and by 1895 the Order's affiliated St. John Ambulance Association was established in Canada. Canadian membership in the Order dates from that time.[74] From 1946 a full Priory within the international order was established in Canada.

Today, The Most Venerable Order of the Hospital of St. John of Jerusalem remains a charitable society that is imbued with the principles of Christianity but membership in a Christian church is no longer a requirement for membership in the Order. Members who adhere to non-Christian religions are eligible for membership in the Order. The Order maintains fraternal relations with the Roman Catholic Order of Malta.

13.34   Societies of Merit

In the decades after the *Nickle Resolution* crystallized the convention that prohibited Canadians from being awarded titles orders ceased to be offered to Canadians even in their non-titular ranks. That left a substantial gap with respect to the ability of Canada to recognize those of its nationals whose merit and devotion to their country deserved some form of public recognition. With the approach of the centennial of confederation in 1967 renewed attention was given to the subject of creating a system of national honours for Canadians. The keystone in what became the national honours system of Canada was the creation during the centennial year of 1967 of the Order of Canada, as the pre-eminent order of state recognizing the merit of individual Canadians.

13.35   The Order of Canada

The highest national honour that a Canadian may now receive for service to Canada is the Order of Canada. The Order of Canada was created on July 1, 1967, as a "society of honour" by Letters Patent issued by Queen Elizabeth II upon the occasion of the centennial of confederation.[75] According to the *Constitution of the Order of Canada* the order consists of Her Majesty Queen Elizabeth II as the Sovereign of the Order, with the Governor General of Canada for the time being as, *ex officio*, the Chancellor and Principal Companion of the Order. The Secretary to the Governor General for the time being is, *ex officio*, the Secretary General of the Order. The Governor General of Canada administers the Order of Canada although the Sovereign retains the power to amend the letters patent which created the order.[76]

There are three classes of the order, a general division for Canadians, an honorary division for the appointment of distinguished foreign citizens, and an extraordinary division for appointments of the members of the Royal Family, Governors General, and their spouses. The Order of Canada exists to honour Canadians for outstanding achievement or service to Canada, or to humanity generally, as well as for distinguished service to particular localities, or in defined fields of activity. Appointments to the order are merit-based and arise after a consideration of merit by an Advisory Council.

There are three ranks within the Order; Companions, Officers, and Members. The Companion rank is intended to honour outstanding achievement and merit of the highest degree for service to the country, or to humanity. The Officer rank honours achievement and merit of a high degree for service to the country or to humanity, while the Member rank honours distinguished service at the local level, or on behalf of a group, or field of activity.

The Companion rank is limited in number to 165 living recipients and no more than 15 may be appointed in any given year. Although there is no maximum number of recipients for the Order and Member classes only 72 Officers and 136 Members may be appointed each year. Appointments to the order are typically made in July and December.

No title is conferred by the Order of Canada but the post-nominal letters CC, OC, or CM (depending upon rank within the Order) may be appended to the recipient's name. Non-Canadians may be made honorary officers of the Order. Members of the Royal Family and former Governors General and their spouses may be appointed to the extraordinary division of the order. There are no posthumous appointments. The badge of the order is a stylized snowflake bearing the Crown, the maple leaf, and the Latin motto *Desiderantes Meliorem patriam* (they desire a better country).

13.36   The Advisory Council of the Order of Canada

A key feature of the structure of the Order of Canada was the creation of an Advisory Council to make recommendations to the Crown for the conferral of the Order of Canada. The intention in creating the Advisory Council was to make a significant departure from the processes that existed before the *Nickle Resolution* when appointments were made (for the most part) on the recommendation of politicians. That structure inevitably injected political considerations into every honour that was granted except military valour honours. Perceived abuses in the process of conferring of such honours helped lead to the *Nickle Resolution,* and the long hiatus in the grant of honours to Canadians. To insulate the process of making recommendations to the Governor General from political considerations, the *Constitution of the Order of Canada* provided for a non-partisan Advisory Council to make merit-based and politically neutral recommendations for appointments to the Governor General.

The Advisory Council consists of the Chief Justice of Canada as the chair, and, as members of the Council, the Secretary to the Governor General, the Clerk of the Privy Council, the Deputy Minister of Canadian Heritage, the Chairperson of the Canada Council, the President of the Royal Society of Canada, the Chairperson of the Association of Universities and Colleges of Canada, and up to seven other members of Canadian society who serve for a term of three years. Of the seven appointees from Canadian society at-large two appointees must have experience in the protective sector (e.g., policing, fire etc.) the sciences (other than medicine), and religious or charitable organizations.

13.37   Appointments to the Order of Canada

The powers of the Advisory Council under section 8 of the *Constitution of the Order of Canada* are recommendatory only. The Council considers nominations to the order (which may be submitted by any person or organization) that are forwarded to it by the Secretary General and submits a list to the Governor General of those persons whom the Advisory Council considers to have displayed the greatest merit. The Advisory Council is a body which operates according to the principles of consensus decision-making although there is no requirement that a proposed nomination to the order be unanimous.[77]

The Governor General has the power to refer matters to the Advisory Council pursuant to section 8 (c) of the *Constitution of the Order of Canada,* and this has been interpreted to mean that the Governor General can refer a proposed appointment back to the Advisory Council for reconsideration. Thus the process that has been created is one that permits a dialogue between the Advisory Council and the Governor General. The whole purpose in the design of the appointments process for appointments to the order was to remove all questions of partisan politics from the process by establishing a neutral advisory body that would make recommendations to the Governor General.

The question that naturally arises is whether the Governor General has a discretion to deny a recommendation for an appointment to the Order of Canada that has been submitted by the Advisory Council. As a matter of law, the Governor General undoubtedly has such a discretion. In the case of *Chauvin v Canada (*2009), FC 1202 (Canada, FC) an applicant sought to set aside a recommendation for appointment made by the Advisory Council as unlawfully made which prompted a motion to strike. In dealing with that motion the Prothonotary in the Federal Court, stated in connection with the legal status of the Advisory Council that:

> . . . the Advisory Council does what its name indicates – it submits to the Governor General a list of nominees in the prescribed categories. The Constitution does not contain any provision that requires the Governor General to accept nominations and the decision to appoint is Her Excellency's alone.[78]

But the question that logically follows is whether the Governor General's legal power to deny an appointment to the Order is constrained by the principles of responsible government. On the one hand it is at least arguable that the Governor General has a residual discretion to decline to accept a recommendation of the Advisory Council. However, the alternative view, and I think the better view, is that while the recommendations of the Advisory Council do not constitute formal constitutional advice that the Governor General must follow under the principles of responsible government, one must also consider that the Advisory Council was established for the purpose of insulating the appointments process from partisan considerations, and thus it replaced the Canadian Ministry in what would otherwise be one of its functions. Therefore, it can be assumed that the removal of the Canadian Ministry from the appointments process was not done with the intention of conferring a personal discretion on the Governor General.

Accordingly, it would be consistent with the intention of the framers of the constitution of the order to state that the Governor General, in addition to his or her power to refer a nomination back to the Advisory Council for further consideration, also possesses a power to deny a recommendation by the Advisory Council for the conferral of the honour. However, the power to overrule the Advisory Council is not a personal discretion, and where the Governor General intends to deny a recommendation made by the Advisory Council, the principles of responsible government requires that the Governor General should ask and obtain from the Canadian Ministry acting as the Privy Council an assurance that the Canadian Ministry will accept political responsibility for the Governor General's decision to reject the Advisory Council's nomination of a person to the Order of Canada.

Appointments to the Order of Canada are made by the Governor General, on behalf of the Sovereign, by an instrument of appointment that is sealed with the seal of the order, following the receipt of a recommendation for an award by the Advisory Committee. The Governor General has the power to elevate a person once appointed to a higher rank within the order after receiving and considering advice from the Advisory Council with respect to the elevation. Generally, the appointment of a person to the Order of Canada will be regarded by the courts as a non-justiciable matter (*Black v Canada (Prime Minister)*, [2001] 54 OR (3d) 215 (Ontario, CA).

13.38   Terminations from the Order of Canada

Resignations and dismissals from the Order of Canada are permissible under the *Constitution of the Order of Canada*. Where a resignation or a dismissal has occurred the insignia of the order must be returned to the Secretary General of the Order. Where a termination of membership occurs through death the insignia of the order does not have to be returned, although the insignia remains the property of the order under section 23(1) of the *Constitution of the Order of Canada*, and remains subject to any ordinance made in respect of the insignia.

A policy has been established for terminations which provides, in section 3 that:

3. The Advisory Council shall consider the termination of a person's appointment to the Order of Canada if

(a) the person has been convicted of a criminal offence; or

(b) the conduct of the person

(i) constitutes a significant departure from generally-recognized standards of public behaviour which is seen to undermine the credibility, integrity or relevance of the Order, or detracts from the original grounds upon which the appointment was based; or

(ii) has been subject to official sanction, such as a fine or a reprimand, by an adjudicating body, professional association or other organization.

A detailed process is set out in the policy which is based on the principles of procedural fairness and fact-finding and involves internal examinations by the Deputy Secretary to the Governor General, the Secretary General of the Order, and, if the allegations are deemed to be of sufficient merit, by the Advisory Council. Once the Advisory Council becomes engaged the member whose appointment to the Order is under review will be given the choice of either resigning or providing written representations with respect to the allegations pertaining to them. If representations are made, the Advisory Council will consider the matter and prepare a written report to the Governor General with findings and recommendations. The Governor General will thereafter act on the report and either confirm the membership of the person under review, or issue an ordinance terminating their membership in the order. There have been six terminations and nine resignations from the Order to date.[79]

The Advisory Council is required to adhere to the procedural obligations in the policy when proceeding to consider a termination of an recipient's membership in the order. However, the procedural protections afforded to a person facing removal of the Order of Canada do not go so far as to entitle them to an oral hearing before the Advisory Council; *Black v Advisory Council of the Order of Canada*, [2012] FC 1234 (Canada, FC).

13.39 The Order of Military Merit

In 1972, letters patent were granted by the Sovereign to provide for the creation of an Order of Military Merit. The purpose of the Crown in creating this Order was to recognize merit in the profession of arms over the course of a military career in the Canadian Armed Forces. The Order of Military Merit is established as a sovereign order, with the Sovereign of Canada as the Sovereign of the Order, and the Governor General as the Chancellor of the Order. However, the Principal Commander of the Order of Military Merit is not the Governor General but rather the senior Canadian military officer, the Chief of the Defence Staff. There are three classes within the Order, a general class to which

Canadians are appointed, an honorary class to which foreign officers may be appointed, and an extraordinary class to which members of the Royal Family and former Governors General, may be appointed.

The purpose of the Order of Military Merit is to recognize exceptional merit and service by persons serving in the Canadian Forces in both the regular and the reserve components. It has the same internal structure as the Order of Canada, with Commanders, Officers and Members constituting the ranks within the order. There is no title but recipients may append the post-nominal letters CMM, OMM, or MMM to their names. There are defined limits on the number of appointments to the Order in any given year. The total annual number of appointments is limited to one-tenth of one percent of the total force strength of the Canadian Forces of which 5 percent may be Commanders, twenty percent may be Officers, and seventy-five percent may be invested as Members.[80]

An Advisory Council has been created pursuant to the *Constitution of the Order of Military Merit* and it consists of the Chief of the Defence Staff as chair of the Council, one member appointed by the Governor General, and four members of the Canadian Forces appointed by the Chief of the Defence Staff. Thus, the nominations to this order of state are very much concentrated in the hands of the military with little outside involvement in the nominations made to the order by civilians.

The Advisory Council recommends members of the Canadian Armed Forces as potential candidates for appointment to the order to the Chief of the Defence Staff. The Chief of the Defence Staff submits proposed appointments to the Governor General who makes the appointments on behalf of the Sovereign by an instrument of appointment that is sealed with the official seal of the order. As with the recommendations of the Advisory Council of the Order of Canada, the Governor General has a discretion to refuse a recommendation of the Advisory Council of the Order of Military Merit but the Governor General should only do so only in accordance with the principles of responsible government, by obtaining the concurrence of the Canadian Ministry and its acceptance of political responsibility for a negative exercise of the Governor General's discretion.

Appointments may be terminated by death, or by a resignation addressed to the Governor General, or termination by an ordinance issued by the Governor General. Unlike the Order of Canada, the *Constitution of the Order of Military Merit* does not set out detailed procedural protections for those persons facing termination from the order. However, basic procedural fairness protections will be implied by the common law with respect to any termination proceeding within the Order of Military Merit.

13.40   The Order of Merit of the Police Forces

After the creation of the Order of Military Merit the police forces in Canada expressed a desire that the protective services be acknowledged within Canada's system of honours. That led to the creation of the Order of Merit of the Police Forces in 2000. The Order is modelled very closely on the Order of Military Merit.[81] The Sovereign is the Sovereign of the Order and the Governor General for the time being is the Chancellor of the Order. The Commissioner of the Royal Canadian Mounted Police for the time being is the Principal Commander of the Order. There are three grades within the Order, Commander, Officer, and Member. Appointments to the Order are made by the Governor General upon receiving a recommendation from an Advisory Council that consists of the President of the National Association of Police Chiefs, the Deputy Commissioner of the Royal Canadian Mounted Police, the Deputy Secretary of the Chancellery of Honours, the head of either the Ontario Provincial Police or La Sûreté du Québec, three municipal/regional police chiefs, and the President of the Canadian Police Association. As with the recommendations of the Advisory Council of the Order of Canada, the Governor General has a discretion to refuse a recommendation of the Advisory Council of the Order of Merit of the Police Services but the Governor General should only do so in accordance with the principles of responsible government by obtaining the concurrence of the Canadian Ministry and its acceptance of political responsibility for a negative exercise of the Governor General's discretion. There is an annual cap on appointments of 1/10 of 1% of the total complement of police personnel in Canada in any given year. Elevations within the order are permissible. Recipients may append the post-nominal letters COM, OOM or MOM to their names depending upon their rank in the order.

13.41 Commonwealth Order

There is one British order open to the Commonwealth of Nations to which Canadians are occasionally appointed, the Order of the Companions of Honour.

13.42 The Order of the Companions of Honour

The Order of the Companions of Honour was created on June 4, 1917, by King George V. Originally limited to fifty living persons it was expanded in 1943 to 65 living persons and an explicit number of appointments were set aside for citizens of the Commonwealth. The order may be conferred on any citizen of the Commonwealth who has demonstrated conspicuous service in a national context. Conferral of this honour is not within the personal gift of the Sovereign but rather is conferred on the advice of Her Majesty's Privy Council of the United Kingdom. For Canadian purposes therefore, it is considered to be a Commonwealth honour rather than a national honour. Therefore, Canadians must have permission from the Crown in Right of Canada in order to accept this honour. In general, appointments to this Order are not made without consultations between the British and Canadian governments. Appointments to this order can, however, be initiated by the Sovereign.

Several Canadians have been honoured with this order since its inception. In recent decades they have generally received the honour for services rendered to the Commonwealth. Canadian recipients have included former Prime Minister John Diefenbaker, a staunch supporter of the Commonwealth, former Prime Minister Pierre Trudeau, who was responsible for initiating the practice of inviting the Sovereign, as Head of the Commonwealth, to attend Commonwealth summit meetings outside of the United Kingdom, Arnold Smith, a Canadian who served as Secretary General of the Commonwealth, and General John de Chastelain, who headed the disarmament and decommissioning commission in Northern Ireland at the end of a period known as the "Troubles," an era of significant strife and violence in Northern Ireland.

13.43   Decorations

Decorations are an honour that represents the recognition of courage and devotion to duty in both a military and a civilian context.[82] Until 1972, Canada used the British system of decorations, which contained at its apex the Victoria Cross for valour as the supreme recognition. In that year, the government created a new set of decorations to recognize bravery. Three decorations were created, the Cross of Valour, the Star of Courage and the Medal of Bravery, with the Cross of Valour initially positioned as the highest Canadian decoration for courage.

The creation of the bravery awards was a significant milestone in the development of a Canadian honours system. The bravery decorations provided a way to commemorate the bravery of Canadians in military and civilian endeavours in a manner that was consistent with the country's desire to have a system of decorations that were uniquely Canadian. However, many Canadians, not least of whom the country's military veterans, thought that there was a significant gap in the new Canadian honours regime because there were no decorations specifically set aside to recognize military valour, i.e., the acts of courage in the face of an enemy. Since before confederation in 1867, acts of military courage had been recognized by the award of military valour decorations of which the Victoria Cross recognized supreme acts of courage, often posthumously. The creation of the new bravery awards in 1972 left the Victoria Cross in limbo, without an explicit decision by the Canadian Ministry to either integrate it into the new system, or to dispense with it as a Canadian honour.

Veterans groups, such as the Royal Canadian Legion, as well members of the public made representations to the Federal Government concerning their desire that the Victoria Cross be retained as Canada's preeminent decoration for military courage. In 1991 Australia had taken the step of creating an Australian version of the Victoria Cross by keeping the exact form of the medal that had been historically used in the days of the Empire. Notwithstanding that Commonwealth precedent however, when the Honours Policy Committee turned its mind to the question of military valour decorations in the early 1990's the Committee proposed that a new decoration be created, the Cross of Military Valour, and the Victoria Cross be consigned to the history books. Resulting public pressure eventually compelled the Mulroney Ministry to intervene politically, and a new recommendation to keep the Victoria Cross was obtained from the Committee. In 1993, the Federal Government, bowing to public desires, confirmed the Victoria Cross as an essential component of the system of Canadian honours, and as the highest decoration for extraordinary acts of valour in the face of the enemy during wartime.[83] As part of this restoration, the Victoria Cross was made a Canadian honour, to be conferred by the Sovereign in right of Canada, following the precedent set earlier by Australia. At the same time that the Victoria Cross was restored to its place as the supreme Canadian honour, the Crown also created two other military valour decorations, the Star of Military Valour and the Medal of Military Valour.

Subsequently, there was a concern within the military that the honours system lacked recognition for short-term, or singular acts of merit. Therefore, by letters patent dated June 11, 1984, Queen Elizabeth II created the Meritorious Service Cross. That decoration is conferred for a military deed or activity carried out in an outstanding professional manner of a rare high standard that reflects great credit or benefit to the Canadian Forces. Amendments in 1991 created a more junior level, the Meritorious Service Medal and both decorations were then opened to civilians by the creation of a civil division. The creation of the civil division allowed for the recognition of great merit by civil servants.[84]

13.44   Military Valour Decorations

In 1993 the Crown created a series of military valour decorations to serve the need of recognizing extraordinary acts of valour and gallantry by Canadians serving in the armed forces during hostilities. There are three decorations in the suite of military valour decorations, the Victoria Cross, the Star of Military Valour and the Medal of Military Valour. The suite of Canadian military valour decorations was modelled on the Australian suite of valour decorations that were established in 1991.[85] Nominations for military valour decorations are made by the Military Valour Decorations Committee, which consists of a representative of the Governor General and five persons who are appointed to the committee by the Chief of the Defence Staff. Thus, like the Order of Military Merit, nominations are very much concentrated in the hands of the military, with very little outside involvement in the nominations for the award of military valour decorations. As with the recommendations of the Advisory Council of the Order of Canada, the Governor General has a discretion to refuse a recommendation of the advisory committee but the Governor General should only do so in accordance with the principles of responsible government by obtaining the concurrence of the Canadian Ministry and its acceptance of political responsibility for the negative exercise of the Governor General's discretion.

13.45   The Victoria Cross

This is the preeminent Canadian honour which takes precedence over every other honour conferred by the Sovereign, or by the Government of Canada or one of its provinces. It was created in 1856 by Queen Victoria to reward conspicuous bravery, daring or pre-eminent acts of valour, or self sacrifice, and devotion to duty in the presence of an enemy by a member of the armed forces. For the first twenty-five years of the decoration it could also be awarded for actions in extreme danger not within the face of an enemy, and one such award was made to a Canadian during the Fenian Insurgency in 1866.[86] Canadian soldiers, sailors, and aircrew have won the Victoria Cross between 94 and upwards of 100 times (depending upon how the calculation is done). Lieutenant Hampton Gray VC, who received his award posthumously for a successful attack on a Japanese destroyer in 1945, was the most recent Canadian to be honoured with the VC.

In 1993, the Victoria Cross was continued as a Canadian decoration within the Canadian system of honours following the precedent set by Australia in 1991. The Victoria Cross is the only British award for gallantry that has been carried over into the new Canadian honours system created during the fifty years following the centennial of confederation in 1967.

The Canadian version of the VC is exactly the same in appearance as the British version except that the words "For Valour" in the British version have been rendered in Latin on the Canadian version as "Pro Valore" and a fleur-de-lys has been added to the scroll work on the decoration. Worn on the breast, and suspended from a crimson ribbon, the Victoria Cross is plain in appearance in comparison to more modern decoration designs but carries great meaning in the Canadian honours system. Perhaps it was intended to be a rather plain decoration without significant embellishments. One British recipient in World War One reported that when he received his VC from King George V in 1915 in a simple cardboard box the King said to him: "I give you this highest decoration of all in this very ordinary box so that the intrinsic value of the medal and the box shall not be more than one penny".[87]

One significant change that Canada made when it continued the imperial decoration as part of its own national system of honours was to make the Victoria Cross a revocable honour. The original British honour was also revocable but that caused some unease over the fact that a supreme act of courage could be recognized and then forfeited by a subsequent character failing. Forfeitures[88] of the Victoria Cross during the nineteenth century included cases where the recipient was found to be a bigamist or a cow thief.[89] King George V took a particularly strong view of the matter and insisted that the forfeiture of the VC be banned. The Private Secretary to the Sovereign reported that: "The King feels so strongly that, no matter the crime committed by anyone on whom the VC has been conferred, the decoration should not be forfeited. Even were a holder of the VC to be sentenced to hang for murder, he should be allowed to wear the VC on the scaffold".[90] As a result of the King's insistence, from 1908 onwards the imperial version of the VC could not be forfeited. However, when Canada continued the Victoria Cross as an honour within the Canadian honours system in 1993, forfeiture was restored.[91]

The criterion for the award of the Canadian VC is essentially the same as the British VC. It is awarded for acts of: "the most conspicuous bravery, a daring or pre-eminent act of valour or self-sacrifice or extreme devotion to duty, in the presence of the enemy".[92] However, there is a broader Canadian definition of an enemy, which now includes not only the military forces of an enemy state but also mutineers, rebels, rioters, and pirates, when they are armed, and Canada does not have to formally declare a state of war to exist in order for the VC to be awarded.[93] Recipients of the Victoria Cross are entitled to place the post-nominal letters VC after their names. This post-nominal honour precedes every other order, decoration, or medal that has been previously or subsequently awarded to the recipient.

13.46   The Star of Military Valour

This decoration was created in 1993 to reward distinguished and valiant service where the recipient has been in the presence of the enemy. It is the second highest military valour decoration. Recipients may place the post-nominal letters SMV or ÉVM after their name.

13.47   The Medal of Military Valour

Created in 1993, as the third-highest recognition of military bravery, the Medal of Military Valour is conferred for valorous actions or devotion to duty in the presence of an enemy. Recipients may place the post-nominal letters MMV or MVM after their name.[94]

13.48   Canadian Bravery Decorations

Bravery decorations may be awarded to Canadians serving in the military or in civilian life for acts of heroism in peace or war.[95] These were the first decorations created when the Federal Government embarked upon creating a Canadian system of honours after the centennial celebrations in 1967. There are three decorations, the Cross of Valour, the Star of Courage, and the Medal of Bravery. Nominations are made by the Canadian Decorations Advisory Committee the members of which are represent the Clerk of the Privy Council, the Secretary to the Governor General, the Commissioner of the Royal Canadian Mounted Police, and the Deputy Ministers of National Defence and Transport. The Governor General may also appoint other members of the Committee.

Appointments are made by the Governor General after considering the advice and recommendations of the Advisory Committee. As with the recommendations of the Advisory Council of the Order of Canada, the Governor General has a discretion to refuse a recommendation of the Advisory Committee but the Governor General should only do so in accordance with the principles of responsible government by obtaining the concurrence of the Canadian Ministry and its acceptance of political responsibility for a negative exercise of the Governor General's discretion.

The Canadian Decorations Advisory Committee has applied a two-year rule to events that form the basis of an award which means that it will not consider acts of bravery that occurred more than two years in the past for a bravery decoration. This rule has been applied as a rule of practice by the Committee and is not a rule of law established in the regulations pertaining to the bravery decorations. The practice of applying a two-year rule was challenged in an action commenced in the Federal Court of Canada. A motion by the Crown to strike that action was denied by a Federal Court Prothonotary who while acknowledging that the Royal Prerogative concerning the grant of honours was not justiciable stated that the issue before the Court was whether the Committee had exceeded the powers granted to it:

> The question at issue then is whether the Committee's decision to apply a time bar, to preclude further examination of the plaintiff's nomination, is an exercise of Crown prerogative which is beyond the scope of review by this Court. To the extent that this calls for a determination of the scope of the Committee's powers by reference to the Letters Patent and the Regulations, it may arguably be subject to review.[96]

On appeal to a judge of the Federal Court the decision of the Prothonotary was upheld. In allowing an application for judicial review from the decision of the Committee to proceed Justice Blanchard stated:

> The principle issue raised in this claim calls for a determination of the scope of the Committee's power by reference to the Letters Patent and the Regulations. The respondent argues that this issue is justiciable. It is not plain and obvious to me that it is not. The matter should be disposed of by a judge who has the benefit of a full and complete hearing on the merits.[97]

Thus although a decision of the Advisory Committee to refuse a nomination for a bravery decoration was beyond judicial review for reasons of justiciability, a refusal to consider by the Committee to consider a nomination based on a procedural rule of its own making could be the subject of a judicial review application on the grounds that the Advisory Committee exceeded the powers conferred on it by the letters patent and the regulations.

13.49   The Cross of Valour

The Cross of Valour is the highest award for bravery and is given for acts of the most conspicuous courage in circumstances of an extreme peril. Recipients may include both civilian and military personnel and they may place the post-nominal letters CV after their names.

13.50   The Star of Courage

The Star of Courage, the second highest bravery decoration, is conferred for acts of conspicuous courage in circumstances of a great peril. Recipients may include the post-nominal letters SC or ÉC after their name.

13.51   The Medal of Bravery

A third decoration, the Medal of Bravery is awarded for courage under hazardous circumstances. The post-nominal letters MB may be used after the recipient's name.[98]

13.52   The Mention in Dispatches

In 1991, the Sovereign created the award of Mention in Dispatches as a continuation of an award that was conferred while Canada used imperial honours: "to recognize valiant conduct, devotion to duty or other distinguished service" by members of the Canadian Forces or individuals working alongside the Forces. Mention in Dispatches may be awarded posthumously.[99] An Oak leaf is worn to commemorate the award of a mention-in-dispatches.

13.53   Meritorious Service Decorations

The Meritorious Service Cross, created in 1984, and the Meritorious Service Medal, created on June 6, 1991, is conferred for a military or civilian deed or activity carried out in an outstanding professional manner of a rare high standard that reflects great credit or benefit to the Canadian Forces (military division) or to Canada (civil division). The post-nominal letters MSC (for the award of the cross) and MSM (for the medal) may be borne by the recipients. Recipients are nominated by a Military Advisory Committee or a Civil Advisory Committee to the Governor General who makes the appointments. As with the recommendations of the Advisory Council of the Order of Canada, the

Governor General has a discretion to refuse a recommendation of the Advisory Committees but the Governor General should only do so in accordance with the principles of responsible government by obtaining the concurrence of the Canadian Ministry and its acceptance of political responsibility for a negative exercise of the Governor General's discretion.

13.54   Medals

Medals are intended to recognize general service and may be presented to everyone who participates with distinction in an activity. They are most often given to the members of military, or para-military organizations, but they are also given to civilians. Sometimes they are also conferred to commemorate an auspicious occasion, such as a royal jubilee, or an anniversary of confederation. Medals falling into the latter category are most often given to civilians but may also be given to military personnel. Medals do not confer the right to use any post-nominal letters.

Medals are the most common honour created and conferred by the Crown in Right of Canada through the Royal Prerogative and fall into several categories.

13.55   Campaign Medals

Medals are awarded to military personnel for their participation in defined military campaigns in a theatre of operations during hostilities. Members of police services and some civilians who accompanied the Canadian military during a particular campaign may also be eligible for a campaign medal. Eligibility is determined by a quantitative measure, usually a minimum number of consecutive days of service in-theatre, or an accumulative period of service in-theatre. A minimum number of air sorties have also been utilized as a measure.

Campaign medals recognized by the Crown in Right of Canada do not only include those that have been created by an exercise of the Royal Prerogative but also include non-Canadian medals issued to Canadians by the United Nations, the North Atlantic Treaty Organization, the International Truce Commissions in Indochina and the Sinai Peninsula of Egypt, and the European Union (primarily for peace-keeping monitoring in the Balkan states).) One Australian medal has been recognized by Canada for service in East Timor.

13.56   Polar Service

The Polar Medal is conferred upon persons who have participated in expeditions or undertakings that have been sanctioned by the Government of Canada in the Arctic or in Antarctica. This medal primarily recognizes scientists and explorers (who may, or may not, be affiliated with the military) who have explored in the remote regions of the country and the Earth.

13.57   Long Service Medals

It was long considered important to recognize lengthy and faithful service in the military and that recognition was extended to the Royal Canadian Mounted Police in the first half of the twentieth century. In the twenty-first century long service medals are presented to a variety of military, police, protective, and other organizations. They include the Canadian Forces Decoration, the Royal Canadian Mounted Police Long Service Medal, the Police Exemplary Service Medal, the Corrections Exemplary Service Medal, the Fire Services Exemplary Medal, the Emergency Medical Services Exemplary Service Medal, the Peace Officer Exemplary Service Medal, the Canadian Coast Guard Exemplary Services Medal, the Sovereign's Medal for Volunteers, the Service Medal of the Order of St. John, and the Canadian Corps of Commissionaires Long Service Medal. All have their eligibility determined by an explicit number of years of service except the Sovereign's Medal for Volunteers, which generally requires sustained service over an extended period of time.

13.58   Volunteer Service

The Sovereign's Medal for Volunteers was created in 2016 to replace the Governor General's Caring Canadian Award and is intended to recognize the dedication and commitment of volunteers across many fields of endeavour. Canadian volunteers who have provided significant, sustained, and unpaid services to both Canadian and foreign communities are eligible for the award.

13.59   Commemorative Medals

A commemorative medal marks some special event and is given to Canadians who have been deemed to have made a significant contribution to Canada. The criteria are flexible and a considerable number of medals have in the past been given to Members of Parliament for distribution to worthy constituents, and so there has been an element of political patronage in the conferral of these honours. The commemorative medals include the Centennial Medal in 1967 and the 125th Anniversary of Confederation Medal in 1992 as well as three royal jubilee medals associated with the reign of Queen Elizabeth II, the Silver Jubilee Medal (1977), the Golden Jubilee Medal (2002) and the Diamond Jubilee Medal (2012).

13.60   Achievement Medal

There is one historic achievement medal in the Canadian honours system.

13.61   The Queen's Medal for Champion Shot

Originally established by Queen Victoria in 1869 for the British Army, and extended to Canada in 1923 this medal rewards achievement in marksmanship. Two medals are awarded annually to both the champion shot of the regular army, and to the champion shot of the militia and RCMP. The original medal was continued as a Canadian medal in 1991 but in appearance it is very similar to the British medal, except for the replacement of the British regnal title by the Canadian regnal title.

13.62   Sacrifice and Loss Medals

Several medals have been created to reflect losses encountered by Canadians in the service of their country.

13.63   The Memorial Cross (The Silver Cross)

The Memorial Cross, which is commonly known by Canadians as the Silver Cross, was created on December 1, 1919, to recognize the agonizing losses of servicemen during World War One. The mother of any soldier, sailor, or pilot who died while on active service in the Imperial Forces in World War One was recognized by the presentation of a sterling silver cross suspended from a purple ribbon worn around the neck.[100] More modern versions of the Silver Cross are suspended from a bar that is attached to clothing with a clip. During World War Two the families of merchant seamen and the families of the Canadian Fire Fighters Corps (United Kingdom) also became eligible to receive the Silver Cross. Perhaps 130,000 Silver Crosses have been issued since the inception of the memorial award.

In the twenty-first century, the loss while serving on active duty in Afghanistan of four female soldiers meant that the surviving relatives of servicewomen also began to receive the Silver Cross. Military personnel can now direct to whom the Silver Cross should be given in the event of their death on active service, which may now be a friend instead of a relative. Up to three Silver Crosses may be given.[101]

13.64   The Memorial Ribbon

This award is provided to close loved ones of a deceased soldier, sailor or aircrew who have been killed in the service of Canada or due to an injury attributable to that service, who have not received the Silver Cross. The ribbon is purple and is crossed and held by a small circular pin with the Silver Cross displayed within it. Up to five Memorial Ribbons may be provided to survivors.

13.65   The Sacrifice Medal

This medal is given to members of the Canadian Forces and civilians deployed in conjunction with the Forces who are killed or wounded during hostilities. For military personnel, it replaced the wound stripes that were formerly worn on the sleeve of their uniform.

13.66   Royal Canadian Mounted Police Memorial Memento

This medal is presented to the next of kin of a member of the RCMP who is slain in the course of his or her duties. Three medals are presented to the spouse of the member and to their mother and father, and if one or more of the three recipients are deceased, the medal is presented to the children of the slain member or, if there are none, to the eldest brother, or sister, of the deceased.

13.67   Legislative Medal

All honours emanate from the Sovereign who is the fount of all honour pursuant to the Royal Prerogative. However, as with other elements of the Royal Prerogative, Parliament has the ability to supplant the Royal Prerogative by legislation. The creation by Parliament of a Canadian Peacekeeping Service Medal in 1997 for Canadians who have served abroad with an international peacekeeping missions represents a unique departure from the typical method for the creation of Canadian honours. This medal was established through a private members public bill which was enacted by Parliament as the *Canadian Peacekeeping Service Medal Act*.[102] As a result of the use of this method, the Sovereign was not directly involved in the creation of the medal, unlike all other Canadian honours.[103]

The statute provides for the recognition of Canadians (both military and civilians) who served at least thirty days with a United Nations peacekeeping mission or another peacekeeping mission. The criterion allows for more Canadians to be recognized than the United Nations service medals that are awarded for the same service, and which are incorporated into the Canadian honours system. The United Nations medals only recognize peacekeeping service of at least 180 days, and thus Canadians serving for shorter periods with a United Nations mission had previously gone unrecognized. As a result of the enactment of this statute many Canadians who had already received a United Nations Medal for peacekeeping service also became eligible for this medal, which meant that their service was honoured twice for the same effort, representing a departure from past Canadian policy with respect to the conferral of honours.

The statute provides that the medal is awarded by the Governor in Council upon the nomination of a person by a Minister of the Crown, and thus nominations for the medal constitute formal constitutional advice to the Governor General.[104] Although the exercise of the Royal Prerogative is preserved by a saving section,[105] the Governor General is expected to follow the formal advice of a

Canadian Minister of the Crown in awarding the medal, in accordance with the principle of responsible government.

13.68   Provincial Orders

Each province and territory has established provincial orders of merit to recognize provincial or territorial citizens who have made a significant contribution to their community. All of the provincial and territorial orders have been created by statute, with the exception of Ontario, which created the Order of Ontario by an order-in-council. None of the provincial or territorial orders carry a title and all are of one class, except the Order of Quebec, which consists of three classes of members, Grand Officer, Officer, and Knight. Post-nominal letters may be appended to the recipient's name (in Quebec, in accordance with the class of the Order of Quebec to which they have been appointed).

The provincial orders are all conferred by the Lieutenant Governors of the provinces or by the Commissioners of the northern territories, except in Quebec where the Order of Quebec is conferred by the Premier of Quebec. In each of the provinces and territories the Lieutenant Governor or territorial Commissioner is the Chancellor of the provincial order, except in Quebec, where there is no chancellor.

The provincial orders have, at the request of the provinces, been incorporated into the Canadian honours system by inclusion within the Order of Precedence that is issued by the Crown in Right of Canada in the exercise of the Royal Prerogative. The territorial orders have not yet been included in the Order of Precedence.

The following are the provincial and territorial orders together with their post-nominal abbreviations:

Order National du Québec, GOQ, OQ, or CQ

Saskatchewan Order of Merit, SOM

Order of Ontario, OOnt

Order of British Columbia, OBC

Order of Prince Edward Island, OPEI

Order of Manitoba, OM

Order of New Brunswick, ONB

Order of Nova Scotia, ONS

Order of Newfoundland and Labrador, ONL

Order of Nunavut, ONu

Order of the Northwest Territories, ONWT

Order of Yukon

The provincial orders carry protocol privileges (e.g., precedence) within the provinces and territories in which they are conferred, and are incorporated into the national *Order of Precedence* maintained by the Federal Government. The process for appointments to the provincial orders generally follows the process established for national orders of merit with recommended nominations submitted to the Lieutenant Governor by an advisory committee, or council. The purpose of the advisory committees is to remove the appointments process from partisan politics.

The Lieutenant Governor, like the Governor General, has a discretion to refuse to accept a nomination but in doing so the Lieutenant Governor should act in accordance with the principles of responsible government by obtaining the agreement of the Executive Council of the province to accept political responsibility for Lieutenant Governor's decision not to appoint an individual to the order.

As with the Governor General, the Lieutenant Governor can delay making an appointment to obtain further information, or to have a discussion about the matter with the advisory committee/council, or to obtain formal constitutional advice from the Executive Council where that is warranted.

13.69   *Provincial Decorations, Medals and Awards*

In addition to provincial orders, the provinces and territories have created a number of decorations, medals and awards to recognize bravery, exemplary service and achievement by provincial and territorial citizens. For the most part, these decorations, medals and awards have been created by provincial or territorial statutory authority. Some of the provincial decorations and medals have been incorporated into the national *Order of Precedence*. In some provinces medals bearing the likeness of the Lieutenant Governor on one side, and the arms of the Lieutenant Governor on the other, have been cast and distributed in lieu of certificates of merit to individuals or organizations that have contributed to their communities.[117]

13.70   *Commonwealth and Foreign Honours*

The Royal Prerogative permits the Crown in Right of Canada to approve or disapprove of the conferral on a Canadian of a Commonwealth or foreign honour. To assist both external governments and Canadians in determining whether an honour may be accepted the government has issued a *Policy Respecting the Awarding of an Order, Decoration or Medal by a Commonwealth or Foreign Government*, last updated in 2015. The policy is designed to:

a) Prevent an external government from affecting the loyalty of Canadian public servants, or military personnel, and

b) Enforce the constitutional custome against the grant of titles to Canadians.

The policy is issued by the Governor General in Council and is consistent with the practice of other states but at the same time is more stringent than other countries. Canada, unlike many other states, does not exchange honours between heads of state or diplomatic representatives. A Minister or Minister of State is prohibited by constitutional practice from accepting a foreign honour.

13.71   Miscellaneous Honours

13.72   Honorific Titles

Under the Royal Prerogative the Crown may grant the use honorific prefix or suffix titles, or post-nominal letters.

13.73   Prefix Titles

On April 2, 1968, Queen Elizabeth II approved the use of the title Right Honourable for life for those persons who have held the offices of Governor General of Canada, Chief Justice of Canada, and Prime Minister of Canada.[106] The prefix title Right Honourable has, at times, also been granted to distinguished members of the Queen's Privy Council for Canada as a special mark of distinction.[107]

Privy Councillors are styled Honourable for life, as are members of the Senate of Canada and the Lieutenant Governors of the provinces. Others, such as Puisne Justices of the Supreme Court of Canada, Justices of the provincial superior courts and the federal courts, Judges of the provincial and territorial courts, the Speaker of the House of Commons, and members of provincial Executive Councils, are entitled to the prefix Honourable during their tenure of office.[108] Permission may be obtained from the Governor General for the retention by superior court Justices of the title Honourable after they have retired from the Bench. Former speakers of the House of Commons and former territorial commissioners may also apply for permission to retain the prefix title Honourable after they cease to hold office.[109]

A Table of Titles To Be Used In Canada is published by the Federal Government from time to time.

13.74   Post-Nominal Letters

In the years following the success of the American Revolution, a large number of American loyalists came to the Canadian colonies as refugees. For their loyalty to the Crown during the revolutionary war, the Governor General of Canada, Lord Dorchester, granted to those refugees, as a hereditary honour, the right to append the honorific initials U.E. (standing for United Empire) to their surnames and to the surnames of their descendants.[110] The order-in-council which established this honour was issued at Quebec and dated November 9, 1789. In requiring a separate register of loyalist landowners and a separate loyalist militia roll to be maintained, the order-in-council stipulated that:

> Those Loyalists who have adhered to the unity of the Empire, and joined the Royal Standard before the Treaty of Separation in the year 1783, and all their children and their descendants by either sex, are to be distinguished by the following capitals, affixed to their names: U.E. alluding to their great principle the unity of the Empire.

Although the honour has not been included in the national honours system, and is now only rarely displayed outside of loyalist organizations, it continues to be perpetuated by loyalist organizations. In the late 1970s it was estimated that some 300-400,000 Canadians may be descended from the original loyalists, and may therefore be entitled to this recognition.[111]

Members of the Queen's Privy Council for Canada are entitled to use the post-nominal letters P.C. (for Privy Councillor) after their names for so long as they remain a member of the council, which, barring any unforseen circumstances, will be for life. Similarly, Canadian barristers and solicitors who are appointed as Queen's Counsel are entitled to use the post-nominal letters Q.C. (K.C. if a male Sovereign is reigning).

13.75 Honorary Offices

By an exercise of the Royal Prerogative the Sovereign may create and confer new offices and titles. In *Skelton v Government of Newfoundland* (1888) Nfld. LR 243 (Newfoundland, SC) the Court, quoting the English legal scholar Blackstone, stated:

> The Sovereign is the fountain of honour, of office and of privilege, and consequently the making and disposing of offices is a prerogative of the Crown, "and as the King may create new titles, so may he create new offices; but with this restriction, that he cannot create new offices with new fees annexed to them, nor annex new fees to old offices, for this would be a tax upon the subject which cannot be imposed except by Act of Parliament.[112]

Of like effect was the judgment of the same court in *Barnes v Government of Newfoundland* (1875) Nfld LR 89 (Newfoundland, SC) where the court adjudicated a claim for wrongful dismissal from an office created by the exercise of the Royal Prerogative without the sanction of the Newfoundland Legislature. There the Court stated:

> There cannot, I think, be any reasonable doubt that the mere appointment was valid, even if unauthorized by an Act of the legislature, and though novel in its character, the Crown having, by its prerogative, the power of creating offices for the discharge of the various functions of government, provided no new tax or burden is imposed upon the subject, and therefore that the complainant was legally the officer designated by his commission, although without pay until a salary should be provided by the legislature.[113]

However, in *Re Corporation of the City of Scarborough and Attorney General for Ontario*, [1997] 32 OR (3d) 526 (Ontario, GD) the power of the Crown in right of the Province of Ontario to act under the Royal Prerogative for the purpose of creating offices and making appointments was held to be subject to limitations. There, the Ontario Legislature had before it a bill to confer power to appoint public trustees in respect of municipal government and to confer power on them with retroactive effect. However, the Crown had proceeded to appoint the trustees before the legislation was enacted and that action was challenged.

On an application for a declaration that the actions of the Crown in appointing the trustees before the bill was enacted was invalid, the Ontario Court held that the appointment of the trustees prior to the enactment of the bill by the Legislature could not be supported by the Royal Prerogative. Such an act would, in the circumstances, be tantamount to conferring on the trustees powers that were only within the gift of the legislature.

Furthermore, the Court held that it was contrary to the principles of responsible government for an order-in-council not to aver to its reliance on the Royal Prerogative where the prerogative was being invoked in unusual circumstances. The absence of any reference to the Royal Prerogative allowed the court to conclude that the impugned order-in-council was not made in reliance upon the prerogative.

13.76   Royal Offices

In accordance with the Sovereign's power to create offices and appoint people to them, the Sovereign has created a number of Canadian offices of honour and made appointments to those offices. Some of the following offices are of a temporary nature, particularly those associated with royal visits to Canada, while others are considered to be permanent.

The Canadian Secretary to the Queen

Aide-de-Camp-General to the Queen

Aide-de-camp to the Queen

Queen's Honorary Physician

Queen's Honorary Surgeon

Queen's Honorary Dental Surgeon

Queen's Honorary Nursing Officer

Queen's Honorary Chaplin

Queen's Police Officer

Duke of Edinburgh's Police Officer

For the purposes of royal visits an Equerry and Ladies-in-Waiting may also be appointed, in addition to aides-de-camp both for the Sovereign and other members of the Royal Family. The Governor General and the Lieutenant Governors of the provinces may also appoint aides-de-camp.

13.77   Honorary Appointments to the Imperial Privy Council

In the past, some distinguished Canadians, especially those who had served in high office, were appointed to the Privy Council of the United Kingdom as a high honour. Prior to and even after the divisibility of the Crown was established in the Commonwealth, a practice existed whereby the Prime Ministers of the dominions were appointed to the Privy Council of the United Kingdom. As well, the Prime Ministers of Canada sometimes recommended to the Sovereign that federal Ministers of the Crown and other Canadians of renown be appointed to the Privy Council of the United Kingdom, as an honour. As a member of the Privy Council of the United Kingdom the recipients of this honour were entitled to use the prefix Right Honourable before their names for life.

In Canada, appointments of Canadian ministers to the Privy Council of the United Kingdom were made as late as the post-war government of Prime Minister Mackenzie King but such appointments ceased just prior to his retirement in 1948. However, Canadian Prime Ministers continued to be appointed to the Privy Council of the United Kingdom up to and including Prime Minister Lester Pearson. Thereafter such appointments ceased.

Appointments of renowned Canadians to the Privy Council of the United Kingdom were rare but Vincent Massey, George Vanier, and Jules Leger, all of whom served as Canada's Governor General were appointed at various times.

No appointments of Canadians have been made since the appointment of Jules Leger in 1979. As a result of the evolution of Canada as a sovereign country, appointments to the Privy Council of the United Kingdom have now ceased.

13.78 Honorary Appointments to the Queen's Privy Council

Appointments of distinguished Canadians who are not politicians to the Queen's Privy Council for Canada, though rare, have been made in the past and perhaps with some greater frequency in the latter half of the twentieth century. Such appointments are regarded as a personal honour and do not involve the person called to the Privy Council in any constitutional duties or responsibilities with respect to the governance of Canada. Membership in the Canadian Privy Council entitles the recipient to the prefix Honourable before their name for life, and the use of the post-nominal letters P.C. (for Privy Councillor).

Appointments of non-politicians to the Queen's Privy Council for Canada have included members of the Royal Family, Premiers of the provinces holding office during Canada's centennial year in 1967, and the Premiers of the provinces at the time of the patriation of the *Constitution Act, 1867* in 1982, former Speakers of the House of Commons, and of the Senate, most former Governors General and former Clerks of the Privy Council (the highest-serving federal public servant) as well as a smattering of other distinguished Canadians including hockey players, artists, and distinguished scientists.

13.79 Honorary Appointments in the Canadian Armed Forces

Honorary appointments in the Canadian Forces consist mainly of Honorary colonelcies. Appointments of Honorary officers are part of the Royal Prerogative with respect to the military. The Sovereign is commander-in-chief of the Land and Naval Militia, and of all Naval and Military Forces of and in Canada, by virtue of section 15 of the *Constitution Act, 1867* and the Royal Prerogative. Pursuant to article I of the *Letters Patent Constituting the Office of Governor General of Canada* the Governor General of Canada is the commander chief in and over Canada.

Most appointments to Honorary positions with Canadian regiments involve the members of the Royal Family. In recent decades the practice within the Army has been to appoint a member of the Royal Family to be Colonel-in-Chief (or Captain-General in the artillery) of both regular and militia regiments of the Canadian Army. (Exceptionally, former Governor General Adriene Clarkson has been appointed Colonel-in-Chief of Princess Patricia's Canadian Light Infantry Regiment.)

Branches of the service may also have a Colonel Commandant and regiments of the Regulars may have a Colonel of the Regiment. The latter appointments are made only upon the recommendation of the units concerned and are for three year terms. The appointments are restricted to former officers of the Canadian Forces. Militia regiments may have Honorary Colonels, or Lieutenant Colonels, who may be either former officers or distinguished citizens.

13.80   Honorary Appointments in the Profession of Law

Within the profession of law, the position of Queen's Counsel (Q.C.), or conseil de la reine (c.r.) also has a long history in Canada, predating confederation itself. The office of Queen's Counsel is conferred upon members of the legal professions who are Barristers, Solicitors, Avocats or Notaires. Originally, a Q.C. was a standing counsel for the Queen, capable of being retained in all matters in which the Sovereign might require legal services. It is intended to be a mark of distinction, denoting eminence at the Bar. Appointments are made by the Crown in Right of Canada through the Royal Prerogative, or by the provinces through the creation of a statutory office and appointments thereto. The Crown in right of a province, in the exercise of its constitutional jurisdiction over the administration of justice in a province, may also grant lawyers precedence at the bar through the grant of letters patent of precedence.

A Q.C. is entitled to precedence in Court over other lawyers who are not Queen's Counsel, and they may wear a silk barristers gown in court, and argue their cases from a closer position to the Bench where courtroom facilities permit. As the title or office is one within the gift of the Crown, a Queen's Counsel appointment must be placed in abeyance while the holder serves as a Judge of one of Her Majesty's Courts, in order to avoid any appearance of a conflict of interest. An appointment as a Q.C. that has been placed in abeyance during a judicial tenure may be resumed upon retirement from the Bench.

The nineteenth century case of *Lenoir v Ritchie*, [1879] 3 SCR 575 (Canada, SC) held that the Governor General could appoint Q.C.s in the exercise of the Royal Prerogative. Federal Q.C.s and c.r.s are appointed by a Commission issued under the Great Seal of Canada pursuant to the Royal Prerogative. The provinces may also confer the designation of Q.C. (c.r. in Quebec) but do so pursuant to statutory authority. In *Attorney General for Canada v Attorney General for Ontario (Queen's Counsel Case)*, [1898] AC 247 (Canada, JC) the Privy Council confirmed that under the combined effect of section 92(1), (4) and (14) of the *Constitution Act, 1867*, the Lieutenant Governor of Ontario could exercise a statutory discretion to appoint lawyers to be a Queen's Counsel. Subsequently, other provinces have enacted legislation creating a provincial office of Queen's Counsel, and have made appointments of lawyers to the honorific office in the exercise of the Royal Prerogative. When a male person is the Sovereign, the designation automatically becomes King's Counsel (K.C.) or conseil de le roi (c.r.).

In recent decades some provinces have ceased to appoint lawyers as Queen's Counsel as a result of changing public perspectives on patronage and on the legal profession itself. However, several provinces continue to confer the honour upon barristers and solicitors of a certain vintage and ability. The Federal Government has occasionally rewarded a few of its own lawyers with this honour in the last quarter-century. The honour, when conferred, is traditionally announced on or about New Years Day.

13.81   Awards

Awards are a type of recognition that fall below a dignity or honour and do not form a part of the formal Canadian Honours system. They do not appear in the Order of Precedence established for honours in Canada by the Crown. However, some honours began or emerged from an earlier award created by the Crown.

From a legal perspective the creation of awards is interesting because they may be justified as either an exercise of the Royal Prerogative, or as an exercise of the natural person powers of the Sovereign, the members of the Royal Family, or the Sovereign's representatives.

13.82   Royal Family Awards

Over time the Royal Family has created several awards to recognize citizens of the Commonwealth and of Canada in various endeavours.

13.83   The Gold Medal for Poetry

Created by King George V in 1933 the Gold Medal for Poetry is awarded by the Sovereign for excellence in poetry as displayed:

a) in a body of work extending over many years; or,

b) in a substantial and exemplary collection published in the year that the award is made to the recipient.

The award is open to citizens of the Commonwealth realms. Recommendations for the award are made by an advisory committee that is appointed by the Poet Laureate of the United Kingdom.

13.84   The Queen's Young Leader Award

The Queen's Young Leader Award is intended to recognize youth between the ages of 18-29 from all Commonwealth nations who are demonstrating community leadership and are seeking to use their abilities to change lives.

13.85   The Duke of Edinburgh's Awards

An award created in 1956 by the royal consort to Queen Elizabeth II, the Duke of Edinburgh Awards are designed to challenge youth between the ages of 14-24 to demonstrate achievement in various aspects of their lives and interests. A program of activities must be followed by the recipients with an emphasis on social interaction and team work in the areas of volunteering, physical fitness through sport, dance, or activities, skills development, travels (nationally or abroad) and for the gold level a short period lived away from home. The Duke of Edinburgh Awards were initially open to all Commonwealth citizens but has now been expanded beyond the Commonwealth to the youth of other, non-Commonwealth countries.

13.86   The Prince of Wales Youth Service Awards

Created in 2015 by the heir to the Throne, Prince Charles, the Prince of Wales Youth Service Awards seeks to recognize the commitment by Canadian youth to transform the world for the better and to inspire Canadian youth to seek a better future. Recipients of the award must have achieved accomplishment in their communities through community service and actions. There are four categories of an award: Community Leaders, Global Leaders, Social Innovators, and Agents of Sustainability.

13.87   The Prince of Wales Award for Sustainable Forestry

The Prince of Wales' Award for Sustainable Forestry was created in 2013 and seeks to encourage the younger members of the Canadian Institute of Forestry – Institut forestier du Canada (CIF-IFC) to dedicate themselves to principled and sustainable forest management practices, stewardship of forestry resources based on scientific principles, and promotion of conservation practices.

13.88   Governor General's Awards

Various Governors General have created a series of annual awards to recognize accomplishment by Canadians in a variety of diverse fields in the academics, the arts, sciences, journalism, the culinary arts, and innovation.

13.89 The Governor General's Academic Medal

The oldest of the awards presented by the Governors General are the Governor General's Academic medals which were created in 1873 by Governor General Lord Dufferin. As the most prestigious academic award in Canadian education the Governor General's Academic Medal recognizes the highest level of achievement for Canadian students. They are awarded to students in high schools, colleges, and universities (undergraduate and post-graduate) with the highest average marks.

A bronze medal is awarded to students who have earned the highest average at the high school level, collegiate bronze to college students (diploma programs) who have earned the highest standing in their community college, silver to university students who have earned the highest standing in an undergraduate program, and gold for university students who have the highest standing at the graduate level.

13.90   Governor General's Literary Awards

One of the best known of the awards given by the Governor General is the Literary Awards, which were created by Governor General Lord Tweedsmuir in 1937. The Governor General's Literary Awards recognize excellence in English-language and French-language literature in fiction, non-fiction, poetry, drama, children's literature, textual and illustrative works, and translation. The administering body for the literary awards is Canada Council for the Arts, which is responsible for the process of adjudication.

13.91   The Michener Award

A creation of Governor General Roland Michener in 1970, the Michener Award recognizes excellence in public service-oriented journalism in all media. The award measures journalistic professionalism, public impacts, and the public benefits of reporting. The administering body for this award is the Michener Awards Foundation, a private foundation.

13.92   The Awards in Commemoration of the Persons Case

The Governor General's Awards in Commemoration of the Persons Case were created by Governor General Edward Schreyer in 1979, in honour of the 50th anniversary of the historic Persons Case in which the Judicial Committee of the Privy Council confirmed that women were persons within the meaning of Canada's constitution. The awards recognize efforts to promote and sustain the equality of women. The administering body for the Person's Case awards is a federal agency, the Status of Women Canada.

13.93   Governor General's Medals in Architecture

The Governor General's Medals in Architecture recognize and celebrate outstanding Canadian architectural design and achievement in recent building projects. The award has been offered intermittently since first being established by Governor General Edward Schreyer in 1982. The administering body for the architectural award is the Royal Architectural Institute of Canada. The adjudicative process is supervised by the Canada Council for the Arts.

13.94   Governor General's Performing Arts Awards

The Governor General's Performing Arts Awards were established by Governor General Ramon Hnatyshyn in 1992 to reward excellence in the performing arts (theatre, dance, classical music, popular music, film, and broadcasting). The administering body for the performing arts awards is the Governor General's Performing Arts Awards Foundation, which is responsible for the process of adjudication.

13.95   Governor General's History Awards

Created in 1996 by Governor General Roméo Leblanc, the Governor General's History Awards recognize excellence in the presentation of Canadian history and heritage. The awards are given in the categories of teaching, scholarship, media, museums, and community programming. The administering body for the history award is Canadian National History Society.

13.96   Governor General's Awards in Visual and Media Arts

The Governor General's Awards in Visual and Media Arts were created by Governor General Roméo LeBlanc in 1999 to recognize Canadian achievement in the visual and media arts. The administering body for the visual and media arts awards is the Canada Council for the Arts, which is responsible for the process of adjudication.

13.97   The Award in Celebration of the Nation's Table

Established by Governor General Michaëlle Jean and her spouse, and first awarded in 2010, The Governor General's Award in Celebration of the Nation's Table celebrates Canadians who inspire Canadians with their passion for Canada's table, including farmers, chefs, cheese makers, researchers, culinary festival organizers, tea makers, teachers, students, hospitality professionals, writers, sommeliers, fishers, hunters and winemakers. An advisory committee makes selections for this award.

13.98   The Governor General's Innovation Awards

The Governor General's Innovation Awards were created in 2016 by Governor General David Johnston to recognize excellence in innovation, encourage the entrepreneurial spirits of Canadian youth, and to foster a culture of innovation. Up to six annual awards are given to individuals, groups, or organizations that are or have made a significant positive impact on Canadian society. The Canada Foundation for Innovation is responsible for the adjudication process.

13.99   Commendation Awards

13.100   The Commander-in-Chief Unit Commendation

The Commander-in-Chief Unit Commendation was created by Governor General Adrienne Clarkson on November 7, 2000, and is awarded by the Governor General to a unit of the Canadian Forces (or a unit of an allied force) that performs an extraordinary feat in hazardous conditions, at a rare high standard of performance. The unit so honoured receives a scroll, insignia and a pennant.[114]

13.101 Vice Regal and Commissioner's Commendation

The Chancellery of Honours designed a commendation for junior staff who serve the Lieutenant Governors of the provinces and the territorial commissioners to recognize acts worthy of commendation. The award is a small gold bar with a badge containing three maple leaves and surmounted by a crown. The insignia is intended for wearing on a jacket or dress on formal occasions.

13.102 The Minister of Veterans Affairs Commendation

The Minister of Veterans Affairs Commendation was created to reward veterans and others who have benefited veterans or helped to sustain remembrance of the achievements and sacrifices of Canada's former soldiers, sailors and aircrew. The commendation consists of a small gold bar and lapel pin that is intended to be worn on formal occasions.

13.103 Order of St. John Commendations

Two commendations have been created by the Order of St. John to acknowledge the contributions made by members of the order. The Chancellor's Commendation acknowledges those within the order who have made a conspicuous contribution at the national level and the Provincial and Territorial Council Commendation acknowledges those who have made a conspicuous contribution at the provincial level.

13.104 Other Awards

13.105 Public Service Long Service Awards

Awards are presented to public servants for faithful service over a number of years. The award system consists of Recognition Certificate signed by the Prime Minister, and by the Deputy Minister of the Department in which the public servant has been employed. The standard long service awards are presented to public servants upon achieving twenty-five, thirty, thirty-five, forty, forty-five and fifty years of service, although some departments do not offer their employees all of the milestones.

To the extent that the control of federal public servants has a prerogative foundation, the Prime Minister may exercise the Royal Prerogative to formally acknowledge the long service of individual public servants through the award of a Recognition Certificate.[115]

A Certificate of Appreciation signed by the Prime Minister, and sealed with the Seal of the Prime Minister of Canada, is also provided to federal public servants upon the occasion of their retirement from the public service.

13.106 Tables of Precedence and Titles

The Royal Prerogative provides for the power to establish an order of precedence for the purpose of state ceremonials, including the display of orders and decorations. From time to time an *Order of Precedence* for Canada is established by an order-in-council. The most recent version is generally available on the website of the Department of Canadian Heritage.

The Royal Prerogative also allows for the creation of a *Table of Titles to be used in Canada*. The most recent version is generally available on the website of the Department of Canadian Heritage.

[1] *Distributing Status: The Evolution of State Honours in Western Europe*, Samuel Clark, McGill-Queen's University Press, Montreal and Kingston, 2016, at page 245 (afterwards "*Clark*")

[2] Ibid. There are still exceptions of course. Armorial bearings and some peerages are capable of descent in the contemporary period.

[3] *Clark*, at page 184; *The Canadian Honours System, Second Edition*, Christopher McCreery, Dundurn, Toronto, 2015, at page 27 (afterwards "*McCreery*")

[4] *McCreery*, at page 32

[5] *The Order of Canada: Its Origins, History, and Development*, Christopher McCreery, University of Toronto Press, Toronto, 2005, at page 21

[6] *Clark*, at page 286

[7] *Clark*, at page 307

[8] *McCreery*, at page 328

[9] Ibid, at page 35

[10] *The Register of Canadian Honours*, Robin Brass et al ed. Canadian Almanac & Directory Publishing Company Limited, Toronto, 1991, at page 9 (afterwards *"Brass et al"*)

[11] There is a useful comparison chart between the former British honours and the current Canadian honours in Appendix 3 in *McCreery*, at page 687.

[12] *The Canadian Honours System*, Christopher McCreery, Dundurn Press, Toronto, 2005, at page 325 (afterwards, *"McCreery, 2005"*)

[13] *McCreery 2005*, at page 42

[14] *Sabha et al v Attorney General*, [2009] 4 LRC 818 (Trinidad and Tobago, JC) per Lord Hope at page 832.

[15] *Operation Dismantle v R*, [1985] 1 SCR 441 (Canada, SC)

[16] The word trinity also conveys strong Christian symbolism but since the name of the country, Trinidad, is the Spanish word for trinity, the proponents of the challenge chose not to attack the symbolism of the word trinity.

[17] at page 835.

[18] *Black v Canada (Prime Minister)*, [2000] 47 OR (3d) 532 at 536 (Ontario, SC)

[19] Ibid, at page 534-535

[20] Ibid, at page 541

[21] [1985] 1 AC 374, [1984] 3 All ER 935 (England, HL)

[22] *Black v Canada (Prime Minister)*, [2001] 54 OR (3d) 215 at paragraphs 60-62 (Ontario, CA)

[23] at paragraph 6

[24] *Letters Patent dated January 28, 1997* (P.C. 1997-123)

[25] Historically the Royal Prerogative power only provided for the grant of hereditary titles but in the United Kingdom that was changed in the mid-twentieth century by statute to permit the grant of life peerages, which are not hereditary. The UK legislation has never had any application to Canada however, as its enactment occurred subsequent to the *Statute of Westminster, 1931*.

[26] *McCreery*, at page 47

[27] This was done for Lord Strathcona, whose peerage in the barony of the United Kingdom was inheritable by his male issue, or failing any male issue of his, to his daughter; *London Gazette*, June 26, 1900, No: 27205. The title passed to his daughter. An earlier peerage that did not provide for inheritance by a daughter upon the failure of male issue became extinct upon Lord Strathcona's death.

[28] See, for example, *The Canadian Almanac & Directory 2017, 170th Edition*, Grey House Publishing Canada, Toronto, 2016.

[29] Lord Pirrie, the head of the Harland and Wolff Shipyard, of Titanic fame, in Belfast, Ireland, was raised from a baron to a viscount in 1921. However, his entire business career had been conducted in the United Kingdom and therefore this grant was clearly a British dignity.

Sir Max Aiken, a businessman from New Brunswick who ran the Canadian War Records Office in London in World War One and subsequently became a business magnate and a media baron in the interwar years in Britain was made a baron in 1917.

Former Prime Minister Richard Bennett was made a viscount in 1941. Bennett's peerage was unusual since he had been Prime Minister until 1935 after which he retired to the United Kingdom in 1938. All of his public service was in Canada and there does not appear to any reason beyond his service to Canada why he would have received such recognition.

A newspaper magnate, Roy Thomson of Toronto, who had extensive media properties in the United Kingdom, was given a barony in 1964, as Lord Thomson of Fleet but at the insistence of the Pearson Ministry he was required to forsake his Canadian citizenship in order to accept the peerage. When his son, a Canadian citizen, subsequently inherited the peerage that inheritance did not offend the policy against Canadians obtaining a title since the peerage was not conferred upon a Canadian but rather was inherited by a Canadian.

Another Canadian media magnate, Conrad Black, who also had extensive media holdings in the United Kingdom was proposed for a peerage by British Prime Minister Tony Blair in 2001. Prime Minister Jean Chretien, objected to the grant of a peerage to a Canadian citizen, forcing Black to renounce his Canadian citizenship, and it was as a British citizen that Conrad Black was elevated to the peerage of the United Kingdom as Lord Black of Crossharbour.

[30] *Debrett's Correct Form*, Patrick Montague Smith, Headline, London, 1992, at page 323; *Black's Law Dictionary, 4th ed.*, Henry Campbell Black, West Publishing Co., St. Paul (Minn.) 1968 (1975).

[31] The designation of an esquire was maintained in the United States of America after the American Revolution and continues to be used today as a formal designation for attorneys, both male and female, particularly those engaged in the practice of litigation.

[32] *The Canadian Heraldic Authority*, Rideau Hall, Ottawa, 1990, at page 6 (afterwards *The Canadian Heraldic Authority*)

[33] *Manchester v Manchester Palace of Varieties Ltd.*, [1955] P 133 at 147 (England, Ct. Chiv.)

[34] *The Canadian Heraldic Authority*, at page 11

[35] *Halsbury's Laws of England 4th ed., Vol. 35 Peerages and Dignities*, at page 599, para. 970.

[36] *The High Court of Chivalry: A Study of the Civil Law in England*, G D Squibb, Clarendon Press, Oxford, 1959, at page 14 (afterwards, *"Chivalry"*)

[37] *Chivalry*, at page 164

[38] The Court of Chivalry's only reported Canadian case fell into this category. *Hocker (Wise) v Holmes* (1634) Cur. Mil. Boxes 7/114 (England, Ct. Chiv.) concerned a case of murder brought by the widow of a man killed in a duel in Newfoundland. The defendant Holmes was found liable and sentenced to death but he was pardoned by King James I.

[39] *Chivalry*, at page 184, fn 2.

[40] A quartering would result from the combination of the arms of the daughter's father with the arms of her husband within the arms borne by the daughter's legitimate male issue (see *Halsbury's Laws of England, 4th ed. Vol. 35*, para. 908.

[41] *Chivalry*, at page 189. For the reference to *Carminow v Scrope* see *Chivalry*, at page 183.

[42] An escutcheon of pretense is a heraldic claim by a husband to be the head of his wife's family when the male line of her family has become extinct. The arms of the wife's family would be displayed in a small shield in the centre of the husband's shield.

[43] *Oldys v Tyllie* (1687), Her. Cas. 59 (England, Ct. Chiv.) Supporters are representational figures that stand on either side of a heraldic shield and appear to support it. It is generally considered to be a mark of special distinction.

[44] *Chivalry*, at page 135.

[45] A reference was made to this court by Lord Mance in *Sabha v Attorney General*, [2009] 4 LRC 818 at 836: "Questions arising about precedence, descent, the right to bear a coat of arms and 'other kindred matters of honour' are technically within the jurisdiction in England of the Court of Chivalry . . . and in Scotland the Court of the Lord Lyon has a jurisdiction over the use of arms backed by criminal sanctions".

[46] *Manchester v Manchester Palace of Varieties Ltd.*, [1955] P 133 at 147 (England, Ct. Chiv.) at page 151.

[47] Such cases commonly occurred in the law of wills and estates. Thus, in *Stubs v Stubs*, [1862] Exch. Rep. 257; 1 H & C 1 (England, Exch. Pleas) the devise in a will of all property by a testator to his widow included the letters patent granting the testator armorial bearings even though she was not the heir to the arms. It was held by Chief Baron Pollock (Baron Bramwell concurring) that other family members had an interest in the patent, and the holder of it could be required to produce it to them for inspection, and they could also enjoin the holder of the letters patent from defacing it, or disposing of it.

[48] As the law of arms is part of the public law of the United Kingdom (though it is separate from the common law) the applicable reception date is October 7, 1763, which is the date of the *Royal Proclamation, 1763*, that asserted British sovereignty and established public government over Canada following the cession of the country to the United Kingdom by France.

[49] The Canadian Heraldic Authority will automatically register the grant of arms made by the authorities in the United Kingdom of Great Britain and Northern Ireland, or the United Kingdom of Great Britain and Ireland, before 1988, as those authorities were the lawful grantors of heraldry to Canadians before the transfer of jurisdiction to grant arms to the Governor General of Canada.

[50] *Chivalry*, at page 189, n2

[51] As the grant of arms is an exercise of the Royal Prerogative, and the prerogative is subject to the *Constitution of Canada*, equal grants to males and females is in accord with the equality provisions of the *Canadian Charter of Rights and Freedoms* which is part of the *Constitution Act, 1982*.

[52] However, a female grantee may request that a lozenge be used in the design of her arms if she wishes to maintain the traditional heraldic rule.

[53] That may be unlikely due to the expense of applying for and arranging for the painting of new differentiated shields on supplemental letters patent.

[54] *Austen v Collins* (1886), 54 LT 903 (England, Ch.). Under the English practice arms can be made the subject of a testamentary bequest but a licence from the Crown is required where the arms are to be transmitted to anyone other than the lawful heirs. This situation can occur where a testator dies without issue and wishes his or her arms to be subsequently borne by a person of the testator's choosing. In England, the Crown may grant a licence for this purpose if the character of the designated heir was suitable to bear arms.

[55] at page 153

[56] Thus, the eldest child will cease to use the mark of cadence assigned to them in the original grant and thereafter use their parent's original coat of arms. Senior officials of the Canadian Heraldic Authority have, in the past, taken the view that the descent of undifferentiated arms should follow bloodlines rather than family lines despite the close historic association of heraldry with family surnames. See Robert D Watt Chief Herald of Canada, *A Bold, Successful National Cultural Experiment: The Canadian Heraldic Authority: Personal Reflections on its First Sixteen Years*, in *Canadian Monarchist News*, The Monarchist League of Canada, Oakville (Ont.), Summer, 2004.

[57] An example of a habendum clause in letters patent granting Canadian arms that shows the designation of a junior male child as the heir of the undifferenced arms of his parent will read: "I, the Chief Herald of Canada, do by these Presents grant and assign to _____ the following arms: _____
... to be borne and used forever hereafter by _____ and by his [or her] descendants with such due and proper differences as may be provided, more particularly by his daughter _____ with the arms debruised of a canton _____ charged with _____, and by his son _____ with the arms debruised of a canton _____ charged with _____ during his father's [or mother's] lifetime, all according to the Law of Arms of Canada."

[58] The custom of the descent of the male parent's surname through the male line of descendants is still prevalent in Canada although there are now other options for surnames. The discretion given by the Canadian Heraldic Authority is not limited to circumstances where the eldest male child is junior to a female child. It can also apply where the parent desires the arms to pass through a junior female child or a junior male child.

[59] This is not a unique circumstance in the law pertaining to dignities. At times when it became clear that a peer would not have male issue a parallel peerage was sometimes created that could be inherited by daughters and then subsequently by her sons. This occurred with respect to Donald Smith, Baron Strathcona and Mount Royal, for whom a second barony was created in 1900 to provide for its inheritance by his daughter upon the failure of Lord Strathcona to produce male issue. An earlier barony created for him in 1897 only provided for succession to the barony by male issue. Upon his death in 1914 the 1897 barony became extinct but his daughter succeeded to the barony created in 1900 as Baroness Strathcona and Mount Royal and following her death the title passed to her male offspring.

[60] *Chivalry*, at page 189

[61] *The Canadian Heraldic Authority*, at page 15

[62] *Clark*, at page 231

[63] Ibid, at page 232

[64] Ibid, at page 287

[65] Quoted in *On Her Majesty's Service: Royal Honours and Recognition in Canada*, Christopher McCreery, Dundurn Press, Toronto, 2008, at page 42 (afterwards "*McCreery, OHMS*")

[66] This family order apparently still exists and Queen Elizabeth II is Sovereign of the Order, although it has had no members since 1981.

[67] *Brass et al*, at page 197

[68] Ibid

[69] Ibid at page 199; *McCreery, OHMS*, at pages 50, 55-56

[70] *Royal Warrant of King Edward VII*, June 23, 1902; Statute, July 25, 1907; Statutes, December 16, 1935, Statutes, November 7, 1969, Statutes (Consolidation and Revision) April 14, 1969, Additional Statute, April 15, 1991, Canadian Order-in-Council PC2010-1499, November 26, 2010.

[71] *British Order, Decorations and Medals*, Donald Hall, Balfour Publications, St Ives (Eng.) 1973 at page 30

[72] *McCreery*, at page 673

[73] *The Insignia and Medals of the Grand Priory of the Most Venerable Order of the Hospital of St. John of Jerusalem,* Charles W Tozer O.St.J., JB Hayward & Son, London, 1975, at pages 15-16.

[74] *McCreery,* at page 328

[75] The letters patent creating the Order of Canada was authorized by Order-in-Council P.C 1967-389.

[76] The original version of the *Constitution of the Order of Canada* provided that it could only be amended through the issuance of new letters patent by the Sovereign but an amending Order-in-Council (1972-809) promulgated June 17, 1972 (*Canada Gazette,* Part 1, 1972, page 1628) provided that the constitution of the order could be amended, revoked or revised by either the Sovereign or by the Governor General of Canada acting on the Sovereign's behalf.

[77] Nor does the informal practice of the Advisory Council to proceed by way of consensus establish a legitimate expectation for a consensus process; see *Chauvin v Canada,* 2009 FC 1202 per Aalto, Prothonotary; "The Advisory Counsel may from time to time establish its own informal rules but following *Chiasson,* any informal rules created by the Advisory Committee, such as a requirement for consensus or for not considering a nominee a second time, are secondary, if not irrelevant. These informal rules, to the extent they exist, do not create any legitimate expectations, as in *Chiasson,* that the Advisory Council must act in a certain manner".

[78] at paragraph 71

[79] *McCreery,* at page 268

[80] *McCreery,* at page 289

[81] *McCreery,* at pages 303-304

[82] *Brass et al,* at page 9

[83] *The Military Valour Decorations,* Fact Sheet H1-1, Public Information Directorate, Government House, Ottawa, 1996 (afterwards *"Military Valour Fact Sheet"*)

[84] In the days of the Empire, civil servants were sometimes recognized by the award by the Imperial Government of the Orders of St. Michael and St. George.

[85] *McCreery,* 367

[86] *McCreery,* at page 88

[87] King George V quoted by Sir John Smyth VC in Hall, *British Orders, Decorations and Medals*, at page 5

[88] There were a total of eight forfeitures prior to 1908.

[89] *Clark*, at page 241

[90] *Clark*, at page 237

[91] *McCreery*, at page 366. This could be a problem for future Canadian governments, as the desire to honour a singularly supreme act of valour in war may have to be reconciled with the fact that complex human beings often exhibit significant personal failings. Perhaps it would be preferable if the Federal Government adhered to the view of King George V on this matter, and recognized forever a supreme act of valour regardless of a recipient's human imperfections.

[92] *Pro Valore, Canada's Victoria Cross*, Chancellery of Honours, Office of the Secretary to the Governor General, Ottawa, undated, at page 23

[93] *McCreery*, at page 366

[94] *Military Valour Fact Sheet*

[95] *Canadian Bravery Decorations Regulations*, 1996 P.C. 1997-123 dated January 28, 1997

[96] *Chiasson v Canada*, [2001] 4 FCR 66, 2001per Aronovitch P. at paragraph 37

[97] *Chiasson v Canada* (2001), 215 FTR 293, per Blanchard J. at paragraph 10

[98] *Brass et al*, at page 205

[99] *The Mention in Dispatches*, Fact Sheet H1-1, Public Information Directorate, Government House, Ottawa, 1996

[100] Some were also granted to the mothers of Canadians killed while serving with U.S. forces.

[101] *McCreery*, at page 597

[102] SC 1997, c. 31

[103] But the Sovereign was involved legislatively in the enactment of the statute, through the granting by the Governor General of Canada of Royal Assent to the bill.

[104] Sections 4(1), and 7.

[105] Section 9

[106] *Mallory*, at page 73

[107] For example, the Honourable Herb Gray, who served in Parliament for four decades and held several ministerial offices, as well as serving as the Leader of the Opposition in the House of Commons, was granted the honorific Right Honourable upon his retirement from Parliament in 2002. The prefix title Right Honourable was also granted to Don Mazankowski, another parliamentarian who served in several ministerial posts.

[108] Nova Scotia has allowed some former members of the Executive Council to retain their prefix title after their cessation of office.

[109] *Table of Titles to be used in Canada*, Revised on June 18, 1993, Government of Canada, Ottawa, 1993 (http://canada.pch.gc.ca/eng/1452187406810) (retrieved August 14, 2017)

[110] *Canadian Almanac and Directory 1995*, Canadian Almanac & Directory Publishing Company, Toronto, 1995, at page 6-44

[111] *Colony to Nation, A History of Canada*, A R Lower, McClelland and Stewart, Toronto, 1977, at page 123

[112] at page 247

[113] at page 91

[114] The Commander-in-Chief Unit Commendation is the highest citation in a suite of commendations that include the Canadian Forces Unit Commendation, the Chief of Defence Staff Commendation, and the Command Commendation. These three latter commendations were not established as an exercise of the Royal Prerogative, or the natural person or corporation sole powers of the Sovereign or the Governor General, and the source of the legal authority for their establishment appears to be programmatic within the Defence Department. They have parallels in the honour system of the United States armed forces with which the Canadian Forces have a close working relationship. The RCMP has also established a Commissioner's Commendation and a Commander's Commendation both, apparently, programmatic creations rather than an award emanating from the Crown.

[115] *Lordon*, at page 95

[116] *The Crown and Canadian Federalism,* D Michael Jackson, Dundurn, Toronto, 2013, at page 176.

[117] "Quebec's Lieutenant-Governor gets stamp of disapproval" *The Globe and Mail,* Toronto, February 4, 2010.

THE COMMONWEALTH

14.1   The Evolution of the Commonwealth of Nations

The Canadian monarchy is one part of a broader monarchy that stretches across the world, encompassing realms in the Americas, Europe, and Oceania. Curiously, most realms within this multinational monarchy represent island nations, and only Canada and tiny Belize are continental countries (although Australia is often described as an island continent). At the present time fifteen overseas realms have maintained their links to the constitutional monarchy of the United Kingdom of Great Britain and Northern Ireland since the date of their independence. Together with the United Kingdom the sixteen realms represent a multinational and multi-cultural constitutional monarchy. All of the sixteen realms are linked within the Commonwealth of Nations, an association of former British colonies that have a shared history, and shared values relating to democracy, the rule of law, and the advancement of human rights.

Although at one time in Canada's constitutional history the Commonwealth of Nations was very much a central part of our constitution, it has now largely moved to the periphery of constitutional law and custom in Canada. Beginning with the Balfour declaration of 1926, the Commonwealth evolved away from a unified entity into the free association of independent states that it has become today. This tendency was further reinforced by the *Statute of Westminster, 1931*, which established the *de jure* independence of the British dominions, and subsequently by the post-war request of an independent India to abandon the monarchy and become a republic within the Commonwealth. At the Commonwealth Heads of Government meeting in London in 1949 the heads of the Commonwealth realms acknowledged and accepted the forthcoming transformation of India from a monarchy to a republic within the Commonwealth of Nations. Afterwards, the Sovereign was recognized with the title of the Head of the Commonwealth but the creation of that office did not imply the exercise of any constitutional functions by the Sovereign in relation to the remaining Commonwealth realms, or the republics that subsequently became Commonwealth members. Thus, the 1949 decision by the Commonwealth heads of government to allow republican membership marked the end of a common monarchical allegiance throughout the Commonwealth.[1] Today, Queen Elizabeth II is the Head of the Commonwealth and a symbol of the free association of its member states but she performs no constitutional functions in relation to that office.

14.2   The Commonwealth Realms

The 1949 London Declaration marked an important change in the Commonwealth structure and consequently in Canadian constitutional law. The Commonwealth of Nations has largely become an instrument of Canadian foreign policy rather than part of Canada's constitutional framework. Nevertheless, a few important political and legal linkages to the Commonwealth remain, not the least of which is the fact that Canada is joined to fifteen other countries in a personal monarchical union through the Sovereign of the United Kingdom. Unlike historical examples of personal monarchical unions however, the Commonwealth realms are not jointly governed. Nevertheless, there is a similar governance framework built around the constitutional monarchy that provides a high degree of institutional commonality amongst the Commonwealth realms.

At one time the Commonwealth realms were referred to as Her Majesty's dominions but that description is no longer appropriate; *R v Ashman*, [1985] 2 NZLR 224 (New Zealand, SC). The expression "dominion" was a Canadian innovation at the time of confederation in 1867 that was intended to reflect the organizing principle of monarchy in the new country without antagonizing the republican sensitivities of the neighbouring United States of America. Over time, the expression "dominion" came to characterize self-governing autonomous states that nevertheless remained subordinate to the sovereignty of the United Kingdom and therefore the expression "dominion" eventually fell out of favour as one by one the dominions became fully sovereign states. Today, the expressions that are best suited is Her Majesty's realms, or the Commonwealth realms, which refer to those Commonwealth states that continue to recognize the Sovereign of the United Kingdom of Great Britain and Northern Ireland as their own national head of state. As of 2017, Her Majesty's realms include: Antigua and Barbuda, Australia, Belize, The Bahamas, Barbados, Canada, Grenada, Jamaica, New Zealand, Papua New Guinea, St. Christopher and Nevis, St. Lucia, St. Vincent and the Grenadines, Solomon Islands, Tuvalu, and the United Kingdom of Great Britain and Northern Ireland.[2]

By Commonwealth convention,[3] any member of Her Majesty's realms which chooses to change its status to a republic (or to a monarchy outside of Her Majesty's realms) must first obtain assurances, either directly, or through the Commonwealth Secretariat, that their continued membership in the Commonwealth of Nations will continue to be recognized. Where such assurances are not obtained, the state concerned will cease to be a member of the Commonwealth upon the date of transformation.[4] The required assurances of the other members of the Commonwealth is ordinarily provided if the abolition of the monarchy occurs in accordance with the constitutional procedures of the state that is proposing to abolish the monarchy. But where a state did not seek, or obtain, the required assurances through the Commonwealth Secretariat, or directly, the membership of that state will cease and the state concerned must apply to rejoin the organization and in doing so it would have to give assurances that it will uphold the values of the Commonwealth, including the preservation of the rule of law, and the advancement of human rights.

14.3 The Inter-Se Doctrine

As a result of the historical evolution of the Commonwealth from the former British Empire, Commonwealth countries did not initially regard themselves as subject to international law in their relations with each other. Relations between them in the past were governed by the *Inter Se* doctrine under which it was held that international law could not apply within the Commonwealth owing to the common allegiance of all Commonwealth states to the Sovereign. This was essentially a legal fiction but one that resulted in Commonwealth states exchanging High Commissioners with each other, instead of Ambassadors. Unlike an ambassador, a high commissioner has a right to meet directly with the head of the government of the host state. However, after the London Declaration of 1949 it was no longer possible to maintain this fiction as India became a republic within the Commonwealth, and many new states also joined the Commonwealth as republics, or as fully sovereign indigenous monarchies. As the organization continued to evolve, the various member states came to regard themselves as governed by international law in respect of their relations with each other, and the *Inter Se* doctrine became defunct. However, the traditional diplomatic practice of exchanging high commissioners instead of ambassadors has continued.

14.4 Commonwealth Conventions

One result of its historical foundations within the former British Empire is that the Commonwealth regulates at least some of the relations between its members states through conventions. Perhaps the most prominent is the convention expressed in the *Statute of Westminster, 1931*, that requires the Commonwealth realms to maintain a high degree of similarity with respect to the royal style and titles of the Sovereign. That convention requires the maintenance of similarity with respect to the royal style and titles in each of the realms without precluding the right of every realm to create a title that is suitable for their own realm. In practice, this has meant that all countries within Her Majesty's realms have recognized the current Sovereign as Queen, and not by some other monarchial title, and they have included a reference in their royal styles and titles to the fact of her sovereignty over the other realms, and to the Sovereign's position as Head of the Commonwealth.[5]

An important feature of Commonwealth conventions which distinguish them from domestic constitutional conventions is that state actors (essentially the

Commonwealth heads of government) may establish conventions for the Commonwealth by agreement between themselves and such Commonwealth conventions can have an instant effect, and thus, unlike domestic constitutional conventions, they do not require a history of public adherence in order to be recognized judicially; *Conacher v Canada (Prime Minister)* (2010), 311 DLR (4th) 678 (Canada, FC).

14.5 The Modern Commonwealth

Today the Commonwealth is an international organization which is founded upon the principles expressed in the London Declaration of 1949, the 1971 Singapore Declaration of Commonwealth Principles, and the 1979 Lusaka Declaration concerning human rights. It sustains a high degree of fraternity among its member states with respect to Commonwealth relations. Its main purposes are to maintain the collegiality and fraternity of those states that were formerly constituent parts of the Empire, to enhance the rule of law, democracy, and human rights, in all the member states, and to assist with national capacity-building, and conflict resolution.

14.6 The Organization of the Commonwealth

Membership in the Commonwealth of Nations is open to any country which was formerly dependent in whole, or in part, upon another member of the Commonwealth.[6] Full membership requires that a state be independent, accept the Sovereign as Head of the Commonwealth and agree to cooperate with other Commonwealth states.[7] Small countries which do not have the resources to participate in all forms of cooperation, especially the biennial Heads of Government meeting, may instead opt for a special membership category. Both Tuvalu and Nauru are special members of the Commonwealth. The Secretary-General of the Commonwealth consults the membership on the admission of new members. For the purposes of Canadian law, member states of the Commonwealth are defined in a schedule to the *Interpretation Act* which the Governor in Council may amend from time to time by order-in-council [(s. 35(2) rep. and re-enacted by SC 1992,c.1, s.91].

A Commonwealth Secretariat was established in London in 1965 to promote cooperation and information exchange between the member countries, and to provide support for the Commonwealth Heads of Government meetings (CHOGMs). The Commonwealth Secretariat is headed by a Secretary-General who has access to heads of government and to the Head of the Commonwealth. Consultation amongst member states occurs on diverse subjects, including international and Commonwealth relations, defence, education, law, finance etc. A legal advisory service is attached to the secretariat. The Commonwealth Foundation is an associated entity, which promotes exchanges amongst professional groups. There are also a variety of other technical and education-related entities under the Commonwealth umbrella.

14.7 The Role of the Judicial Committee of the Privy Council

The Judicial Committee of the Privy Council has continued in its role as a Commonwealth Court. Appeals are taken to the Judicial Committee from the British Crown dependencies (e.g., Jersey, Guernsey, and the Isle of Man), the remaining overseas territories of the United Kingdom (e.g., Anguilla, Bermuda, British Antarctic Territory, British Indian Ocean Territory, British Virgin Islands, Cayman Islands, Falkland Islands, Gibraltar, Montserrat, Pitcairn Islands, St Helena, Ascension, and Tristan da Cunha, Turks and Caicos Islands, Akrotiri and Dhekelia), Commonwealth realms that have not abolished appeals to the Judicial Committee (e.g., Antigua and Barbuda, The Bahamas, Grenada, Jamaica, St Christopher and Nevis, Saint Lucia, Saint Vincent and the Grenadines, and Tuvalu), the associated states of New Zealand (e.g., Niue and the Cook Islands), and member states of the Commonwealth who are not within Her Majesty's realms but who have constituted the Judicial Committee by statute as their final court of appeal in respect to all or some of their national litigation (e.g., Trinidad and Tobago, Kiribati, and Mauritius). In the latter case the Judicial Committee operates solely as a court exercising a statutory jurisdiction, and the Royal Prerogative upon which the Judicial Committee's jurisdiction is otherwise based has no application. There is also one Commonwealth monarchy (Brunei) where the Judicial Committee hears appeals that are made to the local Sovereign in civil law matters.

The role of the Judicial Committee as an expositor of the common law throughout the Commonwealth has thus diminished due to the number of member states which have abolished appeals to it. In 1949, Canada became the first member state of the Commonwealth to abolish all appeals to the Judicial Committee (although there was a transitional period, and the last Canadian judgment of the Judicial Committee was not issued until 1959).[8] The judgments of the Judicial Committee issued prior to the abolition of appeals continue to bind lower courts in Canada under the doctrine of *stare decisis*. Judgments of the Judicial Committee since the abolition of appeals are considered to be of persuasive value only in Canadian courts of law (though they continue to be regarded as high authority). *Stare decisis* does not apply to the Supreme Court of Canada, which is no longer bound by the judgments of the Judicial Committee pronounced prior to the abolition of appeals in 1949, nor by the past judgments of the Supreme Court itself. Nevertheless, the Supreme Court remains reluctant to depart from precedent unless a clear rationale for such a departure exists.

14.8 The Role of the Sovereign as Head of the Commonwealth

422 Crown and Constitutional Law

The role of the Sovereign as Head of the Commonwealth is a symbolic and formal role. Queen Elizabeth II is a symbol of the free association of the member states of the Commonwealth but she exercises no constitutional responsibilities over the member states as a result of her position as the Head of the Commonwealth. Nor does she exercise any executive responsibilities over the Commonwealth Secretariat, or play an executive role at the CHOGMs although she customarily attends those meetings wherever they are held. The custom of having the Head of the Commonwealth attend the biennial Heads of Government meetings held outside the United Kingdom was an innovation began by former Canadian Prime Minister Pierre Trudeau in 1973.[9]

Despite her purely formal role, the Sovereign, as Head of the Commonwealth, does play an important symbolic role in preserving unity in an otherwise disparate organization.[10] As Head of the Commonwealth, the Sovereign may act in Commonwealth matters without taking formal advice from her constitutional advisors in either the Commonwealth realms, or from any other Commonwealth member state.[11] However, by a constitutional convention applicable throughout the Commonwealth realms, the Sovereign does not take a public position in her capacity as Head of the Commonwealth that is at a variance from the public positions of any of her governments in those states for which she is the Head of State.[12]

14.9   Citizenship and Allegiance

Commonwealth citizenship replaced the former category of a British subject in Canadian citizenship law. A person who is the citizen of any Commonwealth state is recognized by Canada as a Commonwealth citizen.[13] However, any benefits flowing from the possession of Commonwealth citizenship in Canada, or in any other Commonwealth state, will depend upon the terms of local laws.

No allegiance is owed by the citizens of any Commonwealth country to the Sovereign solely in her capacity as Head of the Commonwealth. Additionally, the Commonwealth of Nations is not a country but rather is an international organization, and therefore no allegiance is owed to it in its corporate capacity.

[1] *Constitutional and Administrative Law*, O Hood Phillips and Paul Jackson, Sweet & Maxwell, London, 1987, at page 765 (afterwards *"O Hood Phillips"*)

[2] The Commonwealth also includes several indigenous monarchies including Tonga, Brunei, Swaziland, Lesotho, and Malaysia. The remaining states (about 30) follow a republican model of government. None of those countries are included within the meaning of the phrase 'Her Majesty's realms'.

[3] For the United Kingdom, Canada, Australia and New Zealand this convention is embodied in legislation – in the preamble to the *Statute of Westminster, 1931.*

[4] For example, the 1987 biennial CHOGM held in Vancouver, British Columbia, declared on October 16, 1987, that Fiji's membership in the Commonwealth of Nations had lapsed in accordance with Commonwealth conventions upon the overthrow of the monarchy by a military coup d'etat.

[5] These are the minimum elements and it is open for realms to add other elements. For instance, Canada has maintained a reference to the United Kingdom in its royal title, and the current Canadian title also recognizes the Sovereign as the Defender of the Faith.

[6] At the Commonwealth Heads of Government Meeting held in 1995 Mozambique was admitted to the Commonwealth although it did not meet this criterion. Mozambique had, however, previously cooperated with the Commonwealth in imposing sanctions on the rebellious U.K. colony of Southern Rhodesia.

[7] *O Hood Phillips,* at page 761

[8] *An Act to Amend the Supreme Court Act* SC 1949, c. 37, s. 3

[9] *The Queen, The Life of Elizabeth II,* Elizabeth Longford, Alfred A Knopf, New York, 1983, at page 284 (afterwards, "*Longford*")

[10] *Longford,* at page 285

[11] *O Hood Phillips,* at page 763

[12] Ibid, at page 764

[13] *Citizenship Act* RSC, 1985 c. C-29, s. 32 (1) "Every person who, under an enactment of a Commonwealth country other than Canada, is a citizen or national of that country has in Canada the status of a citizen of the Commonwealth." Subsection (2) provides that the concept of Commonwealth citizenship replaces the former status of a British subject. Section 33 extends all benefits of Commonwealth citizenship in Canada to citizens of the Republic of Ireland. The concept of Commonwealth citizenship in Canadian law originated with *The Canadian Citizenship Act* RSC 1952, c. 33, s. 23(2).

CONSTITUTIONAL CHANGE AND THE FUTURE

15.1   The Central Role of the Constitutional Monarchy

The monarchy is the oldest constitutional institution in Canada, established with the original settlement at Quebec in 1608. Originally absolutist in theory and practice under the French regime it was, after the conquest, slowly transformed into a constitutional monarchy under the British colonial regime. Thereafter, monarchical government in Canada became progressively more limited as the power of elected parliaments became more and more prominent in the country's constitutional development.

Since the *Statute of Westminster, 1931*, Canada has had complete domestic control over the future of the monarchical institution and, over time, there has been a 'Canadianization' of the monarchy in this country. Today, notwithstanding its British origins and connections, the constitutional monarchy as it exists in Canada is a Canadian institution. In a highly decentralized federation such as Canada the constitutional monarchy fulfills an important role as one of three unitary elements (along with the judiciary and the *Canadian Charter of Rights and Freedoms*) that provide a core internal constitutional unity to the federal state. The monarchy fulfills an important role as a unitary element of the country's constitutional architecture and, as a constitutional institution, it leans against the centrifugal forces that have the potential to overwhelm the unity of the state.

15.2   Changes in Monarchical Customs and Practices

Changes to the roles and powers of the Sovereign, and the Sovereign's representatives, have occurred over time in Canada, as in the United Kingdom and the other Commonwealth realms, largely through changes in constitutional customs and practices. There is nothing new about this process, which has resulted in a continuing transfer of power from the monarch to the elected parliamentarians at least since the beginning of the Stuart dynasty in British constitutional theory and has continued to the current date. While the constitutional monarchy of Canada continues to occupy a position at the apex of the state the political legitimacy necessary to exercise the powers of the monarchy is vested in constitutional actors who owe their elected positions to the people of Canada.

In the nineteenth century the British political theorist Walter Bagehot first drew a distinction between the dignified portion of the constitution (the monarchy) and the efficient portion of the constitution (the parliamentary democracy). In all of the Commonwealth realms the boundary between these two elements of the constitution has shifted over time, although such changes are now likely to happen only incrementally in the future, as all of the substantive monarchical powers, with the exception of the reserve powers, are now embraced within the conventions of responsible government. Generally speaking, the division of customs and practices between the monarchy and the parliamentarians now evinces little controversy, except where symbolism may be engaged.[1]

15.3   The Changing Role of the Governor General of Canada

In Canada, and in the Commonwealth realms outside of the United Kingdom, there is a boundary where changes to constitutional customs and practices involving the constitutional monarchy still occurs. That is the boundary between the Sovereign and the Sovereign's representatives in Canada or, more particularly, the boundary between the responsibilities of the Sovereign, and the responsibilities of the Governor General of Canada. In Canada, after World War II the role of the Governor General was enhanced by the issuance of the new letters patent which, in the main, transferred the exercise of the Sovereign's powers to the Governor General of Canada. Those powers were later supplemented by the issuance of letters patent in 1988, which transferred the heraldic authority for Canada to the Governor General. More importantly, with the appointment of Vincent Massey as Governor General in 1952 Canadians began to be appointed to the post for the first time since the Marquis de Vaudreuil in the 1750's. As such, the office of Governor General began to represent the country to itself, and to represent Canada to the world. Successive Canadian Ministries have sought to enhance the role of the Governor General, in some instances, by reducing the role performed by the Sovereign.

Thus, beginning in 1970 the Pierre Trudeau Ministry began to press for changes in the procedures by which diplomats accredited to Canada were recognized, and for the issuance of letters of credence and letters of recall by Canada to foreign states with respect to Canadian diplomats. Both the agrément, issued by the Crown to foreign ambassadors accredited to Canada, and the letters of credence, or recall, issued by the Crown to Canadian ambassadors accredited to foreign countries had by constitutional custom been signed by the Sovereign. In 1972 the Federal Government sought to transfer this procedure from the Sovereign to the Governor General but Queen Elizabeth II resisted this change and the matter was temporarily dropped. But it was not abandoned. In 1975 the Trudeau Ministry renewed its request to transfer this authority from the Sovereign to the Governor General and Queen Elizabeth II, after a meeting with the Prime Minister, relented in so far as the agrément was concerned although she declined to surrender her authority to sign the letters of credence, or the letters of recall for Canadian ambassadors. Finally, in 1977, Prime Minister Pierre Trudeau obtained the Queen's consent to transfer the function of signing the letters of credence and recall from the Queen to the Governor General.[2] A final change, which some observers consider to have gone too far in diminishing the role of the Sovereign, occurred in 2004, when the letters of credence and letters of recall were stripped of any reference to the Sovereign in favour of a reference to the Governor General of Canada.[3]

Since the mid-twentieth century, when Canadians began to be appointed once again to the position of Governor General, the appointments of Governors General have fallen into three broad categories, diplomats, former politicians, and non-traditional appointees. Initially, diplomats were appointed, and figures such as Vincent Massey, Georges Vanier, and Jules Leger added Canadian lustre to the position. Former politicians such as Ramon Hnatyshyn, and Roméo LeBlanc, appointed in the waning years of the 20th century, were low-key in their performances in the position and elicited no controversies. The former academic, David Johnston, a non-traditional appointee who served in the early 21st century was a very successful and admired Governor General. Both the diplomatic appointees and Privy Councillors such as Hnatyshyn and LeBlanc, as well as David Johnston, a former law professor, benefited from the knowledge they acquired of Canada's constitutional laws, customs, and practices during their professional careers.

More controversial has been the non-traditional appointments of personalities from the broadcasting arts whom some may have felt lacked a deeper understanding of Canadian constitutional law and practice. The counter-argument in support of the appointments of Governors General from outside the traditional worlds of law, diplomacy, and politics, is that such non-traditional appointees offer an aspirational model for Canadians to emulate.

15.4   Constitutional Amendments to the Offices of the Monarchy

While changes to customs and practices have constitutional implications, they cannot alter the fundamental constitutional offices under the *Constitution Acts 1867-1982*. Any change to the fundamental structure of the constitutional monarchy as it currently exists in Canada can only occur as the result of a constitutional amendment. In the case of the constitutional monarchy a constitutional amendment that would change or abolish the monarchy is especially difficult. Section 41 of the *Constitution Act, 1982*, states:

41. An amendment to the Constitution of Canada in relation to the following matters may be made by proclamation issued by the Governor General under the Great Seal of Canada only where authorized by resolutions of the Senate and House of Commons and of the legislative assembly of each province:

(a) the office of the Queen, the Governor General and the Lieutenant Governor of a province;

....

(e) an amendment to this Part.

Therefore, in terms of constitutional change the monarchy in Canada is much more resistant to constitutional change than the monarchy in the United Kingdom, or perhaps in the other fourteen Commonwealth realms. Unlike the unwritten British constitution, which confers supremacy on the Parliament of the United Kingdom, any change to the monarchy in Canada, including the offices of the Sovereign's representatives in Canada and in each province, requires the assent not only of the House of Commons and the Senate of Canada but also the consent of the legislatures of each province. This unanimity formula for constitutional amendments is intended to ensure that the central features of the government of the country, including the constitutional monarchy, will be immune to changes where significant regional opposition may exist.[4]

As a result of the unanimity formula it would be extremely difficult to change the constitutional powers of the offices of the Sovereign, the Governor General, or the Lieutenant Governors of the provinces, as expressed in the *Constitution Acts, 1867-1982*.[5] Any attempt to transfer the formal powers of the Sovereign contained in the *Constitution Acts 1867-1982* to the Governor General, or to the Prime Minister, or to abandon the monarchy in favour of some other form of state government, such as a republic, would trigger the unanimity formula for constitutional changes.

It should be noted that some aspects of the constitutional monarchy are amenable to changes or supplementation without triggering the amending formula set out in section 41. As noted in the discussion in chapter 3 concerning the changes to the laws of succession, the Parliament of Canada has the capacity, under the residual peace, order and good government clause in section 91 of the *Constitution Act, 1867*, to assent to changes to the succession laws established by the United Kingdom Parliament without affecting the powers of the office of the Sovereign in Canada, and without triggering the unanimity amending formula. It is also possible, in the author's opinion, for the Parliament of Canada to address the need for a regency in the event of the incapacity of a Sovereign, or the accession of a Sovereign of tender years, through actions by the Federal Government, including federal legislation, without triggering the unanimity amending formula. A regency concerns the personal capacity of the Sovereign but it does not affect the constitutional office of the Sovereign.

Likewise, the Parliament of Canada may address the subject of the royal style and titles borne by the Canadian monarchy through legislation without triggering the amending formula in the *Constitution Act, 1982*, because the definition of the royal style and titles is an administrative act which does not fundamentally affect the "office of the Queen". However, the exercise of that power is subject to certain restraints. The creation of a title other than that of Queen or King would affect the office of the Queen as it is established under the *Constitution Acts 1867 – 1982*, and would be beyond the jurisdiction of Parliament to enact without a constitutional amendment. Furthermore, the Commonwealth convention concerning titles which is given formal recognition in the *Statute of Westminster, 1931*, and which does form part of the *Constitution of Canada* defined in the *Constitution Act, 1982*, restricts the Parliament of Canada from enacting changes to the essential elements of the royal title without obtaining the consent of the other Commonwealth realms.

Parliament may also supplement existing royal practices and procedures provided that the existing royal practices and procedures are not abolished, or wholly dispensed with. An example is the enactment by Parliament of the supplementary procedures for granting Royal Assent that were created by the *Royal Assent Act*.[6] The *Royal Assent Act* was careful to supplement the existing procedure for granting Royal Assent in Parliament by also providing the Governor General with the ability to privately assent to a bill in writing at Rideau Hall. But Parliament was careful not to abolish the traditional procedure for Royal Assent involving the formal presence of the Sovereign, the Governor General, or the Deputy of the Governor General in the Senate Chamber of Parliament, and thus avoided the legal risk that such an action might have been subsequently held to have constituted a change to the offices of the Queen and the Governor General, and therefore require a constitutional amendment under the unanimity formula, an outcome which might have also called into question the validity of any laws passed under a new exclusive procedure for Royal Assent. The new supplemental procedure that was created avoided that risk because it did not displace the formal ceremonial procedure which continues to be used twice in each calendar year, and which remains valid for the purposes of expressing the assent of the Sovereign to the enactment of legislation in Parliament.

Thus, the constitutional monarchy is essentially embedded in the framework of the *Constitution of Canada* and the abolition of the institution, or a significant formal change to the institution, is unlikely. Since the beginning of the twenty-first century formal constitutional initiatives of any kind have been largely avoided by Canadian political actors.

15.5   Commonwealth Conventional Restrictions on Changes

The *Statute of Westminster, 1931*, stipulates in its preamble that any change in the succession to the Throne, or to the royal style and titles requires the assent of the Parliament of the United Kingdom and the assent of all other Commonwealth realms. This constitutional convention is applicable to changes initiated by Canada, as well as to changes initiated by any other Commonwealth realm, and thus the convention operates equally upon the Parliaments of Canada, the United Kingdom, and all other Commonwealth realms. Accordingly, Canada cannot change either the succession to the Canadian Throne, or the essential elements of the royal style and titles, which include a reference to the Queen or King, the other realms, and the monarch's position as Head of the Commonwealth.

15.6   The Question of Abolition

In Canada, the debate about the fate of the monarchy has usually revolved around the question of abolition.[7] As we have seen, section 41(a) of the *Constitution Act, 1982* precludes a formal abolition absent the unanimous consent of the House of Commons, the Senate of Canada, and the legislatures of each of the provinces. From a practical perspective, this essentially insulates the constitutional monarchy from abolition in the absence of some extremely powerful political impetus. But could the monarchy be diminished to the point of non-existence through incremental changes to conventions, customs and practices? One author has suggested that upon the demise of Queen Elizabeth II the Governor General in Council could decline to issue an accession proclamation for her successor. Then, over time, through the adaptation of conventions the Governor General could assume all of the powers of the Sovereign, after which the office of the Governor General could be re-styled as the Canadian President.[8] Is such an approach possible under the rule of law? The short answer is no. The last time in English constitutional history that steps were taken to prevent the proclamation of a successor to the King occurred on the morning of January 30, 1649, when the English House of Commons under the control of the Roundheads met to enact a law to prevent the proclamation of King Charles II while King Charles I waited nearby in Whitehall to be executed by beheading at the order of the High Court of the Commonwealth of England.[9] That example only serves to underscore that it would be a revolutionary act in violation of the *Constitution of Canada* to fail to proclaim a new Sovereign upon the demise of a previous monarch. As a matter of common law the demise of a monarch results in the immediate succession of a new monarch – there is no legal interregnum and the accession proclamation is a mere constitutional formality. A new Sovereign automatically succeeds to the Canadian Throne.

In any event, the monarchy in Canada is a unitary constitutional institution and it is very unlikely that all of the provinces would acquiesce to any effort by federal authorities to manufacture unilateral constitutional changes in circumstances where the written constitution clearly calls for the agreement of the provinces. Doubtless, the courts of law would also soon weigh-in on such a clear violation of the *Constitution of Canada* and the rule of law. Only a true revolution could overturn the constitutional government of Canada other than by way of the amending formulas provided for in the *Constitution Act, 1982*.[10] Thus, so long as the rule of law prevails in Canada, it will not be possible to abolish the constitutional monarchy, except in accordance with the amending formula provided for in the *Constitution Act, 1982*.

Should a decision ever be taken to abolish the monarchy in Canada, important questions will have to be answered concerning the kind of state structure that would replace the monarchy and the distribution, or even the continuation, of those legal powers which draw their source from the Sovereign, such as the Royal Prerogative. The removal of the role of the Sovereign as the head of both the federal and provincial governments would also remove an important element of constitutional unity within the Canadian constitution. Consideration would then have to be given to the future roles of the heads of both the federal and the provincial governments in a federal state. It is probable that at least some of the provinces would no longer consider it to be appropriate for the head of the provincial government to be appointed by the Governor in Council, or to retain any of the functions of a federal officer, once the federal and provincial governments ceased to be carried on in the name of one Sovereign.

The obvious choice for a constitutional structure to replace the monarchy in Canada would be a republican form of government. Generally speaking, there are two forms of republican government that could replace monarchical government in Canada. Firstly, the state could be organized along the lines of an executive republic, with political power concentrated in a chief executive elected by either a direct or an indirect popular vote. The chief executive could hold office for a term of years, and be governed by a strict separation of powers principle, but disempowered from the exercise of any type of prerogative power. That is an apt description of the American constitutional model, which has prevailed in the United States of America for more than two hundred years.

A second possibility would involve the organization of the state along the lines of a parliamentary republic, with a chief executive occupying a symbolic role and exercising very limited powers much like the current monarchical representatives. The chief executive could be popularly elected to office, or nominated to office by the executive cabinet and then subsequently confirmed by Parliament. The office of the chief executive under that scenario would likely be limited to a term of years but could possess all or some of the former Royal Prerogatives of the Crown, although it is likely that the prerogative powers to be transferred would have to be explicitly stated in the constitution. Actual power under this model would be exercised by the Prime Minister deriving his or her authority from their command of a majority in the lower house of Parliament. This parliamentary republican model would most closely resemble the existing monarchical form of government in Canada.

From time to time there have been proposals in other Commonwealth realms to abolish their monarchy and to opt for a republican form of government but public support for such a change has generally been limited or not forthcoming. A bitterly fought constitutional referendum on the establishment of a republic in Australia was defeated in 1999. No Commonwealth realm has withdrawn from the monarchy since Mauritius in 1992.

15.7   Canada's Monarchy – A Final Word

The continued survival of the monarchy in Canada is dependent as much upon sentiment as upon constitutional principles. The royal consort of Queen Elizabeth II, the Duke of Edinburgh, once stated in a Canadian speech that:

> The structure of any society depends on the accepting by the community of that structure. The Monarchy exists in Canada for historical reasons, and it exists in the sense that it is a benefit, or was considered to be a benefit, to the country or to the nation.

> If at any stage any nation decides that the system is unacceptable, then it is up to them to change it. I think it is a complete misconception to imagine that the Monarchy exists in the interests of the Monarch. It doesn't. It exists in the interests of the people.[11]

Although some have strongly defended the institution of the monarchy in Canada,[12] others have called for its replacement by a republic,[13] or by a vice-royalty.[14] The status quo appears to be the course favoured by political elites and by the political leadership of the state during the current period.

Other commentators on the role of the monarchy have focused attention on the Sovereign's representatives. Thus it has been suggested that the office of the Governor General should be reformed by instituting prior consultation with the parliamentary opposition before an appointment is made, that the term of office be fixed, that the salary of the Governor General be guaranteed for the length of the term, and that provision be made for impeachment of the Governor General.[15] With respect to the Lieutenant Governors, calls have been made for their appointments to be made on the recommendation of the provinces.[16]

But apart from all such questions of reform or abolition, there remains the fact that for more than four hundred years Canada has been a monarchy and the whole of the country's constitutional evolution has proceeded with the monarchy as the central pillar of the executive institutions of the state. Absent some radical future change to the political structure of the state, the constitutional principles established under the monarchial form of government will likely continue to nourish Canadian constitutional law over the passage of time.

[1] Thus, for example, there were rumblings of disapproval in the United Kingdom when Prime Minister Margaret Thatcher reviewed returning victorious British troops following the Falkland War – an activity which some viewed as a function of the Sovereign rather than a Prime Minister.

[2] *The Crown and Canadian Federalism*, D Michael Jackson, Dundurn, Toronto, 2013, at page 228 (afterwards *"Jackson"*). In both 1975 and 1977 the transfer of responsibilities between the Sovereign and the Governor General were announced publicly during the Christmas – New Years holiday season when the Canadian public was distracted – a clear indication that the Canadian Ministry understood that these changes were politically sensitive.

[3] Ibid, at page 230. Once again, the public announcement of the change was made during the Christmas – New Years holiday season to minimize the public awareness of the change.

[4] Parliament also has the authority to impose restrictions on the ability of Ministers of the Crown to introduce resolutions to amend the *Constitution of Canada* unless conditions stipulated by Parliament have been satisfied (see *An Act respecting constitutional amendments* SC 1996, c. 1, s. 1; *An Act to give effect to the requirement for clarity as set out in the opinion of the Supreme Court of Canada in the Quebec Secession Reference* SC 2000, c. 26, s. 3(2)) but no such restrictions have been created with reference to resolutions pursuant to section 41(a) of the *Constitution Act, 1982*.

[5] See *Re Initiative and Referendum Act*, [1919] AC 935 (Canada, JC) for an example of an unsuccessful pre section 41(a) attempt to alter the powers of the Sovereign's representative in Manitoba.

[6] SC 2002, c. 15

[7] There have been no serious proposals for a patriation of the monarchy by the establishment of a resident monarch in Canada.

[8] *The Governor General and the Prime Ministers*, Edward McWhinney, Ronsdale Press, Vancouver, 2005, chapter 7

[9] *Cromwell, Our Chief of Men*, Antonia Fraser, Granada Publishing, London, 1973, 1977, at page 290

[10] The common law has come to recognize jurisprudential philosophies concerning a constitutional annulment through the creation of new constitutional facts, particularly in the jurisprudence writing of the influential Austrian jurist Hans Kelsen. However, the common law has historically been

strongly influenced by the English jurist John Austin and his theories concerning the recognition and obedience to the legitimate sovereign, although it must be said that Austin's views no longer possess the dominance that they once did. For an example of the competing philosophies of jurisprudence in the area of revolutionary acts see *Madzimbamuto v Lardner-Burke*, [1969] 1 AC 645 (Southern Rhodesia, JC)

[11] Quoted in *Longford*, at page 271

[12] *The Crown in Canada*, Frank MacKinnon, Glenbow-Alberta Institute, Calgary, 1976

[13] See the website of the public advocacy group, the "Citizens for a Canadian Republic" (http://www.canadian-republic.ca/home.html) (accessed August 24, 2017)

[14] A vice-royalty was a suggestion made by the editors of the Globe and Mail newspaper in the 1990's who suggested that the Governor General be the Canadian head of state and that he or she should be elected by the Companions of the Order of Canada. A subsequent editor of the Globe and Mail later described this suggestion as "adventurous" (see *Canada and the Crown: Essays on Constitutional Monarchy*, D. Michael Jackson and Philippe Lagassé, McGill-Queen's University Press, Montreal & Kingston, 2013, at page 72.)

[15] *Dawson*, at page 192

[16] The Premier of Quebec made this suggestion in 1996, following the resignation of Quebec's Lieutenant Governor Jean-Louis Roux.

BIBLIOGRAPHY

(Note: This Bibliography contains reference sources used in both the 1998 edition and the 2017 edition.)

BOOKS:

J H Aitchison, *The Political Process in Canada: Essays in Honour of R. MacGregor Dawson*, University of Toronto Press, Toronto, 1963.

Sir William Anson, *The Law and Custom of the Constitution*, Clarendon Press, Oxford, 1907.

Alan Beddoe (revised by Strome Galloway), *Beddoe's Canadian Heraldry*, Belleville (Ontario), Mika Publishing, 1981.

Pierre Berton, *The National Dream, The Great Railway 1871-1881*, McClelland and Stewart Limited, Toronto, 1974.

Vernon Bogdanor, *The Monarchy and the Constitution*, Clarendon Press, Oxford, 1995.

Sir J G Bourinot, *Manual of the Constitutional History of Canada*, Toronto, Copp Clark, 1901.

Catherine Drinker Bowen, *The Lion and the Throne; The Life and Times of Sir Edward Coke (1552-1634)*, Little, Brown & Company (Canada) Limited, Toronto, 1957.

Peter Boyce, *The Queen's Other Realms: The Crown and Its Legacy in Australia, Canada and New Zealand*, The Federation Press, Sydney, 2008.

Craig Brown, ed. , *The Illustrated History of Canada*, Lester & Orpen Dennys, Toronto, 1987.

Henri Brun, Guy Tremblay and Eugénie Brouillet, *Droit constitutionnel, 5th ed.*, Yvon Blais, Cowansville, Que, 2008.

Kirk Cameron and Graham White, *Northern Governments in Transition*, Institute for Research on Public Policy, Montreal, 1995.

Joseph Chitty, *A Treatise on the Law of the Prerogatives of the Crown: And the Relative Duties and Rights of the Subject*, Butterworths, London, 1820.

Samuel Clark, *Distributing Status: The Evolution of State Honours in Western Europe*, McGill-Queen's University Press, Montreal and Kingston, 2016.

Adrienne Clarkson, *Heart Matters*, Penguin Canada, Toronto, 2006.

Larry Collins and Dominique Lapierre, *Freedom at Midnight*, Avon Books, New York, 1976.

A W Currie, *Canadian Transportation Economics*, University of Toronto Press, Toronto, 1967.

Howard Darling, *The Politics of Freight Rates: The Railway Freight Issue in Canada*, McClelland and Stewart, Toronto, 1980.

Louis B Z Davis, *Canadian Constitutional Handbook; Leading Statements, Principles and Precedents*, Canada Law Book, Aurora (Ontario), 1985.

Robert MacGregor Dawson and Norman Ward, *Dawson's The Government of Canada, sixth edition*, University of Toronto Press, Toronto, 1987.

Albert Venn Dicey, *Introduction to the Study of the Law of the Constitution*, (reprint of the eighth edition), Liberty Classics, Indianapolis (Indiana), 1982.

Ted Ferguson, *Desperate Siege, The Battle of Hong Kong*, Doubleday Canada Limited, Toronto, 1980.

Eugene A Forsey, *The Royal Power of Dissolution in the British Commonwealth*, Oxford University Press, Toronto, 1943.

Antonia Fraser, *Cromwell, Our Chief of Men*, Granada Publishing, London, 1973, 1977.

Nancy Gelber, *Canada in London: An Unofficial Glimpse of Canada's Sixteen High Commissioners 1880-1980*, Canada House, London, 1980.

Donald Hall, *British Orders, Decorations and Medals*, Balfour Publications, St Ives (U.K.) 1973.

George Hambleton, *The Parliament of Canada*, Ryerson, Toronto, 1961.

Peter W. Hogg Q.C., *Constitutional Law of Canada, 2nd ed.*, Carswell, Toronto, 1985.

D Michael Jackson, *The Crown and Canadian Federalism*, Dundurn, Toronto, 2013.

D Michael Jackson and Philippe Lagassé, *Canada and the Crown: Essays on Constitutional Monarchy*, McGill-Queen's University Press, Montreal & Kingston, 2013.

David P Jones and Ann S DeVillars, *Principles of Administrative Law, second edition*, Carswell, Scarborough (Ontario) 1994.

Sir Ivor Jennings, *The British Constitution*, Cambridge University Press, London, 1961.

W P M Kennedy, *Documents of the Canadian Constitution 1759-1915*, Oxford University Press, Toronto, 1918.

Kenneth Kernaghan and David Siegel, *Public Administration in Canada; second edition*, Nelson Canada, Scarborough (Ontario), 1991.

Victor Lal, *Fiji, Coups in Paradise, Race, Politics and Military Intervention*, Zed Books Ltd., London, 1990.

Bora Laskin, *The British Tradition in Canadian Law*, Stevens and Sons, London, 1969.

Lord Lloyd of Hampstead, *Introduction to Jurisprudence*, Stevens & Sons, London, 1972.

Elizabeth Longford, *The Queen, The Life of Elizabeth II*, Alfred A Knopf, New York, 1983.

Paul Lordon Q.C., *Crown Law*, Butterworths, Markham (Ontario) 1991.

A R Lower, *Colony to Nation, A History of Canada*, McClelland and Stewart, Toronto, 1977.

Frank Mackinnon, *The Crown in Canada*, Glenbow – Alberta Institute, Calgary, 1976.

James R Mallory, *The Structure of Canadian Government*, Toronto, Gage, 1984.

Robert Marl and Camille Montpetit, *House of Commons Procedure and Practice*, House of Commons, Ottawa, 2000.

W A Matheson, *The Prime Minister and the Cabinet*, Meuthen, Toronto, 1976.

Christopher McCreery, *On Her Majesty's Service: Royal Honours and Recognition in Canada*, Dundurn Press, Toronto, 2008.

Christopher McCreery, *The Canadian Honours System*, Dundurn Press, Toronto, 2005.

Christopher McCreery, *The Canadian Honours System, Second Edition*, Dundurn, Toronto, 2015.

Christopher McCreery, *The Order of Canada: Its Origins, History, and Development*, University of Toronto Press, Toronto, 2005.

Edward McWhinney, *The Governor General and the Prime Ministers*, Ronsdale Press, Vancouver, 2005.

Jacques Monet, *The Canadian Crown*, Clarke, Irwin & Co., Toronto & Vancouver, 1979.

James Morris, *The Pax Britannica Trilogy; Heavens Command, An Imperial Progress*, The Folio Society, London, 1992.

Duke of Norfolk (pub.), *The Ceremonies to be Observed at the Royal Coronation of Her Most Excellent Majesty Queen Elizabeth II in the Abbey Church of St Peter Westminster on Tuesday the Second Day of June 1953*, published under the authority of the Duke of Norfolk, Earl Marshal of the Realm, London, 1953.

O Hood Phillips, *Constitutional and Administrative Law, 5th ed.*, Sweet & Maxwell, London, 1973.

O Hood Phillips and Paul Jackson, *Constitutional and Administrative Law*, Sweet & Maxwell, London, 1987.

Maurice Ollivier Q.C., *British North America Acts and Selected Statutes*, Queen's Printer and Controller of Stationary, Ottawa, 1962.

Peter Russell and Paul James, *At Her Majesty's Service*, Fontana/Collins, Glasgow, 1986.

John T Saywell, *The Office of Lieutenant Governor*, University of Toronto Press, Toronto, 1957.

Frank R Scott, *Essays on the Constitution, Aspects of Canadian Law and Government*, University of Toronto Press, Toronto, 1977.

Walter S Scott, *The Canadian Constitution Historically Explained*, Carswell, Toronto, 1918.

David E Smith, *The Invisible Crown: The First Principle of Canadian Government*, University of Toronto Press, Toronto, 1995.

G D Squibb, *The High Court of Chivalry: A Study of the Civil Law in England*, Clarendon Press, Oxford, 1959.

Roy Strong, *Coronation: A History of Kingship and the British Monarchy*, Harper Collins, London, 2005.

Gregory Tardi, *The Legal Framework of Canadian Government, A Canadian Guide*, Canada Law Book, Aurora (Ontario), 1992.

Alpheus Todd, *Parliamentary Government in the British Colonies*, Longmans, Green & Co., London, 1894.

Charles W Tozer O.St.J., *The Insignia and Medals of the Grand Priory of the Most Venerable Order of the Hospital of St. John of Jerusalem*, JB Hayward & Son, London, 1975.

Pierre E Trudeau, *Memoirs*, McClelland and Stewart, Toronto, 1993.

Philip Ziegler, *Mountbatten*, Alfred A. Knopf, New York, 1985.

PERIODICAL SOURCES

Steven Chase, "Jean feared 'dreadful crisis' when Harper sought prorogation,", *The Globe and Mail*, Toronto, June 25, 2012.

Henry F. Davis, "Nature of the Privy Council," *Canadian Legal Studies*, Butterworths, Toronto, December, 1968.

John Geddes and Aaron Wherry, "Inside a crisis that shook the nation; Secret meetings, shocking alliances, faulty strategies—and one wonky video camera", *Macleans Magazine*, Toronto, December 11, 2008.

Rhéal Séguin, "Quebec's Lieutenant-Governor gets stamp of disapproval", *The Globe and Mail*, Toronto, February 4, 2010.

Peter Hennessy, "The Monarchy, The throne behind the power", *The Economist*, December 24, 1994, London, page 78.

Adrian Morrow, "Ontario Lieutenant-Governor David Onley shares insights on his seven year term", *The Globe and Mail*, September 22, 2014.

David Mundell, "Legal Nature of Federal and Provincial Governments", *Osgoode Hall Law Journal*, 1960, vol. 2:56.

Warren J Newman, "Grand Entrance Hall, Back Door or Foundation Stone? The Role of Constitutional Principles in Construing and Applying the Constitution of Canada", (2001), 14 *Supreme Court Law Review (2d)*, page 197.

Anne Twomey, "Responsible Government and the Divisibility of the Crown," *Legal Studies Research Paper No. 08/137*, November 2008, The University of Sydney Law School.

Michael Valpy, "Scholars scurry to find implications of royal wedding" *Globe and Mail*, February 11, 2005.

Janet Walker, "Interprovincial Sovereign Immunity Revisited," *Osgoode Hall Law Journal*, 35.2 (1997) page 379.

Robert D Watt Chief Herald of Canada, "A Bold, Successful National Cultural Experiment: The Canadian Heraldic Authority: Personal Reflections on its First Sixteen Years," *Canadian Monarchist News*, The Monarchist League of Canada, Oakville (Ontario), Summer, 2004.

John Willis, *Delegatus Non Potest Delegare*,(1943) 21 Canadian Bar Review, Toronto, 1943, page 257.

GOVERNMENT SOURCES

2017 Confidence and Supply Agreement between the BC Green Caucus and the BC New Democrat Caucus, Victoria (British Columbia), May, 2017.

Department of Canadian Heritage, *Installation of the Governor General of Canada*; February 8, 1995, Ottawa, 1995.

Department of Canadian Heritage, *Introduction of Line of Succession Legislation*, Ottawa, January, 2013.

Department of Foreign Affairs and International Trade (1952), Documents on Canadian External Relations, Queen's Printer for Canada, Ottawa, 1952.

Department of Justice (Canada), *Memorandum on the Office of Lieutenant Governor of a Province: Its Constitutional Character and Functions*, King's Printer, Ottawa, 1937.

Department of Justice *Memorandum on the Office of Lieutenant Governor of a Province: Its Constitutional Character and Functions*, Queen's Printer and Controller of Stationary, Ottawa, 1955.

Government of Canada, *Table of Titles to be used in Canada, (revised on June 18, 1993)*, Ottawa, 1993 (http://canada.pch.gc.ca/eng/1452187406810) [accessed August 14, 2017].

Government of Canada, *Open and Accountable Government 2015, Ottawa, 2015* (http://pm.gc.ca/eng/news/2015/11/27/open-and-accountable-government) [accessed July 10, 2017].

440 Crown and Constitutional Law

Government House, Public Information Directorate, *The Swearing-In of a New Ministry*, Ottawa, 1993.

Government House, Public Information Directorate, *The Swearing-In of Privy Councillors*, Ottawa, circa 1993.

Government House, *Role and Responsibilities of the Governor General*, Ottawa, 1996.

Government House, Public Information Directorate, *The Military Valour Decorations, Fact Sheet H1-1*, Ottawa, 1996.

Government House, Chancellery of Honours, Office of the Secretary to the Governor General, *Pro Valore, Canada's Victoria Cross*, Ottawa, undated (circa 1996).

Government House, Public Information Directorate, *The Mention in Dispatches*, Fact Sheet H1-1, Ottawa, 1996.

Government House, Public Information Directorate, *Programme for the swearing-in of Ministers and Secretaries of State at Government House, June 11, 1997*, Ottawa, 1997.

House of Commons (Canada), *Official Report of Debates of the House of Commons*, Ottawa, Kings Printer, 1945.

Legislative Assembly of New Brunswick, *Installation of Marilyn Trenholme Counsell as Lieutenant Governor of New Brunswick*, Fredericton (New Brunswick), 1997.

Library and Archives Canada, *L S Amery P.C., Memorandum in Despatch No. 3 to the Irish Free State* dated February 6, 1929, LAC File No: RG 25, D1, Vol. 740, File No: 132, 1929.

London Gazette, June 26, 1900, No: 27205, The King's Printer, London.

Minister of Supply and Services, *The Great Seal of Canada*, Ottawa, 1988.

Minister of Supply and Services, *Flag Etiquette in Canada*, Ottawa, 1995.

Office of the Clerk of the House of Commons, *Glossary of Parliamentary Procedure*, Ottawa, 1992.

Privy Council Office, *The Preparation of Legislation*, Ottawa, 1981.

Privy Council Office, *A Guide for Ministers and Secretaries of State*, Ottawa, 2002.

Privy Council Office, *Guidance for Deputy Ministers*, Ottawa, 2003.

Privy Council Office, *Accountable Government: A Guide for Ministers and Ministers of State*, Ottawa, 2011.

Privy Council Office, *Historical Alphabetical List since 1867 of Members of the Queen's Privy Council for Canada*, (http: //www.pco-bcp.gc.ca/index.asp?lang=eng&page=information &sub=council-conseil &doc=members-membres/hist-alphabet-eng.htm). [accessed February 1, 2017].

Public Works and Government Services Canada (Department of), *Guide to the Making of Federal Acts and Regulations*, Ottawa, 1996.

Queen's (King's) Printer for Canada (pub.), *Canada Gazette*, Ottawa, (various dates).

Rideau Hall, *The Canadian Heraldic Authority*, Ottawa, 1990.

Senate of Canada, *Senate Journals 1877*, , Ottawa, 1877.

Senate of Canada, *Senate Procedure in Practice*, Ottawa, June 2015.

Treasury Board of Canada, *Treasury Board Manual* (various), Canada Communications Group-Publishing, Ottawa 1993-94.

LEGAL REFERENCE SOURCES

Henry Campbell Black, *Black's Law Dictionary, 4th ed.*, West Publishing Co., St. Paul (Minn.) 1968 (1975).

Canadian Encyclopaedic Digest, 4th Edition *(Crown)*, Carswell, Toronto 2010.

Halsbury's Laws of England 4th ed., *Vol. 35 Peerages and Dignities*, Butterworth, London, 1994.

Halsbury's Laws of Canada, 1st Edition *(Crown 2017 Reissue)* Lexis-Nexis, Toronto, 2017

Rt. Hon. Earl Jowitt and Clifford Walsh, 2nd ed. by John Burke, *Jowitt's Dictionary of English Law, 2nd ed.*, Sweet and Maxwell, London, 1977.

GENERAL REFERENCE SOURCES

Canadian Almanac and Directory 1995, Canadian Almanac & Directory Publishing Company, Toronto, 1995.

Canadian Almanac & Directory 2017, 170th Edition, Grey House Publishing Canada, Toronto, 2016.

Robin Brass et al ed., *The Register of Canadian Honours*, Canadian Almanac & Directory Publishing Company Limited, Toronto, 1991.

Barbara Law, ed., *Corpus Almanac & Canadian Sourcebook*, Southam, Don Mills (Ontario), 1996.

Patrick Montague Smith, *Debrett's Correct Form*, Headline, London, 1992.

WEBSITE RESOURCES

"Citizens for a Canadian Republic" (website) (http://www.canadian-republic.ca/home.html) [accessed August 24, 2017].

The Canadian Encyclopaedia (website) (http://www.thecanadianencyclopedia.ca/en/) [accessed on various dates]

Wikipedia, The Free Encyclopaedia (website) (https://en.wikipedia.org/wiki/Main_Page) [accessed on various dates]

ABOUT THE AUTHOR

Peter William Noonan was born in Windsor Ontario and graduated from Marlborough Public School, Belle River District High School, and the University of Windsor. He received his Bachelor of Laws degree in 1979 and was subsequently called to the Bar of Her Majesty's Courts in Ontario in April 1981. Later that year he joined the Public Service of Canada as a legal counsel and he spent the next thirty years in the practice of public law with the Government of Canada. He appeared before government tribunals and in the Federal Court, the Federal Court of Appeal, and the Supreme Court of Canada. The author retired from the Department of Justice in 2011 and was subsequently appointed a Member of the Ontario Energy Board until 2015.

Through his professional work the author developed a strong research interest in the constitutional role of the Crown in Canada. From 1996-1998 he researched, prepared, and published the first edition of *The Crown and Constitutional Law in Canada*. Between 1998-2000 he held an appointment as a Sessional Instructor in Crown Law in the Faculty of Law of the University of Calgary. He received a grant of arms from the Canadian Crown in 2015 at a ceremony conducted by the Chief Herald of Canada, and the Saguenay Herald, at the Chancellery of Honours in Ottawa.